Supranational Criminal Prosecution of Sexual Violence:
The ICC and the Practice of the ICTY and the ICTR

The drawing on the cover of this book was made by Grace, a Tutsi woman. She was a victim of multiple rapes during the 1994 genocide in Rwanda at the age of 14. Due to the genocide, Grace has lost her parents and all her four brothers and sisters. As a result of the rapes, Grace is now infected with AIDS.

The drawing depicts her story as well as those of millions of other women worldwide who have become victims of sexual violence as genocide, a crime against humanity or a war crime.

To Leonie and Jef & Freek

SCHOOL OF HUMAN RIGHTS RESEARCH SERIES, Volume 20

The titles published in this series are listed at the end of this volume.

Supranational Criminal Prosecution of Sexual Violence: The ICC and the Practice of the ICTY and the ICTR

Anne-Marie L.M. de Brouwer

INTERSENTIA
Antwerpen – Oxford

This volume is an adapted version of a dissertation defended at Tilburg University on 2 November 2005.

Anne-Marie L.M. de Brouwer
Supranational Criminal Prosecution of Sexual Violence:
The ICC and the Practice of the ICTY and the ICTR

ISBN 90-5095-533-9
D/2005/7849/91

ACKNOWLEDGEMENTS

The idea to write a book on the prosecution of sexual violence before the International Criminal Court (ICC), with the practice of the International Criminal Tribunal for the former Yugoslavia (ICTY) and the International Criminal Tribunal for Rwanda (ICTR) in mind, originated during my LL.M. studies in international human rights law at the University of Essex (UK) in 1998/1999. A subsequent internship at the ICTY in 1999 further strengthened this idea. During this internship, I became further acquainted with the hard reality that sexual violence is an all too common phenomenon in the context of genocide, crimes against humanity or armed conflict. Women, especially, are the victims of these crimes. A strong disbelief and indignation that such horrendous crimes could ever be failed to be properly addressed on the international level (especially in light of the precedents set by the Nuremberg and Tokyo Tribunals) directed me to study to what extent justice can or should be done to victims of sexual violence by the supranational criminal law system.

When I started this study at the Law Faculty of Tilburg University in 2000, the ICTY and ICTR had already been in operation for a few years. The ICTY and ICTR Statutes and Rules of Procedure and Evidence contain better provisions than their Nuremberg and Tokyo counterparts where the interests of victims of sexual violence are concerned. I was intrigued by the question as to whether the ICTY and ICTR *practice* would appropriately take into account concerns of victims of sexual violence. Furthermore, I wanted to explore how the ICC, supported by even more elaborate provisions for victims of sexual violence than the ICTY and the ICTR, could deal with sexual violence prosecution and to what extent it should follow ICTY and ICTR practice. In this book, I have tried not only to study and explain the relevant law and to provide recommendations for a more comprehensive supranational criminal prosecution of sexual violence, but also to give a voice to victims of sexual violence and their suffering.

Completing this study would not have been possible without a great many people. In the first place, a special word of thanks goes to my supervisors, Willem van Genugten and Marc Groenhuijsen, for their support over the last five years. I would like to thank Willem for always having given me the space to grow as an academic: his support to and trust in me, both as a researcher and a lecturer in international (criminal) law, has been truly heartwarming. Marc has always been a very active proponent of victims' rights and his commitment thereto has been a real inspiration to me. I will always treasure our meetings and discussions. I am also indebted to the members of the reading committee: Kelly Askin, Theo van Boven, Cyrille Fijnaut, André Klip and Theo de Roos, for having read and commented on my manuscript. Their writings have been at the basis of this study.

I would also like to express my gratitude to the ICTR, for having given me the opportunity to work there as an intern by assigning me to the Office of the Prosecutor, viz., the *Butare* team, in 2003. This experience gave me many more insights into the prosecution of sexual violence before an international criminal tribunal. Moreover, during this period, I also had the opportunity to visit Rwanda several times; visits which have left an indelible impression on me. I would especially like to thank Richard Karegyesa, Senior Trial Attorney at the ICTR, for our inspirational talks and subsequent e-mail discussions on sexual violence prosecution.

This research could not have been possible without NWO (the Netherlands Organisation for Scientific Research), which provided me with the grant, for which I am truly grateful. I would also like to acknowledge the Schoordijk Institute at the Tilburg University Faculty of Law for their services provided to PhD researchers, and the Netherlands School of Human Rights Research for the many interesting meetings pertaining to human rights issues. As to the finalisation of the manuscript I would like to thank the publisher Intersentia. I would also like to thank Marlene Havens, Michelle Möhl and Charlotte Raaimakers for helping me complete the bibliography. I thank Julie Tims, information specialist at Tilburg University Library, who has been of great help in tracing documents I was unable to find. I would furthermore like to express my sincere gratitude to Grace for her drawing and Jean Gakwandi from Solace Ministries in Rwanda for helping me with finding this drawing for the cover of my book.

Many more people have contributed to this book in one way or another, often only just by inquiring about the progress of my research. Here, I would like to thank Marieke van Eik and Chiseche Mibenge for their support in the final stage of my research. I would also like to thank my colleagues at the Department of European and International Public Law at Tilburg University. Some of them have been instrumental in making life at university even more fun and have become true friends. Margreth de Bonth and Ruben Weigel, who introduced me to the life of '*AIO*-hood'. Saskia Lavrijssen-Heijmans, for her enduring optimism and words of encouragement. Susan Mathews, for her endless interest in my research and for proof-reading some of my chapters. Rianne Letschert, for sharing all ups and downs inherent to writing a PhD thesis; I could not have wished for a better and more caring 'office mate'.

Last but certainly not least, I would like to thank a few people who are very dear to me. I am very grateful to my parents Jef and Leonie and my sister Vanessa, of whom I am proud. I thank them for their continuing support and love. I pay special tribute to Freek, who has supported me during this research in uncountable ways. He helped me put my troubles concerning this study into perspective at times when I needed it most. My gratitude for his love, faith, patience and encouragement cannot be expressed in words.

Anne-Marie de Brouwer
Tilburg/The Hague, September 2005

TABLE OF CONTENTS

Abbreviations

ABiH	Army of Bosnia and Herzegovina
ACHR	American Convention on Human Rights
AI	Amnesty International
AIDS	Acquired Immune Deficiency Syndrome
Art.	Article
AFRC	Armed Forces Revolutionary Council
ARV	Anti-retroviral
ASP	Assembly of States Parties
BiH	Republic of Bosnia and Herzegovina
CAT	Convention Against Torture and Other Cruel, Inhuman or Degrading Treatment or Punishment
CCL	Control Council Law No. 10
CEDAW	Committee on the Elimination of Discrimination against Women
Doc.	Document
DRC	Democratic Republic of the Congo
ECHR	European Convention on Fundamental Rights and Fundamental Freedoms
ECtHR	European Court of Human Rights
EoC	Elements of Crimes
FAR	Forces Armées Rwandaises (Rwandan Armed Forces)
FARG	Fonds d'Assistance aux Rescapés du Génocide
FIND	Fonds d'Indemnisation
FWS	Foča Witness Statements (Prosecution witness pseudonyms)
GC	Geneva Convention
HIV	Human Immunodeficiency Virus
HRW	Human Rights Watch
HVO	Croatian Defence Council (the Croatian Community of HZ-HB armed forces)
HZ-HB	Herzeg-Bosna
IACHR	Inter-American Commission on Human Rights
ICC	International Criminal Court
ICCPR	International Convention on Civil and Political Rights
ICRC	International Committee of the Red Cross
ICTR	International Criminal Tribunal for Rwanda
ICTY	International Criminal Tribunal for the former Yugoslavia
ICTY/R	ICTY and ICTR
ICJ	International Court of Justice
IGO	International Governmental Organisation
ILA	International Law Association
ILC	International Law Commission

ILM	International Legal Materials
IMFTE	International Military Tribunal for the Far East (Tokyo Tribunal)
IMT	International Military Tribunal (Nuremberg Tribunal)
ILO	International Labour Organisation
NGO	Non-Governmental Organisation
MONUC	United Nations Mission in the Democratic Republic of Congo
No.	Number
Nos.	Numbers
Nº	Numéro
OTP	Office of the Prosecutor
p.	page
pp.	pages
para.	paragraph
paras.	paragraphs
PrepCom	Preparatory Commission for the ICC
RPE	Rules of Procedure and Evidence
Res.	Resolution
RPF	Rwandese Patriotic Front
RUF	Revolutionary United Front
RTLM	Radio Télévision Libre de Mille Collines
SC	Security Council
SFRY	Socialist Federal Republic of Yugoslavia
Suppl.	Supplement
UK	United Kingdom
UN	United Nations
UNAMIR	United Nations Assistance Mission for Rwanda
UN Doc	United Nations Document
UNGA	United Nations General Assembly
UNSC	United Nations Security Council
UNSCR	United Nations Security Council Resolution
UNTS	United Nations Treaty Series
US	United States
v.	versus
Vol.	Volume
VPRS	Victims' Participation and Reparations Section
VRS	Bosnian Serb Army
WVSS	Witnesses and Victims Support Section
VWU	Victims and Witnesses Unit

INTRODUCTION

The following account was given by Perpetue,[1] a 20-year-old Tutsi woman who was living in Runda commune, Gitarama prefecture, with her husband, child and sister when the violence broke out in Rwanda in 1994. She hid in neighbouring Taba commune until the militia groups from Taba and Runda communes began working together to find out whom they had missed in the area. Perpetue was soon discovered by the militia. This is her account:

> On April 9, 1994, they found me. I was taken to the Nyabarongo River by a group of Interahamwe. When I got there, one Interahamwe said to me that he knew the best method to check that Tutsi women were like Hutu women. For two days, myself and eight other young women were held and raped by Interahamwe, one after another. Perhaps as many as twenty of them. I knew three of them. Some Interahamwe watched over us while others went to eat and sleep. All the young women killed at that river were raped before being thrown in. I didn't know any of the other women. On the third day, one Interahamwe saw that I was not able to walk anymore. He told me that I had already died and could go. I tried to leave, but I could barely walk. There was blood everywhere and my stomach hurt. I walked towards Kamonyi and found refuge in an old church there. When I was going there, I saw that the Interahamwe had been burning people to death. I saw at least ten burnt bodies.
>
> I was in the church building when the Interahamwe came there on May 15 and told us that it was our turn to be burnt. They took a lot of people outside to kill them. One Interahamwe chose me, but told me that he would protect me so that I would not be burnt to death. He took me to another building near the church and raped me there. Before he raped me, he said that he wanted to check if Tutsi women were like other women before he took me back to the church to be burnt. There were other women being raped there at the same time, maybe ten women and seven young girls. The next day, two Interahamwe watched over us while the others went to kill. The two were complaining they were feeling tired from all the killing. Then, one of them sharpened the end of the stick of a hoe. They held open my legs and pushed the stick into me. I was screaming. They did it three times until I was bleeding everywhere. Then they told me to leave. I tried to stand up, but I kept falling down. Finally I crawled outside. I was naked crawling on the ground covered in blood. I tried to ask someone on the road for help, but they thought I was a madwoman and just ignored me. I finally found a house where they gave me some medicine to apply to the area between my legs. They also gave me some clothes, but because I was bleeding so much the skirt became soaked with blood.

[1] Nowrojee (1996), pp. 57-60. In order to protect Perpetue's safety and privacy, her name was changed in the Human Rights Watch report prepared by Nowrojee.

Perpetue stayed hiding in the bush for about one week until she found two men with a bicycle who were willing to take her to Gisenyi in the north-west part of the country. She thought that if she left the area where she was originally from, she would not be recognised as a Tutsi. Unfortunately, when she arrived in Gisenyi at the end of May, she was recognised by an *Interahamwe* from her home area. He immediately notified the other militia that she was a Tutsi and she was taken to a mass grave.

> I was told to give my clothes to them. The mass grave was for women and girls only and it was being organized by a woman they called Donatha. She had a long knife and cut me immediately behind the knee. One Interahamwe saw me and took me aside along with four other women. He explained to us that all the Gitarama people were going to be killed, but that he would protect us and that we could live with him. He took me to the lake. There, he raped me. I cried out because I was still wounded from before and he was opening all the wounds again. He beat me for crying and gagged my mouth. He told me that I was forbidden to cry because Tutsi had no rights at that moment. He also said that any Tutsi woman from Gitarama would be killed in an even worse way than what he was doing to me. After the rape, I was left alone and naked. I decided to try and escape. I couldn't walk properly and so I was on all fours. When people passed me, I sat down and stopped walking so they wouldn't know that I had been raped because I was ashamed. I crawled like that for two days in the bush. When I urinated, it came out like blood. Black, coagulated blood kept coming out of my vagina.
>
> When I got to the road (later I found that I had been walking south along the Rwanda-Zaire border towards Kibuye) I found a camp – Rubengera camp – which was being run by the French. But I recognized someone there who had killed my family so I left. I survived for three days in the bush before the RPF came. When I saw the RPF fighters, I thought it was the Interahamwe. I told them to kill me because I didn't care anymore. They took me to Kibuye where I was examined by a French doctor and was given medicine, food and clothes. When they gave me underwear, it was so painful that I could not even put it on. I was given medical care from June 1994 to December 1994. I had to sit in medicated baths every day. They offered to send me to France for medical treatment, but I wanted to go back to my home. Since the war has ended, I have not had my monthly period. My stomach sometimes swells up and is painful. I think about what has happened to me all the time and at night I cannot sleep. I even see some of the Interahamwe who did these things to me and others around here. When I see them, I think about committing suicide.

This account by Perpetue, who survived sexual violence during the 1994 genocide in Rwanda, is one out of hundreds of thousands. Her account clearly depicts the cruelty with which wartime sexual violence is inflicted as well as the long-lasting devastating consequences it usually has on the victims. Accounts such as the above lie at the heart of this study.

Following the wars in the former Yugoslavia (Croatia 1991-1995, Bosnia and Herzegovina 1992-1995, and Kosovo 1998-1999) and the genocide in Rwanda (1994), numerous accounts and reports laid bare the widespread and orchestrated basis on which sexual violence had been committed against women and girls, and the dreadful brutality which came with it.[2] Mass rapes and other forms of sexual violence were no isolated events during the conflicts in the former Yugoslavia and Rwanda: during practically every conflict in the world, sexual violence against women has been witnessed on a massive scale. Some examples of conflict situations in the 20th century in which sexual violence has been – or still is being – directed against women make this abundantly clear: Europe during World Wars I and II, the Japanese-held territories in South-East Asia during World War II, Bangladesh, Vietnam, Sudan (especially Darfur), Sierra Leone, the Democratic Republic of Congo (especially the Ituri region), Northern Uganda, Liberia, Algeria, Somalia, Colombia, Peru, Guatemala, Afghanistan, Burma, India (especially Gujarat), Iraq, East Timor, Indonesia, Chechnya – and this list is not exhaustive.

---

[2] For the former Yugoslavia see, *inter alia*, the reports prepared by the Special Rapporteur of the Commission on Human Rights, Tadeusz Mazowiecki, on the situation of human rights in the territory of the former Yugoslavia: UN Commission on Human Rights, *Report on the Situation of Human Rights in the Territory of the Former Yugoslavia Prepared by Mr. Tadeusz Mazowiecki, Special Rapporteur of the Commission on Human Rights, Pursuant to Paragraph 15 of Commission Resolution 199/S-1/1 and Economic and Social Council Decision 1992/305*, A/47/666, 17 November 1992; UN Commission on Human Rights, *Report on the Situation of Human Rights in the Territory of the Former Yugoslavia, Submitted by Tadeusz Mazowiecki, Special Rapporteur of the Commission on Human Rights, Pursuant to Paragraph 15 of Commission Resolution 1992/S-1/1 of 14 August 1992,* E/CN.4/1993/50, 10 February 1993; UN Commission on Human Rights, *Situation of Human Rights in the Territory of the Former Yugoslavia: 5th Periodic Report on the Situation of Human Rights in the Territory of the Former Yugoslavia, Submitted by Tadeusz Mazowiecki, Special Rapporteur of the Commission on Human Rights, Pursuant to Paragraph 32 of Commission Resolution 1993/7 of 23 February 1993*, E/CN.4/1994/47, 17 November 1993; UN Commission on Human Rights, *Situation of Human Rights in the Territory of the Former Yugoslavia: 6th Periodic Report on the Situation of Human Rights in the Territory of the Former Yugoslavia, Submitted by Tadeusz Mazowiecki, Special Rapporteur of the Commission on Human Rights, Pursuant to Paragraph 32 of Commission Resolution 1993/7 of 23 February 1993,* E/CN.4/1994/110, 21 February 1994; UN Commission on Human Rights, *Ninth Periodic Report on the Situation of Human Rights in the Territory of the Former Yugoslavia, Pursuant to Paragraph 37 of Commission Resolution 1994/72 of 9 March 1994 and Economic and Social Council Decision 1994/262 of 22 July 1994,* A/49/641, Annex to *Human Right Questions: Human Rights Situations and Reports of Special Rapporteurs and Representatives*, A/49/641, S/1994/1252, 4 November 1994. See also Amnesty International (1993); Human Rights Watch (1993); Stiglmayer (1993); Beverly (1996); Bassiouni and McCormick (1996); Drakulić (2000); Cavelius (2000); Nikolić-Ristanović (2000); Human Rights Watch (2000a). For Rwanda, see, *inter alia*, African Rights (1995a); Nowrojee (1996); UN Commission on Human Rights, *Report on the Situation of Human Rights in Rwanda Submitted by Mr. René Degni-Segui*, Special Rapporteur of the Commission on Human Rights, under Paragraph 20 of Resolution S-3/1 of 25 May 1994, E/CN.4/1996/68, 29 January 1996; UN Commission on Human Rights, Report of the Special Rapporteur on Violence Against Women, Its Causes and Consequences, Ms. Radhika Coomaraswamy, Addendum, *Report of the Mission to Rwanda on the Issue of Violence Against Women in Situations of Armed Conflict*, E/CN.4/1998/54/Add.1, 4 February 1998; Organization of African Unity, International Panel of Eminent Personalities Report, *Rwanda: The Preventable Genocide*, 2000, Chapter 16; Nowrojee and Ralph (2000), pp. 162-175; Nowrojee (2004a); Survivors Fund (SURF) (2005).

This study deals with the supranational criminal prosecution of sexual violence before the International Criminal Court (ICC or the Court), while taking into account the present practice of the International Criminal Tribunal for the former Yugoslavia (ICTY or the Tribunal) and the International Criminal Tribunal for Rwanda (ICTR or the Tribunal). Before taking a closer look at the supranational criminal prosecution of sexual violence before the Court and the Tribunals, it is useful to consider the historical framework in which the supranational criminal prosecution of sexual violence developed. Such an exercise may contribute to our understanding of the origins of the prosecution of sexual violence and what its current position is at the international level.

1 Sexual violence and supranational criminal prosecutions: Historical development

Despite mass rapes and other forms of sexual violence committed against women in times of conflict, the perpetrators of these crimes have hardly been prosecuted and brought before international criminal tribunals. Four phases can be distinguished with regard to the supranational criminal prosecution of sexual violence: (1) from ancient times to World War II (1939-1945); (2) the World War II period and the establishment of the Nuremberg and Tokyo Tribunals in the 1940s; (3) the establishment of the ICTY and ICTR in the 1990s; and (4) the establishment of the ICC in 1998. The historical development of prosecuting sexual violence before international criminal tribunals, on a substantive and procedural level, is briefly described here.

1.1 From ancient times to World War II

From ancient times throughout the greater part of the Middle Ages, rape was commonly considered a property crime, a crime committed against the man who 'owned' the woman, not a crime against the woman herself. In Ancient Greece, rape was 'socially acceptable behavior well within the rules of warfare, an act without stigma for warriors who viewed the women they conquered legitimate booty, useful as wives, concubines, slave labor or battle-camp trophy'.[3] Rape was thus seen as a reward for the victors, and as such not prosecuted as a crime. The trial of Sir Peter Hagenbach in 1474, before the first known international military court, however, resulted in his conviction for war crimes, including rape, committed under his command.[4] Yet, the conviction remained obscure as Sir Peter Hagenbach was convicted for the rapes because he had not declared war: if war had been declared, the acts would have been allowed.[5] Views on the protection of women during war did not really change during the 16th and 17th centuries. Only a small minority of states and scholars were of the opinion that rape during

[3] Brownmiller (1975), p. 33.

[4] Askin (1997), p. 29. Sir Peter Hagenbach was accused of having instituted a reign of terror in the town of Breisach, without first having declared war. It has, however, been argued that the trial cannot be seen to constitute a precedent for international criminal prosecution of individuals. According to Kittichaisaree (2001, p. 14): 'The twenty-eight judges were drawn from the confederate entities of the Holy Roman Empire, thus depriving the tribunal of its "international" character, and the law applied was, therefore, not "international" law.'

[5] Askin (1997), p. 29.

wartime was a crime deserving prosecution.[6] At the end of the 18th century and during the 19th century, the laws of war slowly changed; that is to say war was only to be conducted against combatants, not against civilians. However, the provisions which were presumably intended to protect women from sexual violence were vague. Phrases such as 'women and children ... shall not be molested in their person' and 'honour and rights of the family should be respected' appeared in the Treaty of Amity and Commerce (1785) and The Declaration of Brussels (1874), respectively.[7] The 1863 Lieber Code, which can be seen as the first national document stating a framework for the laws of war at an international level, firmly prohibited rape in war as a crime punishable by death. The 1864 Geneva Convention (aimed at the protection of persons), revised and extended in 1906 and 1929, and the 1899 and 1907 Hague Conventions (aimed at the reduction of the horrors of warfare) further developed the codification of the laws of war and customs of war. The 1907 Hague Convention IV Respecting the Laws and Customs of War on Land is the most important of the Hague Conventions when it comes to the protection of women in war. Article XLVI of the 1907 Hague Convention IV states: 'Family honour and rights, the lives of persons ... must be respected.'[8] Ideas about sexual violence in wartime thus gradually changed from 'a reward for the victors' to 'a crime against the woman', albeit in very equivocal language.

Another opportunity to prosecute sexual violence before an international criminal tribunal arose after World War I. The War Crimes Commission, set up in 1919 to examine the atrocities committed by Germany and the other Axis powers during World War I, had found substantial evidence on sexual violence and had subsequently included rape and forced prostitution among the violations of the laws and customs of war.[9] During World War I, rape and other forms of sexual violence were in particular directed against women in Belgium and France by the German army. Although efforts to prosecute failed miserably, the enumeration of rape and forced prostitution as violations of the laws and customs of war was further evidence of the recognition of the criminal nature of the crimes.[10]

1.2 The Nuremberg and Tokyo Tribunals

The first international criminal tribunals of real significance emerged with the establishment of the Nuremberg and Tokyo Tribunals, in Nuremberg, Germany, in 1945

[6] Hugo Grotius (1583-1645), for one, concluded that rape committed in peace and wartime should not go unpunished; Askin (1997), pp. 29-33.

[7] Askin (1997), p. 34.

[8] Hague Convention (IV) Respecting the Laws and Customs of War on Land (and Annex Regulations Concerning the Laws and Customs of War on Land), 18 October 1907, 36 Stat. 2277, TS No. 539, reprinted in Roberts and Guelff (2000), p. 67. See also Hague Convention (II) with Respect to the Laws and Customs of War on Land, 29 July 1899, 32 Stat. 1803, TS No. 403, reprinted in Schindler and Toman (1988), p. 63, Article 46 ('Family Honours and Rights'). See also Askin (1997), pp. 38-40.

[9] Askin (1997), p. 42.

[10] Askin (1997), pp. 42-45.

and in Tokyo, Japan, in 1946, respectively.[11] The Nuremberg and Tokyo Tribunals were established after World War II to prosecute the major war criminals of the European Axis countries (in fact, only Germans were tried) and Japan for crimes against peace, war crimes and crimes against humanity (Articles 6 and 5, respectively).[12] War criminals considered to be relatively small fry were instead tried before national military courts run by the victorious nations which, in the case of the European Axis countries were based on Control Council Law No. 10.[13] With the establishment of the Nuremberg Tribunal in 1945, individuals, as opposed to States, were held responsible under international law for the first time ever.[14]

Despite evidence on sexual violence, the reluctance to prosecute sexual violence crimes committed in wartime did, however, not drastically change with the establishment of the Nuremberg and Tokyo Tribunals. Although the provisions on war crimes and crimes against humanity in the Nuremberg Statute did not explicitly refer to rape or other forms of sexual violence, the possibility of prosecuting sexual violence as a war crime was present:

---

[11] See the Charter of the International Military Tribunal for the Trial of the Major War Criminals, Appended to the Agreement for the Prosecution and Punishment of Major War Criminals of the European Axis, 8 August 1945, London, as amended, Protocol to Agreement and Charter, 6 October 1945, 82 UNTS 279 (Nuremberg Charter); Charter of the International Military Tribunal for the Far East, 19 January 1946 (General Orders No. 1), Tokyo, as amended, General Orders No. 20, 26 April 1946, TIAS No. 1589, 4 Bevans 20 (Tokyo Charter).

[12] The Nuremberg Tribunal was set up by the joint effort of the US, France, England and the USSR, and was subsequently accepted by nineteen other nations (Australia, Belgium, Czechoslovakia, Denmark, Ethiopia, Greece, Haiti, Honduras, India, Luxemburg, the Netherlands, New Zealand, Norway, Panama, Paraguay, Poland, Uruguay, Venezuela and Yugoslavia), which contributed to its legality as a new institution enforcing new criminal rules on an international level. The Tokyo Tribunal was, in contrast, solely drawn up by the Americans, who consulted the major Allies only after the Tokyo Charter had been issued. However, in the end, the Nuremberg and Tokyo Charters did not drastically differ.

[13] Nuremberg Trials Final Report Appendix D: Allied Control Council Law No. 10, Punishment of Persons Guilty of War Crimes, Crimes Against Peace and Humanity, 20 December 1945, published in Official Gazette of the Control Council for Germany, No. 3, Berlin, 31 January 1946 (Control Council Law No. 10).

[14] According to the Nuremberg Tribunal: 'Crimes against international law are committed by men, not by abstract entities, and only by punishing individuals who commit such crimes can the provisions of international law be enforced.' See International Military Tribunal, Judgment and Sentences, *American Journal of International Law*, vol. 41, 1947, p. 222. This principle was subsequently endorsed, among other principles, by the 'Principles of International Law Recognized by the Charter of the Nuremberg Tribunal and the Judgment of the Tribunal', unanimously adopted by UN General Assembly Resolution 95(1) of 11 December 1946. See UN General Assembly, *Resolution 95(I) Affirmation of Principles of International Law Recognized by the Charter of the Nürnberg Tribunal,* UN Doc. A/64/Add.1, 11 December 1946. The said principles were subsequently formulated by the International Law Commission and accepted by the UN General Assembly on 12 December 1950. See UN General Assembly, *Resolution 488 (V) Formulation of the Nürnberg Principles*, 12 December 1950, Principle I in particular.

> Rape was specifically prohibited in the Lieber Code [1863] as a serious violation of the laws of war, there was evidence that previous war crime trials had punished belligerents for sex crimes, and the Hague Convention [1907] asserted that 'family honour and rights ... must be respected'. In the IMT (International Military Tribunals) Indictments for 'war crimes,' sexual assault could have fallen within the purview of 'abduction of the civilian population ... into slavery and for other purposes' and as 'devastation unjustified by military necessity.' Sexual assault clearly could have been prosecuted as a war crime under Article 6(b) of the IMT Charter (probably as customary law, certainly as 'ill-treatment'), if the drafters and prosecutors had been so inclined, particularly since sexual assault crimes were included within the evidence submitted to the Nuremberg Tribunal.[15]

To prosecute sexual violence as crimes against humanity also became possible. Article 6(c) of the Nuremberg Charter, on crimes against humanity, could have made the prosecution of sexual violence crimes possible under the heading of 'other inhumane acts',[16] and arguably under 'enslavement' for the sexual enslavement of women for weeks, months and sometimes years on end during World War II. It could even be argued that the provisions on war crimes and crimes against humanity should have been stated in explicit language referring to sexual violence crimes from the start. Rape as a war crime was already outlawed before the Nuremberg Tribunal and rape as a crime against humanity, although a novel crime under international law, merely codified what was criminal already in most municipal codes.[17] On the basis of 'general principles of law', a source of international law, rape and most of the other crimes listed were crimes already recognised by the major legal systems in the world.[18] Rape and other forms of sexual violence, including forced prostitution and forced sterilisation, were committed against women in Europe during World War II on a large scale: while Germans raped Jewish and Russian women and girls in particular, the Russian army when it entered Germany raped German women and girls in some kind of retaliation for what the Germans had done to Russian women.[19] Sexual violence was used by the Axis nations, but Allied forces and civilians also took part in the violation of women.[20] Unfortunately, notwithstanding evidence of sexual violence crimes committed against women in Europe during World War II, the will to prosecute crimes of sexual violence was not strong during the Nuremberg Trial, and again sexual violence was not prosecuted. According to Askin, a possible explanation for the lack of will to prosecute sexual violence during the Nuremberg trials may be found in the fear that the Allies might be

---

[15] Askin (1997), p. 138; see also p. 40. The wording of the war crimes provision reads in part: 'namely, violations of the laws or customs of war. Such violations shall include, but not be limited to, murder, ill-treatment or deportation to slave labor or for any other purpose of civilian population of or in occupied territory, ... or devastation not justified by military necessity.' Sexual violence could have been prosecuted under the war crimes provision, due to its in-exhaustive language and the violations mentioned which leave room for prosecution of sexual violence.

[16] Askin (1997), p. 142; Bassiouni (1992), pp. 86, 125.

[17] Bassiouni (1992), p. 246.

[18] *Ibid.*

[19] For an account of the sexual violence crimes which took place in Europe during World War II, see Askin (1997), pp. 52-61, 71-73, 88-91.

[20] Askin (1997), pp. 52, 59, 61.

prosecuted for sexual violence crimes themselves.[21] Moreover, the lack of female participation in the process leading to the establishment of the Nuremberg Tribunal as well as the lack of legal posts assigned to women may provide further clarification of the disinterest in sexual violence prosecutions.[22] Prosecutions under Control Council Law No. 10, which included rape as a crime against humanity,[23] never took place either.

The Tokyo Tribunal can be seen as the more successful Tribunal of the two when it comes to prosecuting sexual violence. Although – again – no straightforward wording is used in the Statute prohibiting rape or any other sexual violence crimes, rape was charged in the indictment as a war crime, under 'inhumane treatment', 'ill-treatment' and 'failure to respect family honour and rights', and was successfully prosecuted.[24] According to the Prosecution, during the first six weeks of the Japanese occupation of the Chinese city of Nankin, in excess of 20,000 women and girls were raped by Japanese soldiers.[25] Moreover, the Tokyo Tribunal included accounts of sexual violence crimes in the trial testimonies as well as public records.[26] At a national level, a commander of the 14th area army, General Yamashita, was convicted for, *inter alia*, rape under his command.[27] Rape, forced prostitution, sexual slavery and other forms of sexual violence were rampant during World War II in Asia. Around 200,000 women, mostly Korean and Chinese, but also Filipino, Indonesian, Dutch and other women, were held in sexual slavery to provide sexual services to the Japanese military.[28] These women have been euphemistically called 'comfort women'. It is estimated that only 25 percent of the comfort women survived and that most were unable to have children as a consequence of the multiple rapes or the diseases they contracted following the rapes.[29] The only successful trial was the one brought by some 35 Dutch 'comfort women' before the Batavia Military Tribunal in 1948.[30] In recent years, more than 50 actions for damages have been filed against Japan, but all have been dismissed.[31] Until 1992, the Japanese government has denied any responsibility for the sexual slavery system during World War II; and still it has not offered an official apology to the 'comfort women', who are now in their 70s and 80s. Although in 1995 a fund was created in order to compensate the 'comfort women' and give them medical and welfare support, the money did not come from the Japanese government but from private donations.[32] For

---

[21] *Ibid.*, p. 163.

[22] *Ibid.*, pp. 102-103 versus pp. 166-167.

[23] Article II Control Council Law No. 10.

[24] Counts 1, 5 and 12 of the Tokyo indictment. See Askin (1997), p. 180.

[25] Askin (1997), p. 180.

[26] *Ibid.*, pp. 185, 163, 203.

[27] *Ibid.*, pp. 164-203.

[28] See generally Yoshiaki (2000).

[29] Askin (1997), p. 92.

[30] *Ibid.*, pp. 85-87.

[31] BBC News, *Japan Rejects Sex Slave Appeal*, 25 March 2003. Courts have generally held that there are no grounds in international or Japanese law under which individuals could claim compensation from the Japanese government.

[32] *Ibid.* (mentioning that the fund paid 2m yen (USD 19,470) in compensation, plus medical and welfare support, to 285 'comfort women' in the Philippines, South Korea and Taiwan. Medical aid was also given to 79 Dutch women who were forced into having sex by Japanese troops in Indonesia).

this reason, many 'comfort women' declined any compensation from the fund. In a recent decision, Japan announced to close the fund in 2007.[33] Some sort of justice has been done to the 'comfort women' by the mock war crimes tribunal, the Women's International War Crimes Tribunal on Japan's Military Sexual Slavery, held in Tokyo in 2000, which ruled that Japan's late Emperor Hirohito and his government were responsible for forcing women into sexual slavery during World War II.[34] The legally non-binding judgment held that Tokyo owed a full apology and compensation to the 'comfort women', but the judgment remains without any results today.

1.3 The ICTY and the ICTR

Before discussing the creation of the ICTY and the ICTR, the context in which sexual violence occurred in the former Yugoslavia and Rwanda – that is whether it was widespread, organised, and public as well as the nature of the crimes (the types of sexual violence and the level of brutality, but also identification of the victims and the perpetrators) – will be outlined first. Such an overview is necessary to understand the overall picture of how sexual violence took place in the former Yugoslavia and Rwanda and how the Tribunals responded or should have responded to it. In Part I, accounts of survivors of sexual violence who appeared before the Tribunals will be quoted, which further substantiate the reports of sexual violence.

1.3.1 Sexual violence in the former Yugoslavia

The conflict in the former Yugoslavia covers different time spans and geographical areas, that is Slovenia (1991), Croatia (1991-1995), Bosnia and Herzegovina (1992-1995), Kosovo (1998-1999) and Macedonia (2001). Reports of sexual violence during the conflicts in Bosnia and Herzegovina and Kosovo have especially been alarming. Although exact numbers are not available, it is estimated that during the conflict in Bosnia and Herzegovina, between 20,000 to 50,000 women were raped.[35] The majority of the rape victims were Muslim women, who were raped by Serbian soldiers. Men too became victims of sexual violence; they were, for instance, forced to bite off another man's testicles. However, sexual violence was disproportionately directed against women, who were (gang)raped in the streets or in their homes in a plurality of ways, *inter alia*, in front of family members and/or by means of objects such as broken glass bottles, guns and truncheons.[36] One obscure situation in which sexual violence took place was the deliberate creation of 'rape camps'. The aim of such camps was to impregnate the Muslim and Croatian women held captive. Often the women were kept in confinement until it was too late to abort the child. Because of the patrilineal society, in which children inherit their father's ethnicity, the result of the impregnation was the birth of a new generation of Serb children. According to the Women's Group Tresnjevka, more than 35,000 women and children were held in such Serb-run 'rape

---

[33] BBC News, *Japan to End WWII Sex Slave Fund*, 24 January 2005.

[34] See Transcript of Oral Judgment delivered on 4 December 2001 by the Judges of the Women's International War Crimes Tribunal on Japan's Military Sexual Slavery.

[35] See, *inter alia*, Nikolić-Ristanović (1999), p. 67.

[36] *Final Report of the Commission of Experts Established Pursuant to Security Council Resolution 780 (1992)*, S/1994/674, 27 May 1994, Chapter IV, F.

camps'.[37] Many of the Serb rapists acted on official orders to rape women as part of the ethnic cleansing, to displace the targeted ethnic group from the region.[38]

During the Kosovo war of 1998-1999, thousands of Kosovo Albanian women and girls became victims of sexual violence.[39] Rape and other forms of sexual violence was used as a weapon of war and instruments of systematic 'ethnic cleansing': rapes were used deliberately as an instrument to terrorise the civilian population, extort money from families and force people to flee from their homes. According to a report prepared by Human Rights Watch in 2000, the rapes in Kosovo can generally be subdivided into three categories:

> ... rapes in women's homes, rapes during flight, and rapes in detention. In the first category, security forces entered private homes and raped women either in the yard, in front of family members, or in an adjoining room. In the second category, internally displaced people wandering on foot and riding on tractors were repeatedly stopped, robbed, and threatened by the Yugoslav Army, Serbian police, or paramilitaries. If families could not produce cash, security forces told them that their daughters would be taken away and raped; in some cases, even when families did provide money, their daughters were taken away. The third category of rapes took place in temporary detention centers, such as abandoned homes or barns.[40]

Most rapes were gang rapes involving at least two perpetrators. The majority of the perpetrators were Serbian paramilitaries, but also Serbian special police or Yugoslav army soldiers. These paramilitary organisations worked closely together with official government forces, either the Serbian Ministry of the Interior or the Yugoslav army, throughout Kosovo. The Serbian and Yugoslav authorities knew that their paramilitaries had committed rape and used other forms of sexual violence in Bosnia and Herzegovina. Yet, the paramilitaries were deployed to or allowed to operate in Kosovo by the Serbian and Yugoslav authorities apparently without any precautions being taken to prevent their committing further such war crimes. The participation of Serbian and Yugoslav forces in gang rapes renders it unlikely that senior officers were unaware of the assaults. Rapes occurred frequently in the presence, and with the acquiescence, of military officers. Several rape victims actually reported the crimes to Yugoslav military officers. There is no evidence, however, that the Yugoslav army or the Serbian Ministry of the Interior made any attempt to apprehend or punish those responsible for the attacks. There is also no evidence that the Yugoslav Army or Serbian Ministry of Interior took any measures to prevent rape and other forms of sexual violence, such as issuing orders or warning troops that they would be punished for these crimes. Moreover, soldiers, police and paramilitaries often raped their victims in front of many witnesses. In addition to actual rapes that took place in front of others, the process of pulling women out of refugee convoys often occurred in full view of other internally

---

[37] Cited in Netherlands Institute for War Documentation, *Srebrenica – A 'Safe' Area*, Part I, Chapter 9, 10 April 2002.

[38] *Final Report of the Commission of Experts Established Pursuant to Security Council Resolution 780 (1992)*, S/1994/674, 27 May 1994, Chapter IV, F.

[39] The overview of sexual violence in Kosovo is based on the report prepared by Human Rights Watch (2000).

[40] Human Rights Watch (2000), Chapter I.

displaced persons. Since the entry of the NATO-led Kosovo Force, rapes of Serbian, Albanian and Roma women by ethnic Albanians, sometimes by members of the Kosovo Liberation Army, have also been documented.

1.3.2 Sexual violence in Rwanda

During the 100 days of genocide that ravaged the small country of Rwanda in Central Africa from April until June 1994, about 934,000 Tutsi and moderate Hutu were killed,[41] while hundreds of thousands of women and girls were raped and/or experienced any other form of sexual violence. The 1996 report of the United Nations Special Rapporteur on Rwanda, René Degni-Segui, found that 'rape was the rule and its absence the exception'.[42] According to the report, 'rape was systematic and was used as a "weapon" by the perpetrators of the massacres. This can be estimated from the number and nature of the victims as well as from the forms of rape.'[43] According to the Report prepared in 2000 by the Organization of African Unity's International Panel of Eminent Personalities: 'we can be certain that almost all females who survived the genocide were direct victims of rape or other sexual violence, or were profoundly affected by it.'[44] In Degni-Segui's report it was estimated, on the basis of the assumption that 100 cases of rape give rise to one pregnancy and on the basis of an estimated number of pregnancies caused by rape of between 2,000 and 5,000, that in between 250,000 to 500,000 Rwandese women and girls had been raped during the genocide.[45] Although the exact number of victims of sexual violence during the genocide in Rwanda (or during any other conflict, for that matter) will never be fully known,[46] it is clear that the number of women and girls confronted with sexual violence

---

[41] This number was given by the Rwandan government on the occasion of the tenth anniversary to commemorate the genocide (1994-2004). Most reports cite numbers between 500,000 and 800,000 deaths. According to the report prepared by the International Panel of Eminent Personalities, it is difficult to estimate the actual figure of persons who lost their lives, but that 'even if the most conservative figure is used, it still means that over three-quarters of the entire population registered as Tutsi were systematically killed in just over 100 days' (Organization of African Unity, International Panel of Eminent Personalities Report, *Rwanda: The Preventable Genocide*, 2000, para. 14.80).

[42] UN Commission on Human Rights, *Report on the Situation of Human Rights in Rwanda Submitted by Mr. René Degni-Segui*, Special Rapporteur of the Commission on Human Rights, under Paragraph 20 of Resolution S-3/1 of 25 May 1994, E/CN.4/1996/68, 29 January 1996, para. 16.

[43] *Ibid.*

[44] Organization of African Unity, International Panel of Eminent Personalities Report, *Rwanda: The Preventable Genocide*, 2000, para. 16.20.

[45] UN Commission on Human Rights, *Report on the Situation of Human Rights in Rwanda Submitted by Mr. René Degni-Segui*, Special Rapporteur of the Commission on Human Rights, under Paragraph 20 of Resolution S-3/1 of 25 May 1994, E/CN.4/1996/68, 29 January 1996, para. 16.

[46] In the first place, stigmatisation associated with being a victim of rape tends to obstruct women and girls from coming forward to report rape. In the second place, many women were killed following the rape, and forensic research does not show whether someone was raped or not.

runs into the hundreds of thousands.[47] Women may rightly be seen as 'the main victims of the massacres ... since they were raped and massacred and subjected to other brutalities'.[48] While many women were killed following their rapes, the women who managed to survive the genocide were left to experience a living death.

Within the genocidal context of Rwanda, victims of sexual violence were predominantly attacked on the basis of their gender and ethnicity. Thus, mostly Tutsi women and girls, of all ages, were sexually attacked; men only seldom. Of particular influence was the anti-Tutsi propaganda that preceded the 1994 genocide and that called on the Hutu population to be aware of the Tutsi population,[49] which was alleged to constitute a real threat to the Hutu community. In the December 1990 issue of the newspaper *Kangura*, the sexuality of Tutsi women was in particular targeted through the publication of the 'Ten Commandments'.[50] In four out of the 'Ten Commandments', Tutsi women were portrayed as tools of the Tutsi community, as sexual weapons that would be used by the Tutsi to weaken and ultimately destroy the Hutu men.[51] In

---

Finally, when you do have a number, it can generally be assumed that the number of rapes are underreported.

[47] According to the Human Rights Watch report prepared by Nowrojee (1996), the large scale occurrence of sexual violence throughout Rwanda is evidenced by a manifold of sources, *inter alia*: the testimony of rape victims themselves; the testimony of rape victims who also saw others being raped; other witnesses; doctors at the hospitals who had treated hundreds of rape victims; humanitarian organisations with programmes for women; the UN Special Rapporteur's report on the situation of human rights in Rwanda.

[48] UN Commission on Human Rights, *Report on the Situation of Human Rights in Rwanda Submitted by Mr. René Degni-Segui*, Special Rapporteur of the Commission on Human Rights, under Paragraph 20 of Resolution S-3/1 of 25 May 1994, E/CN.4/1996/68, 29 January 1996, para. 12.

[49] In 1994, the print media and radio (largely controlled by Hutu extremists) were the two most important and influential mediums in Rwanda that influenced the Hutu population. Over the weekends, newspapers with hate propaganda directed against the Tutsi were distributed throughout the countryside by urban workers who worked in Kigali during the week. The newspapers were read out to those who were illiterate and they also displayed cartoons offensive to Tutsi. As most households had a radio, the radio was the most important and influential medium through which the Rwandan population received information. The most influential radio station with anti-Tutsi hate propaganda was the Hutu extremists owned 'Radio Télévision Libre des Mille Collines' (RTLM), which began broadcasting in August 1993. See also Green (2002), pp. 733-776.

[50] *Kangura* is Kinyarwanda and literally means 'wake up' and described itself as 'the voice that seeks to awake and guide the majority people [the Hutu]'. *Kangura* was one of the most influential newspapers on hate propaganda directed against the Tutsi population.

[51] Four of the 'Ten Commandments' dealt with Tutsi women specifically, i.e., (1) 'Every Hutu should know that a Tutsi woman, wherever she is, works for the interest of her Tutsi ethnic group. As a result, we shall consider a traitor any Hutu who: marries a Tutsi woman; befriends a Tutsi woman; employs a Tutsi woman as a secretary or a concubine'; (2) 'Every Hutu should know that our Hutu daughters are more suitable and conscientious in their role as woman, wife, and mother of the family. Are they not beautiful, good secretaries and more honest?'; (3) 'Hutu woman, be vigilant and try to bring your husbands, brothers and sons back to reason'; and (4) 'The Rwandese Armed Forces should be exclusively Hutu. The experience of the October [1990] war has taught

addition to such sex-oriented anti-Tutsi propaganda, newspapers also printed cartoons in which Tutsi women, but also the moderate Hutu Prime Minister Agathe Uwilingiyimana, were portrayed as sexual objects.[52] The use of gender hate propaganda thus incited the sexual violence to come.[53] This is most clearly evidenced by statements of the perpetrators which accompanied the rapes, such as 'You Tutsi women think that you are too good for us' and 'Let us see what a Tutsi woman tastes like', referring to the (Hutu-imposed) arrogance of Tutsi women, who were generally considered to be more beautiful than Hutu women. Some rapes were, however, directed at Hutu women who were considered to be moderates; they were married to Tutsi men, protected Tutsi people, or were politically affiliated with the Tutsi. There were also rapes that were directed against women and girls regardless of ethnicity or affiliation with the Tutsi population, and they were especially directed against young or beautiful women. These women were thus primarily attacked on the basis of their gender only, as a result of the prevailing chaos during the conflict. Thus, although both Hutu and Tutsi women were sexually violated, there were considerable differences in the number of assaults as well as the underlying reasons. In addition, also Tutsi men were attacked in a sexual manner, although in significantly smaller numbers than women. Such attacks in particular included mutilation of the genitals, which were often displayed in public.

The perpetrators of the sexual violence were mostly members of the Hutu militia, the *Interahamwe*. But rapes were also committed by military soldiers of the Rwandan Armed Forces (FAR), including the Presidential Guard, and civilians. In some cases, leaders of the militia or the military knew that rapes were being committed. Although no explicit written orders to rape and sexually violate women have been found, there is enough evidence that leaders encouraged or ordered their men to rape Tutsi as well as condoned the acts taking place, without making efforts to stop them. The perpetrators were not only men; also Hutu women committed rapes (using objects) or ordered men to perform acts of sexual violence against Tutsi women.[54] These Hutu women came from all layers of society; even nuns took part.

The types of sexual violence against women and girls in Rwanda included: rape, gang rape, sexual slavery (either collectively or individually through 'forced marriages'), rape by means of objects such as sticks or weapons, often leading to the victims' death, sexual mutilation of, in particular, breasts, vaginas or buttocks or of features considered to be Tutsi such as small noses or long fingers, often during or following the rapes. Acid was also frequently used to mutilate women so as to prevent

---

us a lesson. No member of the military shall marry a Tutsi.' The commandments are quoted in African Rights (1995), pp. 42-43.

[52] An example of such a cartoon is one published in the December 1993 publication of 'Power', in which Tutsi women are portrayed as seductresses and RPF [Rwandese Patriotic Front] allies as they were having sex with the Belgian UN peacekeepers of UNAMIR [United Nations Assistance Mission for Rwanda], which were considered RPF supporters. Another example is the cartoon in which the moderate Hutu Prime Minister Agathe Uwilingiyimana is displayed in various sexual poses with other politicians. See Chrétien (1995), pp. 366, 368. During the genocide, the Prime Minister was shot by a lieutenant of the National Police and her lower body was exposed with a beer bottle protruding from her vagina. See Nowrojee (1996), p. 190.

[53] Green (2002), pp. 733-776.

[54] African Rights (1995b).

them having Tutsi children.[55] Pregnant women were not spared from sexual violence and neither did age matter. On many occasions, the victims were killed following the rapes; those whose lives were spared, were only saved in order to be raped. Many women were raped by men who knew they were HIV positive, and thus sadistically tried to transmit the virus to Tutsi women and their Tutsi families.[56] These forms of sexual violence were no isolated incidents; rather, they were more than once committed and/or in combination with other sexual acts and/or over an enduring or recurring period of time in the course of the genocide. Some women were kept as personal slaves for years after the genocide; they were forced to move to neighbouring countries after the genocide along with their captors. In addition to sexual violence attacks, these women witnessed other crimes committed against their loved ones, such as murder and torture. Many of them lost their houses and property. Such factors contributed to the coercive circumstances under which women were raped.

The rapes and sexual violence took place all over the country. The rapes occurred inside the victims' or perpetrators' houses, but more often they were committed in plain view of others, at sites such as schools, churches, roadblocks, government buildings or in the bush. Often, the bodies of the women were, after the rapes, laid spread-eagled in public view. Considering that the sexual violence occurred on such a massive scale in public, it is difficult to imagine anybody in Rwanda who was not aware of the sexual violence taking place. Compared to other conflicts in the world, the sexual violence in Rwanda stands out in a number of ways: the organised nature of the propaganda that contributed significantly to fuelling sexual violence against Tutsi women, the very public nature of the rapes and the level of brutality towards the women.[57]

The sexual violence was inflicted upon the women with complete impunity, and as a very effective weapon of war. For those who survived the sexual violence, the effects thereof go well beyond the acts themselves as they impact on both the individual and the community the victim belongs to. Victims of sexual violence face physical and psychological harm as well as social isolation. Some were faced with unwanted offspring (Rwanda is a patriarchal society and children therefore take the perpetrator's ethnicity), others resorted to self-induced abortions and many faced infections arising from sexually transmitted diseases, including syphilis, gonorrhoea and HIV/AIDS. To date, in the absence of anti-retroviral drugs, women are still dying of AIDS which they often contracted through the sexual violence they endured during the genocide. Many victims of rape have to deal with the social stigmatisation attached to rape; in some cases, their husbands left them because they had been raped, in other cases, these women have become unmarriageable. Some fear retaliation if they speak out about their ordeal, and some feel guilty that they survived. Ten years after the genocide in Rwanda, the survivors of the rapes are left on their own to deal with their trauma.

---

[55] See the AVEGA-AGAHOZO website, Association of Genocide Widows, under 'history' at http://www.avega.org.rw/englishhome.htm (last visited May 2005).

[56] Organization of African Unity, International Panel of Eminent Personalities Report, *Rwanda: The Preventable Genocide*, 2000, para. 16.19.

[57] According to Nowrojee – an expert in conducting investigations regarding human rights violations during armed conflict, especially with regard to sexual violence – who appeared as an expert witness in *The Prosecutor v. Théoneste Bagosora, Gratien Kabiligi, Aloys Ntabakuze and Anatole Nsengiyumva*, Transcripts, Case No. ICTR-98-41-T, 12 July 2004, p. 34.

1.3.3 Creation of the international criminal tribunals

The ICTY was established in The Hague, the Netherlands, in 1993 and the ICTR in Arusha, Tanzania, in 1994. They were created to be able to hold the major perpetrators accountable for the most serious crimes committed in the former Yugoslavia and in Rwanda, although also low- and mid-level perpetrators have been prosecuted. Both Tribunals are comprised of three organs: Chambers, the Office of the Prosecutor and the Registry. The territorial jurisdiction of the ICTY includes the territory of the former Socialist Federal Republic of Yugoslavia and the temporal jurisdiction is phrased in an open-ended manner, so that the jurisdiction of the Tribunal concerns violations committed 'since 1991'. This created for the ICTY Prosecutor the opportunity to address international crimes committed in Croatia, Bosnia and Herzegovina, Kosovo and Macedonia; not, however, the conflict in Slovenia. The territorial jurisdiction of the ICTR covers Rwanda and its neighbouring States.[58] The ICTR's temporal jurisdiction is restricted, namely to crimes committed between 1 January and 31 December 1994.[59] Both the ICTY and the ICTR were created by the UN Security Council under Chapter VII of the UN Charter in response to the threat to international peace and security in the former Yugoslavia and in Rwanda.[60] This approach had the advantage of being expeditious (as opposed to establishing the Tribunals by treaty) and of being immediately effective as all States would be under a binding obligation to take whatever action was required to carry out a decision taken as an enforcement measure under Chapter VII.[61]

---

[58] According to the *Report of the Secretary-General Pursuant to Paragraph 5 of Security Council Resolution 955 (1994),* UN Doc. S/1995/134, 13 February 1995: 'In extending the territorial jurisdiction of the Tribunal beyond the territorial bounds of Rwanda, the Council envisaged mainly the refugee camps in Zaire and other neighbouring countries in which serious violations of international humanitarian law are alleged to have been committed in connection with the conflict in Rwanda.'

[59] According to the *Report of the Secretary-General Pursuant to Paragraph 5 of Security Council Resolution 955 (1994),* UN Doc. S/1995/134, 13 February 1995, para. 14: 'Although the crash of the aircraft carrying the Presidents of Rwanda and Burundi on 6 April 1994 is considered to be the event that triggered the civil war, the Council decided that the temporal jurisdiction of the Tribunal would commence on 1 January 1994, in order to capture the planning stage of the crimes.'

[60] Security Council Resolution 808, *on the Establishment of the ICTY,* S/RES/808 (1993), 22 February 1993; Security Council Resolution 827, *on the Establishment of the ICTY*, S/RES/827 (1993), 25 May 1993. The full name of the ICTY reads: 'The International Tribunal for the Prosecution of Persons Responsible for Serious Violations of International Humanitarian Law Committed in the Territory of the Former Yugoslavia since 1991.' For the ICTR, see Security Council Resolution 955, *on the Establishment of the ICTR,* S/RES/955, 8 November 1994. Its full name reads: 'the International Criminal Tribunal for the prosecution of persons responsible for genocide and other serious violations of international humanitarian law committed in the territory of Rwanda and Rwandan citizens responsible for genocide and other such violations committed in the territory of neighbouring States between 1 January and 31 December 1994.'

[61] *Report of the Secretary-General Pursuant to Paragraph 2 of Security Council Resolution 808 (1993),* UN Doc. S/25704, 3 May 1993, para. 23. See also Article 29 ICTY Statute and Article 28 ICTR Statute on 'Co-operation and Judicial Assistance'.

The ICTY was established after having considered, *inter alia*, the interim and final reports of the Commission of Experts, set up to examine and analyse the situation in the territory of the former Yugoslavia.[62] In its 1992 interim report, the Commission of Experts concluded that grave breaches and other violations of international humanitarian law had been committed in the territory of the former Yugoslavia, including wilful killing, ethnic cleansing, mass killings, torture, *rape*, pillage and destruction of civilian property, destruction of cultural and religious property and arbitrary arrests.[63] In Resolution 820 of 17 April 1993, the Security Council condemned once again 'all violations of international humanitarian law, including in particular the practice of "ethnic cleansing" and *the massive, organized and systematic detention and rape of women*'.[64] The 1994 Final Report of the Commission of Experts states that 'throughout the various phases of the armed conflicts in the former Yugoslavia, there have been numerous reports of *widespread and systematic rape and other forms of sexual assault*'.[65] The massive scale of the rapes of women thus proved to be one of the impetuses for setting up an international criminal tribunal that was able to try persons on the basis of individual criminal responsibility. For the first time in history, rape was explicitly recognised to have taken place in an armed conflict and, as such, given explicit standing in the ICTY Statute under Article 5(g) as a crime against humanity.

The ICTR was established after the Security Council had reviewed various official United Nations reports which indicated that acts of genocide and other systematic, widespread and flagrant violations of international humanitarian law had been committed in Rwanda.[66] In one of these reports, prepared by the Independent

---

[62] Security Council Resolution 780, *on the Establishment of a Commission of Experts for the former Yugoslavia*, S/RES/780 (1992), 6 October 1992; *Report of the Secretary-General on the Establishment of the Commission of Experts Pursuant to Paragraph 2 of Security Council Resolution 780 (1992)*, S/24657, 14 October 1992. The UN Security Council had already expressed its grave concern with regard to the situation in the former Yugoslavia in a number of Resolutions, *inter alia*: Security Council Resolution 764, *on Bosnia and Herzegovina,* S/RES/764, 13 July 1992; Security Council Resolution 771, *on the Former Yugoslavia*, S/RES/771, 13 August 1992. See also the Final Report of the United Nations Commission of Experts Established Pursuant to Security Council Resolution 780 (1992), *Annex II – Rape and Sexual Assault: A Legal Study*, S/1994/674/Add.2 (Vol.1), 28 December 1994.

[63] *Interim Report of the Commission of Experts Established Pursuant to Security Council Resolution 780 (1992)*, S/25274, 11 February 1993 (emphasis added).

[64] Security Council Resolution 820, *Bosnia and Herzegovina*, S/RES/820, 17 April 1993, para. 6 (emphasis added).

[65] *Final Report of the Commission of Experts Established Pursuant to Security Council Resolution 780 (1992)*, S/1994/674, 27 May 1994, para. 232 (emphasis added) and, in particular, paras. 232-253; Final Report of the United Nations Commission of Experts Established Pursuant to Security Council Resolution 780 (1992), *Annex II – Rape and Sexual Assault: A Legal Study*, S/1994/674/Add.2 (Vol.1), 28 December 1994.

[66] *Preliminary Report of the Independent Commission of Experts Established Pursuant to Security Council Resolution 935 (1994)*, S/1994/1125, 4 October 1994; *Final Report of the Commission of Experts Established Pursuant to Security Council Resolution 935 (1994)*, S/1994/1405, 9 December 1994; *UN Commission on Human Rights, Report on the Situation of Human Rights in Rwanda Prepared by the Special Rapporteur of the Commission on Human Rights, in Accordance*

Commission of Experts, it is noted that 'disturbing reports have been filed ... that document the abduction and *rape* of women and girls in Rwanda during the period of armed conflict in Rwanda'.[67] The Commission considered rape to be both a breach of international humanitarian law and a crime against humanity. In addition, it stated that 'there are clear cases where rape, which undoubtedly constitutes "serious bodily or mental harm", is perpetrated under a responsible command as a systematic policy alongside or as part of a larger policy that is "committed with intent to destroy, in whole or in part, a national, ethnic, racial or religious group, as such"'.[68] The Commission of Experts was thus of the opinion that the sexual violence crimes that had taken place during the Rwandan conflict may have even amounted to the crime of genocide. In subsequent cases brought before the Rwanda Tribunal, sexual violence was indeed charged and successfully prosecuted as genocide. Again, sexual violence crimes were thus recognised to have taken place and, as such, were stated explicitly as 'rape' under the crimes against humanity provision (Article 3(g)) and as 'rape' and 'enforced prostitution' under the war crimes provision of the ICTR Statute (Article 4(e)).

The Statutes of both Tribunals explicitly prohibit rape and can thus be seen as a clear improvement in comparison with their forerunners, the Nuremberg and Tokyo Tribunals, where gender-specific sexual violence crimes had not been included in the Statutes. Prosecutions of and convictions for sexual violence under the specific gender-related crimes in the Statutes have taken place in the Tribunals' existence (rape as a crime against humanity (both ICTY and ICTR) and outrages upon personal dignity, in particular humiliating and degrading treatment, rape, enforced prostitution and any form of indecent assault as a serious violation of Common Article 3 and Additional Protocol II (ICTR only)[69]). Prosecutions and/or convictions have also resulted under other crimes, crimes without any clear reference to sexual violence, such as enslavement, torture, persecution and other inhumane acts as crimes against humanity (both ICTY and ICTR); causing serious bodily or mental harm to members of the group as genocide (both ICTY and ICTR); and torture, inhumane treatment, wilfully causing great suffering or serious injury to body or health as grave breaches (ICTY only); cruel treatment, torture, outrages upon personal dignity, in particular humiliating and degrading treatment, and even rape as an independent crime, as violations of the laws or customs of war (ICTY only); and violence to life, health and physical or mental well-being of persons, in particular cruel treatment such as torture, mutilation or any form of corporal punishment as violations of Common Article 3 to the 1949 Geneva Conventions and Additional Protocol II (ICTR only).[70] The war crimes provisions in the

with Commission Resolution S-3/1 and Economic and Social Council Decision 1994/223, S/1994/1157, Annexes I and II, 13 October 1994.

[67] *Final Report of the Commission of Experts Established Pursuant to Security Council Resolution 935 (1994)*, S/1994/1405, 9 December 1994, para. 136 (emphasis added). Compare the Final Report of the Commission of Experts with the Preliminary Report of the Commission of Experts, in which no mention of any sexual violence crimes committed against women is made.

[68] *Ibid.*, para. 145.

[69] Note that although individuals were charged on this basis, it did not result in any convictions.

[70] See the Chart on sentencing in cases of sexual violence in Chapter 6. Note that there are no convictions under the grave breaches provision for ICTR cases. This is because the Rwandan conflict was deemed internal and as a result the grave breaches provision is not laid down in the ICTR Statute.

ICTY and ICTR Statutes were largely based on the 1949 Geneva Conventions and 1977 Additional Protocols thereto, where rape and other forms of sexual violence were explicitly and implicitly laid down. If sexual violence had not been prosecuted under less explicit provisions on sexual violence in the Statutes, but only under the explicit sexual violence provisions, sexual assaults could not have been prosecuted 'to the fullest extent'.[71]

Not only substantive supranational criminal law has been improved by the establishment of the Tribunals, both Statutes also include certain unprecedented procedural rules on sexual violence which take into account sensitivities when victims of sexual violence are to testify in court. Such a shift in attention to victims' interests and rights can partly be explained by earlier achievements made in this field by the victimology movement, for example by the 1985 UN Victims Declaration and the 1985 Council of Europe Recommendation on the Position of the Victim in the Framework of Criminal Law and Procedure.[72] In order to enhance the participation of victims of sexual violence in court proceedings, the following Articles and Rules of Procedure and Evidence (RPE) common for the ICTY and ICTR were in particular developed: Rule 96 (specifying that the testimony of a victim of sexual violence does not need to be corroborated, that consent is not an issue where coercive circumstances are involved and that evidence on prior sexual conduct is not admitted); Article 22 ICTY Statute/Article 21 ICTR Statute and Rules 69, 75 and 79 (on protective measures during court proceedings in order to protect victims' and witnesses' privacy, dignity and security); and Rule 34 (on the Victim and Witnesses Unit, which may recommend protective measures for victims and witnesses and provide counselling and support, in particular to victims and witnesses of sexual violence).[73] Rule 34 furthermore states that 'due consideration shall be given, in the appointment of staff, to the employment of qualified women'.

In total, the ICTY indicted 162 persons,[74] 58 of whom have been charged with, *inter alia*, sexual violence – thus almost one third of the total number of persons indicted. At the end of the ICTR's mandate (2008-2010),[75] it is foreseen that the Tribunal will have prosecuted between 65 and 70 individuals, 35 individuals of whom

---

[71] Viseur Sellers and Okuizumi (1997), p. 57.

[72] Declaration of Basic Principles of Justice for Victims of Crime and Abuse of Power, UN General Assembly Res. 40/34, 29 November 1985, UN Doc. A/RES/40/34 (1985 Victims Declaration); Recommendation No. R (85) 11 of the Committee of Ministers to Member States of the Council of Europe on the Position of Victims in the Framework of Criminal Law and Procedure, 28 June 1985, Rec. 85(11) E.

[73] The ICTY RPE were first adopted on 11 February 1994, and amended several times, the last time on 11 March 2005, UN Doc. IT/32/Rev.36; the ICTR RPE were first adopted on 29 June 1995, and amended several times, the last time on 21 May 2005.

[74] See ICTY website, *The ICTY at a Glance/Key Figures of ICTY Cases*, at http://www.un.org/icty/cases-e/factsheets/procindex-e.htm (last visited June 2005).

[75] See Security Council Resolution 1503, *on the International Criminal Tribunal for the former Yugoslavia and International Criminal Tribunal for Rwanda*, S/RES/1503 (2003), 28 August 2003, in which the ICTR and ICTY were urged to complete all investigations by 2004, all trials by 2008 and all appeals by 2010. The Resolution also called for a separate Prosecutor for the ICTR.

(thus about half of the total number of indictees) will have been charged with, *inter alia*, crimes of a sexual violence nature.

1.4 The ICC

The creation of an international criminal court became a reality in the summer of 1998. In Rome, the ICC Statute was approved by the United Nations Conference of Plenipotentiaries, 120 States voting in favour, 7 against and 21 abstaining.[76] Following the deposit of ten ratifications on 11 April 2002, bringing the total number of ratifying States to 66 (thus, more than the 60 ratifications required), the ICC received permanent jurisdiction over genocide, crimes against humanity and war crimes as of 1 July 2002.[77] The ICC, which has its seat in The Hague, the Netherlands, is not to replace national courts; it will be complementary to national criminal jurisdictions. The Court will only investigate and prosecute when a State is unwilling or unable to genuinely prosecute. Unlike the *ad hoc* Tribunals, the ICC is based on a treaty created by consensus among States Parties, namely the ICC Statute. Article 5 of the ICC Statute lists the crimes which fall within the jurisdiction of the ICC and which are considered 'the most serious crimes of concern to the international community as a whole', namely genocide, crimes against humanity, war crimes and the crime of aggression.[78] The crimes are defined in Articles 6 (genocide), 7 (crimes against humanity) and 8 (war crimes), and a very detailed description of the crimes is furthermore provided in the Elements of Crimes (EoC), an unprecedented, non-binding document.[79] The Court may exercise its jurisdiction with respect to the crime of genocide, crimes against humanity and war crimes either when the situation is referred to the Prosecutor by a State Party or by the Security Council or when the Prosecutor decides to initiate an investigation on his or her own account and on the basis of information received. However, in the latter case the Prosecutor must obtain the authorisation of the Pre-Trial Chamber before starting the investigation. In the two situations other than Security Council referral, the Court may exercise its jurisdiction only if either the State on the territory of which the suspected crime occurred or the State of which the person suspected of having committed the crime is a national is a State Party to the Statute. If neither is a State Party to the Statute, the Court will not be in a position to investigate the suspected crimes, except if either the State of territoriality or the State of nationality of the suspected person accepts the exercise of jurisdiction of the Court by declaration lodged with the Registrar. Furthermore, only crimes committed after 1 July 2002 are eligible

[76] Among the countries voting against the Court were, *inter alia*, the US and China.

[77] Article 126 ICC Statute.

[78] Agreement on the crime of aggression has not yet been reached: see Article 5(2) ICC Statute. As the crime of aggression is not relevant for the purpose of this study, it will not be further discussed.

[79] Assembly of States Parties, *Elements of Crimes*, adopted by the Assembly of States Parties, First Session, New York, 3-10 September 2002, Official Records, 9 September 2002, ICC-ASP/1/3.

for trial by the Court.[80] As of 1 June 2005, 99 countries are States Parties to the Rome Statute.[81]

Strong debates on gender issues featured in the Preparatory Commission (PrepCom) sessions,[82] six in total, which took place from 1996 to 1998.[83] Increasing attention for gender issues can be noticed when comparing the early documents of the PrepCom (no demonstrable concern for gender issues) with the later PrepCom documents and the final ICC Statute. There was a strong lobby from the Women's Caucus for Gender Justice, composed of approximately 200 women's organisations from all regions of the world, advocating the inclusion of gender and sexual violence crimes as well as fair gender representation in all organs of the Court to be included in the ICC Statute.[84] Major controversies existed with regard to the definition of 'gender' and the crime of 'enforced prostitution'.[85] However, as a result of the Women's Caucus's hard-wrought work, gender was defined in the Statute as referring to the 'context of society', including sociological differences between men and women (Article 7(3) ICC Statute), and paved the way for including a non-discrimination provision including gender (Article 21(3) ICC Statute). Gender furthermore features in the crimes against humanity of persecution, which can be based on gender, and enslavement, which may include trafficking in persons, in particular women and children. Although some opposition existed as to the crime of forced pregnancy, no serious opposition existed as to including the other gender and sexual violence crimes in the ICC Statute, and therefore the ICC Statute addressed, at least on paper, some of the defects in the traditional treatment of sexual violence crimes under international treaties and Tribunals.

With the not self-standing sexual violence crimes of the ICTY and ICTR in mind, the ICC Statute has now explicitly laid down a number of sexual violence crimes unprecedented in supranational criminal law. For the first time, rape, sexual slavery, enforced prostitution, forced pregnancy, enforced sterilisation or any other form of

---

[80] Article 11 ICC Statute. See also Article 24 on non-retroactivity: '1. No person shall be criminally responsible under this Statute for conduct prior to the entry into force of the Statute.'

[81] See ICC website, *Assembly of States Parties/The States Parties to the Rome Statute*, at http://www.icc-cpi.int/asp/statesparties.html (last visited June 2005). Out of the 99 States, 27 are African States, 12 are Asian States, 15 are from Eastern Europe, 20 are from Latin America and the Caribbean and 25 are from Western Europe and other States.

[82] See generally Moshan (1998), pp. 154-184; Steains (1999), pp. 357-390.

[83] *Report of the Preparatory Committee on the Establishment of an International Criminal Court, Proceedings of the Preparatory Committee during March-April and August 1996*, Volume 1, GA 51st Session, Supp. No. 22, A/51/22 (1996), 1 January 1996; *Decisions taken by the Preparatory Committee at its Session held in New York*, 11 to 21 February 1997, A/AC.249/1997/L.5 (1997), 12 March 1997; *Decisions taken by the Preparatory Committee at its Session held in New York*, 4 to 15 August 1997, A/AC.249/1997/L.8/Rev.1 (1997), 14 August 1997; *Decisions taken by the Preparatory Committee at is Session held in New York*, 1 to 12 December 1997, A/AC.249/1997/L.9/Rev.1 (1997), 18 December 1997; *Report of the Inter-Sessional Meeting from 19 to 30 January 1998*, Zutphen, The Netherlands, A/AC.249/1998/L.13 (1998), 4 February 1998 (the report was used as a basis at the sixth PrepCom session from 16 March – 3 April 1998). These documents can be found in Bassiouni (1998).

[84] See Bedont and Hall Martinez (1999), pp. 65-85; Pace and Schense (2001), pp. 718-722.

[85] Steains (1999), p. 366.

sexual violence of comparable gravity were laid down in an international instrument, both as a crime against humanity and as a war crime. Also, sexual violence crimes can now be prosecuted under the crime against humanity of persecution on the basis of gender. Other non-specific sexual violence crimes, such as the crimes against humanity of torture, enslavement and other inhumane acts, can be used as a basis for prosecuting sexual violence crimes as well. The war crimes provision similarly includes such non-specific sexual violence crimes. And, although the genocide provision is copied verbatim from the 1948 Genocide Convention, in the ICC EoC a footnote is attached to this crime in which rape and sexual violence are recognised as falling within the scope of genocide. As regards the *chapeau* or jurisdictional elements of the crimes, the crimes laid down in the ICC Statute differ from the definitions of the crimes used in the ICTY and ICTR Statutes. Even though the genocide provision remains unchanged, the crimes against humanity and war crimes provisions have changed considerably. The *chapeau* of crimes against humanity mentions the additional requirement of 'knowledge of the attack', a requirement which was never set before. The war crimes provision states an additional requirement of 'in particular', in the sense that the court is to have jurisdiction over war crimes 'in particular when committed as part of a plan or policy or as part of a large-scale commission of such crimes'. This seems to imply that single, isolated crimes against women may not easily qualify for trial by the court.

Procedural changes have marked the establishment of the ICC as well. Of particular importance are the Rules of Evidence in cases of sexual violence (specifying that the testimony of a victim of sexual violence does not need to be corroborated, that consent is not an issue where coercive circumstances are involved and that evidence on prior sexual conduct is not admitted), protection and support, participation and reparation. Participation and reparation were not taken into account within the ICTY and ICTR, and can be considered to be great achievements on the supranational criminal law level. For the first time, victims can participate in the supranational criminal proceedings and they can request and be awarded reparation by the Court. In addition, a Trust Fund for victims and their families has been set up. The Victim and Witness Unit within the Court's Registry will be able to provide protective measures, security arrangements, counselling and other appropriate assistance for witnesses, victims and others at risk on account of their testimony. Furthermore, this Unit must include staff with expertise in trauma, including trauma related to crimes of sexual violence. A separate provision on the protection of victims and witnesses requires the Court to take appropriate measures, including proceedings in camera or allowing the presentation of evidence by electronic means, to protect the safety, physical and psychological well-being, dignity and privacy of victims and witnesses, taking into account such factors as age, gender, health and the nature of the crime, particularly where the crime involves sexual or gender violence. Furthermore, the Statute requires that 'fair representation of female and male judges' be taken into account in the selection process (seven out of sixteen judges are women), as well as a fair representation of women and men in the selection of staff in the Office of the Prosecutor and in all other organs of the Court. For the selection of judges, prosecutors and other staff, legal expertise in violence against women or children must be taken into account. The Prosecutor is required to appoint advisers with legal expertise in specific issues including sexual and gender violence. The Prosecutor can refer cases to the ICC *proprio motu*, acting on information from NGOs. This is particularly important for victims of crimes of a sexual nature since it allows Women's NGOs to provide the Prosecutor with information which might not be forthcoming if left to the women victims because of the shame generally attached to these crimes.

1.4.1 Situations pending before the Court

The Prosecutor of the Court has started investigations into three situations, all in Africa, that is to say the Democratic Republic of Congo, the Republic of Uganda and Sudan.[86] The first two countries had referred the situations to the Prosecutor themselves.[87] The situation of Darfur in Sudan had been referred to the Prosecutor by the Security Council.[88] Finally, the Central African Republic also referred its situation to the Court, and the Prosecutor is currently carrying out an analysis in order to determine whether to initiate an investigation.[89] In all four conflicts, mass rape and other forms of sexual violence have taken place, and it is therefore to be expected that sexual violence will be included among the charges in the ICC indictments.[90] It must be noted that a proper conduct of the investigative phase is crucial if sexual violence conduct is to be taken up by the Court.[91]

---

[86] ICC Press Release, *The Office of the Prosecutor of the International Criminal Court Opens its First Investigation*, The Hague, 23 June 2004; ICC Press Release, *Prosecutor of the International Criminal Court Opens an Investigation into Northern Uganda*, The Hague, 29 July 2004; ICC Press Release, *The Prosecutor of the ICC Opens Investigation in Darfur*, The Hague, 6 June 2005.

[87] ICC Press Release, *President of Uganda Refers Situation Concerning the Lord's Resistance Army (LRA) to the ICC*, The Hague, 29 January 2004; ICC Press Release, *Prosecutor Receives Referral of the Situation in the Democratic Republic of Congo*, The Hague, 19 April 2004.

[88] Security Council Resolution 1593, *Reports of the Secretary-General on Sudan*, S/RES/1593 (2005), 31 March 2005.

[89] ICC Press Release, *Prosecutor Receives Referral Concerning Central African Republic*, The Hague, 7 January 2005.

[90] See, *inter alia*, the following reports on sexual violence in the Democratic Republic of Congo: Human Rights Watch (2002); Amnesty International (2004e). On the Central African Republic, see Amnesty International (2004f). On northern Uganda, see Human Rights Watch (2003b). On Sudan, see Amnesty International (2004b); Amnesty International (2004c); Médecins Sans Frontières (2005).

[91] According to the Coalition for Women's Human Rights in Conflict Situations with regard to the situation of the ICTR: 'one of the major stumbling blocks to effective prosecution of sexual violence at the OTP [Office of the Prosecutor] is the lack of attention to this issue by the Investigations division. In particular, we believe that your disbanding of the Sexual Assault Team in the Investigations division of OTP in 2000 has corresponded to a significant decrease in attention to the collection of sexual violence evidence. The leadership in the investigations unit appears to have interpreted your disbanding of this team as a signal to diminish attention to this issue. We are also concerned that investigators continue to receive no training on interviewing methodology for rape victims, and the majority of the investigators are male' (Coalition for Women's Human Rights in Conflict Situations, *Letter to Prosecutor Carla del Ponte*, 12 March 2003). The investigative phase of the Court's proceedings is as such not examined in this study.

1.5 The way ahead

As far as the supranational criminal prosecution of sexual violence is concerned, a real breakthrough came with the establishment of the ICTY and the ICTR. Their existence has made an important contribution to the development of the law and procedure related to sexual violence. But the practice before the Tribunals has also shown the difficulties and gaps as far as prosecuting sexual violence at the international level is concerned. Such insights have nevertheless been useful during ICC Statute negotiations, resulting in substantive and procedural provisions with more attention for the interests of victims of sexual violence than the Tribunals had had before. Apart from this positive input, supranational criminal law and procedure still remains a relatively new area of law, likely to face many unforeseen challenges. As regards sexual violence prosecutions, challenges lie ahead as to the best possible interpretation of the law and procedure to attain in the interest of victims of sexual violence testifying before the Court. This study deals with these challenges.

2 Central question

This study is focused on the supranational criminal prosecution of crimes of a sexual violence nature, notably on the question whether supranational criminal law and procedure are adequate from the perspective of victims of sexual violence. In addition, the legal consequences arising from the supranational criminal law system – sentencing and reparation – are examined from the point of view of victims of sexual violence. The study is therefore divided into three subquestions: (1) How is and how should sexual violence be prosecuted as an international crime, that is as genocide, as a crime against humanity and a war crime?; (2) What is and what should be the trial procedures to be followed in cases of sexual violence in order to enhance the effective participation of victims of sexual violence, without compromising the rights of the defence?; and (3) How are and how should sentences for perpetrator's of sexual violence be determined and what are and what should be the possibilities of receiving reparation for victims of sexual violence stemming from the supranational criminal law system?

The three subquestions will be adressed from the perspective of the supranational criminal law system, that is the criminal law system of the international criminal tribunals – the ICTY and the ICTR – and the ICC.[92] The supranational criminal law system sees to the prosecution of individuals who are alleged to have committed international crimes and is monitored by a global court, with an independent prosecutor and judges from all over the world, applying global provisions and rules. With its roots in the 1990s, the supranational criminal law system is still a relatively new system, in which different law families, traditions and systems have come together, that is national criminal law – common and civil as well as inquisitorial and adversial –, international human rights law and international humanitarian law. Although certain definitions, concepts or issues may be clear in the various law families, traditions or systems, this may not be the case within the supranational criminal law system. Each definition,

---

[92] With the term 'supranational criminal law and procedure' reference is made to the laws and procedures before the Court and Tribunals. In this study, the terms 'supranational criminal law/procedure/prosecution/law system' are used. Supranational criminal law as a system *sui generis* has been used before by Haveman (2003a), pp. 1-8; Haveman (2003b), pp. 9-38.

concept or issue has to be (re-)discussed and (re-)interpreted from scratch, which is all the more difficult because different players from different backgrounds are involved. Although the Statutes, the RPE of the Court[93] and the Tribunals are helpful in finding the law and procedure to be applied, as are the EoC for the ICC, the practice of the Tribunals has not always shown a consistent approach when it comes to interpreting definitions and concepts laid down in their codes. Considering the relatively new phase supranational criminal law and procedure are in, the Tribunals are still searching for the right definitions and procedures to be applied within the global context in which the Tribunals operate. The situation will not be much different for the Court.

In this study, the prosecution of sexual violence within the framework of the new supranational criminal law system is examined. On a substantive supranational criminal law level, elements of crimes of a sexual violence nature need to be redefined. This becomes especially clear when one keeps in mind the way in which the definition of the crime of rape has developed before the Tribunals, amounting to three totally different definitions altogether. What conduct falls under the crime of rape in supranational criminal law? The same question applies, *mutatis mutandis*, to other crimes of a sexual violence nature. On a supranational criminal procedural level, concepts and measures which enhance the effective participation of victims and witnesses of rape and sexual assault in the Court's judicial procedures need to be re-evaluated, without losing sight of the rights of the defence to a fair trial. One may think of the rules promulgated especially for victims of sexual violence, such as those related to evidence, protection and support. The ICC faces the challenge to create a fair and consistent supranational criminal law system, with due regard to sexual violence prosecutions. In terms of prosecuting sexual violence, supranational criminal law is almost without precedent and, as such, the ICC will have to rediscuss the substantive as well as procedural framework in which it operates, with a clear understanding of the context in which wartime sexual violence takes place. Sexual violence during times of genocide, crimes against humanity or war occurs in coercive circumstances and, as such, requires definitions and procedures which match the reality of the nature of the crimes. Does the supranational criminal law system adequately take into account the realities of sexual violence crimes in its substantive law and procedures? In addition to supranational criminal prosecutions resulting in a sentence, victims of sexual violence may be in need of reparation, which will enable them to start building up their lives again after conflict. How does the supranational criminal law system deal, and how should it deal, with their claims for reparation?

3 Terminology

This study deals with victims of sexual violence during times of genocide, crimes against humanity and armed conflict. In order to understand what is meant by 'victims' and 'sexual violence' throughout this study, brief definitions and discussions of these and similar terms are given below.

---

[93] See also Assembly of States Parties, *Rules of Procedure and Evidence*, adopted by the Assembly of States Parties, First Session, New York, 3-10 September 2002, Official Records, 9 September 2002, ICC-ASP/1/3.

3.1 Victims, survivors, witnesses and victim-witnesses

The term 'victims' is defined in Rule 85 of the ICC RPE as follows:

> (a) "Victims" means natural persons who have suffered harm as a result of the commission of any crime within the jurisdiction of the Court;
> (b) Victims may include organizations or institutions that have sustained direct harm to any of their property, which is dedicated to religion, education, art or science or charitable purposes, and to their historic monuments, hospitals and other places and objects for humanitarian purposes.

From this definition it follows that not only natural persons may qualify as victims, but also organisations and institutions.[94] The definition of victims departs from the one given for the ICTY and ICTR, which is restricted to 'a person against whom a crime over which the Tribunal has jurisdiction has allegedly been committed'.[95] The ICC definition of victims is thus broader than its ICTY/R counterpart, in the sense that all who have suffered harm may qualify as victims before the ICC, which may include immediate family members or dependants of those who have suffered harm.[96] Furthermore, the ICC definition truly recognises a victim as a victim from the moment he or she reports the crime, whereas the ICTY/R definition only seems to recognise a victim from the moment the guilt of the accused has been established. The ICC definition of victims should be embraced, as it offers the best possible protection of the rights and interests of the victim, e.g., to be informed of his or her rights and opportunities, to seek redress and to participate in the proceedings.[97]

Where, in this study, reference is made to 'victims', in most cases reference is made to victims who have suffered harm as a result of sexual violence committed against them, as part of the crime of genocide, crimes against humanity or war crimes. Although not necessarily having the same meaning, the words 'victims' and 'survivors' are used interchangeably throughout this study.[98] The term 'witness' or 'victim-witness' is also often used, and refers to the situation in which victims of sexual violence take

---

[94] Rule 85(b) ICC RPE reads 'victims may include', and it will thus be up to the Court to decide on whether or not organisations or institutions are considered as victims in a particular case; they do not automatically qualify as victims. See Fernandez de Gurmendi (2001), p. 433.

[95] Rule 2A ICTY/R RPE.

[96] Although strong opposition existed as to the inclusion of the definition of victim as contained in the 1985 Victims Declaration, the current definition strongly resembles the broad definition of victims laid down in that declaration. For an overview of the negotiations on the definition of victims, see Fernandez de Gurmendi (2001), pp. 427-433.

[97] On this point, see Brienen and Hoegen (2000), p. 30.

[98] A victim may not always be a survivor, especially in cases where victims of sexual violence have died following or as a result of the harm done. According to the Law No. 02/98 of 22/01/1998 establishing a National Assistance Fund for Needy Victims of Genocide and Massacres Committed in Rwanda between October 1, 1990 and December 31, 1994: '"survivor" means a person who survived the genocide and massacres committed in Rwanda between October 1, 1990 and December 31, 1994, consisting in acts meant to: (i) exterminate persons and destroy their property because of their ethnic origin; (ii) exterminate persons and destroy their property because of their opinion or of those of close relatives who were against genocide and massacres.'

part in the trial proceedings as witnesses only, to help the Prosecution and the Defence to discover the truth. This is in particular the situation before the Tribunals. The term 'witness' may however, also refer to a person who has witnessed a crime which, on most occasions in this study, will be a crime of a sexual violence nature. Depending on the context of the sentence, the meaning of the words used will in most cases be obvious.

3.2 Sexual violence and gender crimes

Whilst men may also be targeted for sexual violence during conflict, it is an acknowledged fact that sexual violence primarily and disproportionately affects women, particularly when it rises to the level of genocide, crimes against humanity or war crimes. Before the Tribunals, this is particularly evidenced by the female survivors of sexual violence who constituted the majority of victim-witnesses testifying about their ordeal. Therefore, this study is particularly concerned with female victims of sexual violence. However, though to a far lesser extent, sexual violence has also been used against men during conflict and must therefore not be underestimated;[99] for this reason, male sexual assault has been incorporated in this study. Before the Tribunals, male sexual assault has been charged and succesfully prosecuted.[100] The term 'sexual violence' is used in this study, as it is gender neutral, applying to men, women and children, and it emphasises the sexual element of the violence committed. The term 'sexual violence' has been defined in the ICTR *Akayesu* case, and will also be applied in this study:

> The Tribunal considers sexual violence, which includes rape, as any act of a sexual nature which is committed on a person under circumstances which are coercive. Sexual violence is not limited to physical invasion of the human body and may include acts which do not involve penetration or even physical contact.[101]

Several forms of sexual violence have been explicitly listed in the ICC Statute as crimes against humanity and war crimes, viz. rape, sexual slavery, enforced prostitution, forced pregnancy, enforced sterilisation and any other form of sexual violence.

The term 'gender' has been defined in the ICC Statute in Article 7(3) as follows: '... the term "gender" refers to the two sexes, male and female, within the context of society.' Gender violence is violence that is targeted at women or men because of their sex and/or their socially constructed gender roles. Gender violence may be sexual in

---

[99] See, *inter alia*, Oosterhoff (2000).

[100] See, *inter alia*, Čelebići Judgment, paras. 1039, 1072 (forcing two brothers to commit fellatio on each other and placing a burning fuse cord around the genital areas of a prisoner); Tadić Opinion and Judgment, para. 730 (forcing two prisoners to commit fellatio on each other and to sexually mutilate another prisoner); Todorović Sentencing Judgment, paras. 38-40 (forcing one prisoner to bite another prisoner's penis, ordering prisoners to perform oral sex on each other); Karadžić and Mladić Rule 61 Decision, para. 13 ('... many men were also victims of rape and sexual assault by the Serbian forces. On several occasions, brothers or parents were forced to have sexual contact with one another').

[101] Akayesu Judgment, paras. 598, 688. Rape is here defined as: 'A physical invasion of a sexual nature, committed on a person under circumstances which are coercive.'

nature, but also non-sexual. Gender in this study more precisely points to the gender of the person who has been attacked by means of sexual violence, woman or man, and gender violence is sometimes even a more appropriate term than 'sexual violence' as some crimes of a sexual violence nature can only be committed against women because of their reproductive capacity, such as forced pregnancy. This study therefore mainly deals with those sexual violence crimes which are directed against persons on the basis of their gender. For the purposes of the study, the term 'sexual violence' is used most often and, in most situations, incorporates sexual violence directed against women (or men) on the basis of their gender.

4 Working materials

The ICC Statute, its RPE and the EoC, together with – and compared to – the ICTY and ICTR Statutes, their RPE and case law constitute the primary subjects of research.[102] Some remarks about the status of these legal sources in international law should be made here.

The Court and the Tribunals are governed by their respective statutes, consisting of a 'fusion and synthesis' of the common law and civil law traditions.[103] The statutes qualify as sources of international law in conformity with Article 38 of the Statute of the International Court of Justice (ICJ). Under this provision, the sources of international law include international conventions, international customs, general principles of law, judicial decisions and the writings of the most distinguished publicists.[104] However, the

---

[102] Article 21 ICC Statute ('Applicable Law') reads:

1. The Court shall apply:
   (a) In the first place, this Statute, Elements of Crimes and its Rules of Procedure and Evidence;
   (b) In the second place, where appropriate, applicable treaties and the principles and rules of international law, including the established principles of the international law of armed conflict;
   (c) Failing that, general principles of law derived by the Court from national laws of legal systems of the world including, as appropriate, the national laws of States that would normally exercise jurisdiction over the crime, provided that those principles are not inconsistent with this Statute and with international law and internationally recognized norms and standards.
2. The Court may apply principles and rules of law as interpreted in its previous decisions.
3. The application and interpretation of law pursuant to this article must be consistent with internationally recognized human rights, and be without any adverse distinction founded on grounds such as gender as defined in article 7, paragraph 3, age, race, colour, language, religion or belief, political or other opinion, national, ethnic or social origin, wealth, birth or other status.

Article 22 ICC Statute, furthermore, contains the *nullum crimen sine lege* principle. For a discussion of this principle in relation to the crimes falling under the ICC Statute, see Boot (2002).

[103] Čelebići Judgment, para. 159.

[104] Article 38 of the Statute of the International Court of Justice reads:

list in Article 38 is not exhaustive and other sources of international law, such as decisions of international organisations and *jus cogens*, have been recognised by the ICJ as well.[105] Seen in this perspective, the ICC Statute, created as a treaty by the States Parties, qualifies as a source of international law pursuant to Article 38(1)(a) of the ICJ Statute, i.e., an international convention. The ICC Statute reflects to a considerable extent the *opinio juris* of a great number of States and provides a strong indication of the status of customary international law.[106] 'Notwithstanding Article 10 of the Statute, the purpose of which is to ensure that existing or developing law is not "limited" or "prejudiced" by the Statute's provision, resort may be had *cum grano salis* to these provisions to help elucidate customary international law.'[107] Depending on the matter at issue, the ICC Statute may be taken 'to restate, reflect or clarify customary rules or crystallise them, whereas in some areas it creates new law or modifies existing law'.[108] The ICC EoC elaborate on the elements of the crime of genocide, crimes against humanity and war crimes in minute detail and constitute a document *sui generis* within supranational criminal law. The Elements are not binding on the judges as they '... *shall assist* the Court in the interpretation and application of Articles 6, 7 and 8' and 'amendments thereto [to the EoC] shall be consistent with this Statute'.[109] The Statutes of the Tribunals, on the other hand, were set up by Resolutions of the United Nations Security Council acting under Chapter VII of the UN Charter, and therefore qualify as sources of international law not mentioned specifically under Article 38 of the ICJ Statute, as they are decisions of an international organisation.

The RPE, a merger of common law and civil law elements, cover almost all aspects referred to in the Statutes and are necessary for the operation of the Court and the Tribunals. The difference in the establishment of the Tribunals on the one hand and the Court on the other has resulted in different promulgation of the RPE, which, at least in the case of the ICC, as a treaty should be considered a source of international law. In

---

1. The Court, whose function is to decide in accordance with international law such disputes as are submitted to it, shall apply:
   a. international conventions, whether general or particular, establishing rules expressly recognized by the contesting states;
   b. international custom, as evidence of a general practice accepted as law;
   c. the general principles of law recognized by civilized nations;
   d. subject to the provisions of Article 59, judicial decisions and the teachings of the most highly qualified publicists of the various nations, as subsidiary means for the determination of rules of law.
2. This provision shall not prejudice the power of the Court to decide a case *ex aequo et bono*, if the parties agree thereto.

[105] See further Villiger (1997).

[106] See Kupreškić, Kupreškić, Kupreškić, Josipović, Papić and Santić Judgment, para. 580; Furundžija Judgment, para. 227.

[107] Furundžija Judgment, para. 227.

[108] *Ibid.*

[109] Article 9(1) ICC Statute (emphasis added). Similar wording can be found in paragraph 1 of the 'General introduction' to the EoC.

the case of the Tribunals, the powers to promulgate[110] and amend[111] the procedural and evidentiary rules have been, within certain limits, entrusted to the judges of the Tribunals. The Statute of the Court, on the other hand, provides that the RPE be adopted[112] and amended[113] by a two-thirds majority of the Assembly of States Parties. Whereas the RPE applicable to the Tribunal can, after careful consideration by the judges, be amended to meet the needs of the Tribunal, the rules applicable to the ICC can not be amended or fine-tuned so easily.[114] The RPE are subordinate to the Statute in the case of a conflict between the two.[115]

Case law emerging from the ICTY and the ICTR also serves as an important object of study and qualifies as a source of international law, either as international customary law or as a general principle of law pursuant to Article 38(1)(b) and (c), respectively. In international law, the existence of a rule of customary law needs to be evidenced through State practice and *opinio juris*.[116] If a judgment does not constitute evidence of a customary rule, it may be indicative of the emergence of a general principle of law or be a persuasive authority concerning the existence of a rule or principle.[117] Case law is furthermore explicitly listed as a subsidiary means for the determination of rules of law under Article 38(1)(d) under 'judicial decisions'.

The issue of precedents or *stare decisis* has for the Tribunals been settled by the *Aleksovski* Appeals Chamber judgment. According to this judgment, the legal principle or *ratio decidendi* of the Appeals Chamber decisions are binding upon Trial Chambers in order to ensure a single, unified, coherent and rational body of law.[118] Decisions of Trial Chambers have no binding force on each other, although a Trial Chamber is free

---

[110] Article 15 ICTY Statute; Article 14 ICTR Statute.

[111] Rule 6 ICTY and ICTR RPE.

[112] Article 51 ICC Statute.

[113] Article 51(2) ICC Statute in conjunction with Rule 3 ICC RPE. Article 51(3) contains a temporary exception to the rule, and states '... in urgent cases, where the Rules do not provide for a specific situation before the Court, the judges may, by a two-thirds majority, draw up provisional Rules to be applied until adopted, amended or rejected at the next ordinary or special session of the Assembly of States Parties'.

[114] See further Boas (2000), pp. 270-276.

[115] Article 51(4) and (5) ICC Statute.

[116] In the North Sea Continental Shelf cases the ICJ stated, with respect to customary international law: 'Not only must the acts concerned amount to a settled practice, but they must also be such, or be carried out in such a way, as to be evidence of a belief that this practice is rendered obligatory by the existence of a rule of law requiring it' (*North Sea Continental Shelf Cases (Federal Republic of Germany v. Denmark; Federal Republic of Germany v. The Netherlands)*, Judgment, 20 February 1969, ICJ Reports 1969, p. 3). Similarly, in the case of the Continental Shelf (Libyan Arab Jamahiriya/Malta) the ICJ recalled in paragraph 27 that 'the material of customary international law is to be looked for primarily in the actual practice and *opinio juris* of States' (International Court of Justice, *Case Concerning the Continental Shelf (Libyan Arab Jamahiriya/Malta)*, Judgment, 3 June 1985, ICJ Reports 1985, No. 68, pp. 13-49). See also *Military and Paramilitary Activities in and against Nicaragua (Nicaragua v. US)*, Judgment, 27 June 1986, ICJ Reports 1986, No. 70, pp. 14-140.

[117] Kupreškić, Kupreškić, Kupreškić, Josipović, Papić and Santić Judgment, para. 540.

[118] Aleksovski Appeal Judgment, para. 113.

to follow the decision of another Trial Chamber if it finds that decision persuasive.[119] Yet, judgments of one and the same Trial Chamber are generally taken into consideration and cannot easily be dismissed without sound reason. The ICC Statute has taken up a specific provision on this matter, namely Article 21(2), where it is explicitly stated that 'the Court may apply principles and rules of law as interpreted in its previous decisions'. As far as judgments of the Tribunals are concerned, the Court may apply the rules found therein when these decisions are considered to constitute 'principles or rules of international law' within the terms of Article 21(1)(b) of the ICC Statute.[120] This will especially be true when a reasoning behind a determination made by the Tribunals is directly based on those found in general sources of international law.[121]

International (human rights) treaties and national law and case law have also been consulted. In this study, recourse to national law and case law has mainly been done in connection with such an exercise by the Tribunals themselves, as for instance in the case of the definition of rape, and has not been a study on its own. The approach taken by the *Furundžija* Trial Chamber has been followed in this study, namely when no definition of a crime can be found in international law, a general concept may be derived from the general principles or notions of the subject, common to the major legal systems in the world.[122] In the *Furundžija* case, the Trial Chamber held that such an exercise can only be justified under certain conditions:

> (i) unless indicated by an international rule, reference should not be made to one national legal system only, say that of common-law or that of civil-law States. Rather, international courts must draw upon the general concepts and legal institutions common to all the major legal systems of the world. This presupposes a process of identification of the common denominators in these legal systems so as to pinpoint the basic notions they share; (ii) since 'international trials exhibit a number of features that differentiate them from national criminal proceedings', account must be taken of the specificity of international criminal proceedings when utilising national law notions. In this way a mechanical importation or

[119] *Ibid.*, para. 114.

[120] Boot (2002), p. 393.

[121] *Ibid.*

[122] See Furundžija Judgment, para. 177; see also the Kupreškić, Kupreškić, Kupreškić, Josipović, Papić and Santić Judgment, para. 540. See also Kunarac, Kovač and Vuković Judgment, para. 439: 'The value of these sources [the general principles of law common to the major national legal systems of the world] is that they may disclose "general concepts and legal institutions" which, if common to a broad spectrum of national legal systems, disclose an international approach to a legal question which may be considered as an appropriate indicator of the international law on the subject.' In the Kunarac, Kovač and Vuković Judgment (para. 439) it is made clear that the judges are not looking for definitions, but for general principles, common to a broad range of legal systems: 'In considering these national legal systems the Trial Chamber does not conduct a survey of the major legal systems of the world in order to identify a specific legal provision which is adopted by a majority of legal systems but to consider, from an examination of national systems generally, whether it is possible to identify certain basic principles, or in the words of the Furundžija Judgment, "common denominators", in those legal systems which embody the *principles* which must be adopted in the international context.'

> transposition from national law into international criminal proceedings is avoided, as well as the attendant distortions of the unique traits of such proceedings.[123]

Although general principles of law can be useful in some areas of law that are underdeveloped and where no international law definitions exist, recourse to national laws should thus always be had in a cautious manner with due regard for the reality of the nature of the crimes. An analogy can be drawn here with regard to the transferral of elements of crimes from one body of law, say international human rights law, to another, say international humanitarian law. In order to do so, account has always to be taken of the specific differences that exist between these two bodies of law: 'the role and position of the state as an actor is completely different in both regimes' and 'the part of international criminal law applied by the Tribunal is a penal law regime'.[124] That a definition of an offence is largely a function of the environment in which it develops was made clear in the *Kunarac, Kovač and Vuković* case with respect to the crime of torture. Although recourse was had to the 1984 Torture Convention, the Trial Chamber held, as confirmed on appeal:

> ... the definition of torture under international humanitarian law does not comprise the same elements as the definition of torture generally applied under human rights law. In particular, the Trial Chamber is of the view that the presence of a state official or of any other authority-wielding person in the torture process is not necessary for the offence to be regarded as torture under international humanitarian law.[125]

Therefore, the definitions of crimes at the supranational criminal law level all need to be evaluated and re-evaluated in order to see whether they fit the reality of the crime.

Finally, doctrine has been taken into account as a source of international law (Article 38(1)(d) ICJ Statute). The past few years have seen an abundance of articles and books on the laws and procedures of the International Criminal Tribunals and the Court, not in the least in relation to sexual violence crimes. Overwhelmed at times by the wealth of literature available and emerging on the topic, this study has aimed to include the writings of the most distinguished publicists.

5 Method and Structure

The adequacy of supranational criminal prosecutions of sexual violence will primarily be examined from the point of view of the ICC, the future benchmark for supranational criminal prosecutions, with clear reference to the ICTY and ICTR practice in the field of sexual violence prosecutions. The ICTY and ICTR practice on sexual violence may

---

[123] Furundžija Judgment, para. 178 (with reference to the Separate and Dissenting Opinion of Judge Cassese in the Erdemović Appeal Judgment, para. 5). See also the Appeals Chamber in Blaškić which cautioned against 'the transposition onto the international community of legal institutions, constructs or approaches prevailing in national law' as it 'may be a source of great confusion and misapprehension' (*Prosecutor v. Tihomir Blaškić*, Judgment on the Request of the Republic of Croatia for Review of the Decision of Trial Chamber II of 18 July 1997, Case No. IT-95-14-AR108bis, 29 October 1997, para. 40).

[124] Kunarac, Kovač and Vuković Judgment, para. 470.

[125] *Ibid.*, para. 496. See also paras. 465-497.

be indicative of both the achievements and the shortcomings of the supranational criminal law system when it comes to sexual violence prosecutions. Considering that the ICTY and the ICTR serve as the sole predecessors of the ICC (both in terms of 'playing field' and the influence of the Tribunals' work on the Court's provisions), the ICC may greatly benefit from their experience.

The format of this study varies with the topics and serves the subject of study rather than the other way around. For example, when discussing the definition of rape in supranational criminal law, the ICTY and ICTR case law is discussed first, followed by the definition of rape as given in the ICC EoC. In order to understand the ICC definition of rape, the case law of the ICTY and the ICTR has to be discussed first considering its impact on the elements of and thinking about the crime of rape as laid down in the EoC. The same applies, among other things, for the discussion on anonymity measures and on the way in which such protective measures relate to victims of sexual violence. In light of the ICTY's contribution to solving the issue of anonymity measures, it is important to outline the Tribunal's point of view on anonymity before discussing the provisions on anonymity applicable before the Court. For again other topics, examination of the problem occurs from the perspective of the ICC, most of the time in tandem with relevant experiences of the ICTY and ICTR, if available. As an example, the prosecution of sexual violence as genocide can be mentioned.

The order in which the crimes are dealt with in Part I (genocide, crimes against humanity, war crimes) is inspired by the crimes' order of appearance in the Statute of the ICC. As with all crimes in (supranational) criminal law, a division between *actus reus* and *mens rea* has been made.[126] The following crimes, which specifically refer to sexual violence – rape, sexual slavery, enforced prostitution, forced pregnancy, enforced sterilisation or any other form of sexual violence of comparable gravity – are listed in Article 7(1)(g) (on crimes against humanity) and an identical set of crimes is listed in Articles 8(2)(b)(xxii) and 8(2)(e)(vi) (on war crimes in international and internal armed conflict, respectively). In order not to repeat the same subject matter, these specific sexual violence crimes are only discussed in the Chapter on crimes against humanity, but apply, *mutatis mutandis*, to the relevant paragraphs under the war crimes provision.[127] This decision is supported by the order of appearance of the crimes in the Statute, i.e., the specific sexual violence crimes appear for the first time in the Statute as crimes against humanity and will therefore be discussed exhaustively in Chapter 2 on crimes against humanity only. Individual criminal responsibility for perpetrators of sexual violence crimes is discussed in Chapter 1 and aims to address the main difficulties and possibilities of prosecuting individuals for sexual violence under genocide, crimes against humanity and war crimes.[128] As protective and special measures, on the one hand, and participation, on the other, may come up at similar times during the Court's proceedings, the order of the Chapters in Part II is taken randomly and does not correspond with the order of appearance of these topics in the ICC RPE. Part III deals with the legal consequences of the supranational criminal law system:

126 See also Article 30 ICC Statute ('Mental Element').

127 Initially, these specific sexual violence crimes were negotiated under the war crimes provisions, subsequently transferred and re-adjusted under the crimes against humanity provision. See Robinson (2001c), p. 93.

128 See Article 25 ICC Statute ('Individual Criminal Responsibility'). Individual criminal responsibility is listed in the ICTY and ICTR Statutes under Article 7 and Article 6, respectively.

upon a guilty verdict, the accused will be sentenced and the victim will be entitled to reparation. In both situations – sentencing and reparation – the Chambers exercise relatively wide discretionary powers, which constitutes another argument for discussing the two topics in a separate part of the study.
This study aims at addressing the subject of supranational criminal prosecution of sexual violence from the perspective of substantive law and procedural law, as well as the legal consequences arising from the system. It is divided into four Parts. In Part I, the ways in which sexual violence can be prosecuted under the substantive law of the Court and Tribunals, i.e., genocide, crimes against humanity and war crimes, are examined. In Part II, the procedural issues involved when prosecuting sexual violence before the Court and Tribunals are investigated. In Part III, the sentencing of perpetrators of sexual violence and the reparation possibilities for victims of sexual violence are discussed. Each Part starts with an introduction and concludes with an evaluation. The study concludes with some observations and recommendations as regards the possibilities that exist for a more comprehensive supranational criminal prosecution of sexual violence (Part IV). For ease of reference, an Appendix with ICTY and ICTR judgments on sexual violence has been included in this study.

Part I
Part I concentrates on the supranational criminal prosecution of sexual violence as genocide (Chapter 1), crimes against humanity (Chapter 2) and war crimes (Chapter 3), crimes which are part of the *rationae materiae* jurisdiction of both the Court and the Tribunals. In addition, criminal liability for sexual violence as genocide, crimes against humanity and war crimes is examined within the first two Chapter, with special focus on the difficulties of linking the perpetrator to the sexual violence crime or crimes and prosecutorial strategies still remaining or underexploited. With the creation of the supranational criminal law system, a new or refined meaning had to be attributed to the crimes laid down in the ICC Statute, including the specific sexual violence crimes. In the first part of this study, the conduct which is associated with sexual violence crimes will be examined. In other words, what are the definitions of the crimes listed in the ICC Statute under which sexual violence may be prosecuted? Within the context of the Court, the EoC will be of guidance in determining the definitions of the crimes laid down in the ICC Statute. However, this document is not binding on the judges, and in order to arrive at accurate definitions of crimes of a sexual violence nature at a supranational criminal law level, other sources of law need to be consulted, i.e., international humanitarian law, international human rights law, national criminal law, doctrine and the case law of the Tribunals as far as they are not already represented in the definitions laid down in the EoC. Perhaps even more important from the victim's point of view is the requirement that the definitions of the specific sexual violence crimes are in conformity with the reality of the nature of the crimes.

Part II
Part II focuses on victims and witnesses of sexual violence and their treatment within supranational criminal procedure, notably how to enhance the effective participation of victims and witnesses of sexual violence in the Court's judicial procedures without compromising the right of the accused to a fair trial. Particular attention is given to topics or rules that deal with sexual violence or gender as a relevant factor in the proceedings such as protective and special measures (Chapter 4) and participation in

court (Chapter 5). These topics will in particular be examined from the point of view of the ICC's Statute and RPE. The practice of the Tribunals as regards these issues may help to establish the areas of procedure in which increased sensitisation on gender issues may be needed to enable victims and witnesses to testify. Whereas agreement may exist on many of these topics at the domestic level, they may all need to be rediscussed at the supranational criminal law level. The difficulties wartime survivors of sexual violence are confronted with when giving testimony before the Court about their ordeal must be kept in mind.

Part III
The final part deals with the legal consequences of the supranational criminal law system: sentencing and reparation. With regard to sentencing (Chapter 6), the practice of the Tribunals in determining sentences for convicted persons of sexual violence crimes is reviewed. Which factors are important in arriving at the sentence and do the judges adequately address such factors where the prosecution of sexual violence is concerned? The outcome may influence the sentencing of the ICC. As far as reparation is concerned (Chapter 7), the (best) possibilities for victims of sexual violence of receiving reparation from the Court, stemming from supranational criminal prosecutions, are examined. In light of the harsh physical, psychological and social consequences resulting from wartime sexual violence, including stigmatisation associated with sexual violence and HIV/AIDS, which most heavily impacts on female victims, female victims of sexual violence should be considered a special category of victims in need of reparation.

6 Scope and Limitations

When analysing such a fundamental and vast topic as supranational criminal prosecution of sexual violence, it is essential to set boundaries and make choices. First of all, a choice in criminal justice systems has been made. Supranational criminal law is not only applied at the supranational level, but also at the national and 'semi-international' levels. However, this study is only concerned with supranational criminal law as applied at the supranational level (ICC, ICTY, ICTR). National war crimes trials have merely been noted rather than taken into account as an object of study. This is not to say that the case law and overall experience of the Tribunals and the Court should not serve as guides for national war crimes trials when applying supranational criminal law.[129] As a matter of fact, this may even be a prerequisite if the application of supranational criminal law is ever to be applied in a coherent and fair manner. Semi-international systems such as the UN Special Courts of East-Timor, Cambodia, Kosovo and Sierra Leone have also been left out of this study. The statutes of these courts largely represent the law of the ICTY and ICTR and case law has been scarce; in the case of Sierra Leone so far non-existent. It must be noted here that in the case of the Special Court of Sierra Leone some improvements with regard to the prosecution of

[129] In order to meet the deadline of the Tribunals' completion strategy (2008-2010), in 2005, the ICTY and ICTR have referred a substantial caseload to countries, including the countries where the conflicts originally took place. The courts in these countries could benefit from the experiences, work and practice of the two Tribunals.

sexual violence have been made, both in its statutory provisions and regulations and in its (limited) practice.[130]

A second limitation concerns the scope of the crimes falling within the jurisdiction of the Tribunals and the Court. Whereas crimes against humanity and genocide do not necessarily require a link to armed conflict situations and therefore apply to peacetime situations as well, this study mainly concentrates on sexual violence crimes committed in non-peacetime situations, as was the case during the conflicts in the former Yugoslavia and in Rwanda. The ICC will, however, have the power to address sexual violence crimes committed outside conflict situations, such as large-scale enforced prostitution. Even though this is a welcome development, it is not to be expected that the Court will take up such cases shortly, considering the impact it will have on the sovereignty of State concerned. Rather, it is expected that the Court will first and foremost concentrate on crimes committed during conflict situations.

In the third place, this study is not aimed at providing an unambiguous answer to the question how victims or (victim-)witnesses of sexual violence view the work of the Tribunals and the Court in terms of prosecuting sexual violence. A general answer to such a question seems difficult to give, especially given the fact that each person has a different background, experiences and character, which influences the way in which a victim of sexual violence experiences the proceedings. This study is therefore not concerned with quantitative research, but views and perceptions of individual victims of sexual violence are nonetheless integrated in this study where available and applicable.

Finally, this study does not intend to give an overall account of the conflicts that took place in the former Yugoslavia and in Rwanda (*inter alia* the lead-up to the outbreak of the conflicts, the involvement or, rather, non-involvement of the international community, the non-sexual violence crimes committed, etc.); such studies have been done by others.[131] This study deals with the context in which sexual violence occurred as well as the nature of the crimes, which have both been briefly described in subsections 1.3.1 (the former Yugoslavia) and 1.3.2 (Rwanda) of this Introduction and which will be elaborated upon in Part I, where testimonies of victims of sexual violence are described. It should, above all, be kept in mind that this study is to be seen as forward-looking, focusing on current and future conflicts in which sexual violence is or will be committed and in which the Court may play a part in. The ways in which the Tribunals have generally dealt with sexual violence prosecutions may serve as guidance for the Court in the fulfilment of its mandate.

This study was concluded on 1 July 2005.

---

[130] For example, whereas the ICTY and ICTR Statutes only list 'rape' as a crime against humanity explicitly, Article 2 of the Statute of the Special Court of Sierra Leone lists 'rape, sexual slavery, enforced prostitution, forced pregnancy and any other form of sexual violence' as crimes against humanity. Furthermore, 'forced marriage' is charged against RUF (Revolutionary United Front) and AFRC (Armed Forces Revolutionary Council) indictees as an 'inhumane act' under crimes against humanity for the first time in the history of international law.

[131] See, *inter alia*: African Rights (1995a); Gourevitch (1998); Des Forges (1999); Dallaire (2003); Silber and Little (1997); Burg and Shoup (1999); Gow (2003).

PART I
SEXUAL VIOLENCE IN SUPRANATIONAL CRIMINAL LAW

Q. Les cadavres que vous avez pu observer qui gisaient aux barrages routiers ou dans les différents sites, je voudrais attirer votre attention sur le cadavre des femmes. En ce qui concerne ces cadavres que vous avez pu observer, je voudrais que vous nous donniez plus d'informations.

R. Je ne peux pas vous dire que c'était une procédure normale qu'avaient adoptée les radicaux ou les extrémistes, mais ce qu'on peut dire, c'est que sur de nombreux sites - je parle d'informations que j'ai reçues et qui m'ont été données par les informateurs et que moi-même j'ai pu voir, à savoir qu'il y avait de jeunes filles et de jeunes femmes qu'on couchait par terre et dont les vêtements étaient redressés... remontés sur la tête, et vous pouviez voir du sperme qui a séché, et tout cela pouvait me dire... m'indiquer... permettait de déduire que ces femmes ont été violées. Et il y a toutes sortes de choses qui étaient introduites dans leur vagin. Il y avait des femmes dont les seins avaient été sectionnés, et sur le visage, on pouvait voir les traits horrifiés de ces personnes-là. Toutes ces femmes-là étaient couchées sur leur dos. Il y avait certains hommes qui, également, avaient été mutilés, notamment au niveau de leurs parties génitales. Un certain nombre de femmes ont eu les seins sectionnés, le ventre ouvert. Mais je dirais que de manière générale, sur les sites, on pouvait trouver toute jeune fille et des jeunes femmes qui ont été violées. En tout cas, c'est la déduction qu'on pouvait en faire.

Examination-in-Chief of General Roméo Dallaire, former force commander of UNAMIR in Rwanda in *Le Procureur c. Théoneste Bagosora, Gratien Kabiligi, Aloys Ntabakuze et Anatole Nsengiyumva*, Transcription Caviardee, Affaire Nº ICTR-98-41-T, 20 janvier 2004, p. 32.

Q. With respect to the female corpses, in particular, did you make any observations about any particular characteristics that those corpses may have had?

A. Yes, two things, really. One, when they killed women it appeared that the blows that had killed them were aimed at sexual organs, either breasts or vagina; they had been deliberately swiped or slashed in those areas. And, secondly, there was a great deal of what we came to believe was rape, where the women's bodies or clothes would be ripped off their bodies, they would be lying back in a back position, their legs spread, especially in the case of very young girls. I'm talking girls as young as six, seven years of age, their vaginas would be split and swollen from obviously multiple gang rape, and then they would have been killed in that position. So they were laying in a position they had been raped; that's the position they were in.

Rape was one of the hardest things to deal with in Rwanda on our part. It deeply affected every one of us. We had a habit at night of coming back to the headquarters and, after the activities had slowed down for the night, before we went to bed, sitting around talking about what happened that day, drink coffee, have a chat, and amongst all of us the hardest thing that we had to deal with was not so much the bodies of people, the murder of people -- I know that can sound bad, but that wasn't as bad to us as the rape and especially the systematic rape and gang rape of children. Massacres kill the body and rape kills the soul. And there was a lot of rape. It seemed that everywhere we went, from the period of 19th of April until the time we left, there was rape everywhere near these killing sites.

Examination-in-Chief of Major Brent Beardsley, former executive assistant to General Roméo Dallaire, force commander of UNAMIR in Rwanda, in *The Prosecutor v. Théoneste Bagosora, Gratien Kabiligi, Aloys Ntabakuze and Anatole Nsengiyumva*, Transcripts, Case No. ICTR-98-41-T, 3 February 2004, pp. 51-52.

INTRODUCTION TO PART I

In order to prosecute sexual violence at the supranational criminal law level, sexual violence must be recognised as a constituent crime of genocide, crimes against humanity and war crimes. After all, these international crimes, which shock the conscience of mankind, are the crimes over which the Tribunals and the Court have jurisdiction. Although the historical development of criminalising sexual violence as an international crime has come a long way, a definitive change was brought about by the establishment of the Tribunals. Rape as a crime against humanity was explicitly laid down as an international crime in the Statutes of both Tribunals. Rape was also criminalised in the ICTR Statute as an outrage upon personal dignity under Common Article 3 and Additional Protocol II. Furthermore, in order to be able to prosecute sexual violence to the fullest extent, sexual violence was also prosecuted under other non-specific sexual violence crimes, such as torture. Over time, the ICTY also acknowledged the independent customary war crime status of rape as a violation of the laws or customs of war, punishable under Article 3 of the ICTY Statute. Influenced by these experiences and a strong NGO lobby, the ICC has further worked towards the goal of criminalising crimes of a sexual violence nature; many different types of sexual violence are now explicitly recognised and laid down in the ICC Statute.

Despite the increased recognition of rape and other forms of sexual violence as serious international crimes, it cannot be denied that the supranational criminal system is still a relatively new law system composed of different law families and traditions, a system that is still growing and needs space to grow, and in which therefore no settled definitions of crimes exist. So, how do we construe the correct definition of rape or sexual slavery? Although the (non-binding) Elements of Crimes will be of guidance in determining the definitions of the sexual violence crimes laid down in the ICC Statute, other sources of law will need to be consulted such as international humanitarian law, international human rights law, national criminal law, doctrine as well as the case law of the Tribunals. However, should the definitions of sexual violence crimes not first and foremost fit the reality of the crimes? And has this been taken up at the supranational criminal law level? These questions and related ones are addressed in Part I.

CHAPTER 1
SEXUAL VIOLENCE AS GENOCIDE

1 INTRODUCTION

As the world was shocked by the atrocities committed by the Germans during World War II, the crime of genocide and its participatory forms were laid down in Articles II and III of the 1948 Convention on the Prevention and Punishment of the Crime of Genocide (hereinafter Genocide Convention), respectively. They read:

> Article II
> … genocide means any of the following acts committed with intent to destroy, in whole or in part, a national, ethnical, racial or religious group, as such:
>
> (a) Killing members of the group;
> (b) Causing serious bodily or mental harm to members of the group;
> (c) Deliberately inflicting on the group conditions of life calculated to bring about its physical destruction in whole or in part;
> (d) Imposing measures intended to prevent births within the group;
> (e) Forcibly transferring children of the group to another group.
>
> Article III
> The following acts shall be punishable:
>
> (a) Genocide;
> (b) Conspiracy to commit genocide;
> (c) Direct and public incitement to commit genocide;
> (d) Attempt to commit genocide;
> (e) Complicity in genocide.[1]

Genocide, whether committed in time of peace or in time of war by constitutionally responsible rulers, public officials or private individuals, is a crime under international law which States undertake to prevent and punish.[2] The duty to prevent and thus to act has, however, not been taken on in conflicts such as that in Rwanda, where States showed great reluctance to qualify the situation as genocide.[3] The major substantive

---

[1] Convention on the Prevention and Punishment of the Crime of Genocide, UN General Assembly Res. 260 A (III) (9 December 1948), 78 UNTS 277. The Convention entered into force in 1951 and 137 States are parties to the treaty (status June 2005).

[2] Pursuant to Articles I and IV 1948 Genocide Convention.

[3] In order to prevent the recurrence of tragedies such as the Rwandan genocide, Mr. Juan Mendez (Argentina) was appointed Special Advisor to the Secretary-General on the Prevention of Genocide on 13 July 2004 (UN Press Release, *Juan E. Mendez of Argentina Appointed Special*

provisions of the Genocide Convention, which includes the definition of genocide, is now considered to be part of customary international law.[4] The crime of genocide has, moreover, reached the level of a *jus cogens* norm, derogation from which by States is not permitted.[5]

Advisor on Prevention of Genocide, SG/A/880/BIO/3580, 14 July 2004). Mr. Mendez needs to communicate to the Secretary-General, and through him the Security Council, on potential situations that could result in genocide and make recommendations to prevent or halt genocide (*Outline of the Mandate for the Special Advisor on the Prevention of Genocide,* Annex to Letter dated 2004/07/12 from the Secretary-General addressed to the President of the Security Council, S/2004/567, 13 July 2004). On the role of the Special Advisor on Prevention of Genocide, see further Letschert (2005). Despite the duty to prevent and punish and the appointment of a Special Advisor on Prevention of Genocide, the international community has refrained from taking action in Darfur, Sudan. The United Nations has refrained from labelling the situation in Darfur genocide, because the government's authorities' genocidal intent to destroy a particular group was found to be absent. Instead, an UN report concluded that killings, torture, enforced disappearances and sexual violence were carried out on a widespread and systematic basis and could amount to crimes against humanity and war crimes. See *Report of the International Commission of Inquiry on Darfur to the United Nations Secretary General: Pursuant to Security Council Resolution 1564 of 18 September 2004,* Geneva, 25 January 2005. It is estimated that at least 180,000 people may have died over the past eighteen months; 2,000,000 people have sought refuge in camps in Darfur's main towns; and about 200,000 people have fled to neighbouring Chad. See BBC News, *UN's Darfur Death Estimates Soars*, 14 March 2005. Thousands of women have been raped by government backed armed militia, the Janjawid, including gang rapes, and have been abducted for the purposes of sexual slavery. See, *inter alia*, Amnesty International (2004c); Médecins Sans Frontières (2005).

[4] See International Court of Justice, *Reservations to the Convention on the Prevention and the Punishment of the Crime of Genocide*, Advisory Opinion, ICJ Reports 1951, 28 May 1951, p. 23. See also the Akayesu Judgment, para. 495; Rutaganda Judgment and Sentence, paras. 45-46; Musema Judgment and Sentence, para. 151; and Krstić Judgment, para. 541.

[5] Article 53 ('Treaties Conflicting with a Peremptory Norm of General International Law (*jus cogens*)') of the Vienna Convention on the Law of Treaties (23 May 1969, 1155 UNTS 331) states: 'A treaty is void if, at the time of its conclusion, it conflicts with a peremptory norm of general international law. For the purposes of the present Convention, a peremptory norm of general international law is a norm accepted and recognized by the international community of States as a whole as a norm from which no derogation is permitted and which can be modified only by a subsequent norm of general international law having the same character.' Genocide has been explicitly held to constitute a *jus cogens* norm in, *inter alia*, *Application of the Convention on the Prevention and Punishment of the Crime of Genocide (Bosnia and Herzegovina v. Serbia and Montenegro)*, Further Requests for the Indication of Provisional Measures, 13 September 1993, p. 440; *Final Report of the Commission of Experts Established Pursuant to Security Council Resolution 935 (1994),* S/1994/1405, 9 December 1994, Annex, para. 152. See also, *inter alia*, the Kayishema and Ruzindana Judgment, para. 88; Stakić Judgment, para. 500.

Largely influenced by the nature of the crime in international customary law,[6] several decades later the definition of genocide and its participatory forms were copied verbatim into the Statutes of the ICTY (Article 4) and the ICTR (Article 2).[7] The same applies to the ICC Statute, in which the genocide definition of the 1948 Genocide Convention was adopted, without much controversy,[8] in Article 6.[9] The Tribunals and the Court thus have the power to prosecute persons who committed genocide or any of the participatory forms of genocide.

In the genocide definition, explicit reference to gender as a group capable of being destroyed and sexual violence as a constituent act of genocide is blatantly absent. This can be explained when considering the *travaux préparatoires* to the 1948 Genocide Convention, where no explicit reference was made to rape as a means of committing genocide or to destruction of a group on the basis of gender.[10] While the 1947 Draft Genocide Convention listed 'racial, national, linguistic, religious or political groups of human beings',[11] the 1948 Genocide Convention is confined to 'national, ethnical, racial or religious groups'. A discussion of the question whether women should be considered to constitute a separate group within the framework of the Convention was therefore clearly lacking. As far as the prohibited acts were concerned, the 1947 Draft Genocide Convention referred to 'biological genocide', that is, 'restricting births by: (a) sterilization and/or compulsory abortion; or (b) segregation of the sexes; or (c) obstacles to marriage',[12] a subparagraph which later became paragraph (d), 'imposing measures intended to prevent births within the group'. In the Draft, the listing of the acts was preceded by the sentence '[i]n this Convention, the word "genocide" means a criminal act directed against any one of the aforesaid groups of human beings, with the purpose of destroying it in whole or in part or of preventing its preservation or development'.[13] The phrase 'preventing its preservation or development' refers to the acts of biological genocide; they were omitted in the definitive version of the Genocide Convention. The effects thereof were limited, however, as the paragraph on 'biological genocide', now paragraph (d), ('imposing measures intended to prevent births within the group'),

---

[6] In the UN Report on the establishment of the ICTY, the Secretary-General stated that 'it should apply only those rules of international humanitarian law which are part of customary law beyond any doubt'. The 1948 Genocide Convention was explicitly cited. See Report of the Secretary-General Pursuant to *Paragraph 2 of Security Council Resolution 808 (1993),* UN Doc. S/25704, 3 May 1993, para. 45.

[7] In contrast to the 1948 Genocide Convention, the Statutes of the ICTY and ICTR incorporate the definition of genocide and the participatory forms of genocide in one article, viz. Articles 4 and 2, respectively.

[8] Oosterveld (2001), pp. 41-49; Garraway (2001), pp. 49-55; Rückert and Witschel (2001), pp. 59-70; Steains (1999), p. 363.

[9] In contrast to the ICTY and ICTR, the ICC does not include the participatory forms of genocide in Article 6 on genocide itself, but includes forms of participation in Article 25, which is applicable to genocide as well as to other crimes within the Court's jurisdiction.

[10] See also McDonald (1998), pp. 135-136.

[11] Article I(I) of the First Draft of the Genocide Convention, prepared by the UN Secretariat, May 1947, UN Doc. E/447.

[12] *Ibid.*, Article I(II)(2).

[13] *Ibid.*, Article I(II).

remained and has been interpreted to include the examples mentioned in the 1947 Draft Convention. The phrase 'serious bodily or mental harm', which could have provided the opportunity for including rape and other forms of sexual violence as examples thereof, instead listed examples such as 'subjection to conditions of life which, by lack of proper housing, clothing, food, hygiene and medical care, or excessive work or physical exertion are likely to result in the debilitation or death of the individuals' and 'mutilations and biological experiments imposed for other than curative purposes'.[14] Apart from these observations, no attention was given to rape and other forms of sexual violence as such and how they may achieve the destruction of a group different from biological genocide.

The absence of women as a group and sexual violence as a prohibited act in the genocide definition may give the impression that sexual violence cannot be a means of committing genocide and/or to destroy women as a group through sexual violence. Following the case law of the ICTR in particular, this misunderstanding has been partly remedied. In the *Akayesu* case, rendered in 1998, the judges explicitly recognised that sexual violence can constitute genocide in the same way as any other act, provided that the criteria for the crime of genocide are met.[15] The judgment came exactly fifty years after the 1948 Genocide Convention was adopted; it was the first time that an international criminal tribunal interpreted the elements of the crime of genocide. The Trial Chamber's recognition of rape and sexual violence as genocide was innovative, and confirmed that rape and sexual violence may constitute genocidal acts despite explicit references thereto in the provision on genocide itself. The Trial Chamber did not directly deal with the question of whether women can be destroyed as a group as such, but held that the sexual violence was in particular directed against the female population of the Tutsi group. Once and for all, the *Akayesu* Judgment made clear that 'contrary to popular belief, the crime of genocide does not imply the actual extermination of [a] group in its entirety, but is understood as such once *any* one of the acts mentioned in Article 2(2)(a) through 2(2)(e) is committed with the specific intent to destroy "in whole or in part" a national, ethnical, racial or religious group'.[16] The once upheld assertion that sexual violence crimes do not rise to the level of genocide has thus been firmly repudiated.[17]

Prior to *Akayesu*, it had been argued that recognising 'genocidal rape' would result in the disappearance of the gendered nature of the crime of rape, in particular because the focus would rest on the group rather than on the individual in genocide.[18] Others felt

---

[14] *Ibid.*, Article I(II)(1). The words 'causing serious bodily or mental harm' were at that time referred to as 'injuring their health or physical integrity'.

[15] Akayesu Judgment, para. 731. That sexual violence can be a means to commit genocide was already acknowledged by the ICTY in 1996 in a Rule 61 Hearing. Rule 61 deals with the 'Procedure in Case of Failure to Execute a Warrant', see Karadžić and Mladić Rule 61 Decision, para. 94.

[16] Akayesu Judgment, para. 497 (emphasis added).

[17] See Neier (1998, p. 191), who states: 'though rape is not genocide, it is a terrible crime'. Also in this regard McDonald (1998, p. 136), who asserts that it is difficult to argue that large-scale violence against women destroys a group, in whole or in part, as these acts merely 'contribute to preventing the preservation or development of the group'.

[18] Copelon (1995), p. 199.

that one should take into account the 'intersectionality' of genocidal rape, meaning that women were raped because of their group identity (ethnicity) and because of the beliefs and opinions held amongst Hutu about Tutsi women as women (gender).[19] When the *Akayesu* Judgment established that sexual violence could constitute a means of perpetrating genocide, it basically confirmed the latter view as it was recognised that (1) genocidal rape was found to have been committed against Tutsi women because of both their ethnicity (Tutsi women and Hutu women married to or politically affiliated to Tutsi men) *and* their gender (Tutsi women being depicted as sexual objects, as seductresses, as enemies of the State – unattainable, inaccessible and sexually intriguing women who thought themselves to be better than Hutu women and who believed themselves to be too good to marry Hutu men); (2) although the intent of genocidal rape is to destroy a particular group, the act also causes the infliction of serious physical and mental harm on the victim; the harm done to the individual woman is therefore not neglected. Moreover, rape is considered to be one of the worst ways of inflicting bodily and mental harm upon an individual; and (3) rape and sexual violence can be effective tools to shatter a group, that is to say, rape and sexual violence may achieve the destruction of a group.[20]

When the *Akayesu* Trial Chamber convicted Akayesu, a former mayor of Taba commune (Gitarama), of sexual violence as genocide under the act of '(b) causing serious bodily or mental harm to members of the group', it also provided guidance on the way in which sexual violence can be interpreted as constituting the act described in (d), 'imposing measures intended to prevent births within the group'. Furthermore, the Trial Chamber noted the close connection between sexual violence and killings: the women were often killed following the rapes. For many victims of, and also witnesses to, rape and sexual violence, rape and sexual violence were considered worse than death.[21] The *Akayesu* findings with regard to sexual violence as genocide have been upheld by other Chambers, some of which basically concurred with the *Akayesu* findings (*Kayishema and Ruzindana*; *Rutaganda*; *Bagilishema*; *Krstić*). Other Trial Chambers not only upheld the *Akayesu* findings with regard to sexual violence as genocide, but also convicted the accused for sexual violence as genocide; e.g., *Musema*

---

[19] MacKinnon (1993), pp. 64-65; Nowrojee (1996).

[20] Russell-Brown (2003), pp. 351-352, 371-373. Copelon (1995, p. 199), who was initially dismissive to treat rape and genocide as one crime, later agreed that the Akayesu Judgment did not emphasise the reproductive consequences as the hallmark of rape as a genocidal measure, but instead takes into account the physical and psychological harm inflicted upon the individuals as well. See Copelon (2000), p. 228.

[21] For example, a girl who was taken to the rear of the Butare Prefecture Office to be raped on the orders of Nyamasuhuko, told Witness FAP and the other refugees on return that it was 'better to be killed than to be raped by four or more men'. See *The Prosecutor v. Pauline Nyiramasuhuko, Arsène Shalom Ntahobali, Alphonse Nteziryayo, Sylvain Nsabimana, Elie Ndayambaje and Joseph Kanyabashi*, Transcripts, Case No. ICTR-98-42-T, 11 March 2003, p. 60. In the Musema case, 'Witness N testified before the Chamber that Nyiramusugi, who was left for dead by those who raped her, had indeed been killed in a way. Indeed, the Witness specified that "what they did to her is worse than death".' See Musema Judgment and Sentence, para. 933 (the judgment was quashed on appeal). Jeanne, a rape survivor of the 1994 genocide in Rwanda, said that 'rape is a crime worse than others. There's no death worse than that' (Nowrojee (1996), p. 75).

(under paragraph (b), but quashed on appeal); *Gacumbitsi* (under paragraph (b)); and *Muhimana* (under paragraph (b)). In *Kayishema and Ruzindana*, it was furthermore ruled that rape could also be prosecuted under paragraph (c), 'deliberately inflicting on the group conditions of life calculated to bring about its physical destruction in whole or in part'. Charges of genocidal rape are furthermore recorded in a number of Tribunal cases, some of which are pending (*inter alia, Butare*;[22] *Government I*;[23] and *Milosević*[24]), others are still awaiting trial (*inter alia, Karadžić and Mladić*;[25] *Krajisnik*;[26] and *Kovačević*[27]), and in another case the evidence for a conviction was not established (*Stakić*[28]).

By contrast, in the ICC's (non-binding) Elements of Crimes (EoC), a footnote is attached to the crime of genocide concerning 'serious bodily or mental harm', clarifying that 'this conduct may include, but is not necessarily restricted to, acts of torture, *rape, sexual violence* or inhumane or degrading treatment'.[29] Although the definition of

---

[22] The Prosecutor v. Pauline Nyiramasuhuko and Shalom Ntahobali, Amended Indictment, Case No. ICTR-97-21-I, 1 March 2001. Count 2 (genocide by 'killing' and 'serious bodily or mental harm') and, in the alternative, count 3 (complicity in genocide by 'killing' and 'serious bodily or mental harm').

[23] *The Prosecutor v. Édouard Karemera, Mathieu Ngirumpatse and Joseph Nzirorera*, Amended Indictment, Case No. ICTR-98-44-I, 23 February 2005. Count 3 (genocide by 'serious bodily or mental harm') and, in the alternative, count 4 (complicity in genocide by 'serious bodily or mental harm').

[24] *Prosecutor v. Slobodan Milosević*, Indictment (Bosnia), Case No. IT-01-51-I, 22 November 2001, para. 32. Count 1 (genocide by 'serious bodily or mental harm') or count 2 (complicity in genocide by 'serious bodily or mental harm').

[25] *Prosecutor v. Radovan Karadžić*, Amended Indictment, Case No. IT-95-5/18-I, 28 April 2000, para. 17. Count 1 (genocide by 'serious bodily or mental harm') and count 2 (complicity in genocide by 'serious bodily or mental harm'). *Prosecutor v. Ratko Mladić*, Amended Indictment, Case No. IT-95-5/18-I, 10 October 2002, para. 34. Count 1 (genocide by 'serious bodily or mental harm' and 'conditions of life calculated to bring about its physical destruction') and count 2 (complicity in genocide by 'serious bodily or mental harm' and 'conditions of life calculated to bring about its physical destruction').

[26] *Prosecutor v. Momcilo Krajisnik and Biljana Plavšić*, Amended Consolidated Indictment, Case No. IT-00-39 and 40-PT, 7 March 2002. Count 1 (genocide by 'serious bodily or mental harm' and 'conditions of life calculated to bring about its physical destruction') and/or count 2 (complicity in genocide by 'serious bodily or mental harm' and 'conditions of life calculated to bring about its physical destruction').

[27] *Prosecutor v. Milan Kovačević*, First Amended Indictment, Case No. IT-97-24-I, 28 January 1998. Count 1 (genocide by 'serious bodily or mental harm' and 'conditions of life calculated to bring about its physical destruction') and count 2 (complicity in genocide by 'serious bodily or mental harm' and 'conditions of life calculated to bring about its physical destruction').

[28] *Prosecutor v. Milomir Stakić*, Fourth Amended Indictment, Case No. IT-97-24-PT, 10 April 2002, para. 41 (rape and sexual assault as serious bodily or mental harm constituting genocide, or, alternatively, complicity in genocide) and paras. 48-49. However, the Trial Chamber did not find it proven that the specific intent of genocide was established. See Stakić Judgment, paras. 544-561.

[29] See footnote 3 to Article 6(b) in the EoC (emphasis added).

genocide laid down in the ICC Statute thus has not been revised to include a specific reference to sexual violence among its acts, the footnotes in the EoC were inserted to clarify specific issues or the intention of the drafters, and have the same status as the elements of crimes themselves.[30] The footnote linking rape and sexual violence to 'serious bodily or mental harm' as genocide was directly inspired by the *Akayesu* case.[31] This development clearly shows the universal recognition of sexual violence as a tool to commit genocide and abandons the long-held view of sexual violence crimes as inevitable by-products of war, not capable of reaching the level of genocide. Yet, as mentioned above, the connection between genocide and sexual violence remains unrecognised in the definition of genocide contained in the ICC Statute. Also, no reference is made to gender as a basis for group destruction in the genocide definition of the ICC Statute. Although some States had suggested to extend the list of groups with 'social and political', such attempts were largely refuted on the ground that inclusion of such groups lacked a basis in customary international law, during discussions both of at the Ad Hoc Committee and of the Preparatory Commission.[32] As a result, no proposals were made to include other groups than the four mentioned during the work on the EoC.[33]

In this chapter, the ways in which sexual violence can be prosecuted as genocide will be examined by considering both the *actus reus* and the *mens rea* requirements of genocide. In other words, how can sexual violence destroy a group? Considering the important precedent-setting decisions of the Tribunals, their case law and *obiter dicta* will be discussed in depth. As the ICC employs the same definition of genocide, reference to the ICC and/or its EoC will be made where they either reconfirm or depart from ICTY and ICTR case law. In the final section, gaps in the law concerning the prosecution of sexual violence as genocide will be pointed out and suggestions will be made as regards the potential improvement of such supranational criminal prosecutions.

---

[30] The EoC consist of four parts: a general introduction to the EoC applicable to the whole document; an introduction to the three crimes separately; the (numbered) elements of crimes themselves; and footnotes included throughout the document to clarify specific issues or the intention of the drafters. All four parts enjoy the same status. See Kelt and Von Hebel (2001), p. 17.

[31] The proposal was submitted by France and reference was made to the Akayesu Judgment. See Proposal Submitted by France, *Comments on the Proposal Submitted by the United States of America Concerning Article 6 Crime of Genocide*, PCNICC/1999/WGEC/DP.1, 18 February 1999. See also Garraway (2001), pp. 50-51; Rückert and Witschel (2001), p. 68.

[32] *Report of the Ad Hoc Committee on the Establishment of an International Criminal Court*, G.A. 50th Session, Supp. No. 22, A/50/22 (1995),1 January 1995, para. 61.

[33] Rückert and Witschel (2001), p. 66.

2 THE GENOCIDAL ACTS

The acts (or omissions[34]) which amount to genocide if committed with specific intent are listed in paragraphs (a) to (e) of the definition of genocide and constitute the *actus reus* of the crime of genocide. In this section, it is explained how sexual violence fits the legal requirements of the five acts defined as genocide; however, this will by no means be an exhaustive list of sexual violence acts.[35] Although the *mens rea* of the crime of genocide – 'the intent to destroy, in whole or in part, a national, ethnical, racial or religious group, as such' – will be discussed in the next section, it is relevant to note here that *mens rea* requirements are also incorporated in the *actus reus* of all five acts and will therefore be addressed in this section as well. Furthermore, certain acts of sexual violence which constitute genocide may be fall within different paragraphs at the same time.

2.1 Killing members of the group[36]

The *Akayesu* Trial Chamber noted that many women subjected to sexual violence were murdered thereafter. In this regard, the Trial Chamber determined: 'On the basis of the substantial testimonies brought before it, the Chamber finds that in most cases, the rapes of Tutsi women in Taba, were accompanied with the intent to kill those women. Many rapes were perpetrated near mass graves where the women were taken to be killed.'[37] It was clear to the Trial Chamber that '… the acts of rape and sexual violence, as other acts of serious bodily and mental harm committed against the Tutsi, reflected the determination to make Tutsi women suffer and to mutilate them even before killing them, the intent being to destroy the Tutsi group while inflicting acute suffering on its members in the process'.[38] In this respect, the *Akayesu* Judgment described the killing

[34] All forms of genocide include acts of omission as well. The most obvious act of omission is the one listed under (c), 'deliberately inflicting on the group conditions of life calculated to bring about its physical destruction in whole or in part'. Also less obvious acts can be committed by omission, such as killing. The Trial Chamber in the Kambanda Judgment and Sentence held that: 'Jean Kambanda acknowledges that on 3 May 1994, he was personally asked to take steps to protect children who had survived the massacre at a hospital and he did not respond. On the same day, after the meeting, the children were killed. He acknowledges that he failed in his duty to ensure the safety of the children and the population of Rwanda.' His omission to prevent the killings from taking place, was considered by the Trial Chamber to constitute the crime of genocide. See Kambanda Judgment and Sentence, paras. 39(ix) and 40(1).

[35] See also, *inter alia*, Goldstein (1993); MacKinnon (1993); Chinkin (1994), p. 333; Fischer (1996); Askin (1997), pp. 337-344; Fein (1999); Sharlach (2000); Kalra (2001); and Jones (2002).

[36] Killing and/or murder are also prohibited as crimes against humanity or war crimes. What is stated in this section with regard to sexual violence and murder can also be applied *mutatis mutandis* to killing or murder as a crimes against humanity or a war crime. For example, in the Muhimana Judgment and Sentence (paras. 570-583), the Trial Chamber considered the disembowelment of Pascasie Mukaremera, who was pregnant at the time, by cutting her open with a machete from her breasts to her vagina, murder as a crime against humanity.

[37] Akayesu Judgment, para. 733.

[38] *Ibid.*

of a pregnant woman named Alexia on the basis of testimony given by an eye-witness. This witness testified to having seen the *Interahamwe* take three women to Akayesu, upon which the latter said: 'Take them to Kinihira. Don't you know where killings take place, where the others have been killed?'[39] Upon arrival at Kinihira, the three women were forced by the *Interahamwe* to undress and were told to 'walk, run and perform exercises' so that they could 'display the thighs of Tutsi women'.[40] This took place in front of approximately two hundred people. With regard to the rape of Alexia, the *Interahamwe* said: '"Now, let's see what the vagina of a Tutsi woman feels like." ... Then one person held her neck, others took her by the shoulders and others held her thighs apart as numerous Interahamwe continued to rape her .... When she became weak she was turned over and lying on her stomach, she went into premature delivery during the rapes.'[41] The other two girls were brutally raped as well, one of them bleeding profusely from her private parts. After the rapes, all three women were placed on their stomachs and hit with sticks and killed.[42] If Alexia's baby had been killed as well, with the intent to destroy the future generation of Tutsi, this would have constituted genocidal killing. In Rwanda, a patrilineal society, Tutsi foetuses and babies had to be wiped out before they developed into subversive adults.[43] For example, witness TAQ in the *Gacumbitsi* case was asked by her attacker whether the child she was expecting was a boy or a girl, for he would split open her stomach in order to kill the child if it was a boy.[44] Witness TAQ said she did not know, and her child was therefore spared.[45]

In, *inter alia*, the *Akayesu* and *Kayishema and Ruzindana* Judgments, it was held that the intention to cause death must be present.[46] Premeditation is, however, not necessary.[47] The Trial Chambers noted that the French and English versions of the definition of genocide employ different terminology, namely *meurtre* and 'killing'. The Trial Chambers accepted the more precise French term *meurtre*, which applies to intentional homicide (the English term 'killing' also applies to unintentional homicide).[48] This approach was considered to be the more favourable one to the accused. An example of intentional killing with a sexual component is the case of

[39] *Ibid.*, para. 437.
[40] *Ibid.*
[41] *Ibid.*
[42] *Ibid.*
[43] Organization of African Unity, International Panel of Eminent Personalities Report, *Rwanda: The Preventable Genocide*, 2000, para. 16.1.
[44] Gacumbitsi Judgment, para. 203.
[45] *Ibid.*
[46] Akayesu Judgment, paras. 500-501; Kayishema and Ruzindana Judgment, paras. 101-104.
[47] Semanza Judgment and Sentence, para. 319; Kayishema and Ruzindana Appeal Judgment, para. 151.
[48] Akayesu Judgment, para. 501; Kayishema and Ruzindana Judgment, para. 103. See also: Rutaganda Judgment and Sentence, para. 50; Musema Judgment and Sentence, para. 155; Bagilishema Judgment, paras. 57-58; Semanza Judgment and Sentence, para. 319; Kajelijeli Judgment and Sentence, para. 813; Kamuhanda Judgment, para. 632; Cyangugu Judgment, para. 628.

Ruzindana, who was convicted of sexually mutilating Beatrice, a Tutsi girl of sixteen.[49] Before the Trial Chamber it had been established that Ruzindana had cut off both her breasts with a machete, and subsequently tore open her stomach.[50] Beatrice consequently died.

The Trial Chambers noted, however, that 'all the enumerated acts must be committed with intent to destroy a group in whole or in part'.[51] This would imply that 'there is virtually no difference between the two as the term "killing" is linked to the intent to destroy in whole or in part'.[52] Thus, the case law seems to suggest that the intention to cause death is hardly significant in the presence of the intent to destroy a particular group. Does this nonetheless imply that conduct which is intended to cause harm and thereby to destroy the group, but results in death, is to be prosecuted under (a) killing, or (b) causing serious bodily or mental harm? Sexual violence often indirectly leads to death. Although the perpetrator's intent may have been to rape, in many cases death may have been the indirect consequence of the rape. Especially in situations where women are left to themselves, after having endured multiple rapes by different men, having endured grave physical injuries and having no access to medical facilities whatsoever, death may follow. This will be truer still for vulnerable women, like the young, the old and the sick. A rape camp survivor who testified about a case of sexual violence committed against a young person said: 'I saw about seven or eight little girls who died after they were raped. I saw how they took them away to be raped and then brought them back unconscious.'[53] As the other rape victims were forbidden to assist, the young girls died.[54] Another example is rape by using objects, such as sharpened sticks and bottles. In the *Gacumbitsi* case, Witness TAQ testified about how she and seven other women and girls were raped by more than ten attackers. Witness TAQ, who was pregnant at the time, saw one of the women, Chantal (25 years old), with a stick inserted into her genitals. She died as a result of that act of sexual violence.[55]

In the *Kayishema and Ruzindana* case, the Prosecutor had suggested that acts not intended to cause death might be covered by (a) where death in facts results, provided the requisite specific intent is satisfied. In particular, the Prosecutor held that killing is 'merely the act of causing the death' and this 'would permit, if the need arises, a broadening of the meaning or interpretation' beyond the meaning of *meurtre* which is deliberate 'homicide'.[56] Article 6(a)-1 of the ICC's EoC requires that 'the perpetrator killed one or more persons', and a footnote to this Article states that 'the term "killed" is interchangeable with the term "caused death"'.[57] The term 'killing' is thus synonymous

[49] Kayishema and Ruzindana Judgment, paras. 470, 564.
[50] *Ibid.*, paras. 446.
[51] Akayesu Judgment, para. 501; Kayishema and Ruzindana Judgment, para. 103.
[52] Kayishema and Ruzindana Judgment, paras. 103, as upheld on appeal, Kayishema and Ruzindana Appeal Judgment, para. 151.
[53] Stiglmayer (1994), p. 120.
[54] *Ibid.*
[55] Gacumbitsi Judgment, paras. 200-204, 215, 261.
[56] Kayishema and Ruzindana Judgment, para. 102. The Trial Chamber, however, ruled that, the interpretation of 'killing' should be done in favour of the accused, i.e., the act of killing means unlawful and intentional killing. See Kayishema and Ruzindana Judgment, para. 103.
[57] Footnote 2 to Article 6(a)-1 of the EoC.

with causing death and the victim is in fact dead. According to Rückert and Witschel, the phrase was introduced 'to capture cases where a perpetrator had not "pulled the trigger" himself, but caused the death of a victim in an indirect way'.[58] The use of the phrase 'caused death' seems to leave room for covering unintentional homicide, such as the case where death is an indirect result of sexual violence.

2.2 Causing serious bodily or mental harm to members of the group

The *Akayesu* Trial Chamber found the element 'serious bodily or mental harm' to mean 'acts of torture, be they bodily or mental, inhumane or degrading treatment, persecution'.[59] In the *Kayishema and Ruzindana* Judgment, the phrase was interpreted as 'harm that seriously injures the health, causes disfigurement or causes any injury to the external, internal organs or senses'.[60] Serious mental harm has been construed as 'some type of impairment of mental faculties, or harm that causes serious injury to the mental state of the victim'.[61] The harm suffered may thus be physical, mental or both. 'Causing serious bodily or mental harm' does not necessarily mean that the harm needs to be 'permanent and irremediable'.[62] In respect of 'mental harm', there has been discussion as to whether temporary mental harm would suffice,[63] but the guiding criterion seems to be whether or not the harm caused was sufficiently 'serious', which should be evaluated on a case-by-case basis.[64] In the *Krstić* judgments it was noted that 'serious' harm must involve harm 'that goes beyond temporary unhappiness, embarrassment or humiliation. It must be harm that results in grave and long-term disadvantage to a person's ability to lead a normal and constructive life'.[65]

Following the conviction of Akayesu for sexual violence as genocide, it is now well established that 'serious bodily or mental harm' may include acts of sexual violence and rape, appearing as examples of 'serious bodily or mental harm' in the Tribunals' judgments.[66] This is further reinforced in the EoC of the ICC, in which a

[58] Rückert and Witschel (2001), p. 67.

[59] Akayesu Judgment, para. 504.

[60] Kayishema and Ruzindana Judgment, para. 109.

[61] See, *inter alia*, Gacumbitsi Judgment, para. 291 (with reference to ILC Report (1996), para. 14, under Article 17 of the Draft Code of Crimes).

[62] Akayesu Judgment, para. 502; Kayishema and Ruzindana Judgment, para. 108; Rutaganda Judgment and Sentence, para. 51; Stakić Judgment, para. 516; Gacumbitsi Judgment, para. 291.

[63] In the Kayishema Judgment, the Prosecutor submitted that serious mental harm should include 'more than minor or temporary impairment on mental faculties'. The Prosecutor suggested that 'the inflicting of strong fear or terror, intimidation or threat may amount to serious mental harm'. The Trial Chamber did not rule on this point. See Kayishema Judgment, para. 110. Although the issue came up during the ICC negotiations (Preparatory Committee Meeting, A/AC/249/1998/CRP.8, 2 April 1998), the EoC is silent on the matter.

[64] Kayishema and Ruzindana Judgment, para. 113.

[65] Kristić Judgment, para. 513 (with footnote reference to paragraph 502 of the Akayesu Judgment).

[66] Akayesu Judgment, paras. 688, 731. Concurred with in: Rutaganda Judgment and Sentence, para. 51; Kayishema and Ruzindana Judgment, paras. 108-109; Bagilishema Judgment, para. 59; Musema Judgment and Sentence, para. 156; Kajelijeli Judgment and Sentence, paras. 815-816; Gacumbitsi Judgment, para. 291; Krstić Judgment, para. 513; Stakić Judgment, para. 516;

footnote is attached to the crime of genocide of 'causing serious bodily or mental harm', clarifying that this crime '... may include, but is not necessarily restricted to, acts of torture, *rape*, *sexual violence* or inhumane or degrading treatment'.[67] In the *Akayesu* Judgment it was emphasised that 'rape and sexual violence certainly constitute infliction of serious bodily and mental harm on the victims and are even ... one of the worst ways of inflict[ing] harm on the victim as he or she suffers both bodily and mental harm'.[68] In *Akayesu*, the acts of rape and sexual violence were committed 'solely against Tutsi women, many of whom were subjected to the worst public humiliation, mutilated, and raped several times, often in public, in the Bureau Communal premises or in other public places, and often by more than one assailant. These rapes resulted in physical and psychological destruction of Tutsi women, their families and their communities.'[69]

In another case, involving the accused Gacumbitsi, a former mayor of Rusumo commune (Kibungo Prefecture), Gacumbitsi was found to be responsible for instigating the crime of genocide of 'causing serious bodily or mental harm' through the rape of Tutsi women and girls.[70] While driving around in Rubare cellule, Gacumbitsi had announced by megaphone that Hutu men should have sex with Tutsi girls whom had refused to marry Hutu men.[71] Whoever would resist, he had said, had to be killed in an atrocious manner, that is, by inserting sticks into their genitals.[72] Immediately following his utterance to rape, eight Tutsi women were raped by a group of Hutu men.[73] Of those women, one woman (Witness TAQ) had been heavily pregnant during the rape and had to give birth the same night as a consequence of the rape. Three young girls had been forced to stay with their attackers as 'wives'.[74] In other words, the young girls were forced into sexual slavery.

Muhimana Judgment and Sentence, para. 502. A conviction for sexual violence as genocide under 'causing seriously bodily or mental harm' was also found in the Gacumbitsi Judgment, para. 293; Muhimana Judgment and Sentence, paras. 513, 517-519; and the Musema Judgment and Sentence, paras. 907-908, but the latter was quashed on appeal, Musema Appeal Judgment, para. 194. See also the findings in Karadžić and Mladić Rule 61 Decision, para. 93; and the Furundžija Judgment, para. 172.

[67] See footnote 3 to Article 6(b)-1 in the EoC (emphasis added). As mentioned before, the footnotes in the EoC enjoy the same status as the elements of crimes.

[68] Akayesu Judgment, para. 731. The conclusion that rape causes both bodily and mental harm, is supported by the findings made by the ICTY in the Čelebići Judgment. In that case the Trial Chamber found, while considering whether rape causes the requisite level of severe suffering required for the offence of torture at customary international law that 'the rape of any person to be a despicable act which strikes at the very core of human dignity and physical integrity. ... Rape causes severe pain and suffering, both physical and psychological. The psychological suffering of persons upon whom rape is inflicted may be exacerbated by social and cultural conditions and can be particularly acute and long-lasting' (Čelebići Judgment, para. 495).

[69] Akayesu Judgment, para. 731.

[70] Gacumbitsi Judgment, paras. 291-293.

[71] *Ibid.*, paras. 200, 215.

[72] *Ibid.*, paras. 202, 215.

[73] *Ibid.*, para. 224.

[74] *Ibid.*, paras. 200-204, para. 215.

Muhimana, the former *counseiller* of Gishyita *Secteur* (Kibuye Prefecture), was also convicted of rape as genocide under paragraph b.[75] More specifically, Muhimana was convicted of causing serious bodily or mental harm by taking part in attacks at Mugonero Complex, where he raped Tutsi women and shot at Tutsi refugees. In particular he raped Mukasine Kajongi (after the rape he killed her, spread her legs and said 'everyone passing should see what the vagina of a Tutsi woman looks like').[76] Witness BJ, a young Hutu girl, whom he mistakenly believed was a Tutsi was raped by him (Muhimana had instructed BJ and other girls to undress and lie on their backs so that the men could see the genitals of Tutsi girls[77]) as well as Witness AU, whom he raped twice.[78] Furthermore, while he raped Mukasine Kajongi and Witness AU, soldiers who were with him raped other girls.[79]

In yet another case, Pauline Nyiramasuhuko and Arsène Shalom Ntahobali (the former Minister of Women's and Family Affairs and her son and former *Interahamwe* leader in Butare) have both been charged with sexual violence as genocide, for crimes which allegedly took place in Butare Prefecture.[80] The case is pending, and there is persuasive evidence of sexual violence, which, provided the intent to destroy the Tutsi as a group can be proved, may result in a conviction for genocide. For example, prosecution witnesses FAP, QBP and TA testified about rapes committed against themselves and other women by Arsène Shalom Ntahobali and the *Interahamwe*, at and beyond Butare Prefecture Office, where they had sought shelter.[81] Witness TA testified that, on several occasions, she was gang raped by groups of about seven to eight *Interahamwe* at the Prefecture Office.[82] She also testified that a woman named

[75] Muhimana Judgment and Sentence, paras. 513, 517-519.

[76] *Ibid.*, para. 273. Note that the statement about the vagina of a Tutsi woman was made by the Prosecution Witness and not taken up by the Trial Chamber in its findings.

[77] *Ibid.*, para. 291. Note that the statement about the genitals of Tutsi girls was made by Prosecution Witness BJ and not taken up by the Trial Chamber in its findings.

[78] *Ibid.*, para. 302.

[79] *Ibid.*, paras. 274, 291.

[80] The accused are charged with 'serious bodily or mental harm' as complicity in genocide, in the alternative.

[81] *The Prosecutor v. Pauline Nyiramasuhuko, Arsène Shalom Ntahobali, Alphonse Nteziryayo, Sylvain Nsabimana, Elie Ndayambaje and Joseph Kanyabashi*, Transcripts, Case No. ICTR-98-42-T, 24 October 2002, p. 82; *The Prosecutor v. Pauline Nyiramasuhuko, Arsène Shalom Ntahobali, Alphonse Nteziryayo, Sylvain Nsabimana, Elie Ndayambaje and Joseph Kanyabashi*, Transcripts, Case No. ICTR-98-42-T, 11 March 2003, p. 60; *The Prosecutor v. Pauline Nyiramasuhuko, Arsène Shalom Ntahobali, Alphonse Nteziryayo, Sylvain Nsabimana, Elie Ndayambaje and Joseph Kanyabashi*, Transcripts, Case No. ICTR-98-42-T, 25 October 2001, pp. 52, 53, 67.

[82] *The Prosecutor v. Pauline Nyiramasuhuko, Arsène Shalom Ntahobali, Alphonse Nteziryayo, Sylvain Nsabimana, Elie Ndayambaje and Joseph Kanyabashi*, Transcripts, Case No. ICTR-98-42-T, 25 October 2001, pp. 52, 55, 75-76; *The Prosecutor v. Pauline Nyiramasuhuko, Arsène Shalom Ntahobali, Alphonse Nteziryayo, Sylvain Nsabimana, Elie Ndayambaje and Joseph Kanyabashi*, Transcripts, Case No. ICTR-98-42-T, 29 October 2001, p. 8.

Immacule was raped by Ntahobali after her baby had been thrown away.[83] Witness TN and six other girls were kept in sexual slavery conditions at Shalom's house, where they were raped multiple times by Ntahobali and soldiers for five days.[84] On several occasions, TN was also penetrated using an object, the handle of a brush, which caused her great pain and upon which she started to bleed.[85] On 25 April 1994, after the rapes, Shalom told the soldiers to take the girls and to make them their wives.[86] Witness TN was subsequently taken by one of the soldiers from the group, named Alexis, to a Hutu-controlled refugee camp in Burundi.[87] Upon arrival the soldier told TN that he owned her body and that he could use it as he pleased.[88] She was told to obey his orders otherwise she would be killed.[89] At the refugee camp, Alexis ordered TN to have sex with three other soldiers, which she did.[90] TN managed to escape from the camp and to return to Rwanda. TN testified that she is still suffering from pains in the abdomen, just below the stomach on both sides.[91]

The facts in the *Akayesu*, *Gacumbitsi*, and *Butare* cases establish that sexual slavery was used as a means to commit genocide. In *Gacumbitsi*, the three young girls were taken as 'wives'. In *Butare*, Witness TN and six other girls were kept in collective slavery for five days, after which they were forced to remain with their captors as 'wives'. Witness NN testified in the *Akayesu* case that Rafiki, an *Interahamwe*, picked her from of a group of Tutsi who were about to be killed, to make her his 'wife'.[92] Subsequently, NN had been locked in Rafiki's brother's house for a week, where she was repeatedly raped by different men.[93] Sexual slavery was common in Rwanda: over a third of the women who gave testimony to the Office of the Prosecutor had been held in sexual slavery, either individually or collectively, for periods varying between one day and one month, the majority of women being held captive for over a month.[94] It is

[83] *The Prosecutor v. Pauline Nyiramasuhuko, Arsène Shalom Ntahobali, Alphonse Nteziryayo, Sylvain Nsabimana, Elie Ndayambaje and Joseph Kanyabashi*, Transcripts, Case No. ICTR-98-42-T, 29 October 2001, p. 15.

[84] *The Prosecutor v. Pauline Nyiramasuhuko, Arsène Shalom Ntahobali, Alphonse Nteziryayo, Sylvain Nsabimana, Elie Ndayambaje and Joseph Kanyabashi*, Transcripts, Case No. ICTR-98-42-T, 3 April 2002, pp. 159, 160, 161. It should be noted that Witness TN failed to recognise Ntahobali in court.

[85] *Ibid.*, pp. 156, 157, 158, 159, 160.

[86] *Ibid.*, p. 161.

[87] *Ibid.*, p. 162.

[88] *Ibid.*, p. 163.

[89] *Ibid.*

[90] *Ibid.*

[91] *Ibid.*, p. 165.

[92] Akayesu Judgment, para. 435.

[93] *Ibid.*, para. 436.

[94] Nowrojee (2004a), para. 40. In her expert report Nowrojee (2004a) concludes that the findings in her report prepared for Human Rights Watch (1996) have been further corroborated by OTP witness statements. Nowrojee and Harvey conducted a survey of 405 statements of Rwandan rape victims and witnesses of rape, taken by OTP investigators between 1995-2002 (commonly referred to as the 'OTP Rape Database'). Over a third of these testimonies provided by women to the OTP were thus held in sexual slavery.

estimated that between 250,000 to 500,000 Rwandese women and girls have been raped during the genocide;[95] about 84,000 to 166,000 of these women and girls have thus most likely been held in sexual slavery conditions. Despite the evidence, sexual slavery (both individually through 'forced marriages' and collectively) has not been charged and prosecuted in and of itself as genocide. Although since *Akayesu* it has been ruled that sexual violence, which may include sexual slavery, may amount to genocide, sexual violence does not encompass the true nature of the crime of sexual slavery. For this reason, the genocide definition should be amended to include sexual slavery or, at least, a judicial decision should recognise sexual slavery as a specific form of sexual violence.[96] Further grounds for amending the definition can be found in a 2005 study, in which it is estimated that about 120,000 young girls are presently involved in armed conflicts around the world; they have been abducted and forced to serve as sex slaves (along with household tasks and fighting) to members of the armed groups they are with.[97]

In most, if not all, cases, women and girls continue to suffer from the consequences of the sexual violence they had experienced, long after the conflict had ended. Some of the consequences of sexual violence are:[98] (1) physical consequences such as severe pains and bleeding; loss of consciousness, miscarriage due to rape, the loss of virginity and sexual mutilation; (2) health complications such as general body aches and pains, abdominal aches, ongoing pain from uterine and vaginal mutilation, and general malaise, sexually transmitted diseases and HIV/AIDS; (3) the birth of children from rape, which is likely to cause significant increased mental harm, especially in patriarchal societies where the ethnicity of the child is that of the father, thus the rapist;[99] (4) emotional consequences and trauma such as having to watch one's family members being killed while being raped oneself, being raped in front of family members or a large audience, watching one's baby being thrown away before being raped. Multiple rapes, gang rapes, sexual mutilation and rapes with objects are likely to aggravate the physical and psychological consequences; (5) social consequences, which include isolation, stigmatisation and ostracism, and economic consequences. These include having become unmarriageable, abandonment by family members and/or husband when it is found out that a woman was raped (in some cultures a raped woman is considered violated). Genocidal rape is especially effective if society stigmatises the rape victim.[100] Thus, the consequences of sexual violence may well have the effect of contributing significantly to the destruction of a group in whole or in part.

---

[95] UN Commission on Human Rights, *Report on the Situation of Human Rights in Rwanda Submitted by Mr. René Degni-Segui*, Special Rapporteur of the Commission on Human Rights, Under Paragraph 20 of Resolution S-3/1 of 25 May 1994, E/CN.4/1996/68, 29 January 1996, para. 16.

[96] See also Kalra (2001), p. 210.

[97] Save the Children (2005).

[98] See Nowrojee (1996).

[99] In Rwanda, 'a survey of 304 survivors reported that 35% had become pregnant following rape and it is estimated that between two and five thousand "enfants de mauvais souvenir" (children of bad memories) resulted from rapes committed during the genocide' (Gordon and Crehan (2002), p. 5).

[100] Sharlach (2000).

Although sexual violence may lead to the destruction or partial destruction of the group, this is not strictly required under paragraph (b). The result that the Prosecution is to prove is that one or more victims actually suffered physical or mental harm: if the act has been committed with the requisite mental element, the crime has been committed.[101] This is confirmed in the EoC of the ICC.[102] Nevertheless, as mentioned above, the effects of sexual violence on its victim, group or society as a whole should not be underestimated. Sexual violence may cause the destruction of a group through 'deliberate emotional destruction of a vital part of that group'.[103] If women, the carers of society, become dysfunctional, the survival of the society is threatened.[104] Thus, while the legal requirements only demand proof of the result of serious bodily or mental harm, sexual violence in itself may have the effect of destruction of the group. This is strong evidence for the use of sexual violence as a powerful weapon of warfare.

2.3 Deliberately inflicting on the group conditions of life calculated to bring about its physical destruction in whole or in part

In *Akayesu*, the ICTR held that 'deliberately inflicting on the group conditions of life calculated to bring about its physical destruction in whole or in part, should be construed as the methods of destruction by which the perpetrator does not immediately kill the members of the group, but which, ultimately, seek their physical destruction'.[105] Examples of 'conditions of life' that were given included 'subjecting a group of people to a subsistence diet, systematic expulsion from homes and the reduction of essential medical services below minimum requirement'.[106] The *Kayishema and Ruzindana* Judgment held that '*rape*, the starving of a group of people, reducing required medical services below a minimum, and withholding sufficient living accommodation for a reasonable period' constitute 'conditions of life'.[107] The term 'conditions of life' in the EoC of the ICC 'may include, but is not necessarily restricted to, deliberate deprivation of resources indispensable for survival, such as food or medical services, or systematic expulsion from homes'.[108]

Unlike the crimes defined in paragraphs (a), (b) and (e), the offence of deliberately imposing conditions of life calculated to bring about a group's physical destruction does not require proof of a result. No actual destruction is needed; the intentional infliction of the conditions is sufficient. The methods of destruction used by the perpetrator do not immediately kill the members of the group, but, ultimately, seek their physical

---

[101] Schabas (2000b), pp. 164-165.

[102] Article 6(b)-1 EoC.

[103] Bassiouni and Manikas (1996), pp. 587-588.

[104] *Ibid.*

[105] Akayesu Judgment, para. 505. See also the Kayishema and Ruzindana Judgment, para. 116; Rutaganda Judgment and Sentence, para. 52.

[106] Akayesu Judgment, para. 506. See also the Kayishema and Ruzindana Judgment, para. 115: Rutuganda Judgment, para. 52; Musema Judgment and Sentence, para. 157; Stakić Judgment, para. 517.

[107] Kayishema and Ruzindana Judgment, para. 116 (italics added).

[108] See footnote 4 to Article 6(c)-4 EoC. The footnote was based on the Akayesu finding. See Garraway (2001), p. 52.

destruction.[109] This includes 'circumstances which will lead to a slow death'.[110] The EoC of the ICC do not seem to differ on the issue of *mens rea*.[111]

Although rape was thus specifically mentioned in the *Kayishema and Ruzindana* Judgment as a condition of life 'calculated to bring about its physical destruction', no charges for rape under this heading have been laid down to date. It can be argued, however, that the forms of sexual violence which may be 'causing serious or bodily harm' might also constitute conditions of life calculated to bring about a group's physical destruction. The conditions of life see to the group's physical destruction, not its mental destruction. For example, rape, sexual mutilation, forcible sterilisation, forcible abortion and sexual slavery may all lead to the physical destruction of the group. Especially in patriarchal societies, rape and other forms of sexual violence may result in the destruction of the group, because women may no longer be considered to be marriageable after having had sex with a man from another ethnic group.[112] It has been argued that deplorable detention facilities – which include an atmosphere of fear, terror or depression caused by rape crimes, rapes with the intent to cause such damage that the woman loses her reproductive capacity and intentionally subjecting persons to, for instance, infected water or withholding medicines in order to cause sterility or spontaneous abortion – would also qualify as conditions of life calculated to bring about a group's physical destruction.[113]

One notable 'condition of life' which may ultimately seek the physical destruction of a group is the intentional infection with HIV/AIDS through rape. In Rwanda, many women were raped by men who knew they were HIV-positive and who were sadistically trying to transmit the virus to Tutsi women and their Tutsi families.[114] These rapes were committed with the intent to cause the women to die slowly, hoping that the women would transmit the virus to their partners and unborn children. Paul Kagame, the President of Rwanda, even claimed that the former Hutu government released AIDS patients from the hospitals in order to rape Tutsi women and transmit the virus to them.[115] In Rwanda, 70 percent of the genocide survivors are estimated to have been infected with HIV,[116] and the number of children infected with the virus is also believed

---

109 Akayesu Judgment, para. 505; Kayishema Judgment, para. 116.

110 Kayishema Judgment, para. 115.

111 Article 6(c)-1 and Article 6(c)-4 EoC.

112 Bassiouni and Manikas (1996, p. 587) state: 'in patriarchal societies targeting Muslim women for rape and sexual assault in order to effectively separate Bosnian Muslim women from Bosnian Muslim men may create a condition of life calculated to bring about the group's destruction.'

113 Askin (2004b), p. 66.

114 Organization of African Unity, International Panel of Eminent Personalities Report, *Rwanda: The Preventable Genocide*, 2000, Chapter 16.19. Jones points out that 'it appears that at least some 35% of Rwandese soldiers were HIV-positive before the genocide of 1994 ..., and which may have held true for the *interahamwe* killers and other men who participated in genocidal atrocities' (Jones, A. (2002), p. 82).

115 New York Times Magazine, *A Woman's Work* (by Peter Landesman), 15 September 2002.

116 Amnesty International (2004a), p. 3. In a survey of 1125 female genocide survivors carried out by AVEGA, it was established that some 80 percent remain severely traumatized and that about 70 percent of them have tested HIV positive. See the AVEGA-AGAHOZO website (Association of Genocide Widows) at http://www.avega.org.rw/englishhome.htm (last visited June 2005).

to be very high. The mass rapes during the genocide contributed significantly to the spreading of the virus in Rwanda, particularly as rates of HIV transmission during sexual violence are believed to be high.[117] In light of these disturbing statistics, it is striking that this very effective 'condition of life' aimed at dismembering a group has not (yet) been recognised in the Tribunal's case law. In light of the fact that today's conflicts lie in the heart of the 'AIDS belt' (such as DRC and Angola),[118] the ICC is likely to be presented with cases where rapes were committed with the deliberate intent to destroy a group by means of HIV transmission.

2.4 Imposing measures intended to prevent births within the group

The genocidal act of 'imposing measures intended to prevent births within the group' has been clarified by the Trial Chamber in the *Akayesu* case, where it was held that such measures may include 'sexual mutilation, the practice of sterilization, forced birth control, separation of the sexes and prohibition of marriages'.[119] The Trial Chamber also stated that

> in patriarchal societies, where membership of a group is determined by the identity of the father, an example of a measure intended to prevent births within a group is the case where, during rape, a woman of the said group is deliberately impregnated by a man of another group, with the intent to have her give birth to a child who will consequently not belong to its mother's group.[120]

In this perspective, in the *Karadžić and Mladić* Rule 61 Hearing it was established that 'some camps were specially devoted to rape, with the aim of forcing the birth of Serbian offspring, the women often being interned until it was too late for them to undergo an abortion'.[121] The aim of many of these rapes seemed to be enforced impregnation.[122] The Chamber therefore held that 'the systematic rape of women ... is in some cases intended to transmit a new ethnicity identity to the child'.[123] The *Akayesu* Trial

---

[117] Amnesty International (2004g). The risk of HIV transmission increases up to three-fold when sex is forced, especially for girls and young women because their vaginal tracts are immature and tear easily. See World Health Organization Press Release, *Women and Girls Need Access to AIDS Treatment and Protection from Violence*, 30 November 2004.

[118] Jones, A. (2000), p. 192.

[119] Akayesu Judgment, para. 507.

[120] *Ibid.* As to forced impregnation, Goldstein (1993, p. 24) asserts that it imposes at least temporary measures preventing births within a group, because 'for at least the nine months it takes to carry the rapist's child to term, a woman is incapable of conceiving and bearing a child of her own ethnicity'.

[121] Karadžić and Mladić Rule 61 Decision, para. 64.

[122] *Ibid.*

[123] *Ibid.*, para. 94. In particular, the Chamber came to this conclusion on the basis of the testimony of Christine Cleiren, a member of the Commission of Experts established in 1992 by the Security Council, who was asked to appear before the Tribunal as an *amicus curiae*. She was asked whether rape had been used systematically to change the ethnic character of the population by impregnating women or whether this was done in individual cases. Cleiren answered: 'The

Chamber, finally, also noted that measures intended to prevent births within the group may be physical, but that they may also be mental.[124] As an example, the Chamber cited that rape can be a measure intended to prevent births 'when the person raped refuses subsequently to procreate, in the same way that members of a group can be led, through threats or trauma, not to procreate'.[125] The Trial Chambers of the *Kayishema and Ruzindana* and *Rutaganda* cases fully concurred with the observations of the *Akayesu* Trial Chamber.[126] To date, no act of sexual violence has been charged as a measure 'intended to prevent births within the group'.

In conformity with what has been said in relation to the *mens rea* of conditions of life calculated to bring about the physical destruction of the group, the act of 'imposing measures *intended* to prevent births within the group' does not require a result either.[127] Whether or not the measures succeeded in preventing births within the group is not of primary relevance. This is reconfirmed in the EoC of the ICC.[128] What needs to be proved is that the measures were intentionally imposed and were intended to prevent births within the group.

2.5 Forcibly transferring children of the group to another group

The act of 'forcibly transferring children of the group to another group' was touched upon by the *Akayesu* Trial Chamber, although not in great detail. The Chamber held that 'as in the case of measures intended to prevent births, the objective is not only to sanction a direct act of forcible physical transfer, but also to sanction acts of threats or trauma which would lead to the forcible transfer of children from one group to another'.[129] In the EoC, inspired by *Akayesu*, this is made clear in a footnote to this genocidal act, which states: 'The term "forcibly" is not restricted to physical force, but may include threat of force or coercion, such as that caused by fear of violence, duress, detention, psychological oppression or abuse of power, against such person or persons or another person, or by taking advantage of a coercive environment.'[130] Although the term 'children' was not defined in the Statutes of the Tribunals nor in the Genocide Convention, in the EoC it is stated that for the purposes of this crime, in conformity

---

Commission did not have enough information to verify, let us say, these testimonies, who spoke in these terms. I guess it is possible that both happened. There are indications that it was commanded or that it was planned to do this ... It has to do with the descendency, with the succession. As far as we could see, it meant that producing a child of another ethnic background was an automatic result of the fact that the child would have the ethnic origin of the father.' See *Prosecutor v. Radovan Karadžić and Ratko Mladić*, Transcripts, Case No. IT-95-18-R61 and Case No. IT-95-5-R61, 2 July 1996, p. 400.

[124] Akayesu Judgment, para. 508.

[125] *Ibid.*

[126] Kayishema and Ruzindana Judgment, para. 117; Rutaganda Judgment and Sentence, para. 53.

[127] See also Schabas (2000b), p. 173.

[128] Article 6(d)-4 EoC.

[129] Akayesu Judgment, para. 509. Kayishema and Ruzindana Judgment, para. 118; Rutaganda Judgment and Sentence, para. 54; and Musema Judgment and Sentence, para. 159, concurring.

[130] Footnote 5 to Article 6(e)-1. See Garraway (2001), p. 55.

with the Convention on the Rights of the Child, '[t]he person or persons were under the age of 18 years'.[131]

Under this paragraph, the perpetrator must have had the intent to forcibly transfer children from one group to another, with the actual result, although, following *Akayesu*, threats of such transfer is also included. According to the EoC, the perpetrator knew or should have known that the person or persons were under the age of 18.[132]

To date, no prosecution has been started under this paragraph. An example of such an act might be the case where a woman from a patriarchal society has been raped by a man from outside her group and has become pregnant; the child would then belong to the group to which the man belongs. Transfer thus does not take place in the physical sense of the word, but because the perpetrator creates a new child, the child will, after its birth, belong to its father's ethnic group.[133] Another example is the case where girls are abducted against their will to serve in the army. As mentioned above, globally up to 120,000 girls, some as young as 8 years old, are forced to serve in armed groups.[134] The roles of the girls may vary from actual soldiers to porters, cleaners and cooks, but in almost all cases they are forced to serve as sex slaves or 'wives'. If a girl becomes pregnant from a man of the armed group, who belongs to another group than she does, the child may, after its birth, belong to the group the father belongs to. Moreover, if the girl has been abducted and forced to work as a child soldier at a very young age, the girl may lose or forget her cultural identity and, in a way, if she does not or cannot return to her own group, she has become a member of the other group.

3 The elements common to genocide

For the term genocide to be applicable, not only one of the material genocidal acts must have been committed, but also the *mens rea* or mental element common to all acts must have been fulfilled, that is, the 'intent to destroy, in whole or in part, a national, ethnical, racial or religious group, as such'. This intent requirement consists of three subrequirements: (1) the degree of intent; (2) the destruction of the group, as such; and (3) in whole or in part. The effects of the interpretation of the genocidal intent standard on the prosecution of sexual violence as genocide as well as the question of how to infer intent in relation to genocidal sexual violence will be discussed in this section.

3.1 The degree of intent

The degree of intent required for a crime to constitute genocide is generally characterised as specific intent, also referred to as special intent or *dolus specialis*,

[131] Article 6(e)-5 EoC. See also Garraway (2001), p. 54. It has been pointed out that this crime may not apply to older children, who are less likely to lose their cultural identity, which was what the provision was aimed for. See Schabas (2000b), p. 176. Transfer of adults therefore needs to be prosecuted under crimes against humanity or war crimes, for example, Article 8(2)(b)(viii) ICC Statute, or Article 7(a)(d) ICC Statute.

[132] Article 6(e)-6 EoC.

[133] See further the preceding subparagraph '(d) Imposing measures intended to prevent births within the group', where the Karadžić and Mladić Rule 61 Hearing is discussed.

[134] Save the Children (2005).

which requires that the acts listed in the definition of genocide must have been committed with the 'intent to destroy, in whole or in part, a national, ethnical, racial or religious group, as such'.[135] 'Specific intent' requires that the perpetrator clearly intended the result – thus the crime charged. It is the specific intent that makes genocide unique in the eyes of many; genocide is frequently referred to as the 'crime of crimes' for which life imprisonment is often charged and imposed.[136] However, as far as certain modes of liability are concerned, customary international law seems to be changing as regards the intent standard required for genocide, as is evidenced by the Tribunals' rulings on superior criminal responsibility, complicity to genocide, aiding and abetting in the planning, preparation or execution of genocide and the third variant of 'joint criminal enterprise'. The intent standard for genocide developing beyond *dolus specialis* has, however, not been appreciated by some commentators.[137]

3.1.1 Different modes of liability

In a number of cases, the Prosecutor has held that the mental state required for genocide is different for some modes of liability other than that of a principal under Article 7(1) ICTY Statute or Article 6(1) ICTR Statute.[138] As such differentiation is applicable in cases of crimes against humanity and war crimes, this is not any different for genocide. This means that *dolus specialis* is required with respect to the physical perpetrators and those who order, plan or instigate genocide. However, proof of *dolus specialis* is not required for superiors (Article 7(3) ICTY Statute and Article 6(3) ICTR Statute[139]), accomplices to genocide (Article 4(3)(e) ICTY Statute and Article 2(3)(e) ICTR Statute), aiders and abettors in the planning, preparation or execution of genocide, and participants in a joint criminal enterprise where genocide is a natural and foreseeable consequence of the execution of the common purpose, for instance, a campaign of persecution (variant three of the joint criminal enterprise).

The Prosecutor has consistently held that the degree of intent is satisfied for genocide if '(a) he consciously desired the acts to result in the destruction, in whole or

---

[135] See, *inter alia*, Jelisić Appeal Judgment, paras. 45-46; Krstić Judgment, para. 571; Brđanin Judgment, para. 695; Stakić Judgment, para. 520; Akayesu Judgment, paras. 497-498, 517-521; Kambanda Judgment and Sentence, para. 16; Jelisić Judgment, para. 67; Kayishema and Ruzindana Sentencing Judgment, para. 9; Rutaganda Judgment and Sentence, para. 451; Serushago Sentencing Judgment, para. 15.

[136] See, e.g., Kambanda Judgment and Sentence, para. 16.

[137] See, *inter alia*, Schabas (2001), pp. 125-139; Lyons (2001), pp. 99-124.

[138] Article 7(1) ICTY Statute and Article 6(1) ICTR Statute read: 'A person who planned, instigated, ordered, committed or otherwise aided and abetted in the planning, preparation or execution of a crime referred to in articles 2 to 5 [2 to 4 ICTR Statute] of the present Statute, shall be individually responsible for the crime.'

[139] Article 7(3) ICTY Statute and Article 6(3) ICTR Statute read: 'The fact that any of the acts referred to in articles 2 to 5 [2 to 4 ICTR Statute] of the present Statute was committed by a subordinate does not relieve his superior of criminal responsibility if he [or she] knew or had reason to know that the subordinate was about to commit such acts or had done so and the superior failed to take the necessary and reasonable measures to prevent such acts or to punish the perpetrators thereof.'

in part, of the group, as such; or, (b) he knew his acts were destroying, in whole or in part, the group, as such; or (c) he knew that the likely consequence of his acts would be to destroy, in whole or in part, the group, as such'.[140] Only option (a) corresponds to the *dolus specialis* standard; options (b) and (c) refer to broader notions of general intent. In support of including all options as satisfying the intent requirement for genocide, the following three arguments have been put forward by the Prosecutor: (1) The plain and ordinary meaning of Article 4 ICTY Statute (genocide) does not support the proposition that *dolus specialis* is required;[141] (2) such a proposition also contradicts the case law of the ICTR, where it has been held that an accused is culpable of genocide 'because he knew or should have known that the act committed would destroy, in whole or in part, a group';[142] and (3) the doctrine of *dolus specialis* is peculiar to a few civil law jurisdictions only and cannot easily be transposed to international criminal law.[143] According to the Prosecutor, the intent contained in the definition of genocide is 'special' 'only insofar as its *scope* is concerned; that is, the intent must *include or contain* destruction, in whole or in part, of a national, ethnical, racial or religious group, as such'.[144] The mental standard of genocide is particular in its scope, but general in its

[140] *Prosecutor v. Goran Jelisić,* Prosecution's Appeal Brief (Public Redacted Version), Case No. IT-95-10-A, 14 July 2000, para. 4.9. See also, *inter alia, Prosecutor v. Goran Jelisić*, Pre-Trail Brief, Case No. IT-95-10-T, 19 November 1998, para. 3.1; *Prosecutor v. Duško Sikirica, Damir Došen and Dragan Kolundžija*, Prosecutor's Second Revised Pre-Trail Brief, Case No. IT-95-8-PT, 13 October 2000, para. 143. See also Greenawalt (1999), pp. 2259-2294.

[141] According to the Prosecutor, there is no basis in law to give the mental state formulation in Article 4 a 'special' meaning in conflict with its ordinary meaning of intent: 'Article 31(4) of the 1969 Vienna Convention on the Law of Treaties provides that a "special meaning shall be given to a term if it is established that the parties so intended". The *travaux préparatoires* of the 1948 Genocide Convention, on which Article 4 is based, show a manifest absence of such consensus among the negotiating delegations to give the particular intent formulation in Article II of the Convention the exclusive meaning of *dolus specialis.*' Furthermore, the 'proposition that Article 4 contains a *dolus specialis* requirement reduces the scope of application of the genocide prohibition in a way which undermines the object and purpose of the Statute [(Article 31(1) 1969 Vienna Convention on the Law of Treaties), i.e., to do justice, to deter further crimes and to contribute to the restoration and maintenance of peace]' (*Prosecutor v. Goran Jelisić,* Prosecution's Appeal Brief (Public Redacted Version), Case No. IT-95-10-A, 14 July 2000, paras. 4.11-4.17). See also Greenawalt (1999), pp. 2270-2279.

[142] *Prosecutor v. Goran Jelisić,* Prosecution's Appeal Brief (Public Redacted Version), Case No. IT-95-10-A, 14 July 2000, paras. 4.18-4.21 (with reference to the Akayesu Judgment, para. 520, as upheld in the Rutaganda Judgment and Sentence, para. 48, and Musema Judgment and Sentence, para. 153). As mentioned above, the Prosecutor does not propose a 'should have known' standard to satisfy the intent requirement of genocide.

[143] *Ibid.*, paras. 4.22-4.27 (with reference to *Prosecutor v. Tihomir Blaškić*, Judgment on the Request of the Republic of Croatia for Review of the Decision of Trial Chamber II of 18 July 1997, Case No. IT-95-14-AR108*bis*, 29 October 1997, para. 40; and Erdemović Appeal Judgment, including the Separate and Dissenting Opinion of Judge Cassese, para. 4, on the difficulty of transposing legal institutions, constructs or approaches prevailing in national law to international law).

[144] *Ibid.*, para. 4.20.

degree. In addition to the three arguments above, an interpretation of the genocidal intent requirement broader than *dolus specialis* can be deduced from Article 30 of the ICC Statute, which states that the general mental state requirement encompasses both intent and knowledge. Intent with regard to a consequence, which in the case of genocide is the complete or partial destruction of a group, is defined as 'that person means to cause that consequence or is aware that it will occur in the ordinary course of events'.[145] Similarly, knowledge is defined as meaning 'awareness that a ... consequence will occur in the ordinary course of events'.[146] If this interpretation is correct, options (a), (b) and (c) would certainly all fall within the ambit of the ICC's genocidal intent.

3.1.1.1 Superior criminal responsibility

Three essential elements have been established in the Tribunals' case law by which a superior can be held accountable for the acts of his subordinates, viz. (1) the existence of a superior–subordinate relationship of effective control between the accused and the perpetrator of the crime; (2) the knowledge, or constructive knowledge, of the accused that the crime was about to be, was being or had been committed; and (3) the failure of the accused to take the necessary and reasonable measures to prevent or stop the crime, or to punish the perpetrator.[147] There is no reason why Article 6(3) ICTR Statute or Article 7(3) ICTY Statute would impose a higher intent standard on the crime of genocide: a clear differentiation between the two *mens rea* standards should be made. Indeed, Kambanda, Kayishema, Musema, Imanishimwe, Kajelijeli and Barayagwiza have all been convicted of genocide under Article 6(3) ICTR Statute.[148] The *Cyangugu* case strongly supports the conclusion that a superior need not have specific intent in order to be held liable for genocide pursuant to the doctrine of superior criminal responsibility: contrary to the other cases mentioned, Imanishimwe was convicted, as a superior, of genocide while he was not found guilty for the same acts under Article 6(1), viz. his specific intent to commit genocide had not been established. To date, no convictions for genocide under Article 7(3) ICTY Statute have yet resulted. Although the Trial Chamber in the *Stakić* Rule 98*bis* Decision held that *dolus specialis* is required for responsibility under Article 7(3),[149] the Trial Chamber in *Brđanin* ruled to the contrary and therefore agreed with ICTR case law on the issue.[150] Therefore, the *mens rea* required for superiors to be held responsible for genocide pursuant to Article 7(3) is, following the *Brđanin* ruling, that the superiors knew or had reason to know that their

[145] Article 30(2)(b) ICC Statute.

[146] Article 30(3) ICC Statute.

[147] See, *inter alia*, Bagilishema Judgment, para. 38; Kajelijeli Judgment and Sentence, para. 772; Kamuhanda Judgment, para. 603.

[148] See Kambanda Judgment and Sentence, para. 40; Kayishema and Ruzindana Judgment, paras. 228, 555, 559, 563, 569; Musema Judgment and Sentence, para. 926; Cyangugu Judgment, paras. 653-654, 690, 694-695, 821; Kajelijeli Judgment and Sentence, para. 843; Media Judgment, paras. 973, 977.

[149] *Prosecutor v. Milomir Stakić,* Decision on Rule 98*bis* Motion for Judgment of Acquittal, Case No. IT-97-24-T, 31 October 2002, para. 92 ('It follows from Article 4 and the unique nature of genocide that the *dolus specialis* is required for responsibility under Article 7(3)').

[150] Brđanin Judgment, paras. 719-721.

subordinates (1) were about to commit or had committed genocide and (2) had the requisite specific intent.[151] A similar conclusion may be drawn for the ICC regime: under Article 28 (responsibility of commanders and other superiors, for which negligence is a sufficient ground for liability), a superior may be liable for genocidal acts of his subordinates notwithstanding the lack of *dolus specialis* on his part.[152] After all, genocide is 'the crime with which the superiors associated themselves with, through the deliberate failure to carry out their duty to exercise control'.[153]

No convictions of superiors for genocidal rapes committed by their subordinates have taken place to date. As Gacumbitsi was already found liable under Article 6(1) ICTR Statute, the Chamber did not deem it necessary, given the similarity of the acts charged, to find whether Gacumbitsi also incurred criminal responsibility under Article 6(3) ICTR Statute.[154] Akayesu was not charged under Article 6(3) ICTR Statute; he was charged and convicted under Article 6(1) only – not because he was a physical perpetrator, but because he had abetted in the preparation or execution of inflicting serious bodily and mental harm on members of the Tutsi group.[155] As far as Musema's responsibility under Article 6(3) ICTR Statute was concerned, the Chamber noted that 'the Prosecutor has not established, nor even alleged, that among the assailants who attacked Nyiramusugi there were employees of the Gisovu Tea Factory or other persons who were Musema's subordinates'.[156] Musema was therefore not convicted of genocidal rape under Article 6(3) ICTR Statute, only under Article 6(1) ICTR, although his conviction was later quashed on appeal. It is unfortunate that the Tribunal missed the opportunity here to convict the accused convicted of genocidal rapes committed by his subordinates.

In general, to establish a superior's responsibility for sexual violence may be a rather difficult undertaking especially in cases where there is no evidence or allegation of physical contact between an accused and a rape victim, where the accused is not known to have explicitly incited or ordered the rape, where the physical presence of the accused at a rape scene or other concrete proof of knowledge of rape has not been

---

[151] *Ibid.*, para. 721.

[152] Arnold (2003), pp. 146-149.

[153] Brđanin Judgment, para. 720.

[154] Gacumbitsi Judgment, para. 290. Cumulative convictions under Articles 6(1) and 6(3) ICTR Statute have both been permitted and denied. See Kayishema and Ruzindana Judgment, para. 210 (permitted): 'The finding of responsibility under Article 6(1) of the Statute does not prevent the Chamber from finding responsibility additionally, or in the alternative, under Article 6(3). The two forms of responsibility are not mutually exclusive. The Chamber must, therefore, consider both forms of responsibility charged in order to fully reflect the culpability of the accused in light of the facts.' See Cyangugu Judgment, para. 623 (denied): 'If an accused may be held criminally responsible for a crime under either Article 6(1) or Article 6(3), the Chamber will enter a conviction on the form of responsibility that best characterises the accused's role in the crime. In such an event, the Chamber will consider the other form of responsibility in sentencing in order to reflect the totality of the accused's culpable conduct.' See also Naletilić and Martinović Judgment, paras. 78-81; Krnolejac Judgment, para. 173; Čelebići Appeal Judgment, para. 745; Aleksovski Appeal Judgment, para. 183.

[155] Akayesu Judgment, para. 707.

[156] Musema Judgment and Sentence, para. 889.

established, the nexus between the accused and the crime of rape will not be easy to establish. In such cases, what will need to be proved is the presumption that sexual violence was committed with the intent to destroy a particular group and that the accused knew or must have had reason to know that his subordinates were about to commit genocidal rapes and that he did not use his position to prevent or punish the sexual violence. The findings contained in reports such as 'Shattered Lives' or the OTP Rape Database[157] illustrate that the rapes were so commonplace, often committed with the intent to destroy Tutsi women on the basis of both their ethnicity and their gender, that the accused could not have failed to know that they were occurring with genocidal intent. Especially in light of the media influence in Rwanda, which fuelled the sexual violence committed against Tutsi women, it is hard to believe the accused did not know. Reports and/or the OTP Rape Database could be submitted to the court through a Rule 92*bis* application (proof of facts other than by oral evidence), together with the oral testimonies of some strong victims of sexual violence. In addition, or in the alternative, an expert witness could testify and confirm the findings in the report and/or OTP Rape Database before the Court.[158] Binaifer Nowrojee testified, *inter alia*, before the ICTR *Military I* trial, and for this purpose, her expert report, which summarised her conclusions on the basis of her research done for 'Shattered Lives' and the OTP Rape Database, was admitted.[159]

3.1.1.2 Complicity in genocide

Following the Tribunals' case law, an accused can only be found guilty of complicity in genocide (Article 2(3)(e) ICTR Statute and Article 4(3)(e) ICTY Statute) if the crime of genocide itself has been committed.[160] The principal perpetrator need not have been identified or convicted himself.[161] An accused may furthermore not be convicted of genocide and complicity in genocide for the same acts.[162] Three forms of complicity in

---

[157] As mentioned before, the OTP Rape Database was prepared by Nowrojee and Harvey who conducted a survey of 405 statements of Rwandan rape victims and witnesses of rape taken by OTP investigators between 1995-2002 (this was a sample of a larger number of rape statements collected by OTP). The witness statements were analysed with respect to: the date and location of rapes; the profile of the victims; the perpetrators; the forms of sexual violence (rape, gang-rape, sexual slavery, rape with aggravated violence); statements of intent to target women on the basis of ethnicity; and consequences of rape. The OTP Rape Database confirmed Nowrojee's findings of her previous report prepared for Human Rights Watch in 1996. See the expert report prepared by Nowrojee (2004a), pp. 11-15.

[158] For a more elaborate discussion on the ways in which such evidence can be submitted to court, see Chapter 2.

[159] Nowrojee (2004a).

[160] Akayesu Judgment, paras. 527-531; Musema Judgment and Sentence, paras. 170-173; Stakić Judgment, para. 533.

[161] Akayesu Judgment, para. 531. See also Musema Judgment and Sentence, para. 174; Stakić Judgment, para. 533.

[162] Akayesu Judgment, paras. 468, 532; Musema Judgment and Sentence, paras. 175, 291; Media Judgment, para. 1056; Gacumbitsi Judgment, para. 246; Brđanin Judgment, para. 728. However, Kambanda pleaded guilty to both genocide and complicity in genocide based on the same facts

genocide have generally been recognised: complicity by procuring means, complicity by aiding and abetting and complicity by instigation, forms which have been recognised in most civil law systems.[163]

In the ICTR case law, it has been recognised that specific intent is not required for an accomplice to genocide; only knowledge that the principal was acting with specific intent. According to the *Akayesu* judgment:

> As far as genocide is concerned, the intent of the accomplice is thus to knowingly aid or abet one or more persons to commit the crime of genocide. Therefore, the Chamber is of the opinion that an accomplice to genocide need not necessarily possess the *dolus specialis* of genocide, namely the specific intent to destroy, in whole or in part, a national, ethnic, racial or religious group, as such.
>
> Thus, if for example, an accused knowingly aided or abetted another in the commission of a murder, while being unaware that the principal was committing such a murder, with the intent to destroy, in whole or in part, the group to which the murdered victim belonged, the accused could be prosecuted for complicity in murder, and certainly not for complicity in genocide. *However, if the accused knowingly aided and abetted in the commission of such a murder while he knew or had reason to know that the principal was acting with genocidal intent, the accused would be an accomplice to genocide, even though he did not share the murderer's intent to destroy the group.*[164]

The position on the intent standard for complicity in genocide does not seem to be different for the ICC. Complicity in genocide is found in Article 25(3)(c) of the ICC Statute and reads: 'For the purpose of facilitating the commission of such a crime, *aids, abets or otherwise assists* in its commission or its attempted commission, including

---

and was convicted of both. See Kambanda Judgment and Sentence and Kambanda Appeal Judgment.

[163] Akayesu Judgment, para. 533. The ingredients under common law do not appear to be different. See Akayesu Judgment, para. 537. See furthermore Musema Judgment and Sentence, paras. 177, 179; Bagilishema Judgment, paras. 69-70.

[164] Akayesu Judgment, paras. 540-541 (italics added); also para. 545. See also Musema Judgment and Sentence, para. 183; Bagilishema Judgment, para. 71; Brđanin Judgment, para. 730. Note that the Akayesu Judgment held that the difference between complicity in genocide and aiding and abetting under Article 6(1) is that 'complicity requires a positive act, *i.e.* an act of commission, whereas aiding and abetting may consist in failing to act or refraining from action'. Furthermore, aiding and abetting under Article 6(1) requires specific genocidal intent, whereas complicity in genocide does not. See Akayesu Judgment, paras. 485, 546-548. However, see the Semanza Judgment and Sentence, in which it was held that 'complicity to commit genocide in Article 2(3)(e) refers to all acts of assistance or encouragement that have substantially contributed to, or have had a substantial effect on, the completion of the crime of genocide'. See Semanza Judgment and Sentence, paras. 393, 395. In addition, 'there is no material distinction between complicity in Article 2(3)(e) [complicity in genocide] of the Statute and the broad definition accorded to aiding and abetting in Article 6(1). The Chamber further notes that the *mens rea* requirement for complicity to commit genocide in Article 2(3)(e) mirrors that for aiding and abetting and the other forms of accomplice liability in Article 6(1).' See Semanza Judgment and Sentence, para. 394.

providing the means for its commission.'[165] Although the wording 'for the purpose of facilitating' seems to introduce a subjective requirement stricter than mere knowledge, also under the ICC Statute the aider and abetter does not need to share the genocidal intent of the main perpetrator.[166] This approach is justified by the fact that complicity is a lower form of participation than that of main perpetration, for which a different standard must apply.[167]

As far as sexual violence is concerned, this means that an accomplice to sexual violence may be convicted of complicity in genocide if he was aware that the principal perpetrator of sexual violence was acting with genocidal intent. The accomplice may not himself have had the intent to destroy the group. Complicity to genocidal rape includes acts of assistance or encouragement, such as, holding the victim against the ground, spreading the victim's legs, handing over an object to the perpetrator for insertion into the victim's vagina, words of encouragement to rape or mere presence at the rape scene. To date, no accused has been convicted of complicity in genocidal rapes, either because the accused were already convicted of rape as genocide under Article 6(1) ICTR Statute,[168] or because the case has yet to be decided.

3.1.1.3 Joint criminal enterprise (variant three)

Joint criminal enterprise has become one of the primary modes of liability charged by the Prosecutor, especially in leadership cases. The joint criminal enterprise was for the first time elaborated upon in the *Tadić* case, and is governed by Article 7(1) ICTY Statute or Article 6 ICTR Statute as a form of 'committing'.[169] Although no explicit liability basis can thus be found in the Statutes for the joint criminal enterprise, the object and purpose of the Statute (all offenders of international crimes must be prosecuted) as well as the nature of international crimes (crimes which are often carried out by groups of individuals acting in pursuance of a common criminal design) warrant that also individuals that engage in collective criminality should be held accountable.[170]

---

[165] Italics added.

[166] Arnold (2003), p. 145.

[167] *Ibid.*

[168] Akayesu Judgment, paras. 725-726, 734; Gacumbitsi Judgment, para. 295; Musema Judgment and Sentence, paras. 855, 936.

[169] On 'committing' see Tadić Appeal Judgment, para. 188. Many different names have been used for what now is commonly referred to as 'joint criminal enterprise'. For example, common purpose, common design, and common enterprise. The Trial Chamber in Brđanin and the Appeals Chamber in Milutinović et al. have stressed their preference for 'joint criminal enterprise', a term which is now commonly used throughout the ICTY and ICTR. See *Prosecutor v. Radislav Brđanin and Momir Talić*, Decision on Form of Further Amended Indictment and Prosecution Application to Amend, Case No. IT-99-36, 26 June 2001, para. 24; *Prosecutor v. Milan Milutinović, Nikola Šainović and Dragoljub Ojdanić*, Decision on Dragoljub Ojdanic's Motion Challenging Jurisdiction – Joint Criminal Enterprise, Case No. IT-99-37-AR72, 21 May 2003, para. 36.

[170] Tadić Judgment, paras. 188-192 (with reference in paragraph 190 to the *Report of the Secretary-General Pursuant to Paragraph 2 of Security Council Resolution 808 (1993),* UN Doc. S/25704, 3 May 1993, para. 54: 'The Secretary-General believes that *all* persons who *participate*

Three variants of the joint criminal enterprise have been set out in the *Tadić* case, viz. (1) cases where all co-defendants, acting pursuant to a common design, possess the same criminal intention; (2) the so-called 'concentration camp' cases, which is premised on the idea that in an organised system an accused who holds a certain position of authority within the hierarchy of the system, say a guard, will not easily not be aware of the system of ill-treatment and should therefore be held responsible for the crimes committed within the system; and (3) cases involving a common design to pursue one course of conduct where one of the perpetrators commits an act which, while outside the common design, was nevertheless a natural and foreseeable consequence of the effecting of that common purpose.[171] The essential difference between the first two variants of joint criminal enterprise and the last is that in the first two cases the crime fell within the purpose of the criminal design and all members of the enterprise shared the same intent, whereas in the third variant the crime fell outside the purpose of the criminal plan and the members did not necessarily share the intent with the physical perpetrator of that crime. For this reason, the first two categories have been described as the basic forms of joint criminal enterprise, whereas the third variant has been referred to as the extended form of joint criminal enterprise.[172] The *Tadić* Appeals Chamber summarised the requirements of *actus reus* and *mens rea* of the three variants of the joint criminal enterprise as follows:

> ... the objective elements (*actus reus*) of this mode of participation in one of the crimes provided for in the Statute (with regard to each of the three categories of cases) are as follows:
>
> i. *A plurality of persons.* They need not be organised in a military, political or administrative structure, as is clearly shown by the *Essen Lynching* and the *Kurt Goebell* cases.
>
> ii. *The existence of a common plan, design or purpose which amounts to or involves the commission of a crime provided for in the Statute.* There is no necessity for this plan, design or purpose to have been previously arranged or formulated. The common plan or purpose may materialise extemporaneously and be inferred from the fact that a plurality of persons acts in unison to put into effect a joint criminal enterprise.
>
> iii. *Participation of the accused in the common design* involving the perpetration of one of the crimes provided for in the Statute. This participation need not involve commission of a specific crime under one of those provisions (for example, murder, extermination, torture, rape, etc.), but may take the form of assistance in, or contribution to, the execution of the common plan or purpose.

---

in the planning, preparation or execution of serious violations of international humanitarian law in the former Yugoslavia are individually responsible for such violations.'

[171] *Ibid.*, paras. 193-220.

[172] *Prosecutor v. Radislav Brđanin and Momir Talić*, Decision on Form of Further Amended Indictment and Prosecution Application to Amend, Case No. IT-99-36, 26 June 2001, para. 27.

> By contrast, the *mens rea* element differs according to the category of common design under consideration. With regard to the first category, what is required is the intent to perpetrate a certain crime (this being the shared intent on the part of all co-perpetrators). With regard to the second category (which, as noted above, is really a variant of the first), personal knowledge of the system of ill-treatment is required (whether proved by express testimony or a matter of reasonable inference from the accused's position of authority), as well as the intent to further this common concerted system of ill-treatment. With regard to the third category, what is required is the *intention* to participate in and further the criminal activity or the criminal purpose of a group and to contribute to the joint criminal enterprise or in any event to the commission of a crime by the group. In addition, responsibility for a crime other than the one agreed upon in the common plan arises only if, under the circumstances of the case, (i) it was *foreseeable* that such a crime might be perpetrated by one or other members of the group and (ii) the accused *willingly took that risk.*[173]

The compatibility of the *mens rea* required for a conviction for genocide and the *mens rea* requirement enshrined within the third variant of joint criminal enterprise, the so-called *dolus eventualis*, has been, and still is, heavily debated. According to some, there is no reason why genocidal acts cannot be the natural and foreseeable consequence of a joint criminal enterprise. Others hold that the *dolus eventualis* standard is incompatible with the *dolus specialis* required for the crime of genocide, and might lead to a conviction for genocide without that person ever having had the specific intent to commit genocide himself.[174] The case law of the Tribunals is not all straightforward. In the *Brđanin* case, Brđanin was held to be a member of a joint criminal enterprise whose purpose it was to deport and forcibly transfer the non-Serbs from the Krajina region (Bosnia). According to the Prosecutor, genocide, which included rape and sexual assault allegations, and other crimes were the natural and foreseeable consequence of the deportations and forcible transfer, intended by the participants in the joint criminal enterprise.[175] In a preliminary motion, the Trial Chamber decided that there was, however, no case to answer with respect to genocide, since the specific intent required for a conviction for genocide was incompatible with the *mens rea* standard of the third variant of the joint criminal enterprise.[176] As a response, the Prosecutor filed an interlocutory appeal, arguing that the Trial Chamber had 'confused the *mens rea* required for the offence of genocide with the mental state required to establish responsibility of an accused pursuant to a particular mode of liability'.[177] Thus, in the Prosecutor's view, since all modes of liability require their own *mens rea* standard, the *mens rea* of a mode of liability should be strictly applied. The Appeals Chamber agreed with the Prosecutor and held that 'the Prosecution will be required to establish that it was reasonably foreseeable to the accused that an act specified in Article 4(2) would be

---

[173] Tadić Appeal Judgment, paras. 227-228. See also paras. 193-220.

[174] For instance, see the Stakić Judgment, paras. 530, 558.

[175] *Prosecutor v. Radoslav Brđanin,* Sixth Amended Indictment, Case No. IT-99-36-T, 9 December 2003, paras. 27.3 and 37.

[176] *Prosecutor v. Radoslav Brđanin,* Decision on Motion of Acquittal Pursuant to Rule 98*bis*, Case No. IT-99-36-T, 28 November 2003.

[177] *Prosecutor v. Radoslav Brđanin,* Prosection's Appeal from Trial Chamber's Decision Pursuant to 98*bis*, Case No. IT-99-36-T, 10 December 2003, para. 13.

committed and that it would be committed with genocidal intent'.[178] Surprisingly, the Trial Chamber did not address the joint criminal enterprise and its relationship to the crime of genocide in its judgment. Instead, it relied on more traditional modes of liability, such as aiding and abetting, planning and instigating.[179] The Trial Chamber held that charging the accused with joint criminal enterprise was in this case not 'an appropriate mode of liability to describe the individual criminal liability of the accused given the extraordinarily broad nature of the case, where the prosecution seeks to include within a joint criminal enterprise a person as structurally remote from the commission of the crimes charged in the indictment as the accused'.[180] Thus, the Trial Chamber found that joint criminal enterprise was not to be considered in this type of cases where joint criminal enterprise encompasses such a big area (the removal of Bosnian Muslim and Bosnian Croat inhabitants from the territory of the planned Serbian State) and so many participants and where, consequently, the link between accused and perpetrators is a remote one. According to the *Brđanin* Trial Chamber, what the *Tadić* Appeals Chamber had in mind were somewhat smaller enterprises, such as enterprises restricted to a geographical area or limited to a specific military operation and only to members of the armed forces.[181] The discussion about whether or not the third variant of the joint criminal enterprise as such is compatible with the *mens rea* requirement for genocide has not been closed owing to the *Brđanin* Trial Chamber Judgment; instead, their compatibility seems generally to have been accepted by the ICTR Trial Chamber in the *Government I* case, as the Chamber again recognised that the third variant of the joint criminal enterprise may apply to genocide.[182]

To date, no convictions have yet resulted for genocidal rapes that can be the natural and foreseeable consequence of joint criminal enterprise. However, such convictions may take place in the near future as several accused have been charged therewith, such as Milosević, Mladić and Karemera, Ngirumpatse and Nzirorera (*Government I*). In the indictment related to Bosnia, Milosević has been indicted for participating in a joint criminal enterprise, which had as its purpose the forcible and permanent removal of the majority of non-Serbs, principally Bosnian Muslims and Bosnian Croats, from large areas of the Republic of Bosnia and Herzegovina, through the commission of crimes which are in violation of Articles 2, 3, 4 and 5 of the ICTY Statute.[183] The indictment stipulates that:

---

[178] *Prosecutor v. Radoslav Brđanin,* Decision on Interlocutory Appeal, Case No. IT-99-36-T, 19 March 2004, para. 6.

[179] Brđanin Judgment, paras. 357-377.

[180] *Ibid.*, para. 355.

[181] *Ibid.*

[182] *The Prosecutor v. Édouard Karemera, Mathieu Ngirumpatse, Joseph Nzirorera and André Rwamakuba,* Decision on the Preliminary Motions by the Defence of Joseph Nzirorera, Edouard Karemera, André Rwamakuba and Mathieu Ngirumpatse Challenging Jurisdiction in relation to Joint Criminal Enterprise, Case No. ICTR-98-44-T, 11 May 2004, paras. 46-48 (with reference to the Brđanin Appeals Chamber Decision on Interlocutory Appeal). See also *André Rwamakuba v. The Prosecutor*, Decision on Interlocutory Appeal Regarding Application of Joint Criminal Enterprise to the Crime of Genocide, Case No. ICTR-98-44-AR72.4, 22 October 2004.

[183] *Prosecutor v. Slobodan Milosević*, Indictment (Bosnia), Case No. IT-01-51-I, 22 November 2001, para. 6.

> The crimes enumerated in Counts 1 to 29 of this indictment were within the object of the joint criminal enterprise. Alternatively, the crimes enumerated in Counts 1 to 15 and 19 to 29 were natural and foreseeable consequences of the execution of the object of the joint criminal enterprise and the accused was aware that such crimes were the possible outcome of the execution of the joint criminal enterprise.[184]

On the basis hereof, Milosević may face a conviction for genocidal acts, including sexual violence (as stated in count 1), that were the natural and foreseeable consequences of the joint criminal enterprise of forcibly and permanently removing the majority of non-Serbs from large areas of the Republic of Bosnia and Herzegovina. This means that Milosević could be convicted of sexual violence as genocide, not because he intended such acts to occur, but because he could have foreseen that sexual violence as genocide might take place as a result of his participation in the joint criminal enterprise and he willingly took that risk. Mladić too may be convicted of sexual violence as a means to commit genocide if these crimes are proved to be a natural and foreseeable consequence of the execution of the joint criminal enterprise, that is, the elimination or permanent removal, by force or other means, of non-Serb inhabitants from large areas of Bosnia and Herzegovina.[185] As regards Karemera (former Minister of the Interior), Ngirumpatse (former Minister of Justice) and Nzirorera (former National-Secretary of the MRND), it has been held that they participated in a joint criminal enterprise with the purpose of destroying the Tutsi population of Rwanda.[186] The indictment states that:

> The crimes enumerated in Counts 2, 3, 4, 6, and 7 of this indictment were within the object of the joint criminal enterprise. The crimes enumerated in Counts 3 [Genocide], 4 [Complicity in Genocide, in the alternative], and 5 [Rape as a crime against humanity] were the natural and foreseeable consequences of the execution of the object of the joint criminal enterprise and the accused were aware that such crimes were the possible outcome of the execution of the joint criminal enterprise.[187]

Paragraph 66 (under counts 3 and 4) of the *Government I* Indictment is very clear on the point that sexual violence as a means to commit genocide was a natural and foreseeable outcome of the joint criminal enterprise:

> In Ruhengeri *préfecture* during early – mid April 1994, Kigali-ville *préfecture* during April 1994, Butare *préfecture* during mid – late April 1994, Kibuye *préfecture* during May – June 1994, and Gitarama *préfecture* during April and May 1994, and throughout Rwanda, *Interahamwe* and militiamen raped and sexually assaulted Tutsi women and girls throughout Rwanda, causing them serious bodily or mental harm. Such serious bodily or mental harm inflicted upon Tutsi women and girls was intended to destroy the capacity of

[184] *Ibid.*, para. 8.
[185] *Prosecutor v. Ratko Mladić*, Amended Indictment, Case No. IT-95-5/18-I, 10 October 2002, paras. 20-22, 34.
[186] *The Prosecutor v. Édouard Karemera, Mathieu Ngirumpatse and Joseph Nzirorera*, Amended Indictment, Case No. ICTR-98-44-I, 23 February 2005, paras. 4-16.
[187] *Ibid.*, para. 7.

> persons of Tutsi ethnic or racial identity to sustain themselves physically or psychologically as a group, or to reproduce themselves as a group. Edouard KAREMERA, Mathieu NGIRUMPATSE, and Joseph NZIRORERA were aware that rape was the natural and foreseeable consequence of the execution of the joint criminal enterprise and knowingly and wilfully participated in that enterprise.[188]

As the Tribunals have not rejected the applicability of the third variant of joint criminal enterprise to genocide, some of the accused may be convicted of genocidal rapes, crimes which may well have fallen outside the joint criminal enterprise, but were nonetheless a natural and foreseeable consequence of the enterprise.[189] Much will depend on whether or not the link between the accused and the perpetrators of sexual violence is not found to be a too remote one. Article 25(3)(d) of the ICC Statute does not cover the third variant of joint criminal enterprise, as alternative (ii) requires knowledge of the intention of the group, thus excluding *dolus eventualis*.[190] This may create a gap. However, the ICC may use the case law of the Tribunals in interpreting the concepts listed in Article 25: 'Such an approach warrants not only because the Court has to apply customary international law and general principles pursuant to Article 21 of its Statute, but also in order to develop a coherent and uniform concept of perpetration and participation in international criminal law.'[191]

3.2 Destruction of the group, as such

In *Akayesu*, it was held that intent to destroy a group 'as such' means that the particular prohibited act 'be committed against a specifically targeted group'.[192] For a genocidaire, '... the act must have been committed against one or several individuals, because such individual or individuals were members of a specific group, and specifically because they belonged to this group. Thus, the victim is chosen not because of his individual identity, but rather on account of his membership of a national, ethnical, racial or religious group. The victim of the act is therefore a member of a group, chosen as such, which, hence, means that the victim of the crime of genocide is the group itself and not only the individual.'[193] Whereas for genocide the scope of the intent of the perpetrator includes the destruction of the group, for persecution as a crime against humanity the perpetrator selects his victims because they belong to a specific community, but does not seek to destroy the community as such.[194] The genocide prohibition is aimed at protecting the existence of groups as such. Precisely the danger inherent in the intent to destroy the group as such has given the crime of genocide its specific gravity and the label 'crime of crimes'.

---

188 *Ibid.*, para. 66.

189 For further reading on the joint criminal enterprise and sexual violence prosecutions, see Viseur Sellers (2004), pp. 153-194.

190 Van Sliedregt (2003), p. 108.

191 *Ibid.*, p. 114.

192 Akayesu Judgment, para. 499; see also para. 521.

193 *Ibid.*, para. 521.

194 Jelisić Judgment, para. 79.

The groups enumerated – national, ethnical, racial or religious – have been clarified in the *Akayesu* Judgment. A national group is defined as 'a collection of people who are perceived to share a legal bond based on common citizenship, coupled with reciprocity of rights and duties'.[195] An ethnic group has been defined as 'a group whose members share a common language or culture'.[196] As to 'racial group', the Trial Chamber concurs that 'the conventional definition of racial group is based on the hereditary physical traits often identified with a geographical region, irrespective of linguistic, cultural, national or religious factors' and defines a religious group as 'one whose members share the same religion, denomination or mode of worship'.[197]

On the basis of these definitions, the Tutsi, the Trial Chamber held, were to be regarded as an ethnic group. Such a holding is very odd, however, considering that the Tutsi and Hutu (and Twa) share a common language and culture and would thus together constitute an ethnic group. Therefore, the Tutsi as a separate ethnic group within Rwandan society does not exist. The Trial Chamber could have opted for the Tutsi to fall within the ambit of 'racial group'. The drafters of the Genocide Convention understood racial group to refer to, for instance, the 'Jewish race', the 'English race' and the 'German race'.[198] Instead of referring to the Tutsi as the 'Tutsi race', the Trial Chamber took recourse to other factors that, in their eyes, rendered the Tutsi an ethnic group. In favour of its argument, it referred to Rwandan Law, which identified citizens by ethnic group (until the 1993 Arusha Peace Agreement, the definition of ethnic group was not determined on the basis of law, but on the basis of customary rules which applied patrilineal lines of heredity); identity cards with explicit mention of someone's ethnicity (these were introduced during the Belgian colonial days); witnesses who testified before the Trial Chamber identified themselves by ethnic group, and generally knew to what ethnic group their friends and neighbours belonged; and, finally, the perpetrators viewed the Tutsi as an ethnic group.[199] The fact that the Trial Chamber gave a definition of 'ethnic group' and next determined whether a victim belonged to one or not, indicates that the Trial Chamber opted for an objective approach to the definition of ethnic group. As this did not work in the case of the Tutsi – they did not fit the definitional requirements of 'ethnic group' – it might have been better if the Trial Chamber had opted for a subjective approach straightaway. By taking a subjective approach to the issue the Chamber could have considered the (subjective) views and intentions of the participants at the time.[200] How, for instance, did the perpetrators of the

---

[195] Akayesu Judgment, para. 512 (with reference to ICJ, *Nottebohm* (*Liechtenstein v. Guatemala)*, ICJ Decision, 6 April 1955, ICJ Reports (1955).

[196] *Ibid.*, para. 513.

[197] *Ibid.*, paras. 514 and 515, respectively.

[198] According to Schabas (2001a, p. 541): 'Although modern science now rejects the whole notion of the objective existence of 'races', for the purposes of the Convention the term ought to be construed not only to reflect the intent of the drafters but to ensure as large a protection of vulnerable groups as possible. In this respect, it may be useful to note that the International Convention for the Elimination of All Forms of Racial Discrimination does not limit the scope of 'race' to hereditary physical traits, and defines racial discrimination as 'any distinction, exclusion, restriction or preference based on race, colour, descent, or national or ethnic origin'.

[199] Akayesu Judgment, paras. 170-171.

[200] *Ibid.*, para. 172.

genocide perceive their victims: as Tutsi or as Hutu? How did the victims of the genocide identify themselves? Even so, the Trial Chamber took this subjective approach in the *Kayishema and Ruzindana* Judgment a few months later. Here the Trial Chamber determined that the Tutsi were an ethnic group because they had been so designated by the Rwandan authorities on their identity cards and because the witnesses who testified before the Tribunal stated that they were Tutsi and that those whom they had seen massacred were also Tutsi.[201]

The *Akayesu* Chamber chose the objective approach and, in need of a solution to have the Tutsi fit in to it in some way, considered the intentions of the drafters when including the four groups. It opined that the intention of the drafters of the Genocide Convention was 'patently to ensure the protection of any stable and permanent group'.[202] In particular, it articulated that

> ... the crime of genocide was allegedly perceived as targeting only 'stable' groups, constituted in a permanent fashion and membership of which is determined by birth, with the exclusion of the more 'mobile' groups which one joins through individual voluntary commitment, such as political and economic groups. Therefore, a common criterion in the four types of groups protected by the Genocide Convention is that membership in such groups would seem to be normally not challengeable by its members, who belong to it automatically, by birth, in a continuous and often irremediable manner.[203]

According to the Trial Chamber, the Tutsi constituted such a stable and permanent group.[204]

Reference to gender-based groups within the groups selected for destruction is missing. The *travaux préparatoires* of the 1948 Genocide Convention do not seem to indicate that such inclusion was intended.[205] Nevertheless, if the intention of the drafters of the Genocide Convention 'was patently to ensure the protection of any stable and permanent group', it could be argued that they indirectly contemplated that the groups could be extended accordingly.[206] If this interpretation is correct, women would certainly seem to fulfil the 'stable and permanent group' test.[207] Considering that the genocide definition has not changed since 1948, gender is still not a ground for

---

201 Kayishema and Ruzindana Judgment, paras. 523-525. See also para. 98 on 'the Law', where it is said that: 'An ethnic group is one whose members share a common language and culture; or; a group which distinguishes itself, as such (self identification); or, a group identified as such by others, including perpetrators of the crimes (identification by others).

202 Akayesu Judgment, para. 516.

203 *Ibid.*, para. 511. According to several scholars, it is a misreading of the *travaux preparatoires* to conclude that the drafters' intent 'was patently to ensure the protection of any stable and permanent group'. See Schabas (2001a), pp. 541-543; Verdirame (2000), p. 592; Boot (2002), pp. 429-431.

204 Akayesu Judgment, para. 702.

205 McDonald (1998), pp. 135-136.

206 Akayesu Judgment, para. 516.

207 As stated by McDonald (1999, p. 76): 'gender would seem to be more permanent and less easily changed than religion'. According to Koenig and Askin (2000, p. 25): 'Females constitute a stable and permanent group, and indeed probably constitute the largest group possible.'

genocide, and sexual violence may therefore only amount to genocide if it was targeted against an individual belonging to a national, ethnical, racial or religious group. Before the ICTR, sexual violence against women has therefore been prosecuted as genocide because the women belonged to a larger protected ethnic group, the Tutsi. However, the Tutsi women in Rwanda were targeted on the basis of ethnicity *and* gender. During the times of the rapes, numerous statements were made by the rapists which referred to the sexuality of the Tutsi women or the Tutsi in general. Different rapists throughout the country repeatedly employed the same terminology whilst raping Tutsi women, which is compelling evidence that rapists were acting under a common organisational policy to rape Tutsi women.

Whatever the intention of the drafters at the time of preparing the Genocide Convention, it is recommended that gender be included in the list of target groups protected from genocidal acts.[208] As sexual violence is commonly used as a means to destroy a people, its inclusion would appropriately identify gender as a persuasive basis of genocidal persecution. Sexual violence is a way to destroy people's attachment to their identity; it is a way to destroy people in an intimate way, to shatter the group. Gender as a basis for group destruction has never been seen as such. Women as a group have always been overruled, in particularly at the time of the drafting of the 1948 Genocide Convention. The destruction of women as such has never been seen, but if you see them as part of a particular group, their destruction is obvious.[209] New insights have brought about changes in law and practice before. Indeed, in the ICC Statute gender has been included as a ground for persecution under crimes against humanity and reflects the international community's recognition that discrimination against women at least rises to the level of crimes against humanity. Then why not include gender as a basis for group destruction for the crime of genocide?

3.3 In whole or in part

While the chapeau of the crime of genocide states that the destruction of the group must be 'in whole or in part', it is not required that the group has in fact been wholly or partially annihilated, as long as the acts were committed with specific intent.[210] The terminology 'in part' is generally understood to cover a 'substantial' part, which either means 'a large majority of the group in question or the most representative members of the targeted community'.[211] It has also been held that localised genocide may lead to the destruction of a group 'in part', such as the destruction of a group located within a small geographical area if the perpetrators of the genocide regarded the intended destruction as sufficient to annihilate the group as a distinct entity in the geographic area at issue.[212] On the basis of the above, it can be argued that, if the female population of a group is attacked, the survival of the group may be at stake, even if the attacks are localised.

---

208 Askin (1997), pp. 342-343. For a different opinion, see Schabas (2000b), p. 147.

209 MacKinnon, Seminar on Sexual Violence under International Law, Arusha, 15 November 2003.

210 Akayesu Judgment, para. 497.

211 Jelisić Judgment, para. 82.

212 Jelisić Judgment, para. 83; Kristić Judgment, para. 590.

3.4 Proof of intent

Intent is a mental factor which is difficult to determine. For this reason, and in the absence of a confession from the accused, intent can be inferred from a certain number of presumptions of fact. In the ICTY and ICTR case law, a number of factors that may evidence an accused's genocidal intent were developed, including: (1) the general political doctrine which gave rise to the (prohibited) acts;[213] (2) the general nature of atrocities in a region or a country;[214] (3) the existence of a genocidal plan and the accused's participation in its creation and/or execution;[215] (4) the scale of atrocities committed;[216] (5) the general context of the perpetration and/or repetition of other destructive or discriminatory acts committed as part of the same pattern of conduct, systematically directed against the same group, whether committed by the same offender or by others;[217] (6) the perpetration of acts which violate, or which the perpetrators themselves consider to violate, the very foundation of the group;[218] (7) the degree to which the group was in fact destroyed in whole or in part;[219] and (8) utterances of the accused.[220]

In some of the ICTR cases, rape and sexual violence proved to be evidence of the accused's intent to destroy the Tutsi ethnic group. In Rwanda, many women were targeted because they were Tutsi women: they were sexually violated on the basis of both their ethnicity and gender.[221] The OTP Rape Database demonstrates that 'nearly seven women out of every ten women raped heard explicitly ethnic statements during the rape'.[222] On many occasions, utterances by the accused were made which implied that Tutsi women were sexually arrogant in their sexual refusal of Hutu men, and these statements were repeated throughout Rwanda and indicated a systematic policy to rape Tutsi women.[223] In the *Akayesu* case, Akayesu's genocidal intent was inferred from his speeches: '... calling, more or less explicitly, for the commission of genocide'.[224] He

---

[213] Karadžić and Mladić Rule 61 Decision, para. 94.

[214] Akayesu Judgment, para. 523; Kayishema and Ruzindana Judgment, para. 93.

[215] Note that the Jelisić Appeals Chamber stated that 'the existence of a plan or policy is not a legal ingredient of the crime'. See Jelisić Appeal Judgment, para. 48. According to the Kayishema and Ruzindana Judgment (para. 94): 'although a specific plan to destroy does not constitute an element of genocide, it would appear that it is not easy to carry out a genocide without a plan or organization'. In the Krstić Judgment (para. 572), it became clear that a plan of genocide need not have been formed long before.

[216] Akayesu Judgment, para. 523.

[217] *Ibid.*; Karadžić and Mladić Rule 61 Decision, para. 94.

[218] Karadžić and Mladić Rule 61 Decision, para. 94.

[219] Note that the crime of genocide does not imply the actual extermination of the group in its entirety. See Akayesu Judgment, para. 497; Karadžić and Mladić Rule 61 Decision, para. 92.

[220] See Akayesu Judgment, para. 728; Kayeshima and Ruzindana Judgment, para. 538; Musema Judgment and Sentence, para. 933; Gacumbitsi Judgment, para. 259; Karadžić and Mladić Rule 61 Decision, para. 95.

[221] Nowrojee (2004a), para. 41.

[222] *Ibid.*

[223] *Ibid.*

[224] Akayesu Judgment, para. 729.

also participated in the 'very high number of atrocities committed against the Tutsi, their widespread nature not only in the commune of Taba, but also throughout Rwanda, and to the fact that the victims were systematically and deliberately selected because they belonged to the Tutsi group, with persons belonging to other groups being excluded'.[225] This included acts of rape and sexual violence. Specifically, the Trial Chamber held: 'Sexual violence was an integral part of the process of destruction, specifically targeting Tutsi women and specifically contributing to their destruction and to the destruction of the Tutsi group as a whole.[226] Furthermore:

> The rape of Tutsi women was systematic and was perpetrated against all Tutsi women and solely against them. A Tutsi woman, married to a Hutu, testified before the Chamber that she was not raped because her ethnic background was unknown. As part of the propaganda campaign geared to mobilizing the Hutu against the Tutsi, the Tutsi women were presented as sexual objects. Indeed, the Chamber was told, for an example, that before being raped and killed, Alexia, who was the wife of the Professor, Ntereye, and her two nieces, were forced by the Interahamwe to undress and ordered to run and do exercises '*in order to display the thighs of Tutsi women*'. The Interahamwe who raped Alexia said, as he threw her on the ground and got on top of her, '*let us now see what the vagina of a Tutsi woman [tastes] like*'. As stated above, Akayesu himself, speaking to the Interahamwe who were committing the rapes, said to them: '*don't ever ask again what a Tutsi woman tastes like*'. This sexualized representation of ethnic identity graphically illustrates that tutsi women were subjected to sexual violence because they were Tutsi. Sexual violence was a step in the process of destruction of the tutsi group - destruction of the spirit, of the will to live, and of life itself.[227]

Although Kayishema was not charged with sexual violence himself, evidence concerning sexual violence emerged during trial and was taken into account in the verdict. Kayishema's intent to destroy in whole or in part the Tutsi group as such was evidenced by the number of victims,[228] the persistent pattern of conduct and his utterances.[229] In addition, his position as a Prefect made it highly likely that he could be accused of genocide, as the 'national plan to commit genocide was implemented at *prefecture* levels'.[230] On several occasions, the evidence of sexual violence was explicitly held to contribute to proof of specific intent. The Trial Chamber found evidence of specific intent of genocide in the following: 'Witness F's wife was gang-raped by the Hutus before her children's eyes on 13 April.'[231] Kayishema's intent was proved by the great number of people killed, regardless of gender or age: 'Men and women, old and young, were killed without mercy. Children were massacred before

[225] *Ibid.*, para. 730.
[226] *Ibid.*, para. 731.
[227] *Ibid.*, para. 732 (italics added). See also Kayishema and Ruzindana Judgment, para. 95.
[228] Kayishema and Ruzindana Judgment, paras. 531-533.
[229] Kayishema made remarks such as 'all the dirt has to be removed', 'Tutsi dogs' and 'Tutsi sons of bitches', 'get down to work', referring to the Tutsis. Kayishema and Ruzindana Judgment, paras. 538-540.
[230] *Ibid.*, para. 528.
[231] *Ibid.*, para. 299.

their parents' eyes, women raped in front of their families. No Tutsi was spared, neither the weak nor the pregnant.'[232] Although specific intent was found in a number of other cases, such as in *Semanza*, sexual violence was not charged as genocide.

The Trial Chamber in the *Musema* case affirmed Musema's intent to destroy the Tutsi ethnic group as such, which included acts of sexual violence. The Trial Chamber held that:

> ... on the basis of the evidence presented, it emerges that acts of serious bodily and mental harm, including rape and other forms of sexual violence were often accompanied by humiliating utterances, which clearly indicated that the intention underlying each specific act was to destroy the Tutsi group as a whole. The Chamber notes, for example, that during the rape of Nyiramusugi Musema declared: '*The pride of the Tutsis will end today*'. In this context, the acts of rape and sexual violence were an integral part of the plan conceived to destroy the Tutsi group. Such acts targeted Tutsi women, in particular, and specifically contributed to their destruction and therefore that of the Tutsi group as such. Witness N testified before the Chamber that Nyiramusugi, who was left for dead by those who raped her, had indeed been killed in a way. Indeed, the Witness specified that 'what they did to her is worse than death.[233]

Although Musema was found to incur individual criminal responsibility under Article 6(1) of the Statute, for having raped, in concert with others, a young Tutsi woman and for having abetted others in raping the girl, by his own act of rape and the example he thus set, thus having caused serious bodily and mental harm to a member of the Tutsi group,[234] the Appeals Chamber quashed the conviction on the basis of additional contradictory evidence.[235]

In the *Gacumbitsi* case, genocidal intent was established on the basis of Gacumbitsi's utterances and actions: he incited the Hutu to kill the Tutsi, he personally killed a Tutsi and he instigated the rape of Tutsi women and girls.[236] Gacumbitsi had called on Hutu men to have sex with Tutsi girls who had refused to marry Hutu men, adding that whoever would resist had to be killed in an atrocious manner, that is, by inserting sticks into their genitals.[237] Immediately following his call for rape, eight Tutsi women were raped by a group of Hutu men.[238] Witness TAQ's attacker had asked her if

---

[232] *Ibid.*, para. 532.

[233] Musema Judgment and Sentence, para. 933 (italics added).

[234] With respect to the Prosecutor's argument that Musema was also liable under Article 6(3) of the Statute, the Chamber noted that the Prosecutor had not established, nor even alleged, that among the assailants who attacked Nyiramusugi there were employees of the Gisovu Tea Factory or other persons who were Musema's subordinates. Therefore, the Chamber held that Musema did not incur individual criminal responsibility under Article 6(3) of the Statute for Nyiramusugi's rape. Musema Judgment and Sentence, para. 909.

[235] Musema Appeal Judgment, paras. 193-194.

[236] Gacumbitsi Judgment, para. 259.

[237] *Ibid.*, paras. 200-202, 215, 224, 227.

[238] *Ibid.*, para. 224.

the child she was carrying was a boy or a girl, 'for he would have disembowelled her in order to kill the child if it was a boy'.[239]

In the pending *Butare* trial, the genocidal intent can be inferred not only from the acts themselves – the large-scale sexual violence perpetrated solely against the Tutsi women in Butare – but also from the words expressed against them. Witness QBP testified that on one occasion, when Pauline Nyaramasuhuko arrived at the Butare Prefecture Office, she addressed the soldiers and *Interahamwe* gathered there with the following words: 'I see that there is still much dirt here at the prefecture, such as these Tutsi women who were arrogant and did not want to marry the Hutu before. It is now up to you Hutu to do with them what you like.'[240] Following Nyaramasuhuko's encouragement to rape, Tutsi women were dragged behind the Prefecture Office and some were boarded on a vehicle, while others managed to take shelter in the bush behind the Prefecture Office.[241]

4 Final remarks

The definition of genocide was first laid down in the 1948 Genocide Convention. In the early 1990s, almost half a century later, verbatim copies of the definition of genocide were laid down in the ICTY and ICTR Statutes, and in the ICC Statute in 1998. As no international criminal tribunal had ever interpreted the elements of the crime of genocide before, the Tribunals faced a difficult though challenging task. The Tribunals have wrestled enormously with interpretative questions (and still do so), including the types of acts that should fall within the ambit of the acts that constitute genocide, what the mental standard required for genocide should be, how the mental element of some of the participatory forms should relate to the mental standard of genocide and which groups should qualify for protection under the genocide prohibition. As far as the prosecution of rape and other forms of sexual violence as genocide is concerned, the *Akayesu* Judgment constituted an enormous breakthrough in supranational criminal law. Since it was pronounced in 1998, the assertion that such crimes do not rise to the level of genocide has been firmly repudiated. Even if rape or other forms of sexual violence

---

239 *Ibid.*, para. 203.

240 *The Prosecutor v. Pauline Nyiramasuhuko, Arsène Shalom Ntahobali, Alphonse Nteziryayo, Sylvain Nsabimana, Elie Ndayambaje and Joseph Kanyabashi*, Transcripts, Case No. ICTR-98-42-T, 24 October 2002, p. 85. See also the statements of Witnesses TA and QBP who heard her say, while referring to the Tutsi seeking refuge at the Prefecture Office, 'one didn't want that dirt, and that one should get rid of that dirt' and 'take the women and young girls; rape them before you kill them as before they refused to marry Hutus', respectively. Following the latter statement, women and girls were raped. *The Prosecutor v. Pauline Nyiramasuhuko, Arsène Shalom Ntahobali, Alphonse Nteziryayo, Sylvain Nsabimana, Elie Ndayambaje and Joseph Kanyabashi*, Transcripts, Case No. ICTR-98-42-T, 24 October 2001, p. 109; *The Prosecutor v. Pauline Nyiramasuhuko, Arsène Shalom Ntahobali, Alphonse Nteziryayo, Sylvain Nsabimana, Elie Ndayambaje and Joseph Kanyabashi*, Transcripts, Case No. ICTR-98-42-T, 11 March 2003, p. 54.

241 *The Prosecutor v. Pauline Nyiramasuhuko, Arsène Shalom Ntahobali, Alphonse Nteziryayo, Sylvain Nsabimana, Elie Ndayambaje and Joseph Kanyabashi*, Transcripts, Case No. ICTR-98-42-T, 24 October 2002, pp. 85, 86.

do not lead or are not intended to lead to the death of members of a particular group, it aims to undermine the security and cohesion of the targeted community. Genocidal rape is especially effective if the society stigmatises the rape victim. The implementation of this decision in other cases, despite the evidence concerning genocidal sexual violence (especially in Rwanda), has been minimal, however. To date, after the *Akayesu* case only in the *Gacumbitsi* and *Muhimana* cases were the accused convicted of genocidal rapes. Not recognising sexual violence as genocide when it is, jeopardises the legitimacy of the Tribunals and will make survivors reluctant to give testimony.[242] Sexual violence as genocide is not worse than sexual violence as crimes against humanity or war crimes, but only recognises the crime for what it is. If the ICC wants to gain any credibility among genocidal sexual violence survivors, it should prosecute sexual violence crimes as genocide if the intent to destroy the particular group was present.

4.1 The genocidal acts and the prosecution of sexual violence

The *Akayesu* Judgment was instrumental in bringing about the recognition that acts of sexual violence can be a means to achieve genocide. Absent explicit enumeration of rape and sexual violence, these crimes can be charged under *any* of the five acts, most notably paragraphs (b), (c) and (d). The ICC's EoC contains a footnote at Article 6(b) clarifying that 'serious bodily or mental harm' includes rape and sexual violence. Footnotes were inserted into the EoC to clarify specific issues or the intention of the drafters, and have the same status as the elements of the crimes themselves. Therefore, although the genocide definition remains unchanged in the ICC Statute, by categorising rape and sexual violence under 'serious bodily or mental harm', in the (officially non-binding) EoC, genocidal rape received a more explicit written basis than ever before. Nevertheless, it is suggested here that the *actus reus* of the crime of genocide in the ICC Statute be amended to include explicitly rape and other forms of sexual violence as constitutive genocidal acts. 'Rape, sexual slavery, enforced prostitution, forced pregnancy, enforced sterilization, or any other form of sexual violence of comparable gravity', acts listed as the *actus reus* of crimes against humanity and war crimes in the ICC Statute,[243] may also constitute genocide, and should therefore be listed as acts constituting genocide as well. Explicit inclusion of rape, sexual slavery, enforced prostitution, forced pregnancy, enforced sterilisation or any other form of sexual violence of comparable gravity as genocidal acts would recognise the intrinsic seriousness of the crime. In addition, listing 'rape, sexual slavery, enforced prostitution, forced pregnancy, enforced sterilization, or any other form of sexual violence of comparable gravity' as the constitutive acts of genocide would bring the law in line with crimes against humanity and war crimes, where these sexual violence crimes are already listed.

---

[242] According to MacKinnon (Seminar on Sexual Violence under International Law, Arusha, 15 November 2003), such feelings were expressed by genocide rape survivors whom she represented in their case against Karadžić in the US.

[243] See Article 7(1)(g), on crimes against humanity, and Articles 8(2)(b)(xxii) and 8(2)(e)(vi), on war crimes in international and internal armed conflict, respectively.

As long as no amendments of the genocide definition take place, in light of the Tribunals' recognition that rape and sexual violence are one of the worst ways to inflict physical and psychological harm upon a human being, paragraph (b) concerning 'causing serious bodily or mental harm' seems to be the most straightforward basis to charge genocidal rape prosecutions upon. In addition, although genocide is necessarily a crime committed against a particular group, prosecuting rape and sexual violence under paragraph (b) takes into account the infliction of serious physical and mental harm on the individual woman. The harm done to the female individual of the group is therefore not 'forgotten', a factor which might be less surfacing when genocidal rape is prosecuted under paragraphs (a), (c), (d) and (e). Paragraph (a) refers to killing, (c) to group destruction, while paragraphs (d) and (e) to preventing or restricting births within a group. In the latter two cases, the focus is on the reproductive capacity of the members of the group, not so much on the harm to the individual involved.

One dreadful consequence of sexual violence during conflict is infection with HIV/AIDS, a disease resulting in a slow death and, when inflicted intentionally, such genocidal rape could be prosecuted under paragraph (c), or even (b). The current lack of recognition of HIV/AIDS as a means to commit genocide is a failure of the Rwanda Tribunal in particular, obscuring the historical record in terms of how genocidal rape has taken place in Rwanda (where approximately 70 percent of the rape survivors are infected with HIV/AIDS), thereby essentially denying recognition to victims who obtained HIV/AIDS through sexual violence. Intentional infliction of HIV/AIDS could have been prosecuted under paragraph (c) as 'conditions of life calculated to bring about the group's physical destruction'. In view of other conflicts where HIV/AIDS is or will be used with a genocidal purpose, the ICC should take the use of the intentional infliction of HIV/AIDS into account in its investigational and prosecutorial strategies. A more or less similar observation applies to the prosecution of sexual slavery, either collectively or individually through 'forced marriage'. Despite evidence that women were kept in slavery-like conditions for purposes of sex, no charges were brought before the ICTR for sexual slavery as genocide. By not prosecuting sexual slavery it is denied that sexual slavery occurred and the gravity of the crime is disregarded. In Rwanda, many Tutsi women were forced into marriages and often they, instead of the perpetrators, have been blamed for entering into these 'marriages' by Rwandan society: the general belief is namely that Tutsi women only survived because they collaborated with Hutu men. By not prosecuting these crimes, the Tribunal has further enforced such beliefs. Sexual slavery is not limited to the Rwandan conflict only; sexual slavery has been widespread in, for example, Sierra Leone, Uganda and Sudan as well. In many cases, young girls have been abducted by rebel groups to serve as sexual slaves. If the phrase 'rape, sexual slavery, enforced prostitution, forced pregnancy, enforced sterilization, or any other form of sexual violence of comparable gravity' were to be included in the genocide provision of the ICC, collective and individual sexual slavery could be prosecuted under 'sexual slavery'. Intentional infliction of HIV/AIDS through sexual violence might be prosecuted under 'any other forms of comparable gravity', but preferably through explicitly stating the crime in the genocide provision. In this respect, it is noteworthy that the Rwandan courts have failed to address the intentional infliction of HIV/AIDS through rape and forced marriages or sexual slavery in its 2004 Gacaca Law and in its case law as well.[244]

Since certain acts of sexual violence are covered by several paragraphs and because it is often difficult to distinguish the category in which a particular act should fall, it is important to charge all genocidal forms that may be relevant. If the same conduct is cumulatively charged and the perpetrators cumulatively convicted, this will best reflect the heinous nature of the crimes. For example, rape inflicted by the use of a sharp stick inserted into the victim's vagina, which ultimately led to the victim's death, might best be charged under paragraphs (a) and (b). It seems that the case law of the Tribunals has paved the way for future charges of genocidal rape based on any of the five objective acts, including paragraph (c), under which, *inter alia*, Milosević and Mladić face charges for sexual violence. It is, nevertheless, noteworthy that the Tribunals did not utilise these options to their fullest extent: paragraphs (a) and (c) in the case of HIV/AIDS infection and (d) and (e) in the case of transmitting the rapists' ethnicity to the child have never been used as grounds for sexual violence prosecutions, despite evidence to the contrary. However, if the goal is to bring the law into conformity with the reality of the genocidal sexual violence crimes taken place, the *actus reus* needs to be amended to cover explicit references to rape, rape with the intent to inflict HIV/AIDS, sexual slavery (collectively or individually), enforced prostitution, forced pregnancy, enforced sterilisation or any other form of sexual violence of comparable gravity.

4.2 The elements common to genocide and the prosecution of sexual violence

In order to prosecute successfully sexual violence as a constituent crime of genocide, the intent to destroy, in whole or in part, a national, ethnical, racial or religious group, as such, needs to be proved as well. The specific intent of the principal perpetrator requires *dolus specialis*, but in the case of certain modes of liability (including superior criminal responsibility, complicity in genocide, the third variant of the joint criminal enterprise) another, less severe, mental state threshold is applicable to the accused. There will therefore not be any safe havens for those who planned, instigated, ordered, committed or otherwise aided and abetted in the planning, preparation or execution of a sexual violence crime (principal perpetrators). Nor will there be any safe havens for superiors who knew or had reason to know that their subordinates were about to commit or had committed genocidal rapes and that their subordinates had the requisite specific intent; nor for those complicit in genocidal rapes, if they knew that the principal was acting with specific intent (not necessarily themselves); nor for those participating in a joint criminal enterprise, where the genocidal rapes fell outside the joint criminal enterprise but were foreseeable and natural consequences of the enterprise. Intent to destroy a particular group by means of sexual violence can, for instance, be inferred from speeches or statements calling for rape or from statements by rapists themselves explicating that their reason for rape is the victim's gender and/or ethnicity.

[244] Article 72 of the 2004 Gacaca Law outlaws 'acts of rape or acts of torture against sexual organs'. Furthermore, 'acts of torture against others, even though they did not result into death' and 'dehumanising acts on the dead body' also fall within category 1 crimes. See further Chapter 6 on sentencing.

Even though, in conflict situations, women may be sexually targeted because they belong to one of the four groups mentioned above, and are therefore protected by the genocide prohibition, they are often also targeted because they are women. In *Akayesu*, the Trial Chamber referred to the intent of the drafters of the Genocide Convention and held that their intention was to protect 'any stable and permanent group'. If this is correct, women would certainly come within the groups worthy of protection. Gender persecution is furthermore specifically acknowledged as a crime in the definition of crimes against humanity of the ICC Statute. If gender is found to constitute a basis for persecution, this would seem to indicate States' acknowledgement that women as a group are disproportionately the target of sexual violence. It is time for the international community to recognise genocidal rapes for what they are: rapes directed against women in order to destroy them and the larger community they belong to.

4.3 A proposal for an amended definition of genocide that includes genocidal rape and gender as a group

In light of the nature of genocidal sexual violence crimes that are committed in conflict situations, such as rape with or without the intent to inflict HIV/AIDS, collective and individual sexual slavery, enforced prostitution, forced pregnancy, enforced sterilisation, the absence of clear and unequivocal wording prohibiting sexual violence crimes as genocide and gender as a basis for group destruction is striking. The ICC missed the opportunity to address these concerns, and instead accepted the definition of genocide as it had stood since 1948. Although the unwillingness of some States to amend or expand the definition of genocide may be understandable in light of the international customary nature and *jus cogens* status the crime of genocide had acquired, with the passage of time treaties may need to be amended according to new insights or developments in society. True, in 1948 the drafters of the Genocide Convention did not think about sexual violence as a means to destroy a group on the basis of gender. The present-day reality that sexual violence crimes may work to destroy a group has, however, showed that sexual violence may be a perfect tool to destroy a group. The acceptance that sexual violence may rise to the level of genocide, a *jus cogens* crime, means that sexual violence as genocide has become to be accepted as a *jus cogens* norm as well. For the abovementioned reasons, the ICC Statute needs to be amended to include specific sexual violence crimes and gender as a ground for group destruction.[245] That customary international law is moving on this point is also evidenced from State practice and *opinio juris*. Several States have included sexual violence acts among the *actus reus* of genocide[246] in their national legislations and have

[245] See Articles 121 and 123 ICC Statute on amendments and review of the Statute. The next occasion will be in 2009.

[246] For instance, see the Spanish Penal Code and the Rwandan Gacaca Organic Law No. 16/2004 of 19/6/2004. The Spanish Penal Code, Book II, Title XXIV, Crimes against the International Community, Chapter II: Crimes of genocide – Article 607, which reads in part: '(2) With the prison of fifteen to twenty years, if they *sexually attacked* some of the members [of the group] or produced some of the injuries anticipated in article 149' (italics added, unofficial translation). Article 149 reads: 'The one that it will cause to, by any means or procedure, the loss or the uselessness of a device or main member, or of a sense, the impotence, sterility, one serious

made general references such as 'an identifiable group of persons' among the groups targeted for destruction.[247] Together with doctrine, ICTY/R case law and the argument that a definition should fit the reality of the crime, it seems that amendment of the definition of genocide in the ICC Statute is needed. Such an amendment should preferably be accompanied by an amendment of the definition of genocide contained in the 1948 Genocide Convention (or through an additional Protocol), in order to harmonise the law on genocide in further recognition of the fact that sexual violence may amount to genocide.

The proposed amended definition of genocide in Article 6 of the ICC Statute reads:

> 'Genocide' means any of the following acts committed with intent to destroy, in whole or in part, an identifiable group, as such, including a national, ethnical, racial, religious or gender group:
>
> rape, sexual slavery, enforced prostitution, forced pregnancy, enforced sterilization, or any other form of sexual violence of comparable gravity.
>
> …

'Rape with the intent to inflict HIV/AIDS' might either be added to this list or be included in a separate paragraph.

---

deformidad, one serious somatic or psychic disease, will be punished with the prison sentence of six to twelve years' (unofficial translation). For the Spanish Penal Code, see http://www.preventgenocide.org (last visited June 2005). Article 51 of the Gacaca Organic Law No. 16/2004 classifies the following persons as category 1 criminals: 'the person who committed acts of torture against others, even though they did not result in death, together with his or her accomplices', 'the person who committed acts of rape or acts of torture against sexual organs, together with his or her accomplices', and 'the person who committed dehumanising acts on the dead body, together with his or her accomplices'.

[247] For instance, see the Finnish Penal Code, the French Penal Code (both available at http://www.preventgenocide.org) and the Canadian Crimes Against Humanity and War Crimes Act 2000. The Finnish Penal Code, Chapter 11, Section 6 on genocide, reads in part: 'A person who for the purpose of entirely or partially destroying a race or national, ethnic or religious group or *another comparable group*' (italics added). The French Penal Code, Deliver II – Crimes and Offences Against Persons, Titrate Ier – Felonies Against Humanity, Chapter 1 – Genocide, Article 211-1, reads in part: '[1] Genocide is committing or causing to be committed, in the execution of a prearranged plan leading to the total or partial destruction of a national, ethnic, racial or religious group, or of *a group established by reference to by other arbitrary criterion*' (italics added). The Canadian Crimes Against Humanity and War Crimes Act 2000 states that '"genocide" means an act or omission committed with intent to destroy, in whole or in part, *an identifiable group of persons*, as such, that, at the time and in the place of its commission, constitutes genocide according to customary international law or conventional international law or by virtue of its being criminal according to the general principles of law recognized by the community of nations, whether or not it constitutes a contravention of the law in force at the time and in the place of its commission.'

CHAPTER 2
SEXUAL VIOLENCE AS A CRIME AGAINST HUMANITY

1 INTRODUCTION

Since World War II, crimes against humanity have been differently defined in the Nuremberg Charter, the Tokyo Charter, Allied Control Council Law No. 10 (CCL 10), the ICTY Statute, the ICTR Statute and the ICC Statute.[1] While the Nuremberg and Tokyo Charters defined the *actus reus* of crimes against humanity as murder, extermination, enslavement, deportation, persecution and other inhumane acts, CCL 10 added rape, imprisonment and torture to the list. The same (extended) list appears in the ICTY and ICTR Statutes. In 1998, the Statute of the ICC went even further and added the crime of enforced disappearance of persons, the crime of apartheid, sexual slavery, enforced prostitution, forced pregnancy, enforced sterilisation and any other form of sexual violence of comparable gravity to its list. It is obvious that the ICC Statute has significantly developed the law on crimes against humanity, and it has especially expanded on crimes of a sexual violence nature.

Article 7 of the ICC Statute on crimes against humanity reads, in part:

> (1) For the purpose of this Statute, 'crime against humanity' means any of the following acts when committed as part of a widespread or systematic attack directed against any civilian population, with knowledge of the attack:
>
> (a) Murder;
> (b) Extermination;
> (c) *Enslavement*;
> (d) Deportation or forcible transfer of population;
> (e) Imprisonment or other severe deprivation of physical liberty in violation of fundamental rules of international law;
> *(f) Torture*;
> (g) *Rape, sexual slavery, enforced prostitution, forced pregnancy, enforced sterilization, or any other form of sexual violence of comparable gravity*;
> (h) *Persecution* against any identifiable group or collectivity on political, racial, national, ethnic, cultural, religious, *gender as defined in paragraph 3*, or other grounds that are universally recognized as impermissible under international law, in connection with any act referred to in this paragraph or any crime within the jurisdiction of the Court;
> (i) Enforced disappearance of persons;
> (j) The crime of apartheid;

---

[1] See Article 6(c) Nuremberg Charter, Article 5(c) Tokyo Charter, Article II(1)(c) CCL10, Article 5 ICTY Statute, Article 3 ICTR Statute, and Article 7 ICC Statute, respectively.

(k) *Other inhumane acts of a similar character intentionally causing great suffering, or serious injury to body or to mental or physical health.*[2]

Sexual violence has been prosecuted before the Tribunals on the basis of a number of different categories of crimes against humanity. As the Statutes of the Tribunals only specifically mention rape as a crime against humanity (and in the case of the ICTR also to rape and enforced prostitution as 'outrages upon personal dignity'), in order to use the Statutes to their fullest extent other crimes also served as a basis for prosecution, namely enslavement, torture, persecution and other inhumane acts. As no prosecutions had taken place under CCL 10 for rape as a crime against humanity, the case law of the Tribunals constitutes the first source of insights into the legal boundaries of the definitions of sexual violence crimes constituting crimes against humanity at the supranational criminal law level.

The crimes mentioned plus the 'new' specific sexual violence crimes in the ICC Statute (sexual slavery, enforced prostitution, forced pregnancy, enforced sterilisation and any other form of sexual violence of comparable gravity[3]) form the basis of study in this Chapter. First, the applicable prohibited crimes against humanity will be discussed: enslavement (section 2), torture (section 3), specific sexual violence crimes (section 4), persecution on the ground of gender (section 5) and other inhumane acts of a similar character (section 6), followed by the elements common to all crimes against humanity (section 7) and a short discussion of superior responsibility for sexual violence as a crime against humanity (section 8).

2 Enslavement

The crime of enslavement was already recognised as a crime against humanity in Article 6(c) of the Nuremberg Charter, Article II(1)(c) of CCL 10, Article 5(c) of the Tokyo Charter, Article 5(c) of the ICTY Statute and Article 3(c) of the ICTR Statute. However, these instruments give no definition of the crime. Practice before the Tribunals did not provide a (clear) definition of the crime either.[4] The first case that shed some light on the boundaries of the crime of enslavement as a crime against humanity is the *Kunarac, Kovač and Vuković* case, concluded by the ICTY's Appeals Chamber on 12 June 2002, and will therefore be discussed below.

---

[2] Emphasis added.

[3] The 'new' specific sexual violence crimes can also be found in the war crimes provision of the ICC Statute (Article 8(2)(b)(xxii) and Article 8(2)(e)(vi)). In the war crimes provision 'any other form of sexual violence of comparable gravity' is substituted for 'any other form of sexual violence also constituting a grave breach of the Geneva Conventions' and 'any other form of sexual violence also constituting a serious violation of article 3 common to the four Geneva Conventions', respectively. The specific sexual violence crimes will only be discussed in this Chapter, whereas the legal bases of these crimes as war crimes are further explained in Chapter 3.

[4] The post World War II Tribunals rendered some judgments involving the crime of enslavement. However, the boundaries of the crime were not clearly set. See the cases cited in the Kunarac, Kovač and Vuković Judgment, paras. 523-527.

Based on the wording of the 1926 Slavery Convention in particular,[5] paragraph 2(c) of Article 7 of the ICC Statute defines enslavement as

> … the exercise of any or all of the powers attaching to the right of ownership over a person and includes the exercise of such power in the course of trafficking in persons, in particular women and children.

In the ICC's Elements of Crimes (EoC) the element of enslavement is described as follows:

> 1. the perpetrator exercised any or all of the powers attaching to the right of ownership over one or more persons, such as by purchasing, selling, lending or bartering such a person or persons, or by imposing on them a similar deprivation of liberty. [11] [6]
>
> [11] It is understood that such deprivation of liberty may, in some circumstances, include exacting forced labour or otherwise reducing a person to a servile status as defined in the Supplementary Convention on the Abolition of Slavery, the Slave Trade, and Institutions and Practices Similar to Slavery of 1956. It is also understood that the conduct described in this element includes trafficking in persons, in particular women and children.

The first element of the *actus reus* of the crime of enslavement as a crime against humanity was first elaborated for the *actus reus* of sexual slavery as a crime against humanity.[7] It was subsequently copied to the first element of the crime of enslavement as a crime against humanity. As the background of the element will be discussed in greater detail in subsection 4.2 (sexual slavery), here the most basic aspects of the definition will be discussed. Although the footnote to the first element of enslavement was elaborated in the context of the crime of enslavement first, the footnote will be discussed more in depth in subsection 4.2 (sexual slavery) as well.

Enslavement is defined in the ICC Statute (and copied almost verbatim in the EoC) as 'the exercise of any or all of the powers attaching to the right of ownership over a person ...'. How these powers of ownership can be exercised has been made clear by an illustrative list of examples ('purchasing, selling, lending or bartering … or by imposing on them a similar deprivation of liberty'), which, however, all seem to focus on some sort of commercial benefit. The word 'similar' in the phrase 'similar deprivation of liberty', which refers to the examples given, may give rise to misinterpretation because of the commercial aspect mentioned.[8] For that reason, this phrase was elaborated in this context in footnote 11, which added that 'similar deprivation of liberty' should not be interpreted restrictively.[9] According to footnote 11, 'forced labour',[10] 'reducing a person

[5] In Article 1(1) of the 1926 Slavery Convention the first basic definition of slavery is given, namely 'the status or condition of a person over whom any or all of the powers attaching to the right of ownership are exercised'.

[6] Article 7(1)(c) EoC, element 1.

[7] Compare Article 7(1)(c) EoC, element 1, and Article 7(1)(g)-2 EoC, element 1. See also section 4.2 on 'sexual slavery'.

[8] Robinson (2001), p. 85.

[9] *Ibid.*

to a servile status' (which includes debt bondage, serfdom, forced marriage and child exploitation[11]) and 'trafficking in persons, in particular women and children'[12] may all

[10] 'Forced labour' is defined in Article 2(1) of the Convention Concerning Forced or Compulsory Labour (ILO No. 29), 28 June 1930, 39 UNTS 55, as 'all work or service which is exacted from any person under the menace of any penalty and for which the said person has not offered himself voluntarily'.

[11] According to footnote 11 to the EoC, the term 'servile status' has to be interpreted following the Supplementary Convention on the Abolition of Slavery, the Slave Trade, and Institutions and Practices Similar to Slavery, 7 September 1956, 266 UNTS 3. Following Article 7 of this Convention 'a person of servile status' is 'a person in the condition or status resulting from any of the institutions or practices mentioned in article 1 of this Convention'. Article 1 of the 1956 Supplementary Convention on the Abolition of Slavery, the Slave Trade, and Institutions and Practices Similar to Slavery defines the following 'situations and practices similar to slavery':

(a) Debt bondage, that is to say, the status or condition arising from a pledge by a debtor of his personal services or of those of a person under his control as security for a debt, if the value of those services as reasonably assessed is not applied towards the liquidation of the debt or the length and nature of those services are not respectively limited and defined;
(b) Serfdom, that is to say, the condition or status of a tenant who is by law, custom or agreement bound to live and labour on land belonging to another person and to render some determinate service to such other person, whether for reward or not, and is not free to change his status;
(c) Any institution or practice whereby;
    (i) A woman, without the right to refuse, is promised or given in marriage on payment of a consideration in money or in kind to her parents, guardian, family or any other person or group; or
    (ii) The husband of a woman, his family, or his clan, has the right to transfer her to another person for value received or otherwise; or
    (iii) A woman on the death of her husband is liable to be inherited by another person;
(d) Any institution or practice whereby a child or young person under the age of 18 years, is deliverer by either or both of his natural parents or by his guardian to another person, whether for reward or not, with a view to the exploitation of the child or young person or of his labour.

[12] The following treaties were developed separately and largely independently of the movement to abolish slavery and are generally limited to trafficking for the purposes of forced prostitution and include: International Convention for the Suppression of the White Slave Traffic, 18 May 1904, 35 Stat. 426, 1 LNTS 83, as amended by the Protocol of 4 May 1949, 92 UNTS 19; International Convention for the Suppression of White Slave Traffic, 4 May 1910, III LNTS 278; International Convention for the Suppression of the Traffic in Women and Children, 30 September 1921, as amended by Protocol, 93 UNTS 43; International Convention on the Suppression of the Traffic in Women of Full Age, 11 October 1933, 150 LNTS 431, as amended by the Protocol of 12 November 1947, 53 UNTS 39; Convention for the Suppression of the Traffic in Persons and of the Exploitation of the Prostitution of Others, 2 December 1949, 96 UNTS 272; American Convention on Human Rights, San José, 22 November 1969, OAS Treaty Ser. No. 36, OAS Off.

fall within the definition of enslavement. Enslavement as a crime against humanity has thus been given a broad meaning in the ICC Statute: crimes such as forced labour (including forced domestic labour), forced marriage and trafficking in women and children for the purposes of forced prostitution all fall within the definition of enslavement. In addition, on the basis of the wording perpetrators can be prosecuted for holding women in slavery-like conditions for the sole purpose of sex. This particular situation has been described in the *Kunarac, Kovač and Vuković* case, as will be discussed below, and was found to constitute the crime of enslavement on the basis of wording similar to that in the ICC Statute, namely 'the exercise of any or all of the powers attaching to the right of ownership over a person'. In section 4.2 (sexual slavery), it will be made clear that these examples open the door to prosecuting sexual violence crimes as the crimes against humanity of enslavement or sexual slavery without the need to prove that any financial benefits were gained by the perpetrator or that the persons were confined to a special place.

The *mens rea* requirement for the *actus reus* of enslavement as a crime against humanity is in accordance with the default rule as laid down in paragraph 2 of the General Introduction to the EoC; Article 30 applies, requiring intent, knowledge or both. Thus, the perpetrator intentionally exercised any or all of the powers attaching to the right of ownership over a person.

The *Kunarac, Kovač and Vuković* case was the first case where the ICTY had to deal with the task of defining the crime of enslavement as a crime against humanity. In this case, Kunarac and Kovač, both related to the Bosnian Serb army, were accused of enslavement as a crime against humanity on the basis of their conduct relating solely to the bad treatment of women and children and on the basis of allegations of forced or compulsory labour or service.[13] According to the Trial Chamber,

> Men and women were separated, with many of the men detained in the former KP Dom Prison. The women were kept in various detention centres where they had to live in intolerably unhygienic conditions, where they were mistreated in many ways including, for many of them, being raped repeatedly. Serb soldiers or policemen would come to these detention centres, select one or more women take them out and rape them. Many women and girls, including 16 of the Prosecution witnesses, were raped in that way. Some of these women were taken out of these detention centres to privately owned apartments and houses

Rec. OEA/Ser.L/V/II.23 doc. 21 rev. 6 (1979), Article 6(1); Convention on the Elimination of All Forms of Discrimination Against Women, UN General Assembly Res. 34/180 (18 December 1979), Article 6, reprinted in United Nations, *A Compilation of International Instruments*, UN Doc. ST/HR/1/Rev. 5 (Vol.1/Part 1) (1994), p. 150. See also Hall (1999), pp. 160-161. For an elaborate study on trafficking in persons, see Rijken (2003).

[13] Kunarac was a commander of a reconnaissance unit of approximately 15 soldiers, while Kovač (as well as Vuković) was one of the sub-commanders of the paramilitary police and a paramilitary leader. All were related to the Bosnian Serb army. Kunarac and Kovač were charged for enslavement as a crime against humanity in count 18 and count 22, respectively. See *Prosecutor v. Dragoljub Kunarac and Radomir Kovač*, Amended Indictment, Case No. IT-96-23-PT, 8 November 1999, paras. 10.2 and 10.3 (Kunarac), paras. 11.1-11.6 (Kovač). See also the Kunarac, Kovač and Vuković Judgment, para. 516.

> where they had to cook, clean and serve the residents, who were Serb soldiers. They were also subject to sexual assaults.[14]

For the Trial Chamber to determine what constitutes enslavement as a crime against humanity under customary international law and in the absence of a definition under international law, the Trial Chamber had to consult various international humanitarian and human rights law sources.[15] Particular attention was paid to the 1926 Slavery Convention, which provided in Article 1(1) the first basic definition of slavery, namely ' ... the status or condition of a person over whom any or all of the powers attaching to the right of ownership are exercised'.[16] Similar wording is used in the ICC Statute. In *Kunarac, Kovač and Vuković*, the definition of enslavement as contained in the International Law Commission (ILC) Commentary to the 1996 Draft Code was given as evidence of customary international law.[17] According to the ILC, enslavement is

> ... establishing or maintaining over persons a status of slavery, servitude or forced labour contrary to well-established and widely recognized standards of international law, such as: the 1926 Slavery Convention (slavery); the 1956 Supplementary Slavery Convention

[14] Kunarac, Kovač and Vuković Judgment, paras. 573-574.

[15] *Ibid.*, paras. 519-538. The following sources were, *inter alia*, discussed: the 1926 Slavery Convention (Article 1); the 1956 Supplementary Slavery Convention (Article 7); the 1930 Forced or Compulsory Labour Convention; the 1957 Convention Concerning the Abolition of Forced Labour (Article 1); the 1948 Universal Declaration of Human Rights (Article 4); the 1966 International Covenant on Civil and Political Rights (Article 4(2)); the 1950 European Convention on Human Rights (Article 4); the 1969 American Convention on Human Rights (Article 6); the 1981 African Charter on Human and Peoples' Rights (Article 5); the 1979 Convention on the Elimination of All Forms of Discrimination Against Women (Article 6); the 1989 Convention on the Rights of the Child (Article 11(1)); the 1991 Draft Code of Crimes Against Peace and Security of Mankind (Article 21); the 1996 Draft Code of Crimes Against Peace and Security of Mankind (Article 18); the 1949 Geneva Convention IV (Common Article 3 and Articles 24, 27, 32, 40, 42, 51 and 95); 1977 Additional Protocol I to the 1949 Geneva Conventions (Articles 75, 76(1) and 77); and 1977 Additional Protocol II to the 1949 Geneva Conventions (Articles 4, 5, 17).

[16] The 1926 Slavery Convention also prohibits the slave trade in Article 1(2): 'The slave trade includes all acts involved in the capture, acquisition or disposal of a person with intent to reduce him to slavery; all acts involved in the acquisition of slave with a view to selling or exchanging him; all acts of disposal by sale or exchange of a slave acquired with a view to being sold or exchanged, and, in general, every act of trade or transport of slaves.' According to the Kunarac, Kovač and Vuković Judgment, para. 520, 'the customary international law status of these substantive provisions is evidenced by the almost universal acceptance of that Convention and the central role that the definition of slavery in particular has come to play in subsequent international law developments in this field'.

[17] Kunarac, Kovač and Vuković Judgment, para. 537, states: 'As a body consisting of experts in international law, including government legal advisers, elected by the General Assembly, the work of the ILC, at least in relation to this issue, may be considered as evidence of customary international law.'

(slavery or servitude); the ICCPR (slavery and servitude); and the 1957 Forced Labour Convention (forced labour).[18]

On the basis of its survey of international law sources, the *Kunarac, Kovač and Vuković* Trial Chamber found the *actus reus* of enslavement to consist in

> ... the exercise of any or all of the powers attaching to the right of ownership over a person. The *mens rea* of the violation consists in the intentional exercise of such powers.[19]

According to the Trial Chamber,

> under this definition, indications of enslavement include elements of control and ownership; the restriction or control of an individual's autonomy, freedom of choice or freedom of movement; and, often, the accruing of some gain to the perpetrator. The consent or free will of the victim is absent. It is often rendered impossible or irrelevant by, for example, the threat or use of force or other forms of coercion; the fear of violence, deception or false promises; the abuse of power; the victim's position of vulnerability; detention or captivity, psychological oppression or socio-economic conditions. Further indications of enslavement include exploitation; the exaction of forced or compulsory labour or service, often without remuneration and often, though not necessarily, involving physical hardship; sex; prostitution; and human trafficking. ... The 'acquisition' or 'disposal' of someone for monetary or other compensation, is not a requirement for enslavement. Doing so, however, is a prime example of the exercise of the right of ownership over someone. The duration of the suspected exercise of powers attaching to the right of ownership is another factor that may be considered when determining whether someone was enslaved; however, its importance in any given case will depend on the existence of other indications of enslavement. Detaining or keeping someone in captivity, without more, would, depending on the circumstances of a case, usually not constitute enslavement.[20]

The Trial Chamber furthermore agreed that the factors that need to be taken into account when determining whether enslavement has been committed include

> the control of someone's movement; control of physical environment; psychological control; measures taken to prevent or deter escape; force, threat of force or coercion; duration; assertion of exclusivity; subjection to cruel treatment and abuse; control of sexuality; and, forced labour. ... the mere ability to buy, sell, trade or inherit a person or his or her labours or services ... is insufficient, such actions actually occurring could be a relevant factor for determining enslavement.[21]

With regard to Kunarac, who had taken two girls to an abandoned house in Trnovace (east Bosnia), the Trial Chamber considered the following factors of particular

---

[18] *Report of the International Law Commission on the Work of Its Forty-Eight Session*, A/51/10 (SUPP), 1 January 1996, p. 98.
[19] Kunarac, Kovač and Vuković Judgment, para. 540.
[20] *Ibid.*, para. 542.
[21] *Ibid.*, para. 543.

relevance to the establishment of the crime of enslavement: (1) the girls in question were detained for an extensive period of time, namely six months; (2) the girls had to do everything they were ordered to do, including household chores; (3) Kunarac asserted exclusivity over one of the girls by forbidding any other soldier to rape her; (4) the girls were at the constant disposal of Kunarac and another man; (5) other mistreatments, such as offering one soldier the permission to rape one of the girls at the price of DEM 100; (6) the girls were effectively denied any control about their lives; (7) the girls were not free to go where they wanted to, and if this were the case, they had nowhere to go or hide.[22] The Trial Chamber was satisfied that the girls were kept in the house to be used by Kunarac and another man for sexual services whenever the soldiers returned to the house.[23] Kunarac continuously and constantly raped one of the girls for about two months while she was kept in the house.[24] Similar factors in the establishment of enslavement as a crime against humanity were found to apply in the case of Kovač, who kept two girls in his apartment for a period of more than four months and two other girls for about a week, and then handed them over to other men as it pleased him. The factors concern: (1) the girls were not allowed to leave the apartment without one of the men accompanying them. They were also psychologically detained, because even if they had managed to flee from the apartment, they would have had nowhere to go. They were also aware of the risks involved if they were recaptured; (2) Kovač sold three of the witnesses; (3) twice he handed two of the witnesses over to a group of other soldiers for a period of about two weeks; they were constantly raped by these men; (4) mistreatment such as beating and slapping; (5) his claim of exclusivity over one of the witnesses, whom he raped almost every night he spent in the apartment; (6) the poor living conditions and lack of food; (7) they had to obey every order and do whatever they were told to do, including the household chores, the cooking and the cleaning.[25] The Trial Chamber concluded that

> Kovac's conduct towards the two women was wanton in abusing and humiliating the four women and in exercising his de facto power of ownership as it pleased him. Kovac disposed of them in the same manner. For all practical purposes, he possessed them, owned them and had complete control over their fate, and he treated them as his property. The Trial Chamber is also satisfied that Kovac exercised the above powers over the girls intentionally. The Trial Chamber is satisfied that many of the acts caused serious humiliation, of which the accused was aware.[26]

What is remarkable, however, is that the part of the judgment dealing with the Trial Chamber's findings on enslavement does not always link the sexual violence crimes to the enslavement, and when it does, it only refers to sexual violence crimes as one of the factors in the determination of enslavement. Yet, the prime purpose of the enslavement of these women in Foča was to rape them, not to have them perform household chores.[27]

---

[22] *Ibid.*, paras. 738, 740-742.

[23] *Ibid.*, para. 739.

[24] *Ibid.*, paras. 734, 741.

[25] *Ibid.*, paras. 749-752, 754, 756, 761, 780.

[26] *Ibid.*, para. 781.

[27] De Brouwer (2001), p. 234.

For this reason, the crimes the women had to endure might have been better charged as sexual slavery rather than as enslavement. As the ICTY and ICTR Statutes do not provide an explicit basis for the prosecution of sexual slavery in law and sexual slavery can be considered a form of enslavement, the Trial Chamber had to resort to enslavement as a crime against humanity, taking into account all the factors relevant in establishing the enslavement. Indeed, Kunarac and Kovač were faced with charges of enslavement as a crime against humanity not only for conduct relating to the treatment of women and children, but also on the basis of allegations of forced or compulsory labour or service. What has been established before this Tribunal is that enslavement can include sexual slavery, but also non-sexual slavery practices, such as forced domestic labour. However, when the evidence is so clear that the main purpose of the enslavement of the women was to rape them, not to have them perform some household jobs, the right charge would be sexual slavery, not enslavement. Under the ICC Statute, both options – enslavement and sexual slavery as crimes against humanity – are available. The criminal nature of the sexual exploitation of the women held in slavery-like conditions will best be made clear by charging the crime of sexual slavery as the crime against humanity of sexual slavery, while forced labour, including household chores, would best be charged under enslavement as a crime against humanity.

In appeal, the definition of the crime of enslavement was contested by the appellants Kunarac and Kovač; to no avail, however.[28] Their submission that the definition of enslavement as established by the Trial Chamber was too broad and did not define the elements of the crime was clearly rejected by the Appeals Chamber. According to the Appeals Chamber, the definition of the crime of enslavement reflects customary international law at the time when the alleged crimes were committed.[29] A number of alternative elements for the crime of enslavement were put forward by Kunarac and Kovač. First, the accused must have treated the victim 'as its [sic] own ownership'.[30] The appellants made reference to the definition in the 1926 Slavery Convention and similar subsequent conventions. In the view of the Appeals Chamber, more contemporary forms of slavery are to be subsumed under the traditional concept of slavery, being 'the exercise of any or all of the powers attaching to the right of ownership over a person'. To determine whether a particular situation may be defined as enslavement, the Appeals Chamber takes the non-exhaustive list of factors of the Trial Chamber as a starting point.[31] Second, the victims must have shown a constant and clear lack of consent during the entire period of the detention or the transfer.[32] According to the appellants, the victims testified that they had freedom of movement within and outside the apartment and could therefore have escaped or attempted to change their situation.[33] In addition, according to them the victims were not forced to do

[28] Kunarac, Kovač and Vuković Appeal Judgment, paras. 106-124.

[29] *Ibid.*, para. 124.

[30] *Ibid.*, para. 107.

[31] Kunarac, Kovač and Vuković Judgment, para. 543. The factors that need to be taken into account to determine whether enslavement has been committed are cited above. See also Kunarac, Kovač and Vuković Appeal Judgment, para. 119.

[32] Kunarac, Kovač and Vuković Appeal Judgment, para. 108.

[33] *Ibid.*

household chores but undertook them willingly.[34] The Appeals Chamber did not find lack of consent to constitute an element of the crime of enslavement as the crime is based on claimed rights of ownership.[35] While the concept of consent may be used from an evidential point of view in order to prove that one did not exercise any or all of the powers attaching to the right of ownership, because the victim consented, the Appeals Chamber decided that in the case at hand circumstances rendering it impossible to express consent were present.[36] Thus, circumstances which render it impossible to express consent may be sufficient to presume the absence of consent.[37] The responded referred to, *inter alia*, the following circumstances: '... detention, captivity or psychological oppression'.[38] Third, the victim must have been enslaved for an indefinite or at least for a prolonged period of time.[39] The Appeals Chamber concurred with the Trial Chamber's decision on this matter and found the duration of the detention to be only one of the factors that may indicate the presence of enslavement, but its importance to be dependent on the existence of other indications of enslavement.[40] Fourth, the appellants submitted that the *mens rea* is the intent to detain the victims under constant control for a prolonged period of time in order to use them for sexual acts.[41] Kovač claimed that he accepted the victims in his house in order to transfer them outside of the theatre of the armed conflict.[42] Again, the Appeals Chamber concurred with the Trial Chamber in that the required *mens rea* refers to the *actus reus* of the crime and thus consists in the intentional exercise of a power attaching to the right of ownership.[43]

The judgment in the *Kunarac, Kovač and Vuković* case has made the boundaries of the crime of enslavement as a crime against humanity more clear. Following this judgment, but also following the definition of enslavement in the ICC Statute, the central parameter of the crime concerns 'the exercise of any or all of the powers attaching to the right of ownership over a person'. Even though in the EoC a somewhat restrictive list of examples is given of the exercise of these powers of ownership, the elaborate footnote makes up for this restrictiveness: commercial benefit is not a requirement for enslavement to constitute a crime against humanity. In addition, the ICC has now expanded the definition to include the crime of trafficking in persons, in particular women and children, and forced marriage may also be included.

---

[34] *Ibid.*

[35] *Ibid.*, para. 120. In subsection 4.1 on 'rape', it is also argued that consent should not constitute an element of the crime of rape.

[36] *Ibid.*

[37] *Ibid.*

[38] *Ibid.*, para. 113.

[39] *Ibid.*, para. 109.

[40] Kunarac, Kovač and Vuković Judgment, para. 542; Kunarac, Kovač and Vuković Appeal Judgment, para. 121.

[41] Kunarac, Kovač and Vuković Appeal Judgment, para. 110.

[42] Kovać Appeal Brief, para. 165, as cited in Kunarac, Kovač and Vuković Appeal Judgment, para. 110.

[43] Kunarac, Kovač and Vuković Appeal Judgment, para. 122.

3 TORTURE

Torture as a crime against humanity was explicitly listed in Article II(1)(c) of CCL 10, Article 5(f) of the ICTY Statute and Article 3(f) of the ICTR Statute.[44] No definition of the crime was given in any of these instruments. The case law of the Tribunals has, however, shed some light on the contours of the crime. Only Kunarac, Vuković, Simić and Semanza have been prosecuted for sexual violence conduct as torture as a crime against humanity and been convicted thereof.[45] In the ICC Statute, torture as a crime against humanity is laid down in Article 7(1)(f) and is defined in Article 7(2)(e) as

> ... the intentional infliction of severe pain or suffering, whether physical or mental, upon a person in the custody or under the control of the accused; except that torture shall not include pain or suffering arising only from, inherent in or incidental to, lawful sanctions.

In the EoC, the elements of torture are described as follows:

1. The perpetrator inflicted severe physical or mental pain or suffering upon one or more persons.

2. Such person or persons were in the custody or under the control of the perpetrator.

3. Such pain or suffering did not arise only from, and was not inherent in or incidental to, lawful sanctions.

In footnote 14, attached to the title of the crime against humanity of torture, it is stated: 'It is understood that no specific purpose need be proved for this crime.'

The definition of torture in the ICC Statute has been copied verbatim into the EoC. This definition is different from the definition of torture previously applied under international law, including by the Tribunals, where the 1984 Torture Convention was taken as the leading authority.[46] In Article 1(1) of the 1984 UN Convention against Torture and other Cruel Inhuman or Degrading Treatment or Punishment it is stated:

---

[44] Torture is also laid down in a number of international humanitarian and human rights law treaties, which do not define the crime of torture. Torture is found to be a crime constituting a *jus cogens* norm from which no derogation is permitted. Torture as a war crime is provided for in Articles 8(2)(a)(ii) and 8(2)(c)(i) of the ICC Statute and is further discussed in Chapter 3 on war crimes. Under the Nuremberg and Tokyo Charters, torture was charged under 'other inhumane acts'.

[45] For a short overview of the sexual violence conduct the accused were convicted of with regard to sexual violence as torture as a crime against humanity, see the Appendix.

[46] The ICTR considered the definition of torture as outlined in Article 1(1) of the 1984 Torture Convention to apply to 'any rule of international law on torture, including the relevant provisions of the ICTR Statute' (Furundžija Judgment, para. 160, referring to the Akayesu Judgment, para. 593). Furthermore, 'the definition ... codifies, or contributes to developing or crystallising customary international law' (Furundžija Judgment, para. 160). The definition of torture contained in the 1984 Torture Convention 'reflects a consensus which the Trial Chamber considers to be representative of customary international law' (Čelebići Judgment, para. 459).

> For the purposes of this Convention, the term 'torture' means any act by which severe pain or suffering, whether physical or mental, is intentionally inflicted on a person for such purposes as obtaining from him or a third person information or a confession, punishing him for an act he or a third person has committed or is suspected of having committed, or intimidating or coercing him or a third person, or for any reason based on discrimination of any kind, when such pain or suffering is inflicted by or at the instigation of or with the consent or acquiescence of a public official or other person acting in an official capacity. It does not include pain or suffering arising only from, inherent in or incidental to lawful sanctions.

From this definition the following four elements of torture can be deduced: (1) there must be an act or omission that causes severe physical or mental pain or suffering; (2) the act is inflicted intentionally; (3) for one or more of the following (non-exhaustive) purposes:[47] (a) to obtain information or a confession from the victim or a third person; (b) to punish the victim or a third person for an act committed or suspected of having being committed; (c) for the purpose of intimidating or coercing the victim or the third person; (d) for any reason based on discrimination of any kind; and (4) the perpetrator himself is an official, or acts at the instigation of, or with the consent or acquiescence of, an official or person acting in an official capacity. According to the definition, lawful sanctions are exempted from the definition of torture. These elements were also found to constitute the elements of torture in some of the cases before the Tribunals.[48]

Contrary to previous decisions, the Trial Chamber in the *Kunarac, Kovač and Vuković* case held that the fourth element, official capacity, was not necessarily an element of the crime of torture.[49] The Trial Chamber stated that

> ... the human rights conventions, consider torture *per se* while the Tribunal's Statute criminalises it as a form of war crime, crime against humanity or grave breach. *The characteristic trait of the offence in this context is to be found in the nature of the act*

[47] The Čelebići Trial Chamber considered that 'the use of the words "for such purposes" in the customary definition of torture, indicate that the various listed purposes do not constitute an exhaustive list, and should be regarded as merely representative. Further, there is no requirement that the conduct must be solely perpetrated for a prohibited purpose. Thus, in order for this requirement to be met, the prohibited purpose must simply be part of the motivation behind the conduct and need not be the predominating or sole purpose' (Čelebići Judgment, para. 470).

[48] Akayesu Judgment, para. 594; Čelebići Judgment, para. 494. See also Furundžija Judgment, para. 162 (for the elements of torture in armed conflict).

[49] In the Čelebići Judgment (para. 473) it was held that 'traditionally, an act of torture must be committed by, or at the instigation of, or with the consent or acquiescence of, a public official or person acting in an official capacity. In the context of international humanitarian law, this requirement must be interpreted to include officials of non-State parties to a conflict, in order for the prohibition to retain significance in situation of internal armed conflicts or international conflicts involving some non-State entities.' In the Furundžija Judgment (para. 162), as upheld by the Furundžija Appeal Judgment (para. 111), the Trial Camber noted that under international criminal law relating to armed conflict, torture requires at least one of the persons involved to be a public official or must at any rate have acted in a non-private capacity, for example, as a *de facto* organ of a state or any other authority-wielding power.

> *committed rather that in the status of the person who committed it.* The Trial Chamber concludes that the definition of torture under international humanitarian law does not comprise the same elements as the definition of torture generally applied under human rights law. In particular, the Trial Chamber is of the view that the presence of a state official or of any other authority-wielding person in the torture process is not necessary for the offence to be regarded as torture under international humanitarian law.[50]

Because torture had not been defined in international humanitarian law, the *Kunarac, Kovač and Vuković* Trial Chamber had to take recourse to human rights law in determining the elements of torture. According to the Trial Chamber, 'because of their resemblance, in terms of goals, values and terminology, such recourse is generally a welcome and needed assistance to determine the content of customary international law in the field of humanitarian law'.[51] However, it is not possible to transfer the elements of torture as found in human rights law to international humanitarian law without taking into account the specific differences that exist between these two bodies of law.[52] In particular, the definition of torture in human rights treaties, such as the Torture Convention, was meant to apply at an inter-State level and was thus intended to create obligations for States.[53] A State is obliged to protect its citizens from State-organised or State-sponsored violence, whereas humanitarian law aims at placing restraints on the conduct of warfare so as to diminish its effects on the victims thereof.[54] The nature of the act committed rather than the status of the person who committed it is important in international humanitarian law. In this regard, the Trial Chamber referred to the definition of torture as contained in the provisions on crimes against humanity and war crimes in the ICC Statute, neither of which mention the requirement of official capacity.[55] In addition, the definition of torture in the 1984 Torture Convention was meant to apply only in the context of that Convention, and only to the extent that other international instruments or national laws did not provide a broader or better protection of the individual.[56] The Trial Chamber in the *Kunarac, Kovač and Vuković* case therefore held that the definition of torture contained in Article 1 of the Torture

---

[50] Kunarac, Kovač and Vuković Judgment, paras. 495-496 (italics added).

[51] *Ibid.*, para. 467.

[52] *Ibid.*, paras. 468-471; Furundžija Judgment, para. 162.

[53] Kunarac, Kovač and Vuković Judgment, paras. 470, 482.

[54] *Ibid.*, para. 470.

[55] Kunarac, Kovač and Vuković Judgment, para. 495, fn. 1210, reads: 'Although the ICC Statute does not necessarily represent the present status of customary international law, it is a useful instrument in confirming the content of customary international law. These provisions obviously do not *necessarily* indicate what the state of the relevant law was at the time relevant to this case. However they do provide some evidence of the state *opinio juris* as to the relevant customary international law at the time at which the recommendations were adopted.'

[56] Article 1 of the 1984 Torture convention reads '*For the purposes of this Convention*, the term "torture" means ...' (italics added). Article 1(2) of the 1984 Torture Convention states that this article is 'without prejudice to any international instrument or national legislation which does or may contain provisions of wider application'. See also Kunarac, Kovač and Vuković Judgment, paras. 473, 482.

Convention could only serve as an 'interpretational aid'.[57] The Trial Chamber's conclusion to omit the official capacity requirement has been upheld by the *Kunarac, Kovač and Vuković* Appeals Chamber.[58]

Thus, in the *Kunarac, Kovač and Vuković* case the Trial Chamber held that 'in the field of international humanitarian law, the elements of the offence of torture under customary international law' contain of

(a) The infliction, by act or omission, or severe pain or suffering, whether physical or mental;
(b) The act or omission must be intentional;
(c) The act or omission must aim at obtaining information or a confession, or at punishing, intimidating or coercing the victim or a third person, or at discriminating, *on any ground*, against the victim or third person.[59]

These purposes have, according the *Kunarac, Kovač and Vuković* Trial Chamber, become part of international customary law.[60] The *Furundžija* Trial Chamber also enumerated 'humiliation' as a purpose of torture.[61] The *Čelebići* Trial Chamber considered that 'the use of the words "for such purposes" in the customary definition of torture, indicate [sic] that the various listed purposes do not constitute an exhaustive list, and should be regarded as merely representative. Further, there is no requirement that the conduct must be solely perpetrated for a prohibited purpose. Thus, in order for this requirement to be met, the prohibited purpose must simply be part of the motivation behind the conduct and need not be the predominating or sole purpose.'[62] This wording seems to restrict the *mens rea* of the perpetrator to at least one of the purposes mentioned.

As already briefly mentioned above, the elements of 'purposes' and 'official capacity' have not been listed in the definition of torture as a crime against humanity in the ICC Statute or the EoC. While some delegates favoured inclusion, in the specific context of crimes against humanity it was considered sufficient to require that the

---

[57] Kunarac, Kovač and Vuković Judgment, para. 482.

[58] Even though the issue of official capacity was not raised by both parties, the Kunarac, Kovač and Vuković Appeals Chamber felt it right to address the issue in order not to retain any controversy about the appeal or its consistency with the jurisprudence of the Tribunal. The Appeals Chamber specifically held that '... the definition of torture in the Torture Convention reflects customary international law as far as the obligation of States is concerned, must be distinguished from an assertion that this definition wholly reflects customary international law regarding the meaning of the crime of torture generally. The Trial Chamber in the present case was therefore right in taking the position that the public official requirement is not a requirement under customary international law in relation to the criminal responsibility of an individual for torture outside of the framework of the Torture Convention' (Kunarac, Kovač and Vuković Appeal Judgment, paras. 147-148; also paras. 145-146).

[59] Kunarac, Kovač and Vuković Judgment, para. 497 (italics added); also Kunarac, Kovač and Vuković Appeal Judgment, para. 156.

[60] Kunarac, Kovač and Vuković Judgment, para. 485.

[61] Furundžija Judgment, para. 162.

[62] Čelebići Judgment, para. 470; see also Kunarac, Kovač and Vuković Judgment, para. 654.

person be in the custody or under the control of the perpetrator in order to establish some link of power or control between the perpetrator and the victim.[63] Under the Torture Convention, a human rights instrument dealing with State obligations, a single act of torture qualifies as an international crime provided that it is committed for one of the prohibited purposes and committed with the support or acquiescence of a State official. For the crime against humanity of torture, its status as an international crime is already justified by its connection to a widespread or systematic attack directed against a civilian population.[64] That official capacity is not a requirement for torture to have been committed is also obvious from the wording in the *chapeau* to crimes against humanity. 'Attack directed against any civilian population' means, according to Article 7(2) of the ICC Statute, 'a course of conduct involving the multiple commission of acts referred to in paragraph 1 against any civilian population, pursuant to or in furtherance of a State or organizational policy to commit such attack'. This wording indicates that it is not required that a perpetrator acted in the capacity of a State official or in an official capacity as a representative of a State.[65]

As was held in the *Kunarac, Kovač and Vuković* case, international humanitarian law is aimed at restraining the conduct of warfare in order to diminish its effects on the victims of hostilities. This means that in order to diminish the effects on victims it is not important *who* committed the torturous acts, but the fact that they were committed (whether by State officials, civilians or rebel groups), and, that this needs to be addressed. For similar reasons, there is no official capacity requirement for torture as a crime under the war crimes provisions either.[66]

In contrast to the definition of torture in the war crimes provision in the ICC Statute and its elements elaborated in the EoC, the crime against humanity of torture does not include the purpose requirement. For the war crimes provision, the purpose requirement had been retained as it was found by some delegates to be necessary in order to distinguish torture from the crime of inhumane treatment.[67] In addition, by keeping the purpose requirement in the definition it was probably felt that previous case law of the Tribunals on the matter would be followed.[68] Delegates finally agreed that it was not necessary to include the purpose requirement in the context of crimes against

---

63 Rückert and Witschel (2001a), p. 79; Robinson (2001b), p. 90.

64 Robinson (2001b), p. 92.

65 Boot (2002), pp. 509-510.

66 Dörmann (2001, p. 127), noted that 'the delegations agreed that such a requirement would give the impression that non-State actors would not be covered. This would restrict the crime too much, particularly in non-international armed conflicts involving rebel groups.' See also, in particular, Chapter 3, the section on 'torture' as a war crime.

67 The war crime of 'inhumane treatment' consists of one element only, namely: 'The perpetrator inflicted severe physical or mental pain or suffering upon one or more persons.' This element is similar to the first element of torture as a war crime (and a crime against humanity). Torture as a war crime, however, adds a second element containing the prohibited purposes. For the elements of torture and inhumane treatment, see Article 8(2)(a)(ii).

68 As discussed above, several ICTY Judgments explicitly listed the prohibited purposes of torture. See Kunarac, Kovač and Vuković Judgment, para. 497; Akayesu Judgment, para. 594; Čelebići Judgment, para. 494. See also Furundžija Judgment, para. 162 (for the elements of torture in armed conflict).

humanity. This is laid down specifically in footnote 14, which states that no specific purpose needs to be proved for the crime against humanity of torture. It was argued that, in contrast to Article 8, the crimes against humanity provision in the ICC Statute (Article 7) already contained a specific and clear definition of torture omitting the purpose requirement, which was agreed upon during the Rome Conference.[69] There was consequently no need to depart from that definition in the EoC. Moreover, according to some, case law of the European Court of Human Rights showed that a purpose requirement is not necessary and that the distinguishing feature of torture is its severity of the pain or suffering inflicted.[70] This comes to mind when comparing the crime of torture with other crimes against humanity involving the infliction of pain or suffering to body or mind. The crime of torture is about 'severe' physical or mental pain or suffering, whereas 'other inhumane acts' refers to 'great suffering, or serious injury to body or to mental or physical health'.

Without the requirements of purpose and official capacity, sexual violence crimes fulfil the elements of torture as currently laid down in the ICC Statute and EoC rather easily. What is necessary is that: (1) the perpetrator inflicted severe physical or mental pain or suffering upon one or more persons (element 1); and (2) the person or persons were in the custody or under the control of the perpetrator (element 2). Element 3 requires that 'such pain or suffering did not arise only from, and was not inherent in or incidental to, lawful sanctions'.[71]

The threshold of element 1 is not very high in the context of sexual violence: not only does sexual violence inflict severe physical or mental pain or suffering, it often inflicts both: severe physical and mental pain or suffering. While there are no specific criteria by which to determine the degree of pain required for an act to amount to torture, the Appeals Chamber in the *Kunarac, Kovač and Vuković* case has made it once again clear that sexual violence amounts to torture as it necessarily gives rise to severe pain or suffering, whether physical or mental.[72] A medical certificate to prove the suffering inflicted is therefore not necessary.[73] The term 'custody' in the second element would include any form of detention or imprisonment, including arrest by security forces and other restrictions to liberty such as crowd control by security forces or enforced disappearances.[74] The term 'under the control of the accused' is broader and would include any other form of restraint by another, including enslavement.[75] Situations of sexual violence would thus fall within the terms of 'in the custody' or 'under the control' of the accused. This would also include situations in which the

[69] Robinson (2001b), p. 91.

[70] 'Ireland v. UK, Series A, o. 25 (1976), separate opinion of Judge Fitzmaurice, 129', cited in Robinson (2001b), p. 91.

[71] Robinson (2001b, p. 92) stated that 'since the Elements were to provide a list of items to be proven, exceptions and defences were often not included in the Elements. However, because of the importance attached to this exception by some delegations, it was included as an element.'

[72] Kunarac, Kovač and Vuković Appeal Judgment, paras. 149-150.

[73] *Ibid.*, para. 150.

[74] The term 'custody' is not synonymous with the term 'imprisonment' (Hall (1999), p. 163).

[75] The term 'under the control of the accused' is not synonymous with the term 'other severe deprivation of liberty' (Hall (1999), p. 163).

victims were not physically detained, but had nowhere else to go.[76] Lawful sanctions are not considered to constitute torture (element 3). Lawful here refers to international law or national law which is consistent with international law and standards.[77] In the 1988 Report of the Special Rapporteur on Torture it was stated that the fact that 'sanctions are accepted under domestic law does not necessarily make them "lawful sanctions" in the sense of Article 1 of the Convention against Torture. ... It is international law and not domestic law which ultimately determines whether a certain practice may be regarded as "lawful".'[78] Thus, when a State allows a certain treatment or punishment, this does not mean that it is lawful under international law: sexual violence will never qualify as a lawful sanction as it is prohibited under international law. It may also be argued that stoning a person to death because he or she is gay or stoning a woman to death because she was found to have committed adultery, throwing acid into a woman's face because she refused to marry a man she had not selected herself or female genital mutilations are all forms of torture that under the new definition may be prosecuted as crimes against humanity of torture.[79]

Leaving out the other two requirements makes it clear that (1) random, purposeless or mere sadistic infliction of severe pain or suffering is included among the purposes of torture mentioned; and (2) torture in peacetime by members of armed political groups not connected to any State is included as well.[80] But also civilians and other people not connected to any State organ can be held responsible for committing torture in peacetime as well as wartime. For the prosecution of sexual violence as torture under crimes against humanity, it is thus no longer necessary to prove one of these two requirements. Especially for sexual violence crimes, it should not matter who committed the act or for what purpose.

What has become clear from the deliberations on the definition of torture is that human rights law cannot be copied verbatim into supranational criminal law. The ICC rightly took this notion into account when elaborating the definition of torture as a crime against humanity.

The *mens rea* of torture is covered by Article 30 of the ICC Statute. Thus, the perpetrator intended to inflict severe physical or mental pain or suffering upon one or more persons (element 1). With regard to the word 'severe' in this element, it is, according to paragraph 4 of the General Introduction to the EoC, 'not necessary that the perpetrator personally completed a particular value judgement', 'such person or persons were in the custody or under the control of the perpetrator' (element 2); 'such pain or

---

[76] See the Kunarac, Kovač and Vuković case as discussed above.

[77] See Hall (1999), p. 164.

[78] Report of the UN Special Rapporteur on Torture, UN Doc. E/CN.4/1988/17, para. 42.

[79] See Islam/Shah case (Pakistani women received refugee status in the UK because they were persecuted in Pakistan for having allegedly committed adultery. In reality they were hunted down by their husband and/or family in order to have them killed. In Pakistan women who flee from their home because they are molested disgrace the whole family and are killed because of that. The State of Pakistan tolerates this behaviour and therefore implicitly allows women to be the target of these practices, which it apparently considers 'lawful sanctions'. See *Islam (AP), Regina v. Secretary of State for the Home Department, Immigration Appeal Tribunal and Another ex parte Shah (AP)* (1999), House of Lords.

[80] Hall (1999), p. 164.

suffering did not arise only from, and was not inherent in or incidental to, lawful sanctions' (element 3).

4 Specific sexual violence crimes

In the ICC Statute, crimes of sexual violence are recognised as violent crimes; it is the first time that these crimes have thus been recognised in a supranational criminal instrument. Previously, rape and enforced prostitution had been recognised as crimes under international humanitarian law, though merely as violations of the honour, dignity and reputation of women, not as crimes in and of themselves.[81] This situation gradually changed with the establishment of the ICTY and ICTR, where rape was explicitly included in their Statutes as a crime against humanity. The ICTR furthermore includes rape and enforced prostitution as 'outrages upon personal dignity' as violations of Common Article 3 of the 1949 Geneva Conventions and 1977 Additional Protocol II. In the ICC Statute, not only rape, but also 'sexual slavery, enforced prostitution, forced pregnancy, enforced sterilization, and any other form of sexual violence of comparable gravity' are listed under the crimes against humanity and war crimes provisions.[82] Thanks to the intensive lobby of many Women NGOs in particular, these long-forgotten crimes have finally been recognised by the international community as violent crimes.[83] The elements of the sexual violence crimes were negotiated in the context of the war crimes provisions and subsequently transferred to the crimes against humanity provision in more or less the same wording.[84] The specific sexual violence crimes will be discussed in this Chapter, for the reason that the crimes against humanity provision appears first in the Statute and as such will be discussed first in this study. However, what is said here also applies to the specific sexual violence crimes contained in the war crimes provision (Article 8 ICC Statute). In the next Chapter, on war crimes, for this category of crimes only the legal basis of the crimes will be discussed.

---

[81] Article 27 of 1949 Geneva Convention IV reads 'women shall be especially protected against any attack on their honour, in particular against rape, enforced prostitution, or any form of indecent assault'. Article 75(2)(b) of 1977 Additional Protocol I prohibits 'outrages upon personal dignity, in particular humiliating and degrading treatment, enforced prostitution and any other form of indecent assault'. Article 76(1) of 1977 Additional Protocol I states that 'women shall be the object of special respect and shall be protected in particular against rape, forced prostitution and any other form of indecent assault'. Article 4(2)(e) of 1977 Additional Protocol II is similar to Article 75(2)(b) of Protocol I.

[82] Compare Article 7(1)(g) with Article 8(2)(e)(vi) and Article 8(2)(b)(xxii).

[83] A major contributor to the inclusion of these crimes within the ICC Statute was the Women's Caucus for Gender Justice (now Women's Initiatives for Gender Justice).

[84] A slight difference between the crimes against humanity and the war crimes provision can be found in the second element of Article 7(1)(g), the crime against humanity of sexual violence which refers to conduct of a 'gravity comparable to the other offences in article 7, paragraph 1(g), and Article 8(2)(b)(xxii), which refers to conduct of a 'gravity comparable to a grave breach of the Geneva Conventions.

4.1 Rape

In Article 5(g) of the ICTY Statute and Article 3(g) of the ICTR Statute, rape is listed explicitly as a crime against humanity. No other explicit listing of rape (as genocide or a war crime) can be found, although the ICTR Statute implicitly refers to rape as an example of an 'outrage upon personal dignity' punishable as the war crime of 'Violations of Article 3 Common to the Geneva Conventions and of Additional Protocol II' (Article 4(e)). In addition to the listing of rape in the Statutes of the Tribunals, the crime is implicitly stated as a war crime in international humanitarian law treaties, that is to say, Article 27(2)(b) of the 1949 Geneva Convention IV relative to the Protection of Civilian Persons in Time of War and Article 76(1) of Additional Protocol I and Article 4(2)(e) of Additional Protocol II to the 1949 Geneva Conventions, albeit as an example of a broader, somewhat unattractive and inexplicit category.[85] Moreover, rape as a crime against humanity was made punishable under Article 2(1)(c) of CCL 10.

A definition of rape was, however, not given in any of these instruments, and the attempts in legal practice to arrive at such a definition can be called negligible.[86] Thus, when the judges of the Tribunals were to deal with cases involving rape charges, they had to conclude that no definition of rape existed in international law.[87] For this reason,

[85] Article 27(2)(b) of 1949 Geneva Convention IV reads 'women shall be especially protected against any attack on their honour, in particular against rape, enforced prostitution, or any form of indecent assault'. Article 76(1) of Additional Protocol I reads 'women shall be the object of special respect and shall be protected in particular against rape, forced prostitution and any other form of indecent assault', while Article 4(2)(e) of Additional Protocol II reads 'outrages upon personal dignity, in particular humiliating and degrading treatment, rape, enforced prostitution and any form of indecent assault'.

[86] While rape was included in CCL 10 as a crime against humanity, no prosecutions on this basis followed. An attempt to define the crime of rape (as a war crime) was made by the Temporary Court Martial after World War II in the Batavia case, where 35 Dutch women, who had been victimised in Indonesia during the Japanese occupation, brought their case against twelve Japanese Army officers. The crime of rape was construed as forcibly causing a woman to have 'extra-marital, carnal intercourse' (Case No. 72/1947, Verdict 231, Batavia Case, pp. 2-5 and 16, cited in Viseur Sellers (2001b), pp. 9-10). Although the European Court of Human Rights (ECtHR) and the Inter-American Commission on Human Rights (IACHR) heard the first charges of rape since the Nuremberg and Tokyo trials, the Statutes of the ECtHR and IACHR do not explicitly prohibit rape. Rape was instead characterised as inhumane treatment or as an abrogation of the right to privacy, and by the mid-1990s as torture, but no definition of rape resulted. Contrary to the ICTY and ICTR, the IACHR and ECtHR are limited to hearing complaints against Member States. See further Strumpen-Darrie (2000), pp. 12-13.

[87] See ICTY/R case law discussed in this section. See also the Final Report of the United Nations Commission of Experts Established Pursuant to Security Council Resolution 780 (1992), *Rape and Sexual Assault: A Legal Study*, UN Doc. S/1994/674/Add.2, Vol. I, annex II, para. 2: 'unlike the majority of codified penal law, rape is not precisely defined in international humanitarian law. As a consequence, there is, at present, every reason to interpret this concept broadly as encompassing other sexual assaults.' See also the Final Report of the Special Rapporteur of the Working Group on Contemporary Forms of Slavery, on Systematic rape, Sexual slavery and Slavery-like Practices During Armed Conflict, UN Doc. E/CN.4/Sub.2/1998/13, 22 June 1998,

the concept of the crime of rape was developed through the case law of the ICTY and ICTR, resulting in different definitions. Creating legal definitions only in the final phase of a judicial process, i.e., in the judgments, has, however, been criticised as violating the legality principle.[88] Conversely, the EoC of the ICC specify the elements of the crime of rape in minute detail.[89] As mentioned, it is for the first time in the history of supranational criminal law that the elements of the crime of rape (as of any of the other crimes mentioned in the ICC Statute) are spelled out in an international legal instrument. In the ICC Statute, the crime of rape as a crime against humanity is explicitly referred to in Article 7(1)(g) and as a war crime in international and non-international armed conflicts in Articles 8(2)(b)(xxii) and 8(2)(e)(vi), respectively. In contrast with the Tribunals, the ICC Statute thus explicitly mentions rape as a war crime. A straightforward designation of rape as a form of genocide is still absent, although a footnote in the EoC to the crime of genocide clarifies that rape and sexual violence may fall within its ambit.[90]

The Tribunals convicted the accused Kunarac, Kovač, Vuković, Češić, Akayesu, Musema (but quashed on appeal), Semanza, Gacumbitsi and Muhimana for rape as a crime against humanity.[91] Express mention of rape as a crime constituting genocide, a crime against humanity or a war crime is nonetheless no requirement for prosecution; as long as all the elements of the crime concerned are fulfilled, rape can be prosecuted successfully. For example, convictions within the Tribunals have taken place for rape and other forms of sexual violence as: (1) torture, persecution, enslavement and other

---

paras. 23-24: 'There is no explicit definition of rape in international humanitarian or human rights law ...' Furthermore, '"rape" should be understood to be the insertion, under conditions of force, coercion or duress, of any object, including but not limited to a penis, into a victim's vagina or anus; or the insertion, under conditions of force, coercion or duress, of a penis into the mouth of the victim'. In 1997, the United Nations Division for the Advancement of Women expressed its idea about what to understand by rape in international law and held that 'sex-based crimes be referred to in the Statute of the ICC, but they should not be explicitly defined, so that the legal meaning of these crimes can be informed by the progressive interpretation of international law. In particular, rape in the context of the Statute of the ICC should be left undefined, but the elements of the crime should be understood in the practice of the future Court as forcible penetration of the vulva, anus or the mouth by the penis or of the vulva or anus by any object (United Nations Division for the Advancement of Women, *Report of the Expert Group Meeting*, Toronto, Canada, 9-12 November 1997, EGM/GBP/1997/Report).

[88] Haveman (2002), pp. 263-278.

[89] See the EoC for the elements of rape as a crime against humanity (Article 7(1)(g)-1) and a war crime in international and non-international armed conflicts, respectively (Articles 8(2)(b)(xxii)-1/Article 8(2)(e)(vi)-1).

[90] See footnote 3 to Article 6(b), 'Genocide by causing serious bodily or mental harm', which reads: 'This conduct may include, but is not necessarily restricted to, acts of torture, *rape, sexual violence* or inhumane or degrading treatment (italics added).' Of importance is that the EoC consists out of four parts – a general introduction to the EoC applicable to the whole document; an introduction to the three crimes separately; the (numbered) elements of crimes themselves; and footnotes included throughout the document to clarify specific issues or the intention of the drafters - and all four parts enjoy the same status. See Kelt and Von Hebel (2001), p. 17.

[91] See the overview in the Appendix for the sexual violence conduct committed by each accused.

inhumane acts as crimes against humanity; (2) torture, inhumane treatment and wilfully causing great suffering or serious injury to body or health as grave breaches; (3) torture, cruel treatment, outrages upon personal dignity, in particular humiliating and degrading treatment, and outrages upon personal dignity, in particular humiliating and degrading treatment, rape, enforced prostitution and any form of indecent assault as violations of the laws and customs of war; and (4) causing serious bodily or mental harm as genocide.[92] It may, however, be questioned whether it would not be better to recognise rape for what it is, i.e. the crime of rape, instead of charging rape or other forms of sexual violence under other crimes. As mentioned above, in the ICC Statute this situation has been improved by the explicit recognition of different forms of sexual violence, i.e. rape, sexual slavery, forced prostitution, forced sterilisation, forced pregnancy and any other form of sexual violence of comparable gravity as crimes against humanity and as war crimes.

In order to understand the ICC's elements of the crime of rape (as contained the EoC), the ICTY/R case law – which significantly influenced the ICC definition of the crime of rape – will be discussed first.

4.1.1 ICTY and ICTR case law on the definition of rape

The ICTY and ICTR ruled on the definition of rape in a total of twelve cases.[93] From this flow of case law, three principal definitions of rape emerged, representing three different lines of thinking on the relevant elements of the crime of rape. These standard-setting definitions were advanced in the *Akayesu* (1998), *Furundžija* (1998), and *Kunarac, Kovač and Vuković* (2001/2002) Judgments and were concurred with in subsequent judgments. They will be outlined and commented upon in this subsection in chronological order.

4.1.1.1 The *Akayesu* Judgment

The first case in which judges had to deal with the definition of rape in international law was the *Akayesu* case before the ICTR. Akayesu, a former *bourgmestre* of Taba commune (Gitarama Prefecture, Rwanda), was charged with rape as a crime against humanity (Article 3(g) of the ICTR Statute) and 'outrages upon personal dignity, in particular humiliating and degrading treatment, rape, and any form of indecent assault' as violations of Article 3 common to the 1949 Geneva Conventions and of Article 4(e) of Additional Protocol II (Article 4(e) of the ICTR Statute). In addition, the judges

[92] See further the Chart in Chapter 6 on sentencing, where it is set out who has been convicted of which crimes.

[93] In chronological order: (1) Akayesu Judgment (1998); (2) Čelebići Judgment (1998); (3) Furundžija Judgment (1998) and Furundžija Appeal Judgment (2000), concurring with the Trial Chamber's definition of rape; (4) Musema Judgment and Sentence (2000); (5) Kunarac, Kovač and Vuković Judgment (2001) and Kunarac, Kovač and Vuković Appeal Judgment (2002), quoting and concurring with the Trial Chamber's definition of rape; (6) Kvočka et. al. Judgment (2001); (7) Semanza Judgment and Sentence (2003); (8) Niyitegeka Judgment and Sentence (2003); (9) Kajelijeli Judgment and Sentence (2003); (10) Kamuhanda Judgment (2004); (11) Gacumbitsi Judgment (2004); (12) Muhimana Judgment and Sentence (2005).

examined whether rape and other forms of sexual violence could qualify as genocide. In its judgment of 2 September 1998, the Trial Chamber defined, after noting that there was no commonly accepted definition of the term 'rape' in international law, rape as

> ... *a physical invasion of a sexual nature, committed on a person under circumstances which are coercive.* The Tribunal considers sexual violence, which includes rape, as any act of a sexual nature which is committed on a person under circumstances which are coercive. Sexual violence is not limited to physical invasion of the human body and may include acts which do not involve penetration or even physical contact.[94]

Before the Trial Chamber arrived at this definition of rape, the judges noted that 'while rape has been historically defined in certain national jurisdictions as non-consensual intercourse, variations on the form of rape may include acts which involve the insertion of objects and/or the use of bodily orifices not considered to be intrinsically sexual'.[95] As an example of rape consisting of an act which involves the insertion of an object, the Tribunal cited the act as described by Witness KK in her testimony, namely 'the Interahamwes thrusting a piece of wood into the sexual organs of a woman as she lay dying'.[96] The Chamber furthermore considered that

> ... rape is a form of aggression and that the central elements of the crime of rape cannot be captured in a mechanical description of objects and body parts. The Convention against Torture and Other Cruel, Inhuman and Degrading Treatment or Punishment does not catalogue specific acts in its definition of torture, focusing rather on the conceptual frame work [sic] of state sanctioned violence. This approach is more useful in international law. Like torture, rape is used for such purposes as intimidation, degradation, humiliation, discrimination, punishment, control or destruction of a person. Like torture, rape is a violation of personal dignity, and rape in fact constitutes torture when inflicted by or at the instigation of or with the consent or acquiescence of a public official or other person acting in an official capacity.[97]

---

[94] Akayesu Judgment, paras. 598, 688 (italics added).

[95] *Ibid.*, paras. 598, 686.

[96] *Ibid.*, para. 686.

[97] *Ibid.*, paras. 597, 687. A connection to state-sponsored violence is regrettable as it is now widely accepted that non-state parties can commit torture as well. In the Čelebići case it was found that in the context of international humanitarian law, the requirement that torture must be committed by, or with the acquiescence of, a public official or person acting in an official capacity, 'must be interpreted to include officials of non-State parties to a conflict, in order for the prohibition to retain significance in situations of internal armed conflicts involving some non-State entities' (Čelebići Judgment, paras. 473 *et seq.* See also Kunarac, Kovač and Vuković Judgment, paras. 483-497). The Statute of the ICC similarly recognises that torture, including sexual torture, does not necessarily require state action or authority. Article 7(2)(e) of the ICC Statute states that '"Torture" means the intentional infliction of severe pain or suffering, whether physical or mental, upon a person in the custody or under the control of the accused; except that torture shall not include pain or suffering arising only from, inherent in or incidental to, lawful sanctions.'

The Tribunal thus explicitly rejected a mechanical definition of rape as found in many national laws, and instead chose a definition focusing on the concept of rape, which, in its view, would more accurately provide for the full protection of vulnerable persons in situations of mass violence. In addition, the Tribunal noted 'the cultural sensitivities involved in public discussion of intimate matters and recalls the painful reluctance and inability of witnesses to disclose graphic anatomical details of sexual violence they endured'.[98] In other words, a conceptual definition of rape could preclude situations in which victims have to talk about body parts in minute detail, which in some countries may be culturally forbidden. In the *Akayesu* trial, some witnesses used the term 'rape' without describing what happened to them in terms of body parts involved.[99] As to the second part of the definition of rape – the circumstances which need to be established in order for the physical invasion of a sexual nature to constitute a crime – the Trial Chamber noted that:

> ... coercive circumstances need not be evidenced by a show of physical force. Threats, intimidation, extortion and other forms of duress which prey on fear or desperation may constitute coercion, and coercion may be inherent in certain circumstances, such as armed conflict or the military presence of Interahamwe among refugee Tutsi women at the bureau communal.[100]

The conceptual definition of rape as put forward in the *Akayesu* case is thus broadly formulated: it is not limited to conventional notions of rape requiring penetration, nor does it require 'lack of consent' as an element of the crime of rape, despite its observance of the use thereof in certain national jurisdictions.[101] Rape can thus be understood as including other forms of sexual violence which do not amount to penetration, such as sexual mutilation. Instead of describing the body parts involved, rape is defined as what it does: a physical invasion of a sexual nature. The term 'invasion' points to the perspective of the victim, who is invaded, rather than the perspective of the perpetrator, who penetrates.[102] By defining the crime of rape from a traditionally male point of view, the sexual violence experienced by the victim is disregarded as the definition is limited to 'penetration', thereby excluding other kinds of

---

[98] Akayesu Judgment, para. 687. For example, one victim of rape disclosed that 'she can never go to testify that she was raped, because in doing, she would be forced to mention the sexual organs by their names, which she cannot dare do' (statement of witness VM, quoted in Ingabire (2004), p. 6). Witness TAP in the Gacumbitsi case told the Court that she could not discuss such painful details and asked whether she could write it down instead. She explained that 'things of that nature are not spoken of. Our parents never taught us to speak like that; it was a taboo, which is why I don't want to say those words' (*Le Procureur c. Sylvestre Gacumbitsi,* Transcription Caviardee, Affaire Nº ICTR-2001-64-T, 6 août 2003).

[99] Akayesu Judgment, para. 686: 'The Tribunal notes that many of the witnesses have used the term "rape" in their testimony. *At times*, the Prosecution and the Defence have also tried to elicit an explicit description of what happened in physical terms, to document what the witnesses mean by the term "rape"' (emphasis added).

[100] *Ibid.*, para. 688.

[101] *Ibid.*, paras. 598, 686.

[102] Boon (2001), p. 649.

sexual contact that might be equally devastating to victims.[103] In addition, describing the body parts involved is not done for any of the other crimes: for instance, murder or torture is not defined as 'blood flows', 'arms being chopped off', etc. In the second place, the definition focuses on the concept of coercion, not on the element of consent, which will be discussed below. The decision not to include consent as an element of rape was most likely inspired by the gruesome facts of the case, which left no doubt about the victims' not consenting to sexual violence, as well as by the analogy to the definition of torture, which does not contain the element of consent. When the term 'coercive circumstances' is interpreted broadly, as was done in the *Akayesu* case, coercion is the correct element of the crime of rape in international law: in the context of genocide, crimes against humanity and war crimes, when a sexual act is forced on a person the issue of consent becomes redundant. Although the *Akayesu* definition of rape has been heralded as an important standard,[104] it has also been criticised as being too broad, not specific enough to take into account situations beyond penetration, thereby possibly violating the legality principle.[105] By defining the sexual acts in detail, the *Furundžija* case constituted a clear reaction to such concerns (to be discussed in the next subsection).

The definition of rape as given in the *Akayesu* Judgment was upheld in the *Čelebići* Judgment (1998), *Musema* Judgment (2000), *Niyitegeka* Judgment (2003) and *Muhimana* Judgment (2005).[106] Although, in the *Niyitegeka* case Niyitegeka was acquitted of the charge of rape as a crime against humanity on the basis of insufficient evidence, the Trial Chamber in that case cited the *Akayesu* definition of rape as the leading definition of rape in international law. In the *Čelebići* case, the meaning of rape was considered while determining whether rape may constitute torture, punishable as a grave breach under Article 2(b) of the ICTY Statute and as a violation of the laws or customs of war, punishable under Article 3 of the ICTY Statute and recognised by Article 3(1)(a) common to the four Geneva Conventions of 1949. With regard to the

---

[103] See Thomas and Levi (1999), p. 197: 'A male standard pervades legal definitions of rape, a crime overwhelmingly committed by men against women.' By focusing on non-consensual or forced vaginal penetration, 'legal definitions emphasize the male perspective of the acceptable boundaries of heterosexual sex rather than the victim's experience of sexualized violence'. See also MacKinnon (1991), p. 180: 'The problem is that the injury of rape lies in the meaning of the act to its victim, but the standard for its criminality lies in the meaning of the act to the assailant. ... this means that the man's perceptions of the woman's desires determine whether she is deemed violated.'

[104] Askin (1999, p. 109) stated that 'in Akayesu, the trial chamber articulated a broad and sensible definition of rape and sexual violence'. Amann (1999, p. 199) wrote that 'the Tribunal fashioned a standard that is sufficiently precise and within accepted definitions to give notice to forbidden conduct'. Moghalu (2002, p. 284-286) considers the Akayesu definition of rape 'a revolution in legal thinking' and views the ICTY approach as 'more conservative'.

[105] According to McDonald (1999, p. 77), 'the definition is overly vague and unspecific'. According to Judge Hunt (2004, p. 60), the definitions of rape as established in Akayesu and Furundžija are narrow, whereas the Kunarac, Kovač and Vuković definition is broader.

[106] Čelebići Judgment, paras. 478-479; Musema Judgment and Sentence, paras. 220, 226; Niyitegeka Judgment and Sentence, para. 456; Muhimana Judgment and Sentence, paras. 535-551. The definition of rape was not subject of appeal in any of these cases.

definition of rape, the *Čelebići* Trial Chamber saw 'no reason to depart from the conclusion of the ICTR [in *Akayesu*]'.[107] It found that acts of vaginal and anal penetration by the penis under coercive circumstances clearly constituted rape.[108] In addition, it was explicitly held that fellatio could have constituted rape as well had it been pleaded in the appropriate manner.[109]

In the *Musema* case, the definition of rape was explored in the context of rape as genocide, in particular as 'causing serious bodily or mental harm', and rape as a crime against humanity. The *Musema* Trial Chamber, by adopting the conceptually broad definition of rape as construed in the *Akayesu* case and as followed by the *Čelebići* Trial Chamber judges, once again underlined that '... the essence of rape is not the particular details of the body parts and objects involved, but rather the aggression that is expressed in a sexual manner under conditions of coercion'.[110] The *Musema* Judgment thus clearly rejected the mechanical approach taken by the *Furundžija* Trial Chamber with regard to the definition of rape,[111] which relied on a detailed description of objects and body parts. According to the *Musema* Trial Chamber

> ... the distinction between rape and other forms of sexual violence drawn by the *Akayesu* Judgment, that is 'a physical invasion of a sexual nature' as contrasted with 'any act of a sexual nature' which is committed on a person under circumstances which are coercive is clear and establishes a framework for judicial consideration of individual incidents of sexual violence and a determination, on a case by case basis, of whether such incidents constitute rape. The definition of rape, as set forth in the *Akayesu* Judgment, clearly encompasses all the conduct described in the definition of rape as set forth in *Furundzija*. ...in light of the dynamic ongoing evolution of the understanding of rape [in national jurisdictions] and the incorporation of this understanding into principles of international law, the Chamber considers that a conceptual definition is preferable to a mechanical definition of rape. The conceptual definition will better accommodate evolving norms of criminal justice.[112]

The *Musema* Trial Chamber did not discuss the extent to which national jurisdictions had reformed the definition of rape in their penal codes or the way in which interpretations thereof evolved in national case law. The general trend in national jurisdictions to which they refer, however, is that the crime of rape has been broadened to include, *inter alia*, the penetration of the vagina, anus, mouth or any other orifice (such as the ear, nose or eye) by the penis, any other part of the body (such as the

---

[107] Čelebići Judgment, paras. 478-479.

[108] *Ibid.*, paras. 940, 962.

[109] *Ibid.*, paras. 1065-1066. In Čelebići it was held that forcing two brothers to perform fellatio on one another constituted, at least, a fundamental attack on their human dignity, and constituted inhuman treatment under Article 2 of the Statute, and cruel treatment under Article 3 of the Statute. The Trial Chamber observed *obiter* that the aforementioned act could constitute rape for which liability could have been found if pleaded in the appropriate manner.

[110] Musema Judgment and Sentence, para. 226.

[111] At the time the Musema Judgment and Sentence came out (27 January 2000), the second important definition of rape, as set out in the Furundžija Judgment, was already pronounced (10 December 1998). The Furundžija definition of rape will be discussed in the next subsection.

[112] Musema Judgment and Sentence, paras. 227-228.

fingers or tongue) or an object.[113] Penetration of the mouth or any other orifice generally includes penetration with the penis only.[114] The wording used for the definition of rape in national jurisdictions may either be specific (describing body parts as in *Furundžija*) or unspecific in nature (without specifying body parts as in *Akayesu*).[115] A considerable number of States have thus shifted away from traditional definitions of rape, which tended to focus on vaginal (and sometimes anal and, to a lesser extent, oral) penetration by the penis only.[116] The focus now tends to be on the sexual autonomy of the individual, which can be violated in at least all of the situations mentioned above, having an equally humiliating and traumatic impact on the victim as in 'traditional rape cases'. Considering that these developments have not yet fully crystallised at the national level, the Trial Chamber in *Musema* preferred an open definition of rape to a limited definition of rape with no possibilities of incorporating other forms of sexual violence.

In the *Muhimana* case, the Trial Chamber held that 'coercion is an element that may obviate the relevance of consent as an evidentiary factor in the crime of rape' and therefore seemed to accept that lack of consent should not be an element of the crime of rape.[117] The Trial Chamber furthermore held that the *Kunarac, Kovač and Vuković* and *Akayesu* definitions of rape were not mutually exclusive, but that *Kunarac, Kovač and Vuković* in fact provided 'additional details on the constituent elements of acts considered to be rape'.[118]

---

[113] For an overview of the definition of rape in a number of different States, see, *inter alia*, the Council of Europe, *Legislation in the Member States of the Council of Europe in the Field of Violence Against Women*, EG (2001) 3 rev., Volumes I and II, Strasbourg, November 2002. Belgium, for instance, recognises penetration of the ear, nose, and eyes as constituting rape. See Stevens (2002), p. 452.

[114] However, see the 'Tongzoen' case in the Netherlands (Hoge Raad, Staat der Nederlanden v. T.J., 21 april 1998, *NJ* 1998, 781), where French kissing was considered to constitute rape.

[115] An example of an open ended definition of rape can be found in Article 242 of the Dutch Penal Code, where rape is defined as 'he who by means of violence or another fact or by threats with violence or another act compels another person to undergo acts consisting or including sexual *invasion* of the body, will be punished as guilty of rape with imprisonment of twelve years as a maximum or a fine of the fifth category' (emphasis added and my translation).

[116] A considerable number of countries in the world still define rape as non-consensual or forced vaginal penetration. For instance, see the penal codes of Belarus, the Czech Republic, Georgia, Kazakhstan, Kyrgyzstan, Latvia, Slovakia, Tajikistan, Ukraine, and Uzbekistan in International Helsinki Federation for Human Rights, *Women 2000: An Investigation into the Status of Women's Rights in Central and Sourth-Eastern Europe and the Newly Independent States*, 9 November 2000, pp. 76, 148, 183, 229, 244, 261, 406, 437, 487 and 504. The old definition of rape in the Dutch Penal Code prohibited forcing a woman to have extra-marital carnal intercourse by force or threat of force. This definition of rape was used since 1886 and was only changed since 1 December 1991, when it became clear that rape within marriage could not be prosecuted under the old definition. In addition, the 1886 definition only prohibited rape against women, while men could also be victims of rape. The new definition of rape covers such situations.

[117] Muhimana Judgment and Sentence, para. 546.

[118] *Ibid.*, para. 549; see also paras. 547-551.

As a final note, the *Akayesu*, *Musema* and *Niyitegeka* cases were all brought before Trial Chamber I of the ICTR. Judges Pillay (South Africa), Kama (Senegal) and Aspegren (Sweden), all three sitting on both the *Akayesu* and *Musema* trials,[119] emphatically expressed in the *Musema* case their disapproval of the mechanical definition of rape as it had been established, by that time, in the *Furundžija* case before the ICTY. They underlined the arguments put forth in *Akayesu* for sticking to the *Akayesu* definition of rape, as advanced by themselves.[120] The *Muhimana* case appeared before Trial Chamber III.[121]

4.1.1.2 The *Furundžija* Judgment

On 10 December 1998, only three weeks after the ICTY *Čelebići* Judgment was rendered (which concurred with the *Akayesu* definition of rape), the second principal definition of rape was established in the *Furundžija* case, this time by the ICTY. In defining rape, the Trial Chamber (again) noted that existing international law was not very useful, but that nevertheless some general indications could be discerned from the manner in which rape and other forms of sexual violence were laid down in international law. In particular, the Chamber referred to Article 5 of its Statute on crimes against humanity, where rape is specifically laid down as a separate crime, while other, less grave forms of serious sexual assault are to be prosecuted under 'other inhumane acts'.[122] This difference in emphasis resulted in the conclusion that rape is to be regarded as 'the most serious manifestation of sexual assault'.[123] Next, the Trial Chamber cited the definition of rape as given in *Akayesu* and stated that

> ... no elements other than those emphasised may be drawn from international treaty or customary law, nor is resort to general principles of international criminal law or to general principles of international law of any avail. The Trial Chamber therefore considers that, to arrive at an accurate definition of rape based on the criminal law principle of specificity (*Bestimmtheitgrundsatz*, also referred to by the maxim '*nullum crimen sine lege stricta*'), it is necessary to look for principles of criminal law common to the major legal systems of the world. These principles may be derived, with all due caution, from national laws.[124]

---

[119] In the Niyitegeka trial, the bench was composed of Judges Pillay (South Africa), Møse (Norway) and Vaz (Senegal). Judge Pillay was therefore the only judge sitting in all three trials.

[120] It is noteworthy that, although Judge Pillay originally comes from a common law country (South Africa), she nevertheless chose for a conceptual broad definition of rape within international law. In the Furundžija Judgment it is explained that the *actus reus* of rape in South Africa is viewed as consisting of the penetration, however slight, of the female sexual organ by the male sexual organ. See the Furundžija Judgment, para. 180, especially footnote 209.

[121] The Trial Chamber was composed of judges Khan (Pakistan), Muthoga (Kenya) and Short (Ghana).

[122] Furundžija Judgment, para. 175. The Chamber also referred to the division in the prohibition of rape and 'any form of indecent assault' of women in article 27 of Geneva Convention IV, article 76(1) of Additional Protocol I and article 4(2)(e) of Additional Protocol II.

[123] *Ibid.*

[124] *Ibid.*, para. 177. See also Kunarac, Kovač and Vuković Judgment, para. 439: 'The value of these sources [the general principles of law common to the major national legal systems of the

On the latter issue, the Tribunal held:

> Whenever international criminal rules do not define a notion of criminal law, reliance upon national legislation is justified, subject to the following conditions: (i) unless indicated by an international rule, reference should not be made to one national legal system only, say that of common-law or that of civil-law States. Rather, international courts must draw upon the general concepts and legal institutions common to all the major legal systems of the world. This presupposes a process of identification of the common denominators in these legal systems so as to pinpoint the basic notions they share; (ii) since 'international trials exhibit a number of features that differentiate them from national criminal proceedings', account must be taken of the specificity of international criminal proceedings when utilising national law notions. In this way a mechanical importation or transposition from national law into international criminal proceedings is avoided, as well as the attendant distortions of the unique traits of such proceedings.[125]

The approach taken by the *Furundžija* Trial Chamber thus indicates that when no definition of a crime can be found in international law, a general concept of a definition may be derived from the general principles or notions concerning the subject common to the major legal systems in the world.[126] Thus, the *Furundžija* Trial Chamber approach seems to imply that the *Akayesu* definition of rape was not sufficiently specific, and therefore in violation of the legality principle.

After having examined a number of national laws on rape, the Trial Chamber concluded that different opinions existed as to whether or not rape can be committed against a victim of either sex (or against women only) and whether or not penetration should be an element of the crime of rape (excluding other forms of sexual violence). All national laws surveyed by the Trial Chamber required an element of force, coercion, threat or acting without the consent of the victim, although the wording of the provisions diverged considerably. Some, but certainly not all, national jurisdictions indicated that force or intimidation can be directed against a third person.[127] Despite these types of discrepancy, the Trial Chamber concluded that most legal systems in both common-law and civil-law systems consider rape to be '... the forcible sexual

world] is that they may disclose "general concepts and legal institutions" which, if common to a broad spectrum of national legal systems, disclose an international approach to a legal question which may be considered as an appropriate indicator of the international law on the subject.'

[125] *Ibid.*, para. 178 (the original text includes a reference to the Separate and Dissenting opinion of Judge Cassese in the Erdemović Appeal Judgment, para. 5).

[126] In the Kunarac, Kovač and Vuković Judgment (para. 439), it is made clear that the judges are not searching for definitions, but for general principles, common to a broad range of legal systems: 'In considering these national legal systems the Trial Chamber does not conduct a survey of the major legal systems of the world in order to identify a specific legal provision which is adopted by a majority of legal systems but to consider, from an examination of national systems generally, whether it is possible to identify certain basic principles, or in the words of the *Furundžija* Judgment, "common denominators", in those legal systems which embody the *principles* which must be adopted in the international context.'

[127] For all these different views, see the Furundžija Judgment, para. 180

penetration of the human body by the penis or the forcible insertion of any other object into either the vagina or the anus'.[128] It noted, however, that there was a major discrepancy in the attitudes of States to forced oral sex: in some States it was classified as sexual assault, while in others as rape. Considering this dissimilarity, the Trial Chamber felt it necessary to resort to an examination of the general principles of international criminal law and, if this did not yield a workable result, to an examination of the general principles of international law. The Trial Chamber subsequently referred to the general principle of respect for human dignity when it stated that:

> ... the forced penetration of the mouth by the male sexual organ constitutes a most humiliating and degrading attack upon human dignity. The essence of the whole corpus of international humanitarian law as well as human rights law lies in the protection of the human dignity of every person, whatever his or her gender. The general principle of respect for human dignity is the basic underpinning and indeed the very *raison d'être* of international humanitarian law and human rights law; indeed in modern times it has become of such paramount importance as to permeate the whole body of international law. This principle is intended to shield human beings from outrages upon their personal dignity, whether such outrages are carried out by unlawfully attacking the body or by humiliating and debasing the honour, the self-respect or the mental well being [sic] of a person. It is consonant with this principle that such an extremely serious sexual outrage as forced oral penetration should be classified as rape.[129]

Furthermore, the notion that this finding, namely to charge a person accused of forced oral sex with rape while in some national jurisdictions such a person would be charged with sexual assault, would constitute a breach of the general principle of *nullum crimen sine lege* was well rejected as follows:

> It is not a question of criminalising acts which were not criminal when they were committed by the accused, since forcible oral sex is in any event a crime, and indeed an extremely serious crime. Indeed, due to the nature of the International Tribunal's subject-matter jurisdiction, in prosecutions before the Tribunal forced oral sex is invariably an aggravated sexual assault as it is committed in time of armed conflict on defenceless civilians; hence it is not simple sexual assault but sexual assault as a war crime or crime against humanity. ... His only complaint can be that a greater stigma attaches to being a convicted rapist rather than a convicted sexual assailant. However, one should bear in mind the remarks above to the effect that forced oral sex can be just as humiliating and traumatic for a victim as vaginal or anal penetration. Thus the notion that a greater stigma attaches to a conviction for forcible vaginal or anal penetration than to a conviction for forcible oral penetration is a product of questionable attitudes. Moreover any such concern is amply outweighed by the fundamental principle of protecting human dignity, a principle which favours broadening the definition of rape.[130]

---

[128] *Ibid.*, para. 181.

[129] *Ibid.*, para. 183.

[130] *Ibid.*, para. 184. The Sexual Offences Act 2003 (UK) was reformulated to include forced oral sex as rape based on an argument similar to the one laid down in the Furundžija case, namely that 'forced oral sex is as horrible, as demeaning and as traumatising as other forms of forced penile

On the basis of an evaluation of the national jurisdictions reviewed, the Trial Chamber finally stated the following elements of rape:

(i) the sexual penetration, however slight:
  (a) of the vagina or anus of the victim by the penis of the perpetrator or any other object used by the perpetrator; or
  (b) of the mouth of the victim by the penis of the perpetrator;
(ii) by coercion or force or threat of force against the victim or a third person.[131]

This mechanical definition of rape, focusing on what one body part (of the perpetrator) does to another body part (of the victim), is a departure from the broad definition of rape as established in *Akayesu*.[132] A definition of rape which is too much focused on penetration will exclude other forms of sexual violence as severe as rape. For this reason, and as set out in the previous subsection, the *Akayesu* Trial Chamber rejected the idea of constructing a definition of rape focusing on body parts. Focusing on penetration is in many national jurisdictions challenged as reinforcing stereotypes of sexual violence; moreover, it makes it more difficult for rape victims to build their case as they will have to talk about the anatomical details of the rape itself. On the other hand, it may be held that the *Furundžija* definition of rape is a precise one even if it focuses on penetration. The definition of rape includes the sexual penetration of the woman's vagina or the woman's or man's anus by the penis of the perpetrator or any object used by the perpetrator, as well as the sexual penetration of the mouth of the man

---

penetration' (Home Office, *Setting the Boundaries: Reforming the Law on Sex Offences*, Vol.1, Home Office (2000), para. 2.8.5).

131 Furundžija Judgment, paras. 180 (and accompanying footnotes), 185. The national laws on rape examined concerned the Penal Codes of the following countries: Chile; China; Germany; Japan; Socialist Federal Republic of Yugoslavia; Zambia; Austria; France; Italy; Argentina; Pakistan; India; South Africa; Uganda; New South Wales; The Netherlands; England and Wales; and Bosnia and Herzegovina. In the Final Report a similar conclusion was reached: '"Rape" should be understood to be the insertion, under conditions of force, coercion or duress, of any object, including but not limited to a penis, into a victim's vagina or anus; or the insertion, under conditions of force, coercion or duress, of a penis into the mouth of the victim' (Final Report of the Special Rapporteur of the Working Group on Contemporary Forms of Slavery, on Systematic rape, Sexual slavery and Slavery-like Practices During Armed Conflict, UN Doc. E/CN.4/Sub.2/1998/13, 22 June 1998, para. 24).

132 That the Furundžija definition of rape is more restrictive than the Akayesu definition of rape was emphasised in the Musema Judgment and Sentence, para. 227, in the following words: 'The definition of rape, as set forth in the Akayesu Judgment, clearly encompasses all the conduct described in the definition of rape as set forth in Furundžija.' However, see Strumpen-Darrie (2000, p. 17), who argued that the Furundžija Judgment 'advanced international jurisprudence on rape by expanding the legal definition of rape. ... the ICTY broadened the scope of rape crimes to include forced oral and anal sex'. See also Karagiannakis (1999, p. 489): '... it would seem that the broad, albeit more mechanical definition posited in the *Furundžija* Judgment does not differ in its practical application from the conceptual definition born in the *Akayesu* Judgment and followed and applied in the *Čelebići* Judgment'.

or woman by the penis of the perpetrator. Although, at first sight, these three forms of sexual penetration may be considered to be the only major forms of sexual penetration, it does seem that the definition excludes other forms of sexual penetration, such as penetration of the vagina with the perpetrator's tongue or penetration of the vagina with the fingers of the perpetrator. These are all sexual acts involving the penetration of the vagina, though not by the penis of the perpetrator, the body part that the *Furundžija* definition of rape seems to be focused on. As explained above, several national jurisdictions included such sexual acts consisting of non-penile penetration in their national laws on rape. If the *Furundžija* argument is that certain types of sexual acts are just as humiliating and traumatic for a victim as vaginal or anal penetration, the fundamental principle of protecting human dignity would also favour broadening the definition of rape in these situations, not only in the case of fellatio.[133] Additionally, if this line of thinking is accepted, there seems to be no reason for not accepting certain sexual acts that do not involve penetration, such as sexual mutilation, as a form of rape. By referring to the principle of the protection of human dignity, the *Furundžija* judges seem to have opened the door to a broad interpretation of the definition of rape, instead of closing it, as they intended. Finally, it should also be noted that it is rather remarkable that the Chamber employed the principle of respect for human dignity to establish whether or not fellatio constitutes rape, while initially it held that there was no general principle in international law or international criminal law that could be employed to establish the acts constituting rape within international law and that it had to look to national penal laws instead. It seems that the Tribunal in the *Furundžija* Judgment has been broadcasting rather contradictory messages, basically not knowing the criterion by which to judge which acts do and which acts do not fall within the definition of rape.

Apart from these observations, it may be held that the *Furundžija* definition distinguishes rape from other forms of sexual violence: if such a distinction is not made, what is it that separates rape from other forms of sexual violence? The Trial Chamber in the *Furundžija* case furthermore endorsed a gender-neutral approach as to the victim or perpetrator in rape cases by using words such as 'victim' and 'perpetrator', which should also be interpreted to cover male-to-male and female-to-female violations.[134] As to the circumstances which need to be established in order for the sexual acts to constitute a crime, the *Akayesu* 'circumstances which are coercive' have been replaced by 'coercion or force or threat of force against the victim or a third person', a qualification which should be interpreted to include the same type of circumstances as meant in *Akayesu*. The Trial Chamber furthermore stressed that 'any form of captivity [a situation in which Witness A found herself] vitiates consent'.[135] It is noteworthy that the Trial Chamber in its survey of national laws referred to non-consent as an element of the crime of rape, worthy of including.[136] Without explaining why it chose its

---

[133] In conformity with the reasoning applied for including oral sex in the definition of rape, see Furundžija Judgment, para. 184.

[134] A literal reading of the definition, however, would seem to exclude the most common form of male sexual violence, i.e., forcing two males to perform fellatio on each other. It would appear that 'perpetrator' in the Furundžija definition of rape (see (i)(b)) encompasses victims as well.

[135] Furundžija Judgment, para. 271.

[136] However, the element of consent was based on the England and Wales Sexual Offences Act 1956 to 1992 only. See Furundžija Judgment, para. 180. The use of non-consensual intercourse as

wording – a decision which was possibly instigated by the facts of the case –, the element of consent was thus, again, left out of the definition of rape. In addition, this sentence specifically states that coercion or force or threat of force may also be directed against a third person. This implies that in situations in which the victim is forced to undergo the act of rape because otherwise a relative or acquaintance will be murdered or raped, the perpetrator will be punishable. It should be noted, however, that no other conclusions on these issues – gender-neutral wording and the use of the third person – may be drawn from the *Akayesu* definition of rape.[137]

The definition of rape as given in the *Furundžija* case has not been followed up in subsequent judgments. Instead, a third definition of rape, more or less similar to the *Furundžija* one, was established in the *Kunarac, Kovač and Vuković* case, which was upheld in subsequent cases. This will be discussed in the next subsection.

4.1.1.3 The *Kunarac, Kovač and Vuković* Judgment

On 22 February 2001, the *Kunarac, Kovač and Vuković* Judgment was rendered by the ICTY, establishing the third definition of rape in international law. The *Kunarac, Kovač and Vuković* definition of rape follows the first part of the *Furundžija* definition of rape, i.e. it gives the identical mechanical description of body parts and objects involved. However, according to the Trial Chamber the second part of the definition of rape as established in the *Furundžija* case – '(ii) by coercion or force or threat of force against the victim or a third person' – was, although appropriate to the circumstances of that case, more narrowly stated than required by international law. The Trial Chamber noted that 'in stating that the relevant act of sexual penetration will constitute rape only if accompanied by coercion or force or threat of force against the victim or a third person, the *Furundžija* definition [of rape] does not refer to other factors which would render an act of sexual penetration *non-consensual or non-voluntary* on the part of the victim'.[138] By considering the survey of national laws conducted by the judges in the *Furundžija* case, the Trial Chamber in *Kunarac, Kovač and Vuković* concluded that 'the true common denominator' is the 'violations of sexual *autonomy*'.[139] In other words, in the eyes of the *Kunarac, Kovač and Vuković* judges the definition of rape as established in the *Furundžija* case was too restrictive because it focused on coercion or force only. They argued that the relevance of absence of consent was already noted in the

---

an element of the crime of rape in national jurisdictions was also noticed in the Akayesu Judgment (paras. 598, 686).

137 The definition in the Akayesu case, and as subsequently uphold in the Čelebići and Musema cases, similarly speaks in gender neutral terms, i.e., 'a person', and similarly includes situations in which rapes were made possible by coercion or force directed against a third person, i.e., coercive circumstances are explained as not requiring a show of physical force: 'Threats, intimidation, extortion and other forms of duress which prey on fear or desperation may constitute coercion, and coercion may be inherent in certain circumstances, such as armed conflict or the military presence of *Interahamwe* among refugee Tutsi women at the bureau communal.' For a discussion of the Akayesu definition of rape, see the previous subsection.

138 Kunarac, Kovač and Vuković Judgment, para. 438. See also paras. 440, 457-460.

139 *Ibid.*, para. 440; see also para. 457.

Furundžija case, but mistakenly not incorporated in the definition of rape.[140] The Chamber further substantiated this conclusion by surveying (again!) the major national legal systems in the world focussing on the common principles underlying their definitions of rape. On the basis of this survey, which included more national laws than the survey made in the *Furundžija* case, the Trial Chamber distinguished three broad categories of circumstances which need to be established in order for the acts to constitute a crime:

(i) the sexual activity is accompanied by force or threat of force to the victim or a third party;
(ii) the sexual activity is accompanied by force *or* a variety of other specified circumstances which made the victim particularly vulnerable or negated her ability to make an informed refusal; or
(iii) the sexual activity occurs without the consent of the victim.[141]

Thus, the *Kunarac, Kovač and Vuković* judges held that, besides (threat of) force, the circumstances as indicated in (ii) and (iii) will render the sexual acts criminal as well. With regard to category (ii), the Trial Chamber observed the following 'specified circumstances' in which the victim 'was put in a state of being unable to resist, was particularly vulnerable or incapable of resisting because of physical or mental incapacity, or was induced into the act by surprise or misrepresentation'.[142] As to the first category, one may think of circumstances in which the victim is put in a state of unconsciousness, is drugged or put under psychological pressure. These are all circumstances of a temporary or circumstantial nature. With regard to the second category, circumstances of an enduring or qualitative nature, one may think of mental or physical illness, or minors. The third category refers to situations in which there is no opportunity for informed or reasoned refusal, such as is the case with fraud, surprise or impersonation. It should be noted that, in the context of genocide, crimes against humanity and war crimes, these specified circumstances do not all occur on a similar scale as in peace-time situations (for instance, in the case of impersonation), for which the laws were originally drawn up. Nevertheless, situations which come to mind include the false promises made to women concerning jobs such as housekeeping while they were intended to be used as sexual slaves (the 'comfort women' in Asia in the late

---

[140] *Ibid.*, para. 440. See also the previous subsection.

[141] *Ibid.*, paras. 443-456. The Penal Codes of the countries examined include those from Bosnia and Herzegovina; Germany; Korea; China; Norway; Austria; Spain; Brazil; Sierra Leone; some jurisdictions in the United States of America (New York, Maryland, Massachusetts) (all these Penal Codes refer to the first category: 'force or threat of force'); Switzerland; Portugal; France; Italy; Denmark; Sweden; Finland; Estonia; Japan; Argentina; Costa Rica; Uruguay; The Philippines; California Penal Code, US (all these Penal Codes refer to the second category: 'specific circumstances which go to the vulnerability or deception of the victim'); England; Canada; New Zealand; Australia; India; Bangladesh; South Africa; Zambia; Belgium; and Nicaragua (all these Penal Codes refer to the third category: 'absence of consent or voluntary participation').

[142] Kunarac, Kovač and Vuković Judgment, para. 446.

1940s).[143] It is nevertheless doubtful whether such situations warrant the inclusion of consent as an element of the crime of rape considering that such circumstances are or should be read to be included in the terms coercion, (threat of) force (*Furundžija*) or coercive circumstances (*Akayesu*).

The Trial Chamber concluded that the factors referred to under (i) and (ii) are matters which result in 'the will of the victim being overcome or in the victim's submission to the act being non-voluntary'.[144] For this reason, the basic principle underlying the crime of rape in national laws should be that the sexual activity occurs 'without the consent of the victim',[145] as such laid down in common-law jurisdictions in particular.[146] The Trial Chamber held that

> In practice, the absence of genuine and freely given consent or voluntary participation may be *evidenced* by the presence of the various factors specified in other jurisdictions – such as force, threats of force, or taking advantage of a person who is unable to resist. A clear demonstration that such factors negate true consent is found in those jurisdictions where absence of consent is an element of rape and consent is explicitly defined not to exist where factors such as use of force, the unconsciousness or inability to resist of the victim, or misrepresentation by the perpetrator.[147]

Thus, the judges in the *Kunarac, Kovač and Vuković* case found the element of 'coercion or force or threat of force' as laid down in the *Furundžija* Judgment to be more restrictive than required by international law and concluded that it should be replaced by the all-embracing phrase 'without the consent of the victim'. The third definition of the crime of rape in international law therefore reads:

> ... the sexual penetration, however slight: (a) of the vagina or anus of the victim by the penis of the perpetrator or any other object used by the perpetrator; or (b) of the mouth of the victim by the penis of the perpetrator; where such sexual penetration occurs without the consent of the victim. Consent for this purpose must be consent given voluntarily, as a result of the victim's free will, assessed in the context of the surrounding circumstances. The *mens rea* is the intention to effect this sexual penetration, and the knowledge that it occurs without the consent of the victim.[148]

On appeal, the appellants challenged the definition of rape. According to all three of them, in addition to penetration two additional elements should be showed: 'force or

[143] These kinds of situations could fall under the 'specified circumstance' of 'surprise', but, ideally, such situations should be prosecuted as sexual slavery.
[144] Kunarac, Kovač and Vuković, para. 457; see also para. 452.
[145] According to Smith and Hogan (1999, p. 457): 'the essence of rape is the absence of consent. ... At one time it was stated that the intercourse must have been procured through force, fear or fraud. Some books continued to state the law in these terms until very recently but they have been out-of-date for well over a century.'
[146] Kunarac, Kovač and Vuković Judgment, paras. 453-456. Out of the ten national laws cited, only Belgium belongs to the non-common law jurisdictions.
[147] *Ibid.*, para. 458.
[148] *Ibid.*, para. 460.

threat of force and the victim's "continuous" or "genuine" resistance'.[149] The Appeals Chamber strongly rejected these statements and explicitly concurred with the definition of rape as established by the Trial Chamber.[150] As to the 'genuine resistance' requirement, the judges of the Appeals Chamber held: 'The Appellants' bald assertion that nothing short of continuous resistance provides adequate notice to the perpetrator that his attentions are unwanted is wrong on the law [they did not prove any basis in customary international law] and absurd on the facts.'[151] As to the other assertion, the Appeals Chamber concluded that 'a narrow focus on force or threat of force could permit perpetrators to evade liability for sexual activity to which the other party had not consented by taking advantage of coercive circumstances without relying on physical force'.[152] The detention facilities in which the women were held captive in Foča amounted to 'circumstances that were so coercive as to negate any possibility of consent'.[153] Although the *Kunarac, Kovač and Vuković* Appeals Chamber upheld the Trial Chamber's definition of rape which focused on absence of consent, it seems that it interpreted the *Furundžija* definition of rape incorrectly. In explaining why the definition of rape should include the element of non-consent, it held that the *Furundžija* definition of rape only referred to force or threat of force, while factors other than force could also render an act of sexual penetration non-consensual or non-voluntary on the part of the victim.[154] However, coercion is also mentioned as an element of the *Furundžija* definition of rape and, in fact, precisely the coercive circumstances in the detention facilities led to the conclusion that consent to the rapes could not be presupposed. It would therefore seem that the introduction of non-consent and lack of knowledge of non-consent as advocated by the *Kunarac, Kovač and Vuković* Appeals Chamber is absurd within the context in which rape almost always takes place within supranational criminal law, as evidenced by the facts of all the ICTY and ICTR cases so far, including *Kunarac, Kovač and Vuković*.[155]

In other words, does the wording in both the *Akayesu* (coercive circumstances) and *Furundžija* definitions of rape ((threat of) force and coercion) not cover all situations in which rapes take place within the context of genocide, crimes against humanity and (non-)international armed conflicts if interpreted broadly? Put otherwise, why include the element of consent in the definition of rape? There are a number of reasons why 'absence of consent' should not be an element of the crime of rape in supranational criminal law:

---

149 Kunarac, Kovač and Vuković Appeal Judgment, para. 125.

150 *Ibid.*, para. 128.

151 *Ibid.*, para. 128.

152 *Ibid.*, para. 129

153 *Ibid.*, para. 132. In the Judgment (para. 131) reference is made to German and US national laws in which consent is deliberately left out as an element of the crime of rape in situations of unequal power structures, such as those between prisoners and those watching over them.

154 *Ibid.*, para. 129.

155 In this respect the following remark made by the Appeals Chamber (para. 130) is exemplary and remarkable at the same time: 'While it is true that a focus on one aspect gives a different shading to the offence, it is worth observing that the circumstances giving rise to the instant appeal and that prevail in most cases charged as either war crimes or crimes against humanity will be almost universally coercive. That is to say, true consent will not be possible.'

1. Although 'lack of consent' features in a significant number of domestic legislations (mostly common-law legislations, however, which can hardly qualify as representing most criminal-law systems[156]), national laws were never intended to fit the definition of rape to genocide, crimes against humanity and war crimes situations. It is not possible to transfer the elements of rape as found in national laws into supranational criminal law just like that, without taking into account the specific differences that exist for these two bodies of law.[157] The definitions of rape in national laws were written for peace-time situations, which possibly justifies the inclusion of non-consent, but in the context of genocide, crimes against humanity and armed conflict – in many cases, if not all – acts of sexual violence will have been committed under (threat of) force, coercion or coercive circumstances, and the issue of consent becomes redundant.[158] In the context of oppression or violence, non-consent and the knowledge thereof are highly irrelevant elements of rape for the Prosecutor to prove. Introducing 'lack of consent' into the definition of rape as a crime against humanity (as was done in *Kunarac, Kovač and Vuković*) was both inappropriate and unnecessary in view of the fact that any alleged rape would, in any event, have to be considered as part of a widespread or systematic attack on a civilian population on discriminatory grounds, suggesting the existence of coercive circumstances that negate any possibility of consent. The same applies to rape as genocide or as a war crime, where the jurisdictional requirements of the crimes make the issue of consent irrelevant. Although domestic laws may inform supranational criminal law on the standard of rape, it is suggested to consult those laws which consider consent to be vitiated or irrelevant in situations of unequal power structures.[159] Such circumstances in domestic legal systems are more akin to the context of rape in supranational criminal law and provide a better basis for the

---

[156] Many national Penal Codes refer to 'force, threat of force or coercion' instead of consent. See the examples mentioned in the Furundžija Judgment, para. 180; and the Kunarac, Kovač and Vuković Judgment, paras. 443-445.

[157] In this respect, see the Kunarac, Kovač and Vuković Judgment, paras. 468-471: 'it is not possible to transfer the elements of torture as found in human rights law into international humanitarian law without taking into account the specific differences that exist for these two bodies of law'.

[158] This was confirmed by a Special Rapporteur to the UN Commission for Human Rights, Ms. Gay J. McDougall, in her Final Report, in which it was held that 'the manifestly coercive circumstances that exist in all armed conflict situations establish a presumption of non-consent and negates the need for the prosecution to establish a lack of consent as an element of the crime' (Final Report of the Special Rapporteur of the Working Group on Contemporary Forms of Slavery, on Systematic rape, Sexual slavery and Slavery-like Practices During Armed Conflict, UN Doc. E/CN.4/Sub.2/1998/13, 22 June 1998, para. 25). This observation equally applies to genocide and crimes against humanity situations. See also Kalosieh (2003) and Boon (2001).

[159] See *The Prosecutor v. Sylvestre Gacumbitsi*, Appellant's Brief, Case No. ICTR-2001-64-A, 28 September 2004, pp. 58-59. See also the examples of national laws mentioned in the Kunarac, Kovač and Vuković Appeal Judgment, para. 131 (for example, the situation in which a prison guard has sex with an inmate; in these situations consent is never relevant whether or not the inmate consents).

definition of rape than the search for a common denominator in the majority of legal systems around the world.[160] If omitting non-consent as an element of the crime of rape can be done at the national level, then why not also at the international level, where the conditions may be even more extreme than those addressed by domestic laws?[161]

2. Consent should not be an acceptable element in supranational criminal law because, if one accepts that rape constitutes a form of genocide, or any other crime, by extension this would imply that a victim could consent to genocide. It matters what rape really is, a crime. After all, given the nature of crimes, consent is not accepted either as an element of any of the other crimes inflicting bodily or mental harm listed, such as torture and enslavement.[162] How should we conceive of a person who consents to the infliction of bodily or mental harm? In respect of enslavement, the Appeals Chamber in the *Kunarac, Kovač and Vuković* case expressly rejected proof of lack of consent as an element of the crime since, in its view, 'enslavement flows from claimed rights of ownership'.[163] It is suggested that rape as an international crime is treated in the same way as any other international crime, thereby removing consent as an element of the crime of rape or as a defence if coercive circumstances have been proved.

3. By introducing Rule 96 into the ICTY and ICTR Rules of Procedure and Evidence (RPE), supranational criminal law deliberately left out consent as a relevant issue. According to Rule 96, consent can be accepted as a defence in very limited circumstances only: if the accused can prove the absence of real, threatened or feared violence, duress, detention or psychological oppression against the victim or a third person.[164] This provision was introduced to take into account both the reality

---

[160] See *The Prosecutor v. Sylvestre Gacumbitsi*, Appellant's Brief, Case No. ICTR-2001-64-A, 28 September 2004, p. 58.

[161] *Ibid.*, p. 59.

[162] Viseur Sellers (2001a, p. 285) states that 'there can, of course, never be consent to torture, given the nature of the crime'. During the ICC negotiations, judges of the ICTY suggested that consent is not a legally recognisable defence to sexual crimes that are components of enslavement, torture and genocide because the nature of these crimes preclude consent. See on this latter issue Boon (2001), p. 669.

[163] Kunarac, Kovač and Vuković Appeal Judgment, para. 120.

[164] Rule 96 of the ICTY RPE reads (italics added):

In cases of sexual assault:

i. no corroboration of the victim's testimony shall be required;
ii. *consent shall not be allowed as a defence if the victim:*
   (a) has been subjected to or threatened with or has had reason to fear violence, duress, detention or psychological oppression, or
   (b) reasonably believed that if the victim did not submit, another might be so subjected, threatened or put in fear;
iii. *before evidence of the victim's consent is admitted, the accused shall satisfy the Trial Chamber in camera that the evidence is relevant and credible;*

of sexual violence in situations of mass violence and the need to protect the right of the accused to a fair trial.[165] The Rule is based on the presumption that whether or not the victim consented is an irrelevant question under coercive circumstances. In such a case, the issue of non-consent is irrelevant, and it would seem that consent could hardly be presented as a viable defence at all. However, by bringing in consent through the backdoor of judicial interpretation – consent as an element of the crime of rape –, the Tribunal judges brought back the issue of consent which they initially rejected by including Rule 96 in their RPE.[166]

4. Including consent in the definition of rape can expose victims of sexual violence to painful and humiliating questions which are not relevant in situations where force, coercion or coercive circumstances are present. An inquiry into the victim's conduct and state of mind ('Did you consent?' or other questions to that extent) with the purpose of obtaining explicit evidence of non-consent is offensive and shocking to most victims of sexual violence. It is insulting to most rape victims, especially when a victim has just described the circumstances in which the sexual violence took place, and may lead to revictimisation.[167] Including consent in the definition of rape places the burden on the Prosecutor to prove that there was no consent and thus leads the Prosecutor to inquire with the victim about whether or not she consented. The reaction of Witness 95 in the *Kunarac, Kovač and Vuković* case to the question posed by the Prosecutor, – viz. whether the sexual contact had been against her will – was met with outrage, and is illustrative in this regard: 'Please, madam, if over a period of 40 days you have sex with someone, with several individuals, do you really think that is with your own will?'[168] Witness 95 had just explained to the court that she had been selected for the purpose of rape more than 150 times in a period of 40 days. Putting the question of consent to the witness may therefore in a way give the impression that she is not believed, that in fact she did consent. In the *Kunarac, Kovač and Vuković* case, the judges had requested that the issue of absence of

---

iv. prior sexual conduct of the victim shall not be admitted in evidence.

With regard to the ICC, a similar provision can be found in Rule 70 ICC RPE. The defence of consent is further discussed in Chapter 4 on protective and special measures for victims of sexual violence.

[165] Fitzgerald (1997), p. 642.

[166] Rule 96 was adopted by the ICTY judges on 11 February 1994, several times amended in 1994 and 1995, and now containing the rebuttable presumption that a defence of consent would not be applicable. In the first version of Rule 96 ICTY RPE, it was stated under sub-section (ii) that consent would never be allowed as a defence in cases of sexual violence. Because of fair trial concerns, the rule was changed into the current reading of the provision.

[167] See *The Prosecutor v. Sylvestre Gacumbitsi*, Appellant's Brief, Case No. ICTR-2001-64-A, 28 September 2004, pp. 58-59.

[168] *Prosecutor v. Dragoljub Kunarac, Radomir Kovač and Zoran Vuković,* Transcripts, Case No. IT-96-23-T and IT-96-23/1-T, 25 April 2000, pp. 2235-2236. The Prosecutor recognised in its closing statements that the question was met with 'appropriate outrage' by the rape victim (*Prosecutor v. Dragoljub Kunarac, Radomir Kovač and Zoran Vuković,* Transcripts, Case No. IT-96-23-T and IT-96-23/1-T, 20 November 2000, p. 6281).

consent was brought up, despite the coercive circumstances established by the Prosecutor.[169] Despite the fact that at that time the *Furundžija* definition of rape was still applicable, focusing on coercion and force and threat of force instead, Judge Hunt held that inquiries into consent would serve the 'proper prosecution procedure not to leave matters to implication', also in light of a possible move away from the *Furundžija* definition of rape after the closing of the *Kunarac, Kovač and Vuković* case.[170] The Prosecutor, who had initially not inquired into the issue of consent (because in her view the coercive circumstances were sufficiently established and thus rendered consent irrelevant), subsequently reformulated the question into: 'Was it against your will?'[171] However, if the Prosecutor establishes coercion, force or threat of force, consent should no longer be an issue and lack of consent should instead be inferred by the Judges themselves.[172] The possibility of raising consent as a defence is still possible under the strict conditions laid down in Rule 96 of the RPE, but the burden of proof will in that case be on the defendant.

5. Victims will only perceive the Tribunals and the Court as legitimate if rape is defined in conformity with the reality of the crime. Including consent in the definition of rape is just a tool to silence them: they will not come forward, and justice will not be done to victims of sexual violence, who constitute one of the largest groups of victims in situations of mass violence. If the Tribunals and the Court want to achieve the purpose they were created for in the first place, i.e. to prosecute and try those persons responsible for the most serious violations of international humanitarian law, then they should not introduce the criterion of consent into the definition of rape.

Summarising, although the new definition as established in the *Kunarac, Kovač and Vuković* case may theoretically rule out any possibility of the victim consenting, consent is not an acceptable element in supranational criminal law and its inclusion as an element in the definition of rape in international law must therefore be contested.[173] In

---

[169] *Prosecutor v. Dragoljub Kunarac, Radomir Kovač and Zoran Vuković,* Transcripts, Case No. IT-96-23-T and IT-96-23/1-T, 19 April 2000, pp. 1979-1982.

[170] *Ibid.*, p. 1981.

[171] *Prosecutor v. Dragoljub Kunarac, Radomir Kovač and Zoran Vuković,* Transcripts, Case No. IT-96-23-T and IT-96-23/1-T, 18 May 2000, pp. 3481, 3597-3598, 3601.

[172] If a judge nevertheless insists that the issue of non-consent is raised with the victim (as in the Kunarac, Kovač and Vuković case), the question should be asked in the least offensive wording, such as 'was their any possibility to resist?' In this regard it may also be helpful when preparing the witness for trial to underline that such a question might or will be asked, despite compelling evidence that the sexual intercourse was forceful.

[173] See also the Prosecutor's Pre-Trial Brief I in the Kunarac, Kovač and Vuković case, para. 128: 'lack of consent is not an element of the offence of rape (or any other sexual assault) as defined by the law and rules of the Tribunal, and the existence of force, threat of force, or coercion vitiates consent as a defence' (cited in Kunarac, Kovač and Vuković Judgment, para. 461, footnote 1165). The Trial Chamber, however, submitted that 'the Prosecution, by its emphasis on the need to prove "coercion, force or threats" in the Final Trial Brief (par 754) also apparently favours a narrower definition of what constitutes rape than is indicated by the sources of

the *Kunarac, Kovač and Vuković* case, the Trial Chamber held that some situations would not be covered by the *Furundžija* definition of rape; i.e., mention was made of the victim being brought into a state of being unable to resist, having a physical or mental incapacity or being deceived by surprise or misrepresentation. However, all these acts could and should be covered by the words 'coercion, force, or threat of force' and/or 'circumstances which are coercive', and therefore make inclusion of the element of consent unnecessary.

The mechanical approach to the definition of rape taken in the *Kunarac, Kovač and Vuković* Judgment (2001) and affirmed by the *Kunarac, Kovač and Vuković* Appeal Judgment (2002) was upheld in the *Kvočka et al.* (2001), *Semanza* (2003), *Kajelijeli* (2003) and *Kamuhanda* (2004) Judgments.[174]

The ICTY's *Kvočka et al.* Judgment was rendered on 2 November 2001, some eight months after the definition of rape had been accepted by the *Kunarac, Kovač and Vuković* Trial Chamber. Without much explanation, the Trial Chamber in the *Kvočka et al.* case concurred with the *Kunarac, Kovač and Vuković* definition and emphasised the view of rape as a violation of sexual autonomy.[175] It was furthermore stressed that the holdings 'coercive conditions are inherent in situations of armed conflict [*Čelebići/Akayesu*]' and 'any form of captivity vitiates consent [*Furundžija*]' were accepted.[176] As to the definition of 'sexual violence', it relied on the one established in the *Akayesu* case, viz. 'any act of a sexual nature which is committed on a person under circumstances which are coercive'.[177] On the basis of this definition, the Trial Chamber argued that 'sexual violence is broader than rape and includes such crimes as sexual slavery or molestation', but also sexual acts short of physical contact, such as forced public nudity.[178] In addition, 'sexual violence would also include such crimes as sexual mutilation, forced marriage, and forced abortion as well as the gender related crimes explicitly listed in the ICC Statute as war crimes and crimes against humanity, namely "rape, sexual slavery, enforced prostitution, forced pregnancy, enforced sterilization" and other similar forms of violence'.[179]

In the *Semanza* case (15 May 2003), the judges noted the conceptual broad definition as established in *Akayesu*, but nevertheless argued

international law surveyed in this judgment. The submissions, however, appear to misconceive absence of consent as being some sort of "further element" or "additional" factor rather than a matter which encompasses the narrower range of factors which it cites. (see Prosecutor's Final Trial Brief, pars 755 and 760). As will become apparent, the Trial Chamber does not agree with the Prosecution's submission that proof of force, threat of force or coercion is an element imposed by international law' (cited in Kunarac, Kovač and Vuković Judgment, footnote 1119).

[174] Kunarac, Kovač and Vuković Appeal Judgment, para. 127 (quoting and concurring with the Trial Chamber's definition of rape); Kvočka et. al. Judgment, paras. 177-179; Semanza Judgment and Sentence, paras. 344-346; Kajelijeli Judgment and Sentence, para. 915; and the Kamuhanda Judgment, paras. 709-710.

[175] Kvočka et. al. Judgment, para. 177.

[176] *Ibid.*, para. 178.

[177] *Ibid.*, para. 180.

[178] *Ibid.*

[179] *Ibid.*, footnote 343.

> the comparative analysis in *Kunarac* to be persuasive and thus [the Chamber] will adopt the definition of rape approved by the ICTY Appeals Chamber. In doing so, the Chamber recognises that other acts of sexual violence that do not satisfy this narrow definition may be prosecuted as other crimes against humanity within the jurisdiction of this Tribunal such as torture, persecution, enslavement, or other inhumane acts.[180]

By adhering to the more restrictive *Kunarac, Kovač and Vuković* definition of rape, the *Semanza* Trial Chamber departed from the conceptual approach to the definition of rape applied until then as the standard definition of rape within the ICTR in the *Akayesu* and *Musema* cases. It just so happened that the next day the *Niyitegeka* Judgment was pronounced (by another Trial Chamber), which, remarkably, relied on the conceptual definition.[181]

A similar approach was taken in the *Kajelijeli* Judgment of 1 December 2003. After noting the conceptual definition of rape established in *Akayesu* and adopted in *Musema*, the Trial Chamber held:

> Given the evolution of the law in this area, culminating in the endorsement of the *Furundzija/Kunarac* approach by the ICTY Appeals Chamber, the Chamber finds the latter approach of persuasive authority and hereby adopts the definition as given in *Kunarac* and quoted above. The mental element of the offence of rape as a crime against humanity is the intention to effect the above described sexual penetration, with the knowledge that it was being done without the consent of the victim.[182]

In addition, 'other acts of sexual violence which may fall outside of this specific definition may of course be prosecuted, and would be considered by the Chamber under other categories of crimes for which the Tribunal has jurisdiction, such as *other inhumane acts*'.[183] On 22 January 2004, the *Kamuhanda* Trial Chamber reiterated in almost the same wording the *Kajelijeli* arguments for maintaining the *Furundžija/Kunarac, Kovač and Vuković* definition of rape, after noting the *Akayesu/Musema* approach.[184]

While the *Semanza*, *Kajelijeli* and *Kamuhanda* Judgments seem to have led the ICTR in the direction of the *Kunarac, Kovač and Vuković* mechanical approach to the definition of rape, the recent *Muhimana* Judgment seems to have brought back the balance in the ICTR to 50 (*Akayesu*) – 50 (*Kunarac, Kovač and Vuković*). Kajelijeli and Kamuhanda stood trial before Trial Chamber II, Semanza and Muhimana before Trial Chamber III and Akayesu, Musema and Niyitegeka before Trial Chamber I. The argumentation in the *Kajelijeli*, *Kamuhanda* and *Semanza* Judgments for shifting from the *Akayesu* definition to the *Kunarac, Kovač and Vuković* definition is poor, but seems to be largely influenced by the fact that the *Kunarac, Kovač and Vuković* definition of rape was confirmed by an Appeals Chamber. In the *Gacumbitsi* case, ICTR Trial Chamber III seems, however, not to have taken a clear stand in the discussion on the

---

[180] Semanza Judgment and Sentence, para. 345.

[181] See the previous subsection.

[182] Kajelijeli Judgment and Sentence, para. 915.

[183] *Ibid.*, para. 916.

[184] Kamuhanda Judgment, paras. 705-710.

definition of rape. The Trial Chamber recognised that '... any penetration of the victim's vagina by the rapist with his genitals or with any object constitutes rape, although the definition of rape under Article 3(g) of the Statute is not limited to such acts alone', in this respect relying on both the *Akayesu* and *Kunarac, Kovač and Vuković* Judgments for guidance.[185] However, the Trial Chamber also considered absence of consent when it held that '... the utterances made by the Accused to the effect that in case of resistance the victims should be killed in an atrocious manner, and the fact that rape victims were attacked by those they were fleeing from, adequately establish the victims' lack of consent to the rapes'.[186] Thus, even though the Trial Chamber found that coercive circumstances were present, the Trial Chamber raised the element of non-consent, making it clear that the ICTR judges continue to have difficulty deciding which definition of rape should be the correct one in supranational criminal law. In order to clarify whether or not absence of consent is a constituent element of rape as an international crime, the Prosecutor in *Gacumbitsi* requested the Appeals Chamber to make a decision in this matter.[187] In his brief, the Prosecutor very clearly set out why non-consent of the victim and knowledge of the victim's non-consent are no elements of the crime of rape in international law.

Within the ICTY, a different picture has emerged, with more explicit preference for the mechanical definition of rape. Although the judges of Trial Chamber II in the *Čelebići* case argued for the *Akayesu* definition of rape,[188] such thinking was not upheld by the subsequent Trial Chamber II judges who served in the *Furundžija* and *Kunarac, Kovač and Vuković* cases, as was explained above.[189] In the *Kvočka et al.* case, which took place before Trial Chamber I, the *Kunarac, Kovač and Vuković* view of the definition of rape was upheld.[190] The Appeals Chamber in the *Kunarac, Kovač and Vuković* case has confirmed the *Kunarac, Kovač and Vuković* Trial Chamber's definition of rape.[191] So far, ICTY Trial Chamber III has not yet dealt with interpreting the definition of rape.

---

[185] Gacumbitsi Judgment, para. 321 (with reference (in a footnote) to '*Akayesu*, Judgement (Ch.), paras. 597-598; TPIY, *Kunarac et al.*, Arrêt (App.), paras. 127-133').

[186] *Ibid.*, para. 325.

[187] *The Prosecutor v. Sylvestre Gacumbitsi*, Appellant's Brief, Case No. ICTR-2001-64-A, 28 September 2004, pp. 47-60.

[188] The judges who served in the Čelebići case (Trial Chamber II) were Judge Adolphus G. Karibi-Whyte (presiding, Nigeria), Judge Elizabeth Odio Benito (Costa Rica) and Judge Saad Saood Jan (Pakistan).

[189] The judges who served in the Furundžija case (Trial Chamber II) were Judge Florence Ndepele Mwachande Mumba (presiding, Zambia), Judge Antonio Cassese (Italy) and Judge Richard May (UK). The judges who served in the Kunarac, Kovač and Vuković case (Trial Chamber II) were Judge Florence Ndepele Mwachande Mumba (presiding, Zambia), Judge David Hunt (Australia) and Judge Fausto Pocar (Italy). Judge Mumba was the only judge serving in both the Furundžija and Kunarac, Kovač and Vuković cases.

[190] The judges who served in the Kvočka et. al. case (Trial Chamber I) were Judge Almiro Rodrigues (presiding, Portugal), Judge Fouad Riad (Egypt) and Judge Patricia Wald (US).

[191] The judges who served in the Appeals Chamber in the Kunarac, Kovač and Vuković case were Judge Claude Jorda (presiding, France), Judge Mohamed Shahabuddeen (Guyana), Judge

4.1.1.4 *Intermezzo*

On the basis of this survey of ICTY and ICTR case law, it will have become clear that there are three lines of thinking concerning the definition of rape in international law. The first adheres to a broad conceptual definition of rape (*Akayesu*, upheld in *Čelebići*, *Musema*, *Niyitegeka* and *Muhimana*), the second takes a more restrictive, mechanical approach (*Furundžija*) and the third introduces, in addition to the mechanical description of body parts involved, the element of consent (*Kunarac, Kovač and Vuković* (Trial Chamber and Appeals Chamber), upheld in *Kvočka et al.*, *Semanza* and *Kajelijeli*). Although the *Gacumbitsi* Trial Chamber was not clear on the definition it chose, it appears to have taken the *Kunarac, Kovač and Vuković* definition of rape as it refers to non-consent in the discussion of rape. The second and third lines of thinking – on the basis of a number of national laws thought to comprise the major systems of the world – restrict the definition of rape to penetration of the vagina, anus and mouth by the penis and of the vagina and anus by means of objects. According to the third line of thinking, absence of consent is an element of the crime that needs to be proved. The first definition is more broadly defined and would not preclude forms of sexual violence beyond penetration. In addition, a physical invasion of a sexual nature is deemed to be a crime when committed on a person under coercive circumstances. Thus, no mention is made of non-consent. The Appeals Chamber decision in the *Kunarac, Kovač and Vuković* case seems to direct the Tribunal judges to application of the mechanical definition of rape, which includes 'lack of consent' as an element of the crime. Despite the Appeals Chamber decision, later judgments are still confusing as to the correct standard of rape within supranational criminal law: in the *Niyitegeka* Judgment (2003) and the *Muhimana* Judgment (2005), the *Akayesu* definition of rape was adhered to, while in the *Gacumbitsi* Judgment (2004) reference was made to both the *Akayesu* and the *Kunarac, Kovač and Vuković* definitions of rape in the discussions of the acts constituting rape and of non-consent, implying that this might be an element of the crime of rape.

It is, of course, highly remarkable that so many definitions of rape have emerged from ICTY/R case law. It has been argued that these definitions of rape, established by the Tribunal judges only in the sentencing phase after all the evidence relating to sexual violence had been given, violates the legality principle, according to which punishment is only possible if the crime has been defined in advance (retrospective effect being forbidden), in written law (*lex scripta*) and clearly and unequivocally (*lex certa*).[192] In short, rape as an international crime can only be prosecuted if it was defined in law before the crime took place, however atrocious the crime itself may be. In this way, an individual will know that certain behaviour constitutes a crime and is punishable, the Defence will be able to prepare the accused's case, the judge will not sit in the legislator's seat (separation of powers) and, as a result, the trial will generally be considered fair.

Wolfgang Schomburg (Germany), Judge Mehmet Güney (Turkey) and Judge Theodor Meron (US).

[192] Haveman (2002), pp. 263-278. However, see Amann (1998, p. 199): '... the Tribunal fashioned a standard that is sufficiently precise and within accepted definitions to give notice to forbidden conduct'.

Having said this, it cannot be upheld that rape was not an international crime before the establishment of the Tribunals even if it was not well defined at the time the rapes occurred in the former Yugoslavia and in Rwanda. Rape was laid down in the 1949 Geneva Conventions and its Additional Protocols.[193] The reason why there has been no definition of rape in international law for so long is that the crime was rarely prosecuted, essentially because it was never really considered a crime of violence. Moreover, rape has been recognised as and prosecuted under other crimes, such as torture as a crime against humanity or as a war crime. Such indirect prosecutions evidence that the conduct of the accused was found criminal at the time it was committed. Retrospective effect is therefore not forbidden, considering that rape was not a new crime; it had already been prosecuted under other crimes.[194]

Especially in supranational criminal law, the legality principle has proved to be problematic: not just with respect to the definition of rape, but also with regard to several other crimes or principles.[195] The indefinite nature of the crimes has largely resulted from this relatively new system of law, influenced by common-law and civil-law systems alike, which is still 'growing'. For lack of international treaties defining rape, the Tribunals searched for the common denominator in the definitions of rape in national jurisdictions. Their search was, however, rather one-sided, focusing on common-law jurisdictions in particular and excluding the national laws of the home countries of the accused.[196] In addition, transferring elements from national jurisdictions to an international plane cannot automatically be done without taking into account the different contexts in which the players operate. In *Furundžija*, the Tribunal judges also referred to the fundamental principle of human dignity as a criterion for establishing whether oral sex fell under rape as well. However, if this principle is the standard by which certain acts of sexual violence are measured, the reference to the common denominator of national jurisdictions becomes superfluous, and many more sexual acts should fall under the definition of rape. The question, therefore, is: What is the standard by which undefined crimes should be measured? The answer should be found in the realities of war-time rape.[197] With regard to the definition of rape, the *Kunarac, Kovač and Vuković* definition does not fit into the context of genocide, crimes against humanity and war crimes, where consent should not be considered an element of the definition of rape.

In order to bring law 'into conformity with reason and common sense',[198] the judges of the Tribunals initially had no choice but to decide on the definitions of rape so

---

[193] See subsection 4.1 above.

[194] See Opinion C. Dugard in the Bouterse case (Hoge Raad, Staat der Nederlanden v. D. Bouterse, 18 september 2001, 00749/01 *CW* 2323).

[195] See, for instance, the Čelebići Appeal Judgment, paras. 573-579, on the concept of 'mental incapacity'.

[196] For example, the Rwandan Penal Code of 1977 prohibits defilement, rape, torture and sexual torture, but fails to define these acts. Judicial discretion has lead to inconsistent guilty verdicts: some judgments categorise an act of rape as 'sexual torture', while other judgments reserved this term for acts of sexual mutilation or gang rape. See Human Rights Watch (2004b), p. 32.

[197] See also Boon (2001), pp. 648-655.

[198] McHenry III (2002), p. 1301; McHenry (2002), pp. 212-214 (he refers to the United States Supreme Court in Rogers v. Tennessee, 532 US 451 (2001)).

late in the process. However, in light of the uniformity of the law, the situation is still not satisfactory and the Tribunals should apply only *one* definition of rape. This would prevent that one accused is convicted of rape and another accused is convicted of 'sexual violence', based on the same prohibited sexual acts. Possible solutions to this problem may be found either in the common-law practice of *stare decisis* or in the drafting of clear definitions of crimes in advance in a document such as the EoC.[199] It is suggested here that the *Kunarac, Kovač and Vuković* Appeal Judgment be overruled by the Appeals Chamber in a rape-related case and that the definition of rape as stated in the EoC of the ICC will be the standard definition within supranational criminal law once and for all. As mentioned above, a request to clarify the law as regards the definition of rape has been forwarded to the Appeals Chamber by the Prosecutor in the *Gacumbitsi* case, and the decision of the Appeals Chamber therefore needs to be awaited.[200] Indeed, a clear task lies here with the (Senior) Trial Attorneys, who should advance the *Akayesu* or ICC definition of rape in, for instance, their closing briefs and oral statements, while at the same time explaining to the judges why the chosen definition should be the correct standard within supranational criminal law and not the *Kunarac, Kovač and Vuković* definition of rape.[201]

4.1.2 The ICC's Elements of Crimes on the definition of rape

In the ICC's EoC – which were drafted to *assist* the ICC judges in their application and interpretation of the crimes[202] – rape is described as follows:

1. The perpetrator invaded[15] the body of a person by conduct resulting in penetration, however slight, of any part of the body of the victim or of the perpetrator with a sexual

[199] Haveman (2002), pp. 275-276.

[200] In the Appellant's Brief, the Prosecutor has requested the Appeals Chamber to clarify the law on the definition of rape (as a ground of appeal based on an error of law) arguing for non-consent not to be an element of the definition of rape. If the Appeals Chamber would accept the definition of rape with no reference to non-consent at all, this would not result in a reversal of the Trial Chamber's decision on the rape charges, given the nature of its findings, but it would clarify the law on the definition of rape once and for all. See *The Prosecutor v. Sylvestre Gacumbitsi*, Appellant's Brief, Case No. ICTR-2001-64-A, 28 September 2004, pp. 53, 60.

[201] See, for instance, the Prosecutor's closing brief in the Gacumbitsi trial, in which the Prosecutor clearly outlined why the Akayesu definition of rape should be applied by the ICTR judges and not the Kunarac, Kovač and Vuković definition of rape. See *The Prosecutor v. Sylvestre Gacumbitsi*, The Prosecutor's Closing Brief, Case No. ICTR-2001-64-I, 22 December 2003, pp. 342-352. See also *The Prosecutor v. Mika Muhimana*, The Prosecutor's Closing Brief, Case No. ICTR-95-1B-T, 25 October 2004, pp. 87-89. Although the Prosecutor in the Kajelijeli case did propose the Akayesu definition of rape in its closing brief, the differences which existed between the Akayesu and Kunarac, Kovač and Vuković definitions of rape were not explained. See *The Prosecutor v. Juvénal Kajelijeli*, Closing Brief, Case No. ICTR-98-44A-T, 16 June 2003, pp. 42-44. See also *The Prosecutor v. Eliézer Niyitegeka,* Prosecutor's Final Trial Brief, Case No. ICTR-96-14-T, 13 December 2002, p. 52.

[202] In conformity with Article 9(1) ICC Statute.

organ, or of the anal or genital opening of the victim with any object or any other part of the body.
2. The invasion was committed by force, or by threat of force or coercion, such as that caused by fear of violence, duress, detention, psychological oppression or abuse of power, against such person or another person, or by taking advantage of a coercive environment, or the invasion was committed against a person incapable of giving genuine consent.[16]

[15] The concept of 'invasion' is intended to be broad enough to be gender-neutral.
[16] It is understood that a person may be incapable of giving genuine consent if affected by natural, induced or age-related incapacity. This footnote also applies to the corresponding elements of article 7(1)(g)-3, 5 and 6.

In addition to the elements of rape found in national laws, the case law of the ICTY and the ICTR has significantly influenced the definition of the crime of rape in the EoC of the ICC.[203] This is not very surprising considering the similarity of the cases that are likely to be brought before the ICC and considering the ICTY/R's survey of the definition of rape in international law. ICC delegates made special reference to the *Akayesu, Čelebići* and *Furundžija* Judgments. With the exception of the *Musema* Judgment, the *Kunarac, Kovač and Vuković* and *Kvočka et al.* Judgments had not yet been rendered at the time the EoC were drafted (2 November 2000) and were therefore not taken into account. The ICC definition of rape is a mix of the ICTY/R case law up to that time. Instead of making a clear choice between the *Akayesu, Furundžija* or any other approach to the definition of rape, the ICC definition of rape is confusing at first sight. Overall, however, it can be said that the ICC definition follows more closely the more restrictive *Furundžija* definition of rape;[204] this definition also constituted the starting point in the discussions on the definition of rape within the Preparatory Commission for the ICC.[205]

---

[203] See Rückert and Witschel (2001a), p. 82; La Haye (2001), p. 188, footnote 125. The Final Report of the Special Rapporteur of the Working Group on Contemporary Forms of Slavery, on Systematic Rape, Sexual Slavery and Slavery-Like Practices During Armed Conflict, UN Doc.E/CN.4/Sub.2/1998/13, 22 June 1998, was also taken into account.

[204] See Kittichaisaree (2001), p. 113; Boon (2001), p. 645. However, see Rückert and Witschel (2001a, p. 82), who claim that the ICC definition of rape follows more closely the definition of rape as established in the Akayesu Judgment.

[205] See *Proposal Submitted by Costa Rica, Hungary and Switzerland on Certain Provisions of Article 8 Para. 2 (B) of the Rome Statute of the International Criminal Court, (VIII), (X), (XIV), (XV), (XVI), (XXI), (XXII), (XXVI)*, PCNICC/1999/WGEC/DP.8, 19 July 1999 (rape is defined along the lines of the Furundžija definition of rape); Proposal Submitted by the United States of America, *Draft Elements of Crimes*, PCNICC/1999/DP.4/Add.1, 4 February 1999 (the elements of rape read '2. That the accused intended to attack one or more persons through acts of a sexual nature; 3. That the accused penetrated any part of the body of another persons with the accused's sexual organ, or penetrated the anal or genital opening of another person with any object or other part of the accused's body; 4. That the penetration was committed by force'). Although the US definition of rape is still a mechanical definition, it includes more sexual acts than the definition of rape proposed by Costa Rica, Hungary and Switzerland. Colombia commented upon the proposal of Costa Rica, Hungary and Switzerland by suggesting a broader definition of rape.

As to the first element of the *actus reus* of rape, the wording is mainly based on the mechanical definition of rape as developed in the *Furundžija* case. Although the definition initially concentrates on the *Akayesu* concept of 'invasion', such an invasion needs to result in the penetration of body parts by other body parts or objects, phrasing which is clearly influenced by the *Furundžija* definition of rape as well as by a considerable number of national laws on rape. The element of 'invasion' is thus combined with the element of 'penetration', a compromise reached by the ICC delegates.[206] In this perspective, it should be noted that, although there was considerable support among a number of delegates and NGOs to include 'invasion' instead of 'penetration' in the ICC definition of rape, in the end, a number of influential States argued in favour of the use of 'penetration' as 'invasion' was considered too vague and potentially incompatible with their national laws.[207] Considering, however, that the main focus will be on penetration, the use of the term 'invaded' has become superfluous. The concept of invasion was introduced into the *Akayesu* Judgment precisely because the Trial Chamber did not want to limit the definition of rape to sexual acts involving penetration.

When examining the types of body parts involved, the first part of element 1 refers to the penetration of 'any part of the body of the victim or of the perpetrator with a sexual organ', and the second part of element 1 refers to the penetration of 'the anal or genital opening of the victim with any object or any other part of the body'. It seems that the first part of element 1 refers to vaginal, anal and oral penetration with the penis. In addition, 'any part of the body' may be interpreted as referring to the ears, nose or

---

These comments were, however, not seriously taken up during discussions. See Proposal Submitted by Colombia, *Comments on the Proposal by the Delegations of Costa Rica, Hungary and Switzerland Concerning Article 8, Paragraph 2(b) of the Rome Statute (PCNICC/1999/WGEC/DP.8)*, PCNICC/1999/WGEC/DP.16, 29 July 1999 (the following definition of rape was suggested: '(b) The agent has sexual access to the victim; (c) The agent commits the act through violence or the use of coercion or force or intimidation or the threat of force against the victim or a third person'. It was further explained that: '(a) The expression "penetration" and paragraph 2 (a) and (b) are eliminated, since the expression "to have sexual access to" indicates clearly what the act consists of, without the need for specification which could lower the threshold of protection; (b) In paragraph (c) the word "intimidation" is added so as to include cases in which psychological pressure is exerted on the victim to obtain his or her consent to sexual relations. Also included, with a view to complete protection, is the expression "violence", a generic term which indicates what the act consists of'). See also the reports made by some observer NGOs, which were submitted to the Preparatory Commission and which foresaw in a mechanical Furundžija type of definition as well: International Committee of the Red Cross (1999a); Amnesty International (1999).

206 See La Haye (2001), p. 188; Rückert and Witschel (2001a), p. 82.

207 Twenty-four States were recorded to favour the concept of 'invasion', which they considered to be more neutral. A group of vocal states – including France, the Netherlands, and the United States – argued against its use for the abovementioned reasons and favoured the concept of 'penetration'. On this issue, see Boon (2001), p. 649. See also the reports prepared by some NGOs, in which they argue for the inclusion of the term 'invasion': Women Caucus for Gender Justice (1999); Preparatory Commission for the International Criminal Court; Human Rights Watch (1999).

eyes of the victim. The second part of element 1 seems to refer to situations in which the vagina or anus is penetrated with an object or 'any other part of the body', such as the fingers, hands or tongue of the perpetrator. Excluded from this definition seems to be the penetration of the mouth of the victim with an object, the reason probably being that the sexual aspect is missing in this act. Compared to the *Furundžija/Kunarac, Kovač and Vuković* definition of rape, the ICC's EoC on the crime of rape prohibit more sexual acts. Not only penetration of the vagina, anus and mouth with the penis and penetration of the vagina and anus with an object are included, but also penetration with the fingers (of the vagina or anus), penetration with the tongue (of the vagina, anus and possibly the mouth) and penetration with the penis of any other part of the body are subsumed into the definition of rape. The sexual acts can thus be objectified: the subjective perceptions of the victim and the intentions of the perpetrator with regard to the sexual acts may be treated as irrelevant. On the basis of the ICC's elements of the crime of rape, every penetration of a sexual nature falls within the definition of rape: sexual acts not amounting to penetration, such as intentionally touching another person's body in a sexual manner, are excluded.

From the legality principle point of view, a clear and specific definition of rape, such as in the EoC, will most likely be considered a welcome development.[208] However, the ICC definition is not clearly worded and may lead to confusion. The sentence in part 1, '*the perpetrator* invaded the body of a person by conduct resulting in penetration … of any part of the body *of the victim* or *of the perpetrator* with a sexual organ' is badly drafted and very confusing, to say the least.[209] It is in particular not clear what is meant here by the reference to the second 'perpetrator'. Most likely the drafters of the EoC intended the phrase to include situations in which persons are compelled to perform sexual acts on the compeller himself or on others. Thus, the former perpetrator is in fact the victim of rape, coerced by the real – latter – perpetrator to sexually penetrate him (the latter perpetrator) or to penetrate another ('the victim'). This may include situations in which the victim is compelled to penetrate with his penis the compeller's or a third party's anus, vagina or mouth or the compeller's or a third party's anus or vagina with any body part of the victim or with an object. These situations thus seem to deal in particular with male-to-male (men who compel men to penetrate other men or the compellers themselves) and female-to-female violations (women who compel men to penetrate the female compellers themselves or other women). As was the case in the *Furundžija* and *Kunarac, Kovač and Vuković* definitions of rape, the wording is anything but clear on this point. Moreover, from this definition it is not clear whether it would include, for instance, forced masturbation of the compeller, forced masturbation of the victim him- or herself in front of the compeller and/or others, sexual mutilation, etc. Strict reading of the element would exclude this type of sexual acts, as they do not involve penetration with a sexual organ. Another difficulty relating to the ICC definition of rape is that the definition only refers to persons, leaving out situations in which victims are, for instance, forced to have sex with animals. Although the author has no evidence of such incidents during mass violence, it is suggested that forced sex with animals should be understood to fall within the scope of the ICC definition of rape.

---

[208] See, for instance, Haveman and Wijers (2002), p. 62.
[209] Emphasis added.

The *Akayesu* definition of rape – 'a physical invasion of a sexual nature, committed on a person under circumstances which are coercive' – leaves room to include situations of sexual violence not involving penetration with a sexual organ, such as forced masturbation, sexual mutilation or any other sexual act presently unknown. The ICC definition of rape, however, encompasses all possible forms of rape and should therefore be considered the leading definition of rape in supranational criminal law.[210] The ICC definition of rape is broader than its *Furundžija/Kunarac, Kovač and Vuković* counterpart, but more restrictive than the definition of rape in *Akayesu*. Developments within national jurisdictions with regard to the definition of rape have been taken into account in the ICC definition, but particularly – and most importantly – the realities of rape in times of mass violence. Sexual acts falling short of rape should then be classified as sexual violence, prosecutable under Article 7(1)(g), including 'any other form of sexual violence of comparable gravity'. Considering that all sexual violence crimes mentioned in this section are similar in seriousness, it does not matter under what heading a particular sexual act is prosecuted as long as a crime is prosecuted for what it is. On the contrary, prosecuting the abovementioned sexual acts not involving penetration with a sexual organ as rape would cause injustice to the victims of sexual violence that do meet the ICC definitional requirements of rape and who consider themselves the 'real victims of rape'.[211]

An advantage of the ICC definition of rape is its gender neutrality: it is applicable to victims and perpetrators of either sex.[212] Even though the large majority of victims of sexual violence are women, there is increasing evidence concerning and recognition of male victims of sexual violence in situations of mass violence.[213] Likewise, the majority of perpetrators of sexual violence are men, but women may also be involved in sexual violence crimes, for instance by ordering men to rape other women.[214] The EoC description of rape is thus rightly drafted in gender-neutral terms, using terminology such as 'perpetrator', 'person' and 'victim'. Footnote 15 specifying that 'the concept of

---

[210] According to La Haye (2001, p. 190), the elements of rape were negotiated with the aim of elaborating an expansive definition encompassing all possible forms of rape.

[211] According to Marc Groenhuijsen, Professor of Criminal Law and Procedure and Director of the International Victimology Institute Tilburg (INTERVICT) in the Netherlands, many victims of rape were upset by the Dutch Supreme Court's judgment in the 'Tongzoen' case, where French kissing was accepted as to constitute rape. In their view, to accept French kissing as rape constituted a denial of their own victimisation.

[212] A number of national laws still refer to the female as the victim of rape and the male as the perpetrator of rape.

[213] See, for instance, Oosterhoff (2000). See also the sexual abuse by US and UK soldiers of Iraqi prisoners in Iraq in 2004. See, for instance, BBC News, *US Soldier Jailed for Prison Abuse*, 22 October 2004, in which it is reported that an US soldier, Sgt Ivan Frederick, is sentenced to eight years in prison for, *inter alia*, forcing detainees to masturbate while other soldiers watched and took pictures.

[214] See, for instance, the ICTR Butare case, in which Pauline Nyiramasuhuko (the former Minister of Family and Women's Development) is charged with ordering men to rape women in Butare Province. See also BBC News, *Woman Soldier in Abuse Spotlight*, 7 May 2004, in which Lynndie England is accused of sexual abuse of Iraqi prisoners in an Iraqi prison, Abu Ghraib, near Baghdad.

"invasion" is intended to be broad enough to be gender-neutral' is another indication that the ICC delegations wanted to cover rape by a person of either sex and against a victim of either sex.

The second element of the *actus reus* of rape, the circumstances making the sexual acts criminal, is another example of the mix of ICTY/R case law and domestic laws used for drafting the ICC definition of rape. For 'invasion' to qualify as rape, three types of circumstances are mentioned: (1) 'force, or by threat of force or coercion', which is typical *Furundžija* wording; (2) 'taking advantage of a coercive environment', which resembles *Akayesu* wording; or (3) 'against a person incapable of giving genuine consent', which does not refer to non-consent as applied in the *Kunarac, Kovač and Vuković* definition of rape, but to persons who are legally incapable of giving consent, as is commonly used in national jurisdictions. The in-exhaustive list of examples given for 'coercion' in the second part of the ICC definition includes 'that caused by fear of violence, duress, detention, psychological oppression or abuse of power, against such person or another person'. The examples make it clear that coercion may take place without the use of physical force.

The use of the word 'genuine consent' is clarified in a footnote stating that someone who is 'affected by natural, induced or age-related incapacity' is presumed not to be capable of giving genuine consent.[215] People falling within this category are children, elderly and disabled people and persons under the influence of, for example, drugs.[216] These people are deemed to be incapable of giving genuine consent, and therefore non-consent to rape is presumed. What is important is that the focus of the ICC definition is on the coercive circumstances, not on the lack of consent of the victim.[217] Consent is not an issue when force, threat of force, coercion or coercive circumstances exist, or when the person is incapable of giving genuine consent. With this wording, the EoC seem to have incorporated the views of the *Akayesu* and *Furundžija* Judgments on the types of circumstances that turn sexual acts into criminal acts, and added thereto the factual impossibility of giving consent on the basis of natural, induced or age-related factors.[218] The ICC definition of rape thus moved away from the use and meaning of consent as applied by the *Kunarac, Kovač and Vuković* Trial and Appeals Chamber, which employed non-consent as an element of the crime of rape.

On a final note, the definition of rape covers not only the situation in which the rape may have been committed if the person herself/himself was subjected to the

---

[215] Article 7(1)(g)-1 EoC, footnote 16, p. 12. This footnote also applies for the crimes of enforced prostitution, enforced sterilisation and sexual violence. Some women organisations considered the reference to consent problematic. To add the term 'genuine' to consent was considered to be superfluous, as there is either consent or not. Moreover, Rule 70 of the RPE, on 'Principles of evidence in cases of sexual violence', uses the terminology of 'voluntary and genuine consent'. This may create the impression that the genuine consent which appears in the EoC does not include the concept of being voluntary. See ICC PrepCom Report, March 13-31, 2000. However, according to La Haye (2001, p. 189), 'genuine' is meant to cover concepts such as voluntary and informed consent.

[216] La Haye (2001), p. 189.

[217] *Ibid.* See also Rückert and Witschel (2001a), p. 83.

[218] See also Verrijn Stuart (undated), p. 28.

prevailing circumstances, but also the situation in which another person would have been victimised if the first did not submit to the act(s). The *Furundžija* Judgment mentions 'a third party', while the EoC refer to 'another person'. While it is certainly not problematic to have such an inclusion in the definition of rape, this might already have been concluded from the wording 'coercion, force or threat of force' itself. In fact, the EoC, where explaining the concept of coercion, refer to, *inter alia*, psychological oppression, which would certainly cover these types of situations.

The *mens rea* requirement of Article 30 of the ICC Statute applies to the two elements of the definition of rape as a crime against humanity. Consequently, the perpetrator *intended* to invade the body of a person by conduct resulting in penetration, however slight, of any part of the body of the victim or of the perpetrator with a sexual organ, or of the anal or genital opening of the victim with any object or any other part of the body (element 1); and the perpetrator knew the surrounding circumstances to be that the invasion was committed by force, or by threat of force or coercion, or by taking advantage of a coercive environment, or the invasion was committed against a person incapable of giving genuine consent (element 2).[219] Considering that the definition of rape in the EoC does not include the element of non-consent, knowledge of non-consent as part of the intent requirement thus does not need to be proved by the Prosecutor. The perpetrator's knowledge of the coercive circumstances in which the rapes took place is enough evidence to establish the perpetrator's intent to rape.

To conclude, the judgments that were rendered after the EoC had been adopted show that the Tribunals held on to either the broad *Akayesu* definition of rape or the restrictive mechanical definition of *Kunarac, Kovač and Vuković*, despite the definition of rape laid down in the EoC of the ICC, which takes a middle course between the *Akayesu* and *Kunarac, Kovač and Vuković* definitions.

4.1.3 Some closing remarks on the definition of rape

The EoC, officially a non-binding document, minutely enumerate the elements of the crime of rape. However, since the adoption of the EoC ICTY and ICTR case law has not come to a standstill; it shows the acceptance of various other definitions of rape than are included in the EoC of the ICC. The *Kunarac, Kovač and Vuković* definition of rape was given after the EoC were drafted and constitutes a mechanical definition of rape with a focus on the question whether the victim consented or not, whereas the broader *Akayesu* definition of rape was established before the EoC were drafted and was upheld in judgments delivered after the EoC had been adopted. One important question remains, viz.: Which definition of rape is to be preferred within supranational criminal law, to be applied at all times by the judges of the Tribunals and the ICC?

As explained above, the ICC definition of rape is a mix of the *Akayesu* and *Furundžija* definitions of rape and incorporates domestic law perspectives on the definition of rape. The advantage of the ICC definition is that it is not focused on the issue of consent (as is the case in *Kunarac, Kovač and Vuković*), but on (threat of) force, coercion or coercive environment (as is the case in *Furundžija* and *Akayesu*). Although the judges in the latter two Trial Chambers had noticed that a considerable number of

---

[219] Compare the similarity with the *mens rea* requirement as set out in the Kunarac, Kovač and Vuković Judgment, para. 460, and as cited above.

national laws state 'lack of consent' as an element of the crime of rape, introducing this element into the definition of rape within supranational criminal law was, in their view, unnecessary especially in light of the violent and oppressive contexts in which rapes take place during genocide, crimes against humanity or war, as was also evidenced by the facts of the cases. If the Prosecutor proves the coercive circumstances, non-consent will be presumed. This means that there is no need to inquire into the victim's action or state of mind: questions that might insult victims of rape can thus be avoided. The definition of rape should be applied in consistency with other crimes involving the infliction of physical or mental harm where consent is not considered to be part of the crime, and guidance can be found in those national laws where consent is not accepted as an element of rape because of unequal power structures. The ICC definition also includes a larger number of forbidden sexual acts than the more restrictive *Furundžija/Kunarac, Kovač and Vuković* mechanical description of body parts. The ICC definition is, however, not as broad as the *Akayesu* definition of rape, which makes it easier to distinguish between rape and sexual violence. To distinguish between rape and other acts of sexual violence has in fact been proposed in most of the case law discussed here.[220] Sexual acts falling short of rape should be prosecuted under, for instance, 'any other form of sexual violence of comparable gravity' (Article 7(1)(g) of the ICC Statute), a category which might include, for instance, forced nudity, forced masturbation or forced touching of the body.[221] This is not to say that crimes which are prosecuted under this so-called 'residual category' are less severe than rape or any other of the sexual violence crimes explicitly mentioned in Article 7(1)(g) of the ICC Statute, i.e. these forms of sexual violence should be 'of comparable gravity'. Each situation is different and should be evaluated on the basis of its own merits.

On the whole, the ICC definition of rape is thus more victim-friendly because it does not accept the element of 'lack of consent' and because it recognises more sexual acts as rape than its ICTY counterparts *Furundžija* and *Kunarac, Kovač and Vuković*, whose definitions were upheld by several ICTY/R Trial Chambers. In its wording, the ICC definition of rape takes into account the realities of sexual violence in times of armed conflict, crimes against humanity or genocide to their fullest extent, and therefore the ICC definition of rape, as opposed to the *Kunarac, Kovač and Vuković* definition of rape, should be considered to be the preferred standard within supranational criminal law.[222] The purpose of the Tribunals and the Court is to hear evidence of rape, not to

[220] Akayesu Judgment, paras. 598, 688; Musema Judgment and Sentence, para. 227; Kvočka et. al. Judgment, para. 180; Semanza Judgment and Sentence, para. 345; Kajelijeli Judgment and Sentence, para. 916.

[221] See further section 2.3.6 on 'any other form of sexual violence of comparable gravity'.

[222] However, with regard to the definition of rape, it is noteworthy that Judge Hunt (2004, pp. 60-61) argues that the judges of the ICC should apply the Kunarac, Kovač and Vuković definition of rape, rather than the elements of the crime of rape as laid down in the EoC. According to him, the Kunarac, Kovač and Vuković definition of rape is a broader definition than its more narrowly described counterparts in the Akayesu and Furundžija cases, because Kunarac, Kovač and Vuković focuses on absence of consent by the victim, rather than on coercion, force or coercive circumstances. It should be noted that Judge Hunt served as a Judge in the Kunarac, Kovač and Vuković trial, which possibly explains part of his eagerness to apply the Kunarac, Kovač and Vuković definition of rape within the ICC. McHenry (2002, pp. 218-219) also appears to infer

preclude witness participation by applying definitions of rape which focus on consent.[223] Only when the crime of rape is recognised for what it is, victims of sexual violence will be willing to come forward and justice may be done to them.

4.2 Sexual slavery

The crime of sexual slavery is enumerated among the sexual violence crimes in Article 7(1)(g) of the ICC Statute. The explicit recognition of sexual slavery as a crime against humanity has no statutory precedence as a separate crime in supranational criminal law.[224] Even though the crime of sexual slavery may be seen as a particular form of the crime of enslavement under crimes against humanity,[225] sexual slavery should constitute and is indeed now – by virtue of Article 7(1)(g) of the ICC Statute – recognised as constituting a separate crime.[226] That sexual slavery is a crime separate from that of enslavement and that of enforced prostitution has not always been unequivocal and indisputable.[227] However, to label sexual slavery as sexual slavery instead of mere enslavement is explicit proof of the recognition of the criminal sexual aspect inherent to sexual slavery. In addition, as will be seen below, the enumeration of enforced prostitution among the other sexual violence crimes mentioned in paragraph (g) of Article 7(1) has made the distinction between enforced prostitution and sexual slavery more clear. Moreover, also in times of peace, the ICC will now have the possibility of addressing crimes typified as constituting sexual slavery.[228]

According to the Preparatory Commission for the ICC in its EoC, the elements of sexual slavery include

1. The perpetrator exercised any or all of the powers attaching to the right of ownership over one or more persons, such as by purchasing, selling, lending or bartering such a person or persons, or by imposing on them a similar deprivation of liberty. [18]

2. The perpetrator caused such person or persons to engage in one or more acts of a sexual nature.[229]

---

that the Kunarac, Kovač and Vuković definition of rape should be applied as the standard definition of rape in future supranational criminal prosecutions.

223 In construing the Statutes of the Tribunals, the Appeals Chamber has on a number of occasions pursued a purposive approach, where it has sought to establish the object and purpose of the provisions of the Statute as opposed to narrow construction. See, e.g., Tadić Appeal Judgment, para. 189.

224 The crime of sexual slavery is also explicitly recognised as a war crime in Articles 8(2)(b)(xxii) and 8(2)(e)(vi) ICC Statute.

225 See section 2 on 'enslavement'.

226 Rückert and Witschel (2001a), p. 83.

227 Koenig and Askin (2000): 'It is unclear if sexual slavery is considered an entirely separate crime from enslavement and enforced prostitution.'

228 See Rijken (2003).

229 Article 7(1)(g)-2 EoC. Footnote 17 is attached to the title of the crime and reads as follows: 'Given the complex nature of this crime, it is recognized that its commission could involve more than one perpetrator as a part of a common criminal purpose.'

[18] It is understood that such deprivation of liberty may, in some circumstances, include exacting forced labour or otherwise reducing a person to a servile status as defined in the Supplementary Convention on the Abolition of Slavery, the Slave Trade, and Institutions and Practices Similar to Slavery of 1956. It is also understood that the conduct described in this element includes trafficking in persons, in particular women and children.

The first element of the *actus reus* of the crime of sexual slavery as a crime against humanity requires the exercise of 'any or all of the powers attaching to the right of ownership over one or more persons'. This wording was copied from the definition of enslavement contained in Article 7(2)(c) of the ICC Statute.[230] Because some delegations found the wording too vague, the US proposed to include examples of the way in which the powers of ownership over a person can be exercised.[231] Purchasing, selling, lending or bartering are in this regard illustrative, which is made obvious by the wording used, namely 'such as'. Concerns existed, however, as to the commercial aspect inherent to all of these examples.[232] The use of the word 'similar' in 'a similar deprivation of liberty' also seems to imply that other possible forms of exercising ownership should contain the commercial aspect of the four examples used. In addition, other examples such as recruiting or abducting were not included in the illustrative list, as they were found to define the means of 'obtaining' a person and do not describe directly the exercise of ownership over a person.[233] This is remarkable since the crime of sexual slavery in wartime situations and situations where crimes against humanity take place can – and usually is – committed without any commercial benefit obtained.[234] In order to reject this notion, several delegations therefore insisted that the same footnote as attached to the crime of enslavement as a crime against humanity be added to the crime of sexual slavery.[235] As seen above, the footnote states that 'a similar deprivation of liberty' is to be understood to include forced labour, reducing a person to a servile status (debt bondage, serfdom, forced marriage, child exploitation) and trafficking in persons, in particular women and children.[236] Several of these examples do not necessarily require a form of commercial benefit (debt bondage, forced marriage, child labour) nor confinement to a particular place (debt bondage). The addition of the footnote, which has the same status as the other parts in the EoC, was thus important in order that the crime of sexual slavery not be restricted to commercial transactions only.

---

230 La Haye (2001), p. 191. The element was subsequently copied from the element of sexual slavery as a crime against humanity to the element of the crime of enslavement as a crime against humanity in the EoC.

231 La Haye (2001), p. 191.

232 Following the *ejusdem generis* doctrine the words following 'such as' are to be interpreted in accordance with the common denominator of the words used. The common denominator of the examples used is the commercial exchange involved. This interpretation would restrict the definition of sexual slavery to cases where the captors would receive a pecuniary advantage for holding women sexually enslaved.

233 La Haye (2001), p. 191.

234 Women's Caucus for Gender Justice (2000). See also Human Rights Watch (2000b).

235 La Haye (2001), p. 191.

236 Article 7(1)(g)-2 EoC, footnote 18.

History is replete with examples of women who were deceived or abducted into sexual slavery where no commercial benefit for the perpetrators was involved. In fact, in most wartime circumstances no commercial benefit is obtained at all: in occupied territories, women are often completely at the mercy of their captors. During World War II, approximately 200,000 women from all over the Asia-Pacific region were kept in rape camps (peculiarly called 'comfort stations') and forced to provide sexual services to Japanese soldiers.[237] These women were rarely purchased or sold: they were kidnapped, coerced and deceived into sexual slavery. The sexual violence crimes these women had to endure were never prosecuted: neither by the Japanese government itself,[238] nor by the Tokyo Tribunal. Only in the Batavia (Indonesia) Trial, the case of thirty-five Dutch women victimised in Indonesia was tried against twelve Japanese army officers.[239] In an effort to remedy these failures, a specially convened Tribunal 'The Women's International War Crimes Tribunal 2000 for the Trial of Japanese Military Sexual Slavery' sat in Tokyo from 8 to 12 December 2000. While this Tribunal was a People's Tribunal, organised by Asian women and human rights organisations and supported by international NGOs, and its judgment therefore lacked formal legal force, its moral authority lay in examining the evidence and in developing a lasting historical record for the crimes committed as well as for the presentation thereof in the future. This Tribunal was intended to pave the way for the government of Japan to recognise its full responsibility and to provide redress to the 'comfort women'. Also, acknowledgement of the fact that sexual violence crimes had taken place during World War II and responsibility being assigned to the perpetrators of these crimes would help these women to be able to live their remaining years in peace. In its judgment, sexual slavery was held to have constituted a crime against humanity by 1945 already, when committed on a widespread, systematic or large-scale basis. In this regard, the Tribunal found Emperor Hirohito responsible on the basis of command responsibility.[240] According to the Tribunal,

> sexual slavery is not a new crime but rather a particularly outrageous, invasive and devastating form of enslavement defined as the 'exercise of any or all of the powers of ownership over a person.' Enslavement includes forced or deceptive transfer, forced labor, and other expropriation of a human being as one's property. The conscription of the 'comfort women' as part of the 'material' of war represents the institutionalisation of sexual slavery on an unprecedented scale, rooted in profoundly misogynistic and racist attitudes,

[237] Generally, see Yoshiaki (2000).

[238] Since the 1990s eight court cases have been filed by survivors from South Korea, China, Taiwan, the Philippines and Japan in the Tokyo District Court and other Japanese courts and all survivors lost their law suites.

[239] The defendants were found guilty of war crimes for acts including rape, coercion to prostitution, abduction of women and girls for forced prostitution, and ill-treatment of prisoners. See Sellers (2001).

[240] The Women's International War Crimes Tribunal 2000 for the Trial of Japanese Military Sexual Slavery' in the matter of THE PROSECUTORS AND THE PEOPLES OF THE ASIA-PACIFIC REGION V. EMPEROR HIROHITO et al. AND THE GOVERNMENT OF JAPAN, Summery of Findings, 12 December 2000 (on file with the author), para. 24.

> all too common in the world today, directed at predominantly poor and non-Japanese women of the Asia-Pacific region.[241]

During the conflicts in the former Yugoslavia and Rwanda, some women were kidnapped, detained and repeatedly raped. No financial benefits were involved, but they were forced into sexual slavery. As to the confinement to a particular place, some delegations made clear that 'similar deprivation of liberty' should not exclude situations in which women were not locked in a particular place and therefore 'free to go', but were in fact deprived of their liberty as they had nowhere else to go and feared for their lives;[242] the *Kunarac, Kovač and Vuković* case before the ICTY and the *Akayesu* case before the ICTR have made this clear. Forced marriages were also commonplace. In Rwanda, Hutu men forced women who feared for their children's or their own safety to enter into 'temporary marriages' and to perform sexual and domestic services.[243]

What makes sexual slavery uniquely brutal is the combination of having to endure serial rapes with no possibility of escape and no perceivable end to the violence.[244] Additionally, the crime of sexual slavery may involve more than one perpetrator as part of a common purpose, which makes the sexual slavery one of the most heinous sexual violence crimes.[245]

Because of new developments and insights, it has become clear that many forms of sexual slavery exist. According to the Special Rapporteur on Systematic Rape, Sexual Slavery and Slavery-like Practices in armed conflict 'practices such as the detention of women in "rape camps" or "comfort stations"; forced temporary "marriages" to soldiers; and other practices involving the treatment of women as chattel, are both in fact and in law forms of slavery and, as such, violations of the peremptory norm prohibiting slavery'.[246] The fact that a person was not bought, sold or traded does not in any way defeat a claim of slavery.[247] That the detention of women, which took place without any form of commercial transaction, may constitute the crime of enslavement as a crime against humanity has also been decided in the *Kunarac, Kovač and Vuković* case. It was considered that exchange of money is not an element of the crime, but that it can be taken into account as one of the factors establishing enslavement.[248] Footnote 18 helps to understand that the crime of sexual slavery includes non-commercial sexual slavery situations: debt bondage, forced marriage and child labour do not require a form

---

[241] *Ibid.*, para. 23.

[242] La Haye (2001), pp. 191-192.

[243] UN Commission on Human Rights, *Contemporary Form of Slavery: Systematic Rape, Sexual Slavery and Slavery-like Practices During Armed Conflict: Final Report Submitted by Gay J. McDougall, Special Rapporteur*, E/CN.4/Sub.2/1998/13, 22 June 1998, p. 10 (there are also reports from Myanmar of women and girls who have been raped and otherwise sexually abused after being forced into 'marriage').

[244] Ray (1997).

[245] Article 7(1)(g)-2 EoC, footnote 17.

[246] UN Commission on Human Rights, *Contemporary Form of Slavery: Systematic Rape, Sexual Slavery and Slavery-like Practices During Armed Conflict: Final Report Submitted by Gay J. McDougall, Special Rapporteur*, E/CN.4/Sub.2/1998/13, 22 June 1998, paras. 8, 30.

[247] *Ibid.*, para. 28.

[248] *Ibid.* For a discussion of the Kunarac, Kovač and Vuković case, see section 2.

of purchase, sale, lending or bartering. If the elements of sexual slavery will be interpreted by the Court to include some sort of commercial aspect, certain forms of sexual slavery may be inappropriately prosecuted as enforced prostitution. This is another argument to make clear that the crime of sexual slavery does not necessarily entail a pecuniary benefit for the perpetrator as the difference between sexual slavery and enforced prostitution exists, according to the EoC, precisely in this pecuniary benefit. As explained above, the ICC is not bound to make use of the EoC.

The second part of the *actus reus* of sexual slavery as a crime against humanity refers to the sexual nature inherent to sexual slavery, and distinguishes sexual slavery from enslavement as a crime against humanity. Enslavement as a crime against humanity, however, was the charge for, *inter alia*, sexual violence crimes amounting to sexual slavery in the *Kunarac, Kovač and Vuković* case.[249] While the ICTY and ICTR Statutes only contain enslavement as a crime against humanity (Articles 5(c) and 3(c), respectively), this was the best charge at hand. Even though sexual slavery may be a form of enslavement, under the ICC Statute future sexual slavery cases are preferably charged as sexual slavery, not as enslavement. As argued above, in this way, the criminal aspect of the sexual nature of the crime of sexual slavery will be made clear explicitly.

The *mens rea* of the *actus reus* of sexual slavery is applied according to Article 30 of the ICC Statute. Thus, the perpetrator must have had the intent to exercise 'any or all of the powers attaching to the right of ownership over one or more persons, such as by purchasing, selling, lending or bartering such a person or persons, or by imposing on them a similar deprivation of liberty' (element 1); and the perpetrator must have had the intent to cause 'such person or persons to engage in one or more acts of a sexual nature' (element 2).

4.3 Enforced prostitution

The crime of enforced prostitution is mentioned in the ICC Statute as a crime against humanity for the first time in supranational criminal law.[250] Enforced prostitution is also contained in the ICTR Statute, but then as an 'outrage upon personal dignity' as a violation of Common Article 3 to the 1949 Geneva Conventions and 1977 Additional Protocol II. The elements of enforced prostitution are, according to the EoC:

1. The perpetrator caused one or more persons to engage in one or more acts of a sexual nature by force, or by threat of force or coercion, such as that caused by fear of violence, duress, detention, psychological oppression or abuse of power, against such person or persons or another person, or by taking advantage of a coercive environment or such person's or persons' incapacity to give genuine consent.

[249] For a discussion of the Kunarac, Kovač and Vuković case, see section 2.

[250] Enforced prostitution is laid down in international humanitarian law where the emphasis is put on the immoral attack of the woman's honour: Article 27 of 1949 Geneva Convention IV; Articles 75(2)(b) and 76(1) of 1977 Additional Protocol I; and Article 4(2)(e) of 1977 Additional Protocol II. Enforced prostitution is also laid down as a war crime in Articles 8(2)(b)(xxii) and 8(2)(e)(vi) of the ICC Statute.

2. The perpetrator or another person obtained or expected to obtain pecuniary or other advantage in exchange for or in connection with the acts of a sexual nature.[251]

The first element of the *actus reus* of enforced prostitution as a crime against humanity requires that 'the perpetrator caused one or more persons to engage in one or more acts of a sexual nature'. The forcible circumstances in which the crime may take place are stated in the same way as the provision on rape; non-consent is therefore not an element of the crime of enforced prostitution.[252] The second element of the *actus reus* of enforced prostitution was introduced to be able to distinguish between sexual slavery and other forms of sexual violence.[253] In addition, the majority of the delegations felt that this was also in line with the common understanding of the crime.[254] The element namely refers to the fact that the perpetrator or another person obtained or expected to obtain pecuniary or other advantage in exchange for or in connection with the acts of a sexual nature. With this in mind, it is clear that the situation of the women who were coerced into sexual slavery by the Japanese army during World War II was incorrectly labelled enforced prostitution.

It has been argued by the Special Rapporteur on slavery that in practice sexual slavery encompasses most, if not all forms of forced prostitution.[255] As a general principle it would appear that, in situations of armed conflict, most factual scenarios that could be described as forced prostitution would also amount to sexual slavery and could more appropriately and more easily be characterised and prosecuted as slavery.[256] While the aspect of pecuniary advantages distinguishes enforced prostitution from sexual slavery, in situations of crimes against humanity taking place or situations of armed conflict most of the perpetrators who allowed sexual violence crimes to be committed did so in the absence of any pecuniary advantage received or expected to be received. The sexual services women were obliged to perform equal what is expected of women

---

[251] Article 7(1)(g)-3 EoC. The definition is based on the definition of enforced prostitution as proposed by Special Rapporteur Gay J. McDougall, who stated: 'forced prostitution generally refers to conditions of control over a person who is coerced by another to engage in sexual activity' (UN Commission on Human Rights, *Contemporary Form of Slavery: Systematic Rape, Sexual Slavery and Slavery-like Practices During Armed Conflict: Final Report Submitted by Gay J. McDougall, Special Rapporteur*, E/CN.4/Sub.2/1998/13, 22 June 1998, para. 31). A study prepared by the ICRC and offered to the PrepCom for the ICC defines the *actus reus* of enforced prostitution in similar wording, viz. 'the perpetrator imposed conditions of control over a person and coerced that person to engage in sexual activity' (*Request from the Governments of Belgium, Costa Rica, Finland, Hungary, The Republic of Korea and South Africa and the Permanent Observer Mission of Switzerland Regarding the Text Prepared by the International Committee of the Red Cross on Article 8, paragraph 2(B), (C), and (E) of the Rome Statute of the International Criminal Court*, PCNICC/1999/WGEC/INF.2, 14 July 1999, p. 54).

[252] See subsection 4.1 on 'rape'.

[253] Rückert and Witschel (2001a), p. 84; La Haye (2001), p. 193.

[254] La Haye (2001), p. 193.

[255] UN Commission on Human Rights, *Contemporary Form of Slavery: Systematic Rape, Sexual Slavery and Slavery-like Practices During Armed Conflict: Final Report Submitted by Gay J. McDougall, Special Rapporteur*, E/CN.4/Sub.2/1998/13, 22 June 1998, p. 10.

[256] *Ibid.*

who are kept enslaved for the primary purpose of sex. It was suggested by some delegates that 'the other person' expecting an advantage might be the victim herself or himself, hoping simply to survive.[257] However, exactly because of the coercive circumstances, the women have no choice but to cooperate – if they do not cooperate, they may not survive. For example, in the Democratic Republic of Congo peacekeepers have been defiling girls and women for a banana or a cake.[258] While there may still be cases that fall short of sexual slavery, such as women who are forced to fall back to prostitution because of the economic breakdown of their country after war, most cases of sexual slavery that take place in wartime (or in situations of crimes against humanity) can and should be prosecuted as sexual slavery. It is therefore imperative not to read the commercial aspect into the elements of sexual slavery and thus lift the distinction between sexual slavery and enforced prostitution.

The *mens rea* of the two elements constituting the *actus reus* of enforced prostitution has to be applied in conformity with Article 30 of the ICC Statute. Thus, (1) the perpetrator intended to cause 'one or more persons to engage in one or more acts of a sexual nature by force, or by threat of force or coercion, such as that caused by fear of violence, duress, detention, psychological oppression or abuse of power, against such person or persons or another person, or by taking advantage of a coercive environment or such person's or persons' incapacity to give genuine consent' (element 1); (2) the perpetrator or another person intended to obtain or expected to obtain pecuniary or other advantage in exchange for or in connection with the acts of a sexual nature (element 2).

4.4 Forced pregnancy

The crime of forced pregnancy is among the sexual violence crimes listed in the ICC Statute as a crime against humanity.[259] The crime has no predecessor in supranational criminal law either, although it had already been recognised in a number of documents as constituting a humanitarian and human rights violation.[260]

Negotiations on this crime proved to be difficult, both before and during the Rome Conference. At the last meeting of the PrepCom in March – April 1998, the Holy See

---

[257] La Haye (2001), p. 193.

[258] BBC News, *DR Congo's Shameful Sex Secret*, 3 June 2004: 'Faela is 13 and her son Joseph is just under six months old. Sitting on the dusty ground in Bunia's largest camp for Internally Displaced People (IDP), with Joseph in her arms, she talks about how she ensures that she and her son are fed. "If I go and see the soldiers [of the UN peacekeeping force MONUC] at night and sleep with them then they sometimes give me food, maybe a banana or a cake," she explains. "I have to do it with them because there is nobody to care, nobody else to protect Joseph except me. He is all I have and I must look after him.".'

[259] The crime of forced pregnancy is also laid down as a war crime in Articles 8(2)(b)(xxii) and 8(2)(e)(vi) of the ICC Statute.

[260] The term had been used before in, *inter alia*, the Vienna Declaration and Programme of Action, 12 July 1993, UN Doc. A/Conf.157/23, paras. 18 and 38; the Beijing Declaration and Platform for Action, Fourth World Conference on Women, 15 September 1995, UN Doc. A/Conf.177/20, paras. 114, 132 and 135; and a number of resolutions of the Commission on Human Rights on the Elimination of Violence Against Women between 1995 – 1998, i.e., Res. 1998/52; Res. 1997/44, para. 4; Res. 1996/49, para. 5; Res. 1995/85, para. 5.

proposed to replace the words 'enforced pregnancy' with 'forcible impregnation'.[261] Having the atrocities in Bosnia in mind, where women were raped and held captive until they bore a child of the rapist's (Serb) ethnicity, most delegations found it inadequate to hold on to the term 'forcible impregnation', which refers to forcibly making a woman pregnant, whereas 'enforced pregnancy' was considered a broader concept involving keeping the woman pregnant.[262] Arguments were also made that the crimes of rape and unlawful confinement already sufficiently encompassed the crime of forced pregnancy.[263] Other delegations argued that this way of reasoning denied the criminal nature inherent to forced pregnancy and that it therefore should be treated as a distinct crime.[264] In Rome, the following definition of forced pregnancy was ultimately laid down in paragraph (f) of Article 7(2) of the ICC Statute

> ... the unlawful confinement of a woman forcibly made pregnant, with the intent of affecting the ethnic composition of any population or carrying out other grave violations of international law. This definition shall not in any way be interpreted as affecting national laws relating to pregnancy.

The crime of forced pregnancy proved to be the most contentious of all the gender provisions and one of the most emotionally charged issues in the Rome negotiations.[265] This had mainly to do with the fact that several delegates (among which the Vatican and Ireland) were afraid that the crime of forced pregnancy might impose on national States the obligation to provide women forcibly made pregnant access to abortion.[266] They reasoned that if it is a crime to keep a woman pregnant, then not to allow abortion to a woman forcibly made pregnant would not be an option as it would contribute to the crime of keeping the woman pregnant. In cases of forced pregnancy, women have to make a difficult choice: they can decide to keep the child, who is also the child of a rapist who, in turn, is often of different ethnicity, or decide not to have the child and to have an abortion or decide to give the child up for adoption. It is clear that in both instances, the psychological harm is immense. In the case of the first option, in many societies, in particular patriarchal societies, the woman will be treated as an outcast. The woman and her child will be rejected by society, and she, in turn, may reject her child; she may not regard it as completely her own. The Vatican and other States were worried about the second option, where a woman might want an abortion and the State where she is resident or where she has sought refuge does not permit it. Yet, the intention of those who wanted the crime of forced pregnancy to be included in the Statute was not to interfere with the abortion debates in some countries.[267] Rather, the intention was to acknowledge and to criminalise the crime of forced pregnancy.[268] In order to take away

---

[261] Proposal Submitted by the Holy See, A/AC.249/1998/DP.13, 1 April 1998.

[262] Steains (2000), pp. 366-366. For an overview of the negotiation and adoption of the crime of forced pregnancy at the Rome Conference, see Steains (2000), pp. 357-390.

[263] Steains (2000), p. 367.

[264] *Ibid.*

[265] *Ibid.*

[266] *Ibid.*, pp. 366-367; Bedont and Hall Martinez (1999), p. 9.

[267] Steains (2000), p. 366; Bedont and Hall Martinez (1999), p. 9.

[268] *Ibid.*

the concerns of the Vatican and other States, the last sentence ('this definition shall not in any way be interpreted as affecting national laws relating to pregnancy') was included in the ICC Statute as a compromise.

The EoC describe the element of forced pregnancy as

1. The perpetrator confined one or more women forcibly made pregnant, with the intent of affecting the ethnic composition of any population or carrying out other grave violations of international law.[269]

The crime of forced pregnancy is thus taken over almost verbatim from the ICC Statute to the EoC;[270] the elements of the crime are not elaborated in the EoC.[271] The reason is that the elements of this crime as they had been provisionally adopted did, according to some delegations, not take into account sufficiently the compromise reached in Rome on Article 7(2)(f), in particular the last sentence.[272] According to the EoC, the elements of forced pregnancy should have made a distinction between conduct (confining the pregnant woman), the circumstances (the woman having been made pregnant forcibly) and the element of intent (the intent of affecting the ethnic composition of any population or carrying out other grave violations of international law).[273] It has been argued that, by missing this opportunity, the Preparatory Commission acted contrary to the general structure of the EoC and failed to formulate the elements of this crime with more precision and clarity.[274]

Indeed, the crime of forced pregnancy is – as it stands – narrowly defined. In the first place, the crime only refers to confining a pregnant woman in order to make her bear the child. No mention has been made of the situation in which women are not confined per se, but are raped anyway with the intent of making her pregnant and to bear the child of the rapist's ethnicity.[275] While prosecution under another crime will still be possible (for instance, rape or sexual slavery), this would not take into account the aggravating circumstance within the crime of forced pregnancy: the intent to make the woman pregnant with a child of the rapist's ethnicity. 'Confinement' should therefore be interpreted broadly, including any deprivation of physical liberty no matter

---

[269] Article 7(1)(g)-4 EoC.

[270] According to para. 6 of the General Introduction to the EoC, the requirement of 'unlawfulness' as found in the Statute will not be specified in the EoC.

[271] Paragraph 7 of the General Introduction to the EoC stipulates that the elements of crimes are generally structured in accordance with the following principles: (1) as the elements of crimes focus on the conduct, consequences and circumstances associated with each crime, they are generally listed in that order; (2) when required, a particular mental element is listed after the affected conduct, consequence or circumstance; (3) contextual circumstances are listed last.

[272] La Haye (2001), p. 195. The elements as provisionally adopted concern the following: (1) The accused confined one or more women; (2) Such woman or women had been forcibly made pregnant; (3) The accused intended to keep the woman or women pregnant in order to affect the ethnic composition of a population or to carry out another grave violation of international law.

[273] Rückert and Witschel (2001a), p. 85. Note that the provisional draft included all these elements.

[274] *Ibid.*

[275] Bedont and Hall Martinez (1999), p. 9.

how long. In the second place, formulating the elements might have contributed to the fact that the confinement of the woman and her forced impregnation are two separate acts which are not necessarily committed by the same person.[276] In the third place, the definition of forced pregnancy requires that the woman was made pregnant under forcible circumstances. The circumstance in which a woman became pregnant by consensual sex and is subsequently kidnapped in order to force her to bear a child for sale on the black market would not fall within the crime of forced pregnancy.[277] While, again, such crimes might be prosecuted under other crimes (for instance, sexual slavery), the harm inherent to enslaving a woman with the purpose of having her bear a child that will be sold, has an additional aspect of harm which needs to be recognised. In the fourth place, the phrase 'the intent of affecting the ethnic composition of any population or carrying out other grave violations of international law' is not completely clear. This requirement incorporates an additional *mens rea*: without the specific intent there is not forced pregnancy. The phrase 'carrying out other grave violations of international law' was added to include situations in which women were forcibly made pregnant so that they and their foetuses could be used for medical experiments.[278] This latter form of intent may also constitute, for instance, the crime of genocide.[279] As seen in the previous Chapter, forced pregnancy may also be prosecuted under Article 6(d) 'genocide by imposing measures intended to prevent births'. Attempts by the Vatican to restrict the definition to acts committed for the purpose of ethnic cleansing were successfully resisted.

4.5 Enforced sterilisation

Enforced sterilisation is included in the ICC Statute as a crime against humanity.[280] It is the first time that enforced sterilisation has been laid down in an international treaty. The elements of the crime are:

1. The perpetrator deprived one or more persons of biological reproductive capacity. [19]
2. The conduct was neither justified by the medical or hospital treatment of the person or persons concerned nor carried out with their genuine consent. [20] [281]

[19] The deprivation is not intended to include birth-control measures which have a non-permanent effect in practice.
[20] It is understood that 'genuine consent' does not include consent obtained through deception.

The first part of the *actus reus* of the crime of enforced sterilisation was finally agreed upon as to see to the deprivation of biological reproductive capacity. The definition covers cases of temporary or permanent sterilisation alike and is not restricted to the

[276] Rückert and Witschel (2001a), p. 85.
[277] Bedont and Hall Martinez (1999), p. 9.
[278] *Ibid.*, p. 10; Robinson (1999), fn. 63.
[279] Salzman (1998), pp. 365-366. See also Fischer (1996), pp. 91-133.
[280] Enforced sterilisation is also laid down as a war crime in Articles 8(2)(b)(xxii) and 8(2)(e)(vi) of the ICC Statute.
[281] Article 7(1)(g)-5 EoC.

surgical removal of the reproductive organs: it is to encompass any means or measures which have the effect of depriving a person of his or her biological reproductive capacity.[282] This would certainly include the cutting off or taking out of genitals. Moreover, it may also include cases where women have been raped so viciously that there reproductive system has been destroyed completely. Enforced sterilisation may also amount to the crime of genocide when committed with the specific intent to destroy a particular group in whole or in part. It may in particular be charged either as 'deliberately inflicting on the group conditions of life calculated to bring about its physical destruction in whole or in part' or 'imposing measures intended to prevent births within the group'.[283] Birth-control measures which have a non-permanent effect in practice are not to be subsumed under the definition (according to footnote 19).

The second part of the *actus reus* makes clear that sterilisation as such is not a crime; it becomes a crime when the conduct was neither justified by medical or hospital treatment of the person concerned nor carried out with the genuine consent of this person. In some post-World War II trials, defendants were charged with acts of enforced sterilisation in the context of medical experiments.[284] Footnote 20 expressly affirms that 'genuine consent' cannot be present when consent is obtained through deception.

The *mens rea* of the crime of enforced sterilisation is in accordance with Article 30 of the ICC Statute. Therefore, the perpetrator intended to deprive one or more persons of his or her or their biological reproductive capacity, and he knew that his conduct was neither justified by the medical or hospital treatment of the person or persons concerned nor carried out with their genuine consent.[285]

4.6 Any other form of sexual violence of comparable gravity

The final phrase of Article 7(1)(g) of the ICC Statute is 'any other form of sexual violence of comparable gravity' (hereinafter sexual violence). The category as such has been laid down for the first time in an international instrument. Previously, under the ICTY and ICTR Statutes, the category of 'other inhumane acts' served as a basis for the prosecution of crimes, including sexual violence crimes, falling short of any of the other possible grounds enumerated in the crimes against humanity provision.[286] Here, 'any other form of sexual violence of comparable gravity' serves as a residual category explicitly specifying the aspect of sexual violence.

---

[282] La Haye (2001), p. 196.

[283] Article 6(c) and (d) ICC Statute. See further Chapter 1 on genocide.

[284] 'The Hoess Trial, Supreme National Tribunal, Poland, and the Trial of K. Brandt and Others', cited in *Request from the Governments of Belgium, Costa Rica, Finland, Hungary, The Republic of Korea and South Africa and the Permanent Observer Mission of Switzerland Regarding the Text Prepared by the International Committee of the Red Cross on Article 8, paragraph 2(B), (C), and (E) of the Rome Statute of the International Criminal Court*, PCNICC/1999/WGEC/INF.2, 14 July 1999, p. 55.

[285] Article 7(1)(g)-5 EoC.

[286] 'Other inhumane acts' as crimes against humanity will be discussed in section 6.

According to the EoC, the elements of sexual violence are

1. The perpetrator committed an act of a sexual nature against one or more persons or caused such person or persons to engage in an act of a sexual nature by force, or by threat of force or coercion, such as that caused by fear of violence, duress, detention, psychological oppression or abuse of power, against such person or persons or another person, or by taking advantage of a coercive environment or such person's or persons' incapacity to give genuine consent.

2. Such conduct was of a gravity comparable to the other offences in article 7, paragraph 1 (g), of the Statute.

3. The perpetrator was aware of the factual circumstances that established the gravity of the conduct.[287]

The first element of the *actus reus* makes clear that the crime of sexual violence can be committed in two ways, either by committing an act of a sexual nature against one or more persons or by causing such person or persons to engage in an act of a sexual nature by force or by threat of force or coercion. The examples of coercion given are identical to the ones in the crimes against humanity of rape element and non-consent is therefore not an element of the crime of sexual violence.[288]

The second element of the *actus reus* of the crime of sexual violence requires, in line with the text in the Statute, that the conduct should be of a gravity comparable to the other crimes in Article 7(1)(g) of the ICC Statute.[289] Thus, on its face, it would seem that for a crime to qualify as 'any other form of sexual violence' it has to meet the criteria for the crimes of rape, sexual slavery, enforced prostitution, forced pregnancy and enforced sterilisation. Concerns existed among human rights organisations with regard to the 'comparable gravity' part.[290] This terminology refers to the other crimes enumerated in Article 7(1)(g) (rape, sexual slavery, enforced prostitution, forced pregnancy and enforced sterilisation) and could be interpreted to require some degree of penetration.[291] If such an interpretation is upheld, this will eliminate other equally grave

---

[287] Article 7(1)(g)-6 EoC.

[288] For a commentary on the examples of coercion, see section 4.1 on 'rape'.

[289] Proposals brought forward by the US and a group of Arab States suggested restricting the provision to conduct of a gravity comparable to rape only. See Proposal Submitted by the United States of America, *Draft Elements of Crimes*, PCNICC/1999/DP.4/Add.1, 4 February 1999; *Proposal Concerning the Elements of Crimes Against Humanity Submitted by Bahrain, Iraq, Kuwait, Lebanon, The Libyan Arab Jamahiriya, Oman, Qatar, Saudi Arabia, The Sudan, The Syrian Arab Republic and United Arab Emirates,* PCNICC/1999/WGEC/DP.39, 3 December 1999.

[290] See Women's Caucus for Gender Justice (2000).

[291] This follows from the *ejusdem generis* principle, as discussed above. It is debatable whether the crime of enforced sterilisation involves the act of penetration as contained in the other crimes enumerated in Article 7(1)(g). However, the element of the crime of enforced sterilisation requires for the crime to be committed that 'the perpetrator deprived one or more persons of biological reproductive capacity'. While this may include the surgical removal of the reproductive

acts short of penetration. To take away these concerns, the Women's Caucus for Gender Justice opted for the construction 'conduct of a gravity comparable to any crime against humanity'.[292]

According to the case law of the ICTY and ICTR, sexual violence does not need to include acts which involve penetration or even physical contact. Indeed, forced nudity has been found by both the ICTY and ICTR to constitute the crime of sexual violence. The ICTR formulates the definition of sexual violence in the *Akayesu* case, which was later upheld in the *Kvočka et al.* case, as follows:

> The Tribunal considers sexual violence, which includes rape, as any act of a sexual nature which is committed on a person under circumstances which are coercive. Sexual violence is not limited to physical invasion of the human body and may include acts which do not involve penetration or even physical contact.[293]

Akayesu was found criminally responsible for 'other inhumane acts' as a crime against humanity under Article 3(i) of the ICTR Statute, for 'forced undressing of the victim outside the bureau communal, after making her sit in the mud', 'the forced undressing and public marching of (the victim) naked at the bureau communal' and 'the forced undressing (of three victims) and the forcing of the women to perform exercises naked in public near the bureau communal'.[294] These situations did not involve the sexual penetration of the human body, not even physical contact, but are regarded as most degrading and humiliating for the victims. Also, the *Tadić* and *Niyitegeka* cases resulted in convictions for other inhumane acts as crimes against humanity for, *inter alia*, sexual mutilation.[295]

The ICTY reached a similar conclusion in the *Furundžija* case:

> ... international criminal rules punish not only rape but also any serious sexual assault falling short of actual penetration. It would seem that the prohibition embraces all serious abuses of a sexual nature inflicted upon the physical and moral integrity of a person by means of coercion, threat of force or intimidation in a way that is degrading and humiliating for the victim's dignity. As both these categories of acts are criminalised in international law, the distinction between them is one that is primarily material for the purposes of sentencing.[296]

---

organs (including the cutting off or taking out of genitals), it could also include cases where women have been raped so viciously that their reproductive system has been completely destroyed. In these instances, the penetration as provided for in the other enumerated crimes of Article 7(1)(g) is surely existent. In addition, the insertion of objects in order to sterilise a person can also be seen as penetration. However, for the latter and in other cases, it is best to prosecute the crime for what it is: enforced sterilisation. On 'enforced sterilisation', see also subsection 4.5.

[292] Women's Caucus for Gender Justice (2000). Note that a similar construction can be found in the 'other inhumane acts' category under crimes against humanity as discussed in section 6.

[293] Akayesu Judgment, paras. 598, 688. See also the Kvočka et. al. Judgment, para. 180.

[294] Akayesu Judgment, para. 697.

[295] Tadić Judgment, paras. 729-730; Niyitegeka Judgment and Sentence, paras. 456-467. On 'other inhumane acts of a similar character', see further section 6.

[296] Furundžija Judgment, para. 186.

The conclusion that the 'prohibition', thereby referring to any serious sexual assault falling short of actual penetration, would include all serious abuses of a sexual nature inflicted by means of coercion, threat of force or intimidation seems to be more or less in line with the definition of sexual violence as established in the *Akayesu* case. The approach taken in *Akayesu* to the definition of sexual violence is realistic. Indeed, 'sexual violence' cannot be captured in an enumeration of crimes.

When considering forms of sexual violence other than the specific sexual violence crimes mentioned in Article 7(1)(g) of the ICC Statute, one may think of, *inter alia*, forced nudity, sexual mutilations, sexual molestations and forced abortion. The UN Special Rapporteur on the Situation of Systematic Rape, Sexual Slavery and Slavery-like Practices during Armed Conflict defined 'sexual violence' as

> any violence, physical or psychological, carried out through sexual means or by targeting sexuality. Sexual violence covers both physical and psychological attacks directed at a person's sexual characteristics, such as forcing a person to strip naked in public, mutilating a person's genitals, or slicing off a woman's breasts.[297]

The *Kvočka et al.* Judgment states that

> … sexual violence is broader than rape and includes such crimes as sexual slavery or molestation. … Sexual violence would also include such crimes as sexual mutilation, forced marriage, and forced abortion as well as the gender related crimes explicitly listed in the ICC Statute as war crimes and crimes against humanity …[298]

Forced nudity does not involve sexual penetration or physical contact, and would therefore not qualify as any of the other crimes mentioned in Article 7(1)(g) of the ICC Statute. Also, mutilation of parts of the human body having a sexual connotation (for instance, a woman's breasts or the genitals) could be subsumed within the definition of sexual violence. However, some of the crimes mentioned above (such as sexual slavery) are now explicitly laid down in the ICC Statute as crimes in and of themselves, specifying the criminal nature of the crime explicitly, and should therefore be considered as the grounds to base charges on.

On the basis of this survey of ICTY and ICTR case law, it can be concluded that sexual violence has been found to constitute a broad concept, which includes all possible forms of sexual violence, including rape. However, the crime not necessarily involves a form of penetration or even physical contact. When sexual violence is to be restricted to crimes of a gravity comparable to the other crimes enumerated in Article 7(1)(g), crimes such as forced nudity and sexual mutilation of breasts may not meet this obligation. Even though the drafters may have chosen for this construction in order to abide by the *nullum crimen sine lege* principle, they have restricted the crime of sexual violence too much. Sexual violence, not including rape, has been laid down in the major

---

[297] UN Commission on Human Rights, *Contemporary Form of Slavery: Systematic Rape, Sexual Slavery and Slavery-like Practices During Armed Conflict: Final Report Submitted by Gay J. McDougall, Special Rapporteur,* E/CN.4/Sub.2/1998/13, 22 June 1998, para. 21.

[298] Kvočka et. al. Judgment, para. 180 and footnote 343.

national legal systems in the world as sexual assault for a long time. These laws have never required an element of penetration or physical contact to be a constituent element of sexual assault. Thus, such specificity as now may be required by the 'comparable gravity' wording was not necessary on the basis of the *nullum crimen sine lege* principle at all. Instead of referring to the crimes as enumerated in paragraph (g) solely, the provision should have referred to the article as a whole. Contrary to the 'inhumane treatment' provision contained in Article 7(1)(k), containing a similar residual category applying to the whole article, the reference could have included clear references to the sexual aspect inherent to the crime. The wording used might have been the following: 'Such conduct was of a sexual nature and of a gravity comparable to the other offences in article 7, paragraph 1, of the Statute.' This would also have made the difference with the 'inhumane acts' provision apparent.

As noted above, in the end it will be up to the judges to interpret the crime correctly. It is to be recommended that previous case law on the matter be taken into account. In addition, if the crime of sexual violence is interpreted in a restrictive manner, requiring some form of penetration, there would be no ground for a charge with sexual violence as no prosecution could be conducted on that basis.[299] In that case, the only possible ground for prosecuting such a crime would be the crimes against humanity category of 'other inhumane treatment'. This category does not only refer to the crimes enumerated in Article 7(1)(g), but also refers to all crimes enumerated in the crimes against humanity provision. By also referring to crimes such as deportation or imprisonment, no connection with penetration or physical contact per se is made, which leaves open the possibility of prosecuting sexual violence crimes short of penetration or physical contact under 'inhumane treatment'. However, it would be best to prosecute other forms of sexual violence on the sexual violence ground, as it takes into account more accurately the sexual violence inherent to the crime charged.

The *mens rea* of the crime of sexual violence is partly a clarification of the standard default rule contained in Article 30 of the ICC Statute. Only the first element is governed by the default rule. Thus, the perpetrator intended to commit 'an act of a sexual nature against one or more persons or caused such person or persons to engage in an act of a sexual nature by force, or by threat of force or coercion, such as that caused by fear of violence, duress, detention, psychological oppression or abuse of power, against such person or persons or another person, or by taking advantage of a coercive environment or such person's or persons' incapacity to give genuine consent' (element 1). Element 2 explicitly contains the mental element, which must be seen as either a clarification or a diminution of the requirement of Article 30.[300] What was eventually agreed to is the requirement that 'the perpetrator was aware of the factual circumstances that established the gravity of the conduct' (element 3). The knowledge requirement was generally regarded as opening the door to the defence of mistake of law and thus as a too high threshold. It should also be noted that, in the case of value judgements, 'it is

---

[299] According to the Tadić Appeal Judgment (para. 284), when elaborating on the issue whether all crimes against humanity require a discriminatory intent or solely the crime of persecution, 'it is an elementary rule of interpretation that one should not construe a provision or part of a provision as if it were superfluous and hence pointless: the presumption is warranted that law-makers enact or agree upon rules that are well thought out and meaningful in all their elements'.
[300] La Haye (2001), p. 199.

not necessary that the accused personally completed a particular value judgement, unless otherwise indicated'.[301]

5 Persecution on the ground of gender

The crime against humanity of persecution is laid down in international instruments, such as in Article 6(c) of the Nuremberg Charter, Article 5(c) of the Tokyo Charter, Article 2(1)(c) of CCL 10, Article 5(h) of the ICTY Statute and Article 3(h) of the ICTR Statute.[302] Until recently, the crime had not been clarified in supranational criminal law nor has it been known as such in the world's major criminal justice systems.[303] Persecution has now been defined in the ICC Statute and been clarified in the EoC. The *Tadić* Judgment, which was rendered before the Statute was drafted, significantly contributed to the drafting of the ICC definition of persecution. However, later judgments also did, including the *Kupreškić et al.* Judgment, the *Blaškić* Judgment and the *Todorović* Judgment. In recent years, the prosecution of rape and other forms of sexual violence has often been based on the crime of persecution.

In the ICC Statute, persecution as a crime against humanity is laid down in Article 7(1)(h) and reads:

> Persecution against any identifiable group or collectivity on political, racial, national, ethnic, cultural, religious, gender as defined in paragraph 3, or other grounds that are universally recognized as impermissible under international law, in connection with any act referred to in this paragraph or any crime within the jurisdiction of the Court.

Persecution as a crime is further defined in Article 7(2)(g):

> 'Persecution' means the intentional and severe deprivation of fundamental rights contrary to international law by reason of the identity of the group or collectivity.

Article 7(3) clarifies the term 'gender':

> For the purpose of this Statute, it is understood that the term 'gender' refers to the two sexes, male and female, within the context of society. The term 'gender' does not indicate any meaning different from the above.

---

[301] Paragraph 4 of the General Introduction to the EoC.

[302] Article 6(c) Nuremberg Charter; Article 5(c) Tokyo Charter; Article 2(1)(c) CCL No. 10; Article 5(h) ICTY Statute; and Article 3(h) ICTR Statute, respectively.

[303] Bassiouni (1992), p. 327; Tadić Judgment, para. 694. In international refugee law persecution is also not defined, but the status of refugee is attributed to anyone who '... owing to a well-founded fear of being persecuted for reasons of race, religion, nationality, membership of a particular social group or political opinion is outside the country of his nationality and is unable or, owing to such a fear, is unwilling to avail himself of the protection of that country' (Article 33 of the Convention Relating to the Status of Refugees, Geneva, 28 July 1951, 189 UNTS 137). See also Kupreškić, Kupreškić, Kupreškić, Josipović, Papić and Santić Judgment, paras. 586-589.

According to the EoC, the elements of the crime against humanity of persecution are as follows:

1. The perpetrator severely deprived, contrary to international law,[21] one or more persons of fundamental rights.

2. The perpetrator targeted such person or persons by reason of the identity of a group or collectivity or targeted the group or collectivity as such.

3. Such targeting was based on political, racial, national, ethnic, cultural, religious, gender as defined in article 7, paragraph 3, of the Statute, or other grounds that are universally recognized as impermissible under international law.

4. The conduct was committed in connection with any act referred to in article 7, paragraph 1, of the Statute or any crime within the jurisdiction of the Court.[22] [304]

[21] This requirement is without prejudice to paragraph 6 of the General Introduction to the Elements of Crimes.
[22] It is understood that no additional mental element is necessary for this element other than that inherent in element 6.

In the *Tadić* Judgment, the crime of persecution is defined as follows: '... what is necessary is some form of discrimination that is intended to be and results in an infringement of an individual's fundamental rights. Additionally, this discrimination must be on specific grounds, namely race, religion or politics.'[305] The *Kupreškić et al.* Judgment defines the crime against humanity of persecution as 'the gross or blatant denial, on discriminatory grounds, of a fundamental right, laid down in international customary or treaty law, reaching the same level of gravity as the other acts prohibited in Article 5.'[306] The definition of persecution in the ICC Statute and the EoC is for a large part in line with these definitions. Generally speaking, it can be held that persecution as a crime under international law consists of two components: (1) the intentional severe deprivation of fundamental rights of a person by the commission of certain acts against him; and (2) this deprivation is pointed at an individual or more individuals of a certain group (or a group as such) because he is a member of this group (discriminatory policy). The first element of the *actus reus* of the crime of persecution requires the perpetrator to severely deprive one or more persons of fundamental rights. The deprivation itself is thus directed against one or more individual persons.[307] Discussions on the question whether or not to refer to groups was resolved by the second element, in which the group or collectivity as such was introduced as a possible

[304] Article 7(1)(h) EoC.
[305] Tadić Judgment, paras. 697, 715.
[306] Kupreškić, Kupreškić, Kupreškić, Josipović, Papić and Santić Judgment, paras. 621, 627.
[307] This is in conformity with the Tadić Judgment (para. 697), in which the Trial Chamber held that persecution requires some form of discrimination that is intended to be and results in an infringement of an individual's fundamental rights, in order to prove the need for individual rights to be violated.

target of the perpetrator.[308] The group or collectivity is 'identifiable' on the basis of objective criteria or in the mind of the perpetrator.[309] The phrase 'contrary to international law' is taken verbatim from the definition in the Statute. A footnote attached to it states that the requirement is without prejudice to paragraph 6 of the General Introduction to the EoC. Paragraph 6 renders unnecessary a repetition of whether a particular act is unlawful under international law.

Some uncertainty remains. What are 'fundamental rights' and which acts qualify as a severe deprivation of these fundamental rights? As for the first issue, some delegations favoured an additional requirement of 'universal recognition' to further qualify 'fundamental rights'.[310] While this additional requirement was not retained in the definitive text, their concerns were partially addressed by the introduction to crimes against humanity in the EoC which states that the provisions of Article 7 of the Statute must be strictly construed and that it includes 'conduct which is impermissible under generally applicable international law, as recognized by the principal legal systems of the world'.[311]

The *Kupreškić et al.* Trial Chamber remarked in this context that for an indication of what rights are so fundamental that their infringement may result in persecution, one needs to revert to some of the human rights treaties:

> … drawing upon its earlier discussion of 'other inhumane acts', holds that in order to identify those rights whose infringement may constitute persecution, more defined parameters for the definition of human dignity can be found in international standards on human rights such as those laid down in the Universal Declaration on Human Rights of 1948, the two United Nations Convenants on Human Rights of 1966 and other international instruments on human rights or on humanitarian law. Drawing upon the various provisions of these texts it proves possible to identify a set of fundamental rights appertaining to any human being, the gross infringement of which may amount, depending on the surrounding circumstances, to a crime against humanity. … The Trial Chamber does not see fit to identify which rights constitute fundamental rights for the purposes of persecution. The interests of justice would not be served by so doing, as the explicit inclusion of particular fundamental rights could be interpreted as the implicit exclusion of other rights (*expressio unius est exclusio alterius*). This is not the approach taken to crimes against humanity in customary international law, where the category of 'other inhumane acts' also allows courts flexibility to determine the cases before them, depending on the forms which attacks on humanity may take, forms which are ever-changing and carried out with particular ingenuity. Each case must therefore be examined on its merits.[312]

While it is, according to the Trial Chamber, not in the interest of justice to give an exhaustive list of rights qualifying for fundamental rights, it seems that, at a minimum, fundamental rights are those laid down in the Universal Declaration and the two 1966 Covenants. These human rights treaties deal with civil, political, economic, social and

---

[308] For the discussions, see Rückert and Witschel (2001b), pp. 95-96.

[309] Boot (2002), p. 520.

[310] For the discussions, see Rückert and Witschel (2001b), p. 96.

[311] Paragraph 1 to the introduction of crimes against humanity in the EoC.

[312] Kupreškić, Kupreškić, Kupreškić, Josipović, Papić and Santić Judgment, paras. 621, 623.

cultural rights. Without mentioning the latter, the rights may all be infringed by the crime of persecution according to the *Kupreškić et al.* Judgment.[313] The fundamental rights may at the least include rights which are so fundamental that no derogation from these rights is permitted, also referred to as *jus cogens* norms.[314] Following General Comment no. 24 of the Human Rights Committee, a number of rights contained in the International Convenant on Civil and Political Rights (ICCPR) have acquired this status and reservations to these rights may subsequently not be made by States Parties. Following this General Comment,

> ... a State may not reserve the right to engage in slavery, to torture, to subject persons to cruel, inhuman or degrading treatment or punishment, to arbitrarily deprive persons of their lives, to arbitrarily arrest and detain persons, to deny freedom of thought, conscience and religion, to presume a person guilty unless he proves his innocence, to execute pregnant women or children, to permit the advocacy of national, racial or religious hatred, to deny to persons of marriageable age the right to marry, or to deny to minorities the right to enjoy their own culture, profess their own religion, or use their own language ...[315]

The gross or blatant denial of the fundamental rights not to be engaged in slavery, not to be tortured nor to be subjected to cruel, inhuman or degrading treatment or punishment, on discriminatory grounds is thus a clear case of persecution. This was confirmed in the *Blaškić* case.[316] Sexual violence can thus definitely be used as a method to infringe upon the right not to be held in slavery or the right not to be subjected to torture or to cruel, inhuman or degrading treatment or punishment. That sexual violence amounts to slavery or torture has been established by the Tribunals more than once.[317] A clear fundamental right not to be subjected to sexual violence does not yet exist in these or any other human rights treaties.

This brings one to the second issue: which acts – when applied on one of the discriminatory grounds – can constitute persecution or, in other words, result in a severe deprivation of fundamental rights contrary to international law? Can sexual violence crimes indeed amount to acts constituting persecution? Some guidance can be found in ICTY case law on this matter. According to the *Tadić* Judgment, an act of persecution

---

313 *Ibid.*, para. 615: '(b) In their interpretation of persecution courts have included acts such as murder, extermination, torture, and other serious acts on the person such as those presently enumerated in Article 5. (c) Persecution can also involve a variety of other discriminatory acts, involving attacks on political, social, and economic rights.'

314 See also Boot, Hall and Dixon (1999), p. 167.

315 *General Comment adopted by the Human Rights Committee under Article 40, paragraph 4, of the ICCPR*, No. 24, CCPR/C/21/Rev.1/Add.6, 11 November 1994, para. 8.

316 Blaškić Judgment (para. 220): 'The Trial Chamber considers that infringements of the elementary and inalienable rights of man, which are "the right to life, liberty and the security of person", the right not to be "held in slavery or servitude", the right not to "be subjected to torture or to cruel, inhuman or degrading treatment or punishment" and the right not to be "subjected to arbitrary arrest, detention or exile" as affirmed in Articles 3, 4, 5 and 9 of the Universal Declaration of Human Rights, by their very essence may constitute persecution when committed on discriminatory grounds.'

317 See section 2 ('enslavement'), section 3 ('torture') and subsection 4.2 ('sexual slavery').

may involve crimes enumerated in Articles 2 (grave breaches) and 3 (violations of the laws and customs of war) of the Statute when the elements of persecution are fulfilled.[318] Following the *Kupreškić et al.* case, the other crimes listed in Article 5 (Crimes against humanity) may also be acts constituting persecution.[319] When elaborating on the acts not enumerated in the Statute, the *Tadić* Trial Chamber held that acts of persecution can be of varying severity 'from killing to a limitation on the type of professions open to the targeted group'.[320] It also held that acts of persecution include those of a physical, economic and judicial nature[321] and that persecution not necessarily requires a physical element.[322] Examples of non-physical persecution given by the Trial Chamber included the incitement by means of hate speech and the application of laws in a discriminatory and arbitrary manner.[323] In the *Blaškić* case, it was stated that persecution not only encompasses bodily and mental harm and infringements upon individual freedom, but also acts which appear less serious, for instance acts aimed at property, provided that the victims were selected specifically because of their belonging to a certain community.[324] There are, nevertheless, limits to the acts which may constitute persecution within the meaning of crimes against humanity. The *Tadić* Trial Chamber in this regard mentioned the taking of industrial property.[325] When deciding on which attacks on property can constitute persecution, the Trial Chamber in *Kupreškić et al.* stated that such is the case when the attack results in a comprehensive destruction of the livelihood of a certain population.[326]

Tadić was ultimately convicted of (his role in), *inter alia*, 'the attack on Kozarac and the surrounding areas, as well as of the seizure, collection, segregation and forced transfer of civilians to camps, calling-out of civilians, beatings and killings, which clearly constituted an infringement of the victims' enjoyment of their fundamental rights and these acts were taken against non-Serbs on the basis of religious and political discrimination'.[327] Kupreškić was convicted of persecution by means of 'deliberate and systematic killing of Bosnian Muslim civilians', the 'organised detention and expulsion of the Bosnian Muslims from Ahmici-Santici and its environs' and the 'comprehensive destruction of Bosnian homes and property'.[328] It was found that these acts denied, in a gross and blatant manner, the Muslim citizens their fundamental rights to life, freedom of movement and free enjoyment of their family life and property, respectively.[329] Kupreškić's actions and their consequences were found to be of such a heinous nature that there could be no doubt that they matched in gravity the other crimes in Article 5 of

---

318 Tadić Judgment, para. 700.
319 Kupreškić, Kupreškić, Kupreškić, Josipović, Papić and Santić Judgment, paras. 593-607, 615.
320 Tadić Judgment, para. 704.
321 *Ibid.*, para. 710.
322 *Ibid.*, para. 707.
323 See the cases cited in the Tadić Judgment, paras. 708-709.
324 Blaškić Judgment, para. 233.
325 Tadić Judgment, para. 707 (citing the Flick case).
326 Kupreškić, Kupreškić, Kupreškić, Josipović, Papić and Santić Judgment, paras. 630-631.
327 Tadić Judgment, para. 717.
328 Kupreškić, Kupreškić, Kupreškić, Josipović, Papić and Santić Judgment, paras. 628-631.
329 *Ibid.*, para. 781.

the Statute.[330] Kupreškić clearly attacked his Muslim neighbours solely on the ground of their ethnicity and with the aim of cleansing the village of Muslim inhabitants.[331] Blaškić was found guilty of persecutions against the Muslim civilians of Bosnia on the basis of the following acts: attacks on towns and villages; murder and serious bodily injury; the destruction and plunder of property and, in particular, of institutions dedicated to religion or education; inhuman or cruel treatment of civilians and, in particular, their being taken hostage and used as human shields; and the forcible transfer of civilians.[332]

Following the interpretation of acts as discussed above, sexual violence crimes can thus also be seen as acts – when committed on any of the discriminatory grounds – that can constitute persecution. Sexual violence has been criminalised in the Statutes, and this includes sexual violence without any physical contact. In fact, some judgments have already been rendered in which sexual violence was implied to constitute persecution.

With reference to the 1948 *Justice* case, which had been brought before the US Military Tribunal, the Trial Chamber in *Kupreškić et al.* stated:

> It is probably true to say that the Tribunal regarded as constituting crimes against humanity not merely a series of changes made in the legal system of Germany but a series of such alterations as involved or were pursuant to persecutions on political, racial, or religious grounds, or (perhaps) such as led to the commission of atrocities and offences, including but not limited to murder, extermination, enslavement, deportation, imprisonment, torture, *rape*, or *other inhumane acts* against any civilian population.[333]

In the *Kupreškić et al.* case, the Chamber finally held that persecution 'included acts such as murder, extermination, torture and *other serious acts on the person such as those presently enumerated in Article 5*'.[334] By specifically referring to the other crimes enumerated in Article 5, which include rape and other inhumane acts, the Trial Chamber acknowledged that sexual violence crimes can be used for the persecution of people. In another case, the *Todorović* case, Todorović was convicted of the crime of persecution, including sexual violence, on a guilty plea. In the Plea Agreement, Todorović had agreed that ordering six men to perform fellatio on each other constituted, among other things, the factual basis for his guilty plea.[335] Thereby he pleaded guilty to sexual assault used as a method of persecution, a crime against humanity. In relation to the allegations of sexual assault, he accepted the following account of his conduct:

---

[330] *Ibid.*

[331] *Ibid.*, para. 780.

[332] Blaškić Judgment, p. 267.

[333] Kupreškić, Kupreškić, Kupreškić, Josipović, Papić and Santić Judgment, footnote 895 (Josef Altstötter et al., NMT Vol. III, Notes on the Case, UNWCC, 1948, Vol. VI, pp. 82-83) (emphasis added).

[334] Kupreškić, Kupreškić, Kupreškić, Josipović, Papić and Santić Judgment, paras. 571, 615(b), (d) (emphasis added).

[335] Todorović Judgment, paras. 9, 12.

> Witness A described how he was taken to the police station in Bosanski Samac, where Stevan Todorovic began to beat him and kick him in the genital area. Witness A was then taken over to another man and ordered by Stevan Todorovic to 'bit into his penis'. After that he was beaten again and endured further mistreatment.[336]

> Witness C stated that Todorovic had telephoned and had required him to come to the police station in Bosanski Samac. There, Witness C was beaten for about half an hour. In Witness C's words: 'Only Todorovic and me were present at the office and the beating lasted for about half an hour. After that Witness D was brought to the office and he continued beating both of us. The beating lasted for another hour. After that he ordered us to perform oral sex on each other.[337]

> Witness E described how he was arrested on 9 or 10 May 1992 and taken to the police station in Bosanski Samac. There he was beaten by Stevan Todorovic, among others, for several hours. Witness E stated that: 'After the beating Todorovic ordered us (Witness E and Witness F) to do a blow job on each other. He was laughing when we was doing it.[338]

Fellatio, which is considered to amount to rape, is thus found to constitute a method of persecution. The conviction of Todorović for rape as a form of persecution proved to set into motion a number of convictions for sexual violence conduct as constituting the crime of persecution as a crime against humanity. Convictions for sexual violence as part of several other crimes constituting persecution were rendered for the accused Kvočka, Prcać, Kos, Radić, Žigić, Sikirica, Simić, Plavšić, Stakić, Nikolić, Brđanin, Nahimana, Barayagwiza and Ngeze.[339] The so-called *Media* case (involving the accused Nahimana, Barayagwiza and Ngeze) deserves particular attention. In this case the Trial Chamber held that

> Tutsi women, in particular, were targeted for persecution. The portrayal of the Tutsi woman as a *femme fatale*, and the message that Tutsi women were seductive agents of the enemy was conveyed repeatedly by RTLM and *Kangura. The Ten Commandments*, broadcast on RTLM and published in *Kangura*, vilified and endangered Tutsi women ... By defining the Tutsi woman as an enemy in this way, RTLM and *Kangura* articulated a framework that made the sexual attack of women a foreseeable consequence of the role attributed to them.[340]

It seems that the ICTR and ICTY Prosecutors chose to charge a considerable number of accused with the crime of persecution because the crime adequately covers a broad range of crimes (such as murder, torture, rape, etc.) and therefore each crime does not need to be charged separately.

The third element of the *actus reus* of the crime of persecution states the discriminatory grounds of persecution. These discriminatory grounds distinguish the

---

336 *Ibid.*, para. 38.
337 *Ibid.*, para. 39.
338 *Ibid.*, para. 40.
339 For an overview of the sexual violence crimes committed, see the Appendix.
340 Media Judgment, para. 1079.

crime of persecution from the other crimes against humanity even though the acts may be the same.[341] With the exception of the Tokyo Charter, in the previous international instruments mentioned above reference was made only to political, racial or religious grounds.[342] The 1948 Genocide Convention, however, like the 1991 and 1996 ILC Draft Codes, contains the additional ground of ethnicity, while the 1954 Draft Code contained culture as a basis for persecution.[343] The ICC Draft consolidated text of April 1998 referred to 'social, economic and mental or physical disability grounds'.[344] The *Tadić* Judgment therefore held that 'there are no definitive grounds in customary international law on which persecution must be based'.[345] With the ICC Statute, national, ethnic, cultural, gender or other grounds that are universally recognised as impermissible under international law have for the first time been listed in an international instrument. This is in accordance with the *Tadić* Appeals Chamber decision, in which it was recognised that since the aim of the drafters of the ICTY Statute was to make all crimes against humanity punishable, the discriminatory grounds enumerated in Article 5(h) of the ICTY Statute cannot be exhaustive. According to the Appeals Chamber, '[s]uch an interpretation of Article 5 would create significant *lacunae* by failing to protect victim groups not covered by the listed discriminatory grounds. The experience of Nazi Germany demonstrated that crimes against humanity may be committed on discriminatory grounds other than those enumerated in Article 5(h), such as physical or mental disability, age or infirmity, or sexual preference.'[346] Extension of the list with these discriminatory grounds was considered to bring the ICC Statute into line with the current status of the crime under international law.[347] Yet, the meaning of these different grounds is not always clear.[348] Finally, it is generally accepted that each of the grounds in and of itself is sufficient ground for persecution.[349] In addition, it is not considered necessary to demonstrate that an accused took part in the formulation of a discriminatory policy or practice by a governmental authority.[350]

---

[341] Kupreškić, Kupreškić, Kupreškić, Josipović, Papić and Santić Judgment, para. 607.

[342] The Tokyo Charter did not include religion as a discriminatory ground given its inapplicability to the Pacific war. See Tadić Judgment, para. 711.

[343] *Ibid.*

[344] *Report of the Preparatory Committee on the Establishment of an International Criminal Court*, A/CONF.183/2/Add.1, 14 April 1998, p. 26.

[345] *Ibid.*

[346] Tadić Appeal Judgment, para. 285.

[347] Rückert and Witschel (2001b), p. 95.

[348] See Chapter 1 on genocide. See also Boot (2002, pp. 520-522), in particular on the issue of whether 'universally recognized as impermissible' includes 'social origin, property, and birth, hence social grounds, as well as color'. Furthermore, it is questionable whether States excluded mental or physical disability grounds, economic grounds, and grounds concerning age, which were included in the Draft consolidated text of April 1998.

[349] Tadić Judgment, paras. 712-713: 'The use of the word "and" most likely results from the fact that the Statute attempts to define, in a cumulative sense, the International Tribunal's adjudicatory powers under Article 5. ... and, since there is no clear indication of an intention to deviate from customary international law, it is highly unlikely that the Statute's drafters intended the word "and" to require all three grounds to be present.'

[350] Kupreškić, Kupreškić, Kupreškić, Josipović, Papić and Santić Judgment, para. 625.

Gender is explicitly mentioned in the ICC Statute and is understood to refer 'to the two sexes, male and female, within the context of society'. This definition was hardly negotiated at the Rome Conference.[351] Some delegations favoured the use of the word 'sex' over 'gender'. This attempt was successfully thwarted by the argument that during the preceding decade the United Nations had consistently used the term 'gender' in recognition of the fact that 'gender' encompasses biological and sociological aspects whereas 'sex' only refers to the biological distinction between men and women.[352] Although the term 'gender' incorporates the socially constructed roles of men and women, the phrase 'within the context of society' was included in order to make sure that sexual orientation is excluded from the definition.[353]

The inclusion of gender as a ground for discrimination is a major step forward in the prosecution of gender-based crimes. Previously, a rapist could not be prosecuted for the crime of persecution for the rape of a woman on the basis of her gender solely; he could only be charged with persecution for rape on the basis of any of the other grounds: racial, religious or political background. This narrow range of discriminatory grounds suggested that gender-based persecution was considered to be less important than persecution on the other grounds.[354] Now, that gender has been added to the grounds for persecution, a perpetrator can be found guilty of the crime of persecution when it has been proved that he raped a woman solely for reasons of her being a woman. In situations in which crimes against humanity take place (or during armed conflict) gender-based persecution often occurs.[355] The reasons for committing the sexual violence crimes may also encompass more discriminatory grounds altogether: a woman may be singled out because she or her husband is related to a political party and, cumulatively, because she is a woman. Alternatively, a woman may be raped while her rape is not related to the fact that she is a woman: she may be raped because she is a Muslim, and a Muslim man would have been raped under the same circumstances.[356] However, whatever the reasons of the perpetrator for raping his victim, now the criminal nature of the discriminatory ground of gender is no longer denied. The inclusion of gender as a ground is practical from a prosecutorial point of view as it is not easy, if not impossible, to determine why the sexual violence occurred.[357]

---

[351] For a background to the negotiations, see Steains (2000), pp. 371-375.

[352] *Ibid.*, p. 373.

[353] *Ibid.* According to Boot (2002), 'although the term "gender" has a specific meaning under the ICC Statute as defined in paragraph 3, persecution on gender grounds as the term is generally understood in other international instruments and UN usage may still fall within the jurisdiction of the Court to the extent that such discrimination would be based on one of the "other grounds that are universally recognized as impermissible under international law" or involved "other inhumane acts" within the meaning of paragraph 1(k)'.

[354] Steains (2000), p. 370; Bedont and Hall Martinez (1999), p. 11.

[355] Askin (1997), p. 222, fn. 735: 'In wartime, the woman is often raped because she is a member of the "enemy" side of the conflict. Yet, because "enemy" men are not raped with the frequency as "enemy" women, gender is the primary factor. However, because "non-enemy" women are raped often, but still not with the same frequency as "enemy" women, this distinction cannot be dismissed.'

[356] *Ibid.*

[357] Askin (1977), pp. 354-355.

The fourth element of the *actus reus* requires that the conduct be committed in connection with any act referred to in Article 7(1) of the Statute (murder, extermination, enslavement, rape, etc.) or any crime within the jurisdiction of the Court (war crimes, genocide or aggression). This wording was also used in the Nuremberg and Tokyo Charters, but departs from the formulations in CCL 10 and the ICTY and ICTR Statutes. According to the *Kupreškić et al.* Judgment, the requirement that the conduct be committed in connection with any crime within the jurisdiction of the Court is not in line with customary international law.[358] Similarly, according to the *Tadić* Trial Chamber, 'if there is an infringement of an individual's fundamental right through discrimination on one of the stipulated grounds, then it is not necessary to have a separate act of an inhumane nature to constitute persecution'.[359]

It should also be noted that 'when determining whether particular acts constitute persecution, the Trial Chamber wishes to reiterate that acts of persecution must be evaluated not in isolation but in context, by looking at their cumulative effect. Although individual acts may not be inhumane, their overall consequences must offend humanity in such a way that they may be termed "inhumane". This delimitation also suffices to satisfy the principle of legality, as inhumane acts are clearly proscribed by the Statute.'[360] The Tribunal gives the example of placing restrictions on a particular group to curtail its rights to participate in particular aspects of social life (such as visits to public parks, theatres or libraries). Even though these examples may not in and of themselves amount to persecution, taken together they might. One may also think of, for instance, the treatment of women in some countries, where women are discriminated in many ways which could cumulatively be seen as persecution on the basis of gender.

Generally speaking, the *mens rea* requirement in the case of the crime of persecution is stronger than that in the case of other crimes against humanity, although less strong than in the case of genocide. In the crime of genocide, the criminal intent is to destroy the group or its members; in the crime of persecution, the criminal intent is to forcibly discriminate against a group or members of a group by grossly and

---

[358] In the Kupreškić, Kupreškić, Kupreškić, Josipović, Papić and Santić Judgment (para. 580), the Trial Chamber held that 'to the extent that it is required that persecution be connected with war crimes or the crime of aggression, this requirement is especially striking in light of the fact that the ICC Statute reflects customary international law in abolishing the nexus between crimes against humanity and armed conflict. Furthermore this restriction might easily be circumvented by charging persecution in connection with "other inhumane acts of a similar character intentionally causing great suffering, or serious injury to body or to mental or physical health" under Article 7(1)(k). ... The application of the provisions contained in Part II of the Statute ..., including Article 7 on crimes against humanity, is restricted by Article 10 of the same Statute which provides that "Nothing in the Statute shall be interpreted as limiting or prejudicing in any way existing or developing rules of international law for purposes other than this Statute". This provision clearly conveys the idea that the framers of the Statute did not intend to affect, amongst other things, *lex lata* as regards such matters as the definition of war crimes, crimes against humanity and genocide.'

[359] Tadić Judgment, para. 697.

[360] Kupreškić, Kupreškić, Kupreškić, Josipović, Papić and Santić Judgment, para. 622; also para. 615.

systematically violating their fundamental human rights.[361] However, 'from the viewpoint of *mens rea*, genocide is an extreme and most inhuman form of persecution. When persecution escalates to the extreme form of willful and deliberate acts designed to destroy a group or part of a group, it can be held that such persecution amounts to genocide.'[362]

The *mens rea* of the crime of persecution as described in the EoC is, with the exception of element 4, covered by Article 30 of the ICC Statute. Thus, the perpetrator intended to severely deprive, contrary to international law, one or more persons of fundamental rights (element 1); the perpetrator intended to target such person or persons by reason of the identity of a group or collectivity or intended to target the group or collectivity as such (element 2). It has been argued that element 3, the targeting on the basis of one of the enumerated groups, does not contain a specific mental element, but can be established objectively.[363] Element 4 has been clarified by footnote 22 and should be read as meaning that the perpetrator does not have to be aware of any specific 'connected' acts; it suffices that he or she has the general awareness of the context of the attack directed against a civilian population, as is required in element 6.

6 Other inhumane acts of a similar character

The provision 'other inhumane acts' as a crime against humanity can be found in a number of international instruments: in Article 6(c) of the Nuremberg Charter, Article 5(c) of the Tokyo Charter, Article 2(1)(c) of CCL 10, Article 5(i) of the ICTY Statute and Article 3(i) of the ICTR Statute.[364] The category 'other inhumane acts' enables the prosecution of crimes not prosecutable under any of the other crimes against humanity, thus it is made clear that not all crimes can be covered by the provision.[365] In the past, this provision provided the basis for the prosecution of sexual violence crimes in some cases. In the ICC Statute, the category is stated as 'other inhumane acts of a similar

---

[361] *Ibid.*, para. 751.

[362] *Ibid.*, para. 636.

[363] Rückert and Witschel (2001b), p. 97.

[364] Note that under the Nuremberg and Tokyo Charters the category is not listed last, like in the other instruments, but follows before the crime of persecution. From this it can be inferred that the clause did not refer to persecutions.

[365] According to the Kayishema Judgment, para. 149, 'since the Nuremberg Charter, the category "other inhumane acts" has been maintained as a useful category for acts not specifically stated but which are of comparable gravity'. Similarly, the Blaškić Judgment (para. 237) states that 'as with the underlying crime of "persecution" the sub-characterisation "other inhumane acts" laid down in Article 5(i) of the Statute is a generic charge which encompasses a series of criminal activities not explicitly enumerated'. Both cases refer to the ICRC Commentary on Article 3 common to the Geneva Conventions (Jean Pictet, Commentary on the 1st Geneva Convention of 12 August 1949, Geneva, 1952, p. 54) with regard to the notion of 'humane treatment'. In the ICRC Commentary it was held that '... it is always dangerous to try to go into too much detail – especially in this domain. However much care were taken in establishing a list of all the various forms of infliction, one would never be able to catch up with the imagination of future torturers who wished to satisfy their bestial instincts; and the more specific and complete a list tries to be, the more restrictive it becomes.'

character intentionally causing great suffering, or serious injury to body or to mental or physical health'.[366] According to the EoC, the elements of the crime against humanity of other inhumane acts of a similar character consist in:

1. The perpetrator inflicted great suffering, or serious injury to body or to mental or physical health, by means of an inhumane act.

2. Such act was of a character similar to any other act referred to in Article 7, paragraph 1, of the Statute.[30]

3. The perpetrator was aware of the factual circumstances that established the character of the act.

[30] It is understood that 'character' refers to the nature and gravity of the act.

In the ICC Statute and the EoC, two requirements for the inhumane acts have been added: (1) they must cause 'great suffering, or serious injury to body or to mental or physical health'; and (2) they have to be of a character similar to the other acts in Article 7(1) of the ICC Statute The former addition seems to have been taken from the grave breaches provisions of the Geneva Conventions, which include 'wilfully causing great suffering, or serious injury to body or health'.[367] The two requirements were added in order to arrive at a more precise definition of the crime and thus consistency with the principle of *nullum crimen sine lege*.[368] The distinction between the crime of other inhumane acts and the crime of torture lies in the severity of the suffering: the crime of torture requires 'severe pain or suffering', whereas the crime of inhumane acts requires 'great suffering, or serious injury'.[369]

The wording of Article 7(1)(k) is in line with the practice of the *ad hoc* Tribunals. While not deducible from the text of the ICTY and ICTR Statutes as such, the phrase 'other inhumane acts' has been interpreted by the judges of the ICTY and ICTR to include the above-cited elements. This interpretation is based on the text of Article 7(k) of the ICC Statute as well as the 1996 ILC Commentary on Article 18 of its Draft Code of Crimes, both taking into account the two additional requirements.[370]

The *Kayishema* Judgment, as upheld by the *Blaškić* and *Bagilishema* Judgments, specifically stated:

---

[366] Article 7(1)(k) ICC Statute.

[367] Articles 50, 51, 130 and 147 of the 1949 Geneva Conventions I, II, III and IV, respectively.

[368] Boot, Hall and Dixon (1999), p. 156; Rückert and Witschel (2001c), p. 107; Bassiouni (1992), p. 331.

[369] See also section 3 on 'torture'.

[370] Kayishema Judgment, para. 150; Blaškić Judgment, paras. 241-242; Bagilishema Judgment, para. 91. The 1996 ILC Commentary on Article 18 of the Draft Code of Crimes states: 'The Commission recognized that it was impossible to establish an exhaustive list of the inhumane acts which may constitute crimes against humanity. First, this category of acts is intended to include only additional acts that are similar in gravity to those listed in the preceding subparagraphs. Second, the act must in fact cause injury to a human being in terms of physical or mental integrity, health or human dignity.'

> In relation to the Statute, other inhumane acts include acts that are of similar gravity and seriousness to the enumerated act of murder, extermination, enslavement, deportation, imprisonment, torture, rape, or persecution on political, racial and religious grounds. These will be acts or omissions that deliberately cause serious mental or physical suffering or injury or constitute a serious attack on human dignity.[371]

According to the Chambers in *Kayishema* and *Bagilishema*, the question of which acts amount to inhumane acts should be determined on a case-by-case basis.[372]

That sexual violence crimes fit the elements of 'inhumane acts' is without question. This conclusion follows from the ICTY and ICTR case law as well as from the texts of the ICC Statute and the EoC. In the *Tadić* case, sexual mutilation and other types of severe bodily harm were given as examples of 'other inhumane acts' within the meaning of crimes against humanity.[373] Beatings and acts of violence were found to constitute inhumane acts.[374] In this case, the ICTY Trial Chamber found Tadić guilty of crimes against humanity on the ground of 'inhumane acts' because of his participation in forcing two prisoners to perform oral sexual acts on a third prisoner and forcing one of these two prisoners to mutilate this third prisoner sexually, viz.:[375]

> After G and Witness H had been forced to pull Jasmin Hrnic's body about the hangar floor they were ordered to jump down into the inspection pit, then Fikret Harambasic, who was naked and bloody from beating, was made to jump into the pit with them and Witness H was ordered to lick his naked bottom and G to suck his penis and then to bite his testicles. Meanwhile a group of men in uniform stood around the inspection pit watching and shouting to bite harder. All three were then made to get out of the pit onto the hangar floor and Witness H was threatened with a knife that both his eyes would be cut out if he did not hold Fikret Harambasic's mouth closed to prevent him from screaming; G was then made to lie between the naked Fikret Harambasic's legs and, while the latter struggled, hit and bite his genitals. G then bit off one of Fikret Harambasic's testicles and spat it out and was told he was free to leave. Witness H was ordered to drag Fikret Harambasic to a nearby table, where he then stood beside him and was then ordered to return to his room, which he did. Fikret Harambasic has not been seen or heard of since.[376]

Before the ICTR, Akayesu was found criminally responsible for 'other inhumane acts' as a crime against humanity under Article 3(i) of the ICTR Statute, for 'forced undressing of the victim outside the bureau communal, after making her sit in the mud'; 'the forced undressing and public marching of (the victim) naked at the bureau communal'; and 'the forced undressing (of three victims) and the forcing of the women

---

[371] Kayishema Judgment, para. 151; Blaškić Judgment, paras. 240-243; Bagilishema Judgment, para. 92.

[372] Bagilishema Judgment, para. 92.

[373] Tadić Opinion and Judgment, para. 729. The examples were drawn from the terms of Article 18(k) of the ILC Draft Code.

[374] *Ibid.*, para. 730.

[375] *Ibid.* Tadić was also found guilty on these acts under Article 3(1)(a) of the Statute, cruel treatment, as a violation of the laws or customs of war.

[376] *Ibid.*, para. 206.

to perform exercises naked in public near the bureau communal'.[377] These types of situation do not involve the sexual penetration of the human body and do not even require physical contact. In the *Niyitigeka* case, Niyitegeka was found guilty of other inhumane acts as a crime against humanity for the killing, decapitation, castration of Kabanda and the piercing of Kabanda's skull through his ears with a spike.[378] Kabanda's genitals were subsequently hung on a spike, visible to the public. In addition, Niyitegeka was convicted of other inhumane acts as crimes against humanity for ordering *Interahamwe* to undress the body of a Tutsi woman who had just been shot dead, and to fetch and sharpen a piece of wood, which he then instructed them to insert into her genitalia.[379] The Chamber subsequently held 'that the acts committed with respect to Kabanda and the sexual violence to the dead woman's body are acts of seriousness comparable to other acts enumerated in the Article, and would cause mental suffering to civilians, in particular, Tutsi civilians, and constitute a serious attack on the human dignity of the Tutsi community as a whole'.[380]

It is clear that 'inhumane acts' represents a broad spectrum of crimes when the two additional requirements are fulfilled. No penetration or even physical contact is needed. This also follows from the EoC text. The first element of the *actus reus* of the crime of inhumane treatment requires that the perpetrator inflicted great suffering or serious injury to body or to mental or physical health, by means of an inhumane act. By this wording, it is recognised that not only physical harm constitutes an inhumane act, but also non-physical harm, mental harm, such as forced nudity. This also follows from the second element of the *actus reus* of the crime of inhumane treatment: by requiring that the act was of a character similar to any of the other crimes enumerated in Article 7(1), covering all the crimes constituting a crime against humanity, the crime does not have to be of a physical nature. In a footnote attached to this element, the word 'character' is further explained to refer to the nature and gravity of the act.[381]

Concerns relating to the possible violation of the *nullum crimen sine lege* principle seem to be out of place.[382] The case law of the Tribunals and the ICC's EoC have already considerably contributed to a more specific definition and description of the crime by adding the two requirements as discussed above. The crime of 'other inhumane acts' serves as a residual category and should also be treated in that way. According to the Trial Chamber in the *Kupreškić et al.* case 'the category of "other inhumane acts" also allows courts flexibility to determine the cases before them, depending on the forms which attacks on humanity may take, forms which are ever-

[377] Akayesu Judgment, para. 697.
[378] Niyitegeka Judgment and Sentence, paras. 459-467.
[379] *Ibid.*
[380] *Ibid.*, para. 465.
[381] Gravity is also an element of the crime of sexual violence as discussed above.
[382] Boot (2002, p. 532) stated that Article 7(1)(k) 'contains open-ended terminology, which gives the Court room to decide on the criminality of particular conduct on a case-by-case basis. Furthermore, "other inhumane acts" must be of a character similar to the other crimes enumerated under Article 7, which is also for the Court to decide.'

changing and carried out with particular ingenuity. Each case must therefore be examined on its merits'.[383]

The question is, however, whether it is to be recommended to prosecute sexual violence under this category. Unlike the sexual violence category, it does not explicitly take into account the sexual violence aspect. In future sexual violence cases before the ICC, the category of inhumane treatment should merely serve as a residual category. It has been argued in subsection 4.6 that prosecutions on the ground of sexual violence falling short of any of the specific sexual violence crimes enumerated in Article 7(1)(g) should be prosecuted under 'sexual violence' in the same subparagraph. In this case, the category of 'inhumane treatment' may not be the right category for the prosecution of gender crimes. The only possible obstacle to prosecuting sexual violence on the ground of sexual violence ground is the requirement that the act be of a gravity comparable to the other acts enumerated in the same paragraph.

The *mens rea* of the crime of inhumane treatment as a crime against humanity is in line only with the default rule contained in Article 30 of the ICC Statute for the first element. What is needed is that: (1) the perpetrator had the intent to inflict great suffering, or serious injury to body or to mental or physical health, by means of an inhumane act (element 1); and (2) the perpetrator was aware of the factual circumstances that established the character of the act (element 3). Element 3 thus clarifies the mental aspect of the crime.[384]

7 ELEMENTS COMMON TO CRIMES AGAINST HUMANITY

According to Article 7(1) of the ICC Statute, a crime against humanity, such as rape or sexual slavery, can only be qualified as such 'when committed as part of a widespread or systematic attack directed against any civilian population, with knowledge of the attack'. In paragraph 2 of this Article, 'attack directed against any civilian population' is described as 'a course of conduct involving the multiple commission of acts referred to in paragraph 1 against any civilian population, pursuant to or in furtherance of a State or organizational policy to commit such attack'.[385] The word 'widespread' has generally been used to refer to the scale of the acts perpetrated or the number of victims involved.[386] The term 'systematic' refers to 'the organised nature of the acts of violence and the improbability of their random occurrence. Patterns of crimes – that is the non-

---

383 Kupreškić, Kupreškić, Kupreškić, Josipović, Papić and Santić Judgment, para. 623; see also paras. 563-566.

384 The Kayishema Judgment (para. 153) held in relation to the *mens rea* that 'an accused may be held liable … only where at the time of the act, the accused had the intention to inflict serious mental suffering on the third party, or where the accused knew that his act was likely to cause serious mental suffering and was reckless as to whether such suffering would result. Accordingly, if at the time of the act, the accused was unaware of the third party bearing witness to his act, then he cannot be held responsible for the mental suffering of the third party.' See also Blaškić Judgment, paras. 240-243.

385 See also the Introduction to Article 7 in the EoC.

386 Akayesu Judgment, para. 580. See also, *inter alia*, the Blaškić Judgment, para. 206.

accidental repetition of similar criminal conduct on a regular basis – are a common expression of such systematic occurrence.'[387]

The *Kunarac, Kovač and Vuković* case is illustrative with regard to the interpretation of the *chapeau* requirements of crimes against humanity and rape prosecutions. In this case, the Trial Chamber held that the accused were 'aware that there was an attack on the Muslim civilian population going on, and they willingly took an active part in it. [They] mistreated Muslim girls and women, and only Muslim girls and women, *because* they were Muslims. They therefore fully embraced the ethnicity-based aggression of the Serbs against the Muslim civilians, and all their criminal actions were clearly part of and had the effect of perpetuating the attack against the Muslim civilian population.'[388] In the *Kunarac, Kovač and Vuković* Trial Judgment, it has furthermore been noted that the act alleged, for instance rape, does not need to be committed in a widespread or systematic manner; the act need simply *form part of* a widespread or systematic attack.[389] In other words, the attack directed against the civilian population must be widespread or systematic, not each act forming part of the attack.

The ICC Statute furthermore requires that the accused had 'knowledge of the attack'. The EoC add that this requirement 'should not be interpreted as requiring proof that the perpetrator had knowledge of all characteristics of the attack or the precise details of the plan or policy of the State or organization. In the case of an emerging widespread or systematic attack against a civilian population, the intent clause of the last element indicates that this mental element is satisfied if the perpetrator intended to further such an attack.'[390] In the *Kunarac, Kovač and Vuković* case, the Trial Chamber held that the accused 'knew that Muslim women were specifically targeted, as he himself took several of them to his men and raped some of them himself. In the course of one of these rapes, he expressed with verbal and physical aggression his view that the rapes against the Muslim women were one of the many ways in which the Serbs could assert their superiority and victory over the Muslims. While raping FWS-183, the accused Dragoljub Kunarac told her that she should enjoy being "fucked by a Serb".'[391] Through these acts, the Trial Chamber found that

> the accused Dragoljub Kunarac not only showed that he knew of the attack and knew that his crimes fitted in with or were part of the attack, but he also clearly showed that he intended them to be so. He demonstrated a total disregard for Muslims in general and Muslim women in particular. The accused Kragoljub Kunarac used his bravery in combat to gain the respect of his men, and he maintained it by providing them with women.[392]

---

[387] Kunarac, Kovač and Vuković Judgment, para. 429. See also, *inter alia*, the Blaškić Judgment, para. 203.

[388] Kunarac, Kovač and Vuković Judgment, para. 592; also para. 588. See also, *inter alia*, the Musema Judgment and Sentence, para. 966.

[389] Kunarac, Kovač and Vuković Judgment, para. 417.

[390] Introduction to Article 7 in the EoC.

[391] Kunarac, Kovač and Vuković Judgment, para. 583.

[392] *Ibid.*, para. 585.

It is to be noted that the motives of the accused for taking part in the attack are irrelevant. On the basis of Article 7 of the ICC Statute, a crime against humanity may be committed for purely personal reasons.[393] For example, the accused Zoran Vuković had argued that, even if it were proved that he had raped a woman, he would have done so out of a sexual urge, not out of hatred. The Trial Chamber made it clear however, that 'all that matters in this context is his awareness of an attack against the Muslim civilian population of which his victim was a member and, for the purpose of torture, that he intended to discriminate between the group of which he is a member and the group of his victim'.[394]

8 Superior Responsibility for Sexual Violence as a Crime Against Humanity

Three essential conditions have been established in the Tribunals' case law in order to hold a superior accountable for the acts of his subordinates, viz. (1) the existence of a superior – subordinate relationship of effective control between the accused and the perpetrator of the crime; (2) the knowledge, or constructive knowledge, of the accused that the crime was about to be, was being, or had been committed; and (3) the failure of the accused to take the necessary and reasonable measures to prevent or stop the crime, or to punish the perpetrator.[395] In cases where there is no evidence or allegation of physical contact between an accused and a rape victim, where the accused is not known to have explicitly incited or ordered the rape, where the physical presence of the accused at a rape scene or other concrete proof of knowledge of rape has not been established, the nexus between the accused and the crime of rape will not be easy to establish. In such cases, what will need to be proved is the presumption that the crime was so widespread that the accused must have known about it and did not use his position to prevent or punish the crime. It is therefore argued that the second condition, the knowledge requirement, should be less restrictively interpreted. What needs to be established are conditions 1 and 3, and a commander or superior can thus only evade his responsibility if he demonstrates that he tried to prevent or punish the sexual violence. The knowledge requirement should be met by the historical information that sexual violence takes place in every conflict and, in particular, by the common or public knowledge of the widespread occurrence of gender crimes in armed conflict in the situation at hand. The set-up of an OTP Rape Database, a database similar to the one used at the ICTR, will make it possible for the Court to establish that for each conflict situation, if applicable, rapes were so widespread and so openly conducted that the accused could not not have known about them.

The data in the ICTR OTP Rape Database illustrates that the rapes were so commonplace, so omnipresent, so public that the accused must have known that they were occurring. The data of the OTP Rape Database are admissible as evidence before the ICTR on the basis of a Rule 92*bis* application ('Proof of Facts Other Than by Oral

[393] *Ibid.*, para. 433. See also Tadić Appeal Judgment, paras. 248, 252.
[394] Kunarac, Kovač and Vuković Judgment, para. 816.
[395] See, *inter alia*, Bagilishema Judgment, para. 38; Kajelijeli Judgment and Sentence, para. 772; Kamuhanda Judgment, para. 603. The responsibility of commanders and other superiors is laid down in the ICC Statute in Article 28, for the ICTY in Article 7(3) and for the ICTR in Article 6(3).

Evidence'). In addition, oral testimony and expert testimony can be given if the database is introduced as evidence into the record.

The Rule 92*bis* application has been used by the Prosecutor in the *Government I* case in an attempt to establish widespread and systematic rapes committed throughout the territory of Rwanda.[396] In her motion, the Prosecutor requested the ICTR to admit as evidence the written statements of 51 witnesses in lieu of their oral testimonies and not to require these witnesses to appear for cross-examination.[397] The witness statements were drawn from the OTP Rape Database. The Trial Chamber did not arrive at a substantive discussion of Rule 92*bis*, however. Instead, the Trial Chamber held that the 51 statements could not at all be introduced, because in order to do so Rule 92*bis*(A) requires that a statement must be from a witness.[398] A person becomes a witness in the trial when his/her name has been entered in the Prosecution's list of witnesses filed in the case. What the Prosecutor therefore could have done was to request the Trial Chamber under Rule 73*bis*(E) for leave to add witnesses to their witnesses' list.[399] In light of the time span in which the Prosecutor had made corrections to the witnesses' list and the final witnesses' list of 4 June 2004, adding 51 statements was rather late (two months before the closing of the case). The Prosecutor's motion to establish widespread and systematic rapes in Rwanda was therefore denied without a discussion of whether or not the statements went to prove a matter other than the acts and conduct of the accused.

9 Final remarks

The sexual violence crimes included in the ICC Statute as crimes against humanity have increasingly been recognised as violent crimes in and of themselves. Previous international criminal instruments – CCL 10 and the Statutes of the Tribunals – only mentioned rape as a crime against humanity. The specific sexual violence crimes discussed in this Chapter have also been laid down in the war crimes provision of the ICC Statute (Article 8), and what is said here about the specific sexual violence crimes will therefore apply *mutatis mutandis* to the specific sexual violence crimes as war

[396] *Prosecutor v. Casimir Bizimungu, Justin Mugenzi, Jérôme-Clément Bicamumpaka and Prosper Mugiraneza*, Prosecutor's Motion and Notice Pursuant to rule 92*bis*(E) Showing Widespread and Systematic Rapes Committed Throughout the Territory of Rwanda During the Period Covered by the Temporal Jurisdiction of the Tribunal, 23 September 2004. The Prosecutor's Motion is confidential, but the title of the document is cited in *The Prosecutor v. Casimir Bizimungu, Justin Mugenzi, Jérôme-Clément Bicamumpaka and Prosper Mugiraneza*, Decision on the Prosecutor's Motion and Notice Pursuant to Rule 92*bis*(E), Case No. ICTR-99-50-T, 17 November 2004.

[397] *The Prosecutor v. Casimir Bizimungu, Justin Mugenzi, Jérôme-Clément Bicamumpaka and Prosper Mugiraneza*, Decision on the Prosecutor's Motion and Notice Pursuant to Rule 92*bis*(E), Case No. ICTR-99-50-T, 17 November 2004, para. 1.

[398] *Ibid.*, para. 8.

[399] *Ibid.*, para. 6 (with reference to Prosecutor v. Pauline Nyiramasuhuko et. al., Decision on Prosecutor's Motion for Leave to Be Authorised to Have Admitted the Affidavits Regarding the Chain of Custody of the Diary of Pauline Nyiramasuhuko Under Rule 92*bis*, Case No. ICTR-97-21-T, 14 October 2004, para. 12).

crimes. As far as war crimes are concerned, only rape, enforced prostitution or any form of indecent assault had been prohibited in the 1949 Geneva Conventions and the 1977 Additional Protocols thereto. For the first time at the supranational criminal law level, Article 7 and Article 8 of the ICC Statute explicitly recognise the criminal nature of sexual violence crimes themselves.

Although the crimes of enslavement, torture and other inhumane acts of a similar character have been discussed in this Chapter, these crimes – with the exception of the crime of torture – have become almost redundant in light of the specific sexual violence crimes, such as sexual slavery, rape and the residual category of 'any other form of sexual violence of comparable gravity'. This is different for the crime of torture as a war crime, because torture still requires a purpose, including discrimination on the basis of gender, which in the case of rape could provide an additional charge in order to establish the totality of the accused's conduct.

Some of the crimes against humanity proved to be quite 'new' in the sense that they had never been defined before in international humanitarian law, human rights law or domestic law (sexual slavery, forced pregnancy). For some of the crimes, the drafters of the ICC Statute had to refer to international humanitarian law (enslavement), human rights law (enslavement, torture, sexual slavery) and domestic law (rape) in order to find the definition of a crime against humanity under supranational criminal law. ICTY and ICTR case law also played an important role in this regard. The reason for considering other treaties and laws is that the contours of the crimes in the supranational criminal law system are not clearly established yet. As mentioned, in order to transfer elements from other fields of law to supranational criminal law one must keep in mind the differences that exist between these bodies of law as well as the reality of the nature of the sexual violence crimes as international crimes.

With regard to the definition of rape, the ICC EoC are not focused on the issue of consent (as contained in the *Kunarac, Kovač and Vuković* Appeals Chamber definition of rape), but on force, threat of force, coercion or a coercive environment (as contained in the *Furundžija* and *Akayesu* cases). Lack of consent as an element of the crime of rape (or of any other sexual violence crime, for that matter) is immaterial within the supranational criminal law context, especially in light of the violent and oppressive context in which rapes as genocide, crimes against humanity or war crimes take place, and should therefore be rejected. To a large extent, the Tribunals took recourse to definitions of rape in national laws focusing on consent. However, the definitions of rape in those national laws were never written for the kind of situations the Court and Tribunals deal with and should therefore not be transposed to the supranational criminal law level easily. Introducing the concept of non-consent into the definition of rape would necessarily burden the Prosecutor with inquiring into the victim's state of mind. No matter how they are phrased ('Did you consent?' or 'Was it done against your will?'), questions about consent may insult victims of rape and may cause further traumatisation, especially if such questions are asked after the victim has explained to the court the totality of the sexual violence inflicted upon her and the coercive circumstances in which the sexual violence was committed. If it has been established that a crime has been committed, questions about consent are redundant. As has been explained in Part II, in those (presumably) rare cases in which the Defence may want to advance consent, this is still possible, but the relevance and admissibility of such evidence must first be established in an *in camera* procedure in order to spare the victim from painful propositions which have not been tested first. Including non-consent in the definition of rape is not in agreement with the nature of the crime and will cause victims of sexual violence to shun the Court. The ICC elements of rape have furthermore taken into account a larger number of prohibited sexual acts than as contained in the more restrictive *Furundžija* and *Kunarac, Kovač and Vuković* mechanical descriptions of body parts. The ICC definition of rape focuses not only on penetration of the vagina, anus and mouth with the penis and the penetration of the vagina and anus with an object, but also on penetration with the fingers or tongue and penetration with the penis of any other part of the body. At the same time, the ICC definition is not as broad as the *Akayesu* conceptual definition of rape, which makes it easier to distinguish between rape and sexual violence. The prohibited sexual acts constituting rape in the ICC EoC essentially focus on penetration and leave out sexual acts falling short thereof, such as forced nudity and forced masturbation. The latter sexual acts could then be prosecuted under 'any other form of sexual violence of comparable gravity'. This is not to say that crimes which are prosecuted under that heading are less serious than rape or any other of the explicitly mentioned sexual violence crimes in Article 7(1)(g) of the ICC Statute; the provision reads that these forms of sexual violence should be 'of comparable gravity'. Distinguishing between rape and other forms of sexual violence will make it possible not to cause injustice to those victims of rape who do fit the ICC mechanical definitional requirements of rape and who consider themselves the 'real victims of rape'.

Summarising, the definition of rape as found in the ICC EoC fits the reality of the crime well. The ICC has chosen, on the one hand, for incorporating the element of force, threat of force, coercion or a coercive environment (and not lack of consent) and, on the other hand, for a mechanical approach focusing on penetration (and not for a conceptual approach), albeit not in a restrictive manner. However, the developments with regard to the definition of rape since the coming into force of the EoC have not come to a standstill. Despite the non-uniformity as regards the definition of rape within the ICTY and ICTR, the *Kunarac, Kovač and Vuković* Appeals Chamber definition of rape, which includes the element of non-consent, seems to have been taken as the leading definition within the supranational criminal law context in a majority of cases. This trend should not be followed by the ICC, as the *Kunarac, Kovač and Vuković* definition of rape does not reflect the reality of rapes taking place in situations over which the Court has jurisdiction. If rape is not defined in conformity with the nature of the crime, victims may be reluctant to come forward and testify at the Court. In that case, the crimes committed against them will not be recognised and punished.

As far as the other specific sexual violence crimes are concerned, the EoC have set out a rather workable framework as well. For the first time, sexual slavery has been laid down in an international instrument on the supranational criminal law level, that is, the ICC Statute. Of course, the crime itself is as old as war, one gruesome example being the rape camps during the Japanese occupation of parts of Asia during World War II. However, the criminal nature of the crime has now been explicitly recognised as a crime in and of itself and is as such prosecutable before the Court. The EoC define sexual slavery in conformity with the definition of enslavement (viz. 'exercise any or all of the powers attaching to the right of ownership over one or more persons'), with the addition that the perpetrator caused the victim to engage in one or more acts of a sexual nature. The examples mentioned in the EoC with regard to ownership – purchasing, selling, lending or bartering – might give the impression that some sort of commercial aspect must be involved. However, the footnote attached to the first element of sexual slavery makes it perfectly clear that sexual slavery also includes 'forced labour', 'reducing a person to a servile status' (including forced marriage) and 'trafficking in persons, in particular women and children'. On this basis, it can be concluded that sexual slavery does not necessarily require any financial benefits for the perpetrator or even confinement of the victim to a particular place. Sexual slavery should be distinguished from enslavement, but also from enforced prostitution, which does require that some pecuniary benefit is involved. In the ICTY, the sexual enslavement of women and girls was prosecuted as the crime against humanity of enslavement in the *Kunarac, Kovač and Vuković* case. Although the ICTY had no other option than to prosecute the sexual slavery as enslavement, the ICC will now be able to prosecute sexual slavery directly as sexual slavery, clearly recognising the sexual aspects of the slavery.

Like sexual slavery, enforced prostitution as a crime against humanity has also been included in a supranational criminal law instrument for the first time. Enforced prostitution, however, was already enumerated in Article 4(e) of the ICTR Statute as a violation of Article 3 Common to the 1949 Geneva Conventions and of 1977 Additional Protocol II, albeit no prosecutions on this basis have taken place. According to the ICC EoC, the elements of this crime require the perpetrator to have caused one or more persons to engage in one or more acts of a sexual nature under conditions of coercion (non-consent is not an element of the crime), and he obtained or expected to obtain pecuniary or other advantage in exchange for or in connection with these sexual acts. In situations in which crimes against humanity take place (or situations of armed conflict), it is important to distinguish the crime of enforced prostitution from the crime of sexual slavery. In many situations, the crime may be better charged as sexual slavery rather than as enforced prostitution. In times that genocide, crimes against humanity and war crimes take place, women are frequently captured for the prime purpose of sex without any financial benefits involved. The 'comfort women' were wrongly thought to have been captured for the purpose of enforced prostitution, whereas they were in fact sexual slaves. Situations falling short of sexual slavery are nevertheless prosecutable as enforced prostitution. Especially in times of peace, enforced prostitution takes place quite frequently and has now found a solid basis in supranational criminal law if it can be proven that the crime has taken place within the context of crimes against humanity or war crimes.

As sexual slavery and, partially, enforced prostitution, forced pregnancy was never before laid down in a supranational criminal instrument either. Due to contradictory opinions among ICC delegates, the definition in the ICC Statute and EoC are almost identical. This has left open some uncertainties, including whether confining a woman implies a specific amount of time or whether it includes any deprivation of physical liberty, no matter for how long, and whether confining a woman and forced impregnation are two separate acts not necessarily committed by the same person. It will be up to the judges of the ICC to interpret this crime. The realities of forced pregnancy as a constituent act of genocide, a crime against humanity or a war crime, however, require that no narrow interpretation of the crime of forced pregnancy should be made. In the case of the questions raised above, this means that no specific time frame should be required and that the confinement of the woman and the forced impregnation can be two separate acts committed by different persons.

The crime of enforced sterilisation has also been laid down in a supranational criminal law instrument, that is to say, the ICC Statute, for the first time. The crime concerns the deprivation of a person's biological reproductive capacity without any justified medical reason or this person's genuine consent. The crime would also entail situations in which women were raped so viciously that their reproductive system has been destroyed completely. Especially where women and girls have been raped multiple times by multiple perpetrators, their biological reproductive capacity may be injured beyond healing. Also the cutting off or taking out of genitals may come within the ambit of enforced sterilisation.

The category of 'any other form of sexual violence of comparable gravity' is a sort of rest category for sexual violence crimes not falling under any of the other specific sexual violence crimes mentioned in Article 7(g) or Articles 8(2)(b)(xxii) and 8(2)(e)(vi) (where it is referred to as 'any other form of sexual violence also constituting a grave breach of the Geneva Conventions' and 'any other form of sexual violence also constituting a serious violation of article 3 common to the four Geneva Conventions', respectively). This crime is new in supranational criminal law as well. In the crimes against humanity provision of the Tribunals, a similar rest category is found under 'other inhumane acts', but this category is applicable to all crimes against humanity, not to sexual violence crimes only. For an act to fall within the definition of 'any other form of sexual violence' the ICC EoC require that the perpetrator committed an act of a sexual nature under coercive circumstances (non-consent is not an element of the crime) and that the conduct be of a gravity comparable to the other crimes in Article 7(1)(g) of the ICC Statute. When interpreted strictly, this might lead to the conclusion that all other sexual violence crimes need some degree of penetration. Such an interpretation is unwanted and would not take into account case law by the Tribunals on this matter. According to the case law of the Tribunals with regard to the 'other inhumane acts' category, sexual violence is not limited to physical invasion of the human body, but may include acts which do not involve penetration or even physical contact, like forced nudity. While concerns existed among ICC delegates with regard to the open-ended language contained in this provision, it is not always possible to capture all criminal acts in one definition, especially not in a rest category like this one, being drafted to take into account unforeseeable sexual violence crimes. This is also in conformity with national laws containing open-ended formulations of sexual assault crimes. For this reason, the category of 'any other form of sexual violence of comparable gravity' should not be interpreted restrictively. Furthermore, although the category of 'other inhumane acts' could serve as an additional rest category in cases where sexual violence would not fall under 'any other form of sexual violence of comparable gravity', it is suggested that this should not easily be the case because it would make the category of 'any other form of sexual violence of comparable gravity' completely superfluous. The rest category of 'other inhumane acts' does not take into account the specific sexual nature of the crimes as has been done by the category of 'any other form of sexual violence of comparable gravity'.

Another novelty with specific attention to sexual violence crimes committed on the basis of gender has been introduced at the Court through the crime of persecution. In general, persecution means the intentional and severe deprivation of fundamental rights by reason of a person's connection to a specific group. In a considerable number of cases, the Tribunals charged and convicted accused of the crime of persecution. Such charges and prosecutions are effective as the crime adequately covers a broad range of crimes (murder, torture, rape, etc.) and therefore make it possible for the Prosecutor not to charge each crime separately. For the first time ever, gender has now been added to the list of groups mentioned. Therefore, raping a woman solely for the reason that she is a woman can be prosecuted as the crime against humanity of persecution.

The elements common to crimes against humanity all need to be fulfilled in order for rape or any other form of sexual violence to qualify as a crime against humanity. In ICTY and ICTR case law it has been established that the act of rape or any other form of sexual violence does not need to be committed in a widespread or systematic manner; the act need simply *form part of* a widespread or systematic attack. Such an understanding of the common elements of crimes against humanity certainly facilitates the prosecution of sexual violence, as victims are not always able (they may, for instance, be dead, handicapped, or severely ill) or willing (they may, for instance, feel ashamed or stigmatised and/or fear reprisals) to testify, despite the mass rapes which may have taken place in a particular country or region.

CHAPTER 3
SEXUAL VIOLENCE AS A WAR CRIME

1 INTRODUCTION

The ICTY is authorised to prosecute war crimes under Articles 2 and 3 of the ICTY Statute and the ICTR has been attributed this power under Article 4 of the ICTR Statute. Article 2 of the ICTY Statute grants the Tribunal jurisdiction over grave breaches of the 1949 Geneva Conventions[1] and Article 3 of the ICTY Statute grants the Tribunal jurisdiction over violations of the laws or customs of war.[2] In practice, most war crimes

---

[1] Article 2 of the ICTY Statute ('Grave Breaches of the Geneva Conventions of 1949') reads:

> The International Tribunal shall have the power to prosecute persons committing or ordering to be committed grave breaches of the Geneva Conventions of 12 August 1949, namely the following acts against persons or property protected under the provisions of the relevant Geneva Convention:
>
> (a) wilful killing;
> (b) torture or inhuman treatment, including biological experiments;
> (c) wilfully causing great suffering or serious injury to body or health;
> (d) extensive destruction and appropriation of property, not justified by military necessity and carried out unlawfully and wantonly;
> (e) compelling a prisoner of war or a civilian to serve in the forces of a hostile power;
> (f) wilfully depriving a prisoner of war or a civilian of the rights of fair and regular trial;
> (g) unlawful deportation or transfer or unlawful confinement of a civilian;
> (h) taking civilians as hostages.

[2] Article 3 of the ICTY Statute ('Violations of the Laws or Customs of War') reads:

> The International Tribunal shall have the power to prosecute persons violating the laws or customs of war. Such violations shall include, but not be limited to:
>
> (a) employment of poisonous weapons or other weapons calculated to cause unnecessary suffering;
> (b) wanton destruction of cities, towns or villages, or devastation not justified by military necessity;
> (c) attack, or bombardment, by whatever means, of undefended towns, villages, dwellings, or buildings;
> (d) seizure of, destruction or wilful damage done to institutions dedicated to religion, charity and education, the arts and sciences, historic monuments and works of art and science;
> (e) plunder of public or private property.

charges before the ICTY have been brought under Article 3, as proof of the international character of the conflict under Article 2 has generally been considered difficult, whereas Article 3 merely requires proof that the crime was committed in either an international or an internal armed conflict and was closely related to the armed conflict. No reference to sexual violence as a grave breach or violation of the laws or customs of war can be found in Articles 2 and 3 of the ICTY Statute, although the provisions have been interpreted through ICTY and ICTR case law to cover such acts. There is furthermore no requirement that grave breaches and violations of the laws or customs of war be committed on a widespread or systematic scale: in other words, war crimes may arise from isolated acts.[3] The ICTR Statute, on the other hand, confers on the Tribunal jurisdiction over serious violations of Article 3 common to the 1949 Geneva Conventions and of 1977 Additional Protocol II, as evidenced by Article 4.[4] A grave breaches provision was not included in the ICTR Statute, because the Rwandan conflict has generally been deemed a non-international one. Unlike the war crimes provisions in the ICTY Statute, Article 4(e) of the ICTR Statute refers to acts of sexual

---

It must be noted here (and as will be further explained in this Chapter) that the Appeals Chamber in the *Tadić Jurisdiction Decision* ruled that the non-exhaustive Article 3 of the ICTY Statute needs to be considered a residual clause and all applicable offences may be prosecuted under it provided they are not included in Articles 2 (grave breaches), 4 (genocide) or 5 (crimes against humanity). This resulted in the fact that Common Article 3 of the 1949 Geneva Conventions has been interpreted to come within the ambit of Article 3 of the ICTY Statute. See Tadić Jurisdiction Decision, paras. 89, 91.

[3] Čelebići Judgment, para. 178.

[4] Article 4 of the ICTR Statute ('Violations of Article 3 Common to the Geneva Conventions and of Additional Protocol II') reads:

> The International Tribunal for Rwanda shall have the power to prosecute persons committing or ordering to be committed serious violations of Article 3 common to the Geneva Conventions of 12 August 1949 for the Protection of War Victims, and of Additional Protocol II thereto of 8 June 1977. These violations shall include, but shall not be limited to:
>
> (a) Violence to life, health and physical or mental well-being of persons, in particular murder as well as cruel treatment such as torture, mutilation or any form of corporal punishment;
> (b) Collective punishments;
> (c) Taking of hostages;
> (d) Acts of terrorism;
> (e) Outrages upon personal dignity, in particular humiliating and degrading treatment, rape, enforced prostitution and any form of indecent assault;
> (f) Pillage;
> (g) The passing of sentences and the carrying out of executions without previous Judgment pronounced by a regularly constituted court, affording all the judicial guarantees which are recognized as indispensable by civilised peoples;
> (h) Threats to commit any of the foregoing acts.

violence, that is to say 'rape, enforced prostitution and any from of indecent assault', a phrase that was copied from Article 4(2)(e) of the 1977 Additional Protocol II. Charges concerning sexual violence under Article 4(e) of the ICTR Statute have been laid down in ICTR indictments, although so far there have been no convictions on this basis.

In the ICC Statute, war crimes are defined in one provision, viz. Article 8, which is the longest of the three provisions on crimes in the Statute, containing fifty different subparagraphs in total. The majority of the fifty subparagraphs relate to international armed conflict, even though most contemporary armed conflicts are or have been of a non-international character. Article 8(1) states that the Court 'shall have jurisdiction in respect of war crimes *in particular* when committed as part of a plan or policy or as part of a large-scale commission of such crimes'.[5] Thus, the provision underlines that the Court has jurisdiction in particular over war crimes committed systematically or on a large scale since these are primarily the situations that are of concern to the international community.[6] However, the wording does not expressly exclude isolated war crimes, such as sexual violence, from the Court's jurisdiction.[7] Article 8 essentially divides war crimes into two categories, with a further subdivision of crimes within their respective categories: the first category applies to war crimes committed in international armed conflict and enumerates the grave breaches of the 1949 Geneva Conventions and other serious violations of the laws and customs (paragraphs (a) and (b), respectively), the second category applies to war crimes that occurred in internal armed conflict and enumerates the serious violations of Article 3 common to the four 1949 Geneva Conventions and other serious violations of the laws and customs (paragraphs (c) and (e), respectively). The 'other serious violations of the laws and customs' included for both international and internal armed conflict are based on international humanitarian law treaties, in particular the 1809 and 1907 Hague Conventions and Regulations, the four 1949 Geneva Conventions and the two 1977 Additional Protocols thereto. In respect of sexual violence crimes, Article 8 explicitly lists a number of sexual violence crimes – viz. rape, sexual slavery, enforced prostitution, forced pregnancy, enforced sterilisation and any other form of sexual violence – as 'other serious violations of the laws and customs' applicable in armed conflicts of both an international and internal character (paragraphs (b) and (e), respectively). Although some of these sexual violence crimes were already included in the abovementioned international humanitarian law treaties, the ICC Statute has advanced the law on sexual violence by elaborating on these sources by adding 'new' sexual violence crimes to the war crimes' list.

For the first time in history, a treaty, that is to say, the ICC Statute, explicitly criminalises such an extensive list of sexual violence crimes as war crimes in international and non-international armed conflict, thus recognising that sexual violence crimes are among the most egregious crimes of concern to the international community as a whole. An almost identical list of sexual violence crimes can, moreover, be found in Article 7(1)(g) on crimes against humanity.[8] As mentioned in the Introduction of this study, especially the Women's Caucus for Gender Justice lobbied for their inclusion in the ICC Statute. The negotiations concerning the elements of these sexual violence

---

[5] Italics added.

[6] Von Hebel (2001), p. 110.

[7] *Ibid.*

[8] See Chapter 2 on crimes against humanity.

crimes took quite some time, almost three weeks out of the fourteen weeks allocated to the Preparatory Commission (PrepCom).[9] The crimes were first discussed in the context of war crimes, and further elaborated in the context of crimes against humanity.[10] As with other war crimes, the US and Costa Rican/Hungarian/Swiss proposals formed the starting point of discussion.[11] In addition, ICTY and ICTR case law on sexual violence as well as input from the Women's Caucus for Gender Justice played an important role in shaping the definitions of sexual violence crimes as they now stand.[12] The discussions at the PrepCom meetings 'often touched raw nerves and generally aroused great emotion'.[13] Defining the elements of the sexual violence crimes was, overall, not easy, especially because not much case law on the issue existed, or where it did, it was not always uniform, as in the case of the definition of rape in international law.[14]

The way in which sexual violence may be prosecuted as a war crime under Article 8 of the ICC Statute is the topic of this Chapter. From ICTY and ICTR case law it is evident that sexual violence need not necessarily be prosecuted under specific sexual violence provisions; sexual violence may also be brought under non-specific sexual violence crimes.[15] In light of the almost identical listing of sexual violence crimes in Article 8(2)(b)(xxi), Article 8(2)(e)(vi) and Article 7(1)(g), specific sexual violence crimes have been discussed extensively in the context of crimes against humanity (Chapter 2). In this Chapter, some remarks will be made, in the context of these war crimes provisions, on the legal bases from which the war crimes provisions on sexual violence have drawn as well as their current status in international (humanitarian) law and supranational criminal law (subsections 2.2.2 and 3.2.1).

2 War crimes in international armed conflict

Sexual violence crimes as war crimes in international armed conflict may be prosecuted under either Article 8(2)(a), as grave breaches, or Article 8(2)(b), as other serious violations of the laws and customs.

---

[9] La Haye (2001), p. 186.

[10] *Ibid.*

[11] *Ibid.* See Proposal Submitted by the United States of America, *Draft Elements of Crimes*, PCNICC/1999/DP.4/Add.2, 4 February 1999; *Proposal Submitted by Costa Rica, Hungary and Switzerland on Certain Provisions of Article 8 Para. 2 (B) of the Rome Statute of the International Criminal Court, (VIII), (X), (XIV), (XV), (XVI), (XXI), (XXII), (XXVI)*, PCNICC/1999/WGEC/DP.8, 19 July 1999.

[12] La Haye (2001), p. 186.

[13] *Ibid.*

[14] Dörmann (2004), p. 327.

[15] For a general overview of the ICTY and ICTR Judgments on sexual violence, see the Appendix.

2.1 Grave breaches of the 1949 Geneva Conventions

Article 8(2)(a) of the ICC Statute reproduces the grave breaches that are recognised in the four 1949 Geneva Conventions:

(i) Wilful killing;
(ii) Torture or inhuman treatment, including biological experiments;
(iii) Wilfully causing great suffering, or serious injury to body or health;
(iv) Extensive destruction and appropriation of property, not justified by military necessity and carried out unlawfully and wantonly;
(v) Compelling a prisoner of war or other protected person to serve in the forces of a hostile Power;
(vi) Wilfully depriving a prisoner of war or other protected person of the rights of fair and regular trial;
(vii) Unlawful deportation or transfer or unlawful confinement;
(viii) Taking of hostages.[16]

No reference is made to Articles 11(4) and 85 of 1977 Additional Protocol I, which also include grave breaches and elaborate on them.[17] Grave breaches are considered to be among the most serious violations of international humanitarian law, to which criminal liability is attached. For this reason, in the 1949 Geneva Conventions and 1977 Additional Protocol I universal jurisdiction was imposed on States for grave breaches only.[18] For violations other than grave breaches, States are under the less onerous

[16] The grave breaches provisions can be found in Article 50 of 1949 Geneva Convention I (on wounded and sick in armed forces in the field), Article 51 of 1949 Geneva Convention II (on wounded, sick and shipwrecked members of armed forces at sea), Article 130 of 1949 Geneva Convention III (on the treatment of prisoners of war) and Article 147 of 1949 Geneva Convention IV (on the protection of the civilian population).

[17] Note that grave breaches are not included in 1977 Additional Protocol II.

[18] Each provision preceding the grave breaches provision in the four 1949 Geneva Conventions contains a provision on liability. For example, Article 146 of Geneva Convention IV states: 'The High Contracting Parties undertake to enact any legislation necessary to provide effective penal sanctions for persons committing, or ordering, to be committed, any of the grave breaches ... Each High Contracting Party shall be under the obligation to search for persons alleged to have committed, or to have ordered to be committed, such grave breaches, and shall bring such persons, regardless of their nationality, before its own courts.' See also Article 49 of Geneva Convention I, Article 50 of Geneva Convention II, Article 129 of Geneva Convention III and Article 85(1) of 1977 Additional Protocol I (on the repression of grave breaches). See also the Tadić Jurisdiction Decision, para. 80: 'The grave breaches system of the Geneva Conventions establishes a twofold system: there is on the one hand an enumeration of offences that are regarded so serious as to constitute "grave breaches"; closely bound up with this enumeration a mandatory enforcement mechanism is set up, based on the concept of a duty and a right of all Contracting States to search for and try or extradite persons allegedly responsible for "grave breaches." The international armed conflict element generally attributed to the grave breaches provisions of the Geneva Conventions is merely a function of the system of universal mandatory jurisdiction that those provisions create. The international armed conflict requirement was a

obligation to 'take measures necessary for the suppression' of such acts.[19] The difference between these two categories of crimes basically comes down to, on the one hand, an obligation to prosecute (grave breaches) and, on the other hand, a right to prosecute (other violations). The distinction between grave breaches and other violations is, however, not important in the context of the ICC, because the Statute does not stipulate different consequences for these categories.[20]

Article 8(2)(a) states: 'Grave breaches of the Geneva Conventions of 12 August 1949 ... [are] any of the following acts against persons or property protected under the provisions of the relevant Geneva Convention.' Therefore, an act qualifies as a grave breach, if the act has been committed against a protected person. The ICTY has interpreted Article 4 of 1949 Geneva Convention IV on protected persons in light of present-day interethnic conflicts, stating that the provision should be given a wide scope so that a person may be accorded protected status, notwithstanding the fact that he or she is of the same nationality as his or her captors.[21] The ICC did not further clarify the meaning of protected persons and is thus free to follow ICTY case law on this point. For all grave breaches, the ICC Elements of Crimes (EoC) lists the requirements for the status of protected person and, furthermore, adds an unprecedented element, viz. that the perpetrator 'was aware of the factual circumstances that established that protected status'. Footnote 33 clarifies that the factual knowledge required by the perpetrator of the status of the victim would be limited to the knowledge that the victim belonged to an 'adverse party': knowledge of a victim's nationality is not required.

The grave breaches provisions in the 1949 Geneva Conventions, in particular Article 147 of Geneva Convention IV (protection of civilian persons in time of war), do not explicitly mention rape or any other forms of sexual violence.[22] International humanitarian law failed to recognise the specific harm women face during armed conflict, in particular sexual violence, as grave breaches. The grave breaches definition, drafted primarily by men, reflects the way in which certain groups of men experience armed conflict, such as the prohibition of compelling a protected person to serve in the forces of a hostile power.[23] Because the grave breaches provisions of the 1949 Geneva Conventions was copied into the ICTY and ICC Statutes, Article 2 of the ICTY Statute and Article 8(2)(a) of the ICC Statute do not contain the specific types of harm women

---

necessary limitation on the grave breaches system in light of the intrusion on State sovereignty that such mandatory universal jurisdiction represents. State parties to the 1949 Geneva Conventions did not want to give other States jurisdiction over serious violations of international humanitarian law committed in their internal armed conflicts – at least not the mandatory universal jurisdiction involved in the grave breaches system.'

[19] Article 49 of 1949 Geneva Convention I, Article 50 of 1949 Geneva Convention II, Article 129 of 1949 Geneva Convention III, and Article 146 of 1949 Geneva Convention IV. See also the Tadić Jurisdiction Decision, para. 80, cited in the previous footnote.

[20] Dörmann (2004), p. 128.

[21] Tadić Appeal Judgment, para. 166. Article 4 of Geneva Convention IV (on the protection of civilians) reads: 'Persons protected by the Convention are those who, ... find themselves, ... in the hands of a Party to the Conflict or Occupying Power of which they are not nationals.'

[22] Note that the grave breaches provisions in the 1977 Additional Protocol I do not mention sexual violence either.

[23] Gardam and Jarvis (2001), p. 185.

need to be protected from most of all, viz. rape, sexual slavery and other forms of sexual violence. Despite the omission of an explicit prohibition of sexual violence as a grave breach, sexual violence crimes can be prosecuted under these provisions, as is evidenced by the case law of the ICTY. According to the *Furundžija* Trial Chamber, 'rape may also amount to a grave breach of the Geneva Conventions, ... if the requisite elements are met, and may be prosecuted accordingly'.[24] Further support for treating rape and other forms of sexual violence as grave breaches is found in, *inter alia*, the 1992 *Aide-Mémoire* of the ICRC,[25] the annex to the report of the Yugoslav UN Commission of Experts,[26] the US stand on the issue[27] and the opinions expressed by several legal scholars.[28] The ICTY has even indicted some persons on charges of rape as a grave breach directly.[29] The grave breaches most applicable in terms of supranational criminal prosecution of sexual violence are stated in Article 8(2)(a)(ii) ('Torture or Inhumane Treatment, Including Biological Experiments') and in Article 8(2)(a)(iii) ('Wilfully Causing Great Suffering, or Serious Injury to Body or Health').

2.1.1 Torture or inhuman treatment, including biological experiments

In Article 8(2)(a)(ii) of the ICC Statute, 'torture or inhuman treatment, including biological experiments' are listed as grave breaches.

2.1.1.1 Torture

Torture has been outlawed under treaty law and customary international law, in times of peace and armed conflict, either international or non-international.[30] The prohibition of

---

[24] Furundžija Judgment, para. 172.

[25] ICRC *Aide-Mémoire* of 3 December 1992, cited in Meron (1993), p. 426. The ICTR *Aide-Mémoire* states that rape constitutes the grave breach of 'wilfully causing great suffering or serious injury to body or health'.

[26] Final Report of the United Nations Commission of Experts Established Pursuant to Security Council Resolution 780 (1992), *Annex II – Rape and Sexual Assault: A Legal Study*, S/1994/674/Add.2 (Vol. 1), 28 December 1994, section II. In support of the argument that rape and other forms of sexual violence should be considered to constitute grave breaches, the report refers to the fact that '"inhuman treatment" [as a grave breach] is treatment contrary to article 27 [of 1949 Geneva Convention IV, which states that protected persons are to be treated humanely], which, *inter alia*, expressly prohibits rape and other sexual assaults. Also, the enumeration of the "grave breaches" should be considered exhaustive in form only, not in substance.'

[27] Meron (1993), p. 427.

[28] See, *inter alia*, Cleiren and Tijssen (1994), p. 491; Askin (1997), pp. 308-314.

[29] *Prosecutor v. Ramush Haradinaj, Idriz Balaj and Lahi Brahimaj*, Indictment, Case No. IT-04-84-I, 4 March 2005: 'count 36: A VIOLATION OF THE LAWS OR CUSTOMS OF WAR, Rape, punishable under Articles 2 and 3 and 7(1) of the Statute of the Tribunal.'

[30] In relation to international armed conflict, torture is prohibited in each of the grave breaches provisions of the 1949 Geneva Conventions; with regard to non-international armed conflict, torture is prohibited in Common Article 3 to the 1949 Geneva Conventions. Torture was already outlawed in the Lieber Code (Articles 16 and 80) and the 1907 Hague Regulations (Article 44). In addition to the prohibition of torture in international humanitarian law, there are many

torture has furthermore acquired the status of *jus cogens*,[31] in respect of which all States have *erga omnes* obligations.[32] In the EoC, the elements of the grave breach of torture (which are similar to torture as a violation of Common Article 3 as will be discussed in subsection 3.1.1.2) are defined. The first two elements of torture read:

1. The perpetrator inflicted severe physical or mental pain or suffering upon one or more persons.
2. The perpetrator inflicted the pain or suffering for such purposes as: obtaining information or a confession, punishment, intimidation or coercion or for any reason based on discrimination of any kind.[33]

As torture was not defined in the 1949 Geneva Conventions, the PrepCom had to determine whether the definition of torture in the ICC Statute as regards crimes against humanity (Article 7(2)(e)) would also apply to the context of war crimes. The definition of torture as a crime against humanity does not contain a purposive element or an element of official capacity as laid down in Article 1(1) of the 1984 Torture Convention.[34] Delegates to the PrepCom had diverging opinions on the elements of the

---

international human rights instruments that outlaw torture, *inter alia*, the Universal Declaration of Human Rights (Article 5), the ICCPR (Article 7), the ECHR (Article 3), the ACHR (Article 5(2)) and the African Charter on Human and People's Rights (Article 5). The 1984 Torture Convention also prohibits torture, and this Convention is considered to be part of customary international law; see Furundžija Judgment, paras. 134-142, 160-162; Čelebići Judgment, para. 459. The prohibition of torture is absolute and derogation of the prohibition of torture is not permitted under any circumstances; see, *inter alia*, Article 2(2) of the 1984 Torture Convention, Article 15(2) of the ECHR, Article 4(2) of the ICCPR and Article 27(2) of the ACHR.

[31] Furundžija Judgment, paras. 153-157; Čelebići Judgment, paras. 452-454; Kunarac, Kovač and Vuković Judgment, para. 466.

[32] Furundžija Judgment, paras. 151-152.

[33] EoC, Article 8(2)(a)(ii) – War crime of torture. The elements of the war crime of torture in non-international armed conflict (Article 8(2)(c)(i)) are identical to the elements of torture in international armed conflict discussed here, but different from the elements of torture as a crime against humanity (Article 7(2)(e)). Element 1 is, however, identical to the definition of torture in the Torture Convention and to the definition of torture as a crime against humanity in the ICC Statute. In the ICTY Statute, the elements of torture under the grave breaches provision of Article 2(b) are similar to the ones set forth for torture in Common Article 3 and Article 5(f) as a crime against humanity. In the ICTR Statute, the elements of torture are similar to those in Common Article 3 and Protocol II (Article 4) and to torture as a crime against humanity (Article 3(f)).

[34] Article 1(1) of the 1984 Torture Convention reads: 'For the purpose of this Convention, the term "torture" means any act by which severe pain or suffering, whether physical or mental, is intentionally inflicted on a person for such purposes as obtaining from him or a third person information or a confession, punishing him for an act he or a third person has committed or is suspected of having committed, or intimidating or coercing him or a third person, or for any reason based on discrimination of any kind, when pain or suffering is inflicted by or at the instigation of or with the consent or acquiescence of a public official or other person acting in an official capacity. It does not include pain or suffering arising only from, inherent in or incidental

war crime of torture: some argued that a purposive and/or official capacity element was necessary to distinguish torture from the crime of inhuman treatment, whereas others felt, with reference to the case law of the European Court of Human Rights (ECtHR) on torture, that the severity of the pain or suffering inflicted should be the factor to differentiate between the two crimes.[35] The wording of the elements of the ICC war crime of torture reflects, to a certain extent, the case law of the ICTY: that is to say, the definition incorporates the purposive element by repeating the illustrative list of Article 1(1) of the 1984 Torture Convention, but the reference to official capacity has been left out.[36] It was argued that including the element of official capacity would restrict the crime of torture, particularly in internal armed conflicts involving rebel groups.[37] The *Kunarac, Kovač and Vuković* Appeals Chamber has confirmed this view in its holding that in the context of supranational criminal law official capacity is not an element of

---

to lawful sanctions'; see UN Doc. A/RES/39/46 of 10 December 1984. See Chapter 2 on the crime of torture as a crime against humanity.

[35] Dörmann (2004), p. 45. See for ECtHR case law and the level of severity of pain or suffering required, for instance, '*Ireland v. The United Kingdom*, Publications of the European Court of Human Rights, Series A: Judgments and Decisions, vol. 25, p. 66; 58 ILR 188 at 265', cited in Dörmann (2004), p. 51.

[36] Although at the time of the drafting of the EoC the ICTY had not settled the issue of official capacity completely, in the Čelebići Judgment it was already opined that 'in the context of international humanitarian law, this requirement must be interpreted to include officials of non-State parties to a conflict, in order for the prohibition to retain significance in situations of internal armed conflicts or international conflicts involving some non-State entities'; Čelebići Judgment, para. 473. The Kunarac, Kovač and Vuković Trial Chamber disposed of the official capacity element in its entirety, stating: 'The definition of torture under international humanitarian law does not comprise the same elements as the definition of torture generally applied under human rights law. In particular, the Trial Chamber is of the view that the presence of a state official or of any other authority-wielding person in the torture process is not necessary for the offence to be regarded as torture under international humanitarian law'; see Kunarac, Kovač and Vuković Judgment, para. 496; see also paras. 483-497. This view was concurred with in the Kvočka et al. Judgment, paras. 138-139, and has now been confirmed on appeal in the Kunarac, Kovač and Vuković Appeal Judgment, para. 148 ('The Trial Chamber in the present case was therefore right in taking the position that the public official requirement is not a requirement under customary international law in relation to the criminal responsibility of an individual for torture outside of the framework of the Torture Convention'). Therefore, the Kunarac, Kovač and Vuković Appeals Chamber accepted that the definition of torture in the Torture Convention reflects customary international law, but only as far as the obligation of States is concerned. Compare previous ICTY and ICTR case law, in which it was put forward that the definition laid down in Article 1(1) of the 1948 Torture Convention provides the customary law basis of the elements of torture. See Akayesu Judgment, para. 593, Čelebići Judgment, para. 459, Furundžija Judgment, paras. 161 and 472 and Furundžija Appeal Judgment, para. 111.

[37] Dörmann (2004), p. 46; La Haye (2001), p. 210. Note that the elements of the war crime of torture in non-international armed conflict are identical to the elements of torture in international armed conflict.

the crime of torture.[38] Contrary to ICTY case law, the severity of the crime is, however, no longer a factor in the EoC to distinguish torture from other forms of mistreatment.

As the war crime of torture as defined in the EoC includes the purposive element, the war crime of torture is different from torture as a crime against humanity. According to one commentator, 'no convincing argument was made to explain why the definition of torture as a war crime should be different from the one of torture as a crime against humanity'.[39] One explanation that has been given is that torture in war crimes is committed with the specific purpose of furthering the war effort.[40] As a compromise between those delegates who were in favour of retaining the purposive element and those who wanted to dispose of it, a broad and open-ended purpose element was included in the definition of the war crime of torture, as the main feature distinguishing torture from other forms of inhuman treatment.[41]

2.1.1.1.1 Severe physical or mental pain or suffering

Torture is constituted by an act or an omission giving rise to severe physical or mental pain or suffering.[42] For the purposes of the EoC, the severity of the crime as a factor distinguishing torture from other forms of mistreatment has been removed: element 1 of the crime of torture (as a grave breach and a serious violation of Common Article 3) is similar to element 1 of the crimes of inhuman treatment as a grave breach and cruel treatment as a violation of Common Article 3. By contrast, in ICTY case law, physical or mental pain or suffering that has risen to a certain threshold has been qualified as torture. It has been held that the severity of the crime is one such factor which distinguishes torture from other forms of mistreatment,[43] although the ICTY has admittedly said that, in general, it is difficult to establish when, for instance, inhuman treatment becomes torture.[44] In the *Kvočka et al.* Trial Chamber, objective and subjective examination of the severity of the harm was proposed for the purpose of determining whether torture had been committed.[45] In *Čelebići*, it was held that 'the existence of such a grey area should not be seen as an invitation to create an exhaustive

---

[38] Kunarac, Kovač and Vuković Appeal Judgment, para. 148. See also the Brđanin Judgment, paras. 488-489.

[39] Dörmann (2001), p. 128.

[40] Kittichaisaree (2001), p. 145.

[41] La Haye (2001), p. 210.

[42] See, *inter alia*, Čelebići Judgment, para. 468; Furundžija Judgment, para. 162; Kunarac, Kovač and Vuković Judgment, para. 483.

[43] Čelebići Judgment, para. 468.

[44] *Ibid.*, para. 469.

[45] Kvočka et al. Judgment, para. 143 (subjective criteria included the physical or mental effect of the treatment upon the particular victim and factors such as the victim's age, sex and state of health). See also Brđanin Judgment, para. 484 ('in assessing the seriousness of any mistreatment, the objective severity of the harm inflicted must be considered, including the nature, purpose and consistency of the acts committed. Subjective criteria, such as the physical or mental condition of the victim, the effect of the treatment and, in some cases, factors such as the victim's age, sex, state of health and position of inferiority will also be relevant in assessing the gravity of the harm').

list of acts constituting torture ... As stated by Rodley, "... a juridical definition cannot depend upon a catalogue of horrific practices; for it to do so would simply provide a challenge to the ingenuity of the torturers, not a viable legal prohibition".'[46] As an example of the evolving thinking about torture the forced observance of the repeated rape of a female friend can be mentioned, which was classified torture for the forced observer.[47] In turn, the presence of people forced to observe the rapes, particularly family members, also inflicts severe mental harm amounting to torture on the person being raped.[48] As an exhaustive list of acts that constitute torture is thus not available, nor desirable, guidance may, *inter alia*, be found in ICTY and ICTR case law.[49] However, as mentioned above the ICC EoC do not take into account the severity of the crime as a distinguishing factor, and for that reason it is questionable whether the Court will deal with the issue in the same vein as the Tribunals.

That rape and other forms of sexual violence may qualify as torture has been confirmed in ICTY and ICTR case law.[50] The recognition that sexual violence may constitute torture has been expressed by international and regional human rights organisations as well as in several United Nations reports, from which the Tribunals derived guidance when examining whether sexual violence constitutes the war crime of torture.[51] Rape satisfies element 1 of the crime of torture on the basis that 'rape causes

---

46 Čelebići Judgment, para. 469 (with reference to the Report of the Special Rapporteur, para. 105).

47 Furundžija Judgment, paras. 264-267. See also Kvočka et al. Judgment, para. 149.

48 Kvočka et al. Judgment, para. 149.

49 See, for example, the Čelebići Judgment, paras. 917-924 (beatings to the point of unconsciousness, burning a cross on a person's hand, hitting a person with shovels, suffocating a person by putting a gas mask over his head, applying corrosive powder to a person's body).

50 Akayesu Judgment, para. 597: 'Like torture, rape is used for such purposes as intimidation, degradation, humiliation, discrimination, punishment, control or destruction of a person. Like torture, rape is a violation of personal dignity, and rape in fact constitutes torture when inflicted by or at the instigation of or with the consent or acquiescence of a public official or other person acting in an official capacity.' See also the Čelebići Judgment, para. 495: 'The Trial Chamber considers the rape of any person to be a despicable act which strikes at the very core of human dignity and physical integrity. The condemnation and punishment of rape becomes all the more urgent where it is committed by, or at the instigation of, a public official, or with the consent or acquiescence of such an official. Rape causes severe pain and suffering, both physical and psychological. The psychological suffering of persons upon whom rape is inflicted may be exacerbated by social and cultural conditions and can be particularly acute and long lasting. Furthermore, it is difficult to envisage circumstances in which rape, by, or at the instigation of a public official, or with the consent or acquiescence of an official, could be considered as occurring for a purpose that does not, in some way, involve punishment, coercion, discrimination or intimidation. In the view of this Trial Chamber this is inherent in situations of armed conflict.' See also Furundžija Judgment, paras. 163 and 171; Kunarac, Kovač and Vuković Judgment, para. 655; Kvočka et al. Judgment, para. 561.

51 See, for example, the Čelebići Judgment, paras. 480-493. In these paragraphs, the Trial Chamber refers to, *inter alia,* the decision of the Inter-American Commission in the case of Fernando and Raquel Mejia v. Peru (Annual Report of the Inter-American Commission on Human Rights, Report No. 5/96, Case No. 10.970, 1 March 1996) and the decision of the ECtHR

severe pain and suffering, both physical and psychological. The psychological suffering of persons upon whom rape is inflicted may be exacerbated by social and cultural conditions and can be particularly acute and long lasting.'[52] The Appeals Chamber in the *Kunarac, Kovač and Vuković* case very strongly opined that rape and other forms of sexual violence *necessarily* inflict severe physical or mental pain or suffering in the following words:

> Generally speaking, some acts establish *per se* the suffering of those upon whom they were inflicted. Rape is obviously such an act. The Trial Chamber could only conclude that such suffering occurred even without a medical certificate. Sexual violence necessarily gives rise to severe pain or suffering, whether physical or mental, and in this way justifies its characterisation as an act of torture.[53]

Therefore, 'the assumption of the Appellants that suffering must be visible, even long after the commission of the crimes in question, is erroneous'.[54] What the Appeals Chamber meant was that 'severe pain or suffering, as required by the definition of the crime of torture, can thus be said to be established once rape has been proved, since the act of rape necessarily implies such pain or suffering'.[55] Thus, establishing the elements

---

in the case of Aydin v. Turkey (European Court of Human Rights, Reports of Judgments and Decisions, No. 50 (1997-VI)). Reference is also made to the Report of the Special Rapporteur, Mr Nigel S. Rodley, submitted pursuant to Commission on Human Rights resolution 1992/32, E/CN.4/1995/34 and the report of the United Nations Special Rapporteur on Contemporary Forms of Slavery, i.e., the Final Report submitted by Ms Gay J. McDougall, Special Rapporteur, E/CN.4/Sub.2/1998/13, 22 June 1998.

[52] Čelebići Judgment, para. 495. See also the Kunarac, Kovač and Vuković Judgment, para. 655: 'The acts of the accused caused his victims severe mental and physical pain and suffering. Rape is one of the worst sufferings a human being can inflict upon another' and the Kvočka Judgment, para. 561: '[T]hreat of rape or other forms of sexual violence undoubtedly caused severe pain and suffering ... and thus, the elements of torture are also satisfied.'

[53] Kunarac, Kovač and Vuković Appeal Judgment, para. 150 (with reference in a footnote to the 'Commission on Human Rights, Forty-eight session, Summary Record of the 21st Meeting, 11 February 1992, Doc. E/CN.4/1992, para. 35: '*Since it was clear that* rape or other forms of sexual assault against women held in detention were a particular ignominious violation of the inherent dignity and right to physical integrity of the human being, *they accordingly constituted an act of torture*' (italics added)). In a similar vein, see the Brđanin Judgment, para. 485: 'Some acts, like rape, appear by definition to meet the severity threshold [of torture].' The Kvočka Judgment is less persuasive on this point as it states that 'beatings, sexual violence, prolonged denial of sleep, food, hygiene, and medical assistance, as well as threats to torture, rape, or kill relatives were among the acts most commonly mentioned [by the UN Special Rapporteur on Torture, human rights bodies, and legal scholars] as those *likely* to constitute torture. Mutilation of body parts would be an example of acts *per se* constituting torture' (italics added). See Kvočka et al. Judgment, para. 144.

[54] Kunarac, Kovač and Vuković Appeal Judgment, para. 150. Upheld in the Brđanin Judgment, para. 484.

[55] Kunarac, Kovač and Vuković Appeal Judgment, para. 151. See also the Brđanin Judgment, para. 485.

of the crime of rape automatically fulfils the first element of torture, that is, severe pain or suffering, whether physical or mental. Other forms of sexual violence that may qualify for torture, recognised in ICTY case law, include threats of sexual mutilation,[56] the fears and threats inherent to circumstances of detention where rapes are ongoing and victims are extremely vulnerable to the whim of their captors,[57] and the forced observance of rape committed against a friend or relative.[58] It is noteworthy that the Tribunal in *Čelebići* held that 'whenever rape and other forms of sexual violence meet the aforementioned criteria [on prohibited purposes and official capacity], then they shall constitute torture, in the same manner as any other acts that meet this criteria [sic]'.[59] As explained above, it is nowadays generally understood that under customary international law the requirement of an official link cannot be held to constitute an element of the crime of torture within the context of an armed conflict.[60]

2.1.1.1.2 Prohibited purposes

Element 2 of the war crime of torture in the EoC refers to the same purposes as contained in Article 1(1) of the 1984 Torture Convention, that is to say, 'obtaining information or a confession, punishment, intimidation or coercion or for any reason based on discrimination of any kind'. The wording 'for such purposes as' discloses that other purposes than the ones mentioned may be found in order to convict someone of torture. Similarly, the general trend in ICTY case law is that the list of purposes be retained and that it is not exhaustive.[61] In the *Furundžija* case, the Trial Chamber added 'humiliation' to the list of prohibited purposes, an addition which was held to be warranted by the general spirit of international humanitarian law, viz. to safeguard human dignity.[62] Because rape frequently involves gender-based discrimination, gender discrimination was held to constitute a prohibited purpose with regard to torture in the

---

[56] Furundžija Appeal Judgment, para. 114.
[57] Kvočka Judgment, para. 561.
[58] Furundžija Judgment, paras. 264-267.
[59] Čelebići Judgment, para. 496.
[60] Kunarac, Kovač and Vuković Appeal Judgment, para. 148.
[61] See Čelebići Judgment, paras. 459, 470, 472; Furundžija Judgment, para. 162; Furundžija Appeal Judgment, para. 111. But see the Kunarac, Kovač and Vuković Judgment, para. 485 ('The Trial Chamber is satisfied that the following purposes have become part of customary international law: (a) obtaining information or a confession, (b) punishing, intimidating or coercing the victim or a third person, (c) discriminating, on any ground, against the victim or a third person. *There are some doubts as to whether other purposes have come to be recognised under customary international law.* The issue does not need to be resolved here, because the conduct of the accused is appropriately subsumable under the above-mentioned purposes' (italics added)). It should be noted that the purposes listed in the ICRC Commentary to Article 147 of the Fourth Geneva Convention were far more restricted: here, torture was defined as 'the infliction of suffering on a person to obtain from that person, or from another person, confessions or information' (Pictet (1958), p. 598).
[62] Furundžija Judgment, para. 162; confirmed in Furundijza Appeal Judgment, para. 111. See also Naletilić Judgment, para. 338; Semanza Judgment and Sentence, para. 343.

Čelebići case.[63] In this regard, the *Čelebići* Trial Chamber referred to the work of the Committee on the Elimination of Discrimination against Women (CEDAW) that violence directed against a woman, because she is a woman, is a form of discrimination.[64] The Trial Chamber furthermore pointed out that rapes taking place in a detention camp were often committed with the 'purpose of seeking to intimidate not only the victim but also other inmates, by creating an atmosphere of fear and powerlessness'.[65] In the *Kunarac, Kovač and Vuković* case, the Trial Chamber established that the rapes were committed on the basis of ethnicity and gender,[66] but the Appeals Chamber only stressed ethnicity as the basis of the discrimination.[67] The *Kvočka et al.* Trial Chamber concurred with the *Furundžija* and *Čelebići* Judgments by upholding humiliation and gender discrimination as possible purposes for which torture may be committed.[68] In contrast, the Trial Chamber in the *Krnojelac* case denied that 'humiliation' is a purpose of torture acknowledged under customary international law.[69] The UN Special Rapporteur on Contemporary Forms of Slavery opined that 'in many cases the discrimination prong of the definition of torture in the Torture Convention provides an additional basis for prosecuting rape and sexual violence as torture'.[70] And, as stated in *Čelebići*, 'it is difficult to envisage circumstances in which rape, by, or at the instigation of a public official, or with the consent or acquiescence of an official, could be considered as occurring for a purpose that does not, in some way, involve punishment, coercion, discrimination or intimidation. In the view of this Trial Chamber this is inherent in situations of armed conflict.'[71] It is argued that such purposes are inherent in situations of armed conflict even without the involvement of a person in an official capacity.

It is presumed that the aforementioned purposes are also prohibited when a perpetrator pursues them for purely private motives or reasons, which may in particular be true in cases of rape and other sexual assaults.[72] While rape and other forms of sexual

[63] Čelebići Judgment, para. 493.

[64] *Ibid.*

[65] *Ibid.*, para. 941.

[66] Kunarac, Kovač and Vuković Judgment, paras. 654, 711. On appeal, the Chamber stressed the fact that the victims were Muslim, and does not expressly refer to the fact that in particular the Muslim women and girls were the victims of sexual violence. See Kunarac, Kovač and Vuković Appeal Judgment, para. 154.

[67] On appeal, the Chamber stressed the fact that the victims were Muslim and did not expressly refer to the fact that in particular the Muslim women and girls were the victims of sexual violence. See Kunarac, Kovač and Vuković Appeal Judgment, para. 154.

[68] Kvočka Judgment, para. 154.

[69] Krnojelac Judgment, para. 186. See also the Kunarac, Kovač and Vuković Judgment, para. 485, in which doubts are expressed about other purposes than the ones contained in the Torture Convention.

[70] Čelebići Judgment, para. 493 (with reference to the Final Report submitted by Ms Gay J. McDougall, Special Rapporteur, *Contemporary Forms of Slavery: Systematic Rape, Sexual Slavery and Slavery-like Practices during Armed Conflict*, E/CN.4/Sub.2/1998/13, 22 June 1998, para. 55).

[71] Čelebići Judgment, para. 495.

[72] *Ibid.*, para. 471.

violence may otherwise be labelled 'private' and may be outside the scope of torture, rape and sexual assaults 'could meet the purposive requirements of torture as, during armed conflicts, the purposive elements of intimidation, coercion, punishment or discrimination can often be integral components of behaviour, thus bringing the relevant conduct within the definition'.[73] Accordingly, the Trial Chamber in the *Čelebići* case held that the conduct comprising torture need not be perpetrated solely for a prohibited purpose, but that the prohibited purpose simply be part of the accused's motivation.[74] According to the *Kunarac, Kovač and Vuković* Appeals Chamber, 'if one prohibited purpose is fulfilled by the conduct, the fact that such conduct was also intended to achieve a non-listed purpose (even one of a sexual nature) is immaterial'.[75]

The *mens rea* of element 1 of torture is covered by Article 30 of the ICC Statute. Therefore, the perpetrator intended to inflict 'severe physical or mental pain or suffering upon one or more persons' (element 1). According to the General Introduction to the EoC, 'it is not necessary that the perpetrator personally completed a particular value judgement' in relation to the severity of the pain or suffering.[76] According to ICTY case law, the conduct must be 'deliberate and not accidental'.[77] Furthermore, the Appeals Chamber in the *Kunarac, Kovač and Vuković* case held that

> ... even if the perpetrator's motivation is entirely sexual, it does not follow that the perpetrator does not have the intent to commit an act of torture or that his conduct does not cause severe pain or suffering, whether physical or mental, since such pain or suffering is a likely and logical consequence of his conduct. In view of the definition, it is important to establish whether a perpetrator intended to act in a way which, in the normal course of events, would cause severe pain or suffering, whether physical or mental, to his victims.[78]

Furthermore, the perpetrator intended to inflict 'the pain or suffering for such purposes as: obtaining information or a confession, punishment, intimidation or coercion or for any reason based on discrimination of any kind' (element 2).

2.1.1.1.3 ICTY case law

Sexual violence has been charged as the grave breach of torture in several ICTY cases. To date, two individuals have been convicted of rape as the grave breach of torture, viz. Delić and Brđanin. Delić, deputy commander of the Čelebići camp (central Bosnia and Herzegovina) from approximately May 1992 to November 1992, was convicted of the rape of two women as the grave breach of torture (Article 2(b) ICTY Statute). The same facts served for a finding of guilt under Article 3 of the ICTY Statute, as recognised by Common Article 3(1)(a) (torture) of the 1949 Geneva Conventions. Delić was not convicted of cruel treatment under Article 3 of the ICTY Statute, as recognised by

---

[73] *Ibid.*

[74] *Ibid*, para. 470. See also Kvočka Judgment, para. 153; Kunarac, Kovač and Vuković Appeal Judgment, para. 155.

[75] Kunarac, Kovač and Vuković Appeal Judgment, para. 155.

[76] Paragraph 4 of the General Introduction to the EoC.

[77] Čelebići Judgment, para. 468.

[78] Kunarac, Kovač and Vuković Appeal Judgment, para. 153.

Common Article 3(1)(a) of the 1949 Geneva Conventions, as cruel treatment was charged in the alternative to torture under Article 3 of the ICTY Statute, as recognised by Common Article 3(1)(a). However, on appeal the charges of torture under Article 3, as recognised by Common Article 3(1)(a) of the 1949 Geneva Conventions, were dismissed, as the grave breach of torture under Article 2 of the ICTY Statute was considered more specific than torture under Article 3 of the ICTY Statute.[79] Summarising, Delić was convicted of the grave breach of torture twice (the repeated rape of two women).

In particular, Delić was convicted of the repeated rape of a female detainee, Ms Ćećez, and the repeated rape of another female detainee, Ms Antic, whom he raped both vaginally and anally over a period of six weeks. Ms Ćećez (43 years old at the time) was taken to Čelebići prison camp on 27 May 1992 and was forced to stay there until 31 August 1992. According to the Trial Chamber:

> Upon her arrival at the prison-camp she was taken by a driver, Mr. Dzajic, to a room where a man with a crutch was waiting, whom she subsequently identified as Hazim Delic. Another man subsequently entered the room. Ms. Cecez was interrogated by Mr. Delic, who asked her about the whereabouts of her husband and slapped her. She was then taken to a second room with three men, including Mr. Delic. Hazim Delic who was in uniform and carrying a stick, then ordered her to take her clothes off. He then partially undressed her, put her face down on the bed and penetrated her vagina with his penis. He subsequently turned her over on to her back, took off the remainder of her clothes and again penetrated her vagina with his penis. During this time, Mr. Dzajic was lying on another bed in the same room and the other man present was standing guard at the door of the room. Mr. Delic told her that the reason she was there was her husband, and that she would not be there if he was.[80]

Ms Ćećez was also subjected to multiple rape on the third night of her detention in the prison camp and to further rape in July 1992.[81] The Trial Chamber considered that 'acts of vaginal penetration by the penis under circumstances that were coercive, quite clearly constitute rape', which were intentionally committed by Delić, 'an official of the Bosnian authorities running the prison-camp'.[82] The Trial Chamber furthermore held that

> … there can be no question that these rapes caused severe mental pain and suffering to Ms. Cecez. The effects of the rapes that she suffered at the hands of Hazim Delic are readily

---

[79] Čelebići Appeal Judgment, para. 427 (see counts 18, 19, 21 and 22). See in particular paras. 401-426 of the Čelebići Appeal Judgment for the discussion of cumulative convictions and Chapter 6 on sentencing.

[80] Čelebići Judgment, para. 937.

[81] *Ibid.*, para. 938.

[82] *Ibid.*, para. 940. Note that the Čelebići Trial Chamber accepted the definition of rape as put forward in the Akayesu case. For a discussion of the definition of rape, see Chapter 2 on crimes against humanity.

> apparent from her own testimony and included living in a state of constant fear and depression, suicidal tendencies, and exhaustion, both mental and physical.[83]

Thus, the Trial Chamber found that the elements of the crime of rape easily satisfied the elements of the crime of torture. The purposes of the rapes committed by Delić were held, *inter alia*, 'to obtain information about the whereabouts of Ms. Cecez's husband who was considered an armed rebel; to punish her for her inability to provide information about her husband; to coerce and intimidate her into providing such information; and to punish her for the acts of her husband'.[84] These rapes were not only intimidating Ms Ćećez, but also all other detainees, thus creating 'an atmosphere of fear and powerlessness'.[85] In addition, the violence suffered by Ms Ćećez in the form of rape was inflicted upon her because she was a woman.[86] This, the Trial Chamber found, 'represents a form of discrimination which constitutes a prohibited purpose for the offence of torture'.[87]

The other woman who had to endure sexual violence at the hands of Delić was Ms Antic, a Bosnian Serb woman, who was 44 years old on 15 June 1992 when she was taken to the Čelebići prison camp and from which she was released on 31 August 1992. In support of convicting Delić of rape as the grave breach of torture with regard to Ms Antic, the Trial Chamber found that:

> ... Ms. Antic was raped for the first time on the night of her arrival in the prison- camp. On this occasion she was called out of Building A and brought to Hazim Delic in Building B, who was wearing a uniform. He began to interrogate her and told her that if she did not do whatever he asked she would be sent to another camp or she would be shot. Mr. Delic ordered her to take her clothes off, threatened her and ignored her crying pleas for him not to touch her. He pointed a rifle at her while she took her clothes off and ordered her to lie on a bed. Mr. Delic then raped her by penetrating her vagina with his penis, he ejaculated on the lower part of her stomach and continued to threaten and curse her.[88]
>
> The second rape occurred when Hazim Delic came to Building A and ordered Ms. Antic to go to Building B to wash herself. After doing so, she was led to the same room in which she was first raped, where Delic, who had a pistol and a rifle and was in uniform, was sitting on a desk. She started crying once again out of fear. He ordered her to take her clothes off. She kept telling him that she was sick and asking him not to touch her. Out of fear that he would kill her she complied with his orders. Mr. Delic told her to get on the bed and to turn around and kneel. After doing so he penetrated her anus with his penis while she screamed from pain. He was unable to penetrate her fully and she started to bleed. Mr. Delic then turned her around and penetrated her vagina with his penis and ejaculated on her lower

---

[83] *Ibid.*, para. 942.
[84] *Ibid.*, para. 941.
[85] *Ibid.*
[86] *Ibid.*
[87] *Ibid.*
[88] *Ibid*, para. 958.

> abdomen. After the rape Ms. Antic continued crying, felt very ill and experienced bleeding from her anus, which she treated with a compress, and was provided with tranquillisers.[89]
>
> The third rape occurred in Building A. It was daylight when Hazim Delic came in, armed with hand grenades, a pistol and rifle. He threatened her and she again said that she was a sick woman and asked him not to touch her. He ordered her to undress and get on the bed. She did so under pressure and threat. Mr. Delic then pulled his trousers down to his boots and raped her by penetrating her vagina with his penis. He then ejaculated on her abdomen.[90]

Again, the Trial Chamber found that the *actus reus* of rape (acts of vaginal penetration by the penis and anal penetration by the penis, under circumstances that were undoubtedly coercive) and the *mens rea* of rape (rape was intentionally committed) necessarily fulfilled the elements of torture. The Trial Chamber held that

> ... there can be no question that these rapes caused severe mental and physical pain and suffering to Ms. Antic. The effects of the rapes that she suffered at the hands of Hazim Delic, including the extreme pain of anal penetration and subsequent bleeding, the severe psychological distress evidenced by the victim while being raped under circumstance[s] where Mr. Delic was armed and threatening her life, and the general depression of the victim, evidenced by her constant crying, the feeling that she was going crazy and the fact that she was treated with tranquilizers, demonstrate most emphatically the severe pain and suffering that she endured.[91]

The purpose of these rapes was to intimidate, coerce and punish Ms Antic.[92] At least with respect to the first rape, Delić's purpose was to obtain information from Ms Antic, as it was committed in the context of interrogation.[93] In addition, the violence suffered by Ms Antic in the form of rape was inflicted upon her by Delić because of her womanhood, a form of discrimination which constitutes a prohibited purpose for the offence of torture.[94]

The other case mentioned above which resulted in a conviction for torture as a grave breach by means of sexual violence was the *Brđanin* case. Brđanin, elected First Vice-President of the Association of the Bosanska Krajina Municipalities Assembly in 1991 and appointed President of the Autonomous Region of Krajina (ARK) Crisis Staff in 1992, was found guilty of torture as a grave breach because he aided and abetted members of the Bosnian Serb forces in the commission of, among other crimes, sexual violence crimes amounting to torture in Keraterm, Trnopolje and Omarska camps (Preijdor) as well as in Teslić municipality.[95] In the camps in the Preijdor area, many women were singled out for rape by the commander, guards and soldiers (from outside

---

[89] *Ibid.*, para. 960.
[90] *Ibid.*, para. 961.
[91] *Ibid.*, para. 964.
[92] *Ibid.*, para. 963.
[93] *Ibid.*
[94] *Ibid.*
[95] Brđanin Judgment, paras. 535, 538.

the camp) because they were Muslim women.[96] The purpose of the rapes was therefore to discriminate the detainees on the basis of their gender and ethnicity. The threat of rape (an elderly Bosnian Muslim man was forced to rape a female detainee and was killed afterwards) was also found to constitute sexual assault *vis-à-vis* a female detainee.[97] The following account is from a Bosnian Muslim woman in the Trnopolje camp, who gave testimony before the Tribunal about what had happened to her. Her account was summarised in the Judgment as follows:

> In August 1992, Slobodan Kuruzovic, the commander of Trnopolje camp, personally arranged for a Bosnian Muslim woman to be detained in the same house in which he had his office. During the first night, Kuruzovic entered her room with a pistol and a knife. He took his clothes off and told the woman that he wanted to see 'how Muslim women fuck'. She replied 'You better kill me.' When the woman started screaming, Kuruzovic said 'You are screaming in vain. There's nobody here who can help you.' He started raping her, and when she started screaming, Kuruzovic warned her: 'You better keep quiet. Did you see all these soldiers standing outside? They will all take their turns on you.' He left saying 'See you tomorrow'. The woman was bleeding and spent the whole night crying, wanting to kill herself. Kuruzovic raped that woman nearly every night for about a month. On two occasions, he stabbed her shoulder and her leg with his knife because she resisted against being raped.[98]

The woman thus had to endure repeated rape, for the duration of about one month. That she was singled out as a Muslim woman was clearly expressed in the words of the commander of the camp when he said that he wanted to see 'how Muslim women fuck'. From July to October 1992, a number of Bosnian Muslim women were raped by members of the Bosnian Serb police and the Bosnian Serb Army (VRS) in Teslic municipality. The Trial Chamber found all these rapes to be 'intrinsically discriminatory against these women'.[99] These rapes 'constituted severe pain and suffering amounting to torture, inflicted intentionally on the victims, who were all non-combatants'.[100]

2.1.1.2 Inhuman treatment

Apart from torture, 'inhuman treatment, including biological experiments' is included in Article 8(2)(a)(ii) of the ICC Statute as a grave breach of the 1949 Geneva Conventions. In the EoC, the first element of the war crime of inhuman treatment reads:

> 1. The perpetrator inflicted severe physical or mental pain or suffering upon one or more persons.[101]

---

[96] *Ibid.*, paras. 512-518.
[97] *Ibid.*, para. 516.
[98] *Ibid.*, para. 513.
[99] *Ibid.*, para. 523.
[100] *Ibid.*, para. 524.
[101] EoC, Article 8(2)(a)(ii) – War crime of inhumane treatment. In the ICTY Statute, the elements of inhuman treatment in Article 2(b) are the same as those of inhumane acts in Article 5(i) and the breach of the obligation to provide 'humane treatment' contained in Common Article 3 of the

This element is identical to element 1 of the crime of torture discussed above, and therefore the only factor distinguishing between torture and inhuman treatment is that of one purpose or more purposes. Although the case law of the ICTY suggests that the difference between the two crimes can also be found in the severity of the crime, in the ICC EoC this view is abandoned by the introduction of the aspect that the perpetrator inflicted 'severe' physical or mental pain or suffering for both torture and inhuman treatment. In *Čelebići*, inhuman treatment had been defined as 'an intentional act or omission, that is an act which, judged objectively, is deliberate and not accidental, which causes *serious* mental or physical suffering or injury or constitutes a serious attack on human dignity'.[102] Element 1 of the grave breach of inhuman treatment is furthermore identical to element 1 of the serious violation of Common Article 3 of cruel treatment, as will be discussed below. The *mens rea* of inhuman treatment is covered by Article 30 of the ICC Statute. The perpetrator intended to inflict severe physical or mental pain or suffering upon one or more persons (element 1). According to the General Introduction to the EoC, 'it is not necessary that the perpetrator personally completed a particular value judgement' in relation to the severity of the pain or suffering.[103]

Mucić, Tadić, and Blaškić have all been convicted of sexual violence conduct as inhuman treatment under Article 2(b) of the ICTY Statute, which includes acts of forced fellatio, sexual mutilation (biting off a testicle) and rapes. Mucić, who was the commander of the Čelebići prison camp from approximately May to November 1992, was convicted of the grave breach of inhuman treatment (and cruel treatment under Article 3 of the ICTY Statute, as recognised by Common Article 3(1)(a) of the 1949 Geneva Conventions on the basis of the same facts) for failing his command responsibility when one of his subordinates, Esad Landžo, forced two brothers to perform fellatio on each other in the full view of the other detainees.[104] The *Čelebići* Trial Chamber established that Esad Landžo had ordered the two brothers to remove their trousers and to kneel down upon which one brother had to take the other brother's penis into his mouth for about two to three minutes.[105] The Trial Chamber held that forced fellatio 'constituted, at least, a fundamental attack on their human dignity', which merited prosecution under Article 2(b) and Article 3 of the ICTY Statute.[106] The Trial Chamber further noted that this act 'could constitute rape for which liability could have been found if pleaded in the appropriate manner'.[107] On appeal, only the conviction for the grave breach of inhuman treatment was upheld: the conviction for cruel treatment

Geneva Conventions. Inhuman or degrading treatment is also prohibited in a number of human rights treaties, *inter alia*, the ICCPR (Article 7), ECHR (Article 3), ACHR (Article 5) and CAT (Article 1).

[102] Čelebići Judgment, paras. 543, 544 (italics added).

[103] Paragraph 4 of the General Introduction to the EoC.

[104] Čelebići Judgment, para. 1066.

[105] *Ibid.*, para. 1065.

[106] *Ibid.*, para. 1066.

[107] *Ibid.*

based on the same conduct was dismissed because the grave breach of inhuman treatment was considered to be more specific.[108]

The *Tadić* Appeals Chamber overturned the Trial Chamber's finding that the accused was not guilty of the grave breach of torture or inhumane treatment under Article 2(b) of the ICTY Statute (Count 8) in relation to forcing two male prisoners, G and H, to commit oral sexual acts on Harambašić and forcing one of them to sexually mutilate Harambašić, conduct which took place in the Omarska camp (Opština Prijedor, north-western Bosnia Herzegovina).[109] On the basis of the evidence it was established that witness H was ordered to lick Harambasic's naked bottom and G 'to suck his penis and then to bite his testicles'.[110] This took place while a group of men in uniform was watching, shouting to bite harder.[111] Thereupon, 'Witness H was threatened with a knife that both his eyes would be cut out if he did not hold Fikret Harambasic's mouth closed to prevent him from screaming; G was then made to lie between the naked Fikret Harmabasic's legs and, while the latter struggled, hit and bite his genitals. G then bit off one of Fikret Harambasic's testicles and spat it out and was told he was free to leave.'[112] Harambašić has not been seen since. Tadić, a former Serbian camp guard at, amongst others, Omarska camp, was convicted under Article 7(1) because he aided and abetted the commission of these sexual violence crimes.[113] On the basis of the same facts, Tadić had already been convicted of cruel treatment as a violation of the laws or customs of war (count 10) and inhumane acts as a crime against humanity (count 11) by the Trial Chamber.[114] On appeal, he was additionally convicted of the grave breach of torture or inhuman treatment (count 8), as mentioned above, and the grave breach of wilfully causing great suffering or serious injury to body or health.[115]

In the last case to be discussed here, the *Blaškić* case, the Trial Chamber found that Blaškić, a former General of the Croatian Defence Council (HVO) armed forces, had to have been aware of the rapes that occurred in Rotilj village (Kiseljak municipality) and Dubravica Primary School (Vitez municipality) against Bosnian Muslim women by the HVO soldiers and military police (over which he had effective control) and did not take the necessary and/or reasonable measures required to prevent or punish the perpetrators.[116] For this conduct, the Trial Chamber found Blaškić guilty of inhuman treatment as a grave breach under Article 2(b) and cruel treatment as a violation of the laws or customs of war under Article 3(a).[117] On appeal, in light of the cumulative

---

[108] Čelebići Appeal Judgment, para. 427 (counts 44 and 45). See paras. 401-426 of the Čelebići Appeal Judgment for the discussion on cumulative convictions and Chapter 6 on sentencing.

[109] Tadić Appeal Judgment, para. 171. Whereas the Trial Chamber had ruled that the grave breaches regime of the 1949 Geneva Conventions did not apply, this was overturned by the Appeals Chamber, and thus count 8 was held to be proved.

[110] Tadić Judgment, para. 206.

[111] *Ibid.*

[112] *Ibid.*

[113] *Ibid.*, paras. 237, 730.

[114] *Ibid.*, paras. 726 and 730, and p. 300.

[115] Tadić Appeal Judgment, paras. 171, 327. According to the Tadić Appeals Chamber, the Trial Chamber had erred in its finding that the grave breaches regime did not apply.

[116] Blaškić Judgment, paras. 692, 695, 732-734.

[117] *Ibid.*, VI Disposition.

conviction principle, the grave breach of inhuman treatment was upheld and the violation of the laws or customs of war of cruel treatment dismissed.[118]

2.1.2 Wilfully causing great suffering, or serious injury to body or health

In Article 8(2)(a)(iii) of the ICC Statute, 'wilfully causing great suffering, or serious injury to body or health' is included in the list of grave breaches of the 1949 Geneva Conventions. The EoC contains an almost exact copy of the description of the crime:

1. The perpetrator caused great physical or mental pain or suffering to, or serious injury to body or health of, one or more persons.[119]

In the *Čelebići* case, the Trial Chamber considered that the crime of 'wilfully causing great suffering or serious injury to body or health constitutes an act or omission that is intentional, being an act which, judged objectively, is deliberate and not accidental, which causes serious mental or physical suffering or injury'.[120] The Trial Chamber furthermore held that 'it covers those acts that do not meet the purposive requirements for the offence of torture, although clearly all acts constituting torture could also fall within the ambit of this offence'.[121] The difference between the grave breach of wilfully causing great suffering or serious injury to body or health and the grave breach of inhuman treatment was explained during the *Kordić and Čerkez* case: 'This crime [wilfully causing great suffering or serious injury to body or health] is distinguished from that of inhuman treatment in that it requires a showing of serious mental or physical injury. Thus, acts where the resultant harm relates solely to an individual's human dignity are not included within this offence.'[122] However, the EoC does not seem to incorporate 'human dignity' as an element of the crime of inhuman treatment. The ICC element of the war crime of wilfully causing great suffering or serious injury to body or health incorporated the additional element 'physical or mental' as put forward in the *Čelebići* description of 'wilfully causing great suffering or serious injury to body or health'. The term was only linked to pain or suffering, while the *Čelebići* Trial Chamber also linked it to 'injury'. Some delegates found it, however, difficult to conceive of 'mental injury'.[123] The 1992 *Aide-Mémoire* of the ICRC specifically cited the offence of 'wilfully causing great suffering or serious injury to body and health' as a legal basis for prosecuting rape.[124] The *mens rea* of 'wilfully causing great suffering or serious injury to body and health' requires that the perpetrator intended or consciously accepted to cause great physical or mental pain or suffering to, or serious injury to body or health of, one or more persons (element 1).

The grave breach of 'wilfully causing great suffering, or serious injury to body or health' has been found to cover sexual violence conduct in the *Čelebići* and *Tadić* cases,

[118] Blaškić Appeal Judgment, paras. 633-634.
[119] EoC, Article 8(2)(a)(iii) – War crime of wilfully causing great suffering.
[120] Čelebići Judgment, para. 511. See also Kordić Judgment, para. 245.
[121] Čelebići Judgment, para. 511; also paras. 442-443, 1040.
[122] Kordić and Čerkez Judgment, para. 245.
[123] Dörmann (2001), p. 131.
[124] ICRC *Aide-Mémoire* of 3 December 1992, cited in Meron (1993), p. 426.

and includes such conduct as forced oral sex and sexual mutilation by biting off testicles or by burning a victim by means of a fuse cord tied around the body in the genital area. The accused, Mucić, who was the commander of the Čelebići prison camp from approximately May to November 1992, was found guilty of the grave breach of 'wilfully causing great suffering or serious injury to body or health' (as well as of cruel treatment under Article 3 of the ICTY Statute on the basis of the same facts) as a superior, because his subordinate, Landžo, tied a burning fuse cord around the body of a detainee, Vukasin Mrkajic, in the genital area.[125] When the victim was subsequently forced to put back on his trousers, he set light to the fuse, and was forced to run around between rows of prisoners, screaming from the pain of the burning fuse. As a result, he developed blisters filled with liquid, which later became open wounds, for which he was never given any medical treatment. On appeal, the grave breach of wilfully causing great suffering or serious injury to body or health was upheld and the cruel treatment under Article 3 of the ICTY Statute dismissed.[126] As far as Tadić is concerned, the *Tadić* Appeals Chamber overturned the Trial Chamber's judgment that Tadić was not guilty under Article 7(1) of 'wilfully causing great suffering or serious injury to body or health' as a grave breach under Article 2(b) of the ICTY Statute (Count 9) in relation to forcing two male prisoners to commit oral sexual acts on another prisoner, Harambasic, and forcing one male prisoner to mutilate the other prisoner by biting off one of his testicles.[127] On the basis of this sexual violence conduct, Tadić has been cumulatively convicted under cruel treatment (Article 3 ICTY Statute), inhumane acts (Article 5(i) ICTY Statute), both in first instance, and torture or inhuman treatment (Article 2(b) ICTY Statute), and, as discussed here, wilfully causing great suffering or serious injury to body or health (Article 2(c) ICTY Statute), both on appeal.

2.2 Other serious violations of the laws and customs applicable in international armed conflict

Other serious violations of the laws and customs applicable in international armed conflict which cover sexual violence prosecutions are included in Article 8(2)(b)(xxi), 'Committing outrages upon personal dignity, in particular humiliating and degrading treatment' and, most of all, Article 8(2)(b)(xxii), which expressly lists sexual violence crimes as war crimes in and of themselves. It should, moreover, be mentioned here that, although several subparagraphs of Article 8 frequently concern or affect women, these subparagraphs are generally not applicable in terms of sexual violence prosecutions at the supranational criminal law level.[128]

---

[125] Čelebići Judgment, paras. 1038-1040, 1046-1047, 1285. Note that there was insufficient evidence to convict Mucić for the same act allegedly committed against another detainee, Dusko Bendo. See Čelebići Judgment, para. 1045.

[126] Čelebići Appeal Judgment, para. 427 (counts 38 and 39). For a discussion on cumulative convictions, see paras. 401-426 and Chapter 6 on sentencing.

[127] Tadić Appeal Judgment, para. 171. See for a more elaborate description of the facts the preceding subsection.

[128] See Article 8(2)(b)(i) ('Intentionally directing attacks against the civilian population as such or against individual civilians not taking direct part in hostilities'); Article 8(2)(b)(ii) ('Intentionally directing attacks against civilian objects, that is, objects which are not military objectives');

2.2.1 Committing outrages upon personal dignity, in particular humiliating and degrading treatment

Article 8(2)(b)(xxi) of the ICC Statute prohibits 'committing outrages upon personal dignity, in particular humiliating and degrading treatment' as a serious violation of the laws and customs applicable in international armed conflict. In the EoC the first two elements of the crime read:

> 1. The perpetrator humiliated, degraded or otherwise violated the dignity of one or more persons.[49]
> 2. The severity of the humiliation, degradation or other violation was of such degree as to be generally recognized as an outrage upon personal dignity.[129]
>
> [49] For this crime, 'persons' can include dead persons. It is understood that the victim need not personally be aware of the existence of the humiliation or degradation or other violation. This element takes into account relevant aspects of the cultural background of the victim.

The elements are identical to those of Article 8(2)(c)(ii) – 'Committing outrages upon personal dignity, in particular humiliating and degrading treatment' – as a violation of Common Article 3 in non-international armed conflict. In light of convictions for sexual violence conduct as outrages upon personal dignity under Article 3 of the ICTY Statute, as recognised by Common Article 3 of the 1949 Geneva Conventions, the war crime of 'outrages upon personal dignity' is discussed in subsection 3.1.2 below.

Article 8(2)(b)(iv) ('Intentionally launching an attack in the knowledge that such attack will cause incidental loss of life or injury to civilians or damage to civilian objects or widespread, long-term and severe damage to the natural environment which would be clearly excessive in relation to the concrete and direct overall military advantage anticipated'); Article 8(2)(b)(v) ('Attacking or bombarding, by whatever means, towns, villages, dwellings or buildings which are undefended and which are not military objectives'); Article 8(2)(b)(viii) ('The transfer, directly or indirectly, by the Occupying Power of parts of its own civilian population into the territory it occupies, or the deportation or transfer of all or parts of the population of the occupied territory within or outside this territory'); Article 8(2)(b)(x) ('Subjecting persons who are in the power of an adverse party to physical mutilation or to medical or scientific experiments of any kind which are neither justified by the medical, dental or hospital treatment of the person concerned nor carried out in his or her interest, and which cause death to or seriously endanger the health of such person or persons'); Article 8(2)(b)(xi) ('Killing or wounding treacherously individuals belonging to the hostile nation or army'); Article 8(2)(b)(xvi) ('Pillaging a town or place, even when taken by assault'); Article 8(2)(b)(xxiii) ('Utilizing the presence of a civilian or other protected person to render certain points, areas or military forces immune from military operations'); Article 8(2)(b)(xxv) ('Intentionally using starvation of civilians as a method of warfare by depriving them of objects indispensable to their survival, including wilfully impeding relief supplies as provided for under the Geneva Conventions') and Article 8(2)(b)(xxvi) ('Conscripting or enlisting children under the age of fifteen years into the national armed forces or using them to participate actively in hostilities').

[129] EoC, Article 8(2)(b)(xxi) – War crime of outrages upon personal dignity.

2.2.2 Committing rape, sexual slavery, enforced prostitution, forced pregnancy, as defined in Article 7(2)(f), enforced sterilisation, or any other form of sexual violence also constituting a grave breach of the 1949 Geneva Conventions

There is no treaty precedent in international (humanitarian) law prohibiting as many sexual violence crimes as war crimes in international armed conflict as are laid down in Article 8(2)(b)(xxii) of the ICC Statute so explicitly. The precedents prohibiting sexual violence crimes in international armed conflicts explicitly are Article 44 of the 1863 Lieber Code, Article 27(2)(e) of 1949 Geneva Convention IV and Articles 75(2)(b) and 76(1) of 1977 Additional Protocol I. An implicit prohibition of rape can, moreover, be found in Article 46 of 1907 Hague Convention IV that provides for the respect for 'family honour and rights'.[130] Article 44 of the 1863 Lieber Code reads, in part: 'All wanton violence committed against persons in the invaded country, ... *all rape*, wounding, maiming, or killing of such inhabitants, are prohibited under the penalty of death';[131] Article 27(2)(e) of 1949 Geneva Convention IV reads: 'Women shall be especially protected against any attack on their honour, in particular against *rape, enforced prostitution, or any form of indecent assault*'; Article 75(2)(b) of 1977 Additional Protocol I reads: 'The following acts are and shall remain prohibited at any time and in any place whatsoever, whether committed by civilian or by military agents: ... outrages upon personal dignity, in particular ... *enforced prostitution* ...'; and Article 76(1) of 1977 Additional Protocol I reads: 'Women shall be the object of special respect and shall be protected in particular against *rape, forced prostitution and any other form of indecent assault.*'[132] That rape is outlawed in *any* armed conflict for which one can be held individually criminally responsible was furthermore recognised by the *Furundžija* Trial Chamber when it examined the international customary war crime status of rape:

> The prohibition of rape and serious sexual assault in armed conflict has also evolved in customary international law. It has gradually crystallised out of the express prohibition of rape in article 44 of the Lieber Code and the general provisions contained in article 46 of the regulations annexed to Hague Convention IV, read in conjunction with the 'Martens clause' laid down in the preamble to that Convention. While rape and sexual assaults were not specifically prosecuted by the Nuremberg Tribunal, rape was expressly classified as a crime against humanity under article II(1)(c) of Control Council Law No. 10. The Tokyo International Military Tribunal convicted Generals Toyoda and Matsui of command responsibility for violations of the laws or customs of war committed by their soldiers in Nanking, which included widespread rapes and sexual assaults. The former Foreign Minister of Japan, Hirota, was also convicted for these atrocities. This decision and that of the United States Military Commission in *Yamashita*, along with the ripening of the fundamental prohibition of 'outrages upon personal dignity' laid down in common article 3

[130] 1907 Hague Convention IV Respecting the Laws and Customs of War on Land, 18 October 1907, 36 Stat. 2277, TS No. 539, reprinted in Roberts and Guelff (2000), p. 67.

[131] Instructions for the Government of Armies of the United States in the Field by Order of the Secretary of War, 24 April 1863 (commonly referred to as the 'Lieber Code'), reprinted in Schindler and Toman (1988).

[132] Italics added.

> into customary international law, has contributed to the evolution of universally accepted norms of international law prohibiting rape as well as serious sexual assault. These norms are applicable in any armed conflict.[133]
>
> It is indisputable that rape and other serious sexual assaults in armed conflict entail the criminal liability of the perpetrators.[134]

The *Furundžija* Appeal Judgment reaffirmed that rape is a war crime.[135] On the basis of the abovementioned sources, it is clear that at least rape, under customary international law, has always been a war crime in itself, giving rise to individual criminal responsibility. The Tribunal acknowledged the independent customary war crime status of rape when it convicted Kunarac, Kovač and Vuković of rape as a violation of the laws or customs of war, punishable under Article 3 of the Statute of the Tribunal.[136] Their particular cases with regard to rape convictions under Article 3 of the ICTY Statute will be discussed in subsection 3.2.1.

On the basis of this brief historical overview, the explicit listing of rape and enforced prostitution in Article 8(b)(xxii) and (e)(vi) of the ICC Statute, applicable to international and non-international armed conflict and to which individual criminal liability is attached, means that at last these crimes are now recognised as such. Apart from rape and enforced prostitution, sexual slavery, forced pregnancy and enforced sterilisation are now also explicitly prohibited as war crimes in international armed conflicts, giving rise to individual criminal responsibility. The explicit criminalisation of different forms of sexual violence as war crimes in international (and non-international) armed conflict in and of themselves does away with obscure language such as 'attack on their honour', 'outrages upon personal dignity' and 'special respect', and is an important advancement in international law. In other words, rape, enforced prostitution, sexual slavery, forced pregnancy and enforced sterilisation are independent crimes and no longer need to be characterised as a species of another war crime. Such direct language prohibiting rape, sexual slavery, enforced prostitution, forced pregnancy, enforced sterilisation or any other form of sexual violence also constituting a grave breach of the 1949 Geneva Conventions generally eases the burden of proof on the part of the Prosecutor. The Prosecutor is no longer required to charge rape under a non-specific sexual violence crime, such as inhumane treatment as a grave breach; he or she only needs to prove the elements of the crime itself, say rape, if rape is charged as rape under Article 8(2)(b)(xxii). However, this assumption should not be overrated as it can generally be argued that rape necessarily fulfils the element(s) of the applicable grave breaches.

The phrase 'any other form of sexual violence also constituting a grave breach of the Geneva Conventions' is also better framed than its counterpart 'any (other) form of

---

[133] Furundžija Judgment, para. 168. Note that the Furundžija Judgment did not deal with rape as a war crime on its own, but treated rape as an outrage upon personal dignity as a violation of the laws or customs of war.

[134] *Ibid.*, para. 169.

[135] Furundžija Appeal Judgment, para. 210. See also the Čelebići Judgment, paras. 476-477, for a discussion of rape as a war crime under international customary law.

[136] See subsection 3.2.1.

indecent assault' in Article 27(2)(e) of 1949 Geneva Convention IV and Article 76(1) of 1977 Additional Protocol I as it is more specific and states the source of its prohibition. Moreover, the wording 'also constituting a grave breach of the Geneva Conventions' is of significant importance as it must be understood to emphasise that the sexual violence crimes stated also constitute grave breaches, despite the fact that the Statute fails to enumerate these and other forms of sexual violence in Article 8(2)(a) as grave breaches themselves.[137] The 'grave breach' reference was, moreover, intended to indicate that only serious crimes of sexual violence should fall within this definition.[138] As mentioned before, the omission of listing sexual violence crimes explicitly as grave breaches can be explained by the exact copying of the grave breaches provision from the 1949 Geneva Conventions into the ICC Statute. However, the phrase 'or any other form of sexual violence also constituting a grave breach of the Geneva Conventions' has plainly brought sexual violence crimes on the same level as grave breaches. This may, in turn, lead to compulsory universal jurisdiction for States to repress or prosecute the perpetrators of sexual violence crimes committed in armed conflict.

The material and mental elements of these specific sexual violence crimes were drafted in the same way for war crimes under Article 8(2)(b)(xxii) in international armed conflicts and war crimes under Article 8(2)(e)(vi) in non-international armed conflicts as well as under Article 7(1)(g) for crimes against humanity. The elements were initially drafted under the war crimes provisions and subsequently transposed to the crimes against humanity provision.[139] In this study, the elements of the sexual violence crimes listed specifically have been extensively dealt with in Chapter 2 on crimes against humanity, and will therefore not be repeated here.

2.3 Elements common to war crimes in international armed conflict

There are two elements which are common to all crimes under Article 8(2)(a) and (b), which are: (1) 'the conduct took place in the context of and was associated with an international armed conflict'; and (2) 'the perpetrator was aware of factual circumstances that established the existence of an armed conflict'. As to the first element, the EoC do not define 'international armed conflict'. Footnote 34, however, indicates that it includes military occupation. The phrase 'in the context of' refers to the temporal and geographical scope of the armed conflict, whereas the words 'and was associated with' refer to the nexus between the armed conflict and the conduct of the perpetrator. The first element has been amply discussed in ICTY case law, by which the drafters of the EoC were guided.[140] The second element, 'the perpetrator was aware of factual circumstances that established the existence of an armed conflict', is a new

137 See, *inter alia*, McDonald (1998), p. 140; Steains (2000), p. 364; Bedont and Hall Martinez (1999); Boot (2002), p. 592.

138 Steains (2000), p. 364.

139 Robinson (2001c), p. 93; La Haye (2001), p. 186.

140 See, for example, on the existence of an 'international armed conflict' and the time frame of the armed conflict, in particular, the Tadić Appeals Chamber's Decision on the defence motion for interlocutory appeal on jurisdiction, para. 70, and the Čelebići Judgment, paras. 208-209. See also Dörmann, pp. 17-28, for a discussion of the EoC and ICTY case law on the interpretation of the contextual elements of the grave breaches.

element, never applied in ICTY proceedings. Further guidance on these two elements common to war crimes in international armed conflict are found in the introduction to the war crimes section in the EoC:

> There is no requirement for a legal evaluation by the perpetrator as to the existence of an armed conflict or its character as international or non-international;
> In that context there is no requirement for awareness by the perpetrator of the facts that established the character of the conflict as international or non-international;
> There is only a requirement for the awareness of the factual circumstances that established the existence of an armed conflict that is implicit in the terms 'took place in the context of and was associated with'.

Therefore, in order to be able to convict someone of sexual violence as a grave breach of the 1949 Geneva Conventions or of other serious violations of the laws and customs in international armed conflict, not only the elements of the specific sexual violence or non-specific sexual violence crimes must have been established, but the conduct must also have taken place in the context of and have been associated with an international armed conflict, and the perpetrator must have been aware of factual circumstances that established the existence of an armed conflict.

3 War crimes in non-international armed conflict

Sexual violence crimes as war crimes in non-international armed conflict may be prosecuted under either Article 8(2)(c), as serious violations of Article 3 common to the four 1949 Geneva Conventions, or under Article 8(2)(e), as other serious violations of the laws and customs.

3.1 Serious violations of Article 3 common to the 1949 Geneva Conventions

Article 8(2)(c) of the ICC Statute reproduces the violations of Article 3 common the four 1949 Geneva Conventions:

> (i) Violence to life and person, in particular murder of all kinds, mutilation, cruel treatment and torture;
> (ii) Committing outrages upon personal dignity, in particular humiliating and degrading treatment;
> (iii) Taking of hostages;
> (iv) The passing of sentences and the carrying out of executions without previous judgment pronounced by a regularly constituted court, affording all judicial guarantees which are generally recognised as indispensable.[141]

[141] See Article 3 of 1949 Geneva Convention I (on wounded and sick in armed forces in the field), Article 3 of 1949 Geneva Convention II (on wounded, sick and shipwrecked members of armed forces at sea), Article 3 of 1949 Geneva Convention III (on the treatment of prisoners of war), and Article 3 of 1949 Geneva Convention IV (on the protection of the civilian population). The subject-matter of these articles is the same, that is why they are referred to as Article 3 *common* to the four 1949 Geneva Conventions.

Article 8(2)(d) of the ICC Statute stresses that not all situations of internal violence are covered: 'Paragraph 2(c) applies to armed conflicts not of an international character and thus does not apply to situations of internal disturbances and tensions, such as riots, isolated and sporadic acts of violence or other acts of a similar nature.'[142] According to Article 8(2)(c) of the ICC Statute, the Common Article 3 violations must have been committed against 'persons taking no active part in the hostilities, including members of armed forces who have laid down their arms and those placed hors de combat by sickness, wounds, detention or any other cause', wording derived from Common Article 3. For each serious violation of Common Article 3, the EoC further clarifies: 'Such person or persons were either *hors de combat*, or were civilians, medical personnel, or religious personnel taking no active part in the hostilities'; and: 'The perpetrator was aware of the factual circumstances that established this status.'

In the serious violations of Article 3 common to the four 1949 Geneva Conventions rape or any other forms of sexual violence are not mentioned explicitly, thus they are not mentioned explicitly in the ICC Statute either. In contrast, the ICTR Statute not only includes the serious violations of Common Article 3 in its Article 4, but also the serious violations of Additional Protocol II, and for this reason the ICTR Statute also refers to 'outrages upon personal dignity, in particular ... rape, enforced prostitution and any form of indecent assault'. There has only been one conviction for sexual violence on the basis of Article 4 of the ICTR Statute, that is, for the accused Semanza who (on appeal) was convicted on the basis of Article 4(a) (violence to life, health and physical or mental well-being of persons, in particular ... cruel treatment such as torture, mutilation or any form of corporal punishment).[143] Semanza was convicted of, *inter alia*, instigating the rape and torture of Victim A, conduct for which he had already been convicted under rape and torture as crimes against humanity. However, the Appeals Chamber did not elaborate on how the rape of Victim A fitted into Article 4(a) of the ICTR Statute and therefore this case is not further discussed here.

Under Article 3 of the ICTY Statute, the Yugoslav Tribunal has the power to prosecute persons violating the laws or customs of war. The Appeals Chamber in the *Tadić Jurisdiction Decision* ruled that non-exhaustive Article 3 of the ICTY Statute needs to be considered a residual clause and all applicable offences may be prosecuted under it provided they are not included in Articles 2 (grave breaches), 4 (genocide) or 5 (crimes against humanity).[144] The Appeals Chamber in the *Tadić Jurisdiction Decision* indicated the conditions to be fulfilled for Article 3 to become applicable:

(i) The violation must constitute an infringement of a rule of international humanitarian law.
(ii) The rule must be customary in nature or, if it belongs to treaty law, the required conditions must be met ...

---

[142] See also paragraph 1 of the introduction to the war crimes section in the EoC, where it is stated: 'The elements for war crimes under article 8, paragraph 2(c) and (e), are subject to the limitations addressed in article 8, paragraph 2(d) and (f), which are not elements of crimes.'

[143] Semanza Appeal Judgment, Disposition.

[144] Tadić Jurisdiction Decision, paras. 89, 91.

(iii) The violation must be 'serious', that is to say, it must constitute a breach of a rule protecting important values, and the breach must involve grave consequences for the victim ...

(iv) The violation of the rule must entail, under customary or conventional law, the individual criminal responsibility of the person breaching the rule.[145]

According to the Appeals Chamber, 'it follows that it does not matter whether the "serious violation" has occurred within the context of an international or an internal armed conflict, as long as the four requirements set out above are met'.[146] Therefore, Article 3 enables the Tribunal to prosecute any person guilty of any serious violation in all armed conflicts, thereby preventing that such persons may escape the jurisdiction of the Tribunal. The ICTR has upheld the reasoning in the *Tadić Jurisdiction Decision.*[147] On the basis of the Appeals Chamber's reasoning in the *Tadić Jurisdiction Decision*, it was for the first time held in *Furundžija* that sexual violence can be prosecuted as a violation of the laws or customs of war under Article 3 of the ICTY Statute in all armed conflicts, which in the *Furundžija* case meant torture and outrages upon personal dignity including rape contained in Common Article 3.[148] In addition to the crimes listed in Article 3, the Prosecutor of the ICTY has therefore prosecuted non-listed crimes, such as sexual violence, on the basis of Common Article 3 of the 1949 Geneva Conventions, but also for rape constituting an independent crime, as violating treaty law and customary international law applicable in international and non-international armed conflicts coming within the ambit of Article 3 of the ICTY Statute.[149]

Despite the lack of explicit prohibitions of sexual violence crimes as violations of Common Article 3, sexual violence crimes can be prosecuted under these provisions, as is evidenced by the case law of the ICTY. The violations most applicable in terms of sexual violence prosecutions are Article 8(2)(c)(i), 'Violence to life and person, in particular ... mutilation, cruel treatment and torture', and Article 8(2)(c)(ii), 'Committing outrages upon personal dignity, in particular humiliating and degrading treatment.'

---

[145] *Ibid.*, para. 94.

[146] *Ibid.*, paras. 94 and 102 (with the following reference: 'The International Court of Justice has confirmed that these rules reflect "elementary considerations of humanity" applicable under customary international law to any armed conflict, whether it is of an internal or international character (Nicaragua Case, at para. 218).').

[147] See, *inter alia*, Akayesu Judgment, para. 616; Musema Judgment and Sentence, para. 286; Bagilishema, Judgment, para. 102; Rutaganda Judgment and Sentence, para. 106; Kayishema and Ruzindana Judgment, para. 184; Semanza Judgment and Sentence, para. 370.

[148] *Prosecutor v. Anto Furundžija*, Decision on the Defendant's Motion to Dismiss Counts 13 and 14 of the Indictment (Lack of Subject Matter Jurisdiction), Case No. IT-95-17/1, 29 May 1998. The Defence had argued that torture and outrages upon personal dignity including rape were not covered by Article 3 of the Statute, but by Article 2 (grave breaches) only, as the Prosecutor had argued that the conflict was international in character. See also Furundžija Judgment, paras. 132-133, 169. See also Kunarac, Kovač and Vuković Judgment, para. 436.

[149] Kunarac, Kovač and Vuković Judgment, paras. 400, 405-406; Kunarac, Kovač and Vuković Appeal Judgment, para. 195.

3.1.1 Violence to life and person, in particular murder of all kinds, mutilation, cruel treatment and torture

Article 8(2)(c)(i) of the ICC Statute prohibits 'violence to life and person, in particular, murder of all kinds, mutilation, cruel treatment and torture' as a violation of Common Article 3 of the 1949 Geneva Conventions.

3.1.1.1 Cruel treatment

The first element of the war crime of cruel treatment is elaborated in the EoC (Article 8(2)(c)(i)-3) and reads:

> 1. The perpetrator inflicted severe physical or mental pain or suffering upon one or more persons.[150]

In light of the little difference in meaning between the adjectives 'cruel' and 'inhuman', the element concerning cruel treatment as a violation of Common Article 3 of the 1949 Geneva Conventions is identical to the element concerning inhuman treatment as a grave breach under Article 8(2)(a)(ii).[151] The element is partly borrowed from the *Čelebići* Judgment, which found cruel treatment to constitute 'an intentional act or omission, that is an act which, judged objectively, is deliberate and not accidental, which causes serious mental or physical suffering or injury or constitutes a serious attack on human dignity'.[152] The 'serious attack on human dignity' part is not included for the crime of cruel treatment, but constitutes a crime on its own in Article 8(2)(c)(ii) of the ICC Statute, 'outrages upon personal dignity'. The *Čelebići* Trial Chamber furthermore held that cruel treatment

> ... carries an equivalent meaning and therefore the same residual function for the purposes of common article 3 of the Statute, as inhuman treatment does in relation to grave breaches of the Geneva Conventions. Accordingly, the offence of torture under common article 3 of the Geneva Conventions is also included within the concept of cruel treatment. Treatment that does not meet the purposive requirement for the offence of torture in common article 3, constitutes cruel treatment.[153]

On the basis of the EoC, the factor distinguishing between cruel treatment and torture as violations of Common Article 3 is not the severity of the crime, but purpose. The *mens*

---

[150] Cruel treatment is a serious violation of international humanitarian law covered implicitly by Article 3 of the ICTY Statute pursuant to Common Article 3. The elements of cruel treatment in Article 3 are the same as those of inhuman treatment in Article 2(b) and of inhumane acts in Article 5(i) of the ICTY Statute. Article 4 of the ICTR Statute covers cruel treatment as a violation of Common Article 3 to the Geneva Conventions and Additional Protocol II.

[151] La Haye (2001), p. 209.

[152] Čelebići Judgment, para. 552. The Appeals Chamber in the Aleksovski and Čelebići cases upheld the elements of the crime of cruel treatment; see Aleksovski Appeal Judgment, para. 26, and Čelebići Appeal Judgment, para. 424.

[153] Čelebići Judgment, para. 552.

rea of cruel treatment is that the perpetrator intended to inflict severe physical or mental pain or suffering upon one or more persons.

ICTY case law has resulted in a number of convictions for sexual violence rising to the level of cruel treatment under Article 3 of the ICTY Statute via Common Article 3, among others in the *Čelebići*, *Tadić* and *Blaškić* cases. The sexual violence conduct rising to the level of cruel treatment included rape, including forced fellatio, and sexual mutilation by means of a burning fuse around the body in the genital area or by biting off another person's testicle. The facts of these cases have already been discussed in subsections 2.1.1.2 and 2.1.2, as the sexual violence conduct also resulted in convictions for the grave breaches of inhuman treatment and wilfully causing great suffering. The Appeals Chamber in *Čelebići* ruled that if the same conduct is charged both as inhuman treatment under Article 2 and as cruel treatment under Article 3 or as wilfully causing great suffering under Article 2 and cruel treatment under Article 3, the count under Article 3 should be dismissed.[154] For this reason, the conviction of Mucić for sexual violence conduct was only upheld for the grave breaches of inhuman treatment and wilfully causing great suffering, both under Article 2 of the ICTY Statute.[155] The same reasoning was applied in the *Blaškić* case, where General Blaškić's involvement in the rapes was only upheld for the grave breach of inhuman treatment conviction, but not for cruel treatment as a violation of the laws or customs of war.[156] As the cumulative convictions test was not applied in the *Tadić* case, Tadić was cumulatively convicted of cruel treatment (Article 3), torture or inhuman treatment (Article 2(b)), wilfully causing great suffering or serious injury to body or health (Article 2(c)), and other inhumane acts as a crime against humanity (Article 5(i)) with regard to forcing two male prisoners to commit fellatio on another prisoner and forcing one of them to bite off the other prisoner's testicles. Cruel treatment as a violation of the laws or customs of war, as recognised by Common Article 3(1)(a) of the 1949 Geneva Conventions has been charged in a number of cases.[157]

3.1.1.2 Torture

Article 8(2)(c)(i) of the ICC Statute also prohibits torture as a violation of Common Article 3 of the 1949 Geneva Conventions. The war crime of torture is defined in Article 8(2)(c)(i)-4 of the EoC, the first two elements of which read:

1. The perpetrator inflicted severe physical or mental pain or suffering upon one or more persons.

---

[154] Čelebići Appeal Judgment, paras. 426, 424. For a more elaborate discussion of cumulative convictions, see Chapter 6 on sentencing.
[155] *Ibid.*, para. 427.
[156] Blaškić Appeal Judgment, paras. 633-634.
[157] See, *inter alia*, *Prosecutor v. Ramush Haradinaj, Idriz Balaj and Lahi Brahimaj*, Indictment, Case No. IT-04-84-I, 4 March 2005 (count 37); *Prosecutor v. Rasim Delić*, Indictment, Case No. IT-04-83-PT, 17 March 2005 (count 4); *Prosecutor v. Milan Martić,* Amended Indictment, Case No. IT-95-11, 18 December 2002 (count 9).

2. The perpetrator inflicted the pain or suffering for such purposes as: obtaining information or a confession, punishment, intimidation or coercion or for any reason based on discrimination of any kind.

The elements of the war crime of torture are identical for torture in international armed conflict and torture in non-international armed conflict. Torture as a war crime has been dealt with in subsection 2.1.1.1 above, and for a general discussion of the war crime of torture and rape as torture that subsection may be consulted. In this subsection, the case law that led to convictions for rape as torture pursuant to Common Article 3, via Article 3 ICTY Statute, is described.

Torture has been charged under Article 3 of the ICTY Statute, as recognised by Common Article 3 of the 1949 Geneva Conventions, in several cases. To date, convictions for rape as torture under Article 3 of the ICTY Statute have been pronounced in the *Čelebići, Furundžija, Kunarac, Kovač and Vuković* and *Kvočka* cases. In *Čelebići*, Delić was found guilty under Article 3 of the Statute, as recognised by Common Article 3(1)(a), torture, of the 1949 Geneva Conventions, in view of the repeated rape of a female detainee, Ms Ćećez, including public rape and the repeated vaginal and anal rape of another detainee, Ms Antic, whom he had raped for over a period of six weeks.[158] The same facts served as a basis for a finding of guilt for the grave breach of torture under Article 2(b) of the ICTY Statute, and have been dealt with extensively in subsection 2.1.1.1 above. In light of the cumulative conviction principle, the conviction under Article 3 was dismissed on appeal.

In the *Furundžija* case, Furundžija, the commander of the Jokers, a special unit of the HVO, was also convicted of torture under Article 3 of the ICTY Statute, as recognised by Common Article 3 of the 1949 Geneva Conventions.[159] At the Jokers' Headquarters (Nadioci, central Bosnia and Herzegovina), Furundžija interrogated Witness A, a civilian Bosnian Muslim woman, who was naked, while Accused B (another commander of one of the HVO units) rubbed his knife against her inner thighs and threatened to cut out her private parts if she did not tell the truth in answer to the interrogation by the accused. Furundžija and Accused B's intention was to obtain information which they believed would benefit the HVO. Witness D, a friend of Witness A, was also brought to the room for a confrontation with Witness A, in order to make her confess, and both were beaten with a baton. The accused intended to obtain information about his alleged betrayal of the HVO to the ABiH (the army of Bosnia and Herzegovina) and his assistance to Witness A and her children. Accused B then raped Witness A orally, vaginally and anally and forced her to lick his penis clean. This happened in front of an audience of laughing soldiers. In the meantime, Furundžija continued to interrogate Witness A, and as the interrogation intensified, so did the sexual assaults and the rape. Witness D was forced to watch the rape of Witness A. Although Furundžija had not raped the woman himself, he was found as responsible as his colleague who did rape her as he had facilitated the rapes by allowing them to occur and continue. Furundžija's interrogation of Witness A formed an integral part of the

[158] Čelebići Judgment, para. 943 (Ms Ćećez) and para. 965 (Ms Antic).

[159] The Croatian Community of Herzeg-Bosna (HZ-HB) considered itself an independent political entity inside the Republic of Bosnia-Herzegovina. From at least January 1993 through at least mid-July 1993, the HVO was engaged in an armed conflict with the ABiH.

torture. With respect to Witness D, the physical attacks as well as the fact that he was forced to watch sexual attacks on a woman, in particular, a woman whom he knew as a friend, caused him severe physical and mental suffering.[160] For this conduct, Furundžija, as a co-perpetrator by virtue of his interrogation, was found guilty under Article 7(1) for sexual assault as torture (for the rape of Witness A he was furthermore convicted, as an aider and abetter, of rape as part of outrages upon personal dignity as a violation of the laws or customs of war, recognised by Article 3 of the ICTY Statute).[161] On appeal, the Appeals Chamber rebutted the Appellant's argument that some of the conduct charged did not constitute torture holding that 'it [is] inconceivable that it could ever be argued that the acts charged in paragraph 25 of the Amended Indictment, namely, the rubbing of a knife against a woman's thighs and stomach, coupled with a threat to insert the knife into her vagina, once proven, are not serious enough to amount to torture'.[162] Furthermore, 'it is difficult to ignore the intimidating and humiliating aspects of that scene and their devastating impact on the physical and mental state of Witness A'.[163] The Appeals Chamber affirmed the convictions and sentences.

In yet another case, the one involving the accused Kunarac, Kovač and Vuković, both Kunarac and Vuković were convicted of torture under Article 3 ICTY Statute. Kunarac, a commander of a special volunteer unit of the VRS, was convicted of torture under Article 3 (count 3) for the rapes of women at the House Ulica Osmana Dikica No. 16, the headquarters of a group of soldiers under Kunarac's command. Kunarac himself raped three women (Witnesses D.B., FWS-87, FWS-95[164]) and aided and abetted the (gang) rapes of the same and other women (Witnesses D.B., FRW-75, FWS-50, FWS-87) by soldiers at the house.[165] The rapes took on different forms (oral, vaginal or anal) and were committed against Muslim women who were held captive in the house. The same conduct was also the basis for a conviction for rape under Article 3 of the ICTY Statute as a crime in and of itself (count 4).[166] With regard to the discriminating purpose, the Trial Chamber held that:

> The accused acted intentionally and with the aim of discriminating between the members of his ethnic group and the Muslims, in particular its women and girls. The treatment reserved by Dragoljub Kunarac for his victims was motivated by their being Muslims, as is evidenced by the occasions when the accused told women, that they would give birth to Serb babies, or that they should 'enjoy being fucked by a Serb'. The law does not require that the purpose of discrimination be the only purpose pursued by the offender; it is enough that it forms a substantial part of his *mens rea*. Such was the case with the accused Kunarac.[167]

[160] Furundžija Judgment, paras. 264-267.

[161] *Ibid.*, para. 269.

[162] Furundžija Appeal Judgment, para. 114.

[163] *Ibid.*, paras. 113-114.

[164] The term 'FWS' stands for 'Foča Witness Statements' (Prosecution witness pseudonyms).

[165] Kunarac, Kovač and Vuković Judgment, paras. 630-687.

[166] See subsection 3.2.1. The same conduct furthermore resulted in a conviction of Kunarac, Kovač and Vuković for torture as a crime against humanity (count 1) and rape as a crime against humanity (count 2). See further Chapter 2 on crimes against humanity.

[167] Kunarac, Kovač and Vuković Judgment, para. 654.

In addition, Kunarac was convicted of torture by means of rape of Witness 183 as a violation of the laws or customs of war, punishable under Article 3 of the Statute of the Tribunal and recognised by Common Article 3(1)(a) (torture) of the 1949 Geneva Conventions (count 11).[168] The same conduct also resulted in a conviction for rape as a violation of the laws or customs of war, punishable under Article 3 of the Statute of the Tribunal (count 12).[169] The Trial Chamber found that the following account was proved:

> The three soldiers then took her to the banks of the Cehotina river in Foca near Velecevo, where the accused tried to obtain information or a confession from FWS-183 concerning her valuables while he threatened to kill her and her son. By his attempt to intimidate her, Dragoljub Kunarac also showed his hatred for Muslims, his intention to intimidate her, and his intention to discriminate against Muslims in general, and FWS-183 in particular. All three soldiers raped FWS-183. In the course of the rapes, Kunarac forced her to touch his penis and to look at him. He cursed her. The other two soldiers watched from the car, laughing. While she was raped by Dragoljub Kunarac, FWS-183 heard him tell the other soldiers to wait for their turn. Subsequently, she was raped vaginally and orally by the other soldiers. The rapes resulted in severe mental and physical pain for FWS-183.[170]

Vuković, a subcommander of the military police and paramilitary leader in Foča, was convicted of torture under Article 3 (count 35) for the rape of a 16-year-old girl, FWS-50, who had been taken by Vuković from the Partizan Sports Hall to an apartment where she was subsequently raped.[171] Vuković had told FWS-50 that she was 'lucky in that she was the same age as his daughter, otherwise he would have done much worse things to her'.[172] The rape led to serious mental and physical pain for the victim. Even though the Defence in its Final Trial Brief argued that, even if it were proved that he had raped FWS-50, the rape was committed 'out of a sexual urge, not out of hatred',[173] the Trial Chamber opined that

> all that matters in this context is his awareness of an attack against the Muslim civilian population of which his victim was a member and, for the purpose of torture, that he intended to discriminate between the group of which he is a member and the group of his victim. There is no requirement under international customary law that the conduct must be *solely* perpetrated for one of the prohibited purposes of torture, such as discrimination. The prohibited purpose need only be part of the motivation behind the conduct and need not be the predominant or sole purpose. The Trial Chamber has no doubt that it was at least a predominant purpose, as the accused obviously intended to discriminate against the group of which his victim was a member, ie the Muslims, and against his victim in particular.[174]

---

[168] *Ibid.*, para. 715.
[169] *Ibid.*
[170] *Ibid.*, para. 711.
[171] *Ibid.*, para. 822.
[172] *Ibid.*, para. 814.
[173] *Ibid.*, para. 816.
[174] *Ibid.* This reasoning was upheld on appeal; see Kunarac, Kovač and Vuković Appeal Judgment, paras. 153, 155.

The same conduct formed the basis for a conviction for rape under Article 3 of the ICTY Statute as an independent crime (count 36).[175] The Appeals Chamber upheld the convictions for all the convicted and stipulated that inter-Article and intra-Article convictions with regard to Articles 3 and 5 of the Statute were permissible.[176]

In the *Kvočka et al.* case, Radić, a shift commander of guards at Omarska camp, was found guilty as a co-perpetrator of the joint criminal enterprise of raping a woman, attempting to rape another woman and further sexually intimidating, harassing and assaulting female prisoners for torture as a violation of the laws or customs of war under Article 3 ICTY Statute.[177] Witness K was forced to go to Radić's room, where she was raped by Radić under the coercive circumstance that her children would not be harmed if she agreed to the sexual intercourse.[178] Radić furthermore attempted to rape witness J, but instead ejaculated over her.[179] Although another witness was raped by Radić, this rape was not charged in the indictment and therefore the Trial Chamber did not consider this rape in its determination of guilt. The Trial Chamber did, however, find that this testimony assisted in establishing a consistent pattern of conduct in conformity with Rule 93.[180] A similar reasoning was applied in the case of the sexual harassment in respect of another witness.[181] In respect of Witnesses J, F, Sifeta Susic and Zlata Cikota, it was established that Radić committed sexual violence against them by sexually intimidating, harassing and assaulting them. Among other things he sexually assaulted them by touching their breasts, vaginas and bottoms.[182] He furthermore tried to convince them to have sexual intercourse with him by promising to help them.[183] The discriminatory nature of the rapes was expressed by the Trial Chamber in the following words:

> … the rape and other forms of sexual violence were committed only against the non-Serb detainees in the camp and that they were committed solely against the women, making the crimes discriminatory on multiple levels. Radic did not rape any of the male non-Serb detainees. As recognised in the Čelebići case, raping a person on the basis of sex or gender is a prohibited purpose for the offence of torture.[184]

Whereas the rape of Witness K and the attempted rape of Witness J were readily found to inflict severe pain and suffering, and thus torture, with respect to the other sexual violence the Trial Chamber held:

---

[175] See subsection 3.2.1. The same conduct furthermore formed the basis for a conviction for torture (count 33) and rape (count 34), both as crimes against humanity. See further Chapter 2 on crimes against humanity.

[176] For cumulative convictions, see Chapter 6.

[177] Kvočka Judgment, paras. 559, 578, 761.

[178] *Ibid.*, para. 551.

[179] *Ibid.*, para. 548.

[180] *Ibid.*, para. 556.

[181] *Ibid.*, para. 547.

[182] *Ibid.*, paras. 547-548.

[183] *Ibid.*

[184] *Ibid.*, para. 560.

> In considering whether severe pain and suffering was also inflicted upon the other victims of sexual violence, the Trial Chamber takes into consideration the extraordinary vulnerability of the victims and the fact that they were held imprisoned in a facility in which violence against detainees was the rule, not the exception. The detainees knew that Radic held a position of authority in the camp, that he could roam the camp at will, and order their presence before him at any time. The women also knew or suspected that other women were being raped or otherwise subjected to sexual violence in the camp. The fear was pervasive and the threat was always real that they could be subjected to sexual violence at the whim of Radic. Under these circumstances, the Trial Chamber finds that threat of rape or other forms of sexual violence undoubtedly caused severe pain and suffering to Witness F, Zlata Cikota, and Sifeta Susic and thus, the elements of torture are also satisfied in relation to these survivors.[185]

By concluding that the threat of sexual violence in coercive conditions in a detention camp fulfilled the requirements of torture, the Trial Chamber upheld the *Akayesu* definition of sexual violence, that is 'any act of a sexual nature, which is committed on a person under circumstances which are coercive'.[186] Although Radić was also charged with rape and torture as crimes against humanity, these counts were subsumed into the persecution conviction under Article 5, which included sexual violence.[187] Furthermore, the charge of outrages upon personal dignity as violations of the laws or customs of war based on the same rapes and other forms of sexual violence was dismissed as torture was considered to be the more distinct crime.[188]

Summarising, the case law of the ICTY has recognised that rape and other forms of sexual violence can rise to the level of torture. As rape often disproportionately affects women, discrimination on the basis of gender has been rightly recognised as one of the purposes for which torture can be committed by means of rape. Furthermore, other forms of sexual violence qualifying as torture are threats to sexually mutilate a person, threats to rape someone in conditions of, for instance, detention where victims are subject to the whims of their captors, forced observance of rape committed against a friend or relative and rape in front of a friend or relative who is forced to watch. Clearly, these examples are not exhaustive and other forms of torture by means of sexual violence may be prosecuted in the future; for instance, to force someone to rape one's child while others are watching.

3.1.2 Committing outrages upon personal dignity, in particular humiliating and degrading treatment

Article 8(2)(c)(ii) of the ICC Statute criminalises 'committing outrages upon personal dignity, in particular humiliating and degrading treatment' as a violation of Common Article 3 in non-international armed conflict. The prohibition of 'outrages upon personal dignity' in Common Article 3 has been laid down in a number of other international humanitarian law provisions as well, and some of them were expanded to

---

[185] *Ibid.*, para. 561.
[186] *Ibid.*, para. 559.
[187] *Ibid.*, paras. 573, 579.
[188] *Ibid.*, paras. 577, 579.

include sexual violence conduct: Article 75(2)(b) of 1977 Additional Protocol I states 'outrages upon personal dignity, in particular humiliating and degrading treatment, enforced prostitution and any form of indecent assault' and Article 4(2)(e) of 1977 Additional Protocol II incorporated the same list as found in Article 75(2)(b) of Protocol I, adding the crime of rape.[189] The elements of this crime are identical to those listed under Article 8(2)(b)(xxi), 'committing outrages upon personal dignity, in particular humiliating and degrading treatment' in international armed conflict, but are discussed in this section in light of the case law accumulating from the ICTY and ICTR on rape as an outrage upon personal dignity, which was developed under Articles 4 (Common Article 3 and Additional Protocol II) and 3 (violations of the laws or customs of war), respectively.

In the EoC, this crime is defined as:

1. The perpetrator humiliated, degraded or otherwise violated the dignity of one or more persons.[57]
2. The severity of the humiliation, degradation or other violation was of such degree as to be generally recognized as an outrage upon personal dignity.[190]

[57] For this crime, 'persons' can include dead persons. It is understood that the victim need not personally be aware of the existence of the humiliation or degradation or other violation. This element takes into account relevant aspects of the cultural background of the victim.

Article 8(2)(c)(ii) of the ICC Statute criminalises 'committing outrages upon personal dignity, *in particular* humiliating and degrading treatment', and thus states 'humiliating' and 'degrading treatment' as examples of the crime of 'outrages upon personal dignity'.[191] In the EoC, 'or otherwise violated the dignity of one or more persons' is added, which implies that 'outrages upon personal dignity' can be achieved by any other means that violates the dignity of a person. The footnote attached to element 1 of the crime refers to dead persons and was included to cover case law from World War II, where an accused was convicted of having maltreated dead prisoners of war.[192] The second sentence in the footnote refers to unconscious persons or the mentally disabled, and the last sentence mentions the cultural background of the victim, which may be of influence in establishing whether or not the victim experienced an act as degrading or humiliating.[193] The second element of the crime refers to the degree of severity of the humiliation, degradation or other violation. Through ICTY case law it has become clear that 'outrages upon personal dignity' means that the 'act or omission must cause serious suffering or humiliation'.[194] There is no obligation to list the acts which constitute outrages upon personal dignity.[195] The seriousness of the act need not

[189] See also Article 95 of 1949 Geneva Convention IV and Article 85(4) of 1977 Additional Protocol I.
[190] EoC, Article 8(2)(b)(xxi) – War crime of outrages upon personal dignity.
[191] Italics added.
[192] Dörmann (2004), p. 314 (with reference to World War II case law).
[193] *Ibid.*, p. 315 (with reference to the example of forcing a person to eat something that is prohibited by the religion of that person).
[194] Kunarac, Kovač and Vuković Judgment, para. 503.
[195] Kunarac, Kovač and Vuković Appeal Judgment, paras. 162-163.

cause 'lasting suffering'.[196] According to ICTY case law, the degree of suffering the victim endures must be established on the basis of subjective and objective elements. Thus, whereas the degree of suffering may depend on the victim's temperament or sensitivity (subjectivity), the humiliation to the victim must be so intense that any human being would have experienced it as such (objectivity).[197] In this perspective, element 2 of the EoC contains the requirement that the violation be 'generally recognized as an outrage on personal dignity'. The *mens rea* is covered by Article 30 of the ICC Statute. According to ICTY case law, no specific discriminatory intent or motive is required for the crime of outrages upon personal dignity.[198] Moreover, the perpetrator need not intend to humiliate the victim; it is sufficient that he knew that his act or omission could have that effect.[199] The *Kunarac, Kovač and Vuković* Trial Chamber added the element of knowledge to the *mens rea*, viz. the knowledge that the act could cause serious humiliation, degradation or an affront to human dignity. In practice, the knowledge element seems to be easily met; if an act or omission causes serious suffering or humiliation, 'it would be rare that the perpetrator would not also know that the acts could have that effect'.[200]

The *Kunarac, Kovač and Vuković* Trial Chamber, quoting the *Furundžija* Trial Chamber, held that the jurisdiction to charge rape as an outrage against personal dignity, in violation of the laws or customs of war pursuant to Article 3 was clearly established.[201] Convictions for sexual violence conduct as outrages upon personal dignity resulted in the *Furundžija, Kunarac, Kovač and Vuković* and *Češić* cases. In the first case mentioned, *Furundžija*, the Trial Chamber established that, because of Furundžija's presence and his continued interrogation, Furundžija aided and abetted the rapes committed by Accused B, namely the penetration of Witness A's mouth, vagina and anus with his penis. The Trial Chamber found that

> the rapes and sexual assaults were committed publicly; members of the Jokers were watching and milling around the open door of the pantry. They laughed at what was going on. The Trial Chamber finds that Witness A suffered severe physical and mental pain, along with public humiliation, at the hands of Accused B in what amounted to outrages upon her personal dignity and sexual integrity.[202]

The sexual violence conduct included not only rape, but also threats of sexual mutilation (Accused B had threatened to cut out her vagina) and forced public nudity.

---

196 Kunarac, Kovač and Vuković Judgment, para. 501 (deviating from the Aleksovski Judgment, which required that the act cause lasting suffering). See also Kvočka Judgment, para. 168.

197 Aleksovski Judgment, para. 56; Aleksovski Appeal Judgment, para. 37; Kunarac, Kovač and Vuković Judgment, paras. 504, 507; Kunarac, Kovač and Vuković Appeal Judgment, paras. 162-163.

198 Aleksovski Appeal Judgment, para. 28.

199 Kunarac, Kovač and Vuković Judgment, para. 774.

200 *Ibid.*, para. 512. Upheld on appeal; see Kunarac, Kovač and Vuković Appeal Judgment, para. 166.

201 Kunarac, Kovač and Vuković Judgment, para. 436 (with reference to the Furundžija Judgment, para. 173).

202 Furundžija Judgment, para. 272.

For this conduct, Furundžija, as an aider and abetter, was found guilty of committing outrages upon personal dignity as a violation of the laws or customs of war, recognised by Article 3 of the ICTY Statute.[203] The Appeals Chamber upheld the conviction for sexual violence as a means of committing outrages upon personal dignity.[204] The second case involves Kovač, a defendant in the *Kunarac, Kovač and Vuković* case, who was found guilty of outrages upon personal dignity because Kovač knew that 'having to stand naked on a table, while the accused watched them, was a painful and humiliating experience for the three women involved, even more so because of their young age'.[205] In addition, the 'sexual exploitation of A.B. and FWS-75, in particular their sale, constitutes a particularly degrading attack on their dignity'.[206] During their enslavement in Kovač's apartment, the victims were repeatedly raped, humiliated and degraded.[207]

Češić, a member of the Bosnian Serb Police Reserve unit at the Brčko police station, pleaded guilty to, *inter alia*, the fact that he 'intentionally forced, at gunpoint, two Muslim brothers detained at Luka Camp to perform fellatio on each other in the presence of others'.[208] The forced fellatio, which took place in full view of several guards who were laughing, lasted about 45 minutes.[209] For this conduct, Češić was convicted of humiliating and degrading treatment as a violation of the laws or customs of war under Article 3 as recognised by Common Article 3(1)(c) (count 7) as well as for rape as a crime against humanity under Article 5(g) (count 8).[210]

On the basis of this overview of ICTY case law, it is clear that such conduct as rape, including forced fellatio, threats of sexual mutilation, forced public nudity and sexual exploitation, in particular the sale of women for purposes of sex, are all examples of conduct that amounts to 'outrages upon personal dignity'. Of course, other sexual violence conduct may qualify as outrages upon personal dignity and, on the basis of the EoC, would certainly include the raping of or other forms of sexual violence against dead bodies.

Charges of sexual violence on the basis of outrages upon personal dignity have been laid down in ICTR indictments, but until this date, they have all been dismissed. For example, Akayesu was charged with violations of Article 3 common to the 1949 Geneva Conventions and of Article 4(2)(e) of 1977 Additional Protocol II, as incorporated in Article 4(e) (outrages upon personal dignity, including rape, degrading and humiliating treatment and indecent assault). For a conviction under Article 4 of the ICTR Statute, proof was needed that Akayesu acted for either the government or the RPF in the execution of their respective conflict objectives.[211] However, the Trial Chamber held that the accused was not guilty, finding that it had not been proved

---

[203] *Ibid.*, para. 275.

[204] Furundžija Appeal Judgment, para. 127.

[205] Kunarac, Kovač and Vuković Judgment, para. 773.

[206] *Ibid.*, para. 756. A.B. was sold for DEM 200.

[207] Kovač was convicted of rape, enslavement and outrages upon personal dignity on the basis of the enslavement, rape and other mistreatment of A.B. and FWS-75, although it is not entirely clear which facts support which convictions.

[208] Češić Sentencing Judgment, para. 13.

[209] *Ibid.*, para. 14.

[210] *Ibid.*, para. 107.

[211] Akayesu Judgment, para. 640.

beyond reasonable doubt that the 'acts perpetrated by Akayesu in the Commune of Taba at the time of the events alleged in the Indictment were committed in conjunction with the armed conflict'.[212] It was not established that Akayesu was actively supporting the government's war effort against the RPF. For this reason, all charges under Common Article 3 and Protocol II were dismissed, including the sexual violence charges. A similar conclusion was reached in the *Musema* Judgment, and charges of sexual violence as violations of the laws or customs of war were therefore dismissed as well.[213]

Although there have been no convictions for sexual violence as outrages upon personal dignity by the ICTR, the understanding that sexual violence amounts to an outrage upon personal dignity was not questioned;[214] on the contrary, the elements required to prove 'humiliating and degrading treatment', 'rape' and 'indecent assault' under Article 4(e) of the ICTR Statute were further explained.[215] Other indictments in which sexual violence has been charged under outrages upon personal dignity include the *Butare* case, where Nyiramasuhuko has been charged with this crime.

3.2 Other serious violations of the laws and customs applicable in non-international armed conflict

'Other serious violations of the laws and customs applicable in armed conflicts not of an international character' which cover sexual violence are stated in the very explicit Article 8(2)(e)(vi). Subparagraph (f) furthermore states:

> Paragraph 2(e) applies to armed conflicts not of an international character and thus does not apply to situations of internal disturbances and tensions, such as riots, isolated and sporadic acts of violence or other acts of a similar nature. It applies to armed conflicts that take place in the territory of a State when there is protracted armed conflict between governmental authorities and organized armed groups or between such groups'.[216]

---

[212] *Ibid.*, para. 643.

[213] Musema Judgment and Sentence, para. 947. Semanza was also charged with serious violations of Common Article 3 and Additional Protocol II on the basis of his conduct in relation to acts of rape and sexual violence allegedly occurring at Musha church, Mwulire Hill and Mabare mosque, but the Prosecutor failed to introduce any evidence of the occurrence of rape or other forms of sexual violence at these sites and Semanza was therefore acquitted as regards this count. See Semanza Judgment and Sentence, paras. 537-539.

[214] Akayesu Judgment, para. 688.

[215] Musema Judgment and Sentence, para. 285 ('a) *Humiliating and degrading treatment*: Subjecting victims to treatment designed to subvert their self-regard. Like outrages upon personal dignity, these offences may be regarded as a lesser forms of torture; moreover ones in which the motives required for torture would not be required, nor would it be required that the acts be committed under state authority; b) *Rape*: The specific elements of rape are stated in Section 3.3. on Crime against Humanity in the Applicable Law; c) *Indecent assault*: The accused caused the infliction of pain or injury by an act which was of a sexual nature and inflicted by means of coercion, force, threat or intimidation and was non-consensual').

[216] See also paragraph 1 of the introduction to the war crimes section in the EoC, where it is stated: 'The elements for war crimes under article 8, paragraph 2(c) and (e), are subject to the limitations addressed in article 8, paragraph 2(d) and (f), which are not elements of crimes.'

As mentioned above, an almost similar provision was included in the case of subparagraph (c), and was inserted in order to dissuade the Court from examining a situation which is not considered to have reached the threshold of a non-international armed conflict. Although several subparagraphs contained in Article 8(2)(e) of the ICC Statute may affect the lives of women in non-international armed conflicts,[217] the subparagraph most applicable in terms of sexual violence prosecution before the Court is contained in subparagraph (vi), on 'committing rape, sexual slavery, enforced prostitution, forced pregnancy, as defined in article 7, paragraph 2 (f), enforced sterilization, and any other form of sexual violence also constituting a serious violation of article 3 common to the four Geneva Conventions'.

3.2.1 Committing rape, sexual slavery, enforced prostitution, forced pregnancy, as defined in Article 7(2)(f), enforced sterilisation and any other form of sexual violence also constituting a serious violation of Article 3 common to the 1949 Geneva Conventions

As mentioned in the context of international armed conflict, there is similarly no treaty in international (humanitarian) law that expressly prohibits as many sexual violence crimes as war crimes in internal armed conflict as have been laid down in Article 8(2)(e)(vi) of the ICC Statute. The only provisions prohibiting sexual violence crimes in internal armed conflicts are Article 4(2)(e) of 1977 Additional Protocol II, which prohibits 'outrages upon personal dignity, in particular, humiliating and degrading treatment, *rape, enforced prostitution and any form of indecent assault*', and Article 4(e) of the ICTR Statute, a provision which copied verbatim Article 4(2)(e) of 1977 Additional Protocol II, in further recognition of the customary nature of the crime.[218] Common Article 3 furthermore implicitly prohibits rape under 'torture' and 'outrages upon personal dignity'. As mentioned above, although Common Article 3 strictly speaking applies to internal armed conflicts only, it is generally understood that it is applicable to all armed conflicts.[219] On the basis of these provisions as well as the treaty

[217] Article 8(2)(e)(i) ('Intentionally directing attacks against the civilian population as such or against individual civilians not taking direct part in hostilities'); Article 8(2)(e)(v) ('Pillaging a town or place, even when taken by assault'); Article 8(2)(e)(vii) ('Conscripting or enlisting children under the age of fifteen years into armed forces or groups or using them to participate actively in hostilities'); Article 8(2)(e)(viii) ('Ordering the displacement of the civilian population for reasons related to the conflict, unless the security of the civilians involved or imperative military reasons so demand') and Article 8(2)(e)(xi) ('Subjecting persons who are in the power of another party to the conflict to physical mutilation or to medical or scientific experiments of any kind which are neither justified by the medical, dental or hospital treatment of the person concerned nor carried out in his or her interest, and which cause death to or seriously endanger the health of such person or persons').

[218] Italics added. Article 4(1) of 1977 Additional Protocol II also implicitly prohibits rape and sexual assault by stating that all persons are entitled to respect for their person and honour.

[219] See the ICJ Nicaragua case, para. 218, quoted in the Tadić Jurisdiction Decision, para. 102.

provisions and customary law on rape related to international armed conflict,[220] the Prosecutor successfully prosecuted Kunarac, Kovač and Vuković for rape as a crime in and of itself under Article 3 of the ICTY Statute as applicable in all armed conflicts. Despite the fact that the emergence of the ICC Statute and the explicit standing of rape as an independent crime in all armed conflicts makes tricks such as the one performed before the ICTY redundant, the prosecution of rape as an independent crime has greatly contributed to its inclusion in the ICC Statute; therefore, the relevant case law is discussed below.

In addition to rape and enforced prostitution, sexual slavery, forced pregnancy and enforced sterilisation are now explicitly prohibited in Article 8(2)(e)(vi) of the ICC Statute as war crimes in internal armed conflicts, giving rise to individual criminal liability. The explicit criminalisation of different forms of sexual violence as war crimes in internal armed conflict in and of themselves does away with obscure language such as 'outrages upon personal dignity' and is of major significance in international law.[221] The phrase 'any other form of sexual violence also constituting a serious violation of article 3 common to the four Geneva Conventions' is also better wording than its counterpart 'any form of indecent assault' in Article 4(2)(e) of 1977 Additional Protocol II, as it is more specific and states the source of the prohibition.[222] Moreover, the latter part of that phrase, 'also constituting a serious violation of article 3 common to the four Geneva Conventions', is of major importance as it must be understood to emphasise that the sexual violence crimes stated also constitute violations of Common Article 3, despite the fact that the Statute fails to list these forms of sexual violence as violating Common Article 3 themselves.[223] The 'serious violation of common article 3' reference was, moreover, intended to indicate that only serious crimes of sexual violence should fall within this definition. The direct wording prohibiting 'rape, sexual slavery, enforced prostitution, forced pregnancy ... enforced sterilization, and any other form of sexual violence also constituting a serious violation of article 3 common to the four Geneva Conventions' eases the burden of proof on the part of the Prosecutor. It is no longer required that the Prosecutor charge rape under any non-specific sexual violence crime, such as torture as a serious violation of Common Article 3; instead, he or she only needs to prove the elements of the crime itself, say rape, if rape is charged as rape under Article 8(2)(e)(vi).

The material and mental elements of these specific sexual violence crimes were drafted in the same way for war crimes under Article 8(2)(b)(xxii) in international armed conflicts and Article 8(2)(e)(vi) in non-international armed conflicts as well as under Article 7(1)(g) for crimes against humanity. The elements were initially drafted under Article 8(2)(b)(xxii), and subsequently transposed to the other two provisions. Some minor adjustments in wording were necessary in Article 8(2)(e)(vi) in relation to element 2 of the war crime of sexual violence, viz. the reference 'also constituting a grave breach of the four Geneva Conventions', which was replaced by 'also constituting

---

220 See subsection 2.2.2 above, and, in particular, the Furundžija Judgment, paras. 168-169, Furundžija Appeal Judgment, para. 210, and the Čelebići Judgment, paras. 476-477, for a discussion of rape as a war crime under international customary law in all armed conflicts.

221 See also McDonald (1998), p. 141.

222 *Ibid.*

223 See, *inter alia*, *Ibid.*, p. 140; and Boot (2002), p. 592.

a serious violation of article 3 common to the four Geneva Conventions', thus better accommodating the wording related to war crimes in internal armed conflict. In this study, the specific sexual violence crimes listed have been dealt with in Chapter 2 on crimes against humanity, and will therefore not be repeated here.

In ICTY case law, Kunarac, Kovač and Vuković have all three been convicted of rape as an independent customary war crime. Kunarac has been convicted of rape as an independent customary war crime, that is, a violation of the laws or customs of war, under four different counts. In the first place, Kunarac was convicted of the rapes of women at the House Ulica Osmana Dikica No. 16, where he raped three Muslim women and aided and abetted the (gang) rapes of the same and four other Muslim women by soldiers at the house (count 4).[224] As discussed above, the same conduct was also the basis for a conviction for torture under Article 3 (count 3)[225] and torture as a crime against humanity (count 1) and rape as a crime against humanity (count 2).[226] In the second place, it was established that Kunarac raped FWS-87 in Karaman's house (count 10).[227] This conduct also was the basis for a finding of guilt of rape as a crime against humanity (count 9). In the third place, Kunarac was convicted of raping Witness 183 as a violation of the laws or customs of war (count 12).[228] For the rape of this witness he was also found guilty of torture (count 11).[229] Finally, the Trial Chamber thought it proved that Kunarac, together with two other men (DP6 and 'Gaga'), took FWS-186, FWS-191 and J.G. from the house Ulica Osmana Dikica No. 16 to an abandoned house in Trnovace, where FWS-186 was raped by DP6 and FWS-191 was raped by Kunarac.[230] In particular, FWS-191 was ordered to undress herself and Kunarac then tried to rape her while his bayonet was placed on the table. Kunarac did not succeed the first time, as she was still a virgin and rigid with fear. He, however, 'succeeded in taking away her virginity the next day' and 'rejoiced at the idea of being her "first", thereby degrading her more'.[231] In addition, Kunarac was found guilty of holding FWS-186 and FWS-191 captive for a period of about six months in the house in Trnovace. Kunarac constantly raped FWS-191 for about two months, every time he came to the house, while DP6 continuously raped FWS-186 during her stay in the house. The women were treated as the men's personal property: they had to perform sexual services at their command, perform household chores and meet all other demands. The women had nowhere to go, even if they had attempted to leave the house. Other mistreatments included Kunarac inviting a soldier to the house in order to rape FWS-191 in exchange for DEM 100 and trying to rape her while in his hospital bed in front of other soldiers. Although it could not be held that Kunarac aided and abetted the

224 Kunarac, Kovač and Vuković Judgment, paras. 630-687.

225 See subsection 3.1.1.2 for a more elaborate discussion of the sexual violence conduct underlying the conviction for torture and rape under Article 3 of the ICTY Statute.

226 For a discussion of Kunarac, Kovač and Vuković's conviction for torture as a crime against humanity (count 1) and rape as a crime against humanity (count 2), see Chapter 2 on crimes against humanity.

227 Kunarac, Kovač and Vuković Judgment, para. 704.

228 *Ibid.*, para. 715. See subsection 3.1.1 for a more elaborate discussion of the facts.

229 *Ibid.*

230 *Ibid.*, paras. 718, 727.

231 *Ibid.*, para. 724.

rapes committed by DP6, he was found guilty of aiding and abetting DP6 with respect to his enslavement of FWS-186. For these acts, Kunarac was found guilty of rape as a crime against humanity (count 19), rape as a violation of the laws or customs of war (count 20) and enslavement as a crime against humanity (count 18).[232] Although also charged with outrages upon personal dignity as a violation of the laws or customs of war, Kunarac was not convicted thereof as this was already covered by the other convictions.[233]

Kovač was convicted of rape as a violation of the laws or customs of war on the basis of a plurality of sexual violence conduct (count 24).[234] FWS-75 and A.B. (12 years old) had been detained in Kovač's apartment for about a week. The Trial Chamber held that, at his apartment, Kovač raped both women and assisted other soldiers in raping them. Thereafter they were brought to another apartment where they were constantly raped for about fifteen days by at least ten or fifteen Serb soldiers. Next, they were taken to another apartment where they stayed for about seven to ten days, and rapes continued. Finally, the women returned to Kovač's apartment, where the rapes continued. Kovač eventually sold AB at DEM 200 and handed FWS-75 over to DP1 to be used as sexual slaves. Furthermore, also FWS-87 (15 years old) and A.S. were enslaved at Kovač's apartment for about four months. Kovač reserved FWS-87 for himself and raped her almost every night he spent in the apartment. A.S. was constantly raped by Kostic, and it was held that Kovač substantially assisted Kostic by raping A.S. because he allowed Kostic to stay at his apartment. Another incident involved forcing FWS-87, A.S. and A.B. to strip and dance naked on a table while Kovač watched them and pointed weapons at them. FWS-87 and A.S. were ultimately sold to two Montenegrins. By this conduct Kovač showed to have complete control over the victims' movements, privacy and labour. They had to cook, clean, perform sexual services at Kovač's command, endure degrading treatment, including beatings, and had no possibility of escape. Kovač was also found guilty of this conduct under enslavement as a crime against humanity (count 22), rape as a crime against humanity (count 23), and outrages upon personal dignity as a violation of the laws or customs of war (count 25).[235]

Vuković was convicted of raping a 16-year-old Muslim girl, FWS-50, under Article 3 of the ICTY Statute as an independent crime (count 36).[236] The same conduct resulted in a conviction for torture under Article 3 (count 35).[237]

In other indictments as well charges for rape as a violation of the laws or customs of war were brought.[238]

---

[232] *Ibid.*, paras. 745, 883.

[233] *Ibid.*, paras. 743, 745, 884.

[234] *Ibid.*, paras. 746-782.

[235] *Ibid.*, paras. 782, 886.

[236] See subsection 3.2.1. The same conduct furthermore formed the basis for a conviction for torture (count 33) and rape (count 34), both as crimes against humanity. See Chapter 2.

[237] Kunarac, Kovač and Vuković Judgment, para. 822. See subsection 3.1.1 for a discussion of the facts resulting in a conviction.

[238] See, *inter alia*, *Prosecutor v. Ramush Haradinaj, Idriz Balaj and Lahi Brahimaj*, Indictment, Case No. IT-04-84-I, 4 March 2005 (count 36).

3.3 Elements common to war crimes in non-international armed conflict

The elements which apply to all war crimes in internal armed conflicts are the following two: (1) the conduct took place in the context of and was associated with an armed conflict not of an international character; and (2) the perpetrator was aware of factual circumstances that established the existence of an armed conflict. The phrase 'armed conflict not of an international character' was derived from Common Article 3 and has been further clarified in subparagraphs (d) and (f) cited above. Further guidance on these two elements common to war crimes in internal armed conflict can be found in the introduction to the war crimes section in the EoC, that is (1) There is no requirement for a legal evaluation by the perpetrator as to the existence of an armed conflict or its character as international or non-international; (2) In that context there is no requirement for awareness by the perpetrator of the facts that established the character of the conflict as international or non-international; and (3) There is only a requirement for the awareness of the factual circumstances that established the existence of an armed conflict that is implicit in the terms 'took place in the context of and was associated with'. Therefore, in order to convict a person of sexual violence as a serious violation of Article 3 common to the four 1949 Geneva Conventions or as another serious violation of the laws and customs in non-international armed conflict, not only the elements of the specific sexual violence or non-specific sexual violence crimes must have been established, but also the conduct must have taken place in the context of and be associated with a non-international armed conflict; moreover, the perpetrator was aware of factual circumstances that established the existence of an armed conflict.

4 Final remarks

Article 8 of the ICC Statute prohibits rape, sexual slavery, enforced prostitution, forced pregnancy, enforced sterilisation and any other form of sexual violence also constituting a grave breach of the 1949 Geneva Conventions or any other form of sexual violence also constituting a serious violation of Article 3 common to the 1949 Geneva Conventions, in subparagraphs (2)(b)(xxii) and (2)(e)(vi), respectively. These specific sexual violence crimes have been discussed in Chapter 2. For the first time in history, these sexual violence crimes have been explicitly recognised as war crimes in and of themselves, not as an example of a larger protected category, such as 'outrages upon personal dignity' (in the case of rape, enforced prostitution and any other form of indecent assault). In the case of sexual slavery, forced pregnancy, and enforced sterilisation the crimes had not yet been explicitly recognised at all. Criminalising rape and other forms of sexual violence as crimes in and of themselves underscores the criminal nature of the crimes and does away with ambiguous wording which has long prevented the recognition of sexual violence crimes for what they are, that is, independent crimes. Therefore, in principle, prosecuting sexual violence crimes as war crimes no longer needs to be solely based on non-specific sexual violence crimes, such as the grave breaches of torture, inhuman treatment or wilfully causing great suffering or serious injury to body or health or the violations of Article 3 common to the 1949 Geneva Conventions of cruel treatment, torture or outrages upon personal dignity. Many ICTY/R prosecutions of sexual violence conduct had to be brought under these non-specific sexual violence war crimes provisions. In addition, over time, the ICTY also acknowledged the independent customary war crime status of rape as a violation of the laws or customs of war, punishable under Article 3 of the ICTY Statute, and has even indicted some persons on charges of rape as a grave breach (Article 2) directly. However, the ICC will have both options, that is, specific and non-specific sexual violence charges. Although it may be readily assumed that in future cases rape will first and foremost be charged as the war crime of rape, sexual slavery as the war crime of sexual slavery, and so forth, if the facts of the case require it in order to display the totality of the accused's conduct, it may be significant to charge the accused with specific sexual violence crimes under non-specific sexual violence crimes as well.

For example, according to the ICC's EoC, torture as a war crime (in international and non-international armed conflict) requires proof of severe physical or mental pain or suffering and the existence of one or more prohibited purposes. The existence of one or more prohibited purposes may be an important reason to charge rape as the war crime of torture, in addition to the war crime of rape, in order to stress the totality of the accused's conduct. Rape in armed conflict is often committed in order to obtain information, to punish, to intimidate or to discriminate, purposes which form an integral component of the war crime of torture. The list of prohibited purposes should, moreover, be considered to be non-exhaustive; it should also include such purposes as humiliation and gender discrimination, in conformity with ICTY case law. Rape and sexual violence in armed conflict is often, if not always, perpetrated against women because they are women. The recognition of gender as a purpose of raping underscores that, in times of war, women are disproportionately victims of sexual acts. In fact, in times of armed conflict it is difficult to envisage circumstances in which rape occurs for a purpose that does not, in some way, involve punishment, coercion, (gender) discrimination, intimidation or humiliation. ICTY case law has furthermore stressed that the prohibited purpose needs simply to be part of the accused's motivation, which means that even rapists with purely private motives, who claim to rape out of a sexual urge, may be convicted of rape as the war crime of torture. In addition to the purposive element, the rape conduct also needs to satisfy the element of severe physical or mental pain or suffering. The *Kunarac, Kovač and Vuković* Appeals Chamber held that rape by definition constitutes torture. In *Čelebići* it was, for example, held that 'there can be no question' that the vaginal and anal rapes committed against Ms Antic 'caused severe mental *and* physical pain and suffering'.[239] Therefore, it seems that rape and other forms of sexual violence can qualify fairly easily as torture, as they generally meet the requirements of both the purposive element and the severity of the crime. The requirement that a person in an official capacity should be involved in the torture process has justifiably been left out of the definition of torture as a war crime, in full recognition of the different context in which supranational criminal law operates. This trend was already set in motion by ICTY case law, including the *Kunarac, Kovač and Vuković* Appeal Judgment, and can now, with the accumulation in the disposal of the element in the definition of torture as a war crime in the ICC's EoC, be considered customary law in the context of supranational criminal law. The factor distinguishing between torture and other forms of inhuman treatment can be found in the purposive element and the severity of the crime, but for some crimes, such as the grave breach of inhuman treatment and the serious violation of Common Article 3 of cruel treatment, the purposive element of torture is the only distinguishing factor as the severity of the

239 Čelebići Judgment, para. 964.

crime is identical for all three crimes. In the past, conduct such as forced fellatio, rape and sexual mutilation, including burning a man's genitals and biting off a man's testicles, have all been found to come within the ambit of these other forms of inhuman treatment, although rape (which includes forced fellatio) could arguably have been prosecuted as torture if a purposive element had been found. It should be noted that if sexual violence is prosecuted under the non-specific sexual violence crimes, the severity of the crime and, in the case of torture, the purposes have already been established and can therefore not be taken into account again as aggravating circumstances at sentencing stage, while these elements need to be investigated separately at sentencing stage for some of the sexual violence crimes in terms of aggravating circumstances.[240]

The wording in 'also constituting a grave breach of the Geneva Conventions' and 'a serious violation of article 3 common to the four Geneva Conventions' makes clear that crimes of a sexual violence nature have now been brought to the level of grave breaches and violations of Common Article 3. As grave breaches are commonly referred to as *jus cogens*, sexual violence crimes have now officially reached that level too. However, as the phrase 'also constituting a grave breach of the Geneva Conventions' is placed in the part pertaining to 'other serious violations of the laws and customs applicable in international armed conflict', this may create some ambiguity about the *jus cogens* status of sexual violence crimes as grave breaches in and of themselves. It is therefore argued that the specific sexual violence crimes be listed among the grave breaches themselves. Inclusion would not only recognise the *jus cogens* status of sexual violence crimes as grave breaches in their own right, but it would, despite its implicit recognition, also more explicitly recognise sexual violence crimes as grave breaches.

Although the distinction between grave breaches and other violations in Article 8 of the ICC Statute does, in essence, not create different consequences for the two categories, the distinction is relevant for the national implementation of international humanitarian law. Under customary international law, all war crimes are subject to permissive universal jurisdiction, but the 1949 Geneva Conventions and 1977 Additional Protocol I introduced compulsory universal jurisdiction particularly concerning serious war crimes referred to as grave breaches. Whereas States were not obligated to repress or prosecute sexual violence crimes in the past, Article 8(2)(b)(xxii) of the ICC Statute has at least brought sexual violence crimes on the same level as grave breaches. In other words, sexual violence crimes belong to the top of the hierarchy of serious crimes, and compulsory universal jurisdiction is now officially attached to rape and other forms of sexual violence. However, as most conflicts are internal in character, it is important that compulsory universal jurisdiction is also attached to sexual violence crimes occurring in non-international armed conflicts. After all, the crimes are similar in nature and their occurrence does not depend on the character of the armed conflict. Although the ICC Statute may be seen as reflecting the international customary law status of sexual violence crimes as grave breaches and violations of Common Article 3, further clarification and uniformity of the law may be needed, for instance, by amending the grave breaches and Common Article 3 provisions to include specific sexual violence crimes and by attaching compulsory universal jurisdiction to Common Article 3 violations.

---

[240] On sentencing, see Chapter 6.

As it may sometimes be difficult to establish whether an armed conflict is international or non-international in character, the ICC Prosecutor has the option to prosecute sexual violence under both categories. Especially the prohibition of sexual violence in internal armed conflicts is significant in light of the many contemporaneous conflicts of an internal character. The war crimes provision in the ICC Statute furthermore differs from its counterparts in the ICTY and ICTR Statutes in that it states that war crimes are prosecuted in particular when committed on a systematic or large-scale basis. Whereas before the ICTY, for instance, the isolated rapes perpetrated against Witness A were prosecuted in the *Furundžija* case, the ICC Prosecutor may be more reluctant to take up such isolated events. Although such an approach is understandable in light of its mandate to prosecute the most responsible perpetrators, it is submitted that all serious war crimes need to be evaluated and be taken up by the Court, in as far as possible. Moreover, the distinction between crimes against humanity and war crimes would otherwise become too blurred as well.

Evaluation of Part I

No ICC, ICTY or ICTR treaty can remedy the suffering of victims of rape, sexual slavery, forced pregnancy or any other form of sexual violence taking place as constituent acts of genocide, crimes against humanity or war crimes. Yet, the explicit criminalisation in the ICC Statute of rape, sexual slavery, enforced prostitution, forced pregnancy, enforced sterilisation and other forms of sexual violence as crimes against humanity and war crimes (Articles 7 and 8 of the ICC Statute, respectively) provides another step in the direction of ending impunity for sexual violence on the supranational criminal law level. The need that existed within the Tribunals to charge sexual violence crimes also under non-specific sexual violence crimes no longer exists. Rape and other forms of sexual violence can also be prosecuted as genocide under 'causing serious bodily or mental harm' (Article 6 of the ICC Statute), as explained in a footnote in the EoC on the definition of genocide. In addition, raping a person on the basis of his or her gender can now be prosecuted as the crime against humanity of persecution in the ICC Statute as well. With the exception of the crime of rape and enforced prostitution, these specific sexual violence crimes were never laid down in a treaty on the supranational criminal law level before. Therefore, with the exception of the definition of rape, which has been the subject of study in several ICTY and ICTR cases, most of these crimes had never been defined. The EoC provide meaningful guidance for the ICC judges in the determination of the elements of the crimes but, officially, this document is not binding. Therefore, the main question that was raised was: What are or should be the definitions of the sexual violence crimes in the context of the, relatively young, supranational criminal law system?

On the whole, the specific sexual violence crimes laid down in the ICC Statute and EoC (as crimes against humanity and war crimes) provide a good framework in which sexual violence prosecutions can take place. Yet, in the clear example of the crime of rape, some ICTY and ICTR Chambers have defined the elements of rape as to include non-consent. However, lack of consent as an element of the crime of rape (or of any other sexual violence crime, for that matter) is immaterial within the supranational criminal law context, especially in light of the violent and oppressive context in which rapes as genocide, crimes against humanity or war crimes take place, and should therefore be rejected. To a large extent, the Tribunals based themselves on definitions of rape in national laws focusing on consent. However, the definitions of rape in those national laws were never written for the kind of situations the Court and Tribunals deal with and should therefore not be transferred to the supranational criminal law level easily. In order to recognise the sexual crimes in full and to do justice to the victims of these crimes, the ICC and the Tribunals should take into account the realities of rape and other forms of sexual violence when defining and/or interpreting the crimes over which they have jurisdiction. If rape and other forms of sexual violence are not defined in conformity with the nature of the crime, victims may be reluctant to come forward and testify at the Court. In that case, the crimes committed against them will not be recognised and punished. As long as the ICC keeps the realities of rape, sexual slavery, enforced prostitution, forced pregnancy, enforced sterilisation and any other form of sexual violence in mind, the EoC provide great potential to effectively prosecute sexual violence on the supranational criminal law level. In this respect, it must be noted, however, that the crime of genocide does not explicitly include a similar list of specific sexual violence crimes among its constituent acts, nor does it refer to group destruction on the basis of gender discrimination. Yet, the realities of genocidal rape demand such an inclusion as well. Similarly, although the war crimes provision refers to any other form of sexual violence 'also constituting a grave breach of the Geneva Conventions' or 'a serious violation of article 3 common to the four Geneva Conventions', it does not include rape and other forms of sexual amongst its grave breaches and Common Article 3 subparagraphs directly. As mentioned, in order to recognise rape and other forms of sexual violence as genocide, crimes against humanity and war crimes in all their aspects, the law needs to be amended to take into account the realities with which these crimes are committed. Furthermore, it would add to a coherent and uniform supranational criminal law system as far as sexual violence is concerned.

In order for rape or any other form of sexual violence to qualify as an international crime, the elements common to genocide, crimes against humanity and war crimes need to be fulfilled as well. In ICTY and ICTR case law, the elements common to genocide, crimes against humanity and war crimes have been interpreted rather realistically. In sexual violence cases, the specific intent for establishing genocide, may, in particular, be found in speeches of the accused calling for the rape of women of a particular group, in the disproportionate attack on the members of a particular group and in statements made by the rapists themselves during the sexual attack. As far as crimes against humanity are concerned, the act of rape or any other form of sexual violence does not need to be committed in a widespread or systematic manner; the act need simply form part of a widespread or systematic attack. The elements common to war crimes include that the conduct took place in the context of and was associated with an international or non-international armed conflict, and that the perpetrator was aware of factual circumstances that established the existence of an armed conflict. Furthermore, in order to prove the elements common to war crimes, an unfortunate element has been added in Article 8 of the ICC Statute: war crimes will, in particular, be prosecuted when committed on a systematic or large-scale basis. This would leave serious, yet isolated cases of sexual violence outside the jurisdiction of the Court. It is suggested that, in principle, every serious case of rape, sexual slavery or any other form of sexual violence be taken up by the Court in the fulfilment of its mandate. Of course, accountability for sexual violence can only be found if a person can be linked to the perpetration of the crime. On the basis of the ICTY and ICTR case law examined, it can be said that superior responsibility and the third variant of the joint criminal enterprise could have been used better and differently in order to arrive at comprehensive supranational criminal prosecutions of sexual violence.

PART II
SEXUAL VIOLENCE IN SUPRANATIONAL CRIMINAL PROCEDURE

My parents, my brother and my sister were killed. I'm all alone. My relatives were killed in a horrible fashion. But I survived – to answer the strange questions that were asked by the ICTR. If you say you were raped, that is something understandable. How many times do you need to say it? When the judges laughed, they laughed like they could not stop laughing. I was angry and nervous. When I returned, everyone knew I had testified. My fiancée [sic] refused to marry me once he knew I had been raped. He said, you went to Arusha and told everyone that you were raped. Today I would not accept to testify, to be traumatized for a second time. No one apologized to me. Only Gregory Townsend [the ICTR prosecuting lawyer] congratulated me after the testimony for my courage. When you return you get threatened. My house was attacked. My fiancée [sic] has left me. In any case, I'm already dead.

Witness TA, a victim of multiple rapes during the 1994 genocide in Rwanda, who had testified before the ICTR in 2001, in an interview with Binaifer Nowrojee in 2003, in: Nowrojee (2005).

INTRODUCTION TO PART II

Part II of this study deals with the procedural part of the supranational criminal law system, in particular the protective and special measures available to victims of sexual violence and the participation of victims of sexual violence in court proceedings. Are the rights of victim-witnesses of sexual violence to safety, privacy and dignity, and physical and psychological well-being adequately safeguarded by the protective and special measures available at the ICC? How can the Court meet their needs for safety and confidentiality and prevent retraumatisation when testifying in court without compromising the rights of the accused? A lack of effective protective and special measures may dissuade victims from testifying and, hence, prosecution of the most responsible will in most cases not be possible. The truth may never come out. These issues will be examined in Chapter 4 from the perspective of the ICC, taking into account the ICTY and ICTR experience on confidentiality and anonymity measures as well as on protection from retraumatisation.

Chapter 5 focuses on participatory rights of victims. For the first time in the history of supranational criminal prosecution, the ICC allowed victims to participate in its proceedings as victims. Before the Tribunals, victims only participated in trials as witnesses. To what extent can victims of sexual violence enforce their participatory rights before the ICC? Victims of sexual violence may, more than other groups of victims, suffer from stigmatisation, shame and fear and, for this reason, there is a significant risk that victims of sexual violence will be underrepresented at the trials if no special methods are developed to notify them about the participatory possibilities available at the ICC. Furthermore, having victims of sexual violence participating in court requires that special measures are put in place to facilitate this participation. Chapter 5 deals with the challenges faced by the ICC to effectuate the participation of victims of sexual violence in a gender-sensitive manner and looks back on the 'participation' of victims of sexual violence before the Tribunals.

CHAPTER 4
PROTECTIVE AND SPECIAL MEASURES FOR VICTIMS OF SEXUAL VIOLENCE

1 INTRODUCTION

In the international criminal proceedings of the International Criminal Tribunal for the former Yugoslavia and the International Criminal Tribunal for Rwanda, victims appear as witnesses. Their role in the proceedings is solely aimed at the establishment of the truth. However, as a consequence, several victims and their relatives have experienced intimidation and some of them were even killed. Both Tribunals provide a set of protective measures in order to protect those who are of utmost importance to their proceedings: victims and witnesses. After all, it cannot be expected from victims and witnesses that they will risk their lives, face rejection by their own society or accept exposure to secondary traumatisation as a consequence of their giving testimony. It is very likely that the International Criminal Court will have to deal with similar forms of retaliation. Protective and special measures were therefore also included in the ICC provisions, viz. in Rules 87 and 88, respectively.

In this Chapter, the protective and special measures available to victims appearing as witnesses in cases involving sexual violence will be examined. The central question in this Chapter is whether the rights of victim-witnesses of sexual violence (to safety; privacy and dignity; and physical and psychological well-being) are adequately safeguarded by the protective and special measures available at the ICC? The subject is approached from the perspective of the ICC, whereby the experiences of the ICTY and ICTR have been taken as a reference. Section 2 contains an overview of the different forms of protective measures as well as their rationale. Section 3 provides a brief overview of the most important ICC, ICTY and ICTR provisions on witness protection, especially with regard to victims of sexual violence and the rights of the accused. In the subsequent sections, the protective and special measures available to, in particular, the victim-witness of sexual violence, will be examined: confidentiality measures (section 4), anonymity measures (section 5) and measures that prevent further or increased traumatisation (section 6). The main emphasis in these three sections will be on the effectiveness of the measures for victim-witnesses of sexual violence as well as their (non)potential to conflict with the rights of the accused, in particular his or her right to examine the witness. Section 7 will briefly discuss the Victims and Witnesses Unit (VWU) and its role in protecting and supporting victims and witnesses. Finally, in section 8, some concluding observations will be made and a tentative answer to the central question will be given.

2 THE RATIONALE FOR AND FORMS OF PROTECTIVE MEASURES

The rationale behind the use of protective measures for victims and witnesses within international criminal courts is essentially four-fold: (1) to minimise serious risks to the security of victims and witnesses; (2) to avoid serious incursions of their privacy and dignity; and (3) to reduce trauma associated with giving testimony.[1] In addition, a fourth reason can de discerned: (4) without victims and witnesses, there would generally not even be a trial. Protective measures are therefore necessary in order to establish the truth.

The first reason, to protect the victim's safety, lies in the presumption that victims usually still live in volatile areas and therefore have a reasonable fear of retaliation. Although the conflicts in the former Yugoslavia and Rwanda have come to an end, tensions between the warring groups have remained. This can hardly be surprising given that conflicts neither occur nor disappear overnight: ethnic or any other form of hatred against the other group is usually deeply rooted in a society and goes back years. Tensions are especially hard to avoid in countries where victims and perpetrators are still living within the same borders, such as in Rwanda and the countries on the territory of the former Yugoslavia. Therefore, when a victim is willing to testify before an international criminal tribunal against an accused from another ethnic or religious group, this may well cause the victim, his or her family, or even a whole local community, to become the prime target of reprisals by the accused or his or her sympathisers who do not want the accused to stand trial.[2] The danger for witnesses to testify is even greater where the accused is someone who, during the conflict, used to hold a high position and nowadays still has many friends who care about his welfare.[3] These so-called 'big fishes' are precisely the persons who generally have (or had) to stand trial before the ICTY and ICTR, and this is not different for the ICC.

Hard statistics on numbers of intimidations, threats or killings are not available. Still, there are a number of indications that ICTY witnesses from the former Yugoslavia have been threatened.[4] Also inside the countries of the former Yugoslavia, protection for witnesses who want to testify before national courts is largely unavailable, and victims and witnesses, including rape victims, face intimidations and treats.[5] As far as

---

[1] These goals are recognised, *inter alia*, in the UN Declaration of Basic Principles of Justice for Victims of Crime and Abuse of Power, UNGA Resolution 40/34, 29 November 1985, Article 6(d); and Recommendation No. R (85) 11 on the Position of the Victim in the Framework of Criminal Law and Procedure, Council of Europe, 28 June 1985, C.8, F.15, G.16.

[2] Mumba (2001), p. 360. Please note that witnesses for the Defence may also face intimidations and threats.

[3] *Ibid.*

[4] See, *inter alia*, ICTY Press Release, *Judgement in the Case of The Prosecutor v. Beqa Beqaj*, 5 May 2005 (Beqaj was convicted to four months of imprisonment for contempt of the Tribunal because he wilfully and knowingly interfered with Witness B1 and the administration of justice); New York Times, *Court Rejects Any Liberty for Milosevic, Citing Threats* (by Marlise Simons), 7 March 2002 ('According to the office of the prosecutor, several Balkans-based witnesses scheduled to testify at the trial, which began February 12, have been threatened, and some have received death threats'); *Prosecutor v. Duško Tadić*, Decision on Appellant's Motion for the Extension of the Time-limit and Admission of Additional Evidence, Case No. IT-94-1-A, 15 October 1998, paras. 9, 59 and 62 (it should be noted here that Tadić, a former camp guard, was generally regarded as a 'small fish'); Agence France-Presse, *Trauma and Isolation Await Many Witnesses of UN Court at Home*, 16 January 2004 ('The dire economic situation and the sense of insecurity, especially for victims living in areas where nationalists still hold power, takes a heavy toll on those who testify').

[5] See, *inter alia*, Amnesty International (2003), (2004d) and (2005).

Rwanda is concerned, a number of sources have revealed that witnesses were intimidated, received death treats, were attacked and, in some cases, even killed before or after they had testified before the ICTR.[6] Female victim-witnesses who testified about rape at the Rwanda Tribunal have similarly faced intimidation through verbal harassment or death threats and some had to go into hiding.[7] Killings have also been reported in Rwanda in relation to the national Gacaca trials: genocide survivors who were supposed to testify against the 'small fishes' were killed before the trials had even started in order to deter others from testifying.[8] These cases prove that victims' fears about testifying are well-founded and that threats or killings are not necessarily linked to the high position of the accused.

In order to halt possible threats or killings of victims or witnesses, precautions in the form of protective measures need to be taken. One means of achieving this end is by anonymity. Anonymity measures include the non-disclosure of the victim's or witness's identity to the accused and his counsel. These measures are generally considered to have a far greater potential to conflict with the rights of the accused to a fair trial than those to be discussed next: confidentiality measures. Full anonymity is currently not granted to witnesses appearing before the ICTY or ICTR.

Confidentiality measures are to guarantee that the victim's or witness's identity is not revealed to the public or the press in order to protect a victim's or witness's privacy and dignity. When the public and the media is not aware of who is sitting in the witness box, the victim's name will not be revealed to anyone, except to those sitting in court. This protective measure is especially relevant for victims of sexual violence who, due to publicity, are more vulnerable than others to being rejected by their family or society. In still too many societies, rape victims are looked upon as if they did something wrong, thereby placing the guilt and shame on the victim instead of on the perpetrator. As

---

[6] Hirondelle News Agency, *Prosecution Witness Assassinated in Rwanda*, 20 October 2004 (the Prosecution witness, a confessed genocidaire, was killed at his home in Kaduha (Gikongoro) after he returned from the ICTR, where he had given evidence against Colonel Simba); ICTR Draft Report on Improved Access to Anti-Retroviral Treatment and Psychological Counselling for ICTR Witnesses with HIV/AIDS, prepared by Elsie Effange-Mbella, 2004, pp. 3-4 ('The Office of the Prosecutor has reported a high degree of migration among its witnesses partly in search of comfort and for fear of reprisals. ... Also the dynamics that led to the tragedies in Rwanda are still prevalent and will continue to influence Rwandan communities for many years to come, whether those communities are still living within these territories or are scattered elsewhere in the world. Suspicion and a sense of vengeance are still rampant among Rwandese. This situation makes most witnesses and victims who come to testify before the ICTR live in constant fear of reprisals and threats to their life, property and family. Given the anxiety and the constant fear that continues amongst members of the Rwandan communities, protection and support become the greatest concerns of most people willing to testify before the Tribunal'); International Federation for Human Rights (2002), pp. 8-9; and Coalition for Women's Human Rights in Conflict Situations (1997b).

[7] Hirondelle News Agency, *Survivors Accused 14 Defence Investigators of Genocide Crimes*, 25 March 2002; and Nowrojee (2005).

[8] The New Times, *Gacaca Witnesses Murdered*, 25 April 2005; The New Times, *Survivors' Houses Burnt*, 28-29 June 2004; BBC News, *Genocide Witnesses Being Killed: The Rwandan Government Has Been Urged to Halt the Murder and Intimidation of Potential Witnesses to the Genocide in 1994 During which 800,000 People Died*, 16 December 2003.

explained by Marie Imaculee Ingabire, a women's rights activist from Rwanda, in her report *The Rape of Tutsi Women: A Weapon of the 1994 Genocide* submitted to the ICTR in the *Muhimana* case:

> Sexuality is a taboo in Rwandan culture. Being raped is a major social-cultural problem for a Rwandan girl or woman. In normal times, the Rwandan society does not usually consider a raped woman as a victim who requires compassion and rehabilitation. Society rather looks at her as if she was partly responsible for what happened to her! That is part of the mentality of Rwandans and the women who were raped during the genocide are aware of it. They therefore know that they will always be the objects of stigmatization once they were raped. They know that it is as if they were marked with red iron.[9]

It is therefore not unrealistic that victims of sexual violence experience rejection by their community if they find out about the victim's testimony. For this reason, many victims of sexual violence choose not to testify at all. Ingabire described some of these women's sentiments, representative of thousands of victims of sexual violence, as follows:

- 1. NK: "I had to change homes", she said, "I left my village and I cannot go back there, because everyone there knows that I was raped. I was raped in a school compound where we had gone to hide. Nobody knows what happened to me where I stay now, and you want me to testify and disclose my secret before the entire world? Never".
- …
- 3. RN: She will not testify, because she is married and she does not want her husband, to whom she has never disclosed anything, to know about it.
- 4. JU: She will not testify, because her shame will also spread to her children, who will become everyone's laughing stock.
- 5. RN: She will never go to testify, because if she did so, she would be forced to say that she no longer has a uterus, as a result of the rape. She added: "I no longer consider myself to be a complete human being, I feel so diminished. Is it necessary for the whole world to know? Let me die with my pain, but do not ask me to go and strip myself naked, because I know that those people to whom I will narrate my misfortune have no sympathy for me."[10]

Rejection by your own partner, family and community is thus a good reason why some victims do not want to testify. For those women who do want to testify, however, confidentiality may therefore be a very important protection measure in order to avoid stigmatisation after testimony.[11] However, taking into account the number of threats against and killings of (potential) witnesses in the past, it is questionable whether the

---

[9] Ingabire (2004). Ingabire was scheduled to appear as an expert witness in the Muhimana case but her testimony was dropped at the last minute by the Prosecutor because of bureaucratic delays.

[10] *Ibid.*

[11] It should be noted that not all victims of sexual violence want confidentiality; there are those who do not mind that others hear their story, in fact *want* others to know what happened to them. See also subsection 4.2.

concept of confidentiality offers enough guarantees for the privacy and dignity as well as the safety of those willing to testify before the ICC.

A third reason why witnesses and victims are in need of protective and special measures can be found in the understanding that victims should not suffer unnecessarily from secondary victimisation as a result of testifying. Such measures will be especially important for victims of sexual violence who may find it very painful to recount the terrible details of their ordeal. In order not to increase their trauma, the ICC may allow certain protective and special measures, such as measures that avoid a face-to-face confrontation with the accused in court, restrictions on the questions that the parties may ask the victim as well as restrictions on the manner of questioning, and measures that spare a victim from repeated questioning.

Without protective and special measures, witnesses may be more reluctant to come forward to testify before the ICC. The Court, in its search for truth, is, on the other hand, for a very large part dependent on the testimonies of witnesses. Without extensive documentation about the defendants' war plans,[12] the ICC will have to rely on the testimonies of witnesses. In other words, without witnesses, there will generally be no trial and, without a trial, it will be very difficult to establish the truth. It is therefore also in the interest of the ICC that witnesses receive the best possible protection and support so that they may come forward to testify. This is the fourth reason to have a good set of protection measures.

From the above overview, three main categories of protective measures for victims and witnesses can be discerned, namely, those aimed at: (1) protection from the press and the public, also called confidentiality measures; (2) protection from the accused, also called anonymity measures; and (3) protection from retraumatisation. These measures will be elaborated upon in sections 4, 5 and 6, respectively.

3 WITNESS PROTECTION VERSUS THE RIGHTS OF THE ACCUSED

The main provisions governing the protection of victims and witnesses in the ICC Statute are Articles 68 and 69(2). Rules 87 ('Protective Measures') and 88 ('Special Measures') of the ICC Rules of Procedure and Evidence further elaborate on the appropriate measures that can be taken for the protection of witnesses.[13] Such protective measures must be taken in particular during the investigation and prosecution of such crimes[14] and therefore mainly minimise the risks the witness runs after testimony.

---

[12] In this context, the advantage of the Nuremberg Tribunal is that its records were kept meticulously by the Germans.

[13] The significance of victim and witness protection is recognised on several other occasions in the ICC's RPE. See, *inter alia*, Rules 16-19, Rule 50(1), Rule 52(1), Rule 59, Rule 67, Rule 68, Rule 76(4), Rule 77, Rule 81, Rule 84, Rule 86, Rule 105(3), Rule 106(2), Rule 107(3), Rule 112(4), Rule 119(3), Rule 121(10) and Rule 131(2).

[14] Article 68(1) ICC Statute. With regard to the investigative phase, it should be noted that investigators of the Court must take care not to approach survivors obtrusively. In the initial years of the investigations conducted in Rwanda, Tribunal investigators used very conspicuous vehicles: big white cars with the UN logo on them. Everybody in the neighbourhood would therefore know when they had spoken to a potential witness.

However, even in the post-trial phase, the ICC has taken up certain obligations to ensure victims' and witnesses' safety.[15]

Articles 68 of the ICC Statute requires the Court to take appropriate measures to protect certain well-recognised goals, namely, the safety, dignity and privacy, and physical and psychological well-being of victims and witnesses. In choosing its measures, the ICC must take into account all relevant factors, including age, gender and health, and the nature of the crime, in particular with crimes involving sexual or gender violence or violence against children. The Court hereby explicitly recognised that victims of sexual violence are to be considered vulnerable witnesses who therefore merit special attention when the appropriate protective measures need to be chosen. The ICC Statute is particularly explicit in recognising the need to protect victims of sexual violence in Article 68(2): victims of sexual violence seem to qualify automatically for having any part of the proceedings take place in closed session or for having their evidence presented by use of electronic or other special means. The special needs of victims of sexual violence are also clearly recognised in Rule 88. It provides, *inter alia*, that special measures may be ordered to facilitate the testimony of a victim of sexual violence. Finally, Article 21(3) contains an equality and non-discrimination clause which requires that the application and interpretation of the law must be consistent with internationally recognised human rights, and be without any adverse distinction founded on several enumerated grounds, including gender. The ICC Statute was the first international instrument in which such provisions concerning the protection of victims of sexual violence are formulated so explicitly; the provisions used within the ICTY and ICTR Statutes and RPE are much less specific.

The provisions on witness protection also refer to the rights of the accused: Articles 68(1), (5), and 69(2) all state that the protective measures should not interfere with the rights of the accused, while at the same time acknowledging that these provisions already form an exception to the right of a public hearing and the right to be present in person in court. The drafters of the ICC Statute thus tried to 'balance' victims' rights with the rights of the accused.[16] The rights of the accused are laid down in Article 67 of the ICC Statute. The accused is entitled to a public hearing, a fair hearing conducted impartially and certain minimum guarantees, including: '(b) To have adequate time and facilities for the preparation of the defence and to communicate freely with counsel of the accused's choosing in confidence; ... (e) To examine, or have examined, the witnesses against him or her and to obtain the attendance and examination of witnesses on his or her behalf under the same conditions as witnesses against him or her ....'[17]

Within the ICTY and the ICTR a similar balance between the rights of the accused and those of victims and witnesses can be found.[18] Following Article 21(2) of the ICTY

---

[15] Rules 16(4) and 17 ICC RPE.

[16] Article 64(2) ICC Statute reads: 'The Trial Chamber shall ensure that a trial is fair and expeditious and is conducted with full respect for the rights of the accused and due regard for the protection of victims and witnesses.'

[17] See also Article 6 European Convention on Human Rights and Fundamental Freedoms (1950); Article 14 International Covenant on Civil and Political Rights (1966); and Article 8 American Convention on Human Rights (1969).

[18] See Article 20(1) ICTY Statute and Article 19(1) ICTR Statute. The wording of the provisions is identical to that in Article 64(2) ICC Statute.

Statute (Article 20(2) of the ICTR Statute), the accused shall be entitled to a fair and public hearing with certain well-recognised minimum guarantees, such as the right to examine the witness against him. Yet, the right to a fair and public hearing is made 'subject to Article 22 of the Statute' (Article 21 of the ICTR Statute), which reads:

> The International Tribunal shall provide in its rules of procedure and evidence for the protection of victims and witnesses. Such protection measures shall include, but shall not be limited to, the conduct of *in camera* proceedings and the protection of the victim's identity.

This provision on witness protection can be seen as the predecessor of Article 68 of the ICC Statute. Even though no direct reference can be found in Article 22 of the ICTY Statute (or Article 21 of the ICTR Statute) to the protection of victims of sexual violence, the UN Secretary-General held in his report to the Security Council that such protection should especially be provided in the Rules of Procedure and Evidence for victims and witnesses, 'especially in cases of rape or sexual assault'.[19] In the past, several Trial Chambers have referred to the Secretary-General's Report to substantiate their decisions to grant protective measures where victims of sexual violence were concerned.[20]

Rule 69 ('Protection of Victims and Witnesses'), Rule 75 ('Measures for the Protection of Victims and Witnesses') and Rule 79 ('Closed Sessions') of the ICTY and ICTR RPE further describe the protection available to victims and witnesses and should be read together.[21] On the basis of the above-mentioned provisions, the ICTY Trial

[19] 'In the light of the particular nature of the crimes committed in the former Yugoslavia, it will be necessary for the International Tribunal to ensure the protection of victims and witnesses. Necessary protection measures should therefore be provided in the rules of procedure and evidence for victims and witnesses, *especially in cases of rape and sexual assault*. Such measures should include, but should not be limited to the conduct of *in camera* proceedings, and the protection of the victim's identity' (italics added). See Report of the Secretary-General Pursuant to Paragraph 2 of Security Council Resolution 808 (1993), UN Doc. S/25704, 3 May 1993, para. 108.

[20] See, *inter alia*, *Prosecutor v. Duško Tadić*, Decision on the Prosecutor's Motion Requesting Protective Measures for Victims and Witnesses, Case No. IT-94-1-T, 10 August 1995, para. 46; *Prosecutor v. Zejnil Delalić, Zdravko Mucić, Hazim Delić and Esad Landžo*, Decision on the Motions by the Prosecution for Protective Measures for Prosecution Witnesses pseudonymed "B" through to "M", Case No. IT-96-21-T, 28 April 1997, para. 40; *Prosecutor v. Anto Furundžija*, Decision on Prosecutor's Motion Requesting Protective Measures for Witnesses "A" and "D" at Trial, Case No. IT-95-17/1-T, 11 June 1998, para. 6.

[21] Rule 69(A) ICTY/R RPE states: 'In exceptional circumstances, the Prosecutor may apply to a Trial Chamber to order the non-disclosure of the identity of a victim or witness who may be in danger or at risk until such person is brought under the protection of the Tribunal.' Subparagraph (C) of the same rule states: '*Subject to Rule 75*, the identity of the victim or witness shall be disclosed in sufficient time prior to the trial to allow adequate time for preparation of the defence (italics added).' Rule 75(A) states that 'appropriate measures' may be ordered for the privacy and protection of victims and witnesses, with the qualification that such measures 'are consistent with the rights of the accused'. Finally, Rule 75(B)(iii) states that 'appropriate measures to facilitate the testimony of vulnerable victims and witnesses, such as one-way closed circuit television' may be ordered.

Chamber ruled on the parameters of witness protection and answered the question of whether anonymous witness testimony as a protection measure within the Tribunal is allowed.[22]

4 Protection from the Public or the Press

Article 68(2) of the ICC Statute states that exceptions to the principle of a public hearing can be made in order to protect victims and witnesses. Rule 87 of the ICC RPE, in particular, defines the sort of protective devices which prevent the public or press and information agencies from finding out the identity and address details of the victim, witness or other person at risk on account of testimony given by a witness. Such confidentiality measures are, as mentioned, particularly relevant for victims of sexual violence as they prevent the victim from becoming known in the country or community of origin as a victim of sexual violence. For example, for Witness C, a protected witness in the ICTY *Čelebići* case, the reason for the confidentiality request was 'a desire for privacy, a wish not be publicly associated with the alleged sexual assaults upon his person and that of another'.[23] In many societies, the stigmatisation attached to being a victim of sexual violence is still tremendous. The consequences of having it publicly known that someone was a victim of sexual violence may well cause that person to be rejected by his or her community, family, friends or partner.

Rule 87 is an open-ended provision, thus creating the possibility for other protective measures to be ordered by the Court in the future. Rule 87, however, does not provide for the non-disclosure of confidential details to the accused and his counsel;[24] its scope is limited to non-disclosure to the public or the media. The accused (and his Defence team) can thus still see, hear and confront the victim-witness.

Straightforward confidentiality measures include the withholding of the victim's name of the Court's public records (such as Transcripts, Orders, Decisions, and Judgments); the use of a pseudonym for a victim throughout the proceedings (usually by using letters and/or numbers); and the prohibition of disclosing the identity of the victim by any of the participants in the trial to a third party.[25] Such measures cannot be considered to violate the rights of the accused as the accused and his counsellors are aware of the true identity of the victim in due time before the start of the trial. Rule 87 also provides in the possibility of *in camera* proceedings and the presentation of testimony by electronic or other special means. These two protective measures make an

---

[22] *Prosecutor v. Duško Tadić*, Decision on the Prosecutor's Motion Requesting Protective Measures for Victims and Witnesses, Case No. IT-94-1-T, 10 August 1995. See section 5 for the different interpretations of the ICTY provisions on the possibility of anonymity as a protective measure.

[23] *Prosecutor v. Zejnil Delalić, Zdravko Mucić, Hazim Delić and Esad Landžo*, Decision on the Motions by the Prosecution for Protective Measures for Prosecution Witnesses pseudonymed "B" through to "M", Case No. IT-96-21-T, 28 April 1997, para. 30.

[24] For a discussion of full anonymity, see section 5.

[25] Although not explicitly mentioned in Rule 87 ICC RPE, the Tribunals have on various occasions ordered that the public and media shall not photograph, video record or sketch witnesses who are victims of the conflicts in Rwanda and the former Yugoslavia. It can reasonably be assumed that the Court will also give such orders, when and if necessary, on the basis of non-exhaustive Rule 87.

exception to the general rule that hearings will be held in public, and, in case of live video conferencing, that testimony of a witness must be given in person in court.[26] The latter three protective measures will be discussed in more detail below.

4.1 Non-disclosure of information to a third party

The Prosecutor, the Defence or any other participant in the proceedings are prohibited from disclosing information to a third party revealing the name of the victim, witness or other person at risk on account of testimony given by a witness or any information which could lead to his or her identification. The rule has a broad reach as it prohibits the disclosure of identification details by participants in the proceedings to anyone who was not directly involved in the case. Solely the Prosecutor, Defence and any other participant in the proceedings, such as assistants to the Prosecutor or Defence Counsel including investigators, are allowed to know the true identification details of the victim or witness.

Ordering the non-disclosure of identification details of victims or witnesses is not a violation of the rights of the accused to a fair trial as long as the accused and his counsel as well as those persons assisting them are aware of the true identity of the victim or witness when preparing their case.[27] It is imperative that the chain of people aware of the identity and whereabouts of the victim or witness is kept as small as possible in order not to jeopardise the victim's or witness' privacy or safety. The information must therefore not come into the hands of the allies or supporters of the accused. Practice has revealed that information about witnesses was occasionally leaked via the accused or his counsel and assistants; a practice which may severely jeopardise the witness's privacy or security.[28] It must also be noted that, in some cases, it has been

---

[26] See Articles 64(7), 67(1) and 69(2) ICC Statute.

[27] See, for instance, *Prosecutor v. Dragan Gagović, Gojko Janković, Janko Janjić, Radomir Kovač, Zoran Vuković, Dragan Zelenović, Dragoljub Kunarac and Radovan Stanković*, Decision on Prosecution Motion to Protect Victims and Witnesses, Case No. IT-96-23 and 23/1, 29 April 1998.

[28] According to the report prepared by the International Federation for Human Rights (2002, p. 9): 'Two witnesses returning home from the ICTR were called to report to the Deputy Prosecutor of the Republic and were confronted face to face with a detainee who seemed to know not only their identities and the fact that they had been to Arusha, but was also aware of the content of their statements. Written copies of their statements had apparently been forwarded to him via a defence lawyer who had asked the detainee concerned to present testimony on the same events for the defence. Both these witnesses later received a number of messages containing death threats, and had to seek asylum in Kigali ...' See also New York Times, *Court Rejects Any Liberty for Milosevic, Citing Threats*, (by Marlise Simons), 7 March 2002 ('In addition [to (death) threats], court orders have apparently been violated in the case of two protected witnesses who testified in closed sessions last week. Officials said the nature of their testimony had apparently been leaked by associates of Mr. Milosevic and published in Belgrade news reports'); and the report submitted by Kamuhanda himself, the former Rwandan Minister of Higher Education and Scientific Research, convicted by the ICTR, entitled *Kamuhanda Jean de Dieu, Innocent Mais Condamné*, 11 février 2004. In this report, Kamuhanda explains why he should not have been convicted and reveals names (and names of relatives), address details and the jobs of some persons who appeared as protected witnesses in his trial.

almost impossible to conceal the witness' identity from the public. This is, for example, the case if a victim is known as a survivor and lives in a region where the accused, who is on trial, used to live, and the victim is away for several days or weeks while he or she has never even left the village before.[29] This situation has in particular been the case in Rwanda.

Apart from this, anyone who breaches the rule on non-disclosure of identification details of a victim to a third party can be sanctioned for misconduct before the Court on the basis of Article 71 of the ICC Statute. The sanction may include a fine or the removal of the person who committed the misconduct from the proceedings for a temporary or permanent period.[30] In addition, Article 70 of the ICC Statute ('Offences against the Administration of Justice') contains another form of contempt of court that is aimed to protect witnesses.[31] This includes, under subparagraph (c), 'corruptly influencing a witness, obstructing or interfering with the attendance or testimony of a witness, retaliating against a witness for giving testimony or destroying, tampering with or interfering with the collection of evidence'.[32] The sanction the ICC may impose in these cases is imprisonment to a maximum of five years or a fine, or both.[33] In the *Aleksovski* case before the ICTY, a fine of NLG 10,000 (approximately EUR 4500) was imposed on one of the Defence Counsel for General Blaskić for disclosing information about the identity and occupation of a protected witness in court.[34] The Trial Chamber

---

[29] International Federation for Human Rights (2002, p. 9): 'In most cases the identity was deduced by neighbours who noticed that the person was away at the same time as the radio reported on an ICTR trial concerning events from their region or district.'

[30] See Rules 170-172 ('Misconduct Before the Court Under Article 71') ICC RPE. Rule 171(4) states that the fine may not exceed EUR 2.000, except in cases of continuing misconduct where a new fine may be (cumulatively) imposed for each day the misconduct continues.

[31] See also Rules 162-169 ICC RPE.

[32] These two forms of contempt to protect witnesses were brought together in one provision in the ICTY RPE, i.e., Rule 77, with similar sanctions for both forms. In the ICC Statute and RPE, these forms of contempt are dealt with in separate provisions cumulating in separate sanctions. In other words, if a person is convicted under Article 71 for disclosing the identity of a protected witness, imprisonment cannot be imposed as a penalty. Rule 172, however, provides that if the conduct covered by Article 71 also consititutes one of the offences defined in Article 70, the Court will proceed in accordance with Article 70 and Rules 162-169 and imprisonment can be imposed.

[33] Note that the penalties under the ICC provisions are lower than those under the ICTY provisions: imprisonment with a maximum of five years (ICC) against imprisonment to a maximum of seven years (ICTY); a total amount not exceeding '50 per cent of the value of the convicted person's identifiable assets, liquid or realizable, and property, after deduction of an appropriate amount that would satisfy the financial needs of the convicted person and his or her dependants' (ICC) against fines to a maximum of EUR 100,000 (ICTY).

[34] *Prosecutor v. Zlatko Aleksovski*, Décision Portant Condamnation Pour Outrage Au Tribunal, Case Nº IT-95-14/1-T, 11 décembre 1998. See also Rule 77 ICTY RPE, 'Contempt of the Tribunal', particularly Rule 77(A)(ii), (iv) and (v) ICTY RPE. The latest version of Rule 77 ICTY RPE (amended 17 December 2003) states that the maximum penalty that may be imposed on a person found to be in contempt of the Tribunal is a term of imprisonment not exceeding seven years or a fine not exceeding EUR 100,000, or both. In addition, if counsel is found guilty of contempt of the Tribunal pursuant to Rule 77, the Chamber concerned may also determine that counsel is no longer eligible to represent a suspect or accused before the Tribunal or that such

argued that decisions regarding the protection of witnesses are of primary importance, not only for the protection of the lives of the witnesses, but also for the functioning of the Tribunal. Therefore, all those involved in the work of the Tribunal, including the lawyers, must take all necessary measures to guarantee the absolute respect of protective measures for witnesses. The decision was reversed on appeal, however, on the basis that there was not a 'knowing violation' by counsel of the witness protection order, a requirement under the ICTY provision on contempt.[35] Other contempt of court proceedings have since followed before both Tribunals, in which both witnesses for the Prosecution and Defence have seen their identity revealed, and this raises the question to what extent protected witnesses can really be protected.[36] In one case where a witness's statement was revealed to the media, it was decided that a log was to be kept which would include the names of the persons in possession of the witnesses' statements.[37] In addition, it was held that those persons are under an instruction not to reproduce those statements and to return them when no longer required, on pain of contempt of court.[38] Since then, such orders have been imposed for protected witnesses

---

conduct amounts to misconduct of counsel pursuant to Rule 46, or both. Compare also Rule 77 ICTR RPE, which is much less elaborate on contempt of tribunal proceedings in terms of conduct and sanction.

[35] *Prosecutor v. Zlatko Aleksovski*, Judgment on Appeal by Anto Nobilo against Finding of Contempt, Case No. IT-95-14/1-AR77, 30 May 2001.

[36] See for the ICTR, *inter alia*, *The Prosecutor v. Théoneste Bagosora, Gratien Kabiligi, Aloys Ntabakuze and Anatole Nsengiyumva*, Decision on the Prosecution Motion Ex Parte in the Matter of Violation of the Trial Chamber's Witness Protection Orders, and Contempt of Court, Case No. ICTR-98-41-T, 5 July 2002 (a journalist was accused of contempt of court, but the charges were dismissed; instead, the Trial Chamber referred to the fact that the Prosecutor had violated the order concerning non-disclosure as he had mentioned the profession of a protected witness in a public document); Hirondelle News Agency, *Investigations into Allegations of Interference of Witnesses Ordered*, 27 May 2005 (two employees at the Witness Support and Protection Section were alleged to have attempted to bribe a witness into retracting her testimony against convict Kamuhanda); Hirondelle News Agency, *Rwandan Journalist Cleared of Contempt of Court Charges*, 13 June 2005 (a Rwandan journalist had leaked the names of protected witnesses for the Defence, but because the names were (mistakenly) revealed in open session, it was not held to constitute contempt of court). See for the ICTY, *inter alia*, *Prosecutor v. Beqa Beqaj*, Indictment, Case No. IT-03-66-R77, 21 October 2004. Beqaj, a relative of the accused Musliu in the Limaj et al. case, was charged with contempt, attempted contempt and incitement to contempt of the Tribunal. He was convicted of contempt of the Tribunal and sentenced to four months of imprisonment because he wilfully and knowingly interfered with Witness B1 and the administration of justice. See ICTY Press Release, *Judgement in the Case of The Prosecutor v. Beqa Beqaj*, 5 May 2005. Four other individuals, Ivica Marijacic, Markica Rebic, Stjepan Seselj and Domgaoj Margetic, have been charged with contempt of the Tribunal because they published transcripts of the testimony of a protected witness for the Prosecution in the Zagreb-based weekly publication 'Hrvatski List'. See ICTY Press Release, *Two Indictments for Contempt of the Tribunal Confirmed and Released to the Public*, 27 April 2005.

[37] *Prosecutor v. Tihomir Blaškić*, Decision of Trial Chamber I on the Requests of the Prosecutor of 12 and 14 May 1997 in Respect of the Protection of Witnesses, Case No. IT-95-14, 6 June 1997, para. 10.

[38] *Ibid.*

regularly.[39] While maintaining a log is an essential element in keeping track of those persons possibly capable of leaking relevant information about the protected witness, it may not always be easy to determine who is responsible for such disclosure. In addition, it would seem that the imposition of a fine, a temporary or permanent removal from the courtroom or imprisonment to a maximum of five years in itself may not always offer sufficient safeguards against disclosure of a witness's identity. This may in particular be true for the accused, who possibly awaits a conviction or has been convicted already, as in the case of Kamuhanda, and has 'nothing to lose' by publishing the identification details of the protected witnesses.[40]

4.2 *In camera* proceedings

Article 68(2) of the ICC Statute, together with Rule 87(3)(e) of the ICC RPE, allows any part of the proceedings to be held *in camera*, i.e., without any audience in the public gallery attending the court proceedings. Article 68(2) of the ICC Statute has given victims of sexual violence a strong right and the Court an obligation to conduct any part of the proceedings *in camera* when they have to testify on the sexual violence they endured. In this respect, the ICC Statute contains explicit language – 'shall' – which implies that the Chamber needs to implement *in camera* proceedings automatically when the testimony of a victim of sexual violence is concerned.[41] In such a case, the Prosecutor, the victim or the legal representative, or possibly the VWU, should not have to apply for the *in camera* measure themselves.[42] In this context, the ICC departs significantly from the ICTY and ICTR practice, where protective measures are the exception in all cases, including cases where testimony regarding sexual violence is concerned.[43] Confidentiality measures for victims of sexual violence, including closed sessions, have nevertheless been granted in a number of decisions.[44]

---

[39] See, *inter alia*, *Prosecutor v. Dragan Gagović, Gojko Janković, Janko Janjić, Radomir Kovač, Zoran Vuković, Dragan Zelenović, Dragoljub Kunarac and Radovan Stanković*, Decision on Prosecution Motion to Protect Victims and Witnesses, Case No. IT-96-23 and 23/1, 29 April 1998.

[40] *Kamuhanda Jean de Dieu, Innocent Mais Condamné*, 11 février 2004. As mentioned above, in this report Kamuhanda explains why he should not have been convicted by the ICTR and he reveals names (and names of relatives), addresses and the jobs of some persons who appeared as protected witnesses at his trial.

[41] See also Rydberg (1999), p. 470; and Garkawe (2003), p. 352.

[42] Rule 87(1) ICC RPE. For the role of the VWU in requesting protective measures, see section 7.

[43] Compare Rule 78 ('Open Sessions') and Rule 75(B)(ii) ('Measures for the Protection of Victims and Witnesses') in conjunction with Rule 79(A)(ii) ('Closed Sessions') ICTY/R RPE. See also section 3 above.

[44] See, *inter alia*, *Prosecutor v. Duško Tadić*, Decision on the Prosecutor's Motion Requesting Protective Measures for Victims and Witnesses, Case No. IT-94-1, 10 August 1995; *Prosecutor v. Zejnil Delalić, Zdravko Mucić, Hazim Delić and Esad Landžo*, Decision on the Motions by the Prosecution for Protective Measures for Prosecution Witnesses pseudonymed "B" through to "M", Case No. IT-96-21-T, 28 April 1997; *Prosecutor v. Anto Furundžija*, Decision on Prosecutor's Motion Requesting Protective Measures for Witnesses "A" and "D" at Trial, Case No. IT-95-17/1-T, 11 June 1998.

The explicit wording of Article 68(2) – victims of sexual violence have the right to testify *in camera* – is slightly weakened towards the end of the second sentence: *in camera* proceedings are permitted 'unless otherwise ordered by the Court, having regard to all the circumstances, particularly the views of the victim or witness'.[45] The Defence, who carries the burden of proof here, could, for instance, set out why the protective measure of *in camera* should not be applied in the case at hand. It seems that the best interpretation of this phrase should be that victims' views carry considerable weight when the Chamber needs to decide on whether the hearings will be held in public, rather than *in camera*. Victims of sexual violence do not always want to exclude the public or press from the proceedings. On the contrary, some victims of sexual violence feel they have nothing to be ashamed of and want others to know what happened to them. According to Patricia Viseur Sellers, the Legal Advisor on Gender-Related Crimes at the ICTY, 'most witnesses request confidentiality. ... Meanwhile, some women want to be identified and seen, not only by the defendant but also by the public. "What do I have to be ashamed of and why should I hide?" they might ask.'[46] It is therefore imperative that the options of protective measures available are discussed with the victims before the trial so that they can make an informed choice whether or not to make use of an *in camera* proceeding.[47]

In camera proceedings are generally not seen as a violation of the accused's right to a public and fair trial. The accused's right to examine the witness is retained in closed sessions, as only the public and the press are excluded from the proceedings, not the accused and his Defence team. It has also been held that the public's right to information may yield to confidentiality when protection of victims and witnesses is at stake.[48] Several international treaties also contain provisions to this effect.[49] Moreover, in many national systems, *in camera* proceedings are allowed, and sometimes even obliged when victims of sexual violence are involved, in order to protect the victim's privacy.[50] For example, in Rwanda, Article 38 of the 2004 Gacaca Law provides for an

---

[45] Jones, J.R.W.D. (2002a, pp. 1367-1368) comments that the provision is 'nebulous' leaving the Court to exercise its discretion nonetheless.

[46] Sharratt (1999), p. 70.

[47] Rule 87(1) ICC RPE states that 'the Chamber shall seek to obtain, whenever possible, the consent of the person in respect of whom the protective measure is sought prior to ordering the protective measure'.

[48] *Prosecutor v. Duško Tadić*, Decision on Prosecutor's Motion Requesting Protective Measures for Witness R, Case No. IT-94-1-T, 31 July 1996, para. 6.

[49] Article 14(1) ICCPR and Article 6(1) ECHR state that everyone is entitled to a fair and public hearing. Nevertheless, both Articles provide that the press and the public may be excluded in the interest of morals, public order or national security, where the interests of juveniles or the protection of the private life of the parties so require or where publicity would prejudice the interest of justice.

[50] Brienen and Hoegen (2000), pp. 1132-1134. See also *Prosecutor v. Zejnil Delalić, Zdravko Mucić, Hazim Delić and Esad Landžo*, Decision on the Motions by the Prosecution for Protective Measures for Prosecution Witnesses pseudonymed "B" through to "M", Case No. IT-96-21-T, 28 April 1997, paras. 40-44. In this decision, the Chamber referred to both common law and civil law jurisdictions (England and Wales, Canada, USA, Switzerland, Denmark and Germany) which adopted the position that the identity of an alleged victim of sexual assault should be kept from

(unprecedented) obligation for victims of sexual violence to testify *in camera*. According to the provision, 'the victim chooses among the Seat members for the Gacaca Court of the Cell, one or more to whom she submits her complaint or does it in writing. In case of mistrust in the Seat members, she submits it to the organs of investigations or the Public Prosecution.' Furthermore, 'in case of death or incapacity of the victim, the complaint shall be secretly lodged by any interested party'. Although the effectiveness of the provision still need to be awaited, Mibenge points out that the provision 'effectively relieves the victim of sexual violence from revealing the details of her rape ordeal [to a larger number of judges and to the public] and also protects her from reprisals or other hostile reactions that might threaten her personal security or security as a member of her community'.[51] The provision was inserted as a response to previous intimidations faced by victims of sexual violence as well as incidents where victims of sexual violence were rejected by family members or others who had discovered that the victims were rape survivors of the genocide.

4.3 Testimony presented by electronic or other special means

Article 68(2) of the ICC Statute also mentions the presentation of evidence by electronic or other special means as a way in which the victim's testimony can be withheld from the public or the media. Rule 87(3)(e) of the ICC RPE describes some of the forms which may fall within the ambit of 'electronic or other special means': the use of technical means enabling the alteration of pictures or voice, the use of audio-visual technology, in particular, video conferencing and closed circuit television, and the exclusive use of sound media. The Rule is open-ended; possible future technical developments may therefore be interpreted to come within its ambit.

Some of these measures, such as the alteration of pictures or voice, are obvious: if such measures were not applied in certain circumstances, other confidentiality measures taken would be without any effect and the victim's identity would be revealed after all. It seems that what has been said about *in camera* proceedings above could be applied here as well: Article 68(2) of the ICC Statute contains explicit language when victims of sexual violence are concerned: presentation of evidence by electronic or other special means should be the norm. While video conferencing and (one-way) closed circuit television can be used by victims of sexual violence to protect their identity from the public and the media, the measures may also fulfil other purposes, such as facilitating the testimony of those physically unable to testify in court itself and/or to avoid further traumatisation or retraumatisation. The measure of video conferencing will be discussed here; one-way closed circuit television, primarily a measure to avoid confrontation with the accused, will be discussed in section 6.

4.4 Live video conference link

General provisions permitting the use of (live) video conferencing as a protective measure can be found in Article 68(2) of the ICC Statute and Rule 87(3)(e) of the ICC RPE. If an order for live video conferencing is made, Rule 67 of the ICC RPE ('Live

---

the public, for example by holding the sessions *in camera*. In all these jurisdictions, evidence of sexual assault is considered to be sufficient reason to justify confidentiality.

[51] Mibenge (2005).

Testimony by Means of Audio or Video-link Technology'), stemming from Article 69(2) of the ICC Statute, will apply. The medium makes it possible for victims or witnesses to give testimony through a live video link from a location other than the seat of the Court, usually from a venue within his or her country of residence, via a satellite connection.

Rule 67 of the ICC RPE sets out some procedural guidelines which need to be taken into account when live video conferencing is used. In the first place, the technology should enable the witness to be examined by the Prosecutor, the Defence, and by the Chamber itself, at the time that the witness testifies. In the second place, the Chamber, with the assistance of the Registry, must ensure that the venue chosen for the conduct of the audio or video link testimony is conducive to the giving of truthful and open testimony and to the safety, physical and psychological well-being, dignity and privacy of the witness. These guidelines, which find their precedent in ICTY case law, are to ascertain that the giving of testimony by means of live video broadcasting from a remote area creates a situation as if testimony was given in court.[52]

Within the ICTY and the ICTR,[53] live video conferencing has been allowed under the following conditions: (1) the testimony of the witness must be sufficiently important to make it unfair to proceed without it; (2) the witness must be unable or unwilling to

---

[52] In *Prosecutor v. Duško Tadić*, Decision on the Defence Motion to Summon and Protect Defence Witnesses, and on the Giving of Evidence by Video-Link, Case No. IT-94-1-T, 25 June 1996, para. 22, similar and other guidelines were developed and include: '(1) The party making the application for video-link testimony should make arrangements for an appropriate location from which to conduct the proceedings. The venue must be conductive to the giving of truthful and open testimony. Furthermore, the safety and solemnity of the proceedings at the location must be guaranteed. The non-moving party and the Registry must be informed at every stage of the efforts of the moving party and they must be in agreement with the proposed location. ...; (2) The Trial Chamber will appoint a Presiding Officer to ensure that the testimony is given freely and voluntarily. The Presiding Officer will identify the witnesses and explain the nature of the proceedings and the obligation to speak the truth. He will inform the witnesses that they are liable to prosecution for perjury in case of false testimony, will administer the taking of the oath and will keep the Trial Chamber informed at all times of the conditions at the location; (3) Unless the Trial Chamber decides otherwise, the testimony shall be given in the physical presence only of the Presiding Officer and, if necessary, of a member of the Registry technical staff; (4) The witnesses must, by means of monitor, be able to see, at various times, the Judges, the accused and the questioner: similarly the Judges, the accused and the questioner must each be able to observe the witness on their monitor; (5) A statement made under solemn declaration by a witness shall be treated as having been made in the courtroom and the witness shall be liable to prosecution for perjury in exactly the same way as if he had given evidence at the seat of the International Tribunal.' In this respect, Klip (1996, p. 290) referred to the Tadić case, in which the Defence requested the Tribunal not to allow the presence of a trial attorney at the video conferencing site, as the witness for the Defence feared arrest. Klip noted: 'Although such a presence could indeed seriously hinder the willingness of a witness to cooperate, some form of assurance must exist that the witness is not under pressures outside the view of the camera.' See also Klip (1995), pp. 244-255.

[53] Live video conferencing is mentioned in Rule 71 ('Depositions') and Rule 71*bis* ('Testimony by Video-Conference Link') of the ICTY RPE. For the ICTR, see Rule 71 and Rule 90(A) ICTR RPE.

come to the Tribunal;[54] (3) the accused will not thereby be prejudiced in the exercise of his right to confront the witness;[55] and (4) the practical considerations (including logistical difficulty, expense, and security risks) of holding a deposition in the proposed location do not outweigh the potential benefits to be gained by doing so.[56] Several witnesses have therefore benefited from giving testimony via video conferencing.[57] It remains to be seen what criteria the ICC will take into account in deciding whether or not to make use of live video conferencing. The ICTY and ICTR practice may be helpful in this regard.

It can be said that live testimony by means of audio or video link technology may serve different purposes: not only can it be used as a measure to protect a witness's identity from the public and the press, it can also be invoked when it is physically impossible for a witness to come to court to testify.[58] Especially women who were injured as a consequence of the sexual violence they endured are not always able to undertake the journey to the ICC. In previous ICTY and ICTR Decisions, age and bad health were found to constitute good reasons for witnesses to be unable or unwilling to

---

[54] The first two criteria were developed in *Prosecutor v. Duško Tadić*, Decision on the Defence Motion to Summon and Protect Defence Witnesses, and on the Giving of Evidence by Video-Link, Case No. IT-94-1-T, 25 June 1996, para. 19.

[55] *Prosecutor v. Zejnil Delalić, Zdravko Mucić, Hazim Delić and Esad Landžo*, Decision on the Motion to Allow Witnesses K, L and M to give Their Testimony by Means of Video-Link Conference, Case No. IT-96-21-T, 28 May 1997, para. 17.

[56] *The Prosecutor v. Théoneste Bagosora, Gratien Kabiligi, Aloys Ntabakuze and Anatole Nsengiyumva*, Decision on Prosecutor's Motion for Deposition of Witness OW, Case No. ICTR-98-41-I, 5 December 2001, para. 14.

[57] See further, *inter alia*, *Prosecutor v. Duško Tadić*, Decision on the Defence Motion Requesting Video-Link for Defence Witnesses, Case No. IT-94-1-T, 16 October 1996; *Prosecutor v. Duško Tadić*, Decision on the Defence Motion Requesting Video-Link for Defence Witness Jelena Gajić, Case No. IT-94-1-T, 17 October 1996; *Prosecutor v. Mile Mrkšić, Miroslav Radić, Veselin Šljivančanin and Slavko Dokmanović*, Decision on the Prosecutor's Motion for Deposition Evidence, Case No. IT-95-13a, 11 March 1998; *Prosecutor v. Mile Mrkšić, Miroslav Radić, Veselin Šljivančanin and Slavko Dokmanović*, Decision on the Defence Motions for Video-Conference Link, Case No. IT-95-13a, 29 April 1998; *Prosecutor v. Mile Mrkšić, Miroslav Radić, Veselin Šljivančanin and Slavko Dokmanović*, Decision on Defence Motion for Video Link Conference, Case No. IT-95-13a, 18 May 1998; *The Prosecutor v. Ferdinand Nahimana, Jean-Bosco Barayagwiza and Hassan Ngeze*, Decision on the Prosecutor's Application to Add Witness X to Its List of Witnesses and for Protective Measures, Case No. ICTR-99-52-I, 14 September 2001. See also the media reports on the Simba case, in which it is explained that a number of defence witnesses were allowed to testify via video link from Kigali and the Hague out of security concerns: Hirondelle News Agency, *First Testimonies Via Video Link From Kigali Next Week*, 9 February 2005; Hirondelle News Agency, *Alibi Witness Testifies Via Video Conference From The Hague*, 21 February 2005; Hirondelle News Agency, *Witness Fearing for His Safety Gives Entire Testimony In Camera*, 22 February 2005; Hirondelle News Agency, *Simba Trial Hits Snag as Key Witnesses Refuse to Testify*, 7 March 2005 (explaining that two defence witnesses suddenly refused to testify via video link from Kigali and that 'the security of witnesses in Simba's trial has become a big issue ever since a prosecution witness, Bosco Nyemanzi, was found murdered in his home in October 2004 a short distance from Gikongoro, Simba's hometown').

[58] Brady (2001), p. 455.

travel to the seat of the Tribunal in order to give testimony.[59] In Rwanda, many women contracted HIV/AIDS or a different serious disease as a consequence of the sexual violence committed against them. It has been estimated that between 70 percent and 80 percent of the women surviving the genocide in Rwanda were infected with HIV.[60] If health conditions make it impossible or extremely difficult to give testimony in court, alternative measures, such as giving testimony through live video linkage, should be considered.[61] In fact, a literal reading of Article 68(2) of the ICC Statute requires that testimony by electronic or other special means, such as live video conferencing, is applied to victims of sexual violence automatically. In such cases, both purposes – protection of identity and protection of those physically unable or unwilling to testify in court – can be served.[62] Of course, a victim of sexual violence may also choose to give testimony through live video conferencing because of physically impossibility to attend the trial without any protection from the public or the press.

Within the practice of the ICTY and the ICTR, it is generally accepted that the accused's right to examine the witness against him or her, or to have the witness examined, is not violated by the use of video conferencing.[63] Counsel of the accused can cross-examine the witness and the judges can put questions to clarify evidence given during testimony. In addition, the Chamber may hear the testimony of a witness and can observe the demeanour of the witness whilst giving evidence. Despite this, several ICTY and ICTR Decisions on this matter have expressed a certain preference for testimony in court. Besides practical considerations, it has been held that the witness's credibility may be more difficult to assess when testimony is not given in court.[64] In this

---

[59] *Prosecutor v. Zejnil Delalić, Zdravko Mucić, Hazim Delić and Esad Landžo*, Decision on the Motion to Allow Witnesses K, L and M to give Their Testimony by Means of Video-Link Conference, Case No. IT-96-21-T, 28 May 1997, para. 20; *The Prosecutor v. Théoneste Bagosora, Gratien Kabiligi, Aloys Ntabakuze and Anatole Nsengiyumva*, Decision on Prosecutor's Motion for Deposition of Witness OW, Case No. ICTR-98-41-I, 5 December 2001, para. 16: 'In light of the exceptional circumstances relating to the age and health of the witness, it is understandable that the witness is unable or unwilling to come to the Tribunal.'

[60] See the AVEGA-AGAHOZO, Association of Genocide Widows, website (under 'history') at http://www.avega.org.rw (last visited May 2005). See also Amnesty International (2004a), p. 3; and Save the Children (2002), p. 5.

[61] See also subsection 6.3 on prior recorded testimony.

[62] When a live video link is applied in these circumstances, the measure may have as a side effect that testimony given by vulnerable victims, such as victims of sexual violence, is facilitated. Victims of sexual violence may be afraid to testify in close proximity of the accused and via live video conferencing, even though the witness will still see the accused on the monitor and vice versa, the witness is physically at a distance from the accused. This may prevent any further traumatisation.

[63] *Prosecutor v. Zejnil Delalić, Zdravko Mucić, Hazim Delić and Esad Landžo*, Decision on the Motion to Allow Witnesses K, L and M to give Their Testimony by Means of Video-Link Conference, Case No. IT-96-21-T, 28 May 1997, para. 15; *The Prosecutor v. Ferdinand Nahimana, Jean-Bosco Barayagwiza and Hassan Ngeze*, Decision on the Prosecutor's Application to Add Witness X to Its List of Witnesses and for Protective Measures, Case No. ICTR-99-52-I, 14 September 2001, para. 35.

[64] See, *inter alia*, *Prosecutor v. Duško Tadić*, Decision on the Defence Motion to Summon and Protect Defence Witnesses, and on the Giving of Evidence by Video-Link, Case No. IT-94-1-T,

regard, Klip noted that 'testimony by using video-link could present a sufficient alternative second best option. The guidelines to be followed in case of this testimony all tend to create a situation in which only the location of the witness is different from the courtroom. This corresponds to the rationale behind the use of this technique, to take away an obstacle for testifying.'[65] It will be up to the ICC to determine, when evaluating the evidence as a whole, the weight accorded to the testimony.[66] It could be argued that, with today's technology, it should be possible to assess the demeanour of the witness via a live video link without much difficulty. Rule 67 of the ICC RPE itself prescribes that the witness has to be examined by both parties to the proceedings, as well as by the Chamber, which seems to sufficiently guarantee that the rights of the accused to examine the witness against him or her will not be violated.

5 Protection from the Accused

An anonymous witness is a witness whose identity is withheld *from the accused and (usually) his counsel* in order to protect the witness's safety. This generally means that the accused (and his team) cannot see the witness in court, or, through picture and voice alteration devices, cannot see and hear the real appearance and voice of the witness. Another form of anonymous testimony can be given through hearsay evidence.[67] Anonymity measures go a substantial step further in their protection offered to witnesses when compared to confidentiality measures: the latter only regulate withholding the witness's identity from the press and the public, but not from the accused and his counsel. Granting full anonymity to a witness is highly controversial since it touches upon the rights of the accused to a fair trail, particularly his right to examine the witness against him.

25 June 1996, paras. 11 and 21 (in the decision it is mentioned that it will be easier for judges to evaluate the credibility of a person in court and that witnesses will be less inclined to give false when testifying in court); *Prosecutor v. Zejnil Delalić, Zdravko Mucić, Hazim Delić and Esad Landžo*, Decision on the Motion to Allow Witnesses K, L and M to give Their Testimony by Means of Video-Link Conference, Case No. IT-96-21-T, 28 May 1997, para. 18. This decision states that 'the distance of the witness from the solemnity of the courtroom proceedings and the fact that the witness is not able to see all those present in the courtroom at the same time, but only those on whom the video camera is focused, may detract from the reliance placed upon his or her evidence'.

[65] Klip (1999), p. 226.

[66] See, in particular, Article 69(4) ICC Statute. Article 69(4) reads: 'The Court may rule on the relevance or admissibility of any evidence, taking into account, , the probative value of the evidence and any prejudice that such evidence may cause to a fair trial or to a fair evaluation of the testimony of a witness, in accordance with the Rules of Procedure and Evidence.' See also Article 64(9) and Rule 63(2).

[67] See also subsection 6.3 on prior recorded testimony.

5.1 The ICTY's experience

The ICTY Trial Chamber dealt with the issue of anonymity in the *Tadić* case.[68] In this case, the Prosecutor requested anonymity for some of its witnesses, including two witnesses who had allegedly been forced to participate in acts of sexual mutilation, for fear of reprisals. The Trial Chamber ruled, in a 2-1 majority decision, in favour of anonymity. However, for a request of anonymity to be granted, the Trial Chamber required that the following five conditions were met.

(1) There must be real fear for the safety of the witness or her or his family. The horrendous nature and ruthless character of the crime would justify such fears;
(2) The testimony of the particular witness must be important to the Prosecutor's case. In this respect, it was noted that the Tribunal was heavily dependent on eyewitness testimony and the willingness of individuals to appear before the Trial Chamber to testify;
(3) The Trial Chamber must be satisfied that there is no *prima facie* evidence that the witness is untrustworthy;
(4) The ineffectiveness or non-existence of a witness protection programme: it was noted that the Tribunal did not have a police force available to protect witnesses after trial, nor does it provide for a long-term witness protection programme;
(5) Any measures taken should be strictly necessary. If a less restrictive measure can secure the required protection, that measure should be applied.[69]

In addition to these five criteria, four guidelines were set out that need to be followed in order to ensure that a trial is fair: (1) The judges must be able to observe the demeanour of the witness, in order to assess the reliability of the testimony; (2) The judges must be aware of the identity of the witness, in order to test the reliability of the witness; (3) The Defence must be allowed ample opportunity to question the witness on issues unrelated to his or her identity or current whereabouts, such as how the witness was able to obtain the incriminating information; (4) The identity of the witness must be released when there are no longer reasons to fear for the security of the witness.[70]

However, the *Tadić Protective Measures Decision* to grant anonymity to witnesses under certain prescribed conditions was not well received by everybody. Opponents of full anonymity[71] generally claim that non-disclosure of the identity of the witness to the accused is not allowed on the basis of the ICTY provisions[72] and will result in a

[68] *Prosecutor v. Duško Tadić*, Decision on the Prosecutor's Motion Requesting Protective Measures for Victims and Witnesses, Case No. IT-94-1, 10 August 1995.

[69] *Ibid.*, paras. 62-66.

[70] *Ibid.*, para. 71.

[71] See, *inter alia*, Leigh (1996), pp. 235-238; Leigh (1997), pp. 80-83; Mumba (2001), pp. 359-371; Zappalà (2002), pp. 1330-1333.

[72] Reference is generally made to: (1) the lack of an explicit provision on anonymity in the ICTY Statute or RPE; (2) Article 20(1), which states that a fair trial requires *full respect* for the rights of the accused and *due regard* for the protection of victims and witnesses; and (3) the rights of the accused to a fair trial and to examine the witness against him (Article 21(2) and (4)), which can never be made subject to Article 22, since this would make the trial unfair. In addition, the

conviction of the accused on the basis of tainted evidence. They claim that it is an impossible task to prepare an examination or to cross-examine an adverse witness effectively without knowing that witness's name, background, habitual residence or whereabouts at the time of the events to which he or she testifies. In addition, the rights of the accused are anchored in many domestic laws and international treaties. Allowing anonymity would equate the hard-won constitutional rights of the accused with victims' rights, which are still in the process of being defined. In fact, the terminology often used in this context, of how to 'balance' the rights of the accused with those of witnesses, is inappropriate as it implies that a trial could be slightly unfair. On the contrary, those favouring anonymity[73] generally argue that the ICTY provisions do provide for witness anonymity[74] and state that the rights of the accused are not absolute but need to be balanced against the broader interests of the international community in the pursuit of justice, especially the safety of witnesses. They also refer to a number of national laws, domestic case law and case law of the European Court of Human Rights, which allow, under exceptional circumstances, the use of anonymous witnesses.[75] This development would indicate that the use of the anonymous witness is not prohibited. In addition, Article 21 of the ICTY Statute, the provision on the rights of the accused, is based on Article 14 of the International Convention on Civil and Political Rights (ICCPR), and the ICCPR, in contrast to the ICTY Statute, does not contain provisions on victims' rights. As such, the rights of the accused must be interpreted within the context of an international criminal tribunal, which also has an obligation to protect victims and witnesses. A final point of consideration can be found in the absence of an effective witness protection programme for international criminal tribunals. If protection of victims and witnesses is not guaranteed, they will generally be unwilling to testify, in which case there will neither be a trial nor any truth finding.

As said above, the ICTY Trial Chamber in *Tadić* accepted the possibility of anonymous witness testimony. It held that 'a fair trial means not only fair treatment to

---

wording of Rules 69 and 75 implies that the identity of the witness can only be concealed from the accused until the witness is brought within the protection of the Tribunal or in sufficient time prior to the trial (see also section 3 for the ICTY provisions). See, in particular, the dissenting opinion of Judge Ninian Stephen (Australia) for his interpretation of the relevant ICTY provisions: *Prosecutor v. Duško Tadić*, Separate Opinion of Judge Stephen on the Prosecutor's Motion Requesting Protective Measures for Victims and Witnesses, Case No. IT-94-1, 10 August 1995, pp. 9-15.

[73] See, *inter alia*, Chinkin (1996), pp. 179-212; Momeni (1997), pp. 155-179; and Swaak-Goldman (1997), pp. 215-221.

[74] Reference is generally made to the inprecise phrases in Article 22 ICTY Statute and Rules 75 and 69 ICTY RPE: 'not limited to', 'identity', 'appropriate measures' and 'such as'. Such wording would allow the interpretation that anonymity from the accused is an appropriate protection measure. The 'subject to Rule 75' clause in Rule 69(C) would furthermore suggest that disclosure of the victim or witness's identity in sufficient time prior to the trial is not obligatory when appropriate protective measures, such as anonymity, are ordered under Rule 75 (see also section 3 for the ICTY provisions). See, in particular, the majority decision of Judges Gabrielle Kirk McDonald (USA) and Lal Chand Vohrah (Malaysia) in *Prosecutor v. Duško Tadić*, Decision on the Prosecutor's Motion Requesting Protective Measures for Victims and Witnesses, Case No. IT-94-1, 10 August 1995, for their interpretation of the relevant ICTY provisions.

[75] See the text and accompanying footnotes in subsection 5.2 on 'The ICC: Where to go?'

the defendant but also to the prosecution and to the witness'.[76] It took into account the above-mentioned arguments in favour of anonymity and concluded that the right of the accused to a fair trial would not be compromised if the above-mentioned specified criteria and guidelines were followed. For each and every individual application, the criteria have to be carefully scrutinised and decisions to accord anonymity will therefore not be made lightly. Since the *Tadić Protective Measures Decision* on anonymity, full anonymity to protect witnesses has never been granted again by the ICTY.[77] The ICTR has never even sought recourse to total anonymity to protect its witnesses.[78] The reason not to make use of anonymity measures within the ICTY or the ICTR after *Tadić* is in all probability found in the controversial nature of its application. The application of anonymity as a protective measure became even more controversial when an anonymous witness in the *Tadić* case, Witness L, appeared to be an unreliable witness.[79] Witness L (Dragan Opacić) testified in court that he had been a guard in the Trnopolje camp, and that he had seen the accused Tadić commit murder and rape. It was established by the Defence, however, that Witness L had given false testimony, which he later claimed to have given because he had been trained to do so by the Bosnian government. The Defence had presented evidence concerning Witness L's family circumstances and the death of his father (Witness L had testified that his father had died, but he appeared to be alive).[80] Although such a course of events raises serious concerns, Featherstone noted that 'the circumstances surrounding the evidence of Witness L, and the subsequent request for it to be disregarded, indicate that the defence does have opportunity to investigate the truth of the evidence even of protected witnesses, and that these measures do not unduly hinder a fair trial.'[81] In the end, only one witness has testified at the ICTY under conditions of anonymity.[82] These

---

[76] *Prosecutor v. Duško Tadić*, Decision on the Prosecutor's Motion Requesting Protective Measures for Victims and Witnesses, Case No. IT-94-1, 10 August 1995, para. 55.

[77] However, even though anonymity was not granted in the Blaškić case, it was not precluded either provided there was convincing proof of the five factors enumerated in the 1995 Tadić Protective Measures Decision for each individual application. See *Prosecutor v. Tihomir Blaškić*, Decision on the Application of the Prosecutor dated 17 October 1996 Requesting Protective Measures for Victims and Witnesses, Case No. IT-95-14-T, 5 November 1996. See also *Prosecutor v. Zejnil Delalić, Zdravko Mucić, Hazim Delić and Esad Landžo*, Decision on the Motions by the Prosecution for Protective Measures for Prosecution Witnesses pseudonymed "B" through to "M", Case No. IT-96-21-T, 28 April 1997, paras. 60-63.

[78] Although it seems that the ICTR is not necessarily against the use of anonymity (see *The Prosecutor v. Obed Ruzindana*, Decision on the Motion filed by the Prosecutor on the Protection of victims and witnesses, 4 March 1997), in practice the use of anonymous testimony has not been allowed.

[79] *Prosecutor v. Duško Tadić*, Decision on Prosecution Motion to Withdraw Protective Measures for Witness L, Case No. IT-94-1-T, 5 December 1996.

[80] Featherstone (1997), p. 196. Witness L had given evidence in closed session, which was released in edited form shortly thereafter.

[81] *Ibid.*, p. 197.

[82] This involves Witness H, a witness allegedly forced to participate in acts of sexual mutilation, testifying in the Tadić case. Featherstone (1997, p. 186) mentions, however, that 'the practical arrangements in the courtroom were modified so that defence counsel could view the witness but the accused could not, although he could hear the testimony in the original language and without

developments at the ICTY do not preclude, however, that the matter of anonymity will arise again before the ICC: on the contrary, there is no reason why this would not be the case.

5.2 The ICC: Where to go?

The ICC Statute does not contain a specific provision on anonymity as a protection measure for witnesses. The ICC RPE do not clarify the matter either. This can be explained by its negotiating history: the question of whether anonymous witnesses should or should not be allowed in ICC proceedings was discussed in the ICC Preparatory Commission sessions where it was fiercely debated.[83] Because of its controversial nature, the outcome remained undecided and the drafters have therefore left the issue essentially for the ICC to decide. While it may be preferable to have the provisions amended so as to make the Court's approach to anonymous witnesses clear, this option seems to be unrealistic in the short term given the opposing views during the ICC negotiations on the matter and the requirement that amendments generally need a two-thirds majority of the members of the Assembly of States Parties (ASP).[84] This therefore leads to the question of what the future approach of the ICC on anonymous witnesses will (need to) be: will testimony by an anonymous witness be permitted? From the ICC provisions, it is at least clear that a certain balance between the rights of the accused to a fair trial and those of victims and witnesses to protection has been sought: Articles 64(2), 68(1) and (5), and 69(2) are proof thereof. However, on the basis of these and other provisions, both a negative and a positive answer to the previous question can be given.

Article 68(1) of the ICC Statute requires the Court to 'take *appropriate measures* to protect the safety, physical and psychological well-being, dignity and privacy of victims and witnesses'. Article 68(2) of the ICC Statute states that exceptions to a public hearing are allowed in order to protect victims and witnesses, in particular in cases of sexual violence or when a child is involved. This gives the impression that the rights of the accused, as laid down in Article 67 of the ICC Statute, are not absolute, but should be viewed in context. The Trial Chamber has a certain degree of discretion to order protective measures, and should thereby take into account such factors as age, gender, health and the nature of the crime, but also victims' views. Of particular relevance for the discussion of anonymity is Rule 88 of the ICC RPE. It states that the Chamber may 'order special measures *such as but not limited to* measures to facilitate the testimony of a ... victim or witnesses'. In addition, orders under this rule can be made *ex parte*. It is therefore possible to allow total anonymity as a special measure on

distortion. This was achieved by hearing the evidence of witness H in closed session, adjusting the position of the accused in the courtroom and using screening around the witness box.'

[83] For an account of the proceedings, see Brady (2001), pp. 450-453; and Kreβ (2001), pp. 367-377.

[84] In Articles 51 and 121 ICC Statute, the amendment procedures for the ICC RPE and Statute, respectively, are laid down. The ICC amendment procedure is different from that of the Tribunals, where the power to amend the Rules lies with the judges. Compare Rule 6 ICTY/R RPE.

the basis of Rule 88.[85] However, as mentioned, on the basis of the ICC provisions, the opposite conclusion can be drawn as well.[86]

It is therefore important to look at the topic from a broader perspective. Support for total anonymity can be found in several sources: national laws[87] as well as domestic case law[88] and European case law.[89] Some developments in this field can also be seen on an international level.[90] What appears from this brief overview is that total

[85] See Brady (2001), p. 453. This conclusion is further reinforced by Rule E, the predecessor of Rule 88, which was developed during the International Seminar 'Access of Victims to the International Criminal Court', held to suggest recommendations for rules concerning victims that could be inserted into the Rules of Procedure and Evidence of the ICC. Rule E was negotiated in workshop 3 ('Protection of Victims and Witnesses') of the seminar and states: 'In exceptional circumstances, the Court may order on the request of the parties, victims or their representatives and witnesses, *other special measures* than those listed above [referring to Rule D, the predecessor of current Rule 87(3)]. These measures must be in accordance with the statute' (italics added). See International Seminar 'Access of Victims to the International Criminal Court', Paris, 27-29 April 1999, Report of Workshops, 29 April 1999. What these 'other special measures' should encompass was not specified. However, it has been submitted that the underlying idea of Rule E was that the final decision on whether an anonymous witness is allowed in ICC proceedings is left to the judges' wide discretion and that the witness's identity is known only to the judges and the party seeking the anonymity.

[86] See Brady (2001), p. 453, where she explains, with reference to Article 68(5) ICC Statute, Rule 81(4) and (6) and Rules 87 and 88 ICC RPE, that anonymity for witnesses at trial can be rejected. The provisions could be interpreted to mean that anonymity of the witness is only allowed *before* the commencement of the trial. Within a reasonable time before the start of the trial, the identity should be disclosed to the accused in order to enable him to prepare his case. According to Nicholls (2003, pp. 298-299), the use of anonymous witnesses at trial is prohibited on the basis of the ICC Statute and RPE.

[87] See, *inter alia*, the *Wet getuigenbescherming* 1993 (the Protection of Witnesses Act) and Article 226(a)-(f) of the *Wetboek van Strafvordering* (Code of Criminal Procedure) (The Netherlands); the Evidence (Witness Anonymity) Amendment Act 1997 (NZ) (New Zealand); Article 184(1) and (4) of the Polish Code of Criminal Procedure 1997 (Poland); Article 68(3) of the German Code of Criminal Procedure 1987 (Germany); Section 23(3) of the Criminal Justice Act 1988 (England). In some jurisdictions, anonymous testimony is allowed in court, while in other jurisdictions it is only allowed as 'hearsay evidence', and in some jurisdictions both possibilities are available.

[88] See, *inter alia*, *Jarvie and Another v. The Magistrates' Court of Victoria at Brunswick and Others* (1994), VR 88 (Australia); *R. v. Watford Magistrates' Court ex Parte Lenman* (1993), Crim. L.R. 388 (England); and *R. v. Taylor* (1994), T.L.R. 484 (England).

[89] See, *inter alia*, *Doorson v. The Netherlands*, Judgment, Publications of the European Court of Human Rights, Series A: Judgments and Decisions, Vol. 330, 26 March 1996; *Kostovski v. The Netherlands*, Judgment, Publications of the European Court of Human Rights, Series A: Judgments and Decisions, Vol. 166, 20 November 1989; *Ludi v. Switzerland*, Judgment, Publications of the European Court of Human Rights, Series A: Judgments and Decisions, Vol. 330, 15 June 1992; *Van Mechelen v. The Netherlands*, Judgment, Publications of the European Court of Human Rights, Series A: Judgments and Decisions, Vol. 674, 23 April 1997.

[90] See *Prosecutor v. Duško Tadić*, Decision on the Prosecutor's Motion Requesting Protective Measures for Victims and Witnesses, Case No. IT-94-1, 10 August 1995; Recommendation No. R

anonymity is not categorically barred: neither by civil and common law traditions nor by international (human rights) law. On the contrary, witness anonymity is an accepted means to protect witnesses from retaliation. What is important is that witness anonymity does not necessarily compromise the rights of the accused to a fair trial, including his right to examine the witnesses against him. If conditions and procedural guarantees like those established in the *Tadić Protective Measures Decision* are followed carefully – and which find their basis in the case law mentioned above – a fair trial for the accused can be realised. However, a conviction may not be based either solely or to a decisive extent on anonymous statements.[91]

The examination of an anonymous witness in court should be left entirely in the hands of the judges; questions raised by the Defence Counsel should be discussed with the witness through the mediation of the judge.[92] Such a solution is workable within the ICC system, which takes into account both cross-examination (a common law influence) and the involvement of an active judge (a civil law influence) in its proceedings.[93] The right of the accused to examine the witness against him is one of 'to examine or *have examined*': examination of the witness thus does not necessarily have to be done by the accused or his counsel, but can be conducted by a judge or other court official.[94] As mentioned before, the taking of testimony of an anonymous witness could take place in court, but also during the pre-trial stage in the form of hearsay evidence.

5.3 Some policy considerations in relation to sexual violence crimes

A victim of sexual violence will be eligible for protection by means of anonymity like any other victim or witness with a real fear for his or her safety. The situation is principally not different for victims of sexual violence. Having said this, however, some additional considerations must be taken into account for this group of vulnerable witnesses. In a considerable number of cases that appeared before the ICTY and the ICTR, and most likely will appear before the ICC as well, the accused himself is not the physical perpetrator of the rape or any other form of sexual violence charged. In a situation where the accused was not present when the sexual violence was committed, it seems less relevant for the accused to know the identity of the victim than in situations where the accused himself was the physical perpetrator.[95] Furthermore, at the time of

---

(97) 13 of the European Council's Committee of Ministers to Member States Concerning Intimidation of Witnesses and the Rights of the Defence, 10 September 1997, paras. 10-13; and the Resolution of the International Association of Penal Law, adopted by the International Association of Penal Law at its Budapest session 'The Criminal Justice Systems Facing the Challenge of Organized Crime', 1999, para. 6.

[91] See, *inter alia*, *Doorson v. The Netherlands*, Judgment, Publications of the European Court of Human Rights, Series A: Judgments and Decisions, Vol. 330, 26 March 1996; *Van Mechelen v. The Netherlands*, Judgment, Publications of the European Court of Human Rights, Series A: Judgments and Decisions, Vol. 674, 23 April 1997.

[92] Safferling (2001), p. 288. Counsel of the accused should not question an anonymous witness. This would put an enormous pressure on the client – counsel relationship and there is no guarantee whatsoever that such a witness will not be attacked as a result of his or testimony.

[93] *Ibid.*, pp. 286-291. Compare Articles 64(8)(b) and 69(3) ICC Statute and Rule 140 ICC RPE.

[94] *Ibid.*

[95] Chinkin (2000), pp. 470-471.

the crime, the identity of the rape victim was of no importance to the perpetrator; most victims are namely chosen in a random fashion, without any regard to their identity.[96] While these arguments may be true for many of the crimes falling within the ICC jurisdiction, it can be held that it is even more important to acknowledge these considerations in cases of sexual violence. If victims of sexual violence do not come forward to testify due to the absence of good protection measures, justice for women will remain an unrealisable goal[97] despite legislation acknowledging the nature of the crime.[98] In several ICTR cases, female witnesses were threatened following disclosure of their names and, in one case, a woman's fiancé left her after her testimony was publicised in Rwanda, due to the stigmatisation attached to rape.[99] Such occurrences are a cause for worry, and reveal that the commonly used method of protection within the Tribunals, confidentiality measures, do not always protect the witness from intimidation, threats or even killing.[100] In the case of a victim of sexual violence, there may even be the additional effect of rejection by the victim's own family and friends. This is especially disturbing considering that confidentiality measures for victims of sexual violence were developed to protect them from becoming social outcasts in their countries of residence in the first place. It appears that still too often the identity of the witness leaks out despite its secrecy. In this regard, it must also be noted that rape victims have generally been misinformed about their testimony in court and the confidentiality surrounding it: they are not notified by the Office of the Prosecutor that

---

[96] *Ibid.*

[97] For an account of the traditional silence concerning sexual violence in wartimes, see Brownmiller (1975), pp. 31-113.

[98] Chinkin (2000), pp. 475-476. She refers to the broader interests of the international community in achieving the three objectives for which the Tribunals were established: to do justice, to deter further crimes and to contribute to the restoration and maintenance of international peace.

[99] Coalition for Women's Human Rights in Conflict Situations, Rights and Democracy, and International Centre for Human Rights and Democratic Development, *Letter to Carla del Ponte*, 12 March 2003. See also Hirondelle News Agency, *Survivors Accuse 14 Defence Investigators of Genocide Crimes*, 25 March 2002 ('Ibuka and Avega also cited the case of three women who testified against (Juvénal) Kajelijeli (former Mukingo mayor detained by ICTR) "as victims of sexual violence (amputation of genital organs) infected with HIV." When they returned from Arusha, "their testimonies were taken to Rwanda for the information of detainees co-authors of the genocide with Kajelijeli, and his family members," say the associations. Since then, the women have received death threats. Terrorised, they have ended up seeking refuge in Kigali where they have no homes, close relatives or means of survival'); and Nowrojee (2005).

[100] However, note in this regard the remarks made by Judge Stephen in his dissenting opinion in the Tadić case: 'What does make their case special is the combination of possible social consequences of it becoming generally known in communities in the former Yugoslavia that a woman has been a rape victim and also the often acute trauma of facing one's attacker in court and being made to relive the experience of the rape. The customary protection measures to guard against these two possible consequences are in camera proceedings, devices to avoid confrontation with the accused in court and careful control of cross-examination' (*Prosecutor v. Duško Tadić*, Separate Opinion of Judge Stephen on the Prosecutor's Motion Requesting Protective Measures for Victims and Witnesses, Case No. IT-94-1, 10 August 1995).

the Defence Counsel is provided with their names in accordance with the rules.[101] Instead, the Prosecutor tells them that their identity will be kept confidential, which, although legally correct, gives witnesses the impression that this includes confidentiality from the Defence. Therefore, as long as alternatives to anonymity, such as witness protection programmes, do not protect victims of sexual violence against threats *and/or rejection by their society, family or partner,* anonymity should be considered as a valuable tool for protection.[102] Especially considering that the ICTY Chamber's willingness to grant anonymity in *Tadić* was, to a large extent, based on the lack of a long-term witness protection programme in the country of origin.

5.4 Protection after the trial

The protection possibilities available after testimony in court are relocation and/or domestic witness protection programmes. Both relocation and the set up of protection programmes are heavily dependent on the willingness of the governments concerned.[103] By 2002, the ICTY had managed to conclude eleven formal relocation agreements with States, whereas the ICTR had none, although four countries were willing to cooperate in this perspective.[104] In the past, however, States have on occasion shown to be reluctant to protect witnesses on their return.[105] Relocation, which can be either outside or inside the witness's country of origin, has only been allowed in few cases. For example, in 2002, 35 ICTR witnesses were relocated.[106] The reason for this low number of relocation grants can be found in the enormous sacrifices for the witnesses concerned

[101] Coalition for Women's Human Rights in Conflict Situations, Rights and Democracy, and International Centre for Human Rights and Democratic Development, *Letter to Carla del Ponte*, 12 March 2003; and Nowrojee (2005).

[102] According to Article 226a of the Dutch Code of Criminal Procedure, the examining magistrate may order to hide the identity of the witness from the Defence Counsel and the accused if: (a) the witness justifiably fears for his life; health, security or disruption of *family life*; or socio-economic status, and (b) the witness has declared that he refuses to testify because of threats (my translation and emphasis). The term 'family life' is further explained in the *Memorie van toelichting* (Explanatory Memorandum) to the *Wet van 11 november 1993 tot wijziging van het Wetboek van Strafvordering, the Wetboek van Strafrecht en enige andere wetten (getuigenbescherming)* (Witness Protection Act, amending the Dutch Code of Criminal Procedure), and in which the following examples of 'risk to family life' are mentioned: publicising details which may be disturbing to other family members, such as a homosexuality, biological descent, incestuous or extramarital relationships. The Dutch Code of Criminal Procedure therefore also recognises risks to disruption of family life resulting from the disclosure of identity details as a reason to grant anonymity. See *Wet van 11 november 1993 tot wijziging van het Wetboek van Strafvordering, het Wetboek van Strafrecht en enige andere wetten (getuigenbescherming)*, 11 November 1993, *Staatsblad* 603, pp. 2-3; and *Memorie van Toelichting* (Explanatory Memorandum), Tweede Kamer, vergaderjaar 1991-1992, 22 483, nr. 3, p. 19.

[103] Rule 16(4) ICC RPE on relocation states: 'Agreements on relocation and provision of support services on the territory of a State of traumatized or threatened victims ... may be negotiated with the States by the Registrar on behalf of the Court.'

[104] See Dieng (2002b).

[105] See, for instance, ICTY Yearbook (1995), p. 272.

[106] See Dieng (2002b).

and the high costs involved.[107] As mentioned before, if protective measures, introduced to minimise the risks after trial, do not work and anonymity remains categorically excluded, then at least an effectively functioning witness protection programme or relocation possibilities must be in place, so that the identified witness will not have to fear for his or her life. This could include, under the auspices of the VWU, the establishment of ICC field offices which monitor the security situation in the country concerned and, at the same time, serve as a contact point for victims and witnesses in emergency situations.[108] Article 93(1)(j) of the ICC Statute might be relevant here as it states that States Parties must comply with requests by the Court to provide assistance in relation to investigations or prosecutions, including the protection of victims and witnesses. This provision should enable the ICC to request a State Party to provide various sorts of protection for witnesses on its territory, both before and after testimony.[109] Such a provision did not exist for the ICTY or the ICTR,[110] and could be interpreted for the ICC as to include relocation and witness protection programmes.

6 Protection from Retraumatisation

In the ICTY *Tadić Protective Measures Decision*, the Chamber recognised that 'rape and sexual assault often have particularly devastating consequences' and that 'traditional court practice and procedures have been known to exacerbate the victim's ordeal during trial' which resulted in a general feeling of 'being raped a second time'.[111] The possibility of this so-called 'secondary victimisation' of victims of sexual violence who are to testify in court is nowadays no longer categorically denied. The question remains, however, what kind of protective and special measures for victims of sexual violence are allowed, without obstructing the right of the accused to a fair trial.

In order to facilitate the testimony of sexual violence victims, certain protective and special measures can be applied. In general, measures to protect a victim from increased traumatisation or retraumatisation can be divided into the following four categories: (1) measures that avoid face-to-face confrontation with the accused; (2) measures which, among other things, restrict the questions that may be posed by the parties ('Special Evidentiary Rules'); (3) measures that seek to limit the frequency of questioning; and (4) other measures that facilitate testimony by a witness or victim of sexual violence, such as having a supports person attending the trial and controlling the manner and length of the questioning.

---

[107] Ingadottir, Ngendahayo and Viseur Sellers (2003), pp. 23 and 35 (Table 3). When relocation to another country takes place, the witness and his family members 'must forsake contact with relatives and friends and agree to remain away from their home country for an undetermined period'. Relocation within the country of the witness requires similar actions of the witness, with the advantage that problems with a new culture and language are not present.

[108] Human Rights Watch (2004a), pp. 15-16. See also section 7 on 'The Victims and Witnesses Unit'.

[109] Rydberg (1999), pp. 470-471. Of course, considering the high costs of such protection measures, it is not realistic to require such measures from countries that do not have the financial means to offer such protection.

[110] Compare Article 29 ICTY Statute.

[111] *Prosecutor v. Duško Tadić*, Decision on the Prosecutor's Motion Requesting Protective Measures for Victims and Witnesses, Case No. IT-94-1, 10 August 1995, para. 46.

6.1 Avoiding face-to-face confrontation with the accused

One-way closed circuit television has been laid down in Rule 87(3)(c) of the ICC RPE. The measure allows the witness to give testimony from a room inside the ICC building other than the courtroom itself with the purpose to protect the witness from seeing and therefore directly confronting the accused in court. The parties to the proceedings, including the accused, however, will still be able to hear and see the witness on the television monitors in the courtroom. The measure can be applied together with other measures, such as distortion of the face and voice, to protect the witness's identity from the public and the media. The purpose of this measure is to prevent increased traumatisation or re-traumatisation of the victim by avoiding close proximity to the accused. Such a measure may be of particular importance to victims of sexual assault.[112]

One-way closed circuit television has been laid down in ICTY and ICTR provisions[113] and has generally not been found to obstruct the right of the accused to a fair and public trial.[114] Evidence taken from a remote witness room should be equalled with evidence taken from the courtroom while the counsel of the accused is still permitted to examine the witness.[115] This being said, the ICTY and the ICTR seem to prefer, where possible, alternative methods to one-way closed circuit television which it considers less intrusive to the rights of the accused. This would include the installation of temporary screens in the courtroom itself so that the witness cannot see the accused, but the accused may view the witness via the courtroom monitors.[116] The use of a screen would give the Trial Chamber the benefit of observing the demeanour of the witness directly in court instead of through a monitor.[117]

Rule 87(3)(c) of the ICC RPE, which lays down the possibility of closed circuit television, originates from Article 68(2). Since Article 68(2) seems to indicate an automatic right for victims of sexual violence to *in camera* proceedings or presentation of evidence by electronic or other special means, such as closed circuit television, it can be held that one-way closed circuit television needs to be applied for victims of sexual violence as of right, with the qualification that the victim him- or herself favours such an approach.[118] The relevance of one-way closed circuit television for victims of sexual

---

[112] *Ibid.*, para. 45.

[113] See Rules 75(B)(i)(c) and 75(B)(iii) ICTY/R RPE.

[114] *Prosecutor v. Duško Tadić*, Decision on the Prosecutor's Motion Requesting Protective Measures for Victims and Witnesses, Case No. IT-94-1, 10 August 1995, para. 50; *Prosecutor v. Zejnil Delalić, Zdravko Mucić, Hazim Delić and Esad Landžo*, Decision on the Motions by the Prosecution for Protective Measures for Prosecution Witnesses pseudonymed "B" through to "M", Case No. IT-96-21-T, 28 April 1997, para. 65.

[115] *Prosecutor v. Zejnil Delalić, Zdravko Mucić, Hazim Delić and Esad Landžo*, Decision on the Motions by the Prosecution for Protective Measures for Prosecution Witnesses pseudonymed "B" through to "M", Case No. IT-96-21-T, 28 April 1997, para. 67. See also subsection 4.4, where it is held that giving testimony through a live video link must be considered as creating a situation as if testimony was given in Court.

[116] *Ibid.*, para. 68; *Prosecutor v. Duško Tadić*, Decision on the Prosecutor's Motion Requesting Protective Measures for Victims and Witnesses, Case No. IT-94-1, 10 August 1995, para. 51.

[117] *Ibid.*

[118] See subsection 4.2 for the interpretation of 'automatic right' under Article 68(2) ICC Statute.

violence has not only been highlighted in and applied before ICTY and ICTR cases, it is also accepted and used in several national jurisdictions.[119]

The ICC Statute and RPE do not mention the use of temporary screens in the courtroom as a substitute for closed circuit television. It has been submitted, however, that the use of screens is similar to 'alteration of pictures or voice' mentioned in Rule 87(3)(c)[120] or at least can be subsumed under the open-ended wording 'other special means' mentioned in this Rule. It remains to be seen how the ICC will deal with the protective measure of one-way closed circuit television and the use of temporary screens. Especially in cases of sexual violence where the accused is also the perpetrator of the crime, protection from retraumatisation of the victim may be easier achieved when sitting in a remote witness room than sitting in the courtroom, only protected from the accused by a screen. The stress inherent to such a situation may, in some cases, increase rather than prevent the victim's (re)traumatisation. By physically distancing the accused and the witness from each other, the witness does not have to worry about the possibility of the screen falling over or the accused appearing from behind the screen, even though the likelihood of such occurrences may be negligible in practice. Observing the witness's demeanour in court directly, which is possible when a screen is used in court but not in case of closed circuit television, should not obstruct recourse to the use of one-way closed circuit television: nowadays, with adequate audio-visual technology, the demeanour of the witness can be closely monitored by the parties to the proceedings.

A third option which avoids confrontation between the accused and the witness during testimony given by the latter is the removal of the accused from the courtroom. This option is not mentioned in either Rule 87(3) or Rule 88 and has never been applied before the ICTY or the ICTR. The measure is used in several national jurisdictions,[121] however, and there is no reason why removal of the accused from the courtroom could not be considered as a protective measure for victims of sexual violence in proceedings before the ICC as well. In fact, Rule 88 seems to leave an opening for such a measure to apply.[122] When applied in the right way, the hearing of a witness in the absence of the accused is similar to one-way closed circuit television. If the accused is placed in a separate room with an audio-visual system in effect between him and the courtroom, with the possibility to respond to the witness's statement afterwards, his right to confrontation is not affected. This would also apply to the situation in which the accused is removed from the courtroom, but not his counsel, so that the latter can inform the accused of the victim's statement later and respond to it. An advantage of this measure is that the parties to the proceedings would be able to directly observe the demeanour of the victim.

---

[119] Brienen and Hoegen (2000), p. 1119.

[120] Kreβ (2001), p. 361.

[121] See Brienen and Hoegen (2000), pp. 1118 and 1168; and Kreβ (2001), p. 358, for some examples of jurisdictions that allow the removal of the accused from the courtroom.

[122] Rule 88(1) ICC RPE states: '... a Chamber may, taking into account the views of the victim or witness, order special measures such as but not limited to measures to facilitate the testimony of a ... victim of sexual violence.' See also Kreβ (2001), p. 358.

6.2 Special evidentiary rules

Another way of protecting witnesses and victims of sexual violence from further or increased trauma is restricting the questions that the parties may ask them. Rules 70 ('Principles of Evidence in Cases of Sexual Violence'), 71 ('Evidence of Other Sexual Conduct') and 72 ('In Camera Procedure to Consider Relevance or Admissibility of Evidence') of the ICC RPE contain this obligation. Under these rules, parties are restricted in their questioning with regard to the victim's prior or subsequent sexual conduct or consent to the sexual violence. In addition, Rule 63(4) states that corroboration is not a legal requirement to prove any crime falling within the jurisdiction of the Court, in particular, crimes of sexual violence. The rules are preceded by Rule 96 of the ICTY and ICTR RPE, which was the first rule of this kind within any international tribunal.[123] It formed the basis for discussions on Rules 63(4), 70, 71, and 72 of the ICC RPE. The rules were considered to be some of the most contentious issues in the negotiation of the Rules.[124] Rules 63(4) and 70-72 are placed in Section I of Chapter IV on (the admissibility of) 'Evidence'. While these rules are thus essentially concerned with the presentation of evidence, they also offer certain protective guarantees to victims of sexual violence when testifying.

Before discussing the rules itself, it is important to grasp the significance of the existence of such rules or, in other words, why special evidentiary rules on crimes of sexual violence are needed. In several ICTY cases, it has been attempted to explain the reasons underlying Rule 96.[125] Specific reference has been made to 'the nature of the conflict during which the crimes over which the International Tribunal has jurisdiction

---

[123] Rule 96 ICTY RPE ('Evidence in Cases of Sexual Assault') states:

In cases of sexual assault:

i. no corroboration of the victim's testimony shall be required;
ii. consent shall not be allowed as a defence if the victim:
   (a) has been subjected to or threatened with or has had reason to fear violence, duress, detention or psychological oppression, or
   (b) reasonably believed that if the victim did not submit, another might be so subjected, threatened or put in fear;
iii before evidence of the victim's consent is admitted, the accused shall satisfy the Trial Chamber in camera that the evidence is relevant and credible;
iv prior sexual conduct of the victim shall not be admitted in evidence.

Rule 96 ICTR RPE is almost identical to Rule 96 ICTY RPE; the difference is in subparagraph (i), which reads '*Notwithstanding Rule 90(C)*, no corroboration of the victim's testimony shall be required' (italics added). Rule 90(C) states that in those cases where a child testifies, without understanding the nature of a solemn declaration, a judgment cannot be based on such testimony alone. According to Rule 96(i), in cases of sexual violence, no corroboration is required, even when such a testimony of a child is concerned. See for an analysis of Rule 96, *inter alia*, Viseur Sellers (2001a), pp. 275-290; Fitzgerald (1997), pp. 638-663; and Ni Aolain (1997), pp. 883-905.

[124] For an account of the negotiations on these rules, see Piragoff (2001a), pp. 349-401.

[125] *Prosecutor v. Duško Tadić*, Decision on the Prosecutor's Motion Requesting Protective Measures for Victims and Witnesses, Case No. IT-94-1, 10 August 1995, para. 49, refers in this perspective to the 'consideration of the unique concerns of victims of sexual assault'.

were committed and where appalling allegations have been made of the systematic and mass rape of women'.[126] Indeed, when crimes of a sexual violence nature are committed, under force, coercion or coercive circumstances, as part of genocide, crimes against humanity or war crimes, issues as consent or evidence of prior or subsequent sexual conduct do not seem relevant. In addition, because of 'fear of reprisals, retraumatization and feelings of shame', witnesses are generally reluctant to appear as witnesses before the Tribunal, which formed another good reason for having a special evidentiary rule on sexual violence.[127] The rule can be considered as a major achievement in comparison with several national rules on admissibility of evidence regarding crimes of sexual violence, which tend to discriminate against victims of sexual violence, mostly women, by allowing their credibility to be challenged, and thereby contribute to preventing them from coming forward. Rule 96 must therefore be interpreted 'within a distinctive approach on sexual assault cases by an international tribunal established to do justice, deter future crimes and to contribute to the restoration and maintenance of peace'.[128] The mandate of the ICC requires the Court to take up similar cases of sexual violence as those that appeared or will appear before the Tribunals. The above-mentioned special evidentiary rules will in such cases apply.

6.2.1 Corroboration

The ICC RPE mention corroboration of evidence in subparagraph 4 of Rule 63:

> Without prejudice to article 66, paragraph 3 [ICC Statute: 'In order to convict the accused, the Court must be convinced of the guilt of the accused beyond reasonable doubt'], a Chamber shall not impose a legal requirement that corroboration is required in order to prove any crime within the jurisdiction of the Court, in particular, crimes of sexual violence.

This rule was inspired by Rule 96(i) of the ICTY and ICTR RPE which states that: 'In cases of sexual assault: (i) no corroboration of the victim's testimony shall be required.'[129] The message contained in Rule 63(3) is that corroboration of evidence is not a legal condition to prove any of the crimes within the jurisdiction of the Court. The extra emphasis in this rule on crimes of sexual violence must be viewed against the background of established law and practice in some national jurisdictions that require

---

[126] *Prosecutor v. Zejnil Delalić, Zdravko Mucić, Hazim Delić and Esad Landžo*, Decision on the Prosecution's Motion for Redaction of the Public Record, Case No. IT-96-21-T, 5 June 1997, para. 44.

[127] *Ibid.*, para. 46. See also *Prosecutor v. Duško Tadić*, Decision on the Prosecutor's Motion Requesting Protective Measures for Victims and Witnesses, Case No. IT-94-1, 10 August 1995, para. 46.

[128] *Prosecutor v. Zejnil Delalić, Zdravko Mucić, Hazim Delić and Esad Landžo*, Decision on the Prosecution's Motion for Redaction of the Public Record, Case No. IT-96-21-T, 5 June 1997, para. 47.

[129] Rule 96(i) ICTY/R RPE has been commented on by several ICTY and ICTR Chambers, *inter alia*, Tadić Opinion and Judgment, para. 536; Akayesu Judgment, para. 135; Furundžija Judgment, para. 116; Kayishema and Ruzindana Judgment, para. 70; Musema Judgment and Sentence, para. 45; Aleksovski Appeal Judgment, para. 62; Kunarac, Kovač and Vuković Judgment, para. 566; and Gacumbitsi Judgment, para. 213.

that the testimony of, predominantly female, victims of sexual violence be corroborated.[130] Victims of sexual violence, as opposed to victims of other crimes, used to be (and in some jurisdictions still are) seen as inherently untrustworthy, unreliable witnesses: therefore their testimony needed (or needs) to be corroborated.[131] In order to rebut any speculations on this point, Rule 63(3) explicitly prohibits making a difference between the corroboration requirements of proof for testimony on sexual violence and testimony on any other crime falling within the Court's jurisdiction. Rule 63(3) merely underlines that a victim of sexual violence is as reliable a witness as any other witness to any other crime. This assumption is also in line with the equality and non-discrimination principle laid down in Article 21(3) of the ICC Statute.[132]

Rule 63(3) of the ICC Statute should be understood in relation to the rules on relevance or admissibility of evidence, particularly Article 69(4) of the ICC Statute.[133] The Chamber has the discretion to rule on the relevance or admissibility of any evidence, taking into account the probative value of the evidence and any prejudice that such evidence may cause to a fair trial or to a fair evaluation of the testimony of a witness. When evidence on sexual violence of a single victim is relevant, probative, reliable and credible, a Trial Chamber may convict an accused for the crime charged: corroboration of evidence is not required.[134] For example, in the *Muhimana* case, the Trial Chamber established the rape of BJ by Muhimana and the rapes of two other girls by his companions on the basis of the testimony of BJ exclusively.[135] In situations where testimony, or any other form of evidence including documents,[136] is weak or not totally reliable, corroboration of evidence might be needed for the Chamber in order to 'be convinced of the guilt of the accused beyond reasonable doubt'.[137] When

[130] Piragoff (2001a), p. 355.

[131] In light of Rule 96(i) ICTY RPE, the Trial Chamber in the Tadić Opinion and Judgment, paras. 537 and 539, stated that the corroboration requirement, essentially a civil law requirement, 'is in almost all modern continental legal systems no longer a feature' and concluded that 'there is no ground for concluding that this requirement of corroboration is any part of customary international law'. See also the Kunarac, Kovač and Vuković Judgment, para. 566: 'Rule 96 specifically overrules the requirement which exists or which used to exist in some domestic systems of law that the evidence of a complainant who alleges rape must be corroborated.'

[132] Article 21(3) ICC Statute states: 'The application and interpretation of law pursuant to this article must be consistent with internationally recognized human rights, and be without any adverse distinction founded on grounds such as gender as defined in Article 7, paragraph 3, age, race, colour, language, religion or belief, political or other opinion, national, ethnic or social origin, wealth, birth or other status.' See Piragoff (2001a), p. 355.

[133] See also Article 64(9) ICC Statute and Rule 63(2) ICC RPE.

[134] Akayesu Judgment, para. 135; and Musema Judgment and Sentence, para. 45.

[135] Muhimana Judgment and Sentence, paras. 288-292. See also, *inter alia*, the Gacumbitsi Judgment, paras. 213-215 (on the basis of the testimony of Witness TAQ it was established that 'Witness TAQ and seven other Tutsi women and girls with whom she was hiding' were raped following the instigation of Gacumbitsi to do so. 'One of them, Chantal, died after her genitals had been impaled with a stick, at the instigation of the Accused. Three of the young Tutsi girls were led away forcefully'); Stakić Judgment, paras. 791-806.

[136] Piragoff (2001a), p. 356.

[137] For example, in the Musema case before the ICTR the accused was not convicted of the rape and killing of Immaculée Mukankuzi and the rape and killing of others with her by his men and

corroborating evidence exists, it may help to confirm the testimony of the victim,[138] but it is not a legal requirement as such. Each case therefore has to be assessed on its own merits, without any significance being attached to the victim's sex or the nature of the crime.

6.2.2 Consent

Rules 70 and 72 of the ICC RPE deal with the issue of consent to sexual violence and its (in)admissibility into evidence, respectively.

Rule 70 ICC RPE reads:

> In cases of sexual violence, the Court shall be guided by and, where appropriate, apply the following principles:
>
> (a) Consent cannot be inferred by reason of any words or conduct of a victim where force, threat of force, coercion or taking an advantage of a coercive environment undermined the victim's ability to give voluntary and genuine consent;
> (b) Consent cannot be inferred by reason of any words or conduct of a victim where the victim is incapable of giving genuine consent;
> (c) Consent cannot be inferred by reason of the silence of, or lack of resistance by, a victim to the alleged sexual violence;
>
> ...

Rule 70 is an expression of the understanding that consent to sexual violence cannot be inferred under the circumstances described in subparagraphs (a) to (c). Considering the circumstances apparent in situations of armed conflict, crimes against humanity or

---

on his orders because of lack of corroborated evidence. It was held: 'While the Chamber found the testimony of Witness J to be generally credible, it is deeply troubled by this unexplained inconsistency regarding the rape of her daughter. Without any reasonable explanation, the Chamber must question the accuracy of the account. The Chamber believes that there is likely to be a reasonable explanation, based on its evaluation of the witness. However, recalling the high burden of proof on the Prosecutor and the lack of any other evidence to corroborate the account of Witness J, the Chamber cannot find beyond reasonable doubt that the allegations have been established relating to the rape and killing of Immaculée Mukankuzi by Musema and the rape and killing of others with her by his men and on his orders.' Musema Judgment and Sentence, paras. 844-845.

[138] In the Furundžija Judgment, para. 116, it was mentioned: 'The witness's manner in court was convincing and although her testimony, in accordance with Rule 96 of the Rules, requires no corroboration, the Trial Chamber notes that the evidence of Witness D does confirm the evidence of Witness A in this regard.' See also, *inter alia*, Čelebići Judgment, para. 936 ('The Trial Chamber finds the testimony of Ms. Cecez, and the supporting testimony of Witness D and Dr. Grubac, credible and compelling, and thus concludes that Ms. Cecez was raped by Mr. Delic, and others, in the Čelebići prison-camp') and para. 957 ('Despite the contentions of the Defence, the Trial Chamber accepts Ms. Antic's testimony, and finds, on this basis, and the supporting evidence of Ms. Cecez, Witness P and Dr. Petko Grubac, that she was subjected to three rapes by Hazim Delic').

genocide, in many cases, acts of sexual violence will have been committed under force, coercion or coercive circumstances which negate any apparent consent, including where the victim was silent or did not resist to the act. Consent can likewise not be inferred where a person is incapable of giving genuine consent, due to 'natural, induced or age-related incapacity'.[139] Whereas subparagraph (b) refers to situations where a person is incapable of giving genuine consent due to natural, induced or age-related incapacity, subparagraphs (a) and (c) refer to situations where a person, in normal circumstances, would be capable of giving genuine consent. The Rule is a manifestation of the non-discrimination and equality provisions of Article 21(3), and of the obligations in Article 68(1), to protect victims and witnesses, and further guidance to a Chamber on the application of Article 69(4): in determining the relevance, admissibility, value or weight of evidence, stereotypes and biases about victims of sexual violence, particularly women, are not permitted.[140] The principles laid down in Rule 70 are merely aimed to direct the Chamber to arrive at such a conclusion.

In the Elements of Crimes, no explicit reference to non-consent as an element of the crime of rape or any other form of sexual violence is laid down.[141] Whereas, before the ICTY and the ICTR, a certain development emerged to include the element of consent in the definition of rape, in particular, on the basis of the *Kunarac, Kovač and Vuković* Appeal Judgment,[142] the ICC has not followed this direction and has only

[139] For the interpretation of 'incapable of giving genuine consent', see, for instance, Article 7(1)(g)-1 ICC Elements of Crimes (EoC), crime against humanity of rape, footnote 16. 'Natural, induced or age-related incapacity' refers, *inter alia*, to situations where a person is mentally incapable, unconscious, drugged, or senile.

[140] Piragoff (2001b), p. 399.

[141] See the ICC EoC for the elements of rape as a crime against humanity (Article 7(1)(g)-1) and a war crime (Articles 8(2)(b)(xxii)-1/Article 8(2)(e)(vi)-1):

1. The perpetrator invaded the body of a person by conduct resulting in penetration, however slight, of any part of the body of the vicim or of the perpetrator with a sexual organ, or of the anal or genital opening of the victim with any object or any other part of the body.
2. The invasion was committed by force, or by threat of force or coercion, such as that caused by fear of violence, duress, detention, psychological oppression or abuse of power, against such person or another person, or by taking advantage of a coercive environment, or the invasion was committed against a person incapable of giving genuine consent.

See also the elements of the war crime of enforced prostitution (Article 8(2)(b)(xxii)-3/Article 8(2)(e)(vi)-3); the war crime of sexual violence (Article 8(2)(b)(xxii)-6/Article 8(2)(e)(vi)-6); the crime against humanity of enforced prostitution (Article 7(1)(g)-3); and the crime against humanity of sexual violence (Article 7(1)(g)-6) in the EoC. See also Chapter 2.

[142] Rape has been defined differently by different ICTY and ICTR Chambers. In the Akayesu Judgment, para. 688, the Trial Chamber defined rape as 'a physical invasion of a sexual nature, committed on a person under circumstances which are coercive'. The following judgments concurred with this definition of rape: Čelebići Judgment, paras. 478-479; Musema Judgement and Sentence, paras. 220 and 226; Niyitegeka Judgement and Sentence, para. 456; and Muhimana Judgment and Sentence, paras. 535-551. In the Kunarac, Kovač and Vuković Appeal Judgment,

referred to consent where it concerns a person who is incapable of giving genuine consent. As such, the definition of rape (or any of the other crimes of a sexual violence nature) refers to force or threat of force, but also to coercion, such as that caused by fear of violence, duress, detention, psychological oppression or abuse of power, or by taking advantage of a coercive environment. Thus, where force or threat of force, coercion or coercive circumstances are apparent and the jurisdictional requirements of crimes against humanity, war crimes or genocide are fulfilled, the issue of consent cannot be introduced into evidence. Including consent in the definition can expose victims of sexual violence to painful and humiliating questions which are not relevant in situations where force, coercion or coercive circumstances are present. An inquiry into the victim's conduct and state of mind ('did you consent' or other questions to that effect) with the purpose to obtaining explicit evidence of non-consent is offensive and shocking to most victims of sexual violence. It is insulting to most rape victims, especially after the witness has described the circumstances in which the sexual violence took place. Including consent in the definition of rape places the burden on the Prosecutor to prove that there was no consent and thus leads the Prosecutor to inquire with the victim about whether or not she consented. The reaction of Witness 95 in the *Kunarac, Kovač and Vuković* case to the question posed by the Prosecutor if the sexual contact was against her will, was met with outrage: 'Please, madam, if over a period of 40 days you have sex with someone, with several individuals, do you really think that is with your own will?'[143] Witness 95 had just explained to the court that she was selected for the purpose of rape more than 150 times in a period of 40 days. Putting the question of consent to the witness may therefore create the impression that she is not believed and that she did consent. In the *Kunarac, Kovač and Vuković* case, the judges had in fact requested that the issue of absence of consent was brought up, despite the coercive circumstances established by the Prosecutor.[144] Despite the fact that, at that time, the *Akayesu* and *Furundžija* definitions of rapes were the only definitions available, focusing on coercion, force and threat of force instead, Judge Hunt held that inquires into consent would serve 'proper prosecution procedure not to leave matters to implication' also in light of a possible move away from the Furundžija definition of

para. 127 (quoting and concurring with the Trial Chamber's definition of rape), the Appeals Chamber defined rape in mechanical terms with non-consent as an element of the crime. In the Semanza Judgment and Sentence, paras. 344-346; Kajelijeli Judgment and Sentence, para. 915; and the Gacumbitsi Judgment, paras. 321, 325 (the Trial Chamber in this case seems to accept that non-consent is an element of the crime of rape, but is not very clear on this point, however) this definition is upheld. In addition, the Furundžija definition of rape may be said to be in between the Akayesu and Kunarac, Kovač and Vuković approaches to rape as it does not refer to consent, but gives a mechanical description of the acts falling within the definition of rape. For an analysis of the definition of rape, see Chapter 2.

143 *Prosecutor v. Dragoljub Kunarac, Radomir Kovač and Zoran Vuković*, Transcripts, Case No. IT-96-23-T and IT-96-23/1-T, 25 April 2000, pp. 2235-2236. In the closing statements, the Prosecutor recognised that the question was met with 'appropriate outrage' by the rape victim. See *Prosecutor v. Dragoljub Kunarac, Radomir Kovač and Zoran Vuković*, Transcripts, Case No. IT-96-23-T and IT-96-23/1-T, 20 November 2000, p. 6281.

144 *Prosecutor v. Dragoljub Kunarac, Radomir Kovač and Zoran Vuković*, Transcripts, Case No. IT-96-23-T and IT-96-23/1-T, 19 April 2000, pp. 1979-1982.

rape after the closure of the *Kunarac, Kovač and Vuković* case.[145] The Prosecutor, who had initially not inquired into the issue of consent (because, in her view, the coercive circumstances were sufficiently established and thus rendered consent irrelevant) subsequently re-formulated the question into 'was it against your will?'[146] However, questions about non-consent will likely result in victims becoming reluctant to come forward, which will prevent that justice for sexual violence victims is done. Luckily, the ICC has not included consent as an element of the crime of rape or any other form of sexual violence in its Elements of Crimes document.[147] This will allow the Prosecutor to focus on the coercive circumstances and will prevent the issue of consent being raised by the Prosecutor. The possibility of advancing consent is still possible under strict circumstances laid down in Rule 72 of the ICC RPE, but the burden of proof will then rest with the Defence.

Despite the acknowledgements that consent is not easily of any significance in the sort of cases that appear before the ICC, a procedural mechanism has been developed to scrutinise situations in which consent may nevertheless be relevant. Rule 72 states that if a party wants to introduce or elicit, including by means of the questioning of the victim or witness, evidence that the victim consented to an alleged crime of sexual violence, an *in camera* procedure will be held to determine whether such evidence is relevant or admissible. Subparagraph (2) of Rule 72 lays down the procedure and states:

> In deciding whether the evidence referred to in sub-rule 1 is relevant or admissible, a Chamber shall hear in camera the views of the Prosecutor, the defence, the witness and the victim or his or her legal representative, if any, and shall take into account whether that evidence has a sufficient degree of probative value to an issue in the case and the prejudice that such evidence may cause, in accordance with article 69, paragraph 4. For this purpose, the Chamber shall have regard to article 21, paragraph 3 [the non-discrimination and equality principles], and articles 67 [rights of the accused] and 68 [rights of victims and witnesses], and shall be guided by principles (a) to (d) of rule 70, especially with respect to the proposed questioning of a victim.

Thus, in order to restrict the admission of evidence of consent to cases where the evidence is relevant, the *in camera* procedure will first be followed in order to determine the probative value and prejudice of the evidence. It is submitted here that, during such an *in camera* procedure, the accused should first be interrogated in order to establish relevance and credibility before the defence of consent can be advanced through propositions to the victim. The victim is not present during the *in camera* procedure.[148] This shields the victim from confrontation with painful propositions that

---

145 *Ibid.*, p. 1981.

146 *Prosecutor v. Dragoljub Kunarac, Radomir Kovač and Zoran Vuković*, Transcripts, Case No. IT-96-23-T and IT-96-23/1-T, 18 May 2000, pp. 3481, 3597-3598, 3601.

147 For a discussion of non-consent as an element of the crime of rape, see Chapter 2.

148 According to Piragoff (2001b, pp. 416-417), the text of subparagraph 2 does not require that a witness be heard *in camera*. This was not considered during the negotiations in the Preparatory Commission either. The representations of counsel may be sufficient in most cases. However, the subparagraph does not preclude the hearing of a witness *in camera* either. Hearing a witness *in camera* may even convince the Chamber that the evidence should not be admissible, thereby avoiding the need to subject the witness to needless examination in the public courtroom.

have not been tested first. The rule thus tends to protect victims of sexual violence from a painful examination in court where consent should not at all be an issue, while upholding the accused's right to present evidence of consent in cases where consent does matter. To repeat, it is almost surreal to imagine situations in which victims of sexual violence in periods of genocide, crimes against humanity or war crime could have consented to the act and it is therefore to be expected that consent is not likely to be an issue in the proceedings before the ICC.

Rule 72 of the ICC RPE is based on Rule 96(ii) and (iii) of the ICTY and ICTR RPE. In pertinent part, Rule 96 states:

> In cases of sexual assault:
>
> ...
>
> (iii) consent shall not be allowed as a defence if the victim:
> (a) has been subjected to or threatened with or has had reason to fear violence, duress, detention or psychological oppression, or
> (b) reasonably believed that if the victim did not submit, another might be so subjected, threatened or put in fear;
>
> (iv) before evidence of the victim's consent is admitted, the accused shall satisfy the Trial Chamber in camera that the evidence is relevant and credible;
>
> ...

Rule 96(ii) and (iii) of the ICTY and ICTR RPE seems more victim-friendly than its counterpart in Rule 72 of the ICC RPE in the sense that it includes more firm language: 'consent shall not be allowed as a defence if' as opposed to the Chamber 'shall be guided by principles (a) to (d)'. It must be noted that initially Rule 96 did not allow a defence of consent to be made at all. However, out of fair trial concerns, the rule was quickly amended to not completely exclude the possibility for the Defence to raise the issue of consent.[149] This is also the underlying reason for Rule 72 of the ICC RPE.[150] So far, Rule 96 has not been applied before either Tribunal. However, once in the experience of the ICTY, Rule 96 was skilfully circumvented by the accused. In the *Kunarac, Kovač and Vuković* case, Kunarac brought up the issue of consent by asserting 'mistake of fact', that is, that he believed that Witness D.B. consented to the sexual intercourse because she took part in it in an active way. However, the Trial Chamber did not accept his assertion and held that:

> The Trial Chamber, however, accepts the testimony of D.B. who testified that, prior to the intercourse, she had been threatened by "Gaga" that he would kill her if she did not satisfy the desires of his commander, the accused Dragoljub Kunarac. The Trial Chamber accepts D.B.'s evidence that she only initiated sexual intercourse with Kunarac because she was afraid of being killed by "Gaga" if she did not do so.

[149] Viseur Sellers and Okuizumi (1997), p. 53.

[150] See Scheffer (1999) on the US position in this regard ('... the United States' position has been that the perpetrator has a fundamental right to present a defense. In other words, a lack of consent cannot simply be inferred or assumed').

> The Trial Chamber rejects the evidence of the accused Dragoljub Kunarac that he was not aware of the fact that D.B. only initiated sexual intercourse with him for reasons of fear for her life. The Trial Chamber regards it as highly improbable that the accused Kunarac could realistically have been "confused" by the behaviour of D.B., given the general context of the existing war-time situation and the specifically delicate situation of the Muslim girls detained in Partizan or elsewhere in the Foca region during that time. As to whether or not he was aware of the threat by "Gaga" against D.B., the Trial Chambers finds it irrelevant as to whether or not Kunarac heard "Gaga" repeat this threat against D.B. when he walked into the room, as D.B. testified. The Trial Chamber is satisfied that D.B. did not freely consent to any sexual intercourse with Kunarac. She was in captivity and in fear for her life after the threats uttered by "Gaga".[151]

In the *Kunarac, Kovač and Vuković* case, the issue of consent was thus raised despite the coercive circumstances the victims of rape and sexual slavery were in. In the *Furundžija* case, consent was not an issue and the Trial Chamber remarked, in this perspective, that 'consent was not raised by the Defence, and in any case, Witness A was in captivity. Further, it is the position of the Trial Chamber that any form of captivity vitiates consent.'[152]

6.2.3 Prior or subsequent sexual conduct

Rule 71 of the ICC RPE states:

> In the light of the definition and nature of the crimes within the jurisdiction of the Court, and subject to article 69, paragraph 4, a Chamber shall not admit evidence of the prior or subsequent sexual conduct of a victim or witness.

Rule 70(d) of the ICC RPE furthermore reads:

> Credibility, character or predisposition to sexual availability of a victim or witness cannot be inferred by reason of the sexual nature of the prior or subsequent conduct of a victim or witness.

Rule 71 is an acknowledgement of the presumption that prior or subsequent sexual conduct cannot be admitted into evidence either. The nature of the crimes laid down in the Statute do not justify challenging the victim's prior or subsequent sexual conduct. To admit such evidence would 'lead to a confusion of the issues' essentially trying 'to call the reputation of the victim into question' and would only bring 'further distress and emotional damage to the witness'.[153] This assumption is also in line with the equality and non-discrimination clause laid down in Article 21(3) of the ICC Statute. Unlike the ICTY and ICTR Rule, the current provision does not totally forbid the

---

[151] Kunarac, Kovač and Vuković Judgment, paras. 645 and 646.

[152] Furundžija Judgment, para. 271.

[153] *Prosecutor v. Zejnil Delalić, Zdravko Mucić, Hazim Delić and Esad Landžo*, Decision on the Prosecution's Motion for Redaction of the Public Record, Case No. IT-96-21-T, 5 June 1997, para. 48. The Trial Chamber made specific comments on Rule 96(iv).

introduction of evidence of prior or subsequent sexual conduct.[154] Rule 71 includes the phrase 'subject to Article 69, paragraph 4', which implies that even though prior or subsequent sexual conduct is generally not relevant or admissible, a different conclusion might be drawn on the basis of Article 69(4) which requires that the probative value of the evidence and any prejudice that such evidence may cause to a fair trial or to a fair evaluation of the testimony of a witness needs to be taken into account. However, evidence on prior or subsequent sexual conduct has no probative value nor causes any prejudice to a fair trial or a fair evaluation of the testimony of a witness. It has therefore been argued that a proper reading of Rule 71 implies that the Chamber should be guided by the general rule that prior or subsequent sexual conduct cannot be admitted into evidence, and that the evidence can be fully evaluated in light of Article 69(4) only in exceptional circumstances.[155] However, if evidence of prior or subsequent sexual conduct were considered relevant or admitted, it could never be used for the purposes of inferring that the victim or witness is of bad character, lacks credibility or is predisposed to sexual availability. Such inferences are excluded under Rule 70(d). In essence, the reference to Article 69(4) in Rule 71 is unfortunate, as prior or subsequent sexual conduct should never be admitted into evidence as this would 'lead to a confusion of the issues' as once stipulated by the ICTY Trial Chamber in the *Čelebići* case. Furthermore, Rule 70(d) seems to make any admissibility of prior or subsequent sexual conduct to call into question the reputation of the rape victim on the basis of Article 69(4) redundant.

6.3 Prior recorded testimony

As mentioned before, Article 69(2) of the ICC Statute recognises that the testimony of a witness may also be given outside court. In this regard, the second sentence explicitly makes reference to 'viva voce (oral) or recorded testimony of a witness by means of video or audio technology, as well as the introduction of documents or written transcripts'. A similar provision can be found in Rule 71 of the ICTY and ICTR RPE.[156] Recorded testimony may be introduced at trial as a substitute for the direct testimony of the witness to spare the witness of sexual violence from repeated questioning.[157] So far,

[154] *Ibid.* In this case, the Chamber held that if an act is deemed 'prior sexual conduct' under Rule 96(iv), its exclusion is not 'susceptible to waiver' by any of the parties or the victim. The case concerned abortion.

[155] Piragoff (2001b), pp. 407-408.

[156] Under Rule 71 ICTY RPE a deposition can be taken for use at the trial in the interest of justice. Rule 71 ICTR RPE adds the requirement of 'exceptional circumstances' thereto. This requirement was removed from Rule 71 ICTY RPE and the phrase 'whether or not the person whose deposition is sought is able physically to appear before the Tribunal to give evidence' was added in order to make depositions more common and to expedite trials. See May and Wierda (2002), p. 183. See also Rule 92*bis* ('Proof of Facts other than by Oral Evidence') as regards written statements.

[157] See Kreβ (2001), pp. 362-363; and Brady (2001), pp. 455-456. In addition, in several national jurisdictions (the Netherlands, Belgium and most Swiss cantons) witnesses are, as a rule, not required, to testify in court; examination by both parties takes place during the pre-trial stages. In this way, the number of times witnesses are questioned is reduced. See Brienen and Hoegen (2000), pp. 1125-1127.

Rule 71 of the ICTY and ICTR RPE has never been applied for this reason, and it remains to be seen whether this will happen before the ICC.

In light of Rules 88 and 68, this is not unrealistic. Rule 88 allows for special measures to be taken to, *inter alia*, facilitate the testimony of victims of sexual violence. The rule is open-ended, and prior recorded testimony, as laid down in Rule 68, could qualify as such a special measure as it would spare a victim of sexual violence from being called before the ICC in order to give testimony again. This presumption is further reinforced by Rule 112 which specifies the procedure of questioning a suspect by audio- or video-recording. Moreover, it provides, in subparagraph (4), that audio- and video-recording can also be used for other persons, including victims of sexual or gender violence, where it 'could assist in reducing any subsequent traumatization'. The matter could possibly also be brought within the ambit of Article 56, which provides 'unique investigative opportunities' to take testimony from a witness who 'may not be available subsequently for the purposes of a trial'. The Prosecutor must inform the Pre-Trial Chamber of such a decision. The question is whether this provision can be invoked when testimony is only taken once to spare a victim of sexual violence from further traumatisation or increased traumatisation.

The rights of the accused are guaranteed under both Article 56 and Rule 68, apparently inspired by Article 69(2), which states that the use of prior recorded testimony 'shall not be prejudicial to or inconsistent with the rights of the accused'. Subparagraph (a) of Rule 68 states that the recorded testimony can only be introduced at trial if both the Prosecutor and the Defence had the opportunity to examine the witness during the recording itself.[158] Article 56(1)(b) states that the Trial Chamber 'may take measures as may be necessary to ensure the efficiency and integrity of the proceedings and, in particular, to protect the rights of the defence'. This most likely refers to the right of the accused and/or his counsel to examine the witness during the taking of testimony as well. In addition, a judge may be present when the testimony is taken.[159] In order to safeguard the witness from incursions upon his or her safety, privacy and dignity, and physical and psychological well-being, relevant protective measures could be imposed during the recording of the testimony, including keeping the witness's identity from the public or the press and possibly even the accused.

It is noteworthy that Rule 68 can also be invoked if a crucial witness dies after the taking of the pre-recorded testimony but before the start of the trial.[160] The same presumption could be extended to apply to a witness who is too sick to come to court, but also too sick for having his testimony tested by cross-examination by live video

---

[158] Rule 68(b) ICC RPE concerns the situation in which a witness whose testimony was previously recorded is present before the Trial Chamber. In such a situation, the Trial Chamber may allow the presentation of the previously recorded audio or video testimony of that witness if he or she does not object to the submission of the previously recorded testimony and the Prosecutor, the Defence and the Chamber have the opportunity to examine the witness during the proceedings.

[159] Article 56(2)(e) ICC Statute. In Rule 68(a) ICC RPE, the presence of a judge during the recording of the witness's testimony is not mentioned. The recorded testimony may, however, be admitted into evidence. From the perspective of the accused, it would perhaps be recommendable to conduct the recordings under the supervision of a judge or another court official as well.

[160] Brady (2001), p. 456.

conferencing.[161] Severe illness, such as HIV/AIDS, and death as a consequence thereof, are not uncommon in situations of armed conflict or genocide in which victims have undergone multiple rapes or were held in sexual slavery for weeks or sometimes months on end. The use of such prior recorded testimony at trial, with the condition that both parties would have had the opportunity to examine the witness during the recording, might achieve that valuable testimony is later not easily set aside in court.

The relevance or admissibility of the evidence, like that of any other evidence, will be determined in accordance with the conditions set forth in Article 69(4). If the Prosecutor seeks to introduce the pre-recorded testimony as evidence in court, the judges will be in the position to see the recorded testimony themselves and accord weight to it accordingly.[162]

6.4 Other special measures

Other special measures aimed at preventing further or increased traumatisation relate, *inter alia*, to the manner of questioning, the length of time of questioning and the possibility to have a supports person attend the trial during the testimony of the witness. Rule 88 refers to some of these measures. As the rule is worded in an open-ended way, it offers possibilities to include other measures as well, such as the removal of the accused from the courtroom and the taking of prior recorded testimony.[163]

6.4.1 Attendance of counsel, legal representative, psychologist or family member

Rule 88(2) specifically mentions the possibility of the attendance of 'a counsel, a legal representative, a psychologist or a family member ... during the testimony of the victim or witness'.[164] The rule acknowledges that victims may be in need of legal advise and/or psychological support during trial. For victims of sexual violence, it may be very comforting to have the nearby support of a close relative or psychologist during testimony in court. A counsel or legal representative may be important for a witness as well, for instance, in order for the counsel to intervene when bullying questions are asked.

---

[161] See subsection 4.4 on live video conferencing.

[162] Introducing oral testimony or transcripts into evidence may have the disadvantage that the demeanour of the witness cannot be assessed. However, it can be submitted that, if the accused retains his right to examine the witness or have the witness against him examined, the evidence may still be introduced at trial. In the Tadić case, the use of and weight attributed to deposition evidence was indirectly referred to. It was held that 'the evidentiary value of testimony provided by video-link, although weightier than that of testimony given by deposition, is not as weighty as testimony given in the courtroom. Hearing of witnesses by video-link should therefore be avoided as far as possible.' *Prosecutor v. Duško Tadić*, Decision on the Defence Motion to Summon and Protect Defence Witnesses, and on the Giving of Evidence by Video-Link, Case No. IT-94-1-T, 25 June 1996, para. 21.

[163] See subsections 6.1 and 6.3 above.

[164] See also Rules 16-18 ICC RPE on the responsibilities of the VWU in respect of victims and witnesses. See also Rule 34 ICTY/R RPE.

6.4.2 Manner and length of questioning

Rule 88(5) also explicitly states that '... a Chamber shall be vigilant in controlling the manner of questioning a witness or victim so as to avoid any harassment or intimidation, paying particular attention to attacks on victims of sexual violence'. The judges' right to intervene during the witnesses' testimony is further confirmed in Article 64(8)(b) and (9) of the ICC Statute and Rule 140(2) of the ICC RPE.[165] The RPE of the ICTY and ICTR contain similar provisions.[166] In respect of the ICTR, an international fact-finding mission to collect information on the role and position of victims concluded in 2002 that most witnesses who testified before the ICTR were upset by the cross-examination conducted by Defence Counsel, in particular, the way in which the questions were asked.[167] Many witnesses felt they had been 'treated with scorn, considered to be liars, cheats, mentally disturbed or fools, and feeling that they, in turn, had been accused'.[168] They mentioned that the judges rarely intervened, or only did so to point out that the witness had to answer the question. This attitude seems to be largely influenced by the judges' background as regards legal system (civil or common law) as well as the personality of the judge.[169] Rwandan genocide survivors organisations, IBUKA ('Remember') and AVEGA-AGAHOZO ('Association of Genocide Widows') in particular, have raised the embarrassing nature of the questions put forward by the Defence to victims of sexual violence, which, according to them, included such questions as 'Did you touch his sex? Did you take pleasure in the act? Why did you not interrupt the act if you did not find pleasure in it?'[170] Another example is the *Butare* case, where Witness TA, a victim of multiple rapes by multiple perpetrators, was asked, *inter alia*, the following questions by the Defence: 'Did you see his penis?', 'Did you touch Shalom's [the accused's] penis?', 'How was it introduced into your vagina?', 'Now on the earlier first occasion I asked you whether you had seen Shalom's penis, do you remember that? ... Are you able to tell the Judges of this

---

[165] The wording of Rule 140(2)(c) seems, however, to suggest that a judge's questioning of a witness preferably takes place before or after the questioning by the parties to the proceedings.

[166] Rule 75(C) ICTY RPE states: 'A Chamber shall, whenever necessary, control the manner of questioning to avoid any harassment or intimidation.' Rules 85 and 90(F) and (H) further acknowledge that judges may intervene. See also Rule 46(A), in which it is stated that a Judge or a Chamber may warn Defence Counsel if the conduct of counsel is offensive or abusive.

[167] International Federation for Human Rights (2002), p. 8. The mission interviewed seven of the approximately 500 witnesses (two-thirds of whom were witnesses for the Prosecution). Therefore, no general conclusions can be drawn from these interviews, although some indication concerning certain issues can be inferred, in particular as the concerns of these witnesses were substantiated by other sources.

[168] *Ibid.* 'A number of witnesses had been asked if they had been paid to testify, whether Ibuka, Avega [survivors' groups] or the government had asked them to say one thing or another, or were criticised for not being present at the scene when the events occurred.'

[169] Heikkilä (2004), p. 115. Heikkilä further mentions that 'as a whole, the judges have, however, shown a tendency to stress the parties' right to determine the manner in which they conduct their cases, and have thus not often called into question the witness questioning tactics of the parties.'

[170] Hirondelle News Agency, *Survivors Accused 14 Defence Investigators of Genocide Crimes*, 25 March 2002. The treatment of rape victims in this manner caused AVEGA-AGAHOZO and IBUKA to suspend cooperation with the ICTR for a while.

Chamber whether he was circumcised or not?'[171] The Defence Counsel also insinuated that she could not have been a victim of rape because she was smelling as a result of not having been able to take a bath for a long time.[172] At the end of one of the Defence Counsellor's cross-examination, he practically called her a liar when he asked TA: 'Is it true and possible that these things that you have testified to before the Chamber did not happen to you, but were suggested to you?'[173] Although the President of the Trial Chamber remarked that the latter question was 'impressive', no further attention was given to it by the judges.[174] Moreover, the examination of Witness TA became well-known, in particular, because of the 'laughing judges'. During TA's cross-examination about the rapes, the judges suddenly started to laugh. Whatever the reason for their behaviour,[175] it is obvious that, during trial, a judge is not supposed to laugh, especially not during testimony of a victim of multiple rapes who had the courage to come and testify at the Tribunal. Del Ponte reportedly had said that the 'laughing judges' incident was '"scandalous", and that she was surprised by the passivity of the presiding judge'.[176] She also submitted that the 'prosecution should also be doing more to stop such incidents occurring. "It is important that the prosecutor in court can try to protect him (the witness) from an aggression [in particular, referring to a Defence allegation that a witness was lying]," she said.' When Witness TA agreed to speak to Binaifer Nowrojee (an expert in conducting investigations into human rights violations during armed conflict, especially with regard to sexual violence) more than a year after she gave testimony at the ICTR, she said:

---

[171] *The Prosecutor v. Pauline Nyiramasuhuko, Arsène Shalom Ntahobali, Alphonse Nteziryayo, Sylvain Nsabimana, Elie Ndayambaje and Joseph Kanyabashi*, Transcripts, Case No. ICTR-98-42-T, 31 October 2001, pp. 67, 69, 70, 100, respectively.

[172] *Ibid.*, pp. 60-63, 65, 89.

[173] *The Prosecutor v. Pauline Nyiramasuhuko, Arsène Shalom Ntahobali, Alphonse Nteziryayo, Sylvain Nsabimana, Elie Ndayambaje and Joseph Kanyabashi*, Transcripts, Case No. ICTR-98-42-T, 1 November 2001, p. 68.

[174] *Ibid.*, pp. 68-69. See also the Gacumbitsi case (*Le Procureur c. Sylvestre Gacumbitsi*, Transcription Caviardee, Affaire N° ICTR-2001-64-T, 6 août 2003), where the Defence Counsel implied that Witness TAP lied about the rape by Gacumbitsi. The Trial Chamber replied that the Defence should not make any such allegations. On several occasions, Witness TAP said 'All I know is that I am not lying' and needed breaks. In the Military II trial, the Defence Counsel for Bizimungu, the former Rwandan army chief-of-staff, 'repeatedly challenged the witness [who alleged she had been the victim of gang rape at the hands of soldiers and Interahamwe] by suggesting she was a liar and a member of a genocide survivors' association named IBUKA, which he termed as a "laboratory" where "a bunch of Tutsi extremists [work] who fabricate stories to have Hutus convicted."' In response, Judge Asoka de Silva intervened. See Hirondelle News Agency, *Judge Intervenes to Quell Heated Exchange in Soldiers' Trial*, 21 June 2005.

[175] According to a Trial Attorney at the ICTR, the judges were not laughing about Witness TA, but they were laughing about the Defence Counsel's conduct in court.

[176] Hirondelle News Agency, *Rwanda Tribunal's Witness Protection in Question* (by Julia Crawford), 10 December 2001.

> My parents, my brother and my sister were killed. I'm all alone. My relatives were killed in a horrible fashion. But I survived – to answer the strange questions that were asked by the ICTR. If you say you were raped, that is something understandable. How many times do you need to say it? When the judges laughed, they laughed like they could not stop laughing. I was angry and nervous. When I returned, everyone knew I had testified. My fiancée [sic] refused to marry me once he knew I had been raped. He said, you went to Arusha and told everyone that you were raped. Today I would not accept to testify, to be traumatized for a second time. No one apologized to me. Only Gregory Townsend [the ICTR prosecuting lawyer] congratulated me after the testimony for my courage. When you return you get threatened. My house was attacked. My fiancée [sic] has left me. In any case, I'm already dead.[177]

Thus, not only did Witness TA feel victimised for a second time, because of the publicity given to the case, she was abandoned by her fiancé and she was receiving threats. On the basis of the above, it is important that, during the examination of witnesses, judges use their right to intervene in order to stop unnecessary, repetitive or bullying questions. In addition, Trial Attorneys should also more strongly object to such questioning methods used by Defence lawyers. Rules that prevent victims of sexual violence from being exposed to such a manner of questioning do not affect the right of the accused to a fair trial, as the guarantee of a fair trial does not contain a right to intimidate or harass witnesses.[178]

The length of time a witness is questioned can be a cause for further or increased traumatisation as well. If a witness has to give evidence for days on end (sometimes spread over several weeks), this can be a very tiring experience, especially where questions are repeated by different counsellors in a joint trial. An example of a lengthy questioning by both the Prosecutor and, especially, the Defence, is, again, the examination of Witness TA in the ICTR *Butare* trial.[179] Witness TA was questioned for a day and a half by the Prosecutor and subsequently seven more days by the different counsellors for the accused.[180] Yet, some of the accused were not charged with rape, so why should counsel of these accused pose (similar) questions related to the rape to the witness? While this example is not representative of the overall court proceedings concerning the length of time witnesses are questioned, it nevertheless reveals very unsatisfactory treatment of a victim-witness of sexual violence.

Within the ICTY and the ICTR, the judges have the right to control the examination in time, as the questions posed should be effective for the ascertainment of the truth and should avoid needless consumption of time.[181] In addition, other rules relate to cross-examination which must be limited to points raised in the examination-in-chief or matters affecting the credibility of the witness; and, if the Trial Chamber deems it advisable, it may permit enquiry into additional matters, as if on direct

[177] Nowrojee (2005).

[178] Mumba (2001), p. 367.

[179] In the Butare trial (Case No. ICTR-98-42), six accused are standing trial, two of whom (Pauline Nyiramasuhuko, former Minister of Family and Women Welfare, and her son, Arsène Shalom Ntahobali) are accused of sexual violence crimes.

[180] Diplomatie Judiciaire, *Témoin Non Protégé*, Décembre 2001, No. 80, pp. 14-17.

[181] Rule 90(F) ICTY RPE.

examination.[182] Judge Pillay, in a response to the allegations by the press concerning Witness TA, articulated the judges' 'delicate task of balancing the rights of an accused to a fair trial with the need to protect victims and ensure the integrity of judicial proceedings':

> The length of time that a witness has to undergo examination by counsel is often a result of other decisions such as the number of accused who are joined in an indictment and the number of accused who are implicated by the testimony of a witness. While there is no hard and fast rule determining the length of a witness' testimony, the Trial Chambers are concerned to ensure that the examination of witnesses is confined to matters relevant to the facts in issue in the trial.[183]

The provisions under the ICC are less explicit on this point. There is no longer a requirement to seek the permission of the court to examine on relevant matters not dealt with in the witness's testimony. In addition, Rule 140 encourages the Trial Chamber to question the witness either before or after questioning by either party.

Nevertheless, Article 64(8)(b) and (9) specify that the presiding judge may give directions for the conduct of the proceedings and take all necessary steps to maintain order in the course of a hearing. Rule 88(5) furthermore requires that a Chamber shall control the manner of questioning so as to avoid any harassment or intimidation, paying particular attention to attacks on victims of sexual violence. Judges should therefore ensure that the examination is focused on matters relevant to the facts of the case, without unnecessarily repetitive and distressing questions. Only questions which are relevant for the establishment of the truth matter. Once it has been established that the victim was raped, that a crime was committed, unnecessary and victim-harassing questions (such as 'Did you touch his penis?') are superfluous and are only asked to attack the dignity of the victim or to re-victimise the victim.

6.5 Guidelines on treatment of victims of sexual violence in court

In situations of mass sexual violence, where rapes are often committed multiple times by multiple perpetrators in a number of different ways, the more aggressive common law approach to cross-examining witnesses is certainly not appropriate in the proceedings of the Tribunals. On the contrary, it is offensive to ask a victim of rape who has just recounted her ordeal such an unnecessary and intimidating question as to whether her rapist's penis was circumcised or not. It has therefore been suggested that the more victim-friendly civil law approach to victims of sexual violence should be used in the proceedings of the Tribunals and ICC. As counsel of the accused come from all over the world and therefore either have a common law or a civil law background (and therefore different ways of dealing with cross-examination of witnesses), it is imperative that one uniform approach to cross-examination of victims of sexual

---

[182] Article 90(H) ICTY RPE.

[183] ICTR Press Release, *Statement of Judge Pillay, President of the Tribunal*, ICTR/INFO-9-3-07, Arusha, 14 December 2001. In her statement, Judge Pillay said: 'It is noted that on 31 October 2001, the Presiding Judge intervened no less than 159 times to focus or advance the cross-examination of defence counsel. It is also noted that at various times, the Presiding Judge asked counsel to be sensitive in their examination of the witness.'

violence is chosen and implemented in order to protect rape victims from re-victimisation. However, also prosecutors and judges have shown reluctance when it comes to making intervention when rape victims were offensively addressed by Defence Counsel, which may partly be influenced by their common or civil law background as well. In order to formalise one uniform approach to the treatment of victims of sexual violence in court, a protocol or a set of guidelines for this purpose should be established. These guidelines will set out the proper conduct of all parties to the proceedings when cases of sexual violence are concerned. The experiences before the Tribunals have shown that such guidelines are no luxury in cases of sexual violence. Too often, victims of sexual violence have felt victimised all over again as a consequence of the trial proceedings.

What issues should be dealt with in such guidelines on the treatment of victims of sexual violence? As far as the Prosecutor is concerned, the guidelines should indicate that he or she should have knowledge of and stick to the relevant facts to present the case in a good and brief manner. This will prevent the Defence from asking many insignificant questions.[184] In the second place, the Prosecutor should prepare the rape victim to the kind of questions that may be put to her, so that she knows what to expect during trial. The Prosecutor should make it clear that certain painful questions will necessarily have to be asked by him, but that this is important in order to establish the truth. In the third place, the Prosecutor will have to intervene more actively when insensitive questions are put by Defence Counsel to the victim, to protect the victim from further victimisation.

For Defence Counsel, the guidelines would necessarily entail that they will not be allowed to re-victimise the rape victim by posing questions irrelevant for the establishment of the truth. Cross-examination should be limited to the establishment of the truth, without unduly harassing victims of sexual violence with indecent questions, which undermine the dignity of the victim. Questions previously posed by Defence Counsel in proceedings before the Tribunals such as 'Did you touch his penis?' and 'Was his penis circumcised?' are clearly inappropriate and irrelevant in the determination of the truth. Once it has been established that rape or any other form of sexual violence has been committed, there is a crime, and such questions are highly irrelevant. It must be noted that a 'Proposal for a draft Code of Professional Conduct for counsel before the International Criminal Court' seems to address these concerns.[185]

---

[184] In the Butare case, the Trial Attorney gave the Defence Counsel the opportunity to raise many questions with Witness TA, mainly because he himself had questioned Witness TA for one and a half day, thereby prolonging the examination-in-chief. In this respect, it should be noted that, before the ICTY and ICTR, cross-examination is to be limited to points raised in the examination-in-chief. This requirement has not been taken over by the ICC. That the Trial Attorney in the Butare case did not know how to deal with Witness TA, a rape victim, became obvious when, at first, he did not know whether and how to question the witness as to what had happened to her in anatomical terms. The Trial Attorney used words such as 'attack' and 'treatment' to refer to the rape. See *The Prosecutor v. Pauline Nyiramasuhuko, Arsène Shalom Ntahobali, Alphonse Nteziryayo, Sylvain Nsabimana, Elie Ndayambaje and Joseph Kanyabashi*, Transcripts, Case No. ICTR-98-42-T, 25 October 2001.

[185] Proposal for a draft Code of Professional Conduct for counsel before the International Criminal Court, ICC-ASP/3/11/Rev.1, 27 August 2004. It seems that the term 'counsel' should be

Article 29 of the draft Code ('Relations with Witnesses and Victims') reads: '1. Counsel shall refrain from intimidating, harassing, or humiliating witnesses or victims or from subjecting them to pressure in any manner or form within or outside the courtroom; 2. Counsel shall have particular consideration for victims of sexual, physical or psychological violence; children; the elderly and the disabled.' Misconduct of counsel will be sanctioned with: '(a) Admonishment; (b) Public reprimand with an entry into counsel's personal file; (c) Payment of a fine of up to 30,000; (d) Suspension of the right to practise before the Court for a period not exceeding two years; (e) Permanent ban on practising before the Court with striking off the list of counsel.'[186] The draft Code will be considered for adoption by the ASP.[187]

For judges, the guidelines would have to set out that they should actively intervene when Defence Counsel do not abide by these guidelines. In other words, they should take a more active role in controlling the proceedings. Such guidelines do not violate the rights of the accused to a fair trial, as cross-examination will not become insignificant; rather, cross-examination will be allowed to the extent that the truth is established, without crossing the boundaries of decency. The power to control the proceedings has in fact been given to the judges in Article 64(8)(b) and (9) and Rule 88(5). The judges could furthermore use their power to control the manner of questioning of a witness as to avoid any harassment or intimidation (Rule 88(5)) and to prevent questions of consent to be raised by the Defence, which is not allowed under Rule 72. Of course, in order for the guidelines to have any meaningful effect, they should be distributed and implemented by means of, for example, regularly held training workshops for judges, trial attorneys and counsel for the defence.

7 The Victims and Witnesses Unit

An important actor in the safeguarding of victims' and witnesses' rights is the VWU. This Unit was set up within the Registry and provides:

> *in consultation with the Office of the Prosecutor*, protective measures and security arrangements, counselling and other appropriate assistance for witnesses, victims who appear before the Court, and others who are at risk on account of testimony given by such witnesses. The Unit shall include staff with expertise in trauma, including trauma related to crimes of sexual violence.[188]

The Unit not only provides protection, but also support which may include practical arrangements related to the transfer of the witness to the ICC; psychological and medical care; and compensation for lost wages and daily allowance. The Unit's role in relation to victims of sexual violence is explicitly addressed in Rule 17(2)(b)(iii), where it is said that the Unit has to take gender-sensitive measures to facilitate the testimony of

---

interpreted as referring to counsel for the defence and legal representatives for victims in accordance with Article 2 of the draft Code and Article 2 of the Regulations of the Court.

186 *Ibid.*, Article 42(1)

187 The next occasion for the ASP to meet and to discuss the draft Code will be during the fourth session of the ASP, 28 November – 3 December 2005, The Hague, The Netherlands.

188 Article 43(6) ICC Statute (emphasis added). See also Rules 16-18 ICC RPE. For the VWU of the ICTY and ICTR, see common Article 34 ICTY/R Statute and Chapter 7.

victims and witnesses at all stages of the proceedings.[189] In addition, the Unit needs to train the Court and the parties in issues of trauma, sexual violence, security and confidentiality.[190] An obligation which naturally implies that staff with expertise in trauma, including trauma related to crimes of sexual violence is employed within the Unit.[191] The VWU also formulates short and long-term protection plans and cooperates with and advises States on the application of protective and support measures.[192] The protection and support offered is thus not only restricted to the investigative and trial phase itself.[193] However, as the ICC will most likely not be concerned with one conflict only, monitoring victims and witness protection will require an enormous effort from different actors in the field. In order to safeguard victims and witnesses from retaliation, the Unit needs to work closely with, *inter alia*, ICC field offices (that monitor the security situation in a country), NGOs or IGOs,[194] and governments. The VWU also needs to work closely with the Prosecutor, who usually establishes the first contact with the victim. According to the ICC provisions, the Unit merely has an advisory role towards the Prosecutor where protection or support is concerned.[195] It has been argued, however, that the two organs of the Court need to work closely together from the earliest moment of contact with a victim or witness, that is, in the investigative phase.[196] Such collaboration should include, *inter alia*, an evaluation of security issues and an assessment of necessary protection measures.[197] Such collaboration is necessary throughout the court proceedings and extends to the post-trial phase.[198]

8 Final remarks

The protection offered by the ICC runs throughout all the phases of the court proceedings, from the investigative phase extending to the post-trial phase. Victims and witnesses appearing as witnesses may, depending on their situation, be in need of

[189] See also Rule 16(1)(d) on the Registrar's responsibilities.

[190] Rule 17(2)(a)(iv). The Unit has to train its own staff with respect to victims' and witnesses' security, integrity and dignity, including matters related to gender and cultural sensitity.

[191] Rule 19 ICC RPE in conjunction with Article 43(6) ICC Statute.

[192] Rule 17 ICC RPE. See also subsection 5.4 on protection after the trial, and the possibilities of relocation and domestic witness protection programmes.

[193] In conformity with Article 68(1) ICC Statute.

[194] In conformity with Rule 18(e) ICC RPE. Cooperation with NGOs is very important because they also offer support, counselling or specialist medical and psychological care for victims and witnesses.

[195] Compare Articles 43(6), 68(1) and (4) and Rules 87 and 88. It is disputed whether the role of the Unit should not also include standing to request protective measures, instead of an advisory role only. The VWU in the ICTY has such a request option. On this issue, see Rydberg (1999), Brady (2001) and Ingadottir, Ngendahayo and Viseur Sellers (2003). In addition, it is held that its neutrality (in relation to defence witnesses) is undermined by requiring consultation with the Office of the Prosecutor. See Jones, J.R.W.D. (2002b), p. 280.

[196] See Human Rights Watch (2004a), pp. 6-7.

[197] *Ibid.* The Memorandum also refers to the requirement that investigators have experience in dealing with victims of sexual violence in order to prevent retraumatisation.

[198] See, in particular, Rule 16(4) and subsection 5.4 on protection after the trial, for the possible ways to contribute to an effective post-trial protection programme.

protective and special measures. The protective and special measures offered by the ICC safeguard certain well-recognised goals, that is to say, the safety, dignity and privacy, and the physical and psychological well-being of the victim-witness. These goals may be safeguarded by measures such as anonymity, confidentiality and measures aimed at preventing retraumatisation, respectively. Some of these measures can be applied cumulatively while others may serve more interests at the same time. The framework laid down in the ICC Statute and Rules of Procedure and Evidence takes into account both the rights of the accused (in particular his right to examine or have examined the witness against him) and the rights of victims and witnesses to protection. The ICC provisions show a clear concern for both actors, although sometimes, like in the situation of anonymity, with room for considerable ambiguity. In choosing the appropriate measure, the ICC has furthermore bound itself to take into account such relevant factors as age, gender and health, and the nature of the crime, in particular crimes involving sexual or gender violence or violence against children. Article 21(3) of the ICC Statute, the non-discrimination and equality provision, needs to be taken into account as well when looking for the appropriate measure to apply. The VWU plays a central role as it has the task of providing protection and support (including psychological and medical care) to victims, and gives extra care to victims of sexual violence.

To what extent can the protective and special measures serve the interests of victims of sexual violence? As far as confidentiality measures (protection from the public and the press) for the benefit of victims of sexual violence are concerned, they are more far-reaching than the confidentiality measures offered under the ICTY and ICTR framework. As opposed to the latter, on the basis of Article 68(2) of the ICC Statute, victims of sexual violence have an automatic right to conduct their testimony *in camera* or to present it by electronic or other special means, such as by means of video conferencing or one-way closed circuit television. A proper reading of the provision should direct the ICC to allow such protection where the victim-witness of sexual violence agrees to such a measure. This means that the different protective measures need to be explained to victims of sexual violence for them to make an informed decision on whether or not to make use of them. Some protective measures, such as live video conferencing, can be particularly useful to victims of sexual violence as they may not only prevent identification of the victim by the public or the press, but may also be useful in those cases where a victim is physically unable to testify in court. This is of interest, in particular, to those victims of rape who contracted a severe disease as a result of the sexual violence inflicted, such as HIV/AIDS. Although not all rape victims may want to have their identity protected from the public and the press, most rape victims before the ICTY and ICTR wanted to have their identity hidden from the public and the press out of concern for stigmatisation and rejection by their own family and community. A change of public opinion about rape victims may in some societies be a very welcome development in order to lift the stigmatisation attached to rape victims. Only then may some rape victims feel that they do not need to conceal their identity from the outside world and will they be able to speak freely about what happened to them. Yet, beliefs about victims of sexual violence are often deeply rooted in society and do not change overnight. Such changes may therefore not come in time for those rape victims who want to testify in court. Yet, giving public attention to the issue and making people aware that not the rape victim is to blame but the rapist will hopefully set into a motion a change of thought about rape victims so that they will be truly recognised as victims of crime.

The ICC should especially be attentive to violations of court orders on the non-disclosure of information to third parties, where much of the problem of leaking identity details of witnesses seems to concentrate. Victims of sexual violence are often not informed about the possibility that this might happen. Often they were told that confidentiality would be provided for, but they were not explicitly told that this means that their identification details are passed on to the accused and his Defence team in accordance with the rules. In a number of cases, this has led to threats, and some rape survivors had to seek refuge. Victims of sexual violence should be able to make a well-informed choice on whether or not to testify in court. In other words, they should be able to know the risks attached to testifying. These risks need to be carefully explained. In this regard, it must also be noted that it is sometimes extremely difficult to prevent the identity details of a witness from becoming known. In villages where everybody knows everybody, it is extremely hard to cover up a survivor's absence during a trial of an accused from the same village, especially if people are usually almost never away for a few days or weeks.

It remains to be seen what the ICC will decide on the issue of anonymity. On this point, the provisions are not clear and leave room for speculation. Given the difficult negotiations during the Preparatory Commission sessions without any clear answer to the question of whether anonymity as a protective measure is allowed, except that both a positive and a negative answer is possible under the ICC provisions and (inter)national (human rights) law, the ICC will have to follow either route. However, if concerns for safety as well as privacy and dignity remain very real, the ICC should not immediately refuse anonymity. When special criteria and guidelines are followed, anonymity as a protective measure can be granted without violating the rights of the accused, especially his right to examine the witness or to have the witness examined. For victims of sexual violence, the additional concern exists that, as long as protective measures do not have the effects they should have, they will not come forward and justice will (continue to) be denied for this category of victims. In order to grant any significance to legislation penalising sexual violence crimes, the ICC should not prevent this already very vulnerable group of victims from testifying. Such reasoning is also in line with the equality and non-discrimination provision. Only when survivors of sexual violence are able to speak out against the crimes committed against them will their harm be truly recognised.

Some of the security concerns raised may be taken away if effective post-trial protection is offered. This can be realised through relocation and/or domestic witness protection programmes. It is important to develop a workable approach in order to protect victims and witnesses from threats or killings. This requires extensive collaboration between different actors, such as the Prosecutor, the Registry, the VWU, ICC field offices, NGOs and IGOs, and governments. In the past, however, States have not always been very cooperative as regards witness protection. It is argued here that, for each situation taken up by the Court, at least one ICC contact office should be set up in the country concerned where victims and witnesses could go to in case of intimidation or threats.

Another category of protective and special measures seeks to prevent further or increased traumatisation of the rape victim giving testimony. Avoiding direct confrontation with the accused in court is one such measure and can consist of one-way closed circuit television, the use of a screen in court or removal of the accused from the courtroom. Another possibility is giving testimony by means of prior recorded testimony, which may spare the victim from repeated testimony in court. Like live video conferencing, both options have the 'disadvantage' that the victim's demeanour cannot always be directly assessed. However, the measures are not prohibited and the weight given to such evidence should, as for any evidence, be evaluated in light of Article 69(4) of the ICC Statute. The special evidentiary rules on sexual violence crimes restrict admitting consent and prior or subsequent sexual conduct into evidence and therefore protect the victim of sexual violence from retraumatisation in court as well. Admitting such evidence would subject the witness to unnecessary, humiliating questions, and may only be accepted in very limited circumstances. In light of the nature of the crimes, it seems very unlikely that a situation exists in which consent or prior or subsequent sexual conduct can ever be successfully raised. In addition, in contrast to the developments within the ICTY and the ICTR, the definition of rape or any other form of sexual violence in the ICC's Elements of Crimes fortunately does not explicitly include the element of consent. Such an inclusion is not relevant in cases of this nature and could keep victims of sexual violence away from testifying in court as it places the Prosecutor in the position to inquire into the issue of consent with the victim. The special evidentiary rules also acknowledge that corroboration of evidence is not a requirement for any crime, in particularly not with regard to crimes of sexual violence. The evidentiary rules thus specifically acknowledge that biases against victims of sexual violence, in particular women, are not accepted and clearly imply that they are as reliable as any other witness. This is again in line with the equality and non-discrimination provision. Other measures in the category of special measures include such issues as the manner of questioning, the length of time of the questioning, and allowing a supports person to attend the proceedings. As the practice before the Tribunals has shown some discouraging practices towards the treatment of victims of sexual violence during trial, it is argued that a set of guidelines need to be established which deals with the conduct of parties during the testimony of a victim of sexual violence. Such guidelines would be particularly practicable if they set out one common approach towards the treatment of victims of sexual violence. This is necessary as judges, prosecutors and defence lawyers come from different regions all over the world with different legal backgrounds and therefore have different approaches to addressing victims of sexual violence. Taking into account the nature of the sexual violence committed, it is not at all appropriate to address rape victims in an aggressive way and not to intervene if this happens. In short, for the Prosecutor, the guidelines would need to indicate that he or she will have to intervene during trial when rape victims are asked unnecessary or humiliating questions by Defence Counsel. Before trial he or she will need to prepare victims as to the kind of evidence he or she needs to elicit from them in order to make his or her case. The Prosecutor will have to make the victim understand that, although he or she understands that such questions may be painful, the questions need to be posed in order for the establishment of the truth. For the Defence, this means that aggressive, irrelevant questioning of the rape victim is not allowed. Cross-examination needs to operate in between the boundaries of establishing the truth and respect for the rape victim. Questions as to whether or not she touched his penis are irrelevant for the establishment of the truth and may cause secondary victimisation for the victim concerned. For judges, the guidelines would need to emphasise that they have to actively control the proceedings and step in when Defence lawyers approach the rape victim with unnecessary, irrelevant or intimidating questions. On the basis of the ICC provisions, the judges are given such a power. It is important that victims of sexual violence are treated with respect. Only then will they come forward and testify before the ICC and will present and future generations know about the crimes that were committed against them.

CHAPTER 5
PARTICIPATION OF VICTIMS OF SEXUAL VIOLENCE IN THE PROCEEDINGS

1 INTRODUCTION

The ICC will be the first court in the history of supranational criminal prosecutions to allow victims to participate in its proceedings as victims. In this role, victims may make representations to the Pre-Trial Chamber upon examination by that Chamber of the Prosecutor's request for authorisation to proceed with an investigation; submit observations to the Court in proceedings with respect to jurisdiction or admissibility; present, either themselves or through a legal representative, their views and concerns, where their personal interests are affected. The situation before the Tribunals, as mentioned in the preceding Chapter, is very different: before the Tribunals, victims can only participate in the trial as witnesses. Before the Tribunals, victim-witnesses or witnesses cannot participate in the proceedings of their own accord, but must be invited to do so by one of the parties; may only speak within the limits of examination and cross-examination; cannot have a lawyer present at his hearing; have no access to the evidence; and are not kept informed of the proceedings. This approach is premised on the idea that the Tribunals first and foremost need to punish perpetrators of serious violations of international humanitarian law and the principle that the interests of the Prosecutor (who is charged with bringing the case and seen to be a guardian of victims' concerns) and the rights of the accused (fair and expeditious trial) need to be safeguarded. Basically, the approach of treating victims as mere witnesses in the criminal process largely corresponds with the practice of the majority of common law jurisdictions.[1]

The ICC approach to victim participation is, on the other hand, largely drawn from civil law jurisdictions, which, on the whole, allow victims to participate in trial proceedings, albeit in different forms or degrees. Victim participation at the Court had been advocated by the representatives of some governments, in particular France, and several NGOs, such as Amnesty International, Human Rights Watch and Redress.[2] Victim participation, furthermore, was already recognised in the 1985 *Declaration of Basic Principles of Justice for Victims of Crime and Abuse of Power*.[3] By making

---

[1] See generally Brienen and Hoegen (2000).

[2] For the negotiating history of the RPE on participation, see, for instance, Bitti and Friman (2001), pp. 457-459.

[3] Paragraph 6(b) of the Declaration of Basic Principles of Justice for Victims of Crime and Abuse of Power (annexed to UN General Assembly Resolution 40/34 of 29 November 1985, UN Doc. A/RES/40/34 (hereafter 1985 Victims Declaration)) reads: 'The responsiveness of judicial and administrative processes to the needs of victims should be facilitated by: ... (b) Allowing the views and concerns of victims to be presented and considered at appropriate stages of the proceedings where their personal interests are affected, without prejudice to the accused and consistent with the relevant national criminal justice system.'

victim participation a possibility on the supranational criminal law level, it was hoped that a contribution could be made to the Court's restorative role.[4] Especially in light of the Yugoslav and Rwanda Tribunals' experiences, where the focus had been on retributive justice and victims had therefore been denied participatory rights, victim participation at the Court was felt justified by the need to fill these lacunae. It was generally felt that victim participation would bring the proceedings closer to the ones who had suffered as a result of the crimes.

The ICC faces real challenges with regard to victim participation as it has to act without real precedent: although some developments at national jurisdictions may be helpful in determining how to deal with victim participation at the Court, on the whole, these national courts have not dealt with large numbers of victims, a situation which will most likely arise before the Court. As such, the Court will also have to take into account that, because of the potentially large number of victims who want to participate, their involvement is not detrimental to an impartial, expeditious and fair trial. For this reason, victim participation has largely been left within the overall control of the judges. It is therefore up to the judges to determine, on a case-by-case basis, when and in what manner victims' right to participation will be exercised.

Although the recognition of victim participation on the supranational criminal law level must be considered a real asset in the fight for victims' rights, such rights are meaningless if they cannot be enforced by victims. In particular vulnerable groups of victims, like children and victims of sexual violence, may find it difficult to enforce their participatory rights at the Court. Victims of sexual violence, more than other groups of victims, may suffer from stigmatisation, shame and fear. For this reason, they may run the risk of being underrepresented at the Court if no special methods are developed to notify this group of victims about the possibilities of participation at the Court. Furthermore, having victims of sexual violence participating at the Court requires that special measures are put in place to facilitate their participation. This Chapter deals with the ways in which victims of sexual violence have 'participated' at the Tribunals and the challenges faced by the Court to effectuate victim participation in a gender-sensitive manner.

2 Victim participation at the ICTY and the ICTR

As mentioned above, victim participation is not provided for under the ICTY and ICTR regime.[5] In trial proceedings before the Tribunals, victims only participate as witnesses. This limited role for victims was underlined by President Jorda in his speech of May 2001 where he held that 'the International Tribunal [cannot] hear the tens of thousands of victims. Only those considered useful towards the establishment of the truth are invited to testify.'[6] Thus, victims are only called to the witness stand if their testimony

---

[4] In trying to achieve restorative justice, the Court has also made reparation to victims a possibility. Reparation to victims of sexual violence is discussed in Chapter 7.

[5] As noted by Tochilovsky (1999, p. 348), this situation contrasts sharply with the situation in the countries on the territory of the former Yugoslavia where victims have certain participatory rights in the criminal proceedings.

[6] ICTY Press Release, *The ICTY and the Truth and Reconciliation Commission in Bosnia and Herzegovina*, JL/P.I.S./591-e, The Hague, 17 May 2001.

corroborates the arguments the Prosecutor is trying to prove. The reasons why true participation of victims was not provided for in the Tribunals' Statutes or RPE was explained by Morris and Scharf:

> In preparing the Statute, consideration was also given to authorizing the appointment of a separate counsel for the victims to protect their interests. This would be similar to the concept of *parties civil* employed in many civil law countries. However, the proposal was not accepted for several reasons. First, the Prosecutor is entrusted with the responsibility for protecting the interests of the international community in ensuring the prosecution and punishment of the perpetrators. In this respect, the victims' interests would be coextensive with those of the international community and would be adequately protected by the Prosecutor. The victims' interest in obtaining compensation is not within the jurisdiction of the International Tribunal which was established for the purpose of prosecuting and punishing the persons responsible for the atrocities. Furthermore, the participation of counsel for the victim as a third party to the criminal proceedings could lead to interference with the case presented by the Prosecutor or divert the attention of the court from the relevant issue in the criminal proceedings thereby prolonging the trial. To the extent that a victim's interests are not considered to be adequately represented by the Prosecutor, it may be possible to bring such interests to the attention of the Trial Chamber or the Appeals Chamber with respect to relevant issues by means of an *amicus curiae* brief.[7]

However, victims' interests and those of the Prosecutor may not always coincide. For example, whose interests does the Prosecutor take into account when entering into a plea agreement with the accused by dropping the count on rape in exchange for a guilty plea on the other counts, as was done in the *Serushago* case before the ICTR and in the case of *Predrag Banović* before the ICTY?[8] Surely not those of the rape victims, one would imagine. And what to say about the situation in which evidence of the accused's responsibility for sexual violence is available, but charges of sexual violence are absent in the indictments in spite of that.[9] And what about those cases in which the Prosecutor did not file for an appeal on the rape acquittals, as happened in the ICTR cases of *Kajelijeli* and *Kamuhanda*? In these kinds of situations, the Prosecutor may be preoccupied with other interests than the legitimate concerns of victims. The argument that victim participation would furthermore prolong the trial is contradicted by the many

---

[7] Morris and Scharf (1995a), p. 167.

[8] In the Serushago case, Serushago pleaded guilty to genocide and the crimes against humanity of murder, extermination and torture, but not to rape as a crime against humanity. The count of rape as a crime against humanity was subsequently withdrawn by the Prosecutor. See Serushago Sentence, para. 4. For Predrag Banović, see the Banović Sentencing Judgment, paras. 9-19.

[9] The accused include Kanyabashi, Ndayambaje, Ntezirayayo and Nsabimana (Butare case). In a letter of the Coalition for Women's Human Rights in Conflict Situations, Rights and Democracy and the International Centre for Human Rights and Democratic Development to Prosecutor Carla del Ponte, it is argued that evidence is available to charge the accused Kanyabashi, Ndayambaje, Ntezirayayo and Nsabimana of the Butare case for sexual violence. See Coalition for Women's Human Rights in Conflict Situations, Rights and Democracy, and International Centre for Human Rights and Democratic Development, *Letter to Carla del Ponte*, 12 March 2003.

– in particular civil law – jurisdictions where victim participation works fine, without significant delays for the trial concerned.[10] In addition, instead the serenity of the hearings being disrupted by third party intervention, victim participation may contribute to the establishment of the truth and making the proceedings more transparent. Focusing solely on the prosecution of perpetrators, without any attention to victims' interests, has therefore often been considered to be a rather narrow point of view.[11] Although the Prosecutor, Carla del Ponte, raised the issue of victim participation (together with the issue of compensation) before the Security Council in November 2000, welcoming any change in the Tribunals' Statutes for a provision on victim participation, no such change has ever been made.[12] In light of the minimal attention and response to the issue, such a change in the Tribunals' Statute or Rules of Procedure and Evidence is not to be reasonably expected before the Tribunals close down. Yet, although victims do not participate in the proceedings of the Tribunals as commonly understood, the following three situations of 'victim participation' deserve to be mentioned and further explored, that is, victims 'participating' in the trial proceedings through victim impact statements (subsection 2.1), victims 'participating' in the trial proceedings through *amicus curiae* intervention (subsection 2.2) and victim 'participation' by addressing the Prosecutor directly (subsection 2.3). The focus in this section will be on victims of sexual violence 'participating' in the Tribunals' proceedings in this sense.

2.1 Victim impact statements

A victim impact statement 'provides the victim with an opportunity to inform the court of how the offence has affected him or her physically, mentally or otherwise'.[13] Without participatory rights, victims have no right to submit victim impact statements to the

---

[10] Participation in national jurisdictions does not overall lead to delays in the proceedings. For those situations in which this may nevertheless be the case, most national jurisdictions provide for the possibility to stay the participatory rights of victims. See generally Brienen and Hoegen (2000).

[11] See, *inter alia*, Donat-Cattin (1999a).

[12] In the relevant section, Del Ponte stated: 'Nor should we forget the role of victims in the justice process. The voices of survivors and relatives of those killed are not sufficiently heard. Victims have almost no rights to participate in the trial process, despite the widespread acceptance nowadays that victims should be allowed to do so. And those remarks apply equally to the Yugoslav Tribunal, where the position of victims is no better, and where the accused have also amassed personal fortunes at the expense of their country and its citizens. ... I would therefore respectfully suggest to the Council that present system falls short of delivering justice to the people of Rwanda and the former Yugoslavia, and I would invite you to give serious and urgent consideration to any change that would remove this lacuna in our process' (ICTY Press Release, *Address to the Security Council by Carla del Ponte, Prosecutor of the International Criminal Tribunals for the Former Yugoslavia and Rwanda, to the UN Security Council*, JL/P.I.S./542-e, The Hague, 24 November 2000). See also the Victims Compensation and Participation report prepared by the Rules Committee, 2000.

[13] United Nations Office for Drug Control and Crime Prevention, Center for International Crime Prevention, *Handbook on Justice for Victims: On the Use and Application of the Declaration of Basic Principles of Justice for Victims of Crime and Abuse of Power*, New York, 1999, p. 39.

Trial Chamber themselves. However, at times, both Tribunals have accepted victim impact statements submitted by the Prosecutor. Initially there was no legal basis to submit such statements to the Chamber, but nowadays the basis thereof can be found in Rule 92*bis* ('Proof of Facts Other Than by Oral Evidence') which reads, in part:

> (A) A Trial Chamber may admit, in whole or in part, the evidence of a witness in the form of a written statement in lieu of oral testimony which goes to proof of a matter other than the acts and conduct of the accused as charged in the indictment.
>
> (i) Factors in favour of admitting evidence in the form of a written statement include but are not limited to circumstances in which the evidence in question:
>
> ...
>
> d) concerns the impact of crimes upon victims.[14]

Victim impact statements are mainly provided for purposes of sentencing as they may impact the sentence imposed. Such statements go towards the degree of suffering endured by the victims, which, as recognised in the *Krstić* Judgment, is a component of the gravity of the crime[15] and can also be considered in aggravation of the crime.[16] Although a few victim impact statements have been submitted by the Prosecutor to the Chamber,[17] only one such victim impact statement of a victim of sexual violence can be found, that is, in the ICTY *Čelebići* case. The reference to the victim impact statement can be found in the judgment itself where it is stated:

> Before the first rape of Milojka Antic, Hazim Delic threatened her and told her that, if she did not do whatever he asked, she would be sent to another prison-camp or shot. He then forced her to take her clothes off at gunpoint, ignored her pleas for mercy and cursed and threatened her while raping her. The following day he compounded her fear and suffering by stating "... [w]hy are you crying? This will not be your last time". This rape was followed by two others, one of which involved painful and physically damaging anal penetration. These were committed by Hazim Delic when he was armed, in total disregard of his victim's pleas for mercy. Ms. Antic testified as to the effect these crimes had on her, including feelings of misery, constant crying and the feeling that she had gone crazy. *In a victim impact statement submitted by the Prosecution for the purposes of sentencing, she stated, "[t]he wounds that I carry from the rapes in Celebici will never go away".*[18]

---

[14] Rule 92*bis* was adopted on 1 December 2000 and 13 December 2000 for the ICTY, and on 5-6 July 2002 for the ICTR.

[15] Krstić Judgment, paras. 701-703.

[16] See further Chapter 6 on sentencing.

[17] See, e.g., Tadić Sentencing Judgment, para. 4; Todorović Sentencing Judgment, para. 53. See also *Prosecutor v. Mile Mrkšić, Miroslav Radić, Veselin Šljivančanin and Slavko Dokmanović*, Scheduling Order, Case No. IT-95-13a, 8 June 1998; and *Prosecutor v. Vidoje Blagojević and Dragan Jokić*, Transcripts, Case No. IT-02-60, 22 July 2003.

[18] Čelebići Judgment, para. 1263 (footnotes omitted and italics added).

Thus, in this case, the Prosecutor had inquired with the victim about the consequences of the rapes and forwarded the victim impact statement to the Chamber for consideration of sentencing. However, as mentioned, submitting victim impact statements of survivors of sexual violence seems to be the exception rather than the rule. Although the impact of sexual violence on the victim is sometimes raised by the Prosecutor during examination,[19] the Office of the Prosecutor does not seem to have made such an inquiry part of its prosecutorial strategy to pursue justice for rape victims. An example of an inquiry into the impact of the sexual violence on the victim can be found in the *Butare* case, in which a Trial Attorney asked Witness TN about the consequences of the repeated rapes she endured during the 1994 genocide:

Q. Can you tell this court what the effect of
these acts on you, were?
A. Yes, there were scars, because very often I
have kidney pains, Madame.
THE INTERPRETER: (English booth)
And witness -- the interpreter says the
witness touched him at the level of his
kidneys.

BY MS. ADEBOYEJO:
Q. Can the witness stand up and demonstrate to
the court exactly what part of the body she
is referring to?
MR. PRESIDENT:

[19] See, e.g., *The Prosecutor v. Pauline Nyiramasuhuko, Arséne Shalom Ntahobali, Alphonse Nteziryayo, Sylvain Nsabimana, Elie Ndayambaje and Joseph Kanyabashi*, Transcripts, Case No. ICTR-98-42-T, 29 October 2001, pp. 109-111 (Witness TA). In some cases, the impact of the crime is brought up by the victim-witness him or herself in the course of answering the questions posed by the Prosecutor. See, e.g., *Le Procureur c. Sylvestre Gacumbitsi,* Transcription Caviardee, Affaire N° ICTR-2001-64-T, 6 août 2003 (Witness TAP explained that, as a consequence of the rapes by Gacumbitsi, including the use of a truncheon which was inserted into her vagina several times followed by vaginal penetration, she now suffers from periods that last a whole month); and Čelebići Judgment, paras. 938, 959.

Yes, can she do that. It is safe where she
is, she can stand, if she may. Right there
she should not move.

THE WITNESS:
Yes, I suffer very often at this level.

MR. PRESIDENT:
How would you describe it, Counsel, the area
she has pointed out?

MS. ADEBOYEJO:
I believe it is the lower abdominal level.

MR. PRESIDENT:
On both sides.

MS. ADEBOYEJO:
On both sides. Let the record so reflect.

MR. PRESIDENT:
Yes. The lower --

MS. ADEBOYEJO:
Abdominal level. Just below the stomach, on
both sides.

MR. PRESIDENT:
On both sides of the stomach. Yes, let the
record so reflect. She may sit down.

BY MS. ADEBOYEJO:

Q. Witness, can you tell this court if you lost any family members during this period, yes or no.

A. Yes, Madame, I did lose some members of my family.

Q. Without stating their names can you state their relationship to you?

A. My parents, Madame, my brother and my paternal uncle, Madame.

Q. These pains that you have described, that you have in your lower abdominal level have you asked for medical assistance or gone to see a doctor for these pains?

A. No, Madame. I never went to see a doctor because many people do not know that I was a victim of rape of that manner, Madame.[20]

Witness TN thus explained to the court what the effects of the crime had had, and still have, on her health. In cases where a victim-witness is able to withstand the trauma of a question inquiring into the effects of the sexual violence upon her, questions to that effect should be raised by the Trial Attorney in order to establish a clear record on the effects of genocidal or war time rape on victims. As a Trial Attorney is not obliged to inquire into the effects that rape, sexual slavery or other forms of sexual violence have had on the victims and to subsequently introduce victim impact statements for the purposes of sentencing, the physical and psychological injuries inflicted on victims of sexual violence, including HIV/AIDS infection, may remain hidden. In addition, other

[20] *The Prosecutor v. Pauline Nyiramasuhuko, Arséne Shalom Ntahobali, Alphonse Nteziryayo, Sylvain Nsabimana, Elie Ndayambaje and Joseph Kanyabashi*, Transcripts, Case No. ICTR-98-42-T, 3 April 2002, pp. 164-166.

consequences will not come to light either, such as social-cultural (for example, in some cultures, a raped woman becomes unmarriageable and/or will be isolated from her family) and economic consequences (for example, the stigmatisation of being a rape victim with HIV/AIDS will make it difficult to find a job, to get a loan or to rent a house). If victim impact statements are not used, the often lasting consequences of the rapes on these women will never be recognised and their continuous suffering will continue to be ignored. In addition, as a result of the overall prosecutorial approach not to make use of victim impact statements, the impact of a crime upon a victim may not be taken into account during sentencing. As concluded in Chapter 6 on sentencing, this has indeed been the case in the majority of cases dealing with sexual violence. It may be true that, once rape has been established, the adverse impact on the victim is tacitly understood by the Judges, as once put forward in the *Akayesu* and *Musema* cases,[21] but this does not mean that the effects of the crime always clearly feature in the Tribunals' judgments or sentences when these effects are not properly addressed.

2.2 *Amicus curiae* submissions

Rule 74 ('Amicus Curiae'), common to the ICTY and ICTR Rules of Procedure and Evidence, reads: 'A Chamber may, if it considers it desirable for the proper determination of the case, invite or grant leave to any State, organization or person to appear before it and make submissions on an issue specified by the Chamber.'[22] It can therefore be argued that *amicus curiae* submissions, to a certain extent, allow for some form of victim participation, as victims and their representatives may appear as *amici* before the Tribunals.[23] The ICC has also made provision on *amicus curiae* submissions.[24]

Over the years, numerous *amicus curiae* briefs have been submitted to the Chambers of both Tribunals by States, organisations or persons, either spontaneously or by general invitation of the Chamber.[25] Those briefs dealt with a number of different issues, such as the right of the accused to choose his counsel and the scope of Article 3 Common to the four 1949 Geneva Conventions and of 1977 Additional Protocol II.

---

[21] Akayesu Judgment, paras. 142-144; Musema Judgment and Sentence, paras. 100-101 (Paragraph 100 reads as follows: 'Many of the witnesses who testified before the Chamber in this case have seen or have experienced terrible atrocities. They, their family or their friends have, in many cases, been the victims of such atrocities. The trauma that may have arisen, and may continue to arise, from such experiences is a matter of grave concern to the Chamber. The Chamber notes that recounting and revisiting such painful experiences is likely to be a source of great pain to the witness, and may also affect her or his ability fully or adequately, to recount the relevant events in a judicial context. The Chamber has, accordingly, considered the testimony of those witnesses in this light').

[22] See also ICTY, *Information Concerning the Submission of Amicus Curiae Briefs*, IT/122, 27 March 1997.

[23] Morris and Scharf (1995a), p. 167. See also Heikkilä (2004), p. 155.

[24] Rule 103 ICC RPE.

[25] For an overview of *amicus curiae* applications filed with the ICTY and ICTR, see the lists provided at the website of the McGill University: http://www.law.mcgill.ca/justice/documents-en.htm.

Victim participation through the use of the *amicus curiae* institution has also been dealt with. In the *Bagasora* case, the government of Belgium sought the Tribunal's authorisation to testify, as *amicus curiae*, on, among other things, 'the right of Belgians or their rightful claimants, prejudiced by the massacres committed in 1994 in Rwanda, *to appear before the Tribunal as plaintiffs and not as mere witnesses*, in accordance with Rule 23(3) of the Statute [on penalties] and Rules 105-106 of the Rules of Procedure and Evidence [on restitution of property and compensation to victims, respectively]'.[26] In its decision on the Belgian request on victim participation, the Trial Chamber held that the Belgians, or their rightful claimants, could not appear before the Tribunal as plaintiffs as the only parties to the trial are the Defence and the Prosecution.[27] The Rwandan government also asked to appear as *amicus curiae* in the *Bagasora* case on behalf of Rwandan citizens and to request, *inter alia*, the restitution of stolen property to their rightful owners and to call additional witnesses.[28] In its request, the Rwandan government noted that 'the fact that victims do not appear in the international trial is a major obstacle to national reconciliation'.[29] However, in its decision of October 2004, the Chamber denied the application made by the Rwandan government for the following reasons:

> As Rule 105 envisions a special hearing on restitution which only takes place after a judgment of conviction that specifically includes findings on the unlawful taking of property, the application is premature at this stage. Moreover, the Indictments do not allege that the Accused unlawfully took property. That being the case, the request does not show how the proposed submissions regarding restitution to victims are relevant to the issues to be decided or how they would assist the proper determination of the case. The general problem of the unlawful taking of property in Rwanda is unrelated to the specific facts at issue in this trial.[30]

[26] *The Prosecutor v. Théoneste Bagasora*, Amicus Curiae: Letter from Geert Muylle to Mr. Agwu Ukiwe Okali, Case No. ICTR-96-7-T, 10 February 1998, para. 3 (italics added).

[27] *The Prosecutor v. Théoneste Bagasora*, Decision on the Amicus Curiae Application by the Government of the Kingdom of Belgium, Case No. ICTR-96-7-T, 6 June 1998. Similar statements were made by the Defence and Prosecution. For the Prosecutor, see *The Prosecutor v. Théoneste Bagasora*, Prosecutor's Memorial (In Response to the Motion Filed by the Kingdom of Belgium on 10 February 1998 to Appear at the Trial and Lead Evidence as *Amicus Curiae)*, Case No. ICTR-96-7-T, 10 February 1998. This memorial was, however, withdrawn by the Prosecutor shortly thereafter: *The Prosecutor v. Théoneste Bagasora*, Withdrawal of Prosecutor's Memorial (In Response to the Motion Filed by the Kingdom of Belgium on 10 February 1998 to Appear at the Trial and Lead Evidence as *Amicus Curiae)*, Case No. ICTR-96-7-T, 9 March 1998.

[28] *The Prosecutor v. Théoneste Bagasora*, Request to Appear Before the Tribunal and to Testify as Amicus Curiae in the Case of Théoneste Bagasora and Others, Case No. ICTR-96-7-T, 20 April 1998. The government of Rwanda sought the following rights to be granted: 'the right to access to the case file before the hearing; the right to make opening statement as a party; the right to propose witnesses; and the right to make applications to the Trial Chamber and to appear before it as well a to request restitution after a guilty verdict'.

[29] *Ibid.*

[30] *The Prosecutor v. Théoneste Bagasora, Gratien Kabiligi, Aloys Ntabakuze and Anatole Nsengiyumva,* Decision on Amicus Curiae Request by the Rwandan Government, Case No.

Furthermore, the Trial Chamber held that 'the production of evidence falls within the jurisdiction of the Office of the Prosecutor'.[31] Although Prosecutor Del Ponte once seemed to support the idea of victim participation, as she stated in June 2000 that she would 'discuss with judges the idea of allowing victims to present themselves through a lawyer in an Amicus Curiae procedure',[32] true victim participation has not materialised at the Tribunals. On the basis of these decisions, it can be concluded that the Tribunals have rejected victim participation through the use of the *amicus curiae* institution as this would interfere with the role of the parties to the proceedings, in particular the role of the Prosecutor, who alone is responsible for the prosecution of suspects. This does not mean that victim concerns cannot be presented via the *amicus curiae* procedure to a Trial Chamber in any way. However, from the decisions on Rule 74, it can be concluded that victim concerns can be raised if the proposed submissions are relevant to the case and assist the Chamber in the proper determination of the case.[33] It is up to the Chamber to decide upon the *amicus curiae* submissions' relevance.

To what extent has the use of the *amicus curiae* institution been helpful to victims of sexual violence in the sense that their views and concerns have been presented before the Tribunals? In a number of cases, *amicus curiae* briefs were filed by women's organisations and/or individuals to the Trial Chambers of the Tribunals in support of victims of sexual violence and their concerns. The cases discussed in this section are *Akayesu, Ntagerura, Bagambiki and Imanishimwe* (the so-called *Cyangugu* case), and *Furundžija*.[34] In both the *Akayesu* and *Cyangugu* cases, the Coalition for Women's Human Rights in Conflict Situations, made up by many different human rights organisations and scholars (hereafter the Coalition), applied to file *amicus curiae* briefs to the respective ICTR Trial Chamber on a similar issue.[35] In these briefs, the Coalition

ICTR-98-41-T, 13 October 2004, para. 6. In a similar vein, the Trial Chamber had rejected the request made by African Concern on the restitution of property to victims, i.e., *Prosecutor v. Théoneste Bagasora, Gratien Kabiligi, Aloys Ntabakuze and Anatole Nsengiyumva*, Decision on Amicus Curiae Request by African Concern, Case No. ICTR-98-41-T, 23 March 2004.

[31] *The Prosecutor v. Théoneste Bagasora, Gratien Kabiligi, Aloys Ntabakuze and Anatole Nsengiyumva*, Decision on Amicus Curiae Request by the Rwandan Government, Case No. ICTR-98-41-T, 13 October 2004, para. 7.

[32] Diplomatie Judiciaire, *Compensating Victims With Guilty Money*, Interview with Carla del Ponte, The Hague, 9 June 2000.

[33] See, *inter alia*, *The Prosecutor v. Alfred Musema*, Decision on an Application by African Concern for Leave to Appear as Amicus Curiae, 17 March 1999, para. 2.

[34] Not discussed here is the *amicus curiae* brief submitted by Copelon, Gaer and Green in the Tadić case with regard to the failure to treat rape as an indictable offence. Due to the brief, Copelon (2000, p. 229) argues that the issue of sexual violence was taken up, in particular by (the female) Judge Odio-Benito. In the Tadić case, *amicus curiae* briefs were also filed with respect to anonymity measures for protected witnesses. The briefs and the issue of anonymity are discussed in Chapter 4 on protective and special measures.

[35] *The Prosecutor v. Jean-Paul Akayesu*, Amicus Curiae Brief submitted by the Coalition for Women's Human Rights in Armed Conflict Situations, Amicus Brief Respecting Amendment of the Indictment and Supplementation of the Evidence to Ensure the Prosecution of Rape and Other Sexual Violence Within the Competence of the Tribunal, Case No. ICTR-96-4-T, 29 May 1997; *The Prosecutor v. Samuel Imanishimwe, Emmanuel Bagambiki and André Ntagerura*, Amicus

called upon the judges to exercise their supervisory authority in order to have the Prosecutor review the evidence of sexual violence and to subsequently address the lack of charges on sexual violence in the indictment. The briefs were filed following evidence on sexual violence that had emerged during trial. The Trial Chamber in the *Cyangugu* case, however, rejected the Coalition's brief and held that granting the *amicus curiae* application would be 'tantamount to transgressing upon the independence of the Prosecutor and impugning the integrity of the Tribunal as an arbiter of international criminal law'.[36] The Trial Chamber furthermore held that 'the Amicus Application raises an issue that is not under consideration by the Trial Chamber and is not a live issue in the case. Further, the Prosecutor has indicated that she intends to file a new indictment against the Acccused Bagambiki and Imanishimwe alleging acts constituting rape.'[37] In response, the Coalition filed a request for reconsideration of the Trial Chamber's decision, stating that the dismissal of the *amicus curiae* interprets Rule 74 in a restrictive way. Such a narrow interpretation would 'deprive Trial Chamber III, including the defendants and the Prosecutor, of the opportunity to receive views from interested non-parties to the proceedings on significant issues. Moreover, it could have a deleterious effect on the development of international humanitarian law because such a rule would disproportionately affect on underrepresented interests, such as women's organizations, the very organizations which have advocated for the development of the law in areas traditionally ignored by the entire range of legal institutions.'[38] The Coalition's motion was dismissed as the Chamber held that 'review is an exceptional measure that may be invoked *where a new and potentially decisive fact has been discovered*'.[39] The judges held this not to be the case here. In the *Akayesu* case, the judges had been presented with similar issues as in the *Cyangugu* case. Testimony of sexual violence appeared during the course of the trial. In particular due to Judge Pillay's initiative, the only female judge, to inquire further with Witnesses J and H about the rapes they had witnessed and, in the case of Witness H, had experienced herself (although both witnesses were originally called by the Prosecutor to testify about other crimes), the Trial Chamber decided that subsequent investigations into the

---

Curiae Brief Submitted by the Coalition for Women's Human Rights in Armed Conflict Situations, Amicus Curiae Brief Respecting the Need to Include Sexual Violence Charges in the Indictment, Case No. ICTR-99-46-T, 1 March 2001.

[36] *The Prosecutor v. André Ntagerura, Emmanuel Bagambiki and Samuel Imanishimwe*, Decision on the Application to File an Amicus Curiae Brief According to Rule 74 of the Rules of Procedure and Evidence Filed on Behalf of the NGO Coalition for Women's Human Rights in Conflict Situations, Case No. ICTR-99-46-T, 24 May 2001, para. 22.

[37] *Ibid.*, para. 20.

[38] *The Prosecutor v. Samuel Imanishimwe, Emmanuel Bagambiki and André Ntagerura*, Request for Reconsideration of the Decision on Amici's Application to File an Amicus Curiae Brief According to Rule 74 of the Rules of Procedure and Evidence Filed on Behalf of the NGO Coalition for Women's Human Rights in Conflict Situations, Submitted by The Coalition for Women's Human Rights in Armed Conflict Situations, Case No. ICTR-99-46-T, 12 July 2001.

[39] *The Prosecutor v. Samuel Imanishimwe, Emmanuel Bagambiki and André Ntagerura*, Decision on the Coalition for Women's Human Rights in Conflict Situation's Motion for Reconsideration of the Decision on Application to File an Amicus Curiae Brief, Case No. ICTR-99-46-T, 24 September 2001, para. 9.

occurrence of sexual violence had to be undertaken by the Prosecutor.[40] Subsequent findings of more evidence of sexual violence to which the accused Akayesu could possibly be linked, ultimately made the Prosecutor amend the indictment to include charges of sexual violence. The Chamber substantiated its approval for amendment by stating that 'the investigation and presentation of evidence relating to sexual violence is in the interest of justice'.[41] Although the Trial Chamber never ruled on the *amicus curiae* brief as such, it can be reasonably assumed that the brief significantly contributed to the Trial Chamber's decision and the Prosecutor's subsequent amendment of the indictment to include charges of sexual violence.[42]

What was the reason why different decisions were made in these two more or less similar cases in which the Coalition on Women's Human Rights in Conflict Situations tried to present concerns of victims of sexual violence? The answer must mainly be sought in the exercise of discretion practised by the Judges and Prosecutors and the different procedural context prevailing in the two cases. In the *Akayesu* case, the Prosecutor basically supported the *amici* and asked for an amendment to include sexual violence charges as also supported by the Trial Chamber, whereas in the *Cyangugu* case, the Prosecutor opposed the *amicus curiae* and did not file for an amendment.[43] In *Cyangugu*, the Prosecutor had submitted a motion to add charges of rape as a crime against humanity against both Bagambiki and Imanishimwe in December 1999, but the Prosecutor withdrew her request on 14 February 2000. All this happened before the trial had even started. According to the Prosecutor, it was decided to withdraw the rape

---

[40] Akayesu Judgment, para. 417. See Copelon (2000, p. 225) for the role played by Judge Pillay.

[41] Akayesu Judgment, para. 417.

[42] *Ibid.*, where the Trial Chamber does not explicitly acknowledge the role played by the *amicus curiae* intervention to amend the indictment to include charges of rape: 'The Chamber notes that the Defence in its closing statement questioned whether the Indictment was amended in response to public pressure concerning the prosecution of sexual violence. The Chamber understands that the amendment of the Indictment resulted from the spontaneous testimony of sexual violence by Witness J and Witness H during the course of this trial and the subsequent investigation of the Prosecution, rather than from public pressure. Nevertheless, the Chamber takes note of the interest shown in this issue by non-governmental organizations, which it considers as indicative of public concern over the historical exclusion of rape and other forms of sexual violence from the investigation and prosecution of war crimes. The investigation and presentation of evidence relating to sexual violence is in the interest of justice.' But see the News Release of the Coalition of Women's Human Rights in Conflict Situations, *Rwanda: Akayesu Sentencing a Victory for Women's Rights*, 2 October 1998 ('The charges of rape were only added to the Akayesu indictment mid-trial, following concerted pressure by non-governmental organizations and an amicus curiae brief filed by this Coalition in May 1997'); and Copelon (2000), pp. 225-226.

[43] For the Cyangugu case, see *The Prosecutor v. André Ntagerura, Emmanuel Bagambiki and Samuel Imanishimwe*, Prosecutor's Response to Application for Leave to File an Amicus Brief, Case No. ICTR-99-46-T, 8 May 2001; *The Prosecutor v. André Ntagerura, Emmanuel Bagambiki and Samuel Imanishimwe*, Prosecutor's Response to a Request for Reconsideration of the Decision of the Application to File an Amicus Curiae Brief by Coalition for Women's Human Rights in Conflict Situations, 7 September 2001.

charges as this was 'in the best interests of an expeditious trial'.[44] As a result, when the *amici* filed their brief during trial, the Prosecutor could not be expected to reintroduce charges of sexual violence she had previously decided to drop.[45] In an attempt to make up for this, the Prosecutor announced that she would indict the accused later on, with regard to sexual violence only. Yet, the *Cyangugu* Judgment has already been pronounced and no separate indictment on sexual violence specifically has been presented by the Prosecutor since then. Has justice been served with regard to the Cyangugu victims of rape? In an interview with Nowrojee, a Cyangugu rape victim said:

> We helped the ICTR [prosecutor's staff] to find the rape victims in this area. They even interviewed a rape victim who was HIV positive dying in her hospital bed. We are angry and disappointed that the ICTR, after making us talk about all the humiliating things that were done to us, they did not bring rape charges. What has the ICTR really done since it started? It has cared better for the *interahamwe*. If the tribunal does not change its approach to give value to women, then it's not worth it for us to work with them. Women have so many other things to worry about. Why should we waste our time with the tribunal. Many

---

[44] *The Prosecutor v. André Ntagerura, Emmanuel Bagambiki, Samuel Imanishimwe and Yussuf Munyakazi*, Notice of the Prosecutor to Withdraw All Pending Motions, Case No. ICTR-99-46-T, 14 February 2000. According to Nowrojee (2005): 'the late arrival of the request to amend was reportedly not received kindly by the judges who viewed it as yet another delay of many by the prosecutor. Shortly after, Del Ponte was called in for a meeting by the judges. In December 1999, following her meeting with the judges, the prosecutor, without explanation, ordered her team to withdraw the rape amendment, which had yet to be ruled on by the judges. At that meeting, Del Ponte reportedly said when announcing that the rape charges would be dropped: "I can do this because I am a woman. If I were a man, there would be a fuss."' Because of incidents like this, Del Ponte's position as a Prosecutor, strongly pursuing the investigation and prosecution of sexual violence, was severely questioned by the Coalition. When the issue of her reappointment as a Prosecutor came up, the Coalition requested the Secretary-General, Kofi Annan, not to reappoint her because of this reason. See Coalition for Women's Human Rights in Conflict Situations, *Letter to Kofi Annan, Secretary General of the United Nations, Concerning the Reappointment of Carla del Ponte as Prosecutor of the International Criminal Tribunal for Rwanda*, 24 July 2003.

[45] Yet, in an oral hearing of 13 February 2001 (pp. 92-93), the Prosecutor contended that rape can be subsumed within the crime of genocide, a crime which is already charged, despite that allegations of rape were made in the indictment. However, in an oral hearing of 14 February 2001 (pp. 104-105), the Chamber ruled that 'the Prosecutor cannot lead evidence on a crime that is not charged'. At the late stage of the proceedings, and in light of the previous decision not to charge the accused with rape, 'the accused will not have been afforded adequate and proper opportunity to prepare a defence against the allegations of rape'. See *The Prosecutor v. André Ntagerura, Emmanuel Bagambiki and Samuel Imanishimwe,* Transcripts, Case Nos. ICTR-99-10A-T, ICTR-97-36-T, ICTR-99-46-T, 13 February 2001; and *The Prosecutor v. André Ntagerura, Emmanuel Bagambiki and Samuel Imanishimwe,* Transcripts, Case Nos. ICTR-99-10A-T, ICTR-97-36-T, ICTR-99-46-T, 14 February 2001.

women have AIDS and are starting to die. Today we buried a woman. Last week, another. Last month, another. Women here have so many problems, and no one to go to.[46]

AVEGA-Cyangugu (the Association of Genocide Widows in Cyangugu) had previously helped ICTR staff members in collecting testimonies of rape victims and they had promised to come forward and testify about the rapes which had taken place in Cyangugu during the genocide, and which they held were committed under the leadership of Bagambiki, Imanishimwe and Ntagerura.[47] Yet, both the judges and the Prosecutor decided to use their discretionary powers in the interest of an expeditious trial rather than in the interest of victims of sexual violence, that is, in the interest of justice. Given the availability of evidence in the Prosecutor's possession, it is unlikely that amending the indictment at that point would have caused serious delays to the trial or compromised the rights of the accused since the trial had not even begun. As both the judges and the Prosecutor were not cooperative towards the Coalition in respect of amending the indictment to better serve the rape victims of Cyangugu, the *amici* were finally not able to achieve their purpose by submitting their brief under Rule 74. The *Cyangugu* case is therefore a prime example of a case where victims' interests and those of the Prosecutor did not coincide.

The third and final *amicus curiae* intervention with regard to victims of sexual violence discussed here concerns the *Furundžija* case. In this case, two *amicus curiae* briefs were submitted to the Tribunal, challenging the Trial Chamber's decision to re-open the case and to make Witness A (a victim for whose rape Furundžija had incurred responsibility) available for cross-examination on any medical, psychological or psychiatric treatment or counselling which she had received.[48] The Tribunal moreover ordered that the Prosecutor disclose any documents of relevance to the issue of medical, psychological or psychiatric treatment of Witness A. This decision was made on the basis of the Defence's motion that he had been prejudiced by the non-disclosure of Witness A's rape counselling records. One of the *amici*, the Coalition for Women's Human Rights in Conflict Situations, held in its brief that the Trial Chamber's decision did not properly take into account the rights of Witness A to equality, privacy, and security of the person as well as to witness protection. In this respect, the brief set out that: (1) gender discrimination fundamentally informs requests for disclosure of confidential records in cases of sexual violence; (2) requests for disclosure are most often founded upon irrelevant and prejudicial rape myths and discriminatory attitudes toward women who are victims of sexual assault; (3) the cross-examination of survivors of sexual violence on confidential records risks unwarranted and severe intimidation

[46] Nowrojee (2005).

[47] *Ibid.* See also the Coalition for Women's Human Rights in Conflict Situations, *Sexual Violence in Cyangugu: A Testimonial* (by Monique Kankera), undated.

[48] Coalition for Women's Human Rights in Conflict Situations, *Amicus Curiae Brief Respecting the Decision and Order of the Tribunal of 16 July 1998 Requesting that the Tribunal Reconsider its Decision Having Regard to the Rights of Witness "A" to Equality, Privacy and Security of the Person and to Representation by Counsel*, Case No. IT-95-17/1-T, 5 November 1998; and Center for Civil and Human Rights, Notre Dame Law School, *Amicus Curiae Brief on Protective Measures for Victims or Witnesses of Sexual Violence and Other Traumatic Event*, 6 November 1998.

and revictimisation of these witnesses, thus jeopardising both their mental and physical integrity; and (4) the disclosure of counselling records profoundly affects (a) women's equal rights to access to justice and (b) the goal of bringing perpetrators of sexual violence in armed conflict before the two International Criminal Tribunals. The brief also referred to the *Tadić Protective Measures Decision*, in which it was said that a fair trial not only means fair treatment of the defendant but also of the witnesses. Although the *amici* submitted their briefs just before the re-opening of the case (and leave to intervene was moreover granted),[49] the Trial Chamber did not look into the merits of the briefs as they were considered to have been filed with the court at too late a stage. With this decision, the Chamber set an unwelcome precedent which heavily invades the rights of victims of sexual violence to privacy, equality, security and protection. The interests of Witness A were set aside in this case by judicial discretion in favour of the accused, without even considering the merits of the *amicus curiae* briefs.[50]

2.3 Directly approaching the Office of the Prosecutor

Another way to draw the Tribunals' attention to victims of sexual violence and their concerns can be exercised by directly approaching the Office of the Prosecutor. This can be done, for instance, by sending letters to the Prosecutor directly, which has the advantage of being a quick method to draw the Prosecutor's attention to victims of sexual violence and their plight. Again, the Coalition for Women's Human Rights in Conflict Situations has been a pioneer in this regard. In two cases, the Coalition requested the Prosecutor's attention for sexual violence crimes, that is, in the *Milosević* and *Muvunyi* cases. In the *Milosević* case, the Coalition sent a letter to Prosecutor Del Ponte on 14 August 2001 regarding the urgent need to include charges of sexual violence in the indictment against Milosević at the ICTY.[51] At that time, an indictment against Milosević with regard to his involvement in Kosovo had already been drafted and did not include charges of sexual violence. In the letter, the Coalition asked attention for the historic failure to prosecute sexual violence crimes and requested that Milosević be charged with sexual violence as these crimes were equal in gravity to other crimes and evidence for his accountability in these crimes was readily available. The Coalition members noted that 'the victims of these crimes deserve justice'. In October 2001, Prosecutor Del Ponte informed the Coalition that charges of sexual

---

[49] Coalition for Women's Human Rights in Conflict Situations, *Application to File an Amicus Curiae Brief in the Case of the Prosecutor v. Anto Furundzija*, Case No. IT-95-17/1-T, 5 November 1998; *Prosecutor v. Anto Furundžija*, Order Granting Leave to File *Amicus Curiae* Brief, Case No. IT-95-17/1-T, 10 November 1998; *Prosecutor v. Anto Furundžija*, Corrigendum to Order Granting Leave to File *Amicus Curiae* Brief, Case No. IT-95-17/1-T, 11 November 1998; *Prosecutor v. Anto Furundžija*, Order Granting Leave to File *Amicus Curiae* Brief, Case No. IT-95-17/1-T, 11 November 1998.

[50] The Tribunal finally established that 'there is no reason why a person with PTSD cannot be a perfectly reliable witness'. See Furundžija Judgment, para. 109.

[51] Coalition for Women's Human Rights in Conflict Situations, *Letter to Carla del Ponte, Prosecutor, Regarding the Urgent Need to Include Charges of Sexual Violence in the Indictment against Milosevic*, 14 August 2001.

violence had been included in the Croatia and Kosovo indictments against Milosević.[52] In November 2001, the indictment on Bosnia was released and Milosević was also charged with sexual violence in this indictment.[53]

Again, this time with regard to a case pending before the ICTR, the Coalition for Women's Human Rights in Conflict Situations addressed Prosecutor Jallow in a letter dated 8 February 2005.[54] In this letter, the Coalition discussed the *Muvunyi* case – during the genocide Muvunyi had been the commander of military operations for Butare and Gikongoro – and the Prosecutor's motion to drop the rape charges in this case. The Coalition requested the Prosecutor to withdraw or modify the Prosecutor's motion with regard to the sexual violence charges and instead to renew investigations on sexual violence, thereby pointing to the ICTR's shameful record on sexual violence prosecutions in general. Evidence which linked Muvunyi to sexual violence existed, the Coalition argued, so how could the Prosecutor fail to prosecute Muvunyi for sexual violence and thus inflict great injustice upon Rwanda's survivors of rape, in particular the women survivors in Butare and Gikongoro? A few days later Obote-Odora, Special Assistant to the Prosecutor, responded to the Coalition's letter and provided the following reason for dropping the rape charges against Muvunyi: 'Some of the Prosecution witnesses cannot be traced while other Prosecution witnesses have refused or declined to testify. It serves no purpose to proceed with charges that the Prosecutor will not be able to prove beyond reasonable doubt, not because the crimes were not committed, but because Prosecutions witnesses refuse or decline to testify, or cannot be traced either because they have died or changed residence without leaving forwarding addresses.'[55] In the Tribunal's decision on the Prosecutor's motion to drop the rape charges by amending the indictment, the motion was denied by the Trial Chamber.[56] The Chamber held that the withdrawal of count 4 (rape as a crime against humanity) and count 5 (other inhumane acts as a crime against humanity) were unnecessary: instead of amending the indictment, the Prosecutor could have simply declared, at the opening of the trial, that he would not present any evidence on these counts.[57]

---

[52] Coalition for Women's Human Rights in Conflict Situations News Release, *Women's Group Congratulate ICTY on Charges of Sexual Violence Against Slobodan Milosevic*, 29 October 2001. For Kosovo, see: *Prosecutor v. Slobodan Milosević, Milan Milutinović, Nikola Šainović, Dragoljub Ojdanić and Vlajko Stojiljković*, Second Amended Indictment, Case No. IT-99-37-PT, 29 October 2001 (the initial indictment stems from 24 May 1999 and the first amended indictment was issued on 29 June 2001, both indictments did not include charges of sexual violence). For Croatia, see: *Prosecutor v. Slobodan Milosević*, Indictment (Croatia), Case No. IT-01-50-I, 8 October 2001 (the indictment was first amended on 23 October 2002 and again on 28 July 2004. Sexual violence is still part of the charges).

[53] *Prosecutor v. Slobodan Milosević*, Indictment (Bosnia), Case No. IT-01-51-I, 22 November 2001 (the indictment was amended on 21 April 2004. Sexual violence is still part of the charges).

[54] Coalition for Women's Human Rights in Conflict Situations, *Letter to Prosecutor Hassan Jallow*, 8 February 2005.

[55] Letter from Dr. Alex Obote-Odora, Special Assistant to the Prosecutor, to Ms. Brunet, 11 February 2005.

[56] *The Prosecutor v. Tharcisse Muvunyi*, Decision on the Prosecutor's Motion for Leave to File an Amended Indictment, Case No. ICTR-2000-55A-PT, 23 February 2005.

[57] *Ibid.*, paras. 31 and 34.

Furthermore, it was held, the Prosecutor did not provide any legal justification for the withdrawal of the counts at this late stage of the proceedings, while he could have requested such an amendment when the indictment was last amended in 2003 on the basis of the same statements available at that time.[58] The Trial Chamber stated that although, in certain cases, the withdrawal of counts 'may be a gesture inuring to the benefit of the Defence ... this is not always so'.[59] The Trial Chamber went on to state that

> [i]n the present case, with just a few weeks left before the trial is due to commence, the Chamber observes that the Defence has likely expended time and resources preparing to defend the charges which are now proposed to be withdrawn. This raises questions of not just inconvenience, but of double jeopardy in the sense of the right of an accused to have cleared, once and for all, any criminal accusation against him or her. The Chamber notes, particularly, that the Defence opposes the motion in its entirety, including this proposal to withdraw the two counts.[60]

Very confusingly, the Prosecutor, for some reason, decided to go ahead with the charges of rape in the *Muvunyi* case. In his opening statement of 28 February 2005, Chief Prosecutor Jallow stated that 'Muvunyi had done nothing to either stop the acts by his subordinates or punish them for raping Tutsi women'.[61] Despite earlier remarks that victims of sexual violence were not willing or available to appear as witnesses in the trial (which made the Prosecutor file the motion to withdraw the rape charges), Senior Trial Attorney Adeogun-Phillips of the *Muvunyi* case allegedly said that he intended 'to call at least twenty witnesses to prove allegations of rape against the former army officer'.[62] He further stated that 'the defence [would] regret it', thereby referring to the Defence's dismissal of the motion to withdraw the charges of rape.[63]

It is difficult to judge the impact of such correspondence as the letters sent by the Coalition, aiming to draw the Prosecutor's attention to victims of sexual violence and their quest for justice, on the prosecutorial strategy involving sexual violence. The relevance and need to stress and present rape victims' concerns to the Prosecutor cannot be underestimated. For example, in the case of the ICTR, the record shows that rape charges were not brought in 70 percent of the cases in which judgments had been delivered, despite the widespread and systematic occurrence of sexual violence during the Rwandese genocide, and that, of the remaining 30 percent of cases in which rape charges were brought, 20 percent had resulted in acquittals and only 10 percent in rape

---

[58] *Ibid.*, para. 30.
[59] *Ibid.*, para. 28.
[60] *Ibid.*, para. 29.
[61] Hirondelle News Agency, *ICTR/Muvunyi – New Genocide Trial Opens in Arusha*, 2 March 2005.
[62] Hirondelle News Agency, *ICTR/Muvunyi – Prosecutor to Call 20 Witnesses on Rape Charges Against Former Officer*, 5 March 2005. See further, *inter alia*, Hirondelle News Agency, *ICTR/Muvunyi – Witness Describes Horror of Being Raped by Soldiers*, 9 June 2005.
[63] Hirondelle News Agency, *ICTR/Muvunyi – Prosecutor to Call 20 Witnesses on Rape Charges Against Former Officer*, 5 March 2005.

convictions.[64] However, despite the urgency to present victims' concerns, the Prosecutor will still be in a position to exercise his or her discretionary powers in choosing which crimes will be prosecuted and which will not. Thus, sending letters to the Prosecutor is a meaningful and absolutely necessary way to point out to the Prosecutor his or her responsibility to prosecute sexual violence vigorously, thereby giving a voice to victims of sexual violence who otherwise may see the violations committed against them not pursued at all. However, the method as such makes it clear once again that victims have no true participatory rights in the proceedings at all.

3 Victim participation at the ICC

Unlike its predecessors, the ICC Statute affords victims of crime the right to participate in the proceedings. Participatory rights of victims are explicitly found in the following three provisions: (1) Article 15(3) of the ICC Statute, which stipulates that 'victims may make representations to the Pre-Trial Chamber in accordance with the Rules of Procedure and Evidence', if the Prosecutor submits a request for the authorisation of an investigation with the Pre-Trial Chamber; (2) Article 19(3) of the ICC Statute, which reads, in part, that 'victims may ... submit observations to the Court' if the Prosecutor seeks a ruling from the Court regarding a question of jurisdiction or admissibility; and (3) Article 68(3) of the ICC Statute, which is a more general rule providing that 'where the personal interests of the victims are affected, the Court shall permit their views and concerns to be presented and considered at stages of the proceedings determined to be appropriate by the Court and in a manner which is not prejudicial to or inconsistent with the rights of the accused and a fair and impartial trial. Such views and concerns may be presented by the legal representatives of the victims where the Court considers it appropriate, in accordance with the Rules of Procedure and Evidence.'[65] Other provisions in which victim input plays a role can be found in Article 15(2) where it is indirectly said that victims ('other reliable sources') may submit information to the Prosecutor so that the Prosecutor can initiate investigations *proprio motu*; Articles 75(3) and 82(4) allow victims to make representations before reparations orders are adopted and may appeal against an order for reparations;[66] and Article 65 makes it possible for the Court not to accept a guilty plea where the 'interests of the victims' so require. In addition to the ICC Statute, other or extended provisions on victim participation can be found in Section III (Rules 85-93) of the ICC RPE, Chapter 5 (Regulations 86-88) of the Regulations of the Court, and Section 2 (Regulations 107-128) of the Draft Regulations of the Registry. On 1 June 2005, the ICC informed the public via its website that it had received applications on 26 May 2005 for the participation of victims in the proceedings concerning the situation in the Democratic Republic of Congo.[67] This was the first statement of the Court with regard to victim participation.

---

[64] Coalition for Women's Human Rights in Conflict Situations, *Letter to Prosecutor Hassan Jallow*, 8 February 2005.

[65] The language contained in Article 68(3) strongly suggests the influence of the wording contained in Article 6(b) of the 1985 Victims Declaration.

[66] The rights of victims to request and to be awarded reparation are dealt with in Chapter 7.

[67] ICC, *Order Regarding Request for Additional Information (Concerning Applications for Participation of Victims). Confidential and Ex-parte*, 1 June 2005 (the victims had requested that

How can victims of sexual violence realise their participatory rights within the ICC proceedings? In order to have victims of sexual violence – often girls and women who may suffer disproportionately from fear, shame and stigmatisation – to fully benefit from their right to participation, extra attention should be given to them. This Chapter deals in particular with the question of what special procedures or measures could be instituted to ensure that women who suffered sexual violence can participate in the Court's proceedings.

3.1 Notification

The ICC Statute and RPE oblige the Court to notify victims about participation possibilities at different stages of the proceedings. In the first place, there is an obligation to notify victims irrespective of whether victims have indicated their wish to participate in proceedings. This is, for example, the case with regard to the publication of the reparation proceedings.[68] On the other hand, there are also obligations to notify victims who have already participated in the proceedings or communicated with the Court about a situation.[69] Such is the case with regard to the decision of the Prosecutor not to initiate an investigation or not to prosecute[70] or where the Court decides to hold a hearing to confirm the charges.[71] In the latter case, Rule 92(8), however, also stipulates that the Registrar *shall* take measures necessary to give 'adequate publicity' to the proceedings. The Registrar may, for this purpose, seek the cooperation of relevant State Parties and the assistance of intergovernmental organisations. In addition, in cases where the Prosecutor seeks to initiate investigations *proprio motu*, the Prosecutor *may*, in addition to notifying victims who have already participated in the proceedings or communicated with the Court, 'give notice by general means in order to reach groups of victims if he or she determines in the particular circumstances of the case that such notice could not pose a danger to the integrity and effective conduct of the investigation or to the security and well-being of victims and witnesses'.[72] On the basis of these provisions on notification, the Court has been given considerable flexibility to handle notification demands. However, if the Court decides to confirm charges and the start of the trial will therefore follow soon, the Court is held to give adequate publicity to the case in order to reach as many victims as possible who may have an interest in participating in the proceedings.

Notification about the possibilities of participation is instrumental if participation at the Court is ever to materialise. Because the Court is geographically far removed from the countries and victims concerned, information about participation in the

---

their identity, and any information that could lead to their identity, remain *ex parte*, thus non-disclosed to parties and the public. In response, the Pre Trial Chamber requested the applicants to submit additional information concerning the request for non-disclosure of their identity).

[68] Rule 96(1) ICC RPE.

[69] See, *inter alia*, Rules 50(1) and 59(1)(b) ICC RPE.

[70] Rule 92(2) ICC RPE.

[71] Rule 92(3) ICC RPE.

[72] Rule 50(1) ICC RPE. Note that the Prosecutor, in the first place, 'shall inform victims, known to him or her or to the Victims and Witnesses Unit, or their legal representatives'. See also Rule 92(8) ICC RPE.

proceedings does not easily reach the people whom it may concern. For this reason, information about victims' participatory rights needs to be disseminated as early as possible in the proceedings, without compromising victims' privacy and security concerns. Information on what the Court can do for victims and what victims can do within the Court's proceedings is essential in building a positive relationship with them. It is the Registrar's responsibility to provide notice or notification to victims or their legal representatives and to assist them in participating in the different phases of the proceedings.[73] In practice, the Victims Participation and Reparations Section (VPRS), which is part of the Registry, is responsible for the content and implementation of the victims' outreach campaigns. Therefore, the VPRS has prepared information materials about victims' rights and how victims should access the VPRS. The information materials consist of:

Standard application forms which will be used to contact and solicit information from victims applying for participation and requesting reparation;

An informational booklet accompanying the application forms and explaining the rights of victims before the Court (to be consulted by victims before filling in the standard application forms);

A manual for lawyers, civil society organizations and academic institutions to provide clear guidance on ICC proceedings;

Training materials and programmes.[74]

The aim of these materials prepared by the VPRS is 'to facilitate the realization of the participation and reparation rights afforded to victims by providing accessible and comprehensive information regarding these rights. These materials help to manage expectations among victims, to indicate further sources of support and assistance, to address questions and to clear up misconceptions.'[75] In addition, the materials are held to 'respond to the particular needs of victims (for example in cases where the victim is a child, has been the victim of a crime of sexual violence or torture, or has suffered the loss or disappearance of a loved one)'.[76] The VPRS will disseminate the materials in different ways, including by means of 'public announcements; conferences and workshops; web sites; posters; brochures; print advertisements; radio and TV spots and fact sheets'.[77] Although an outreach programme exists and some information about the ICTR proceedings is available at the ICTR outreach building in Kigali, such information has not reached most of the population in the rural areas.[78] Getting the

[73] Rule 16(1)(a) and (c) ICC RPE.

[74] Assembly of States Parties, *Report on Participation of and Reparations to Victims*, 25 August 2004, ICC-ASP/3/21, Third Session, The Hague, 6-10 September 2004, para. 6.

[75] *Ibid.*, para. 5.

[76] *Ibid.* The author has not been able to get a hold of the materials.

[77] *Ibid.*, para. 7.

[78] Nowrojee (2005).

information about the Court and what it can do for victims to the people for whom it may be relevant will be a real challenge.

The VPRS helps the Registrar to meet the obligation of Rule 16(1)(d) of the ICC RPE, which explicitly provides that the Registrar must take into account 'gender-sensitive measures to facilitate the participation of victims of sexual violence at all stages of the proceedings'. Article 68(1) of the ICC Statute is also of relevant to victims of sexual or gender violence as the provision states that:

> The Court shall take appropriate measures to protect the safety, physical and psychological well-being, dignity and privacy of victims and witnesses. In so doing, the Court shall have regard to all relevant factors, including age, gender and health, and the nature of the crime, in particular, but not limited to, where the crime involves sexual or gender violence, or violence against children.

Special attention for the participatory rights of victims of sexual is important, as stigmatisation and shame may prevent them from being underrepresented at the Court. In order for victims of sexual violence to equally benefit from the right to participation, the Court will have to reach out to international and national or local women's groups working in situations being analysed or investigated by the Prosecutor. These agencies may help in explaining victims' rights and assist them in applying for participation (and reparation) in a sensitive and appropriate manner. Such efforts are currently undertaken by the VPRS and attempts are made to include training on gender issues with those in the field who will work with the victims of sexual violence.[79] However, although the situation in northern Uganda has been formally investigated as of July 2004, the Women's Initiative for Gender Justice revealed that, in November 2004, the majority of the people did not know much about the Court, or even that it existed at all.[80] As a result, for those persons who did hear about the Court, many misconceptions and much misinformation about the Court existed. To prevent the notification obligation about victim participation from becoming an empty promise, the law in the books should not remain just there.

3.2 Application for participation

Following Rule 89(1), victims may submit applications for participation in writing to the Registrar.[81] Such applications may also be made by 'a person acting with the consent of the victim, or a person acting on behalf of a victim, in the case of a victim who is a child or, when necessary, a victim who is disabled'.[82] This provision may fulfil the needs of some victims of sexual violence, e.g., those who suffer from a severe

[79] ICC Newsletter, *Registry: VPRS – Gender Sensitivity*, June 2005, #4, p.6.

[80] Women's Initiative for Gender Justice Press Release, in Collaboration with Isis-WICCE and Ugandan Women Activists, without title, 23 November 2004 ('It seems that neither the Ugandan state nor the International Criminal Court cared to consult with or raise awareness about the ICC among the people of Northern Uganda').

[81] Rule 102 ICC RPE furthermore contains the possibility to make communications other than in writing.

[82] Rule 89(3) ICC RPE.

illness (for example HIV/AIDS) or a disability as a consequence of the rapes. The Registrar submits the application to the Chamber as well as to the Prosecutor and the Defence for consideration. The application can be rejected by the Chamber or on the application of the Prosecutor or the Defence if the person concerned is not a victim (Rule 85) and/or if the applicant's personal interests are not affected (Rule 68(3)).[83]

3.3 Forms of participation

If the application is accepted, the Chamber must specify the proceedings and manner in which participation is considered appropriate.[84] However, the Chamber is always allowed to modify this decision later on in the trial.[85] This leaves the final decision on how victims can participate in the overall control of the judges, so that they can react to different or unforeseen circumstances in the proceedings. Written submissions are allowed, including victim impact statements, and the Court may also seek the views of victims with regard to, for instance, an amendment of the charges.[86] The Chamber may even seek the views of other victims, officially not participating in the proceedings.[87] Rule 89(1) gives a small hint of how victim participation may take place, that is, by making opening and closing statements. Victims or their legal representatives may furthermore be present in the courtroom when the decision of the Trial Chamber concerning admissibility and jurisdiction, the criminal responsibility of the accused, the sentence and reparations are pronounced.[88] Other provisions give the impression that participation is largely left to participation by the legal representative. Although the legal representatives are entitled to attend and participate in the proceedings (participation in hearings, right to make observations and to question witnesses, experts and the accused), their participation remains subject to the discretion of the Court. In particular, the Chamber, when deciding on a legal representative's request to questioning, must take into account 'the stage of the proceedings, the rights of the accused, the interests of witnesses, the need for a fair, impartial and expeditious trial'.[89] These provisions give the impression that oral presentation by the legal representative will be the exception rather than the rule.[90]

3.4 The right to be informed

Information about the criminal procedure is generally considered to be of major importance to victims: it will make them feel respected and recognised by the

---

[83] Rule 89(2) ICC RPE.
[84] Rule 89(1) ICC RPE and Article 68(3) ICC Statute.
[85] Rule 90(1) ICC RPE.
[86] Timm (2001), p. 298. See further Rule 93 ICC RPE and, for instance, Rule 128 ICC RPE ('Amendment of the Charges').
[87] Rule 93 ICC RPE.
[88] Rule 144(1) ICC RPE. Rule 144(2) ICC RPE furthermore states that copies of these decisions shall be provided to all participants in the proceedings.
[89] Rule 91(3)(b) ICC RPE.
[90] Garkawe (2001), p. 281.

authorities.[91] The 1985 UN Declaration states, in Principle 6(a), that 'the responsiveness of judicial and administrative processes to the needs of victims should be facilitated by: (a) Informing victims of their role and the scope, timing and progress of the proceedings and the disposition of their cases, especially where serious crimes are involved and where they have requested such information.'[92] The ICC RPE recognise the right to information of victims or their legal representatives who have successfully applied to participate by informing them of: (1) the proceedings before the Court, including the date of hearings and any postponements thereof, and the date of delivery of the decision; and (2) requests, submissions, motions and other documents relating to them.[93] In addition, they may be allowed to consult the record of the proceedings.[94]

As mentioned before, victims appearing before the Tribunals as witnesses have no legal right to be informed about the particulars of the criminal procedure. This situation has been widely felt by victims to be unsatisfactory. For example, communications between the ICTR and Rwandese who testified before the Tribunal have been meagre. Rape victims and women's groups complain that their contact with the ICTR is minimal and lacks follow-up.[95] They do not get any information about the status of their cases. Many of them feel used by the Tribunal: once they have given testimony, they are no longer needed. One notable exception of good follow-up practice was the time when ICTR staff members went to Taba to explain the sentence imposed on Akayesu, the former mayor of Taba commune and the first person to be convicted by the Tribunal.[96] The explanation of the sentence to the local people 'clearly contributed to a sense of accomplishment and empowerment expressed by one of the Akayesu rape witnesses who felt that she had made a contribution: I am still ready to testify again to tell the world what happened. It is important for the world to know. Thousands were raped and don't dare say it. We gave courage to others who haven't spoken. We dared to speak, to say what happened.'[97] Although such initiatives seem to be relatively low profile and straightforward, it is striking that the Tribunal has largely refrained from informing witnesses about the outcome of trials. The ICTY, when possible, informs witnesses who

---

[91] United Nations Office for Drug Control and Crime Prevention, Center for International Crime Prevention, *Handbook on Justice for Victims: On the Use and Application of the Declaration of Basic Principles of Justice for Victims of Crime and Abuse of Power*, New York, 1999, p. 35.

[92] See also Recommendation No. R (85) 11 of the Committee of Ministers to Member States of the Council of Europe on the Position of Victims in the Framework of Criminal Law and Procedure, Rec. 85(11) E, 28 June 1985, which reads: '... date and place of the hearing ... and how the victim can find out the outcome of the case'.

[93] Rule 92(5) ICC RPE.

[94] Rule 131(2) ICC RPE.

[95] Nowrojee (2005).

[96] *Ibid.* Furthermore, Adeogun-Phillips, the Senior Trial Attorney in the Muhimana case, told Hirondelle News Agency that they had intended 'to bring the victims to Arusha to attend Muhimana's Judgment but had been dissuaded from doing so for fear of divulging their identities. "We are making a recording of the judgment that will be made available to them in Rwanda before the end of this week."' Hirondelle News Agency, *Muhimana Gets Life Sentence for Multiple Rapes in Rwanda Genocide*, 28 April 2005.

[97] Nowrojee (2005).

came to testify at the Tribunal of the sentences imposed on the accused.[98] The ICTY set up an outreach programme in 1999 and offices have since been set up in Sarajevo (Bosnia and Herzegovina), Zagreb (Croatia), Pristina (Kosovo) and Belgrade (Serbia and Montenegro).[99] As part of the programme, victims across the region have been addressed, especially those whose communities were most affected by the crimes under the Tribunal's jurisdiction.[100] For example, on 9 October 2004, a meeting was held in the town of Foča, where Tribunal staff members (including investigators and prosecutors) explained to the local population their work in relation to the crimes committed in Foča, and in particular they discussed the rapes and sexual enslavement of Muslim women and girls.[101] The Tribunal has undertaken such initiatives in order to better 'explain at a grass-roots level its method of operations, its decisions and what facts have been proved beyond a reasonable doubt in order to promote local visibility of justice served, prevent revisionism and foster reconciliation'.[102] Although the explanation of the *Kunarac, Kovač and Vuković* case came a few years after the Trial and Appeal judgments in this case had been rendered, the ICTY has clearly taken up the issue of communicating the work done at the Tribunal with those who were affected by the crimes committed. In light of similar geographical and communicating constraints which the ICC is likely to face in informing victims and witnesses who participated in proceedings at the Court, the ICC will need to make sure that these people receive regular updates about the proceedings, including the content of the judgment. It is a good development that the rights of victims to such information are clearly laid down in the ICC provisions.

3.5 Legal representation

Victims are free to choose a legal representative.[103] However, if the number of victims is large, the Chamber may request the victims to choose a common legal representative or representatives.[104] It is very likely that a large number of victims may want to participate in the trial and a common legal representative may prove helpful in these situations for the effectiveness of the proceedings. The Registrar will provide a list of counsel to the victims or suggest one or more common legal representatives himself. If victims are unable to choose a common legal representative, the Chamber may request the Registrar to choose one or more. In choosing a common legal representative, Rule 90(4) stipulates that the Chamber and Registry shall take steps to ensure that the 'distinct interests of the victims, particularly as provided in article 68, paragraph 1, are represented' and that 'any conflict of interests is avoided'. Article 68(1) refers in

[98] ICTY Third Annual Report (1996), para. 122.

[99] ICTY Eleventh Annual Report (2004), para. 316. See generally Vohrah and Cina (2001), pp. 547-557.

[100] ICTY Eleventh Annual Report (2004), para. 320.

[101] Human Rights Watch (2004c); ICTY Press Release, *Foca Conference: Bridging the Gap Between the ICTY and Communities in Bosnia and Herzegovina*, RC/P.I.S./901-e, The Hague, 13 October 2004.

[102] ICTY Eleventh Annual Report (2004), para. 320.

[103] Rule 90(1) ICC RPE.

[104] Rule 90(2) ICC RPE.

particular to victims of sexual or gender violence and children as they are victims who might have distinct interests that must be taken into account. This requirement may have an effect on, *inter alia*, the number of representatives that should be chosen and on the particular qualifications that would be desirable when choosing the representative for a certain group of victims.[105] The qualifications for legal counsel representing victims of sexual violence should include, among other things, experience in working with victims of (mass) sexual violence and/or experience in trauma counselling. Furthermore, female victims in particular may feel more comfortable liaising with a representative who is of the same sex. As victims of sexual violence may require special, gender-sensitive treatment, separate legal counsel for (a group of) victims of sexual violence may be needed.[106] Moreover, for some victims of sexual violence, it may be helpful to appoint a legal representative who comes from their country or region, speaks their language (which may not be any of the official Court languages) and understands the conflict situation the victims come from. Such a person may also be appointed as an assistant to the legal representative.[107] On the basis of Rule 90(6), a legal representative of a victim must have the same qualifications as a legal counsel for the defence.[108] Although it was debated whether particular qualifications should be required for legal representatives of victims, in particular for vulnerable victims like victims of sexual violence, this idea was rejected as the issue was already covered by paragraph 4.[109] If victims cannot pay for a common legal representative themselves, they may receive assistance, including financial assistance, from the Registry.[110]

4 Final remarks

On the supranational criminal law level, the ICC is the first Court to provide victims with the right to participate in the Court's proceedings, often through a legal representative. The ICTY and ICTR experience has shown that the Prosecutor's interests do not always coincide with those of victims, so the ICC provisions are more victim-friendly. Before the ICTY and the ICTR, the interests of victims of sexual

---

[105] Bitti and Friman (2001), p. 464.

[106] Victims Rights Working Group (2003). See also Article 9(2) of the 'Proposal for a draft Code of Professional Conduct for counsel before the International Criminal Court', in which it is stated that: 'In his or her relations with the client, counsel shall take into account the client's personal circumstances and specific needs, in particular where counsel is representing victims of torture or of physical, psychological or sexual violence, children, the elderly or the disables' (ICC-ASP/3/11/Rev.1, 27 August 2004).

[107] Rule 22(1) ICC RPE.

[108] Rule 22 ICC RPE stipulates the qualifications of counsel for the defence, which include competence in international or criminal law and procedure as well as the necessary relevant experience in criminal proceedings (as a judge, prosecutor, advocate, etc.) and excellent knowledge of and fluency in at least one of the working languages of the Court.

[109] Bitti and Friman (2001), p. 464. Bitti and Friman refer to the proposal submitted by Costa Rica (PCNICC/2000/WGRPE(6)/DP.6, 23 March 2000), in which it was suggested that particular experience should be required of a legal representative of victims of sexual violence, child victims and victims with disabilities.

[110] Rule 90(5) ICC RPE.

violence have, on several occasions, lost out against the Prosecutor's interests. For example, in the *Cyangugu* case, the Prosecutor decided not to prosecute the accused for sexual violence despite evidence in its possession. Time constraints in dealing with the Prosecutor's case load proved to be a decisive factor in taking this decision. While some mechanisms, such as *amicus curiae* interventions and directly addressing the Office of the Prosecutor, have been very helpful in addressing victims' concerns and bringing the situation out in the open, their effectiveness is dependent on a number of issues, in particular judicial and/or prosecutorial discretion, which may not always take into account the concerns of those who are the victims of the crimes concerned. Furthermore, the *amicus curiae* institution or addressing the Prosecutor directly is very much dependent on *amici* who care enough to take up the plight of victims and is therefore an *ad hoc* mechanism. The same is true for the victim impact statements which were occasionally forwarded by the Prosecutor to the Chamber for sentencing purposes, but where, again, victims do not have a right to submit such statements themselves. As a result, the impact of the crime, in the case of victims of sexual violence, has not been taken into account by the Chambers in a consistent and coherent manner.

This unsatisfactory situation for victims has now been remedied at the Court. At least victims can now, among other things, make opening and closing statements to tell their story. This will enable victims of sexual violence to take steps to have the effects of the rapes recognised and taken into account for sentencing purposes. Victims also have the right to be informed about the progress of the proceedings and may be present when the Court reaches its verdict or, alternatively, are notified thereof when they cannot be there. In case of a guilty plea, victims and their interests are taken into account as well, and the Court may decide not to accept the plea if their interest so dictate. Their views may also be sought where the indictment may be amended. These are just a few examples of victim participation recognised in the ICC Statute and Rules and where, in the past, victims of sexual violence have experienced difficulties in getting their voices heard. It is therefore no longer solely the Prosecutor who looks after victims' interests. In light of the complexity of cases, with potentially large numbers of victims participating, the Court will be able to control the manner of participation and has the flexibility to make changes whenever appropriate. In most situations, a legal representative will be assigned to victims or a common legal representative if the number of victims is very large.

Like all victims, victims of sexual violence will be able to participate in the ICC proceedings. The Court has acknowledged that special arrangements for this group of victims must be made. In particular Article 68(1) of the ICC Statute and Rule 16(5) of the ICC RPE specify in this obligation. These provisions require that participation of victims of sexual violence should be conducted in gender-sensitive circumstances which take into account the well-being, dignity and safety of the victim. For this category of victims to participate, it is important to notify them about the participation possibilities and the special (gender-sensitive) arrangements that have been put into place. Precisely because of the stigmatisation, shame and fear disproportionately attached to these crimes, victims of sexual violence need extra attention so that they will be able to realise their participatory rights to the fullest extent. International, national or local women's organisations in the countries concerned will be instrumental in making victim participation of victims of sexual violence a reality. They will be able to locate victims of sexual violence and help them with submitting their applications for participation in the Court's proceedings. If victims of sexual violence suffer from diseases as a result of the sexual violence committed against them and are not capable of making the application themselves, someone else can do this for them. Although the situation before the ICC is better in terms of participatory rights laid down in the legal instruments, if victims are not reached, they will not come. Victims need to be informed about their participatory rights and the circumstances should be such that they can exercise their rights in good conditions. For victims of sexual violence this means, *inter alia*, that they may be represented by a legal representative with experience in dealing with victims of sexual violence and/or trauma counselling.

Evaluation of Part II

The subject of inquiry in Chapter 4 was the extent to which the protective and special measures can serve the interests of victims of sexual violence. The confidentiality measures (protection from the public and the press) which can be applied to victims of sexual violence before the ICC are more far-reaching than those applied before the ICTY and the ICTR. As opposed to the Tribunals, before the ICC, victims of sexual violence have an automatic right to give their testimony *in camera* or to have it presented by electronic or other special means, such as by means of videoconferencing or one-way closed circuit television. A proper reading of the provision should direct the Court to allow such protection where the victim-witness of sexual violence agrees to such a measure herself. However, as long as stigmatisation and rejection by family and community members is a real problem for survivors of sexual violence, confidentiality measures will in most cases be needed to shield rape survivors from these unwelcome effects. The practice before the Tribunals has shown, however, that court orders on non-disclosure have been violated and identity details of victims have been leaked. In addition, it is not always easy to hide a survivor's absence, when an accused of the same town stands trial before the Tribunal. In Rwanda, victims of sexual violence have faced threats and intimidation and have been forced to seek refuge in another part of the country. Another, more controversial, possibility which the Court may provide and which was discussed in Chapter 4 is the protection of victims and witnesses by means of anonymity measures. The ICC provisions and the negotiations on this issue have not been conclusive and the issue is therefore left to be decided by the Court. If concerns for safety as well as privacy and dignity continue to exist, the Court should not immediately refuse anonymity. When special criteria are applied and guidelines are followed, anonymity as a protective measure can be granted without violating the rights of the accused, especially the accused's right to examine witnesses or to have them examined. With victims of sexual violence, the additional concern exists that, as long as protective measures and post-trial protection do not have the desired effects, victims will not come forward and justice will (continue to) be denied for this category of victims. Another category of protective and special measures is aimed to prevent further or increased traumatisation of the rape victim giving testimony. Avoiding direct confrontation with the accused in court is one such measure and can consist of one-way closed circuit television, the use of a screen in court, or removal of the accused from the court room. Another possibility is giving testimony by means of prior recorded testimony, which may spare the victim from having to repeat the testimony in court. The special evidentiary rules on sexual violence crimes restrict admitting consent and prior or subsequent sexual conduct into evidence and therefore protect the victim of sexual violence from retraumatisation in court as well. Admitting such evidence would subject the witness to unnecessary, humiliating questions, and may only be accepted in very limited circumstances. In light of the nature of the crimes, it seems almost extremely unlikely that a situation will arise in which consent or prior or subsequent sexual conduct may be raised. The special evidentiary rules also acknowledge that corroboration of evidence is not a requirement for any crime, particularly not with regard to crimes of sexual violence. The evidentiary rules thus specifically acknowledge that biases against victims of sexual violence, in particular women, are not accepted and that they are as reliable witnesses as any other witness. Other special measures include such issues as the manner of questioning, the duration of the questioning, and allowing a supports person to attend the proceedings. As the practice before the Tribunals has shown some discouraging practices towards the treatment of victims of sexual violence during trial, it is argued here that a set of guidelines needs to be established which deals with the conduct of parties during the testimony of a victim of sexual violence. Such guidelines are particularly important as they set out one common approach, for judges, Prosecutors and Defence Counsel alike, towards the treatment of victims of sexual violence. A code of conduct may be helpful to direct all parties, which all have different legal backgrounds and therefore different approaches in dealing with witnesses in court, to a proper treatment of victims of sexual violence during testimony. It is important that victims of sexual violence are treated with respect. Only then will they come and testify at the Court and will the record reflect the crimes that were committed against them.

In Chapter 5, the participatory rights of victims of sexual violence was dealt with. True participation of victims has not been possible before the Tribunals. Although it has sometimes been argued that the Prosecutor would take the victims' interests into account at the Tribunals, the interests of the Prosecutor and victims obviously do not always coincide. Victims of sexual violence have experienced this on a number of occasions. For example, despite evidence in the Prosecutor's possession, sexual violence was not prosecuted in a few cases and, in other cases, guilty pleas were agreed with the accused, with charges for sexual violence being dropped in exchange. Although mechanisms such as *amicus curiae* interventions and directly addressing the Office of the Prosecutor have been very helpful in giving attention to victims' concerns and bringing the situation out into the open, their effectiveness is dependent on a number of issues, in particular judicial and/or prosecutorial discretion, which may not always take into account the concerns of those who are the victims of the crimes concerned. In addition, victim impact statements have only been forwarded by the Prosecutor to the Chamber for sentencing purposes on a few occasions. The victims themselves have no right to submit victim impact statements. In the case of victims of sexual violence, the impact of the crime has, on the whole, not been taken into account by the Chambers in a consistent and coherent manner. This situation has been remedied at the ICC. At least victims can now, among other things, make opening and closing statements to tell their story, their interests are taken into account in cases where a guilty plea will be entered, their views may also be sought where the indictment may be amended, etc. The ICC provisions furthermore require that participation of victims of sexual violence should be conducted in gender-sensitive circumstances which take into account the well-being, dignity and safety of the victim. For victims of sexual violence this means, *inter alia*, that they may be represented by a legal representative with experience in dealing with victims of sexual violence and/or trauma counselling. First of all, it will be very important that victims of sexual violence are notified about the participation possibilities at the Court. As victims of sexual violence often disproportionately suffer from stigmatisation, shame and fear, they need extra attention as far as notification is concerned. International, national or local women's organisations in the countries concerned will be instrumental in making participation in court proceedings of victims of sexual violence a reality. They will be able to locate victims of sexual violence and help them with submitting their applications for participation to the Court.

PART III
SEXUAL VIOLENCE AND THE LEGAL CONSEQUENCES OF THE SUPRANATIONAL CRIMINAL LAW SYSTEM

'I am disappointed with the sentences – given everything that they have done. I no longer believe in those sentences and will not testify before the tribunal.'

Witness 96, a witness in the ICTY *Kunarac, Kovač and Vuković* case who testified about the sexual violence that had been committed in and around Foča (Bosnia and Herzegovina), in an interview with the Dutch television channel AVRO, as quoted in: Institute for War & Peace Reporting, *Foca Rape Case* (by Mirko Klarin and Vjera Bogati), Issue 210, 28 February 2001.

'It makes me sad to hear them call me a 'genocide survivor.' I am not a survivor. I am still struggling [to survive].'

S.K., a victim of rape during the 1994 genocide in Rwanda without any form of reparation, Kanzenzi district, Rwanda, 20 February 2004, quoted in: Human Rights Watch (2004b), p. 1.

'People detained in Arusha and those imprisoned for genocide and rape are getting anti-retroviral drugs, why is it that we who suffered such heinous crimes through which we were infected with the illness, don't have access to those drugs?'

Console Mukanyirigira, the coordinator of AVEGA, an association of genocide widows in Rwanda, in: Internews, *When Justice Takes Too Long* (by Mary Kimani), 1 September 2003.

Introduction to Part III

The legal consequences of the supranational criminal law system include sentencing and reparation. This part of the proceedings is especially important as a victim of sexual violence may see the violation labelled publicly as a crime and see the perpetrator condemned by the international community and punished. A victim of sexual violence will see herself acknowledged by the community as an innocent victim who deserves reparation. In other words, sentencing and reparation are closely linked. The Chambers have relatively wide discretionary powers as concerns both sentencing and reparation.

Sentencing in cases of sexual violence within the supranational criminal law context is the subject of Chapter 6. What factors are important in determining the sentence and do the Tribunal judges adequately address these factors when the prosecution of sexual violence is concerned? The outcome may influence the sentencing practice on sexual violence before the ICC. Whereas the first section in Chapter 6 describes matters related to sentencing within the supranational criminal law system in a general manner, subsequent sections will cover sentencing in relation to sexual violence in particular.

The ICC does not only aim for retributive justice, but also seeks restorative justice. Reparation, a novelty within the supranational criminal law context, will be discussed in Chapter 7. How can victims obtain reparation within the supranational criminal law system and how are victims of sexual violence best served by the reparation possibilities available at the Court and/or from the Trust Fund for victims and their families? In Chapter 7, the needs of wartime victims of sexual violence and their families, followed by an examination of the Tribunals' failure to provide adequate reparation to victims of sexual violence are discussed, concluding with a section on the ICC's possibilities in this area. In addition to a Court order on reparation following a conviction, the Trust Fund for victims and their families may be in a position to give victims of sexual violence interim relief.

CHAPTER 6
SENTENCING IN CASES OF SEXUAL VIOLENCE

1 INTRODUCTION

Although sentencing received little attention during the initial years of the ICTY's and the ICTR's existence, due to its visibility as the closing part of the Tribunals' criminal proceedings, the attention for sentencing issues has, commensurate with the volume of sentences handed down, increased significantly. In part, this development is to be attributed to the sentencing policy of the Tribunals, which some have characterised as somewhat inconsistent. For instance, Biljana Plavšić (a former Serbian Representative to the Presidency of the Socialist Republic of Bosnia and Herzegovina) received a prison sentence of 11 years, whereas a relatively smaller fish, such as Duško Tadić (a former camp guard), received a prison sentence of 25 years. Moreover, whereas Plavšić received a prison sentence of 11 years on the basis of a guilty plea, Kambanda (the former Prime Minister of Rwanda), who entered a plea of guilty as well, was given life imprisonment. Nevertheless, the Tribunals have held that sentencing is a discretionary decision and that it is inappropriate to set down a definitive list of sentencing guidelines.[1] In other words, each case needs to be evaluated on the basis of the circumstances of that case. For people to have confidence in the supranational criminal law system, as with any criminal law system, it is therefore important that the sentencing argumentation of each and every judgment is persuasive.

This Chapter focuses on sentencing in cases of sexual violence. The main question is: how have sentences by the ICTY and ICTR in cases of sexual violence been determined and, on the basis of these findings, is there any reason to change the approach to sentencing adopted by these Tribunals and the ICC? In other words, how persuasive have the Tribunals been in their sentencing argumentation with respect to sexual violence? In order to give an answer to these questions, an examination was conducted of the sentencing determinants of the ICTY, the ICTR and the ICC on the basis of their sentencing provisions and purposes (section 2), as well as of the Tribunals' sentencing practice and determinants with regard to sexual violence (sections 3 and 4, respectively). A short exposé on sentencing in general is necessary for the discussion of sentencing in relation to sexual violence in particular. The issue of cumulative convictions in relation to sexual violence and informing victims of sexual violence who testified before the court will also be addressed.

2 SENTENCING

The Statutes and Rules of Procedure and Evidence of both the Tribunals and the Court contain provisions on sentencing, the latter in a more elaborate manner than the former.

[1] Krstić Appeal Judgment, para. 242.

2.1 The ICTY and the ICTR

The ICTY Statute deals with sentencing in Articles 23 and 24, supplemented by Rules 87 and 101 of the ICTY RPE in particular. Identical provisions, applicable to those found guilty for their involvement in the Rwandan 1994 genocide, can be found in the ICTR Statute and RPE.[2] Pursuant to these rules, the Trial Chambers pronounce judgment and impose sentences and penalties on persons convicted of serious violations of international humanitarian law, in short: war crimes, crimes against humanity and genocide.[3] A judgment must be rendered by a majority of the judges of the Trial Chamber, and is delivered by the Trial Chamber in public accompanied by a reasoned opinion in writing, to which separate or dissenting opinions may be appended.[4] The Tribunals do not have separate sentencing hearings and do not issue separate sentencing decisions: evidence related to sentencing must be raised during trial.[5] The penalty which the Trial Chamber is allowed to impose is limited to imprisonment (with a maximum of life imprisonment)[6] and thus excludes other forms of punishment, such as the imposition of the death penalty, penal servitude or a fine.[7] In addition to (life) imprisonment, the return of any property and proceeds acquired by criminal conduct may be ordered.[8]

The manner in which sentences are imposed is laid down in Rule 87(C) of the ICTY RPE and reads:

> If the Trial Chamber finds the accused guilty on one or more charges contained in the indictment, it shall impose a sentence in respect of each finding of guilt and indicate whether such sentences shall be served consecutively or concurrently, unless it decides to exercise its power to impose a single sentence reflecting the totality of the criminal conduct of the accused.

---

[2] Articles 22 and 23 ICTR Statute and Rules 87 and 101 ICTR RPE.

[3] Article 23(1) ICTY Statute; Article 22(1) ICTR Statute.

[4] Article 23(2) ICTY Statute; Article 22(2) ICTR Statute.

[5] Rules 85-87 ICTY and ICTR RPE. Under the old Rules 85 and 100 (UN Doc. IT/32/Rev.12 (1997)), determination of an appropriate sentence was considered after a defendant had pleaded guilty or the Trial Chamber had rendered a guilty verdict: information of assistance for determining the sentence could then be submitted by the parties to the Chamber. See, on this issue, Keller (2001). Keller argues that the current procedure, instituted to save time and money in particular, is contrary to the rights of the accused. For example, a witness does not have to come back twice and can testify about the guilt of the accused and the effects of the injury during trial, when the finding of guilt or innocence of the accused is not yet determined.

[6] Article 24(1) ICTY Statute in conjunction with Rule 101(A) ICTY RPE; Article 23(1) ICTR Statute in conjunction with Rule 101(A) ICTR RPE. It is noteworthy that imprisonment for 'the remainder of the convicted person's life' is laid down in the Tribunals' RPE, as promulgated by the judges, instead of the Tribunals' Statutes, which only stipulate that the penalty be limited to imprisonment.

[7] See Kambanda Judgment and Sentence, para. 10; Serushago Sentence, para. 12; Rutaganda Judgment and Sentence, para. 448.

[8] Article 24(3) ICTY Statute; Article 23(3) ICTR Statute. See further Chapter 7 on reparation to victims of sexual violence, para. 3.1.1. on restitution of property and proceeds.

The ICTR Statute does not explicitly refer to the imposition of single sentences, but merely states that a sentence for each count on which the accused is found guilty should be given.[9] The ICTY and ICTR practice reveals that sentences are either imposed as one single sentence[10] or that sentences given for multiple counts are to be served concurrently, which means that only the highest sentence has to be served,[11] but not consecutively.[12] The judges have regularly held that it is within their discretion to choose the appropriate manner of imposing sentences.[13] Previous versions of Rule 87 of the ICTY RPE did not contain the possibility to impose single sentences,[14] but an ICTY Appeals Chamber has ruled that imposing single sentences was never prohibited as such by the Rules or unknown in the practice of the Tribunals:[15] the new Rule 87(C) has 'simply confirmed the power of a Trial Chamber to impose a single sentence'.[16]

Other issues related to sentencing concern cumulative convictions,[17] credit for time served,[18] appeal of sentences,[19] enforcement of sentences,[20] and pardon, commutation of sentences or early release of convicted persons.[21]

---

[9] Rule 87(C) ICTR RPE states: 'If the Trial Chamber finds the accused guilty on one or more of the counts contained in the indictment, it shall also determine the penalty to be imposed in respect of each of the counts.'

[10] See, *inter alia*, the sentences imposed on Kambanda; Musema; Ntakirutimana and Ntakirutimana; Niyitegeka; Nahimana, Barayagwiza and Ngeze; Gacumbitsi; Blaškić; Kunarac, Kovač and Vuković; Kvočka, Kos, Radić, Žigić and Prcać.

[11] See, *inter alia*, the sentences imposed on Akayesu, Semanza, Tadić and Furundžija.

[12] Although the Trial Chamber in the Semanza case ruled that Semanza was to serve both concurrent and consecutive prison terms, see the Appendix.

[13] See, *inter alia*, Kambanda Appeal Judgment, paras. 101-102; Musema Judgment and Sentence, para. 989; Ntakirutimana and Ntakirutimana Judgment and Sentence, para. 917; Niyitegeka Judgment and Sentence, para. 483; Media Judgment, para. 1104.

[14] See Rules 101(C) and 87(C) ICTY RPE (18th edition, 2 August 2000). Rule 101(C) states: 'The Trial Chamber shall indicate whether multiple sentences shall be served consecutively or concurrently.'

[15] Kunarac, Kovač and Vuković Appeal Judgment, paras. 339-344. Reference was made to the Blaškić Judgment, in which a single sentence was imposed for all the crimes of which the accused was found guilty.

[16] *Ibid*, para. 344. In Blaškić, it was furthermore held that the imposition of a single sentence does not entitle the Tribunal to impose a single sentence arbitrarily. See Blaškić Appeal Judgment, para. 680.

[17] See further section 5 on cumulative (charges and) convictions in this Chapter.

[18] Rules 101(C) ICTY RPE and 101(D) ICTR RPE read: 'Credit shall be given to the convicted person for the period, if any, during which the convicted person was detained in custody pending surrender to the Tribunal or pending trial or appeal.'

[19] The Appeals Chamber may revise the sentence if it is satisfied that there has been a discernible error in the Trial Chamber's exercise of discretion in imposing sentence. See, for instance, the Aleksovski Appeal Judgment (Aleksovski's sentence was revised from 2.5 years to 7 years imprisonment) and the Krnojelac Appeal Judgment (Krnojelac's sentence was revised from 7 to 15 years). In the Blaškić case, the Appeals Chamber lowered the sentence imposed on Blaškić by the Trial Chamber considerably, namely, from one single sentence of 45 years to a single sentence

of 9 years. Before the ICTR, Kajelijeli's sentence of life imprisonment was reduced on appeal to 45 years in prison because of irregularities during his arrest and detention. Semanza's sentence of 25 years was increased to 35 years on appeal because he had ordered, rather than aided and abetted, massacres of Tutsi.

[20] Article 27 ICTY Statute; Article 26 ICTR Statute; Rule 103 ICTY and ICTR RPE. Article 27 ICTY Statute reads: 'Imprisonment shall be served in a State designated by the International Tribunal from a list of States which have indicated to the Security Council their *willingness* to accept convicted persons. Such imprisonment shall be in accordance with the applicable law of the State concerned, subject to the supervision of the International Tribunal' (italics added). The ICTR Statute is similar in wording, but adds in Article 26 that the sentences may also be served in Rwanda. Without their own prison facilities, the ICTY and ICTR are thus highly dependent on cooperating States willing to let ICTY/R convicts serve their prison terms on their territory. See further on this issue Tolbert and Rydberg (2001), pp. 533-543. Agreements on the enforcement of sentences have been concluded by the ICTY with ten States: i.e., Germany (*ad hoc* agreements in respect of Tadić and Kunarac), Italy (1997), Finland (1997), Norway (1998), Sweden (1999), Austria (1999), France (2000), Spain (2000), Denmark (2002); United Kingdom (2004). See http://www.un.org/icty. The ICTR has signed agreements on enforcement of sentences with six states: i.e., Mali (1999), Benin (1999), Swaziland (2000), France (2003), Italy (2004) and Sweden (2004). See http://www.ictr.org. The ICTR Prosecutor is currently studying whether use can be made of the Mpenga Prison in the Butare Province in Rwanda. See ICTR Newsletter, June 2004. There has been much criticism on the difference in prison facilities in different countries. For example, while Plavšić was transferred to a prison in Sweden, which is known for 'its plush suites with color TV, and facilities including a sauna, horseback riding, a solarium, and salsa dancing lessons', other less developed countries may not have such luxury prison facilities. See Askin (2004a), p. 58.

[21] Article 28 ICTY Statute; Article 27 ICTR Statute; Rules 123-125 ICTY RPE; Rules 124-126 ICTR RPE; ICTY, *Practice Direction on the Procedure for the Determination of Applications for Pardon, Commutation of Sentence and Early Release of Persons Convicted by the International Tribunal*, IT/146, 7 April 1999. Article 28 ICTY Statute reads: 'If, *pursuant to the applicable law of the State in which the convicted person is imprisoned*, he or she is eligible for pardon or commutation of sentence, the State concerned shall notify the International Tribunal accordingly. The President of the International Tribunal, in consultation with the judges, shall decide the matter on the basis of the interests of justice and the general principles of law' (italics added). Article 27 ICTR Statute contains similar wording, emphasising even more that pardon or commutation of sentences can only be allowed if the interests of justice and the general principles of law so dictate. Rules 123 ICTY and 124 ICTR RPE provide further guidance and state: 'In determining whether pardon or commutation is appropriate, the President shall take into account, *inter alia*, the gravity of the crime or crimes for which the prisoner was convicted, the treatment of similarly-situated prisoners, the prisoner's demonstration of rehabilitation, as well as any substantial cooperation of the prisoner with the Prosecutor.' For example, in conformity with the law in Finland, Furundžija was granted early release on 17 August 2004, after serving two-thirds of his sentence. In arriving at this decision, the President took into consideration 'the gravity of the offences committed by Mr. Furundžija', that he 'is resolved to be integrated into society, exhibited good behaviour in detention, and has a strong attachment to his family', and 'as reported by the Finnish authorities, Mr. Furundžija has accepted the judgment he received as fair and has *expressed remorse for the suffering of victims*' (italics added). See ICTY Press Release,

One essential question remains, that is, how are sentences for those found guilty of serious violations of international humanitarian law determined? Neither the Statutes nor the RPE of the two Tribunals contain a hierarchical list of crimes which link the crimes to specified sentences. Instead, they enumerate several factors that should be taken into account by the Trial Chambers when determining the term of imprisonment: in particular they must take into account (1) the general practice regarding prison sentences in the courts of the former Yugoslavia or Rwanda, as the case may be;[22] (2) such factors as the gravity of the crime and the individual circumstances of the convicted person;[23] and (3) any aggravating or mitigating circumstances.[24] The ICTY and ICTR Statutes and RPE do not provide any further details as how these factors should be interpreted. On the contrary, the judges exert wide discretionary powers when it comes to interpretation.[25] In many Tribunal cases, it has been indicated that taking these factors into account is not mandatory nor is the list of factors exhaustive and that sentencing is a matter of individualising the penalty considering the totality of the

Anto Furundzija Granted Early Release, CT/P.I.S./877e, 30 July 2004. Much criticism exists as to the procedure of early release: whereas convicts of the ICTY are generally released after spending two-thirds of their sentence on the basis of the laws of the countries where they fulfil their prison term, ICTR convicts have generally served their prison terms in Mali, and Mali does not have mandatory review as a part of their legal system. A convicted person can furthermore be eligible for early release if this is specified in the judgment by special clause. Such a clause was included for the first – and so far only – time in the Stakić Judgment (para. 463) and reads in part: 'The *then competent court* (Rule 104 of the Rules) shall review this sentence and if appropriate suspend the execution of the remainder of the punishment of imprisonment for life and grant early release, if necessary on probation, if: (I) 20 years have been served ...' (italics added). A possible explanation of the insertion of this clause may be the composition of the Stakić bench, which was composed of three civil judges. Much uncertainty in this field still exists: for instance, which authority decides on early release (the 'then competent court' or the 'national authority') after the Tribunals' mandate has expired and how can it be that someone with life imprisonment, like Stakić, can have his sentence reviewed after 20 years and possibly be set free, while someone else, like Jelisić, who received a prison term of 40 years, may possibly remain in prison for a longer period of time, likely after he has served two-thirds of his sentence? On this and other related issues, see Kok (2003), pp. 1059-1071.

[22] Article 24(1) ICTY Statute; Article 23(1) ICTR Statute; Rule 101(B)(iii) ICTY and ICTR RPE.

[23] Article 24(2) ICTY Statute; Article 23(2) ICTR Statute; Rule 101(B)(ii) ICTY and ICTR RPE.

[24] Rule 101(B)(i) and (ii) ICTY and ICTR RPE (as far as the mitigating circumstances are concerned, the provision stipulates that it includes the substantial cooperation with the Prosecutor by the convicted person before or after conviction). In addition, Rule 101(B)(iv) makes mention of 'the extent to which any penalty imposed by a court of any State on the convicted person for the same act has already been served, as referred to in Article 10, paragraph 3, of the Statute' as a factor relevant in determining sentence.

[25] The judges at the Nuremberg and Tokyo Tribunals were even given more discretion as they were allowed to impose any sentence they determined to be 'just', which included the death penalty. See Article 27 of the IMT Charter; Article 16 of the Tokyo Charter and Article II(3) of Control Council Law No. 10. The Nuremberg judges found 'just' twelve death sentences (including one in absentia) and the judges of the Tokyo Tribunal sentenced seven accused to death. See Beresford (2001), pp. 36-37.

circumstances.[26] How these factors have been interpreted with respect to crimes of a sexual violence nature will be discussed in section 4 on 'sentencing determinants' below.

Not only the above-mentioned factors play a role in constructing the appropriate sentence in every case: the objectives or purposes of punishment are, naturally, also very relevant. Attributing more weight to one sentencing purpose or another may influence the length of a sentence considerably. The Statutes and RPE of the Tribunals do not specify the reasons underlying the sentences for genocide, crimes against humanity or war crimes. However, ICTY and ICTR case law shows a myriad of sentencing purposes stemming from national criminal law and procedure, in particular, retribution, general and specific deterrence, rehabilitation, and protection of society.[27] This case law also reveals that, on the whole, retribution and general deterrence are among the sentencing purposes found to be most significant.[28] The term 'retribution' is used in the sense that the perpetrator is punished for what he did and that he gets a sentence proportionate to the crimes he committed. Retribution is therefore not to be understood as fulfilling a desire for revenge but as duly expressing the outrage of the international community at these crimes.[29] General deterrence implies that others will be dissuaded by committing similar crimes, and works best if people see that punishment for such crimes in fact results. In other words, impunity for international crimes no longer exists, and perpetrators will be brought to account. One of the main purposes of a sentence imposed by an international criminal tribunal is, as put forward in the *Nikolić* Sentencing Judgment, to 'influence the legal awareness of the accused, the surviving victims, their relatives, the witnesses and the general public in order to reassure them that the legal system is implemented and enforced. Additionally, the process of sentencing is intended to convey the message that globally accepted laws and rules have to be obeyed by everybody.'[30] In this regard, 'the educational task of punishment is

---

[26] See, *inter alia*, Rutaganda Judgment and Sentence, paras. 458-459; Ruggiu Judgment and Sentence, paras. 34-35; Kambanda Judgment and Sentence, paras. 29-31; Kayishema and Ruzindana Judgment, paras. 3-4.

[27] General deterrence serves to dissuade people from committing crimes; specific deterrence is aimed to deter the convicted person from recidivism; retribution or 'just deserts' provides punishment that must be proportionate to the crime's gravity and the moral guilt of the perpetrator; rehabilitation is aimed at the convicted person's treatment, re-education, or social reintegration; and, finally, protection of society is aimed at neutralising the convicted person. See, *inter alia*, Erdemović Judgment, para. 60; Kayishema and Ruzindana Judgment, para. 2; Ntakirutimana and Ntakirutimana Judgment and Sentence, paras. 882 and 887. See generally Nemitz (2001), pp. 87-101, for a discussion of the different sentencing purposes.

[28] See, *inter alia*, Rutaganda Judgment and Sentence, para. 456; Kambanda Judgment and Sentence, para. 28; Musema Judgment and Sentence, para. 986; Furundžija Judgment, para. 288; Naletilić and Martinović Judgment, para. 739; Simić Judgment, para. 33. In the Brđanin Judgment, it was held that the other aims (rehabilitation, social defence and restoration) have not yet achieved the same dominance as retribution and deterrence, even though they are important for achieving the goals of the Tribunal. Instead, such purposes have tended to be dealt with as mitigating or aggravating factors. See Brđanin Judgment, para. 1092.

[29] Aleksovski Appeal Judgment, para. 185.

[30] Nikolić Sentencing Judgment, para. 139.

especially important in international criminal law, considering that this area of law is rather new and that it needs to be "implanted" in the minds of the public all over the world'.[31] Arguably, general deterrence works better for high level perpetrators than for low level perpetrators. In addition, the United Nations Security Council determined that ending impunity by prosecuting those most responsible, thereby promoting national reconciliation and restoring peace, is among the main objectives of the Tribunals' existence.[32] However, it is anything but easy to unite the sentencing purposes with goals such as establishing national reconciliation and peace. For instance, given the distance between the Tribunals and the territory and people of Rwanda and the former Yugoslavia, it is questionable whether the Tribunals are at all able to achieve national reconciliation and peace. The crimes that were committed in Srebrenica and Kosovo a few years after the establishment of the Tribunals are proof of this. Perhaps the ICTY and ICTR were saddled with goals they were never able to live up to from the start.[33] Moreover, supranational criminal punishment is not the only mechanism which can be deployed to respond to large-scale crimes which shock the conscience of mankind. Depending on the goal or goals to be achieved, other mechanisms, such as a Truth and Reconciliation Commission, may be more appropriate.[34] This being said, it can be argued that the reason of the Tribunals' existence, as well as its purpose of sentencing, should instead be found primarily in the confirmation or imposition of the norm, that is, that the international community does not tolerate the commission of international crimes and that such crimes will be punished.[35]

2.2 ICC

The ICC Statute deals with sentencing matters in Articles 76, 77, 78 and 80, which provisions are further elaborated in Rule 145 of the ICC Rules of Procedure and Evidence in particular. The sentence must be pronounced in public and, wherever possible, in the presence of the accused.[36] A Trial Chamber may consider all relevant evidence in one procedure, but, unlike the Tribunals, the ICC Statute also provides the possibility of a separate sentencing procedure.[37] From Article 78(3) of the ICC Statute, it follows that, if a person has been convicted of more than one crime, the Court must pronounce a sentence for each crime and a joint sentence specifying the total period of

---

[31] Nemitz (2001), p. 127. Nemitz calls it 'affirmative general prevention', which, together with just deserts, should be the principal sentencing purposes in international criminal law.

[32] Security Council Resolution 827, *on the Establishment of the ICTY*, S/RES/827 (1993), 25 May 1993; Security Council Resolution 955, *on the Establishment of the ICTR*, S/RES/955, 8 November 1994. These objectives have also been recognised in case law: see, *inter alia*, Ruggiu Judgment and Sentence, paras. 32-33; Stakić Judgment, para. 891.

[33] Van Genugten (1995), p. 56.

[34] See further Haveman (2004), pp. 67-78.

[35] Kok and Van der Wilt (2004), pp. 60-63. See also Groenhuijsen (2004b), pp. 281-284.

[36] Article 76(2) ICC Statute.

[37] Article 76(2) ICC Statute states: '[T]he Trial Chamber *may* on its own motion and *shall*, at the request of the Prosecutor or the accused, hold a further hearing to hear any additional evidence or submissions relevant to the sentence, in accordance with the Rules of Procedure and Evidence' (italics added). See further Keller (2001), p. 74.

imprisonment. The total period of imprisonment can be *no less* than the highest individual sentence pronounced and may not exceed 30 years imprisonment, or a sentence of life imprisonment must be imposed. This practice reflects the totality of the perpetrator's criminal conduct well, because every conviction is part of and adds to the final sentence, and it has been argued that this practice should also be applied by the Tribunals.[38]

Thus, the Court may impose either: (1) imprisonment for a specified number of years, which may not exceed a maximum of 30 years; or (2) a term of life imprisonment when justified by the extreme gravity of the crime and the individual circumstances of the convicted person.[39] Rule 145(3) adds that the extreme gravity of a crime and the individual circumstances of the convicted person must be evidenced by the existence of one or more aggravating circumstances. ICC judges are thus forced to make a choice between two alternatives; the first alternative – imprisonment for a fixed number of years – being the most obvious option. The second alternative – life imprisonment – is only to be considered if the conditions mentioned (the extreme gravity of the crime and the individual circumstances, as evidenced by the existence of one or more aggravating circumstances) are fulfilled. The ICC thus has to differentiate between cases in which life imprisonment and cases in which temporary imprisonment may be imposed. The imposition of life imprisonment requires a higher threshold, namely, the finding of 'extreme gravity' of the crime, rather than the more general requirement of 'gravity' of the crime required for imprisonment for a fixed number of years.[40] It appears that the ICC, in contrast to the sentencing provisions of the Tribunals, provide some degree of specificity in this context, even though a rather broad discretion for the judges remains preserved.[41] In addition to imprisonment, the ICC can impose a fine or a forfeiture of proceeds, property and assets derived from the crime.[42] The imposition of a fine is new in the supranational criminal law context. Moreover, under the ICC regime, there is no link to national laws as a means to determine the sentence, thereby aiming to ensure a uniform penalties regime for all persons convicted by the Court.[43] As such, the Court will start with a clean slate, without having to worry about discrepancies in national jurisdictions on sentencing matters.[44]

Closely linked is the issue on national penalties and their imposition in national courts. Under pressure of several countries, the ICC Statute now contains a provision that, in national proceedings, States are allowed to impose the penalties prescribed by their national laws.[45] Sentences imposed by the ICC do not in any way affect these national penalties. This rule is troublesome in that it allows national courts in countries where the death penalty still exists to impose such a penalty, whereas the death penalty is precluded from both the Tribunals and the ICC sentencing regime. Different

---

[38] Nemitz (2001), pp. 125-126.

[39] Article 77(1) ICC Statute.

[40] Article 78(1) ICC Statute.

[41] Fife (1999a), p. 990.

[42] Article 77(2) ICC Statute. See further Chapter 7 on reparation to victims of sexual violence, section 4 on the ICC.

[43] Fife (1999a), p. 986.

[44] See further subsection 4.1 on general prison sentencing practice in national courts.

[45] Article 80 ICC Statute. See also Fife (1999b), pp. 1009-1014.

sentences for principal perpetrators – commonly prosecuted before the ICC and the Tribunals – and executioners – commonly prosecuted before national courts – creates a rather odd situation. For example, in Rwanda, the death penalty was executed on 24 April 1998, when 22 individuals were publicly executed by firing squad.[46] These persons were considered to be among the masterminds of the genocide.[47] Although more death sentences have been pronounced since this date,[48] no executions have followed since. None of the convicts sentenced to death were charged and convicted of sexual violence. It is hoped that sentences imposed by the ICC – limited to (life) imprisonment – will be an impetus for national courts to pursue the ICC sentencing example. In the long run, this will hopefully lead to a uniform sentencing practice for international crimes within both national and international courts, including preclusion of the death penalty.

Like the Tribunals, the ICC regime includes provisions related to credit for time served,[49] appeal and revision of sentences,[50] the enforcement of sentences[51] and review by the Court concerning reduction of sentences.[52]

---

46 BBC news, *Rwanda Going Ahead with Genocide Executions*, 24 April 1998. See also the commentary by Amnesty International on the execution of the 22 individuals: Amnesty International (1998).

47 Among the 22 convicts was Froduald Karamira, the former vice-president of the Mouvement Démocratique Républicain (MDR), convicted on charges of genocide and incitement to commit genocide. See Hirondelle News, *Analysis: Confronting Genocide with Country's Regular Courts* (by Gabriel Gabiro), 17 September 2003.

48 In a judgment dated 1 August 2003, 105 individuals (out of 142 accused) from Gikonko district (Butare) were convicted, of which 11 were sentenced to death. See Hirondelle News, *Analysis: Confronting Genocide with Country's Regular Courts* (by Gabriel Gabiro), 17 September 2003.

49 Article 78(2) ICC Statute.

50 Article 81(2) in conjunction with Article 83 ICC Statute (a sentence may be varied if the sentence is found to be disproportionate to the crime); Article 84 ICC Statute (a sentence may be revised under circumstances as prescribed in paragraph 1). See also Rules 150-153 ICC RPE (appeals against sentences) and Rules 159-161 ICC RPE (revision of sentence).

51 Articles 103-111 ICC Statute. Article 103(1)(a) ICC Statute reads: 'A sentence of imprisonment shall be served in a State designated by the Court from a list of States which have indicated to the Court their *willingness* to accept sentenced persons' (italics added). In paragraph (4), it is further stated: 'If no State is designated under paragraph 1, the sentence of imprisonment shall be served in a prison facility made available by the *host State*' (italics added). See also Rules 198-216 ICC RPE.

52 Article 110 ICC Statute states that the Court alone has the right to decide any reduction in sentence. Review of sentences may only take place when the person has served two-thirds of the sentence, or 25 years in the case of life imprisonment. Reduction of the sentence is possible if certain factors are present. See also Article 105 ICC Statute and Rules 223-224 ICC RPE. Compare the ICC situation with the practice before the Tribunals as explained above in subsection 2.1 on the ICTY and ICTR.

The sentencing determinants are laid down in Article 78(1) of the ICC Statute, which reads:

> In determining the sentence, the Court shall, in accordance with the Rules of Procedure and Evidence, take into account such factors as *the gravity of the crime and the individual circumstances of the convicted person.*[53]

This formulation is similar to the formulation contained in Articles 24(2) and 23(2) of the ICTY and ICTR Statutes, respectively.[54] Like the Statutes of the Tribunals, the ICC Statute is unclear as to how 'the gravity of the crime' and 'the individual circumstances of the convicted person' are to be understood. Moreover, the formulation used ('in accordance with the RPE' and 'such factors as') indicates that these two factors are not the only ones to be taken into account. Rule 145 of the ICC RPE ('Determination of Sentence') clarifies what other factors may be of importance, much more elaborately than its ICTY and ICTR counterparts, and reads:

> 1. In its determination of the sentence pursuant to article 78, paragraph 1, the Court shall:
>
>   (a) Bear in mind that the totality of any sentence of imprisonment and fine, as the case may be, imposed under article 77 must reflect the culpability of the convicted person;
>   (b) Balance all the relevant factors, including any mitigating and aggravating factors and consider the circumstances both of the convicted person and of the crime;
>   (c) *In addition to the factors mentioned in article 78, paragraph 1* [gravity of the crime and individual circumstances], give consideration, *inter alia*, to the extent of the damage caused, in particular the harm caused to the victims and their families, the nature of the unlawful behaviour and the means employed to execute the crime; the degree of participation of the convicted person; the degree of intent; the circumstances of manner, time and location; and the age, education, social and economic condition of the convicted person.
>
> 2. *In addition to the factors mentioned above*, the Court shall take into account, as appropriate:
>
>   (a) *Mitigating circumstances such as*:
>
>   (i) The circumstances falling short of constituting grounds for exclusion of criminal responsibility, such as substantially diminished mental capacity or duress;
>   (ii) The convicted person's conduct after the act, including any efforts by the person to compensate the victims and any co-operation with the Court;

---

[53] Italics added.

[54] As discussed above in subsection 2.1 on the ICTY and ICTR.

(b) *As aggravating circumstances:*

(i) Any relevant prior criminal convictions for crimes under the jurisdiction of the Court or of a similar nature;
(ii) Abuse of power or official capacity;
(iii) Commission of the crime where the victim is particularly defenceless;
(iv) Commission of the crime with particular cruelty or where there were multiple victims;
(v) Commission of the crime for any motive involving discrimination on any of the grounds referred to in article 21, paragraph 3;
(vi) *Other circumstances which, although not enumerated above, by virtue of their nature are similar to those mentioned.*

3. Life imprisonment may be imposed when justified by the extreme gravity of the crime and the individual circumstances of the convicted person, as evidenced by the existence of one or more aggravating circumstances.[55]

Like the Tribunals, the ICC's starting point was that no clear-cut sentences could be imposed on persons convicted of international crimes: sentencing guidelines were therefore not wanted. Although this was opposed by representatives of some countries, others felt that considerable discretion for the judges was needed to balance all the relevant factors on a case-by-case basis.[56] One commentator wrote that there were several reasons why ultimately an open list of sentencing factors was preferred:

> [O]ne could never pinpoint the exact punishment in years, months and days. Often different courts would differ in the determination of the sentence even in countries where there is a closed list. And it was pointed out that there might well be factors originally not foreseen but very important in a concrete case. So it was found necessary to achieve the right balance between specificity and flexibility.[57]

Therefore, the factors mentioned in Rule 145(1)(c) 'characterize the commission of the crime in a general manner without it necessarily being considered as mitigating or aggravating in nature'.[58] In other words, these factors can either aggravate or mitigate the accused's conduct, depending on the case at hand. This provision is open-ended, as signalled by the use of the words '*inter alia*'. Furthermore, in contrast to the sentencing provisions of the two Tribunals, the ICC has specifically enumerated the aggravating circumstances which should be taken into account when determining the penalty. Yet, the provision leaves scope for other aggravating circumstances not enumerated in the provision, but nevertheless of a similar nature, to be taken into account. Likewise, the mitigating circumstances mentioned are not exhaustive as evidenced by the use of the words 'such as', and, as in the case of the Tribunals, include cooperation with the Court.

---

[55] Italics added. For the negotiation history on Rule 145, see Fife (2001), pp. 557-565.
[56] Peglau (2001), p. 146.
[57] *Ibid.*
[58] *Ibid.*, p. 147.

Sentencing purposes are not explicitly mentioned in the ICC Statute or RPE itself. Some guidance can be found in the Preamble to the ICC Statute, which refers to retribution and deterrence by stating 'that the most serious crimes of concern to the international community as a whole must not go unpunished and that their effective prosecution must be ensured'. Furthermore, States Parties are 'determined to put an end to impunity for the perpetrators of these crimes and thus to contribute to the prevention of such crimes'. In addition, Rule 145(1)(a) lays down the principle that the sentence must always reflect the culpability of the convicted person. In other words, a sentencing factor such as general deterrence can never be given full priority.[59] Although it is hoped that, over time, deterrence of the crimes over which the ICC has jurisdiction is possible, this may, unfortunately, not be a realistic scenario. Thus, as with the ICTY and ICTR, the objectives of the ICC and its purposes of sentencing should be found in the confirmation or imposition of the norm, that is to say, that the international community does not tolerate the commission of international crimes and that such crimes must be punished. This purpose is explicitly laid down in the final phrase of the ICC Preamble, where it is stated that the State Parties are 'resolved to guarantee lasting respect for and the enforcement of international justice'.

3 The sentencing practice for sexual violence

What is the sentencing practice of the Tribunals with regard to sexual violence? First the Tribunals' statistics on sentencing will be given, followed by some preliminary results on the ways in which sexual violence has been prosecuted as well as the sentencing ranges imposed for sexual violence.

3.1 Sentencing statistics

Since the establishment of the ICTY, the Chambers have rendered judgment in 36 cases, involving 56 accused.[60] Of these 56 accused, 51 persons have been found guilty[61] and received (final) prison sentences ranging from 3 years to life imprisonment.[62] From these 51 individuals, 21 have been convicted, *inter alia*, for their involvement in crimes of a sexual violence nature – Tadić, Delić, Mucić, Furundžija, Blaškić, Kunarac, Kovač, Vuković, Todorović, Kvočka, Prcać, Kos, Radić, Žigić, Sikirica, Simić, Plavšić, Stakić,

---

[59] *Ibid.*, pp. 147-148.

[60] See 'The ICTY at a Glance'/'Key Figures of ICTY Cases' at http://www.un.org/icty (last visited May 2005).

[61] *Ibid.* Two accused were acquitted by the Trial Chamber, namely, Z. Delalić and D. Papić (confirmed on appeal). Three accused were acquitted by the Appeals Chamber, namely, Z. Kupreškić, M. Kupreškić, and V. Kupreškić.

[62] Kolundžija received a prison sentence of three years for persecution as a crime against humanity on the basis of a plea agreement (four other counts were dropped). Stakić is the only person who has received life imprisonment so far, i.e., for four counts of crimes against humanity and one count of violations of the laws and customs of war.

Nikolić, Češić and Brđanin[63] – which resulted in sentences ranging between 5 years and life imprisonment.[64] By 2008-2010,[65] the ICTY intends to have tried 128 to 138 individuals,[66] of which approximately 58 have been charged, *inter alia*, with crimes of a sexual violence nature, i.e., almost half of the total number of persons that will have been tried before the ICTY.[67] It must be observed that, for some of these 58 individuals, the indictment was withdrawn due to a lack of evidence against the accused,[68] the sexual violence charges were dropped in the course of a guilty plea,[69] or the case transferred to the national courts.[70] In addition, a few accused of sexual violence have died.[71]

---

[63] See sentencing Chart on sexual violence in this section and the Appendix for the charges on which these accused were convicted and the sentences they received. Note that several of these accused were also acquitted of some of the sexual violence crimes charged.

[64] Final sentences of five years imprisonment for sexual violence were handed down for D. Prcać (Kvočka et al. case) and M. Simić (who received two specific sentences of 5 years imprisonment for torture as a crime against humanity – of which one count included sexual violence – to run concurrently). A sentence of 28 years was handed down for Kunarac (Kunarac, Kovač and Vuković case).

[65] See Security Council Resolution 1503 (S/RES/1503 (2003)), adopted on 28 August 2003, in which the ICTR and ICTY were urged to complete all investigations by 2004, all trials by 2008 and all appeals by 2010.

[66] 128 Accused have appeared before the Tribunal and 10 accused are still at large. In total, the ICTY has indicted 162 individuals since its inception, of whom some have died or have had their indictment withdrawn. See 'The ICTY at a Glance'/'Key Figures of ICTY Cases' at http://www.un.org/icty (last visited May 2005).

[67] The following persons have been indicted by the ICTY for sexual violence (some of them have already been convicted): Duško Tadić, Delić, Mucić, Furundžija, Blaškić, Kunarac, Kovač, Vuković, Todorović, Kvočka, Prcać, Kos, Radić, Žigić, Simić, Sikirica, Plavšić, Stakić, Nikolić, Češić, Brđanin, Milosević, Rajić, Prlić, Stojić, Praljak, Petković, Corić, Pusić, Mladić, Karadžić, Meakić, Gruban, Fustar, P. Banović, N. Banović, Knezević, Zelenović, Gagović, Janjić, Stanković, Janković, Haradinaj, Balaj, Brahimaj, R. Delić, Stanisić, Seselj, Krajisnik, Pavković, Lazarević, Djordjević, Lukić, Talić, Raznjatović, Bralo, Martić, Dusan Tadić. It should be noted that, in the absence of ICTY statistics on sexual violence charges in particular and the changes in charges contained in indictments over time, it is difficult to state with certainty that the number of 58 persons is the exact number of people charged with sexual violence.

[68] See *The Prosecutor v. Banović, Banović, Fustar and Knežević*, Decision on Motion by the Prosecution for Withdrawal of Indictment against Nenad Banović, Case No. IT-95-8/1-PT, 10 April 2002. For a commentary on the withdrawal of this indictment, see De Brouwer (2005), pp. 135-138.

[69] See the Banović Sentencing Judgment. On the basis of a guilty plea, Predrag Banović was convicted to eight years in prison.

[70] *The Prosecutor v. Radovan Stanković*, Decision of Referral of Case Under Rule 11*bis*, Case No. IT-96-23/2-PT, 17 May 2005 (appeal pending). The Stanković case, which deals with charges of sexual violence only (Stanković was originally indicted in June 1996 with Zelenović, Janković, Kunarac, Kovač, Vuković, Gagović and Janjić (Foča case)), forms the first referral before the Tribunal of one of its indictments to a national court, i.e., the internationally composed War Crimes Chamber of the State Court of Bosnia and Herzegovina. Stanković, a 23-year-old Bosnian

The Rwanda Tribunal has a smaller number of accused in its dockets. Since the Tribunal was established, the Chambers have rendered judgment in nineteen cases, involving 25 accused.[72] Of these 25 individuals, 22 have been found guilty[73] and

---

Serb infantry soldier at the time, has been charged with the enslavement of nine non-Serb women and girls over a three-month period of time, and with the rape of two of the women. The Referral Bench was satisfied that neither the level of responsibility of the accused (he did not hold a leadership position) nor the gravity of the crimes alleged in the indictment (the crimes are limited in scope both geographically and temporally, and also in terms of the number of victims affected) were factors that would make a referral to the national authorities of Bosnia and Herzegovina inappropriate. The Referral Bench decided to grant the Prosecutor's Motion for referral to the authorities of Bosnia and Herzegovina, having: (1) considered the question of compatibility of the laws of Bosnia and Herzegovina with the Tribunal's Statute; (2) reviewed the laws applicable to the events in 1992 in Bosnia and Herzegovina; (3) reviewed the prospects for the accused to receive a fair trial before the War Crimes Chamber of the State Court of Bosnia and Herzegovina; (4) satisfied itself that adequate measures were in place for the protection of witnesses, and (5) satisfied itself that the death penalty would not be imposed. With regard to Janković, who was initially jointly indicted with Zelenović, Stanković, Kunarac, Kovač, Vuković, Gagović and Janjić for sexual violence crimes primarily (Kunarac, Kovač and Vuković case), the Prosecutor filed an 11*bis* motion on 29 November 2004 requesting that a Trial Chamber be appointed to review the Prosecution's request to refer the case to the authorities of Bosnia and Herzegovina, but on 14 March 2005, Janković was transferred to the ICTY Detention Unit and, on 18 March 2005 he had his initial appearance before the court. See ICTY Press Release, *Gojko Jankovic Transferred to ICTY Detention Unit*, JP/MOW/948e, 14 March 2005; ICTY Press Release, *Initial Appearance of Gojko Jankovic Scheduled for 18 March 2005*, CVO/MOW/PA213e, 16 March 2005.

71 Gagović and Janjić are deceased. They were originally indicted in June 1996 with Zelenović, Stanković, Kunarac, Kovač, Vuković, and Janković (Kunarac, Kovač and Vuković case). Talić (Krajina case) also died.

72 The Trials conducted in the *first mandate* of the ICTR (May 1995 - May 1999) led to six judgments involving the following seven accused: J-P Akayesu, Bourgmestre of Taba (2 September 1998); J. Kambanda, Prime Minister (4 September 1998, guilty plea); O. Serushago, Businessman and Interahamwe Leader (5 February 1999, guilty plea); C. Kayishema, Prefect of Kibuye, and O. Ruzindana, Businessman (21 May 1999, joinder); G. Rutaganda, Businessman and Second Vice-president of Interahamwe (6 December 1999); A. Musema, Businessman (27 January 2000). The first trial at the ICTR started in January 1997, following the arrival of the first accused to Arusha in May 1996, arguably explaining (in part) its slow start. The judgments in the cases of the first mandate are now final. The trials conducted during the *second mandate* (May 1999 - May 2003) led to nine judgments involving the following fourteen accused: G. Ruggiu, RTLM Journalist (1 June 2000, guilty plea); I. Bagilishema, Bourgmestre of Mabanza (7 June 2001); G. Ntakirutimana, Doctor, and E. Ntakirutimana, Pastor (21 February 2003, joinder); L. Semanza, Bourgmestre of Bicumbi (15 May 2003); E. Niyitegeka, Minister of Information (15 May 2003); J. Kajelijeli, Bourgmestre of Rukingo (1 December 2003); F. Nahimana, RTLM Director, H. Ngeze, Kangura Editor, and J-B Barayagwiza, Director Ministry of Foreign Affairs (3 December 2003, joinder 'Media case'); J. Kamuhanda, Minister of Culture and Education (22 January 2004); A. Ntagerura, Minister of Transport, E. Bagambiki, Prefect of Cyangugu, and S. Imanishimwe, Lieutenant in FAR (25 February 2004, joinder 'Cyangugu case'). Note that, when compared with the first mandate, the number of accused convicted in the second mandate was

received (final) prison sentences ranging from six years imprisonment to life imprisonment.[74] Out of these 22 convicts, eight individuals – Akayesu, Semanza, Niyitegka, Nahimana, Barayagwiza, Ngeze, Gacumbitsi and Muhimana – were sentenced, among other things, for their involvement in crimes of a sexual violence nature, either under Article 6(1) or Article 6(3) or both.[75] Although Musema was initially convicted of sexual violence, his conviction was quashed on appeal. Four other individuals – Bagilishema, Niyitegeka, Kajelijeli and Kamuhanda – were acquitted of sexual violence charged[76] whereas, in some other cases, evidence of sexual violence only emerged during trial and, for this reason, was not taken into account in sentencing.[77] Additionally, in yet another case – involving the accused Serushago – where sexual violence was charged and the accused pleaded guilty, the plea bargaining agreement included the withdrawal of the sexual violence crimes charged.[78] Furthermore, in some cases, charges of sexual violence were withdrawn before the start of the trial.[79] Finally, for some trials, NGOs had documented the accused's

---

doubled. The trials held during the *third mandate* (2003-2007), so far, include sentences for the following individuals: S. Gacumbitsi, Bourgmestre of Rusumo commune (17 June 2004); E. Ndindabahizi, Minister of Finance (15 July 2004); V. Rutaganira, Councillor in Gishyita Commune (14 March 2005, guilty plea); M. Muhimana, Councillor (28 April 2005). See ICTR Fact Sheet No. 1 'The Tribunal at a Glance' at http://www.ictr.org (last visited May 2005). See also: Completion Strategy of the International Criminal Tribunal for Rwanda, 19 November 2004 (on file with the author). Situation as of 1 May 2005.

[73] Three individuals were found not guilty and were therefore acquitted: i.e., I. Bagilishema, A. Ntagerura, and E. Bagambiki.

[74] A sentence of six years imprisonment was handed down for V. Rutaganira who pleaded guilty to extermination as a crime against humanity. Sentences of life imprisonment have been given in a number of cases, *inter alia*: J-P. Akayesu, J. Kambanda, C. Kayishema, G. Rutaganda, A. Musema, E. Niyitegeka, F. Nahimana, H. Ngeze, J. Kamuhanda and E. Ndindabahizi.

[75] See sentencing Chart on sexual violence in this section and the Appendix for the charges on which these accused were convicted and the sentences they received. Note that several of these accused were also acquitted of some of the sexual violence crimes charged.

[76] Bagilishema was charged with, among other crimes, rape as a serious violation of Article 3 Common to the Geneva Conventions and Additional Protocol II, but was acquitted on all counts and released. The decision was upheld on appeal. J. Kajelijeli and J. Kamuhanda were found not guilty for rape as a crime against humanity. The Prosecutor did not appeal Kajelijeli's nor Kamuhanda's acquittal for rape. E. Niyitegeka was acquitted for rape as a crime against humanity. He was, however, found guilty for the sexual mutilation of a dead man and woman under other inhumane acts as a crime against humanity.

[77] See the cases of C. Kayishema & O. Ruzindana and G. Rutaganda, in which evidence of sexual violence came up during trial, was subsequently included in the records, but did not result in a conviction thereof.

[78] See the Serushago case, in which the accused pleaded guilty to genocide and murder, extermination and torture as crimes against humanity, but not to rape as a crime against humanity. The count of rape as a crime against humanity was subsequently withdrawn by the Prosecutor.

[79] This happened in respect of E. Bagambiki and S. Imanishimwe in the so-called 'Cyangugu case' (note that E. Bagambiki was acquitted by the Trial Chamber on all counts and that a commitment was made to open new proceedings against Bagilishema and Imanishimwe to

responsibility for sexual violence, but charges of sexual violence were not included in ICTR indictments even so.[80] On the basis of these numbers, the ICTR record on rape convictions is poor: with regard to rape as genocide and/or a crime against humanity, only four persons (one sixth of the total number of judgments rendered) were convicted (Akayesu, Semanza, Gacumbitsi and Muhimana), and the number is the same for rape acquittals (Musema, Kajelijeli, Kamuhanda and Niyitegeka). These poor rape conviction results are striking in light of the hundreds of thousands of rapes committed during the genocide. The length of sentences imposed for sexual violence crimes ranges between seven years and life imprisonment.[81] By the end of the ICTR's mandate (2008-2010), the Tribunal hopes to have prosecuted an approximate number of 89 individuals, although more realistic numbers indicate that the total number of persons tried will be between 65 and 70.[82] From the approximate 71 persons who appeared, are appearing, or

---

prosecute them for sexual violence only, but this was never done), and with regard to T. Renzaho, F. Karera and L. Rusatira.

[80] The accused include Kanyabashi, Ndayambaje, Ntezirayayo and Nsabimana (Butare case). See critique by the Coalition for Women's Human Rights in Conflict Situations in their letter to Prosecutor Carla Del Ponte, 12 March 2003.

[81] Semanza received a sentence of seven years imprisonment for the specific count of rape as a crime against humanity, which was upheld on appeal. A sentence of life imprisonment was given in the case of J-P. Akayesu where sexual violence was charged, among other charges, as a form of genocide. Muhimana received a sentence of life imprisonment for genocide, which included sexual violence conduct, and life imprisonment for rape as a crime against humanity.

[82] In addition to the 19 judgments mentioned above, 7 trials are in progress, involving a total of 24 accused: i.e., Pauline Nyiramasuhuko, Minister of Family and Women's Affairs, and A.S. Ntahobali, Interahamwe Leader, and S. Nsabimana, Prefect of Butare, and A. Nteziryayo, Prefect of Butare, and J. Kanyabashi, Bourgmestre of Ngoma, and E. Ndayambaje, Bourgmestre of Muganza (joinder, 'Butare case'); T. Bagosora, Director of Cabinet, Ministry of Defence, and G. Kabiligi, Brigadier-General FAR, and A. Ntabakuze, Battalion Commander FAR, A. Nsengiyumva, Lieutenant-Colonel FAR (joinder, 'Military I case'); C. Bizimungu, Minister of Foreign Affairs, and J. Mugenzi, Minister of Health, and J. Bicamumpaka, Minister of Commerce, and P. Mugiraneza, Minister of Civil Service (joinder, 'Government II case'); E. Karemera, President of National Assembly, S-G of MRND, and M. Ngirumpatse, Minister of Interior, V-P of MRND, J. Nzirorera, Minister of Education, and A. Rwamakuba, D-G of Ministry of Foreign Affairs, President of MRND (joinder, 'Government I case'); A. Simba, Lieutenant Colonel; A. Ndindilyimana, Chief of Staff of Gendarmerie Nationale, and F.-X. Nzuwonemeye, Commander of the 42nd Battalion, and I. Sagahutu, Second-in-command of the Reconnaissance Battalion, and A. Bizimungu, Chief of Staff of Rwandan Army (joinder, 'Military II case'); A. Seromba, Catholic Priest. Furthermore, 17 accused are waiting for their trial to commence at the UN Detention Facility in Arusha (5 cases will be transferred to national jurisdictions for trial); 14 indictees are at large, but the Prosecutor intends to transfer four accused to national jurisdictions for trial; and 16 other targeted investigations were ongoing, but have been completed by the end of 2004. This brings the total number of individuals who will be tried before the ICTR to about 89 people. The actual number of people tried will depend on the ICTR's ability to locate the suspects and the willingness of States to cooperate with the Tribunal. In addition, some of the suspects may have died. It is therefore to be expected that the number of trials will involve less that twenty-six persons from the latter two groups (ten and sixteen). It has

still have to appear before court,[83] 35 individuals (i.e., half of the indictments) have been charged with, among other things, crimes of a sexual violence nature.[84]

Sentences for sexual violence have thus been handed down for a number of individuals tried before the ICTY (21) and ICTR (9). In the Appendix, a short overview of these ICTY and ICTR judgments on sexual violence can be found. In addition, the sentencing results on sexual violence have been taken up in the Chart on the next page (for abbreviations of the different convicts, see table below).

Abbreviations ICTY and ICTR Convicts

ICTY Convicts				ICTR Convicts	
Tad	Tadić	Kos	Kos	Aka	Akayesu
Del	Delić	Rad	Radić	Mus	Musema
Muc	Mucić	Zig	Žigić	Sem	Semanza
Fur	Furundžija	Sik	Sikirica	Niy	Niyitegeka
Bla	Blaškić	Sim	Simić	Nah	Nahimana
Kun	Kunarac	Pla	Plavšić	Bar	Barayagwiza
Kov	Kovač	Sta	Stakić	Nge	Ngeze
Vuk	Vuković	Nic	Nikolić	Gac	Gacumbitsi
Tod	Todorović	Ces	Češić	Muh	Muhimana
Kvo	Kvočka	Brd	Brđanin		
Prc	Prcać				

been estimated that, by 2008, the Tribunal may have completed trial involving between 65 and 70 persons. Furthermore, 41 cases (including the five detainees awaiting trial and the four indictees still at large) – not falling within the leadership category, but still important enough to be tried – will be transferred to Rwanda and other national jurisdictions for adjudication. This measure was found necessary in order to comply with the completion strategy and to support the rule of law in Rwanda. These figures have been compiled from statistics listed in the ICTR Fact Sheet No. 1 'The Tribunal at a Glance' (http://www.ictr.org), the ICTR Newsletter No. 8, June 2004, and the Completion Strategy of the International Criminal Tribunal for Rwanda, 19 November 2004. Situation on 1 May 2005.

[83] This number is based on the 25 persons who have already been tried, the 24 persons whose trial is pending, the 17 persons awaiting trial, and the 10 accused at large. Five persons awaiting trial will, however, be prosecuted before a national court, but it is not clear who these persons are and whether they were charged with sexual violence. Situation on 1 May 2005.

[84] The following persons have been indicted by the ICTR for sexual violence (some of them have already been convicted or acquitted): J-P. Akayesu, A. Musema, L. Semanza, E. Niyitegeka, F. Nahimana, J-B. Barayagwiza, H. Ngeze, J. Kajelijeli, J. Kamuhanda, S. Gacumbitsi, M. Muhimana, P. Nyiramasuhuko, A.S. Ntahobali, C. Bizimungu, A. Bizimungu, A. Ndindlilyimana, F-X. Nzuwonemeye, I. Sagahutu, P. Bisengimana, J. Mpambara, S. Bikindi, J.B. Gatete, J. Nzabarinda, A. Bizimana, E. Karemera, C. Nzabonimana, M. Ngirumpatse, A. Rwamakuba, J. Nzirorera, F. Kabuga (at large), P. Mpiranya (at large), I. Bagilishema and O. Serushago. Sexual violence charges were withdrawn before the start of the trial with regard to E. Bagambiki, S. Imanishimwe, T. Renzaho, F. Karera and L. Rusatira.

Chart on Sentencing in Cases of Sexual Violence

CONVICTS	Tad	Del	Muc	Fur #	Bla	Kun #	Kov #	Vuk #	Tod	Kvo	Prc	Kos	Rad	Zig	Sik
GENOCIDE (ARTICLE 4 ICTY STATUTE AND ARTICLE 2 ICTR STATUTE)															
(a) killing															
(b) bodily or mental harm															
(c) conditions of life															
(d) preventing births															
(e) transferring children															
CRIMES AGAINST HUMANITY (ARTICLE 5 ICTY STATUTE AND ARTICLE 3 ICTR STATUTE)															
(c) enslavement						x	x*								
(f) torture						x*		x*							
(g) rape						x*,x-,x	x*	x*							
(h) persecution									10	x	x	x	x	x	15
(i) other inhumane acts	10*														
GRAVE BREACHES OF THE GENEVA CONVENTIONS OF 1949 (ARTICLE 2 ICTY STATUTE)															
(b) torture		15*,15-													
(b) inhumane treatment	9*		7-		x										
(c) wilfully causing great suffering or serious injury to body or health	9*		7*												
rape as an independent crime															
VIOLATIONS OF THE LAWS OR CUSTOMS OF WAR (ARTICLE 3 ICTY STATUTE / COMMON ARTICLE 3(A), (C))															
3(a) violence to life and person, in particular … cruel treatment …	9*		_7*;7-_		_x_										
3(a) violence to life and person, in particular … torture …		_15*,15-_		10*		x*,x+		x*					x		
3(c) outrages upon personal dignity, in particular, humiliating and degrading treatment				8*			x*								
rape as an independent crime						x*,x-, x+,x	x*	x*							
VIOLATIONS OF ARTICLE 3 COMMON TO THE GENEVA CONVENTIONS AND OF ADDITIONAL PROTOCOL II (ARTICLE 4 ICTR STATUTE)															
4(a) violence to life, health and physical or mental well-being of persons, in particular … cruel treatment such as torture, mutilation or any form of corporal punishment															
4(e) outrages upon personal dignity, in particular humiliating and degrading treatment, rape, enforced prostitution and any form of indecent assault															
rape as an independent crime															
SENTENCE	25	18	9	10	9	28	20	12	10G	7	5	6	20	25	15G

x : one single sentence has been imposed for, *inter alia*, the crime(s) marked with x
number : the number of years imposed for each count
number/x : count dismissed on appeal
: individual charged with sexual violence solely
• : conviction for sexual violence quashed on appeal

Sim	Pla	Sta	Nic	Ces	Brd	Aka	Mus •	Sem	Niy	Nah	Bar	Nge	Gac	Muh	CONVICTS
GENOCIDE (ARTICLE 4 ICTY STATUTE AND ARTICLE 2 ICTR STATUTE)															
															(a) killing
						Life	x						x	Life	(b) bodily or mental harm
															(c) conditions of life
															(d) preventing births
															(e) transferring children
CRIMES AGAINST HUMANITY (ARTICLE 5 ICTY STATUTE AND ARTICLE 3 ICTR STATUTE)															
															(c) enslavement
5;5								10*							(f) torture
				x		15	x	7*					x	Life	(g) rape
	11	x	20		x					x	x	x			(h) persecution
						10			x						(i) other inhumane acts
GRAVE BREACHES OF THE GENEVA CONVENTIONS OF 1949 (ARTICLE 2 ICTY STATUTE)															
					x										(b) torture
															(b) inhumane treatment
															(c) wilfully causing great suffering or serious injury to body or health
															rape as an independent crime
VIOLATIONS OF THE LAWS OR CUSTOMS OF WAR (ARTICLE 3 ICTY STATUTE / COMMON ARTICLE 3(A), (C))															
															3(a) violence to life and person, in particular … cruel treatment …
															3(a) violence to life and person, in particular … torture …
				x											3(c) outrages upon personal dignity, in particular, humiliating and degrading treatment
															rape as an independent crime
VIOLATIONS OF ARTICLE 3 COMMON TO THE GENEVA CONVENTIONS AND OF ADDITIONAL PROTOCOL II (ARTICLE 4 ICTR STATUTE)															
								*10**							4(a) violence to life, health and physical or mental well-being of persons, in particular ... cruel treatment such as torture, mutilation or any form of corporal punishment
															4(e) outrages upon personal dignity, in particular humiliating and degrading treatment, rape, enforced prostitution and any form of indecent assault
															rape as an independent crime
5G	11G	(Life)	20G	18G	(32)	Life	Life	35	Life	(Life)	(35)	(Life)	(30)	(Life)	SENTENCE

*/-/+ : cumulative conviction on the basis of the same conduct
Sentence : includes both Trial Chamber and Appeals Chamber sentence
(Sentence) : appeal pending
G : conviction on the basis of a guilty plea
[hatched] : not applicable

3.2 Sentencing results

The Chart on sentencing in cases of sexual violence, read together with the case law overview on sexual violence in the Appendix and the Chapters contained in Part I addressing the sexual violence convictions in more detail, show that many different forms of sexual violence have been prosecuted before the Tribunals as genocide, crimes against humanity and war crimes (sexual mutilations (including of corpes) and threats thereof; oral, anal and vaginal rapes; multiple and gang rapes; sexualised torture; sexual slavery; persecutional rapes based on gender and/or ethnicity; forced nudity and rapes with objects). Often, similar acts have been prosecuted under different counts. Furthermore, sexual violence was committed against both men and women; someone can be held responsible for rape as an individual or a superior, even if that person is not the physical perpetrator himself; and that responsibility can also be attributed if the rapes occurred as a natural and foreseeable consequence of a joint criminal enterprise.

The differences and similarities in sentencing between the ICTY and ICTR become clear as well. Firstly, within the ICTR, sexual violence has been successfully prosecuted as genocide, accumulating in sentences of 30 years or life imprisonment. This is not the case before the ICTY, but the ICTY has laid down charges of sexual violence as genocide, and convictions may therefore still be rendered in the future. Secondly, both Tribunals have a considerable number of convictions for sexual violence as a crime against humanity. The many convictions for sexual violence as persecution stand out, especially the ones within the ICTY, where the accused were convicted on the basis of a guilty plea for persecution, used as a catch-all category covering a broad range of crimes, including rape and other forms of sexual violence. Thirdly, whereas the ICTY has seen relatively many convictions for sexual violence as grave breaches and violations of the laws and customs of war, the ICTR has only convicted one person of sexual violence as a war crime. The ICTR cannot prosecute individuals for grave breaches (as the conflict is deemed internal), and, although the armed conflict in Rwanda was internal and meets the requirements of Common Article 3 as well as Additional Protocol II thereto, it has on the whole been difficult to prove that an accused actively supported the war effort. The only conviction for sexual violence on the basis of Article 4(a) of the ICTR Statute was made on appeal in the *Semanza* case.

Within each Tribunal some observations on sentencing in cases of sexual violence can be made as well. In this respect, it should be noted that, within the ICTY, more convictions for sexual violence under Article 3 (violations of the laws or customs of war) have been made, than under Article 2 (grave breaches). This tendency can be explained by the fact that proof of the international character of the conflict under Article 2 has generally been considered difficult, whereas Article 3 requires proof that the crime was committed in either an international or internal armed conflict and was closely related to the armed conflict. In addition, as said above, many convictions resulted on the basis of persecution as a crime against humanity, including, among other charges, sexual violence. Summarising, the ICTY has found individuals guilty of sexual violence as crimes against humanity, grave breaches and violations of the laws or customs of war, but not genocide. The ICTR has rendered judgments on sexual violence as constituting genocide and crimes against humanity, and only once on the basis of Article 4 (violations of Article 3 Common to the Geneva Conventions and of Additional Protocol II).

3.2.1 Sentencing ranges

Drawing any meaningful conclusions as to the sentencing ranges for sexual violence from the overview in the Appendix, the Chart on sentencing in cases of sexual violence, and the description of the crimes as found in Chapters 1-3 needs to be done in a very cautious manner for the following reasons:

1. The case law on sexual violence within the supranational criminal setting is still minimal (a total of 29 convicts only) and the number of individuals convicted of (more or less) similar crimes is even less. For this reason, the sexual violence conduct which formed the basis for each charge proven (e.g., other inhumane acts as crimes against humanity) needs to be weighed against the sexual violence conduct proven for the same charge in another case (e.g., other inhumane acts as crimes against humanity). Only if the intensity of the crime is reasonably similar in both situations, meaningful conclusions may be drawn from such a comparison.

2. In most cases, no specific sentences were given for individual counts, but instead single sentences of a fixed term or life imprisonment were imposed to describe the totality of the accused's conduct. In addition, in most of the cases in which single sentences were imposed, sexual violence only formed part of the crimes comprising the total sentence, thus making it difficult to point out the impact of the sexual violence conduct on the composite sentence. An exception would be those cases in which a single sentence was given for one proven count only, but most of these convictions were made on the basis of a guilty plea for persecution as a crime against humanity, which usually accommodates a plurality of crimes. Another exception could be found for those cases which deal with sexual violence only and where the single sentence is the result of multiple convictions on the basis of the same conduct. If the underlying conduct does not consist of more than one type of criminal conduct, the composite crime based on a multiplicity of convictions may be slightly more severe than in the case of one conviction for one count only, but the difference will be minimal. Despite these reservations, it is at least possible to ascertain general ranges of sentences for the specific sentences imposed.[85]

[85] In the Semanza Judgment and Sentence (paras. 563-564), the Chamber made such an effort: '... the practice of awarding a single sentence for the totality of an accused's conduct makes it difficult to determine the range of sentences for each specific crime. [Yet] it is possible to ascertain general ranges of sentences ... Principal perpetrators convicted of either genocide or extermination as a crime against humanity, or both, have been punished with sentences ranging from fifteen years' imprisonment to life imprisonment. Secondary or indirect forms of participation have generally resulted in a lower sentence. ... *In the jurisprudence of the two Tribunals, rape as a crime against humanity has resulted in specific sentences between twelve years [Kunarac] and fifteen years [Akayesu].* Torture as a crime against humanity has been punished with specific sentences between five years and twelve years. Murder as a crime against humanity has been punished by specific fixed term sentences ranging from twelve years to twenty years. In other cases, convictions for these crimes have formed part of a single sentence of a fixed term or of life imprisonment for the totality of the conduct of the Accused' (italics added). See also the Gacumbitsi Judgment, para. 354.

3. Both the role or responsibility of the convict and the mitigating and aggravating circumstances involved have a considerable bearing on the final sentence imposed and differ per case. A study on sentences imposed by the ICTY indicated that, generally speaking, persons with high-level responsibility received longer sentences than low-ranking individuals; that some aggravating circumstances, such as the magnitude of the crimes committed and the zeal with which they were committed resulted in lengthier sentences, and that the mitigating circumstance of the guilty plea in particular tended to reduce the length of the sentence.[86] These factors have to be taken into account when sentencing ranges for sexual violence are explained in this and the following section.

With these provisos, some preliminary observations can be made with regard to sexual violence as genocide, a crime against humanity, a grave breach, a violation of the laws or customs of war and a violation of Article 3 Common to the Geneva Conventions and of Additional Protocol II, which will be discussed below.

3.2.1.1 Sexual violence as genocide

Sexual violence constituting serious bodily or mental harm qualifying as genocide has resulted in sentences of life imprisonment (Akayesu, Musema and Muhimana) and a sentence of 30 years (Gacumbitsi). It should be noted, however, that Musema's conviction for sexual violence was quashed on appeal and that sex crimes in the *Akayesu*, *Musema*, *Gacumbitsi* and *Muhimana* cases were not the only crimes which led to convictions of genocide resulting in a life term or 30 years imprisonment. However, given the large number of genocide convictions leading to high fixed sentences or life imprisonment, it can be readily assumed that such sentences are imposed also if the underlying crimes concern sexual violence only. The Trial Chamber in *Akayesu* specifically held that rape and sexual violence 'constitute genocide in the same way as any other act as long as they were committed with the specific intent to destroy, in whole or in part, a particular group, targeted as such'.[87] Indeed, in the *Muhimana* case, the evidence consisted for the most part of sexual violence, which led to a sentence of imprisonment for the remainder of Muhimana's life as a result of his conviction for rape as genocide.

3.2.1.2 Sexual violence as a crime against humanity

Enslavement: so far, only Kunarac and Kovač have been sentenced for sexual violence constituting the crime against humanity of enslavement, namely, to 28 and 20 years, respectively. When comparing the sentences received by Kunarac and Kovač and the sentence received by Vuković (12 years), who was cumulatively convicted for raping a 15-year-old girl, it may be argued that a conviction for enslavement by means of sexual

---

[86] Meernik and King (2003), pp. 747-748. According to this study, the average sentence for high level individuals is 381 months, for medium level individuals 180 months, and for low level individuals 156,6 months.

[87] Akayesu Judgment, para. 731.

violence bears significantly on the final sentence imposed. Whereas Vuković 'only' raped a 15-year-old girl, Kovač and Kunarac repeatedly raped women, whom they enslaved, forced to dance naked, and lent and sold to others. Although none of these men occupied high level positions, those the Tribunals primarily aim to prosecute, the *Kunarac, Kovač and Vuković* Trial Chamber made clear that 'lawless opportunists should expect no mercy, no matter how low their position in the chain of command may be'.[88] This raises the question to what extent the sentences would have been more severe in cases where the accused were the political or military masterminds behind the conflicts and atrocities.

Torture: In the *Simić* case, a conviction for torture as a crime against humanity was rendered on the basis of a guilty plea for Simić's threats to mutilate a man's penis, which was punished with five years imprisonment. Semanza received a sentence of ten years for instigating torture by rape, but the conviction also included torture other than rape, making it difficult to establish the sentence for the rape conviction separately. Vuković raped a 15-year-old girl and for this conduct he was multiply convicted, including rape as torture, and received a single sentence of twelve years. Although Kunarac was also convicted of torture as a crime against humanity on the basis of multiple rapes and aiding and abetting others to gang rape women, the conviction forms part of a number of other convictions, and therefore no conclusions may be drawn from it. Thus, sentences for torture have been rendered ranging from five to a maximum of twelve years. The difference in sentencing can be explained by the underlying conduct (threat to sexually mutilate and rape, which in one case included other forms of torture). Furthermore, Simić received 5 years on the basis of a guilty plea. Being the physical perpetrator of rape (Vuković) or the instigator (Semanza) did not seem to bear significantly on the sentence imposed.

Rape: specific sentences for rape as a crime against humanity have been imposed in three cases resulting in 7 years (Semanza), 15 years (Akayesu) and life imprisonment (Muhimana). As Semanza and Akayesu shared quite some similarities (both were mayors and instigated the rape of Tutsi women and neither of them physically committed rape), the difference in sentence may be explained by the number of victims. However, whereas the Prosecutor in the *Akayesu* case had requested life imprisonment for the multiple rapes committed at Taba commune and 15 years was awarded instead, Muhimana was convicted for a plurality of rapes committed by himself and others whom he aided and abetted. This difference in sentencing is striking. Furthermore, Vuković was cumulatively convicted of rape as a crime against humanity on the basis of the rape of a 15-year-old girl for which he received a 12-year sentence. Other cases in which convictions for rape as a crime against humanity were rendered only formed part of a larger package of crimes. Therefore, sentences for rape as a crime against humanity have resulted in 7 years to life imprisonment.

Persecution: sentences have been rendered of between 5 years and life imprisonment. Although there were 10 cases in which individuals were convicted of persecution as a crime against humanity, which incorporated, among other crimes, sexual violence, the accused were convicted of a number of other crimes as well, which makes it difficult to attach any conclusions to these results at all. In addition, in four

---

[88] ICTY Press Release, *Judgement of Trial Chamber II in the Kunarac, Kovac and Vukovic Case*, JL/P.I.S./566-e, 22 February 2001.

cases – Todorović (10 years), Sikirica (15 years), Plavšić (11 years) and Nikolić (20 years) – persecution formed the only count on which the accused were convicted. In these four cases, other factors influenced the outcome of the sentences considerably, such as the mitigating circumstances (guilty plea and cooperation with the Prosecutor).

Other inhumane acts: resulted in sentences of 10 years. The *Tadić* and *Akayesu* cases are the only ones with specific convictions on this charge. In *Niyitegeka*, the conviction for other inhumane acts formed part of many other crimes of which Niyitegeka was convicted. The crimes involved included oral sex, forced nudity and sexual mutilation.

3.2.1.3 Sexual violence as a grave breach

Torture: Delić was convicted of torture as a grave breach twice, each time for raping one woman multiple times, which cumulated in two sentences of 15 years. Brđanin was also convicted of sexual violence as the grave breach of torture, but this conviction was part of a broader set of crimes he was convicted of.

Inhumane treatment: both Mucić (7 years) and Tadić (9 years) were convicted of sexual violence as inhumane treatment for forcing prisoners to commit fellatio on each other: Mucić as a superior, Tadić for aiding and abetting. Additionally, Tadić was held responsible for the fact that one prisoner was ordered to sexually mutilate another prisoner's testicle. Blaškić was also held responsible as a superior for rapes as inhumane treatment, but the conviction formed part of a set of other crimes.

Wilfully causing great suffering or serious injury to body or health: Tadić was convicted under this heading for forcing two prisoners to commit fellatio on each other and for having one of them sexually mutilate another prisoner's testicle (9 years) and Mucić was convicted for ordering the placement of a burning fuse cord around the genital areas of two detainees (7 years).

3.2.1.4 Sexual violence as a violation of the laws or customs of war

Cruel treatment: sentences of 7 and 9 years were awarded for this crime. The convictions were based on forcing persons to commit fellatio on each other (Mucić, 7 years), forcing a person to place a burning fuse cord around the genital areas (Mucić, 7 years) and forcing persons to commit fellatio on each other and to sexually mutilate another person (Tadić, 9 years).

Torture: sentences range between 10 years and 15 years. Furundžija was convicted of torture as a co-perpetrator of the rape of a woman by his colleague and for the forced observance of this rape by a male friend of the woman (10 years), and Delić was convicted for subjecting two women to multiple rapes himself (15 years, twice). Vuković was cumulatively convicted for the rape of a 15-year-old girl, which included a count of torture as a violation of the laws or customs of war, which resulted in a 12-year sentence. From other cases, no meaningful conclusions can be drawn.

Outrages upon personal dignity, in particular humiliating and degrading treatment: the only specific conviction so far rendered accumulated in a sentence of 8 years for Furundžija as an aider and abetter in the rape of a woman and the forced observance of this rape by a male friend. From other cases, no meaningful conclusion may be drawn for this crime.

Rape as an independent crime (Article 3 of the ICTY Statute): although Kunarac, Kovač and Vuković were convicted under this heading, the counts formed part of a single sentence, and therefore no conclusions can be drawn as to the sentence range. An exception would be the sentence imposed on Vuković, as it was based on multiple conviction on the basis of the same conduct consisting of the rape of a 15-year-old girl, resulting in a sentence of 12 years.

3.2.1.5 Sexual violence as a violation of Article 3 common to the 1949 Geneva Conventions and of 1977 Additional Protocol II

Violence to life, health and physical or mental well-being of persons, in particular cruel treatment such as torture, mutilation or any form of corporal punishment (Article 4(a) of the ICTR Statute): on appeal, Semanza was convicted under this heading for, *inter alia*, instigating the rape and torture of Victim A. Although the Appeals Chamber did not clearly stipulate the sentence under this count, the conviction was made on the basis of the law on cumulative convictions: before the Trial Chamber, the same conduct had led to convictions for rape and torture as crimes against humanity resulting in sentences of 7 and 10 years, respectively.

Outrages upon personal dignity, in particular rape, enforced prostitution and any form of indecent assault (Article 4(e) of the ICTR Statute): no convictions have been made for this crime.

3.2.1.6 Preliminary results

On the basis of the overview in the Appendix and the Chart, read together with Chapters 1-3, certain sentencing ranges for sexual violence emerge. Genocide, including sexual violence, generally leads to life imprisonment or a considerable number of years in a fixed sentence. Convictions for, among other charges, (sexual) enslavement have had a considerable influence on the ultimate sentence, which has resulted in 28 and 20 years imprisonment so far. Torture as a crime against humanity, including sexual violence, has led to sentences of between 5 (threat to sexually mutilate) and 12 years (rape), depending on the conduct. People convicted of rape as a crime against humanity have been sentenced to between 7 and 15 years imprisonment, which sentence was most likely influenced by the number of victims. Persecution incorporating, among other crimes, sexual violence, has led to sentences of between 5 years and life imprisonment. Sexual mutilation, forced oral sex and forced nudity were the basis of convictions under other inhumane acts as crimes against humanity and resulted in two sentences of 10 years each. Torture as a grave breach has led to sentences of 15 years twice for the repeated rapes of two detained women. Inhumane treatment as a grave breach has resulted in two specific sentences of 7 (forced fellatio) and 9 years (forced fellatio and sexual mutilation). The grave breach of wilfully causing great suffering or serious injury to body or health similarly resulted in two sentences of 7 (sexual mutilation) and 9 years (forced fellatio and sexual mutilation). Cruel treatment, including sexual violence, as a violation of the laws or customs of war has been sentenced within the ICTY with 7 years twice (forced fellatio, sexual mutilation) and 9 years (forced fellatio and sexual mutilation). Torture, including sexual violence, as a violation of the laws or customs of war has led, at the ICTY, to sentences of between 10 and 15 years imprisonment. Outrages upon personal dignity, in particular humiliating and degrading treatment, has resulted in the ICTY in an 8-year sentence for rape. Rape as an independent crime under Article 3 of the ICTY Statute has resulted in a 12-year sentence. Within the ICTR, one conviction was rendered on the basis of Common Article 3 and Additional Protocol II, that is, Article 4(a) of the ICTR Statute on the basis of the law of cumulative convictions and resulted in a sentence of 10 years. No convictions have been made on the basis of Article 4(e) of the ICTR Statute.

It is further noteworthy that some of the above-mentioned conduct formed the basis of multiple convictions, some of which were quashed on appeal. In the cases where specific sentences for each count were given, no or not much difference exists for the same conduct charged under different international crimes (genocide, crimes against humanity and war crimes) or within the international crime itself. For example, Delić was convicted of rape as the grave breach of torture as well as of torture as a violation of the laws or customs of war resulting in sentences of 15 years under each heading. The same goes for Mucić. Tadić received similar sentences for the same conduct, although the sentence for other inhumane acts as a crime against humanity was raised with one year. Therefore, whether the conduct was charged and sentenced under grave breaches or violations of the laws or customs of war did not affect the length of the sentence. However, the same conduct charged as a crime against humanity slightly raised the length of the sentence imposed. Furundžija's sentence as a co-perpetrator of rape and the forced observance thereof was two years higher in the case of torture as a violation of the laws or customs of war when compared with the sentence given for outrages upon personal dignity as a violation of the laws or customs of war. The difference within one category of crime, violations of the laws or customs of war, can be explained by the fact that the underlying crime of torture requires a purposive element and a higher threshold for the severity of the crime not necessarily required under outrages upon personal dignity.

To conclude, it must be stressed again that drawing any meaningful conclusions from the practice of sentencing in cases of sexual violence within the two Tribunals is a very arduous task. Some preliminary results can nevertheless be given, but primarily on the basis of specific sentences given for specific counts, as well as the single sentence imposed on Vuković based on cumulative convictions on the basis of the rape of one girl. The results of this comparative sentencing Chart serves as a first step to clarify the sentencing practice on sexual violence within both Tribunals, but further judgments on sexual violence must be handed down before a definitive conclusion on this issue may be made. Further research on this topic is therefore recommended. As the ICC works with a sentence for each crime and a joint sentence specifying the total period of imprisonment, insight into how the Tribunals have dealt with sentences for sexual violence might be helpful for the Court in addressing these crimes. Although the ICC Statute enumerates several sexual violence crimes not listed in the ICTY and ICTR Statutes, that is to say, sexual slavery, forced prostitution, forced sterilisation and forced pregnancy as crimes against humanity and war crimes, the ICTY and ICTR sentencing practice in respect of crimes more or less similar to some of the crimes mentioned (for instance, enslavement within the ICTY and ICTR and sexual slavery within the ICC) may be of significance to ICC sentencing practice with respect to these 'new' crimes.

4 SENTENCING DETERMINANTS

As previously explained, the Tribunals take several factors into account when determining the sentence: that is, the general practice regarding prison sentences in the courts of the convicted person's home country; (2) the gravity of the crime and the individual circumstances of the convicted person; and (3) any aggravating or mitigating circumstances.

4.1 General prison sentencing practice in national courts

In determining the appropriate sentence, the ICTY and ICTR take into account the general prison sentencing practice in the courts of the former Yugoslavia and Rwanda, respectively. The recourse to national sentencing practice was inspired by the principle of legality, which prohibits retroactive offences and penalties. In other words, no person accused can claim that, at the time the crimes were committed, he or she was unaware of the criminal nature of his or her acts and the severity of the penalties sanctioning them.[89] Nevertheless, the ICTY and ICTR provisions are unclear as to whether reference should be made to the prison terms set out in penal laws or to the actual practice of local courts, and at what point in time.[90] The issue seems to have been clarified by the ICTY, which has stipulated on several occasions that 'it is difficult to identify such 'general practice' in the absence of a functioning judiciary during the period in question, especially in relation to those crimes heard before this Tribunal. Rather, Trial Chambers should take into account the applicable written law and today's practice – if any – of courts of the States in the territory of the former Yugoslavia in relation to serious violations of International Humanitarian Law'.[91]

The Tribunals have generally consulted the actual sentencing practice of local courts as well as the relevant laws of the former Yugoslavia and Rwanda, that is, the

[89] See, e.g., the Erdemović Judgment, para. 40.

[90] It is noteworthy that the Rwandan Organic Laws Nos. 8/96, 40/2000, 33/2001 and 16/2004, as discussed below, were drafted *after* the genocide had taken place in Rwanda. Prior to the 1994 genocide, Rwanda had no such legislation. Although the 1949 Geneva Conventions, the 1977 Protocols and the 1948 Genocide Convention had all been ratified and published in the Official Gazette, no implementing legislation of these treaties was ever enacted. Even so, Article 15(2) ICCPR states that nothing may prejudice the trial and punishment of any person for any act or omission which, at the time it was committed, was criminal according to the general principles of law recognised by the community of nations. In addition, although the reference to a law which was not applicable at the time the events took place is unfortunate, it has been held that neither the Statute of the ICTR nor its Rules suggest a time frame for the appreciation 'general practice'. On this issue, see Schabas (1997), p. 476; Schabas (2000a), pp. 526-527.

[91] Nikolić Sentencing Judgment, para. 148; Tadić Judgment in Sentencing Appeals, para. 21; Kupreškić Appeal Judgment, para. 418; Jelisić Appeal Judgment, para. 117; Čelebići Appeal Judgment, para. 813. However, in the Kunarac, Kovač and Vuković Judgment, the Trial Chamber refused to consider a case because it had been tried by a post-1992 Bosnia and Herzegovinian court, and was therefore found to be irrelevant. See Kunarac, Kovač and Vuković Judgment, para. 835.

former Socialist Federal Republic of Yugoslavia (SFRY) Criminal Code (1977)[92] as well as laws enacted later, such as the 2003 Criminal Code for the entity of Bosnia and Herzegovina (BiH) and the Republika Srpska within the State of BiH and the Brčko District enacted by the Office of the High Representative,[93] and the Rwandan Organic Law on the Organisation of Prosecutions for Offences Constituting the Crime of Genocide or Crimes Against Humanity No. 8/96 (1996).[94] In 2001, the Rwandan Organic Law No. 8/96 (1996) was replaced by the Gacaca Organic Law No. 40/2000 and modified by law No. 33/2001, and further amended by the Gacaca Organic Law No. 16/2004.[95] This means that, since the adoption of the latter two, the 1996 Organic Law has been applied to pending cases only.

As to the sentencing practice in local courts, it is possible to be very brief. In Rwanda, there had not been any trials before 1994 involving the sort of crimes prosecuted before the Rwanda Tribunal. In the former Yugoslavia, two significant trials for genocide had taken place, that is, *Milhailovic et al.* in 1946 and *Artukovic* in 1986, in which several of the accused were sentenced to death.[96] There were no cases on war crimes prior to the outbreak of the war in the former Yugoslavia.[97] Therefore, on the basis of this small amount of information, the actual practice of local courts before the outbreak of the conflicts in the former Yugoslavia and Rwanda proved to be of no or only little significance to the Tribunals in determining sentences. As discussed below, the practice on sentencing after the conflicts is minimal as well, although progressing.

---

[92] The former Socialist Federal Republic of Yugoslavia Criminal Code (1977), published in the Official Gazette of The Socialist Federal Republic of Yugoslavia, No. 44/1977 (hereafter SFRY Criminal Code), adopted by the Federal Assembly on 28 September 1976, and in force since 1 July 1977. The Criminal Code of the Socialist Republic of Bosnia and Herzegovina, published in the Official Gazette of the Socialist Republic of Bosnia and Herzegovina, No. 16/77, did not contain provisions on war crimes or crimes against humanity and is therefore not assessed.

[93] For details about this criminal code, see the Nikolić Sentencing Judgment, para. 154.

[94] Organic Law No. 8/96 of 30 August 1996 on the Organization of Prosecutions for Offences Constituting Genocide or Crimes against Humanity Committed since 1 October 1990 of 30 August 1996, published in the Gazette of the Republic of Rwanda, 35th year, No. 17, 1 September 1996 (hereafter Rwandan Organic Law No. 8/96).

[95] Organic Law No. 40/2000 of 26/01/2001 Setting up 'Gacaca Jurisdictions' and Organizing Prosecutions for Offences Constituting the Crime of Genocide or Crimes against Humanity Committed Between October 1, 1990 and December 31, 1994 (hereafter Gacaca Organic Law No. 40/2000); Organic Law No. 33/2001 of 22/6/2001 Modifying and Completing Organic Law No. 40/2000 Setting up 'Gacaca Jurisdictions' and Organizing Prosecutions for Offences Constituting the Crime of Genocide or Crimes against Humanity Committed Between October 1, 1990, and December 31, 1994. These laws were amended by the Organic Law No. 16/2004 of 19/6/2004 Establishing the Organisation, Competence and Functioning of Gacaca Courts Charged with Prosecuting and Trying the Perpetrators of the Crime of Genocide and Other Crimes Against Humanity Committed Between October 1, 1990, and December 31, 1994 (hereafter Gacaca Organic Law No. 16/2004).

[96] In the Milhailovic et al. case, a majority of the defendants were sentenced to death and executed; in the Artukovic case, the accused was sentenced to death but died in prison of natural cause. See Cors and Fisher (1997), cited in: W.A. Schabas (1997), p. 476.

[97] Kunarac, Kovač and Vuković Judgment, para. 835.

The relevant national criminal laws contain provisions on penalisation and sentencing in cases of serious violations of international humanitarian law, including sexual violence.[98, 99] The SFRY Criminal Code stipulates in Articles 141 and 142(1) that

[98] For the former Yugoslavia, see Article 142(1) ('War Crimes Against the Civilian Population') in Chapter XVI of the SFRY Criminal Code ('Criminal Acts Against Humanity and International Law'), which states that 'whoever in violation of rules of international law effective at the time of war, armed conflict or occupation, orders that civilian population be subject to killings, torture; inhumane treatment ..., immense suffering or violation of bodily integrity or health ...; *forcible prostitution or rape*; application of measures of intimidation and terror, ... other illegal arrests and detention ...; forcible labour ... or who commits one of the foregoing acts, *shall be punished by imprisonment for not less than five years or by the death penalty*' (italics added). Rape and forcible prostitution are thus explicitly criminalised under Article 142(1). In addition, sexual violence crimes can also be prosecuted under any of the other crimes mentioned, such as torture, inhumane treatment, and immense suffering or violation of bodily integrity or health. This article gives effect to the provisions of the Geneva Convention Relative to the Protection of Civilian Persons in Time of War of 12 August 1949 and its Protocols, which are incorporated in Article 2 ICTY Statute (Tadić Sentencing Judgment, para. 8). Article 141 of the SFRY Criminal Code penalises genocide, and similarly prescribes imprisonment of not less than five years or the death penalty. The SFRY Criminal Code does not include a specific provision on crimes against humanity. However, certain crimes enumerated in Article 142 are similar to certain crimes against humanity, including rape, and arguably would have attracted similar sentences. On this latter point, see Simić Judgment, para. 46; Češić Judgment, para. 103; and, in particular, *Prosecutor v. Radovan Stanković*, Decision of Referral of Case Under Rule 11*bis*, Case No. IT-96-23/2-PT, 17 May 2005, para. 39 ('This provision of the SFRY CC [Article 142(1)] would also appear applicable to the conduct under the other two counts of rape cumulatively charged as crimes against humanity by Counts 2 and 6 of the present Indictment. The acts of the Accused charged in the present Indictment as enslavement in Counts 1 and 5 [as crimes against humanity] would also appear to be within the scope of the provisions of Article 142(1) which make illegal detention and forcible labour war crimes.' The Criminal Code of Bosnia and Herzegovina of 2003 (or BiH CC) entered into force on 1 March 2003, is applicable to the Federation of BiH as well as the Republika Srpska, and proscribes the crimes against humanity of enslavement and rape under Article 172, and the war crime against civilians of rape under Article 173. In part, Articles 172 (Crimes Against Humanity) reads: '(1) whoever, as part of a widespread or systematic attack directed against a civilian population, with knowledge of such an attack perpetrates any of the following acts: ... (c) Enslavement; ... (g) Coercing another by force or by threat of immediate attack upon his life or limb, or the life or limb of a person close to him, to sexual intercourse or an equivalent sexual act (rape); ... (k) Other inhumane acts of a similar character intentionally causing great suffering, or serious injury to body or to physical or mental health, *shall be punished by imprisonment for a term not less than ten years or long-term imprisonment*' (italics added). Article 173 (War Crimes Against Civilians) reads, in part: '(1) whoever in violation of rules of international law in time of war, armed conflict or occupation, orders or perpetrates any of the following acts: ... (c) ... inhuman treatment ... immense suffering or violation of bodily integrity or health; .... (e) Coercing another by force or by threat of immediate attack upon his life or limb, or the life or limb of a person close to him, to sexual intercourse or an equivalent sexual act (rape); ... *shall be punished by imprisonment for a term not less than ten years or long-term imprisonment*' (italics added). For further discussion of these provisions, see body text. See

references in: *Prosecutor v. Radovan Stanković*, Decision of Referral of Case Under Rule 11*bis*, Case No. IT-96-23/2-PT, 17 May 2005, para. 42, and the Nikolić Sentencing Judgment, para. 158. Genocide is prohibited in Article 171 and carries sentences of imprisonment for at least 10 years or long-term imprisonment. The Criminal Code of Croatia of 1997/98 prohibits rape as a war crime in Article 158(1) by *imprisonment for not less than 10 years or by long-term imprisonment, the latter being between 20 and 40 years* (Article 53(2)). Genocide is prohibited in Article 176 *by 10 years to long-term imprisonment*. Crimes against humanity are not defined. The Criminal Code of the Former Yugoslav Republic of Macedonia of 1996 prohibits rape as a war crime in Article 404(1), which is punished with *at least 10 years or life imprisonment*. Crimes against humanity are not defined in the Criminal Code of Macedonia, but genocide is, and imprisonment for at least 10 years or life imprisonment is imposed by Article 403. The Basic Criminal Code of Serbia of 2003 criminalises rape as a war crime in Article 142(1) with punishment for *not less than 5 years or long-term imprisonment of 40 years*. Genocide is prohibited in Article 141 with the same sentencing range and crimes against humanity as such are not laid down in the code. The sentencing ranges of the latter situation apply to Montenegro as well. For a detailed overview of the laws and sentences applicable to rape as a war crime, a crime against humanity and genocide in the countries in the territory of the former Yugoslavia, see the report prepared by Sieber (2004), pp. 30, 43, 47, 51, 56, 59, 60.

[99] For Rwanda, see Articles 2 and 14 of the Rwandan Organic Law No. 8/96, which provides for the penalisation and sentencing of those accused on the basis of their culpability in the crimes committed or the sort of crimes perpetrated. Four categories of accused are differentiated. Included in the first category are the masterminds of the genocide (planners, organisers, supervisors and leaders), persons in positions of authority, persons who exhibited excessive cruelty and *perpetrators of sexual torture. All such persons are to be punished by the death sentence*. The second category covers perpetrators, conspirators or accomplices in criminal acts, for whom the prescribed penalty is life imprisonment. Included in the third category are persons who, in addition to committing a substantive offence, are guilty of other serious assaults upon the person. Such persons face a short-term imprisonment. The fourth category is that of persons who have committed offences against property. The Gacaca Organic Law No. 40/2000 has maintained this division of categories of accused and crimes, including sexual violence crimes, described as 'rape or acts of torture against person's sexual parts', as category 1 offences (Article 51), but the penalties that can be imposed differ (Articles 68-75). Persons falling within the first category receive the *death penalty or life imprisonment* (Article 68); Persons falling within category two receive a sentence of 25 years imprisonment or life imprisonment (Article 69); Persons falling within category three offences receive a prison term of between five and seven years (Article 70); and persons falling within category four offences are liable to civil reparation of damages caused to the other people's property (Article 71). Perpetrators falling within categories 2 and 3 can receive a considerable reduction of their sentence if they confess and plead guilty to the crime(s) they committed and this is accepted. The degree of reduction depends on the time of their confession: e.g., if a confession is made prior to the Gacaca jurisdiction making up the list of perpetrators of genocide, the sentence reduction is, for instance, 7-12 years imprisonment for category 2 offences; if the confession is made when the list was already drawn up and the person already indicted, the sentence reduction is, for instance, 12-15 years imprisonment for category 2 offences (Article 69). In addition to a reduction of the sentence, half of the sentence will be served in custody and the rest will be commuted into community service. Excepted from this scheme are those who did not confess or whose confession was not accepted under category 2: they receive a

genocide and war crimes – the latter with explicit reference to forced prostitution and rape – must be punished with *imprisonment of not less than five years or the death penalty.*[100] The Code further states that the death penalty can be replaced with a maximum prison sentence of 20 years.[101] In fact, capital punishment was abolished by constitutional amendment in 1977, the new maximum sentence being 15 years, except for crimes punishable with the death penalty, committed under 'particularly aggravating circumstances' or causing 'especially grave consequences', in which cases the maximum term of imprisonment was 20 years.[102] Yugoslavia does not allow life imprisonment as a replacement for the death penalty as it considers lifelong detention a form of cruel, inhuman and degrading punishment.[103] Therefore, *the maximum sentence for rape in the former Yugoslavia was 20 years imprisonment and no less than 5 years.* After the conflict in the former Yugoslavia, the new countries in the territory of the former Yugoslavia (Bosnia and Herzegovina, Croatia, Macedonia, Serbia and Montenegro) all enacted new criminal codes. For example, in March 2003, the Office of the High Representative enacted a new Criminal Code for the entity of BiH and the Republika Srpska within the State of BiH and the Brčko District.[104] According to this Code, crimes against humanity (Article 172) and war crimes (Article 173) must be punished by *imprisonment for a term not less than ten years or long-term imprisonment.* 'Long term imprisonment', the maximum sentence available, is defined as 20 to 45 years imprisonment.[105] If no long-term imprisonment is imposed, the maximum sentence cannot exceed 20 years of imprisonment.[106] Rape as a war crime or when committed as part of a widespread or systematic attack against civilians may therefore be punished with *10 to 20 years or 20 to 45 years imprisonment.*[107] The sentencing norms on rape as an international crime for the other countries in the territory of the former Yugoslavia vary as follows: 10 years to long-term imprisonment, i.e., 20 to 40 years imprisonment (Croatia), 10 years to life imprisonment (Macedonia), 5 years to

---

prison sentence of 25 years or life imprisonment. Although category 1 perpetrators can also have their sentence reduced, this is only possibly through confession and a guilty plea before their names are published on the category 1 list (Article 56 in conjunction with Article 68). In such a case, a sentence of 25 years or life imprisonment may be pronounced. Under Rwandan Organic Law No. 8/96, penalty reduction is also possible; see Articles 15 and 16. In general, the number of years imprisonment which may be imposed after reduction is similar under both laws. The main differences can be found in the possibility for reduction of sentences for category 1 offenders if confession is made before indictments are issued and the possibility to serve part of the sentence as community service. Both are allowed under the Gacaca Law, not Rwandan Organic Law No. 8/96. Gacaca Organic Law No. 16/2004 further amended the 2000/2001 Law. For a discussion of the 2004 law, see the body text where this law is discussed in relevant part.

[100] In conformity with Articles 141 and 142(1), as cited above.

[101] Article 38(1) SFRY Criminal Code.

[102] See the Official Gazette of the FRY, No. 37, 16 July 1993, p. 817.

[103] Schabas (2000a), p. 527.

[104] See the Nikolić Sentencing Judgment, para. 154.

[105] Article 42 2003 BiH Criminal Code.

[106] Article 53(2)(b) 2003 BiH Criminal Code.

[107] Articles 172 and 173 2003 BiH Criminal Code.

long-term imprisonment, i.e., 40 years (Serbia), and 5 years to long-term imprisonment, i.e., 40 years (Montenegro).

Although sexual violence, including rape, can thus be prosecuted under national laws, only a handful of the perpetrators have been brought to justice in the national jurisdictions, despite the widespread nature of the sexual violence committed.[108] On the basis of the foregoing, the sentences that the ICTY would be able to impose for sexual violence as a war crime, a crime against humanity or genocide, with the norms of the countries in the former Yugoslavia in mind, vary considerably per country and *range from 5-40, 10-20, 10-40, 20-45 and 10 to life imprisonment*. With regard to the difference in sentencing length of the old 1977 law and the new 2003 BiH Criminal Code (both restricted to a fixed term of imprisonment) and the Tribunal's possibility to impose life imprisonment, the Tribunal stated that it has 'primacy *vis à vis* national jurisdictions in the former Yugoslavia and is therefore not bound to apply the more lenient penalty under these jurisdictions'.[109] In other words, the Tribunal judges have the discretion to impose life imprisonment if the circumstances of the case so require.[110] However, how the difference in sentencing laws (the 1977 law enacted at the time when the crimes were committed and more recent laws) will influence sentences imposed on ICTY cases referred to the national jurisdictions is unclear. The case of *Stanković*, in which the accused is charged, *inter alia*, with enslavement and rape, is the first case to be transferred to the State Court of Bosnia and Herzegovina by the ICTY.[111] As it will be left to the State Court to determine the applicable law, sentences imposed for sexual violence conduct may vary with those of the Tribunal.[112]

---

[108] Amnesty International (2004d). Amnesty International furthermore points out that threats against women are very real and that protective measures (as well as support) should be in place, for otherwise impunity will continue to be the rule. In addition, they argue that national laws on rape as crimes against humanity need to be adjusted in order to reflect international criminal law developments, such as the ICTY ruling that coercive circumstances negate consent.

[109] Nikolić Sentencing Judgment, para. 165, upheld in Nikolić Judgment on Sentencing Appeal, paras. 84-86. The Defence argued that the principle of *lex mitior* should have been applied in the case at hand, i.e., if the law relevant to the offence of the accused has been amended, the less severe law should be applied. The principle is enshrined in national and international law treaties, including Article 24(2) ICC Statute.

[110] In the Nikolić Judgment on Sentencing Appeal, it was made clear that the principle of *lex mitior* applies to the Statute of the International Tribunal only. 'Accordingly, if ever the sentencing powers conferred by the Statute were to be amended, the International Tribunal would have to apply the less severe penalty.' However, 'allowing the principle of *lex mitior* to be applied to sentences of the International Tribunal on the basis of changes in the laws of the former Yugoslavia would mean that the States of the former Yugoslavia have the power to undermine the sentencing discretion of the International Tribunal's judges'. See Nikolić Judgment on Sentencing Appeal, paras. 85 and 84, respectively.

[111] *The Prosecutor v. Radovan Stanković*, Decision of Referral of Case Under Rule 11*bis*, Case No. IT-96-23/2-PT, 17 May 2005.

[112] *Ibid.*, para. 46. The Referral Bench states here, in part: 'In summary, Article 4(1) of the BiH CC [the Criminal Code of Bosnia and Herzegovina of 2003] would suggest that the SFRY CC, as it was in force in 1992, would be applied to each of the alleged criminal acts of the Accused should this case be referred [i.e., sentences between 5 and 20 years]. The submissions we have

Rwandan Organic Law No. 8/96, on the other hand, imposes the *death penalty* on individuals convicted on the basis of category 1 offences, which includes the masterminds of the genocide and perpetrators of 'sexual torture'.[113] The inclusion of sexual violence as a category 1 crime was long and contestably debated in Parliament.[114] Initially, it was rejected that rape could ever be a constituent part of an international crime such as genocide.[115] Furthermore, the term 'sexual torture' was chosen in order to comprise the rape of women as well as forms of mutilation of men's sexual organs, and therefore pointedly avoided the recognition of gender-based violence directed primarily against women.[116] With the coming into effect of the Gacaca Organic Law in 2000, sexual violence crimes, described as 'rape or acts of torture against person's sexual parts', remained punishable as category 1 crimes, deserving the *death penalty or life imprisonment.*[117] The Gacaca Organic Law which entered into force in 2004 similarly prescribes the *death penalty or life imprisonment* for 'acts of rape or acts of torture against sexual organs'.[118] The latter two laws more appropriately take into account the terrible experiences of women during the genocide by explicitly referring to rape, a crime which in Rwanda clearly is seen as committed by men against women.[119] Furthermore, 'acts of torture against others, even though they did not result into death' and 'dehumanising acts on the dead body' also came to fall within category 1 offences and provided an opening for the prosecution of sexual violence as well.

Despite the recognition of the extreme severity of the crime of rape as a category 1 crime, this is in sharp contrast with the extraordinarily small number of persons tried for sexual violence in Rwanda itself, especially considering that rapes were committed on a large scale during the genocide.[120] While the category 1 suspects (between 2,133 and

---

received canvass the possibilities, however, that in respect of some or all of the alleged criminal acts of the Accused, other provisions of the BiH CC or general principles of international law might be applied pursuant to Articles 4(2) and 4a respectively of the BiH CC [i.e., sentences of 20 to 45 years or even life imprisonment as provided for by the ICTY RPE].'

[113] In conformity with Articles 2 and 14 Rwandan Organic Law No. 8/96. The death penalty has been pronounced in a number of trials and was executed once in respect of 22 individuals. See subsection 2.2 above.

[114] Mibenge (2005).

[115] *Ibid.*

[116] *Ibid.*

[117] Article 51 Gacaca Organic Law No. 40/2000.

[118] Article 72 in conjunction with Article 51 Gacaca Organic Law No. 16/2004. Genocide perpetrators who confessed before their names appeared on the list, enjoy commutation of penalties, namely, *twenty-five to thirty years of imprisonment* (Article 72 in conjunction with Article 55 Gacaca Organic Law No. 16/2004).

[119] Mibenge (2005). Articles 358-362 of Rwanda's Penal Code provide that rape requires sexual penetration of the sexual organs, anus or mouth, by a male sexual organ or, in some cases, by another object. Following the definition, the perpetrator is male and the victims can be either male or female.

[120] If the total number of category 1 suspects is around 2,133-3,000 (see body text), this implies that only a very limited number of perpetrators of sexual violence are prosecuted before national courts, especially considering the large scale on which sexual violence crimes were committed (implying that multiple perpetrators were involved) and the fact that not all of these category 1

3000)[121] are tried by magistrates in the conventional courts, the categories 2 and 3 suspects (between 80,000 and 100,000, which number may be running into the hundreds of thousands with the official start of Gacaca courts in 2005),[122] whose involvement is considered slightly less serious, are tried in traditional community courts, called Gacaca, by locals trained as judges with proven integrity.[123] The Rwandan government decided to reinstall the Gacaca courts in order to speed up trials and sentencing, while at

---

suspects are charged with sexual violence crimes. The reasons why sexual violence is not prosecuted on a larger scale in Rwanda can be found in the following: (1) victims of sexual violence often find it very difficult to report the sexual violence they endured in public, because of shame, trauma, and fear of becoming a social outcast; (2) victims are afraid of reprisals from those they accuse or their families and friends; (3) perpetrators of sexual violence are generally unwilling to confess to sexual violence as this implies they will be prosecuted as category 1 offenders, which means they will receive the harshest sentence available; and (4) some victims do not know the identity of their attackers and some rapists may have died. On the reluctance of survivors of sexual violence to speak up, see Hirondelle News Agency, *Silent Victims of Rwanda's Genocide* (by Gabriel Gabiro), 21 November 2003. In June 2004, the Gacaca Organic Law was amended in order to protect the identity of genocide rape victims by providing them with the possibility to record their testimony on video camera. With this change, it is hoped that rape victims will be motivated to come forward. See IRIN, *Rwanda: Traditional Courts Inaugurated*, 24 June 2004. For some statistics on the extraordinarily small number of cases in which sexual violence has been prosecuted in Rwanda, see Human Rights Watch (2004b), pp. 18-20 (only 32 of over 1000 judgments examined (including 51 defendants of which 31 were convicted over the period 1996-2003) included charges of rape or sexual torture). See also African Rights (2004), pp. 76-78.

[121] See the official website of Rwanda at http://www.rwanda1.com (last visited July 2004) and Hirondelle News Agency, *Analysis: Confronting Genocide with Country's Regular Courts* (by Gabriel Gabiro), 17 September 2003. Gabiro mentions that this number is likely to increase as Gacaca courts re-categorise all suspects and indict new ones.

[122] Currently, around 80,000-100,000 persons are still in jail awaiting their trial: beginning 2003, some 20,000 prisoners (mostly the aged, the sick, those who were minors during the genocide, and those uninvolved in planning the genocide) were provisionally released. See BBC News, *Rwanda Still Searching for Justice*, 30 March 2004. The number of prisoners detained does not necessarily represent the total number of people involved in the genocide. That number is arguably even higher, considering that more people have been incriminated wherever Gacaca sessions were ongoing. 'Official estimates indicate that when investigations are completed later this year, at least 700,000 Rwandans will be listed as suspects for crimes related to the genocide. That is about one in every eleven inhabitants of 'the land of a thousand hills'.' See Hirondelle News Agency, *Villagers Flee as Genocide Courts Press On*, 25 April 2005.

[123] The final phase, the establishment of Gacaca courts throughout the country, was inaugurated on 24 June 2004. In the two preceding years, 751 (out of 9,010) Gacaca courts had operated during a pilot phase in different cells over the country. During this period, lists were drawn up of victims and their supposed perpetrators. See Hirondelle News Agency, *Gacaca Tribunals Officially Launched in Rwanda*, 24 June 2004. The official trials commenced on 10 March 2005 nationwide and, at the peak of operations, it is estimated that about 12,000 courts will be running in Rwanda. See Hirondelle News Agency, *On Day One of Trials, Gacaca Courts Deliver First Genocide Judgements*, 11 March 2005.

the same time trying to contribute to national reconciliation through the involvement of the Rwandan population in the trials.[124] The perpetrators falling in the second category (murderers, attempted murderers and those who caused serious bodily harm) receive 25 to 30 years of imprisonment, whereas those falling within category 3 (property crimes) are sentenced to civil reparation for the damage they have caused to victims.[125] A sentence for a category 2 offender may be reduced by a considerable number of years if this person confessed, pleaded guilty, repented and apologised,[126] but the reduction of a sentence only applies to a category 1 convict if his confession, guilty plea, repentance and apology were made before publication of his name on the category 1 list.[127] In the latter case, the sentence may be reduced to *25 years to 30 years of imprisonment.*[128] Although this sentence is still high, the rule was institutionalised with the hope that category 1 offenders, including those who raped, will confess to their crimes. For persons falling within category 2, the possibility exists that half of the sentence will be served in custody and that the rest will be commuted into community service.[129]

The ICTR, on the other hand, cannot impose the death penalty and may only have recourse to the *prison* sentences applicable in Rwanda,[130] which includes imprisonment up to 30 years or life imprisonment. As far as sexual violence crimes are concerned, the ICTR could, with reference to Rwandan law, impose life imprisonment (on those who did not confess and were found guilty). Although a sentence of 25 years up to 30 years, for those who confessed before publication of his or her name on the category 1 list of perpetrators, is also an option under Rwandan law, this scenario is not readily applicable before the ICTR. Sentences for sexual violence as violations of international humanitarian law are thus assessed differently under the criminal codes of the former Yugoslavia (5 to 20 years under the 1977 Criminal Code and 5-40, 10-20, 10-40, 20-45 and 10 to life imprisonment under the various criminal codes of the countries of the former Yugoslavia today) and Rwanda (25-30 years or life imprisonment).

According to ICTY and ICTR case law, the reference to the general practice regarding prison sentences in the courts of the former Yugoslavia and Rwanda to

[124] In this respect, it is noteworthy, that since the start of the first Gacaca trials in March 2005, thousands of Rwandans suspected of participation in the 1994 genocide have reportedly fled the country to neighbouring Burundi, Uganda, and the Democratic Republic of Congo or have moved to other parts of the country. See Hirondelle News Agency, *Villagers Flee as Genocide Courts Press on*, 25 April 2005; Hirondelle News Agency, *Six Hundred Flee to Burundi Over Gacaca*, 19 April 2005; Hirondelle News Agency, *Over 80 People Flee Rwanda as Gacaca Trials Begin*, 14 March 2005. Furthermore, 700 of the 200,000 Gacaca judges have been accused of taking part in the genocide and were asked to resign and some were immediately arrested. See Hirondelle News Agency, *700 Hundred Gacaca Judges Accused of Taking Part in the Genocide*, 17 March 2005.

[125] Articles 73 and 75 Gacaca Organic Law No. 16/2004.

[126] Article 73 Gacaca Organic Law No. 16/2004.

[127] Article 72 in conjunction with Article 55 Gacaca Organic Law No. 16/2004.

[128] *Ibid.*

[129] Article 73 Gacaca Organic Law No. 16/2004. Note that those who did not confess or whose confession was not accepted under category 2, receive a prison sentence of 25 to 30 years, without the possibility to serve half their sentence as community service.

[130] Kambanda Judgment and Sentence, para. 22.

determine an appropriate sentence must be viewed as a guiding, but not binding, tool to determine the penalty.[131] Even though the reference to the general prison sentencing practice in national courts was largely influenced by the legality principle, confronted with the restriction in length of sentences[132] and a limited national sentencing practice with regard to the sort of crimes prosecuted before the Tribunals, the judges ruled that the general practice could only serve as a guiding tool for determining sentences.[133] In cases where the Chambers divert from the national sentencing practice, they need to explain their reasons for doing so.[134] However, given the length of the sentences imposed by the ICTY and ICTR, it is questionable whether the Tribunals are not actually more influenced by their national sentencing practice than they generally claim to be.[135] With a few exceptions, the ICTY has not given higher sentences than those that would have been awarded in the former Yugoslavia itself under the 1977 SFRY Criminal Code.[136] The ICTR, on the other hand, has convicted a considerable number of people for genocide, imposing life imprisonment.[137] This is in line with the penalties

---

131 The wording contained in the relevant provisions – 'have recourse to' and 'take into account' respectively – indicate that the Tribunals are not bound to follow the sentencing practice of the former Yugoslavia or Rwanda. For the ICTR, see Kambanda Judgment and Sentence, paras. 11, 18, 22-24, 41; Serushago Sentence, para. 18, 30; Ruggiu Judgment and Sentence, para. 31; Rutaganda Judgment and Sentence, para. 454; Musema Judgment and Sentence, para. 984. For the ICTY, see Tadić Appeal Judgment, 26 January 2000, para. 21; Blaškić Judgment, 3 March 2000, paras. 759-760; Čelebići Appeal Judgment, paras. 813, 816; Jelisić Appeal Judgment, paras. 116-117; Todorović Sentencing Judgment, para. 107; Kunarac, Kovač and Vuković Appeal Judgment, para. 377.

132 The most severe sentence in the former Yugoslavia was 20 years of imprisonment under the law applicable at the times the crimes were committed, and 45 years in more recent laws (Bosnia and Herzegovina Federation and Republika Srpska) with the exception of life imprisonment in Macedonia. In Rwanda, the highest sentence is life imprisonment. For certain categories of perpetrators or crimes, sentences may be reduced significantly on a guilty plea and sometimes half of the sentence may be served as community service.

133 See, *inter alia*, Erdemović Sentencing Judgment, para. 35.

134 Dragan Nikolić Appeal Judgment, paras. 68-69.

135 See Beresford (2001), p. 49.

136 For such an exception, see Kunarac, Kovač and Vuković Judgment, para. 859. The Trial Chamber in this case, primarily concerned with sexual violence crimes, referred to the SFRY Criminal Code, but concluded, in particular in relation to Kunarac and Kovač, that 'the scale of their offences calls for a consideration of sentences of higher than 20 years to be imposed'. In the Kunarac, Kovač and Vuković Judgment, the Trial Chamber did not look at laws enacted after the conflict. It is noteworthy that, although Kunarac received a prison term of 28 years, Kovač eventually received a prison term of 20 years. See also, *inter alia*: Stakić Judgment, para. 463 (life imprisonment); Kristić Judgment, para. 727; Krstić Appeal Judgment (46 years; reduced to 35 years on appeal). The length of these sentences approach the sentences as laid down in the new criminal codes enacted after the conflict.

137 In Kayishema and Ruzindana, the Trial Chamber held that 'the general practice regarding prison sentences in Rwanda presents one factor supporting this Chamber's imposition of the maximum and very severe sentences, respectively' on Kayishema and Ruzindana. Kayishema and Ruzindana Judgment, paras. 6-7.

prescribed under Rwandan Law, although it should be noted that the crime of genocide, referred to as the 'crime of crimes', has been more frequently prosecuted before the ICTR than before the ICTY.[138] As far as sexual violence crimes are concerned, the opposite is true: the Tribunals seem to be influenced by the national sentencing practice only marginally. With a few exceptions, the sentences imposed by the Tribunals for sexual violence crimes are more lenient than would have been the case if prosecution had taken place in the national courts. In the former Yugoslavia, rape as a war crime or genocide is punished with imprisonment of between 5 and 20 years under the old law or even up to 40 or 45 years or life imprisonment under more recent laws, and, in Rwanda, the death penalty or life imprisonment is the rule[139] when it comes to punishing sexual violence as genocide or as a crime against humanity. As the sentencing margin under the law of the former Yugoslavia is rather broad, it is difficult to draw any significant conclusions as to what sentences would have been imposed for sexual violence if it had ever been charged as genocide or a war crime before or after the outbreak of the conflict.[140] A survey of the ICTY sentences imposed reveals that the specific sentences for sexual violence crimes range between 5 and 15 years imprisonment, with most crimes sentenced between 7 and 10 years. The sentences imposed on Kunarac and Kovač – 28 and 20 years, respectively, including convictions for repeated rapes and sexual enslavement – are an exception. Here it should be noted that these cases involved many charges on sexual violence only and thus the sentences comprised the total conduct of the accused.[141] As to the cases in which single sentences were imposed, and sexual violence thus formed only a part of the crimes of which the accused was convicted, it is remarkable that, for 7 out of 13 accused, the sentences were rather lenient and ranged between 5 and 12 years imprisonment.[142] When comparing the sentencing ranges for sexual violence imposed by the ICTY with, for instance, the sentencing range for rape in peacetime set out in the criminal codes of the countries in the former Yugoslavia – generally speaking 3 to 10 or 15 years – it seems that the ICTY

---

[138] So far, the only person convicted of genocide is the Bosnian Serb General Krstić, for his involvement in the Srebrenica killings in July 1995. He received a prison term of 46 years, which was reduced to 35 years on appeal. This judgment seems at odds, at least if a hierarchical approach to crimes and sentences is presumed (see section below), with the conviction of Stakić, a Bosnian Serb doctor, for crimes against humanity for which he received a sentence of life imprisonment.

[139] In Rwanda, the sentence of 25 years imprisonment may only be imposed if someone confesses before being indicted. Such an occurrence has been negligible in the ICTR practice so far.

[140] However, an inquiry into the present-day sentencing practice in the countries of the former Yugoslavia revealed that sentences for rape as a crime against humanity, on the basis of one case scenario (a 35-year-old male who commits rape against detainees under his authority), would have ranged from 5 to 12 years, with an average sentence of 9.8 years as opposed to 6.9 years in peacetime. See Sieber (2004), pp. 67-69.

[141] Kunarac, Kovač and Vuković Judgment, para. 859.

[142] The seven accused include Prcać, Kos, Kvočka, Blaškić, Todorović, Plavšić and Vuković. The other five accused include Sikirica (15 years), Radić (20 years), Žigić (25 years), Stakić (life) and Brđanin (32 years).

sentencing practice does not drastically differ from the latter.[143] Perhaps the ICTY sentencing practice is even more influenced by the sentencing practice for sexual violence in times of peace than it is by the rape as a war crime, a crime against humanity and genocide provisions. Yet, in the *Kunarac, Kovač and Vuković* Judgment, while discussing sentencing, the Trial Chamber held that the 'testimony [of an expert witness] largely centred on rape committed during peacetime and is therefore of little relevance'.[144] Up to the *Muhimana* Judgment, the Rwanda Tribunal had only imposed life imprisonment for sexual violence as (one of the crimes constituting) genocide; in cases where sexual violence formed part of several other crimes cumulating in a single sentence, sentences varied between 30 years and life imprisonment. In the latter case, it is difficult to draw any conclusions as to the effect of the sexual violence conviction on the sentence. Specific sentences of 7 to 15 years were imposed when sexual violence was charged as a crime against humanity, despite the fact that the Rwandan law provides for the death penalty or life imprisonment. The *Muhimana* Judgment, however, was the first case in which rape as a crime against humanity led to a sentence of life imprisonment. Again, when comparing the sentencing ranges for sexual violence imposed by the ICTR with the sentencing ranges for rape provided in the Penal Code of Rwanda – 5 to 10 years, or 10 to 20 years if the rape is committed against a person under the age of sixteen and which may be doubled in case of aggravating circumstances – it seems that also ICTR sentences, overall, do not drastically differ from (or, in case of rape of minors, not even approach) the sentences prescribed under the Rwandan Penal Code applicable in times of peace.[145] The conclusion that both

---

[143] The Criminal Code on the level of the entity of Bosnia and Herzegovina-Federation of 1 August 2003 reveals that rape (in peace time) carries a sentence of *between one and ten years of imprisonment* (Article 203(1)). Paragraph 2 stipulates: 'If the criminal offence has been committed in a particularly cruel or degrading manner or if on the same occasion more instances of sexual intercourse or sex acts tantamount to sexual intercourse were performed by more perpetrators, the perpetrators shall be punished by *imprisonment for a term between 3 and 15 years*.' The latter situations will commonly take place during war time situations. More or less comparable sentence ranges are imposed by the Criminal Code of the Republika Srpska of 1 August 2003. Article 221 of the Criminal Code of the Federation of Bosnia and Herzegovina of 22 November 1998, however, stipulated that the perpetrator be punished by *imprisonment for not less than three years and 10 years maximum*. Sentences for rape in peacetime in other countries of the former Yugoslavia (Serbia, Macedonia, Croatia, and Montenegro) vary between 1 and 10 years imprisonment. For the above-mentioned references, see the report prepared by Sieber (2004), pp. 40-41, 43-44, 46, 50, 54-55, 58-59, 60. The provision on rape in peacetime is set out in Article 88 of the Criminal Code of the Socialist Republic of Bosnia and Herzegovina of 10 June 1977, which stipulated that the penalty for rape is *not less than one and not more than 10 years of prison*. The provisions on rape for the criminal codes of the other republics (Macedonia, Slovenia, Serbia, Croatia, Montenegro) and autonomous regions (Kosovo and Vojvodina) in the former Yugoslavia included similar formulation. See the references to the rape provisions in the Sieber report (2004), pp. 33, 40-41, 43-44.

[144] Kunarac, Kovač and Vuković Judgment, para. 835.

[145] Under the Rwandan Penal Code, rape is punishable by a sentence of five to ten years or ten to twenty years (for a rape committed against a minor under sixteen years of age), which may be doubled for certain prescribed aggravating circumstances, such as the position of authority of the

ICTY and ICTR sentences for sexual violence approximate sentences for sexual violence in peace time, rather than sentences for sexual violence as genocide, a crime against humanity or a war crime, raises the question of whether sexual violence in times of war is actually acknowledged for what it is. Furthermore, although this should have been the case, explicit reasons were not generally given for the Chambers' departure from the national sentencing laws or practices for sexual violence as genocide, a crime against humanity or a war crime in the cases examined.

As mentioned before, the ICC does not provide a link to national laws as a means to determine the sentence. In this way, the Court aims at ensuring a uniform penalties regime for all persons convicted by the Court. The Court will not have to worry about restrictions imposed on sentencing in national jurisdictions, and, in light of the many different national laws and sentencing practices on sexual violence crimes,[146] such an approach might indeed be more practical. Sentences for sexual violence as international crimes are relatively severe in a considerable number of national jurisdictions and the crime of rape is internationally recognised as one of the worst crimes that can be inflicted upon another human being.[147] The ICC should bear this in mind when determining sentences. Taking into account the case law of the Tribunals, which shows that often sentences for sexual violence were similar to those that would have been imposed in national jurisdictions in times of peace, the ICC should be particularly careful not to underrate sexual violence crimes but rather acknowledge the features inherent to sexual violence as a crime of genocide, a crime against humanity or a war crime. On the basis of the sentencing practice for sexual violence, the ICTY and ICTR, with the exception of the *Muhimana* Judgment, have clearly failed to address the

---

accused, the multiplicity of perpetrators or the seriousness of the physical harm. These circumstances are most likely present in times of war. See Articles 360-361 of the Rwandan Penal Code, which read: 'Article 360: Est puni d'un emprisonnement de cinq à dix ans celui qui aura commis un viol. Est assimilé à la violence, le fait d'abuser d'une personne qui, par l'effet d'une maladie, par l'altération de ses facultés ou par toutes autre cause accidentelle, a perdu l'usage de ses sens ou en a été privé par quelque artifice. Si le viol a été commis sur la personne d'un enfant âgé de moins de seize ans, le coupable sera puni d'un emprisonnement de dix à vingt ans. Si le viol a causé la mort de la personne sur laquelle il a été commis, le coupable sera puni de mort. Article 361: Le maximum des peines portées par les articles 558 à 361, sera doublé: 1° si les coupables sont les ascendants de la personne sur laquelle l'infraction a été commise ; 2° s'ils sont de la classe de ceux qui ont autorité sur elle; 3° s'ils sont ses instituteurs ou ses employés à gages ou les employés de la personne ci-dessus indiquée; 4° si l'infraction a été commise, soit par fonctionnaires publics, des représentants de l'autorité ou des ministres d'un culte qui ont abusé de leurs fonctions pour la commettre, soit par les médecins, chirurgiens accoucheurs envers les personnes confiées à leurs soins; 5° si le coupable a été aidé dans l'exécution de l'infraction par une ou plusieurs personnes; 6° si l'infraction a causé à la victime une altération grave de sa santé.'

[146] On the basis of a survey of 12 domestic jurisdictions and sentences imposed for rape as a crime against humanity or war crime, Pickard suggested that an individual convicted of such a crime should be imprisoned for ten to twenty-eight years (the mean of the sentences imposed in these domestic jurisdictions). Daniel B. Pickard (1997), p. 161. See also the law on rape in the comparative study of the criminal codes of 23 countries in the Sieber report (2004), pp. 106-113, which indicates that the sentencing ranges are broad.

[147] See, *inter alia*, the Kunarac, Kovač and Vuković Judgment, para. 655.

severity of sexual violence crimes as international crimes. This practice should not be adopted by the Court.

4.2 The gravity of the crime

Articles 24(1) and 23(1) of the ICTY and ICTR Statutes, respectively, as well as Article 78 of the ICC Statute refer to the gravity of the crime as one of the main factors to establish the sentence. In the Tribunals' case law, the gravity of the crime has been labelled the 'litmus test'[148] or the 'primary consideration' for imposing sentences.[149] Neither the provisions nor ICTY and ICTR case law specify, however, what is to be understood by 'the gravity of the crime'. For example, what factors influence the 'gravity of the crime' and what (other) factors should be considered as aggravating and mitigating circumstances and how do the latter circumstances relate to the gravity of the crime?[150] It is submitted that the gravity of the crime should be determined by the harmfulness of the crime and the culpability of the offender as expressed in the commission of the crime and that these two elements are only affected by those aggravating and mitigating circumstances concomitant with and directly influencing the commission of the crime.[151]

4.2.1 The chapeau *of the crime*

The gravity of the crimes falling within the jurisdiction of the Tribunals and the ICC is, among other things, expressed in the jurisdictional elements of the crimes, also referred to as the *chapeau*. For instance, the underlying crime of rape can be prosecuted as a war crime, a crime against humanity, or genocide. However, to successfully prosecute rape under any of these crimes, different jurisdictional requirements have to be proven. For genocide, this implies that the specific intent requirement needs to be fulfilled, that is, the intent to destroy, in whole or in part, a national, ethnical, racial or religious group as such. The perpetrator does not only desire, for instance, the bodily or mental harm of one or more persons but rather aims at the destruction of an entire group or part of it through the use of sexual violence. For the specific intent element, the perpetrator is considered to be more blameworthy. To be a member of this group places someone in an especially harmful position with not much chance to escape the sexual attack.

In the case of crimes against humanity, the sexual violence needs to have been committed as part of a widespread or systematic attack against the civilian population and, moreover, the perpetrator must have been aware of the broader context in which

---

[148] Čelebići Judgment, para. 1225.

[149] Čelebići Appeal Judgment, para. 731; Naletilić and Martinović Judgment, para. 718.

[150] See, *inter alia*, Musema Judgment and Sentence, para. 1001; Rutaganda Judgment and Sentence, paras. 466-473; Serushago Sentence, paras. 27-42; Furundžija Judgment, paras. 281-284.

[151] Nemitz (2001), pp. 109-111. Nemitz refers to several common and civil law jurisdictions as well as ICTY case law, the Blaškić (para. 765) and Čelebići Judgments (para. 1218), which distinguish between specific material circumstances directly affecting the gravity of the crime and specific personal circumstances of the offender which are relevant for the individualisation of the sentence.

the sexual violence crimes were committed. Again, civilians are very vulnerable: the contextual element of a widespread or systematic attack implies a higher risk for potential victims. In addition, although the specific intent to destroy the members of a certain group may be absent, the perpetrator acted with knowledge of a widespread or systematic attack, which aggravates his intent, as he knew that his criminal behaviour contributed to the attack and to a higher risk for potential victims.[152]

Finally, grave breaches of the 1949 Geneva Conventions and violations of the laws and customs of war incorporate crimes requiring a nexus with an armed conflict. It is exactly in war time situations that victims are particularly vulnerable. Although the jurisdictional requirements of genocide or crimes against humanity are not needed for a crime to constitute a war crime, the ICC Statute now imposes on war crimes the jurisdictional requirement 'in particular when committed as part of a plan or policy or as part of a large-scale commission of such crimes',[153] thereby resembling the wording used for crimes against humanity.

4.2.2 A hierarchy of crimes?

As neither the Tribunals' Statutes nor RPE rank the various crimes, and thereby the sentences to be handed down for each crime, contradictory views on whether or not a hierarchy of crimes exists have occupied the minds of the judges ever since the coming into existence of the two Tribunals. Several scholars have argued that there is a hierarchy of crimes on the basis of the *chapeau* of the crimes; thus, the jurisdictional elements provide a ranking of, first, genocide, second, crimes against humanity and, last, war crimes.[154] Analysis of the ICTY's and ICTR's sentencing policy seems to reveal that indeed such a ranking of crimes exists. Research on the length of ICTY sentences clarifies that sentences imposed for war crimes are significantly shorter (a median sentence of 120 months) than those imposed for crimes against humanity (with a median sentence of 180 months).[155] Sentences handed down for genocide have accumulated in some of the longest sentences, including life imprisonment.

Although there seems to be a theoretical acceptance of a hierarchy of crimes as well as a seemingly (coincidental?) practical application thereof by the ICTY, it has

---

[152] There seems to be a division between persecution as a crime against humanity and other crimes against humanity. In respect of the gravity of the crime, the Todorović Trial Chamber stated that 'persecution is the only crime enumerated in Article 5 of the Statute which requires a discriminatory intent, and which, by its nature, may incorporate other crimes. The Blaškić Trial Chamber stated that the crime of persecution, on account of these distinctive features, justifies a more severe penalty.' See Todorović Sentencing Judgment, para. 32.

[153] Article 8 ICC Statute.

[154] See, *inter alia*, Danner (2001), Frulli (2001), Nemitz (2001) and Carcano (2002).

[155] See the empirical and doctrinal research conducted by Meernik and King (2003) on the sentencing determinants of the ICTY. They conclude that, in contrast to what judges argue in their opinion, a ranking among the crimes does exist: '[G]enocide is treated differently from crimes against humanity and war crimes, and crimes against humanity are punished more severely than war crimes.' Of course, there are some exceptions to the rule: see, for instance, Sikirica Sentencing Jugment, para. 245, where the accused Kolundžija received a sentence of three years for persecution as a crime against humanity.

been argued that the seriousness of the crimes does not depend on such a ranking and consequently does not always result in similar hierarchical differences in the length of sentences imposed. Instead, the seriousness of the crime largely depends on the circumstances of the case. In the *Krstić* case, the Trial Chamber expressed it like this:[156]

> Assessing the seriousness of the crimes is not a mere matter of comparing and ranking the crimes in the abstract. It has been argued that crimes against humanity and war crimes are equally serious and that "there is in law no distinction between the seriousness of a crime against humanity and that of a war crime [...]".[157] No Chamber has yet ruled on the ranking of crimes in a case where an individual has been found guilty of genocide. It can also be argued, however, that genocide is the most serious crime because of its requirement of the intent to destroy, in whole or in part, a national, ethnic, racial or religious group, as such. In this sense, even though the criminal acts themselves involved in a genocide may not vary from those in a crime against humanity or a crime against the laws and customs of war, the convicted person is, because of his specific intent, deemed to be more blameworthy. However, this does not rule out the Trial Chamber's duty to decide on the appropriate punishment according to the facts of each case. Genocide embodies a horrendous concept, indeed, but a close look at the myriad of situations that can come within its boundaries cautions against prescribing a monolithic punishment for one and all genocides or similarly for one and all crimes against humanity or war crimes. A murder, whether qualified as a crime against humanity, a war crime or an act of genocide, may be a graver offence than imposing serious bodily or mental harm upon an individual. In this regard, the Trial Chamber ascribes to the approach taken by the Appeals Chamber that "[t]he level [of penalty] in any particular case [be] fixed by reference to the circumstances of the case."[158]

Thus, the Tribunals must assess the gravity/seriousness of the crimes in light of their individual circumstances and consequences, thereby taking into account quantitatively the number of victims and qualitatively the suffering inflicted on the victims[159] as well as the form and degree of the participation of the accused in the crimes.[160]

In other words, the gravity of the crime is also influenced by the underlying crime. For example, a rape or a murder may be considered to be more serious than pillaging a

---

[156] Krstić Judgment, para. 700.

[157] The attached footnote states: '*Tadic* Sentencing Judgement III, para. 69 and the Separate Opinion of Judge Shahabuddeen. The Appeals Chamber, and subsequently Trial Chambers confirmed this assertion. *Furundzija* Judgement, paras 240 to 243; *Kunarac* Judgement, para. 851. In the opposite sense, *See* Separate Opinion of Judge Cassese appended to the *Tadic* Sentencing Judgement III, para. 14, where it is stated that crimes against humanity are more serious than war crimes because of "a whole pattern of criminality" within which they are committed and the intent of the perpetrator of the crime who must be aware of the said pattern. Also *See* the Joint Separate Opinions of Judge McDonald and Judge Vohrah appended to *Erdemovic* Appeal Judgement, paras 20 *et seq.* and Separate and Dissenting Opinion of Judge Li appended to the *Erdemovic* Appeal Judgement, paras 19 *et seq. See* also the Declaration of Judge Vohrah appended to the *Furundzija* Appeal Judgement, in particular paras 5 *et seq.*'

[158] The attached footnote states: '*Tadic* Sentencing Judgement III, para. 69'.

[159] Krstić Judgment, para. 701, with reference to Čelebići Judgment, para. 1226.

[160] Kupreškić Judgment and Sentence, para. 852.

town. In *Semanza*, such a differentiation on the basis of the underlying crimes against humanity was made when the Trial Chamber held that,

> in the jurisprudence of the two Tribunals, rape as a crime against humanity has resulted in specific sentences between twelve years [Vuković] and fifteen years [Akayesu]. Torture as a crime against humanity has been punished with specific sentences between five years and twelve years. Murder as a crime against humanity has been punished by specific fixed term sentences ranging from twelve years to twenty years. In other cases, convictions for these crimes have formed part of a single sentence of a fixed term or of life imprisonment for the totality of the conduct of the Accused.[161]

In other words, some underlying crimes are generally considered to be more serious than others. Whereas rape as a crime against humanity was sentenced with 12 and 15 years, murder as a crime against humanity invoked sentences from 12 to 20 years. However, this does, not imply that one case of rape may be less serious than another case of murder, although, on the whole, murder attracts a more severe sentence. As the gravity of the crime needs to be determined on the basis of the facts of each case, is not possible to say beforehand that acts of sexual violence charged and recognised as war crimes are less severe than sexual violence as crimes against humanity, which are again less severe than acts of sexual violence charged and recognised as genocide. Summarising, when the gravity of the crime is considered, the circumstances particular to each case need to be considered, which includes, among other things, the seriousness of the underlying crime, including the number of victims and the suffering inflicted on the victims, the elements common to the underlying crimes, and the participation of the accused.

The overview of sexual violence cases shows that rape, torture and other inhumane acts prosecuted as crimes against humanity have generally attracted similar sentences as rape and other forms of sexual violence prosecuted under the grave breaches or violations of the laws or customs of war provisions. Whereas rape and torture as crimes against humanity attracted sentences of 5 to 15 years imprisonment, rape as torture, inhumane treatment, or wilfully causing great suffering as a grave breach attracted sentences ranging from 7 to 15 years and rape as torture, cruel treatment or outrages upon personal dignity and rape as an independent crime, both as violations of the laws or customs of war, likewise resulted in sentences of 7 to 15 years. As far as sexual violence is concerned, it is fair to say that the theory of a ranking of crimes does not seem to have been applied in cases involving sexual violence. Although such a conclusion corresponds with the general belief among the Tribunal judges that no hierarchy of crimes exists or should exist, it is striking that sexual violence crimes have apparently been differently appreciated by the Tribunals than other crimes, as the empirical research conducted on ICTY sentencing revealed that sentences imposed for war crimes are on the whole shorter than for crimes against humanity.

---

[161] Semanza Judgment and Sentence, paras. 563-564. It should be noted that, although the Semanza Trial Chamber was obviously referring to the 12-year sentence imposed on Vuković, this was not a specific sentence in the real sense of the word, but a sentence based on cumulative convictions based on the same conduct.

Only three cases explicitly mentioned the gravity of sexual violence when discussing the gravity of the crime. In the *Kvočka et al.* case, the Trial Chamber noted that 'the sexual violence inflicted upon the women' was considered a factor in assessing the gravity of the crimes.[162] The Češić Trial Chamber mentioned 'the family relationship [two brothers were forced to perform fellatio on each other] and the fact that they were watched by others make the offence of humiliating and degrading treatment particularly serious. The violation of the moral and physical integrity of the victims justifies that the rape be considered particularly serious as well.'[163] The third case involves Muhimana, where the Trial Chamber made a general comment about the seriousness of the crimes committed, that is, 'genocide and murder and rape as crimes against humanity rank among the gravest of crimes. The Chamber has no doubt that principal perpetrators of such crimes deserve a heavy sentence.'[164] Despite the fact that many judgments deal with a plurality of crimes, it is peculiar that so little attention is paid to the seriousness of sexual violence crimes when the gravity of the crime is discussed. This is in particular so because the Tribunals have recognised on a number of occasions that 'rape is one of the worst sufferings a human being can inflict upon another' and can cause 'victims severe mental and physical pain and suffering'.[165] Furthermore, in the *Stakić* Judgment, it was held that 'for a woman, rape is by far the ultimate offence, sometimes even worse than death because it brings shame on her'.[166]

4.3 Aggravating and mitigating circumstances

The ICC enumerates a number of aggravating and mitigating circumstances in Rule 145 which can be taken into account when determining the sentence. The Tribunals, on the other hand, with the exception of cooperation with the Prosecutor as a mitigating factor, do not list such circumstances and have instead developed a wide array of aggravating and mitigating circumstances through their case law. Aggravating circumstances are those 'circumstances directly related to the commission of the offence charged and to the offender himself when he committed the offence, such as the manner in which the offence was committed'.[167] If a particular circumstance is included as an element of the offence under consideration, it will not also be regarded as an aggravating factor.[168] Mitigating circumstances generally refer to the accused's conduct after the crime was committed, such as his cooperation with the Prosecutor, but also factors influencing the accused's culpability during the commission of the crime, such as duress, are considered.

Aggravating circumstances taken into account by the Tribunals include: (1) the magnitude of the crime, which includes the number of victims; (2) the zeal in committing the crime; (3) the heinousness of the crime; (4) the duration of the crime; (5) the discriminatory intent; (6) the vulnerability of the victims; (7) the youth of the

---

[162] Kvočka et al. Judgment, para. 702.
[163] Češić Judgment, para. 35.
[164] Muhimana Judgment and Sentence, para. 603.
[165] Kunarac, Kovač and Vuković Judgment, para. 655. See also Čelebići Judgment, para. 495.
[166] Stakić Judgment, para. 803.
[167] Kunarac, Kovač and Vuković Judgment, para. 850.
[168] Brđanin Judgment, para. 1096.

victims; (8) the trauma of the surviving victims; (9) the abuse of trust or personal authority; (10) the failure to punish those committing crimes; (11) disrespectful courtroom demeanour; the intimidation of witnesses;[169] (12) personal gain; and (13) the level of responsibility.[170] The ICC has now enumerated several of these aggravating circumstances in Rule 145, which includes (1) any relevant prior criminal convictions for crimes under the jurisdiction of the Court or of a similar nature; (2) abuse of power or official capacity; (3) commission of the crime where the victim was particularly defenceless; (4) commission of the crime with particular cruelty or where there were multiple victims; (5) commission of the crime for any motive involving discrimination on any of the grounds referred to in Article 21, paragraph 3; (6) other circumstances which, although not enumerated above, by virtue of their nature are similar to those mentioned. Over the years, the following mitigating circumstances have been accepted by the judges in the Tribunals: (1) guilty plea; (2) cooperation with Prosecutor;[171] (3) remorse; (4) voluntary surrender; (5) no prior criminal record; (6) assistance to victims; (7) no active participation; (8) family; (9) youth; (10) old age; (11) not a present threat; (12) redeemability; (13) subordinate rank; (14) prison would be far away; (15) context of actions; (16) cooperation with Defence Counsel; (17) post-conflict conduct.[172] Rule 145 of the ICC RPE contains the following mitigating circumstances: (1) The circumstances falling short of constituting grounds for exclusion of criminal responsibility, such as substantially diminished mental capacity or duress; (2) The convicted person's conduct after the act, including any efforts by the person to compensate the victims and any cooperation with the Court. As mentioned before, the formulation of Rule 145 makes it perfectly clear that both the aggravating and mitigating circumstances enumerated are not exhaustive. The Tribunals' judges have consistently held that aggravating circumstances should be proven beyond a reasonable doubt and mitigating circumstances only on the balance of probabilities.[173]

4.3.1 Circumstances relevant for sexual violence crimes

To date, in only three cases (of a total of twenty), the relationship between sexual violence and aggravating and mitigating circumstances has been dealt with in greater detail. The most pertinent example is the *Kunarac, Kovač and Vuković* case, in which the accused were charged with sexual violence crimes exclusively and sentenced to 28, 20 and 12 years in prison, respectively. In respect of Kunarac, the following aggravating circumstances were considered: (1) the accused played a leading organisational role in the crimes he was held responsible for and had substantial influence over some of the

[169] Čelebići Judgment, para. 1244; Kayishema and Ruzindana Judgment, para. 17. However, this factor does not relate to the commission of the crime and to the offender himself when he committed the offence. Therefore, such a circumstance should instead be treated as negating remorse as a possible mitigating factor and should be treated as a form of contempt of court. See Kunarac, Kovač and Vuković Judgment, para. 854.

[170] Meernik and King (2003), pp. 739-742. See also Beresford (2001), pp. 54-63.

[171] The only mitigating factor specifically laid down in the RPE, i.e., Rule 101(B)(ii) ICTY and ICTR RPE.

[172] Meernik and King (2003), pp. 742-746. See also Beresford (2001), pp. 64-82.

[173] Čelebići Appeal Judgment, para. 763; Kunarac, Kovač and Vuković Judgment, para. 847.

other perpetrators: the criminal culpability of those leading others is higher than those who follow; (2) the youthful age of some of the victims, which ranged between 15 and a half and 19 years old; (3) the commission of the offences over an extended period of time in relation to certain of his victims: for instance, Witnesses FWS-191 and FWS-186 were enslaved for 2 months;[174] (4) the involvement of more than one victim; (5) the commission of some of the offences by more than one perpetrator at the same time: for instance, Kunarac's aiding and abetting in the rape of FWS-75 by about 15 soldiers and the rape of FWS-87 by three soldiers; (6) the discriminatory grounds – ethnic and gender discrimination – upon which Kunarac committed those offences other than torture, which was committed for discriminatory purposes; and (7) the offences were committed against particularly vulnerable and defenceless women and girls.[175] As mitigating factors were accepted: Kunarac's voluntary surrender, his substantial cooperation with the Prosecutor in giving two statements, and his statement of remorse, namely, that he felt guilty about the fact that FWS-75 was gang-raped while he was raping D.B. in an adjoining room.[176] His statement of remorse, namely, that he understood that D.B. was not acting of her own free will was contradicted by his subsequent testimony that she seduced him, and was therefore not accepted.[177] It was not accepted either that he played a rather insignificant role, given the serious nature of the crimes and the vulnerability of the victims. In other words, as a low level perpetrator, it is also possible to receive a high sentence, a sentence which fits the gravity of the crime. Several of the aggravating factors attributed to Kunarac were taken into account for Kovač as well: namely, (1) the youth of the victims, that is, 12 and 20 years; (2) the duration of the crimes, that is, 4 months in relation to FWS-87 and A.S. and 1 month with respect to FWS-75 and A.B; (3) the vulnerability of the victims; and (4) the magnitude of the crimes, that is, the involvement of more than one victim.[178] No mitigating circumstances were accepted with respect to Kovač. With regard to the third person, Vuković, as aggravating circumstances were cited the youthful age of the victim (15 and a half years old) and the vulnerability of the girl.[179] As far as mitigating circumstances were concerned, the Trial Chamber did not accept that Vuković apparently relented from carrying out worse crimes against FWS-50 because she was about the same age as his daughter, 'for the same reason that the possibility that any accused might have committed more or worse offences should not be so considered'.[180] On appeal, all three accused made submissions arguing that not all aggravating and mitigating circumstances were dealt with by the Trial Chamber or were erroneous in nature.[181] Submissions on aggravating circumstances included, *inter alia*, allegations that certain aggravating factors raised were elements of crimes rather than aggravating

[174] The term 'FWS' stands for 'Foča Witness Statements' (Prosecution witness pseudonyms).
[175] Kunarac, Kovač and Vuković Judgment, paras. 863-867.
[176] *Ibid.*, paras. 868-869.
[177] *Ibid.*, para. 869.
[178] *Ibid.*, paras. 874-875.
[179] *Ibid.*, para. 879.
[180] *Ibid.*, para. 880.
[181] Kunarac, Kovač and Vuković Appeal Judgment, paras. 350-362 (Kunarac); paras. 378-390 (Kovač); paras. 403-409 (Vuković).

factors[182] and that the age of certain victims was too high to be considered eligible for aggravation of the sentence.[183] Mitigating circumstances raised by the accused included, *inter alia*, lack of serious consequences for the raped victims,[184] help to other Muslims in the conflict,[185] and the alleged relationship and protection offered to raped victims.[186] The Appeals Chamber dismissed all arguments raised by the three accused, with the exception of 'family life' as a mitigating factor. However, although the Appeals Chamber ruled that 'family life' should have been taken into account as a mitigating factor (Kunarac is a father of three children and Vuković is married and has two children), the number and severity of the crimes directed the judges not to change the length of the sentences, thus attributing only relative weight to 'family life' as a mitigating factor.[187]

The second case clearly addressing the aggravating factors in relation to the sexual violence committed is the *Muhimana* case. Muhimana was convicted to life imprisonment on each count, which included rape as serious bodily or mental harm as genocide and rape as a crime against humanity. He personally committed many rapes of women whom he believed to be Tutsi and aided and abetted others in raping. In aggravation, the Trial Chamber, thereby consulting the aggravating factors for the crime of rape in the Rwandan Penal Code in effect in 1994,[188] found the following factors of

---

182 Kunarac, Kovač and Vuković Appeal Judgment, paras. 352, 356, 357, 382, 383, 405. For example, the Defence argued that duration is an element of the crime of enslavement, rather than an aggravating factor. The Appeals Chamber found it not to be an element of the crime, but a factor in the proof of the elements of the crime.

183 Kunarac, Kovač and Vuković Appeal Judgment, paras. 354-355, 381, 405. The Appeals Chamber found that there is an inherent discretion to consider the victim's age (19 years) as an aggravating circumstance considering its closeness to the protected age of special vulnerability, namely, 18 years old.

184 Kunarac, Kovač and Vuković Appeal Judgment, paras. 361 (Kunarac); 409 (Vuković). In respect of Vuković, the Appeals Chamber recalled that 'the rape of FWS-50 led to serious mental and physical pain for the victim' and further added that 'force or compulsion was used prior to rape'.

185 Kunarac, Kovač and Vuković Appeal Judgment, para. 408. The Appeals Chamber held that Vuković's help to other Muslims 'does not change the fact that he committed serious crimes against FWS-50. If he is to be punished for his acts against FWS-50, it is to these acts that any possible mitigating factors should be linked.'

186 Kunarac, Kovač and Vuković Appeal Judgment, para. 390. The Appeals Chamber concurred with the Trial Chamber's findings that 'the relationship between the Appellant and FWS-87 was not one of love, but "rather one of cruel opportunism on Kovač's part, of constant abuses and domination over a girl who, at the relevant time, was only about 15 years old". The Trial Chamber also finds that the Appellant "substantially assisted Jagos Kostic in raping A.S".'

187 Kunarac, Kovač and Vuković Appeal Judgment, paras. 362, 366, 408, 413.

188 Aggravating factors for the crime of rape under the Rwandan Penal Code in effect in 1994 concern: 'where the victim is a child under sixteen years of age; where the crime is committed by a civil servant, a public official who has used his position in order to commit the rape; if the perpetrator was assisted in the execution of the crime by one or more persons; if the crime has caused serious harm to the victim's health.' Cited in the Muhimana Judgment and Sentence, para. 606 (with reference to Articles 360-361 of the Rwandan Penal Code).

significance: the young age of the victim (Witness BJ was only 15 years old when Muhimana raped her); the presence of others while Muhimana raped Tutsi women, a factor which was held to compound the public humiliation (others, such as *Interahamwe*, were present, assisted, or participated in ten of the rapes committed by Muhimana); the violent and cruel nature of the conduct (while raping Witness AU, Muhimana repeatedly banged her head against the ground); the public humiliation ('after raping two young Tutsi women in his house, Mika Muhimana led them out, paraded them naked, and invited onlookers to look at their naked bodies'); the cutting of a pregnant woman from her breasts down to her genitals and the removal of her baby, who died soon afterwards; and the atrocious crimes committed against Tutsi women, calculated to degrade and humiliate them.[189] Reference was also made to his position as a *conseiller*, that he was a well-known person in the Gishyita commune, and that he occupied a position of influence in the community: instead of using, or attempting to use, his position within the community to promote peace and reconciliation, he actively participated in the atrocities.[190] The Trial Chamber also observed that 'Muhimana's actions have left many dead and others traumatized or with physical disabilities'.[191] No mitigating factors were found.

The third case which addressed the aggravating circumstances in combination with sexual violence of which the accused was convicted is the *Nikolić* case. In aggravation, the Trial Chamber accepted the vulnerability of the victims at Sušica camp, who were powerless, and the fact that 'women and girls were taken out at nights to be sexually abused and some of them never came back'.[192] In the second place, the depravity of the crimes, including the immediate and long term effects of the conditions in the camp on the victims, were taken into account. The Chamber found it 'hard to imagine how murder, torture and sexual violence could be committed in a harsher and more brutal way than employed by the Accused, assisted by others'.[193] Furthermore,

> [t]he Accused abused his personal position of power especially *vis à vis* the female detainees of Sušica camp. He personally removed and returned women of all ages from the hangar, handing them over to men whom he knew would sexually abuse or rape them. Witness SU-032 believes had they resisted, they would have been liquidated. Witness SU-032 would have to agonize throughout the day, knowing what was to be her fate in the coming night.[194]

The long term effects included physical and severe emotional distress. Survivors were extremely traumatised by being forced to watch other detainees beaten, tortured or executed. The fear of being next was very stressful as well. According to the Trial Chamber:

---

[189] Muhimana Judgment and Sentence, paras. 606-613.
[190] *Ibid.*, para. 604.
[191] *Ibid.*, para. 615.
[192] Nikolić Sentencing Judgment, para. 185.
[193] *Ibid.*, para. 186.
[194] *Ibid.*, para. 194.

Witness SU-032, who was sexually assaulted at the camp, testified about what she felt after the assault and what the assault made on her son: I felt miserable, degraded. I wanted to be a good mother, the best I could. I wanted my child to grow up in a beautiful family, but that couldn't be any more. I felt humiliated as a woman and as a mother by the very fact that I was there in that camp in that situation. [...] It's been 11 years now, but my son is still pensive, introverted, sad and he knows what had happened to me. He is withdrawn. He doesn't like talking to anyone. He's sad. He often tells me that he doesn't like living anymore. He tells me that he often thinks of suicide. [...] [He] was eight years old when we arrived at the camp.'[195]

As a third aggravating factor, the multiplicity of victims is mentioned. 'Although most of the detainees were not direct victims of the Accused's brutal acts of murder, torture and sexual violence ..., each and every detainee of the camp was an immediate victim of the more insidious forms of abuse, specifically the inhumane living conditions and the atmosphere of terror created by murders, beatings, sexual violence and other mental and physical abuse.'[196] The Trial Chamber found a substantial reduction of the sentence warranted in light of his guilty plea, expression of remorse, reconciliation and the disclosing of additional information to the Prosecution. Nikolić was sentenced to 23 years, which was reduced to 20 years on appeal.

In other cases where sexual violence came up, no reference to aggravating and mitigating circumstances specifically related to sexual violence was taken into account in the judgment at all (Tadić; Delić/Mucić (Čelebići); Blaškić; Kvočka, Kos, Radić, Žigić and Prcać (Kvočka *et al.*); Plavšić; Semanza; Nahimana/Ngeze/Barayagwiza (Media); Sikirica; Stakić and Brđanin). In some other cases, mention was made of aggravating circumstances applicable to sexual violence specifically, but only to a certain extent, and no mitigating factors directly linked to sexual violence were mentioned. In the *Akayesu* and *Musema* cases, aggravating factors in relation to sexual violence were only brought to light in conjunction with the role played by the accused, whereas the *Furundžija*, *Niyitegeka*, *Gacumbitsi*, *Simić*, *Češić* and *Todorović* cases in particular discussed the cruelty inherent to sexual violence.

Thus, the level of responsibility of the accused and the abuse of trust by the accused were mentioned in the *Akayesu* case, where the Trial Chamber held that Akayesu's 'status as *bourgemestre* made of Akayesu the most senior government personality in Taba and in this capacity he was responsible for protection of the population and he failed in this mission. ... He ... cautioned and supported through his presence and acts, the rape of many women at the bureau communal.'[197] He betrayed the confidence that the population placed in him and used his power as *bourgemestre* to commit the crimes.[198] The aggravating circumstances were considered to outweigh the mitigating factors.[199] In the *Musema* case, a similar finding was made: '[T]he aggravating factors outweigh the mitigating factors, especially as on several occasions Musema personally led attackers to attack large numbers of Tutsi refugees and raped a

195 *Ibid.*, para. 203.
196 *Ibid.*, para. 206.
197 Akayesu Sentencing Judgment (without paragraphs).
198 *Ibid.*
199 *Ibid.*

young Tutsi woman. He [Musema] knowingly and consciously participated in the commission of crimes and never showed remorse for his personal role in the atrocities.'[200]

Like Kunarac, Kovač and Vuković, Furundžija was similarly charged with and convicted for sexual violence solely and sentenced to 10 years in prison. The following aggravating circumstances were considered by the Trial Chamber in respect of Furundžija: (1) the particularly vicious instances of torture and rape, i.e., the heinousness of the crimes and the zeal with which they were committed; (2) his active role as a commander of the Jokers, i.e., his responsibility; and (3) the fact that Witness A was a civilian detainee and at the complete mercy of her captors, i.e., the vulnerability of the victim.[201] Although Furundžija did not himself perpetrate acts of rape, he 'played a role every bit as grave as the person who actually inflicted the pain and suffering'.[202] Young age – he was 23 years old at the time – was not accepted as a mitigating factor by the Trial Chamber. Neither were the factors that Furundžija had no previous convictions and that he is a father of a young child: the Trial Chamber observed that such factors apply to many accused and therefore cannot be given any significant weight in a case of a gravity such as that of Furundžija's.[203] On appeal, no challenges were made with regard to the aggravating and mitigating factors. In the *Todorović* case, Todorović pleaded guilty to the count of persecution as a crime against humanity, which included, *inter alia*, ordering six men to perform fellatio on each other at the police station in Bosanski Šamac. Todorović's role as Chief of Police in Bosanski Šamac and the manner in which several of the offences were carried out were considered as aggravating factors.[204] Todorović's direct participation in the crimes, as well as his abuse of his position of authority and of people's trust in the institution, clearly constituted an aggravating factor.[205] The Trial Chamber went on to state that 'the fact that he might, initially, have been reluctant to take on the position as Chief of Police does not negate the significance of his abuse of such a superior position. However, the TC also recognised that, while the position of Chief of Police is a relatively senior one, Todorović was not in the very highest levels of the overall hierarchy in the conflict in the former Yugoslavia, nor was he one of its architects'.[206] As to the manner in which Todorović committed the offences, the Trial Chamber held that that 'demonstrated particular cruelty'.[207] The Chamber referred to the beatings of Witnesses C and E and that they 'were forced to perform fellatio on other prisoners'.[208] Todorović's guilty plea, cooperation with the Prosecutor and expression of remorse substantially reduced his sentence.[209] In the *Simić* case, Simić was held responsible for the torture of Safet Hadzialiagic, which included beatings and threats that his penis would be cut off. The

---

[200] Musema Judgment and Sentence, para. 1008.
[201] Furundžija Judgment, para. 283.
[202] *Ibid.*, para. 281.
[203] *Ibid.*, para. 284.
[204] Todorović Judgment, paras. 59 and 66.
[205] *Ibid.*, para. 61.
[206] *Ibid.*, para. 62.
[207] *Ibid.*, para. 63.
[208] *Ibid.*, para. 64.
[209] *Ibid.*, para. 95.

barrel of a gun was pushed into his mouth and he also had to endure gunshots fired over his head. The Trial Chamber held that 'although the mistreatment inflicted by Milan Simić upon his victims did not happen over a prolonged period of time, the manner and methods used render them despicable. The sexual, violent, and humiliating, nature of the acts are therefore considered in aggravation, as it would certainly have increased the mental suffering and feeling of degradation experienced by the victims.'[210] In another case, Češić was convicted of ordering forced fellatio on two brothers in a detention camp. The vulnerability of the victims as well the humiliation suffered by them were considered as factors in aggravation. The Trial Chamber stressed that the humiliation suffered by the victims was exacerbated 'because they were brothers and because guards were present, watching and laughing'.[211] For Niyitegeka, the following aggravating circumstances were, among other factors, taken into account 'the fact that the Accused joined in the jubilation over the killing, decapitation and castration of Kabanda ...; The cruel and insensitive disregard for human life and dignity shown by the order given by the Accused to *Interahamwe* to insert a sharpened piece of wood into the genitalia of the dead Tutsi woman on the road in Kibuye ....'[212] The Chamber found the aggravating circumstances to outweigh the mitigating circumstances. Finally, as aggravating circumstances in the *Gacumbitsi* case were recognised his role as *bourgmestre*, his abuse of trust, his failure to prevent or punish the perpetrators of the crimes and 'the seriousness of the crimes committed, particularly genocide, but also the particularly atrocious rapes that some victims suffered, further constitute aggravating circumstances'.[213] All circumstances of the case considered, Gacumbitsi was given an 'exemplary sentence' of 30 years imprisonment.[214]

This overview shows that, in the majority of cases in which the accused were convicted for sexual violence, aggravating factors specifically focusing on sexual violence were not addressed in the judgment, or only marginally. However, given the nature of sexual violence crimes, certain aggravating factors will be present in many cases of sexual violence:[215] for example, the magnitude of crimes, involving more than one victim of sexual violence; the zeal in committing crimes, including sexual violence committed by multiple perpetrators, the cruelty with which the sexual violence was committed, and sexual violence in front of an audience; the heinousness of the sexual violence crimes; the duration of the sexual violence; the discriminatory intent, including the commission of sexual violence on the basis of gender or ethnicity; the vulnerability of the victims, including the use of force, coercion or threats against the victim or others, by keeping someone in detention, or if the victim simply had no where else to go; the youth of the victims; the repeated nature of the crimes; the trauma of surviving victims and others, including the physical and emotional scars inherent to sexual

[210] Milan Simić Judgment, para. 63.

[211] Češić Judgment, paras. 52-54. The humiliation was only considered for the count of rape as a crime against humanity, as humiliation was already considered as an element of the crime of humiliating and degrading treatment as a violation of the laws or customs of war.

[212] Niyitegeka Judgment and Sentence, para. 499.

[213] Gacumbitsi Judgment, para. 345.

[214] *Ibid.*, paras. 355-356.

[215] This is not to say that these aggravating factors are not also applicable for many of the other crimes falling within the jurisdiction of the Tribunals and Court.

violence, such as pregnancy and HIV/AIDS resulting from the sexual violence inflicted, but also social isolation and economic hardship.[216] Several of these aggravating factors are listed in Rule 145 of the ICC RPE, and for those aggravating factors not enumerated, it could be argued that they fall within the ambit of subparagraph (6), that is, 'other circumstances which, although not enumerated above, by virtue of their nature are similar to those mentioned above'.

It is noteworthy that the trauma experienced by surviving victims of sexual violence has, to date, only been raised twice, in the *Simić* and *Nikolić* cases, despite the myriad of consequences generally resulting from sexual violence. Even the *Kunarac, Kovač and Vuković* case, a case solely dealing with sexual violence crimes, does not mention the trauma or harm caused to the victims, victims who have experienced tens to hundreds of rapes in a period of weeks or months, locked up in houses and nowhere to go. In addition, although the *Muhimana* Judgment makes a general reference to Muhimana's actions as traumatising for victims or leaving them with physical disabilities,[217] nowhere is it explicitly stated that these factors have been taken into account in aggravation of the sexual violence crimes. This is the more remarkable given the Trial Chamber's reference to the Rwandan Penal Code, which does make reference to the aggravating factor 'if the crime [rape] has caused serious harm to the victim's health'.[218] Moreover, the Prosecutor in *Muhimana* had explicitly called for the effect of Muhimana's actions on the lives of victims – 'medical, psychological, social and economic wounds' – to be taken into account in aggravation of his crimes.[219] Similarly, the effect of the crime on third parties – for instance, being forced to watch your own daughter and/or wife being raped before your eyes – was, for some time, not acknowledged as a factor in aggravation of the crime,[220] whereas the ICC has now made such an opening by referring to 'the harm caused to the victims *and their families*' as a

[216] In the Kunarac, Kovač and Vuković case, the aggravating circumstances as accepted by the courts in the former Yugoslavia were summarised as follows: (1) the youthful age of the victims of sexual crimes; (2) rapes committed with ethnically based motives; (3) rapes committed against detainees (4) rapes committed against physically weak persons who could not defend themselves; (5) rapes entailing multiple victims; (6) rapes at gunpoint. See Kunarac, Kovač and Vuković Judgment, para. 835. See also Green (1994, p. 171), proposing aggravating circumstances for rape (based on the Yugoslavian law on rape and aggravating circumstances accepted) to be taken into account by the ICTY. Aggravating circumstances accepted under the Rwandan Penal Code include the young age of the victim, the position of authority of the accused, and the severity of the physical harm. See Articles 360-361 of the Rwandan Penal Code.

[217] Muhimana Judgment and Sentence, para. 615.

[218] *Ibid.*, para. 606 (with reference to Article 361 of the Rwandan Penal Code).

[219] *Ibid.*, paras. 595, 600.

[220] The Prosecutor in the Kunarac case raised the effect of sexual violence on others, but it was rejected by the Trial Chamber holding that such effects are irrelevant to the culpability of the offender, but that consideration of the consequences of a crime upon the victim who is directly injured by it is, however, always relevant to the sentencing of the offender. See Kunarac, Kovač and Vuković Judgment, para. 852. However, in Furundžija, a man was forced to watch the rape of a female friend, and this was recognised to cause him severe physical and mental suffering (as part of the crime of torture) (para. 267). See also Groenhuijsen (1996) on this issue.

factor to be taken into consideration in determining the sentence.[221] However, with the *Češić* Sentencing Judgment, a shift in the case law of the Tribunals seems to have taken place, as it was recognised, in this case, that the impact on the victim's relatives and friends is among the factors to be taken into account when evaluating the inherent gravity of a crime.[222] The repetitiveness of the rapes is another factor which has not been taken into account as a factor in aggravation in those judgments where it could have been found, such as in the *Kunarac, Kovač and Vuković* case. In the latter case, the victims were not raped once, but on a repeated basis, over and over again, in different forms. Each time that a victim is raped (whether orally, anally or vaginally) should count as a separate rape, which should be taken into account in aggravation.[223] Other examples in which the repetitive nature of the rapes should have been considered include the *Akayesu* and *Muhimana* cases, as the evidence revealed that some of the victims were raped several times, often by a multiplicity of perpetrators over a longer period of time (which are aggravating factors as well). Finally, gender as a basis of discrimination or as a component of vulnerability should be given more attention in the evaluation of aggravating circumstances in cases where sexual violence is concerned as sexual violence is disproportionately committed against women.

A considerable number of the above-mentioned factors were applied to the three accused in the *Kunarac, Kovač and Vuković* case, although, as explained, not all relevant aggravating factors were sufficiently dealt with. That the *Kunarac, Kovač and Vuković* case emphasised the aggravating circumstances directly related to sexual violence is in principle no surprise given that this case dealt with sexual violence only. This does not mean, however, that, in cases where the accused is charged with other crimes besides sexual violence, less attention should be given to aggravating circumstances. For instance, the *Akayesu* case dealt with many instances of sexual violence and it could be argued that all of the above aggravating factors applied to the events described in the judgment, but none of them were addressed in the judgment: only the role Akayesu played in relation to the sexual violence was brought up. It is important that judgments contain aggravating factors in order to fully describe the perpetrator's conduct. In addition, in the Tribunals' work, aggravating circumstances have been considered time and time again in order to preclude any leniency stemming from mitigating circumstances.[224]

---

[221] Rule 145(1)(c) ICC RPE (italics added).

[222] Češić Judgment, paras. 38-39, 43-44 (with reference to Krnojelac Appeal Judgment, para. 260). However, the Trial Chamber held that the Prosecution did not put forward enough evidence to establish that the suffering was to be attributed solely or mainly to the sexual assault.

[223] Askin (2003b), p. 816. Askin explains that although the indictments do not charge each incident of rape as a separate crime, and it would be difficult to do so given that many were raped by multiple perpetrators in seemingly endless numbers of violations, the repetitive nature of the rapes must be taken into account during sentencing.

[224] Although the Tribunals have acknowledged on several occasions that express consideration of aggravating circumstances is not necessary for the sort of crimes adjudged before the Tribunals, their policy has been to consider them in order to preclude any leniency of sentences. See, *inter alia*, Erdemović Judgment, para. 45; Ruggiu Judgment and Sentence, para. 46. Furthermore, the study conducted by Meernik and King reveals that, as to be expected, a link between aggravating circumstances and the length of sentences generally exists: (a) individuals cited for one or more

By and large, mitigating circumstances are general in nature (more so than aggravating circumstances), applicable to all sorts of crimes or situations, not particularly sexual violence crimes. Mitigating circumstances directly related to sexual violence have therefore been rare. In the *Kunarac, Kovač and Vuković* case, some mitigating circumstances directly linked to sexual violence were raised but none accepted, with the exception of one expression of remorse by Kunarac. From the *Kunarac, Kovač and Vuković* and *Furundžija* cases, it follows that mitigating factors – such as age, family life, prior criminal record, help to others, expressions of remorse and having played only an insignificant role – did not have any substantial effect on the sentence length for sexual violence crimes. In those cases, the balance between the mitigating factors and the seriousness of the sexual violence committed, including the aggravating factors, tipped in favour of the latter, thus precluding any leniency in sentences.[225] For the other cases on sexual violence not focused on sexual violence only, it is difficult to say anything significant on the relationship between mitigating circumstances and sentences imposed, except that factors such as a guilty plea and cooperation with the Prosecutor seem to have had a substantial effect on the sentence length.[226]

4.3.2 Conduct not charged in the indictment, false defences and disrespectful courtroom behaviour

Especially in cases of sexual violence, evidence thereof may come up during trial that was not included in the indictment[227] or, if it was, the charges only related to other acts of sexual violence directed against the witness by the accused. During the *Kunarac, Kovač and Vuković* trial, the Prosecutor came to face the latter situation, that is, evidence of additional rapes committed against FWS-50 (a 15-year-old girl) and FWS-75 by Vuković, not charged in the indictment.[228] In order to expedite the proceedings, the Prosecutor decided not to amend the indictment mid-trial. Instead, the Prosecutor wanted to consider in aggravation of Vuković's crimes 'all acts and omissions that were part of the same course of conduct or common scheme or plan as the offence of

---

aggravating circumstance(s) received longer average sentences than those who where not so cited, and, (b) the magnitude of the crime(s) and the zeal with which the accused committed the crime(s) also resulted in higher sentences. See Meernik and King (2003), pp. 741-742. That the number of aggravating factors influences the length of the sentence is also evidenced by Rule 145 ICC RPE, which requires the existence of one or more aggravating factors before life imprisonment can be imposed.

[225] The role played by Furundžija, however, seems to have had a substantial effect on the sentence imposed as argued above.

[226] See, *inter alia*, the Todorović and Plavšić cases.

[227] See, *inter alia*, the Gacumbitsi case, in which Witness TAP testified during trial that she was raped by Gacumbitsi himself. Gacumbitsi was, however, only charged with instigating rape.

[228] Kunarac, Kovač and Vuković Judgment, paras. 796 and 814. According to the Indictment, Vuković raped Witness FWS-75 in a classroom at Foča High School. However, FWS-75 testified that she was raped by Vuković behind the locked kitchen door in Kovač's apartment, not at Foča High School. Witness FWS-50 testified in court that she was raped at Buk Bijela for the first time, but this incident was not charged in the indictment.

conviction to be relevant for purposes of sentencing'.[229] The Trial Chamber did not accept this line of argument and held:

> Even assuming, however, that the Defence was put on notice to put its case with respect to such uncharged acts and omissions, that those uncharged offences were established beyond reasonable doubt and that they can be said to be part of the same plan as the offence of conviction, the Trial Chamber would not allow such an uncharged crime being used as an aggravating circumstance. The reason is this: an offender can only be sentenced for conduct for which he has been convicted. ... Mitigating and aggravating circumstances should of course also be considered when imposing sentence. Mitigating circumstances not directly related to the offence, such as co-operation with the Prosecutor, an honest showing of remorse and a guilty plea, may be considered. However, the position with respect to aggravating circumstances is quite different. Only those circumstances directly related to the commission of the offence charged and to the offender himself when he committed the offence, such as the manner in which the offence was committed, may be considered in aggravation. In other words, circumstances not directly related to an offence may not be used in aggravation of an offender's sentence for that offence. To permit otherwise would be to whittle away the purpose and import of an indictment. Either the Prosecutor should charge such conduct as an offence, or, where it is not directly related to another charged offence, she should desist from citing such conduct as an aggravating factor. The Trial Chamber understands that the multiplicity of humanitarian law violations committed during an armed conflict as part of a common criminal scheme often cannot be succinctly captured in an indictment. Considerations of fairness to the accused and judicial economy, however, outweigh the wish to have each and every crime committed during a war brought to light and adjudged in whatever way – that is something which this International Tribunal simply cannot do.[230]

In the *Semanza* case, the Prosecutor again submitted that allegations of criminal activity by the accused, not charged in the indictment, should be considered as aggravating factors in sentencing.[231] The *Semanza* Trial Chamber ruled, in line with the *Kunarac, Kovač and Vuković* Judgment, that this is contrary to the purposes of the indictment.[232]

---

[229] Kunarac, Kovač and Vuković Judgment, para. 848.

[230] *Ibid.*, para. 850.

[231] The allegations included killing, beheading, driving a vehicle over the bodies of wounded people, ordering to shoot Tutsi seeking refuge at his home, and threatening to cut a victim's nose off. Semanza Judgment and Sentence, para. 566.

[232] Semanza Judgment and Sentence, para. 570: 'It would circumvent the proper course of justice to rely on allegations of further uncharged criminality to increase the sentence of the Accused. Where the Prosecutor has reliable evidence of criminal activity falling within the jurisdiction of the Tribunal, then she may choose to include those matters in the indictment against an accused. Where such matters arise only during the trial, the Prosecutor may request to have the indictment amended to include the new allegations. Having failed to include these crimes in the indictment, the Prosecutor should not be permitted to achieve a similar effect by having them considered as aggravating factors. In these circumstances, the Chamber will not place any reliance on criminal acts outside the scope of the Indictment and on which it has not made any factual findings.'

There are two reasons why evidence of sexual violence may come up so late in the trial process. The first reason is linked with the three phases in the process in which evidence is taken: (1) during the investigation phase, the investigator takes down a written witness statement; (2) during the mission conducted by the Prosecutor, a trial attorney meets the witness to verify the witness statement and the witness's ability and willingness to testify before the court; and (3) during the witness's stay in the safe house, a few days before the start of the trial, the witness meets again with a trial attorney, not necessarily the same person as during the mission, to verify the statement once again. Since, in all these phases, different persons talk to the witness, sometimes over a considerable time span, it may happen that evidence on sexual violence does not come up, especially if the investigator or trial attorney does not confront the witness with it. The second reason why evidence of sexual violence does not always come up early in the process is to be found in the nature of the crimes committed. For various reasons, including trauma, stigmatisation and feelings of shame, victims of sexual violence may be reluctant to talk about the sexual violence they went through.

Despite the plausibility of the arguments outlined above, in all fairness to the accused, evidence of sexual violence which comes up during trial not laid down in the indictment cannot be taken into account in aggravation of the sentence. To do so would circumvent the purpose of the indictment. New sexual violence evidence may nevertheless show 'a consistent pattern of conduct' and may therefore be 'admissible in the interests of justice' in conformity with Rule 93.[233] In other words, although the accused may not be convicted on the basis of this evidence, it may support other evidence on sexual violence and the role of the accused therein. Another option is just to amend the indictment to include the sexual violence count, which, in all fairness to the victim, is the most proper way to act. The victim should not suffer from a faulty investigation.

In the *Kunarac, Kovač and Vuković* case, another aggravating factor was raised by the Prosecutor. The accused Kunarac and Kovač alleged that they were legitimately involved with two of the witnesses, instead of raping them. Kunarac claimed that he was seduced into intercourse by the 19-year-old D.B., whereas Kovač held that he had a relationship with FWS-87. The alibis as such were rejected by the Trial Chamber, but the Chamber did say that such defences 'are part of the legitimate conduct of the accused's defence, unless the Prosecutor can establish that it was not legitimately raised'.[234] In order to prove a false defence, 'the Prosecutor would have to show that Defence counsel and the accused acted in collusion, for example, that the accused instructed or counselled that line of defence. To hold otherwise would mean the attribution of counsel's conduct to the accused.'[235] The Trial Chamber found no false defences to exist with regard to Kunarac and Kovač.

If it is established that a false defence has been raised, such as the 'girlfriend alibi', such an illegal defence could be viewed as an aggravating circumstance. Perhaps it would even be better to regard such a false defence as negating remorse as a possible

233 Kvočka et al. Judgment, paras. 547 and 556.
234 Kunarac, Kovač and Vuković Judgment, para. 853.
235 *Ibid.*

mitigating factor as it clearly shows any lack of remorse on the part of the accused.[236] In addition, such behaviour is in contempt of court. Apart from all this, it is remarkable that such false defences were raised in the *Kunarac, Kovač and Vuković* case. In light of Rule 96, the raising of defences which concern the victim's consent to the sexual intercourse are restricted. Only if it can be established *in camera* that no force, coercion or any other forms of threats were present may such defences be raised. It seems that the *Kunarac, Kovač and Vuković* case was full of evidence on coercive and forceful circumstances surrounding the sexual violence crimes and the Trial Chamber should thus not have admitted the 'girlfriend alibis' in the first place.

Disrespectful courtroom behaviour, such as laughing during the testimony of a rape victim, was another factor to be taken into account, according to the Prosecutor in the *Kunarac, Kovač and Vuković* case. The Trial Chamber, however, ruled that such behaviour showed a lack of remorse and was therefore treated as negating remorse as a possible mitigating factor, not as an aggravating factor.[237]

5 CUMULATIVE (CHARGES AND) CONVICTIONS

The issue of cumulative charges and convictions deals with the question of whether an accused may be charged with and convicted of more than one offence for the same conduct. The ICTY Appeals Chamber in the *Čelebići* case argued that cumulative charging is allowed as 'prior to the presentation of all of the evidence, it is not possible to determine to a certainty which of the charges brought against an accused will be proven. The Trial Chamber is better poised, after the parties' presentation of the evidence, to evaluate which of the charges may be retained, based upon the sufficiency of the evidence.'[238] Subsequently, in various cases, cumulative convictions for the same conduct have been allowed by the two Tribunals when the following criteria were met: (1) the offences charged have different material elements – an element is materially distinct from another if it requires proof of a fact not required by the other;[239] (2) the offences are designed to protect different values, or (3) it is necessary to record convictions on each offence in the indictment in order to describe fully what the accused did.[240] Thus, while the accused may be convicted twice, he is not punished more than once for the same conduct. However, the prejudice that an offender will or may suffer because of cumulative convictions based on the same conduct has also been acknowledged and needs therefore to be taken into account when a sentence is imposed.[241]

---

[236] Compare this situation with the situation of disrespectful courtroom behaviour discussed below.

[237] Kunarac, Kovač and Vuković Judgment, para. 854.

[238] Čelebići Appeal Judgment, para. 400; Musema Appeal Judgment, para. 369; Semanza Judgment and Sentence, para. 408.

[239] If the relevant provisions do not each have a materially distinct element, the Trial Chamber must select the more specific provision: Čelebići Appeal Judgment, para. 413.

[240] Akayesu Judgment, para. 468; Čelebići Appeal Judgment, paras. 412-413; Kunarac, Kovač and Vuković Judgment, para. 547; Kupreškić Judgment, paras. 668-748.

[241] Prejudice that may arise from cumulative convictions includes the social stigmatisation inherent in being convicted of an additional crime for the same crime and the risk that, under the

Cumulative convictions for sexual violence were entered in the *Tadić, Čelebići, Furundžija, Kunarac, Kovač and Vuković* and *Semanza* cases,[242] but cumulative convictions on sexual violence were discussed in a comprehensive manner only in *Čelebići* and *Kunarac, Kovač and Vuković*. In *Kunarac, Kovač and Vuković*, cumulative convictions under Articles 3 (violations of the laws or customs of war) and 5 (crimes against humanity) of the ICTY Statute on the basis of the same acts (inter-article convictions) were allowed. Both Article 3 and Article 5 contain materially distinct elements not contained in the other: Article 3 contains a nexus requirement, so there must be a close link between the acts of an accused and the armed conflict, and Article 5 requires a widespread or systematic attack directed against a civilian population.[243] Thus, regardless of the underlying crimes contained in Articles 3 and 5, convictions under both articles based on the same conduct are allowed. Cumulative convictions that were accepted in the *Kunarac, Kovač and Vuković* case involved:

> convictions for rape under both Articles; convictions for torture under both Articles; convictions for enslavement under Article 5 and outrages upon personal dignity under Article 3; convictions for rape under Article 5 and torture under Article 3; convictions for rape under Article 3 and torture under Article 5; and convictions for enslavement under Article 5 and rape under Article 3.[244]

The Trial Chamber also allowed cumulative convictions for rape and torture under either Article 3 or Article 5 based on the same conduct (intra-article convictions). As the elements of rape and torture each contain one materially distinct element not contained in the other – rape requires sexual penetration, while torture requires that harm be inflicted for a prohibited purpose – convictions for both crimes on the basis of the same acts have been allowed.[245] Cumulative convictions for enslavement and rape as crimes against humanity were also allowed because enslavement, even if based on sexual exploitation, is a crime distinct from rape: rape requires sexual penetration, while enslavement requires ownership of another person.[246] The Trial Chamber did not clarify whether, in respect of the same conduct, it is allowed to cumulatively convict a person accused of rape as a war crime not enumerated in Article 3 and of outrages upon

---

law of the State enforcing the sentence, the eligibility of a convicted person for early release will diminish where it depends upon the number or nature of the convictions entered. Čelebići Appeal Judgment, paras. 403-405; Čelebići Judgment on Sentence Appeal, para. 25; Kunarac, Kovač and Vuković Judgment, para. 551: Kunarac, Kovač and Vuković Appeal Judgment, para. 169. See also the Separate and Dissenting Opinion of Judge David Hunt and Judge Mohamed Bennouna annexed to the Čelebići Appeal Judgment.

242 See Chart on sentencing in cases of sexual violence in subsection 3.1.

243 Kunarac, Kovač and Vuković Judgment, para. 556.

244 Kunarac, Kovač and Vuković Judgment, para. 556; Kunarac, Kovač and Vuković Appeal Judgment, para. 167.

245 Kunarac, Kovač and Vuković Judgment, para. 557; Kunarac, Kovač and Vuković Appeal Judgment, paras. 188-196; Semanza Judgment and Sentence, para. 506 (Semanza was cumulatively convicted for instigating both rape and torture as crimes against humanity on the basis of the same facts).

246 Kunarac, Kovač and Vuković Appeal Judgment, para. 186.

personal dignity as a violation of Common Article 3 to the Geneva Conventions.[247] In addition, the *Kunarac, Kovač and Vuković* Trial Chamber did not address the possibility of cumulative conviction for rape as a customary war crime under Article 3 and any of the grave breaches under Article 2.

The situation is different for multiple convictions based on the same acts under the grave breaches and violations of the laws or customs of war provisions. Although the accused Delić and Mucić (*Čelebići* case) were initially cumulatively convicted of crimes falling under Articles 2 (grave breaches) and 3 (violations of the laws or customs of war) based on the same acts, these cumulative convictions were overturned on appeal. The Appeals Chamber upheld the Article 2 convictions and dismissed the Article 3 convictions: the crimes did not contain materially distinct elements.[248] The crimes under Article 2 contained an additional element, the protected person requirement, and therefore only the Article 2 convictions were upheld.[249] The Appeals Chamber remitted the case to a Trial Chamber to discuss whether a different sentence should be imposed following the dismissal of cumulative convictions.[250] The new Trial Chamber concluded that this was not the case, since the totality of the accused criminal conduct had not been reduced by the dismissal of the cumulative convictions.[251] In the *Blaškić* case, the cumulative conviction under Article 3, cruel treatment, was, for a similar reason, quashed on appeal, in favour of a conviction under Article 2, inhumane treatment.

Summarising, cumulative convictions should be allowed with the condition that only the total weight of the accused's guilt is reflected in the sentence. The accused should not be prejudiced by receiving a higher sentence for multiple convictions based on the same conduct than in situations where such multiple convictions were not rendered.[252] The use of cumulative convictions is important because it recognises that wartime rape occurs in different contexts, for different reasons, with various impacts.

7 Final remarks

Given the fact that tens of thousands of people were raped during the 1994 genocide, the ICTR record on convictions for rape and other forms of sexual violence is poor: only 8 out of a total of 25 persons prosecuted were found guilty of sexual violence, only 4 of them for rape as genocide and/or crimes against humanity. In addition, 4 accused were acquitted of rape charges. The ICTY convicted 21 individuals of sexual violence conduct out of a total of 56 persons prosecuted, only 4 of them for rape as a crime against humanity. However, on top of these meagre results (at least as far as the ICTR is

---

247 Kunarac, Kovač and Vuković Judgment, para. 556.

248 Čelebići Appeal Judgment, paras. 424-426. The crimes concerned were 'wilfully causing great suffering or serious injury to body or health' (Article 2) and 'cruel treatment' (Article 3); torture (Article 2) and torture (Article 3); 'inhuman treatment' (Article 2) and 'cruel treatment' (Article 3).

249 *Ibid.*

250 *Ibid.*, para. 431.

251 Čelebići Sentencing Judgment, para. 42, upheld by Čelebići Judgment on Sentence Appeal, para. 27.

252 Ntanda Nsereko (2002), pp. 66-67.

concerned), the sentences imposed do not always seem to reflect the seriousness of the crimes committed. A close evaluation of the factors influencing the sentences imposed for sexual violence conduct on the supranational criminal law level has resulted in some remarkable observations.

In the first place, a closer look at the sentencing practice in the national courts of the former Yugoslavia and Rwanda showed that, with the exception of Muhimana's conviction, specific sentences imposed by the Tribunals for sexual violence as international crimes approximated sentences imposed for sexual violence as national crimes, as if the sexual violence conduct over which the Tribunals have jurisdiction were committed in peacetime situations instead of in times of conflict. Although the general sentencing practice on international crimes in the accused's country is officially not binding, the majority of sentences the Tribunals have imposed in cases of sexual violence generally do not even approach that sentencing practice. This finding gives the impression that the seriousness of sexual violence as genocide, a crime against humanity or a war crime has been severely undermined by the Tribunals when imposing sentences for sexual violence. In addition, the Tribunal judges repeatedly held that the national prison sentencing practice must be seen as a guiding, not a binding, tool to determine the sentence and the Chambers committed themselves to explaining their reasons if they thought it necessary to diverge from the national sentencing practice. Yet, in most cases examined, no explicit reasons were given for the Chambers' departure from the national sentencing laws or practices with regard to sexual violence as genocide, a crime against humanity or a war crime.

In the second place, the gravity of the sexual violence crimes need to be assessed in the light of their individual circumstances and consequences, taking into account quantitatively the number of victims and qualitatively the suffering inflicted on the victims as well as the form and degree of the participation of the accused in the crimes. However, the gravity of rape and other forms of sexual violence is often not explicitly mentioned as such. Out of a total of 20 ICTY and ICTR cases dealing with sexual violence, the gravity of rape or sexual violence was mentioned in only three cases (that is, in the *Kvočka et al.*, *Češić* and *Muhimana* cases). This is remarkable, in light of the Tribunals' recognition, on a number of occasions, that 'rape is one of the worst sufferings a human being can inflict upon another' and can cause 'victims severe mental and physical pain and suffering'.[253] In the *Stakić* Judgment, it was held that 'for a woman, rape is by far the ultimate offence, sometimes even worse than death because it brings shame on her'.[254]

In the third place, the aggravating circumstances relevant to sexual violence are in a considerable number of cases addressed to a certain extent or not at all. Again, only in 3 cases out of a total of 20 were the aggravating circumstances broadly discussed (that is, in the *Kunarac, Kovač and Vuković*, *Muhimana* and *Nikolić* cases), and even in these cases, not all aggravating factors that could have been applicable were covered. This practice is at odds with the large number of aggravating factors which are often applicable when it comes to sexual violence committed in conflict situations, such as the magnitude of the crimes, the zeal in committing the crimes, including a multiplicity of perpetrators, the heinousness of the sexual violence crimes, the duration of the sexual

253 Kunarac, Kovač and Vuković Judgment, para. 655. See also Čelebići Judgment, para. 495.
254 Stakić Judgment, para. 803.

violence, the discriminatory intent, including the commission of sexual violence on the basis of gender and/or ethnicity, the vulnerability of the victims, the youth of the victims, the repeated nature of the crimes, and the trauma of surviving victims and others, including the physical and emotional scars inherent to sexual violence, such as pregnancy and HIV/AIDS resulting from the sexual violence inflicted, but also social isolation and economic hardship. Failure to state such aggravating factors may severely impact the sentence imposed. The disillusionment of some of the survivors by the sentences imposed in the *Kunarac, Kovač and Vuković* case was obvious in this perspective. Nezira Zolota of the Sarajevo association of former camp inmates said: 'We are shocked with the verdict. Justice has not been done, as the three received a minimum punishment for what they have done.'[255] In a similar vein, Witness 96, a witness who testified herself in the *Kunarac, Kovač and Vuković* case, stated: 'I am disappointed with the sentences – given everything that they have done. I no longer believe in those sentences and will not testify before the tribunal.'[256] When certain crucial aggravating factors, such as the trauma and repetitiveness of the rapes, are not taken into account, such reactions certainly cannot come as a surprise.

The reactions to the sentence imposed on Muhimana, on the other hand, were very different. Marie Immaculee Ingabire, a women's rights activist from Rwanda, who was scheduled to appear as an expert witness in the case but was dropped at the last minute by the Prosecutor because of bureaucratic delays, praised the ICTR's decision of life imprisonment for Muhimana: 'This is very good news. It sends a message that sexual violence constitutes a very serious crime against humanity.'[257] She continued: 'Women will now come forward willingly and testify on the acts of sexual violence they suffered during the genocide. In the past, they had been reluctant because they thought they would be ridiculing themselves in public and yet it would amount to nothing.'[258] Muhimana was sentenced to life imprisonment for raping 7 women and girls (6 Tutsi girls and one Hutu girl who he mistakenly believed was a Tutsi) and aiding and abetting others to rape a total of 5 Tutsi women and girls, under both genocide and crimes against humanity. The Trial Chamber explicitly referred to the gravity of sexual violence and also discussed the aggravating circumstances in relation to sexual violence. It must be noted, however, that the Trial Chamber missed out on some important aggravating factors (especially the repeated nature of some of the rapes, the trauma inflicted on the victims and the multiplicity of perpetrators), even though this did not seem to affect the sentence imposed.

Summarising, only on the basis of all the circumstances of the case can a just sentence be imposed, reflecting the totality of the defendant's conduct. Victims of sexual violence want to see the violation labelled publicly as a crime and see the perpetrator condemned by the international community and punished. However, if the totality of the criminal conduct is not reflected in the sentence, justice may not prevail

---

255 The Guardian, *Mass Rape Ruled a War Crime*, by Andrew Osborn, Brussels, 23 February 2001.

256 Institute for War & Peace Reporting, *Foca Rape Case*, by Mirko Klarin and Vjera Bogati, Issue 210, 28 February 2001.

257 Hirondelle News Agency, *Muhimana Gets Life Sentence for Multiple Rapes in Rwanda Genocide*, 28 April 2005.

258 *Ibid.*

for those survivors of sexual violence who had the courage to come forward and testify at the Tribunal. This may, in turn, lead them and other victims of sexual violence not to appear before the Tribunal in any other cases involving charges of sexual violence.

In light of the above, the *Semanza* Appeal Judgment is of interest. In this case, the Prosecutor explicitly appealed against the sentence of 7 years for instigating rape imposed on Semanza by the Trial Chamber, a sentence which the Prosecutor found 'manifestly inadequate'.[259] According to the Prosecutor, the sentence should instead be *no less* than 10 years because of the gravity of the crime, the sentences imposed for rape in other Tribunal cases and the sentencing practice in Rwanda. In addition, the Prosecutor held that it appeared that the Trial Chamber was guided by the fact that instigation is a form of indirect participation, likely to result in a lesser sentence than if Semanza had been the principal perpetrator. In response to the first three issues raised, the Appeals Chamber ruled that the Trial Chamber had acted within its discretion and, with regard to the latter issue, that it carried no weight.[260] Although the Appeals Chamber held that the arguments raised by the Prosecutor were not convincing enough to determine that the Trial Chamber made a discernible error in imposing the 7-year sentence, the question is what other arguments the Prosecutor could have raised to make the judges of the Appeals Chamber understand that the 7-year sentence for Semanza was too lenient given the gravity of the crime of rape. The 7-year sentence did not accurately take the gravity and aggravating circumstances into account and approached (or not even approached) sentences given for rape on the basis of sentences imposed on perpetrators of rape in peacetime situations instead of genocide. In Rwanda, the sentence for rape is 5 to 10 years, and 10 to 20 years in those cases where the victims are under the age of sixteen, which sentence may be doubled if certain prescribed aggravating circumstances can be found.

Given the (relatively speaking) small number of sexual violence cases and the many different forms of sexual violence that will appear before the Court, the judges need to have wide discretion in exercising their sentencing powers: sentencing guidelines are not a practical tool in establishing sentences before the ICC. Article 78(1) and Rule 145, both dealing with the sentencing determinants, give the Court sufficient grip to come to good sentencing results. Sexual violence charged as a war crime is not automatically less serious than sexual violence charged as a crime against humanity, and the latter as less serious than sexual violence charged as genocide, resulting in sentences matching the ranking of the crimes. The ICTY and ICTR practice shows, with the exception of *Muhimana*, that sentences imposed for sexual violence prosecuted as a war crime and a crime against humanity are more or less the same. However, in order not to lose sight of the seriousness of sexual violence crimes, the ICTY and ICTR

---

[259] *The Prosecutor v. Laurent Semanza*, Prosecution Appeal Brief, Case No. ICTR-97-20-A, 1 September 2003, paras. 6.42-6.50. It is furthermore not clear whether the Prosecutor always appealed the specific sentences imposed for sexual violence by the Trial Chamber if worth pursuing. See, for example, the Respondent's Brief of the Prosecution (Public Version) in the Furundžija case, 30 September 1999, in which the Prosecutor seemed to agree with the sentences imposed on Furundžija.

[260] Semanza Appeal Judgment, paras. 390-395. It should here again be noted that the Appeals Chamber will only substitute a sentence if a Trial Chamber made a discernible error in exercising its discretion or failed to follow applicable law. The burden of proof is on the moving party.

practice reveals that extra care is needed when the gravity of sexual violence and the aggravating circumstances are examined. It is to be hoped that the explicit mention of the aggravating circumstances in Rule 145, such as 'the harm caused to the victims and their families' and discrimination on the basis of gender, will contribute to the fact that such circumstances, in contrast to the ICTY and ICTR practice, cannot be easily overlooked in cases of sexual violence. If the seriousness of rape and other forms of sexual violence is not taken into account in the sentence imposed, this will give the impression that sexual violence crimes and those who have suffered as a result are not taken seriously. As the ICC will start with a clean slate, in principle, with no recourse to the national prison sentencing practice in national courts, there needs to be a certain degree of consistency in sentences imposed from the very beginning. The ICC judges will therefore not only have to explain the sentences that are imposed for each specific count, but they will also need to justify them relative to other sentences in similar cases. Since the sentencing practice of the ICC may become the standard to be applied in sentencing the most serious crimes in countries around the world, it is important that the sentences are substantiated persuasively and are similar in more or less similar cases.

CHAPTER 7
REPARATION TO VICTIMS OF SEXUAL VIOLENCE

1 INTRODUCTION

Victims' rights to reparation have been widely recognised at both the national level and the international level. At the national level, reparations have been enforced through civil and/or criminal proceedings and/or provided by national compensation schemes and programmes; at the international level, reparations have mainly been awarded through mass claims mechanisms, international courts and tribunals, and various trust funds. In many situations, the enforcement of victims' rights to reparation through such mechanisms proved extremely difficult and many victims have therefore been left without reparation despite gross violations of human rights and international humanitarian law committed against them.[1] As this Chapter is primarily concerned with reparation within the supranational criminal law system, all other reparation

[1] For example, see the foreword by Theo van Boven, the former Special Rapporteur of the UN Commission on Human Rights on Torture (2001-2004), in Redress (2003), in which he expounds upon the remaining difficulties that victims' face in obtaining reparation at the domestic level: 'However, as the findings of the present project clearly demonstrate, domestic law and practice fall far below the international standards to which countries have committed themselves. In a study I carried out in an earlier capacity as Special Rapporteur on the right to reparation I commented that "... large categories of victims of gross violations of human rights, as a result of the actual contents of national laws or because of the manner in which these laws are applied, fail to receive the reparation which is due to them. Limitations in time, including the application of statutory limitations; restrictions in the definition of the scope and nature of the violations; the operation of amnesty laws; the restrictive attitude of courts; the incapability of certain groups of victims to present and to pursue their claims; lack of economic and financial resources: the consequences of all these factors, individually and jointly, is that the principle of equality of rights and due reparation of all victims are not implemented". (UN doc. E/CN/4/Sub.2/1993/8, para: 124). After the turn of the century, now some ten years later, the plight of victims has remained largely unchanged, in spite of continuous efforts by international monitoring mechanisms to bridge the gaps between international standards and national performance. Thus, as far as reparation for victims of torture is concerned, the then Special Rapporteur on Torture, Sir Nigel Rodley, reported in the year 2000 to the fifty-fifth session of the United Nations General Assembly that in response to his requests to Governments for information on the nature and amount of any compensation made to victims of torture or his/her relatives, he had rarely received details regarding reparation (UN doc. A/55/290). As his successor I cannot but confirm Sir Nigel's findings, which still reflect the actual state of affairs that the rights of victims are largely ignored.'

mechanisms that exist in the fields of national and international law will not be discussed here.[2]

Within the field of supranational criminal law and procedure, the notion that international justice should address not only traditional retributive justice, that is to say, the punishment of the offender, but also restorative justice, that is to say, providing compensation to victims for their injuries (as well as allowing victims to participate in the proceedings), has gained increasing recognition. The manner in which the Tribunals and the ICC uphold victims' rights to reparation will be discussed in this Chapter. In the context of this study, attention will specifically be given to victims of sexual violence and their access to reparation, thereby taking into account the reasons why survivors of sexual violence in particular are in need of reparation.

Although awards of reparation to victims of crimes falling within the Tribunals' jurisdiction have been almost non-existent, the lack of restorative justice to survivors in Rwanda and the former Yugoslavia did lead to a general awareness that reparation to victims is of great importance in order to achieve recovery of and justice to victims. As a result, one of the major breakthroughs in the sphere of supranational criminal prosecution has come with the establishment of the ICC, which provides in a directly enforceable reparation mechanism for victims of genocide, crimes against humanity and war crimes. The ICC offers the first supranational criminal law regime that allows victims to file claims against and be awarded reparation by individual perpetrators of crimes falling within the jurisdiction of the Court. In addition, a Trust Fund for victims and their families has been created. The Trust Fund is innovative as, in principle, it can meet victims and witnesses' needs for rehabilitation and support in an early phase of the Court proceedings, thus without awaiting the Court's judgment. Before the ICTY and the ICTR, victims generally appear as witnesses only and therefore do not have standing themselves in restitution matters, nor are the Tribunals allowed to award compensation to victims directly. Support services are only provided in small amounts, usually over a short period of time, and do not meet the needs of most victims.

It should be noted here that the reparation system provided for in the ICC Statute and RPE is largely based on the criminal procedure adopted by numerous judicial systems founded on civil law as well as on the Declaration of Basic Principles of Justice for Victims of Crime and Abuse of Power (1985)[3] and the Basic Principles and Guidelines on the Rights to a Remedy and Reparation for Victims of Violations of International Human Rights and Humanitarian Law (2000) (hereinafter the 'Van Boven/Bassiouni Principles'),[4] which laid the groundwork for reparation in international

---

[2] For a general overview of reparation mechanisms on the national and/or international level, including a discussion of the difficulty to enforce victims' rights to a remedy under these mechanisms see, *inter alia*, Brienen and Hoegen (2000), Ingadottir, Ferstman and Kristjanjsdottir (2003), Zegveld (2003), Gillard (2003) and Hoffman and Riemann (2004).

[3] Declaration of Basic Principles of Justice for Victims of Crime and Abuse of Power, annexed to UNGA Resolution 40/34 of 29 November 1985.

[4] The 'Basic Principles and Guidelines on the Rights to a Remedy and Reparation for Victims of Violations of International Human Rights and Humanitarian Law', annexed to the Final Report of the Special Rapporteur, Mr. M. Cherif Bassiouni, *The Right to Restitution, Compensation and Rehabilitation for Victims of Gross Violations of Human Rights and Fundamental Freedoms*, UN Doc. E/CN.4/2000/62, 18 January 2000. The Principles were the outcome of revisions of earlier

law. In this Chapter, the term 'reparations' will be used to include 'restitution, compensation and rehabilitation' as well as 'other forms of remedy', in line with Article 75(1) of the ICC Statute and Rule 94(1)(f) of the ICC RPE, respectively. The phrasing of Article 75(1), '...reparations to, or in respect of, victims, including restitution, compensation and rehabilitation', aims to reflect the Van Boven/Bassiouni Principles, as evidenced by a footnote in the final report of the Working Group on Procedural Matters.[5] According to the Basic Principles and Guidelines on the Right to a Remedy and Reparation for Victims of Gross Violations of International Human Rights Law and Serious Violations of International Humanitarian Law (2005), adopted by the Commission on Human Rights in April 2005, the terms 'restitution', 'compensation' and 'rehabilitation' should be understood as:

> 19. Restitution should, whenever possible, restore the victim to the original situation before the gross violations of international human rights or serious violations of international humanitarian law occurred. Restitution includes, as appropriate: restoration of liberty, enjoyment of human rights, identity, family life and citizenship, return to one's place of residence, restoration of employment and return of property.
> 20. Compensation should be provided for any economically assessable damage, as appropriate and proportional to the gravity of the violation and the circumstances of each case, resulting from gross violations of international human rights law and serious violations of international humanitarian law, such as:

---

drafts of, in particular, the 'Draft Principles on the Right to Restitution, Compensation and Rehabilitation for Victims of Gross Violations of Human Rights and Fundamental Freedoms', annexed to the Final Report Submitted by Mr. Theo van Boven, Special Rapporteur, *Study Concerning the Right to Restitution, Compensation and Rehabilitation for Victims of Gross Violations of Human Rights and Fundamental Freedoms*, UN Doc. E/CN.4/Sub.2/1993/8, 2 July 1993 (first version); The Administration of Justice and the Human Rights of Detainees: *Revised Set of Basic Principles and Guidelines on the Right to Reparation for Victims of Gross Violations of Human Rights and Humanitarian Law*, Prepared by Mr. Theo van Boven Pursuant to Sub-Commission Decision 1995/117, UN Doc. E/CN.4/Sub.2/1996/17, 24 May 1996 (second version); Question of the Human Rights of All Persons Subjected to Any Form of Detention or Imprisonment, *Basic Principles and Guidelines on the Right to Reparation for Victims of Violations of Human Rights and International Humanitarian Law*, UN Doc. E/CN.4/1997/104, 16 January 1997 (third version). On 13 April 2005, the Commission on Human Rights, during its sixty-first session, adopted in a resolution the 'Basic Principles and Guidelines on the Right to a Remedy and Reparation for Victims of Gross Violations of International Human Rights Law and Serious Violations of International Humanitarian Law' and recommended that States take them into account, promote respect thereof and bring them to the attention of members of the executive bodies of government. See E/CN.4/2005/L.48, with 'Basic Principles and Guidelines on the Right to a Remedy and Reparation for Victims of Gross Violations of International Human Rights Law and Serious Violations of International Humanitarian Law' annexed (hereinafter the Basic Principles and Guidelines on Reparation).

[5] See footnote 5 to Article 73 on reparations to victims in the final report of the Working Group on Procedural Matters, A/CONF.183/C.1/WGPM/L.2/Add.7, 13 July 1998. See also Bonneau (2004). Moreover, the Basic Principles and Guidelines on Reparation also refer to Article 75 of the ICC Statute in its Preamble.

(a) Physical or mental harm;
(b) Lost opportunities, including employment, education and social benefits;
(c) Material damages and loss of earnings, including loss of earning potential;
(d) Moral damage;
(e) Costs required for legal or expert assistance, medicine and medical services, and psychological and social services.

21. Rehabilitation should include medical and psychological care as well as legal and social services.[6]

It may also be argued that the footnote reference to the Van Boven/Bassiouni Principles as well as the reference to 'other forms of remedy' in Rule 94(1)(f) implies that also the measures of satisfaction and guarantees of non-repetition are covered by the term 'reparation'.[7] Although the Van Boven/Bassiouni Principles impose obligations on States as well as persons, legal persons or other entities to provide reparation,[8] it should be noted that some of the reparative measures mentioned in this document can only be realised by States, not by a person convicted by the Court.[9] Therefore, if a person is held liable for reparation, restitution will most likely cover 'restitution of assets, property or other tangible items' (Rule 94(1)(d)) and rehabilitation will in most cases be achieved through monetary awards, for example, for medical and psychological care as well as legal and social services. Restitution, compensation and rehabilitation are discussed in this Chapter in light of the needs of wartime victims of sexual violence in particular.

2 A SPECIAL NEED FOR REPARATION TO VICTIMS OF SEXUAL VIOLENCE

The need for reparation to victims of sexual violence during and in the aftermath of genocide, crimes against humanity and armed conflict is readily apparent. In addition to the devastating physical, psychological, social and economic consequences women and

---

[6] Principles 19, 20 and 21 of the Basic Principles and Guidelines on Reparation, respectively. It should be noted that in the field of victimology the terms 'restitution', 'compensation' and 'assistance' are used differently. See the 1985 Declaration of Basic Principles of Justice for Victims of Crime and Abuse of Power, annexed to UN General Assembly Resolution 40/34 of 29 November 1985, paras. 8, 12 and 14 in particular.

[7] See footnote 5 of the final report of the Working Group on Procedural Matters, A/CON.183/C.1/WGPM/L.63/Rev.1. See also Bonneau (2004). The term 'satisfaction' should be understood to include, for instance, a public apology and commemorations and tributes to the victims. The term 'guarantee of non repetition' includes, for instance, measures to prevent the recurrence of past violations, such as the dissemination of information about past violations. See further Principles 22 and 23, respectively, of the Basic Principles and Guidelines on Reparation.

[8] Principle 15 of the Basic Principles and Guidelines on Reparation reads, in pertinent part, 'In accordance with its domestic laws and international legal obligations, a State shall provide reparation to victims for acts or omissions which can be attributed to the State and constitute gross violations of international human rights law or serious violations of international humanitarian law. In cases where a person, a legal person, or other entity is found liable for reparation to a victim, such party should provide reparation to the victim or compensate the State if the State has already provided reparation to the victim.'

[9] See also Timm (2001), p. 303.

girls generally face, they often contract sexually transmitted diseases, including HIV/AIDS, face unwanted pregnancies and health complications resulting from botched abortions, and suffer sexual mutilation and other injuries, such as fistulas, uterine problems, vaginal lesions and scarring. Injuries to reproductive organs, unwanted pregnancies as well as diseases such as HIV/AIDS are typical consequences that victims of sexual violence have to face, most of them women, and they thus deserve separate attention when it comes to reparation.

The virtual unavailability of proper health care and counselling during and in the aftermath of mass sexual violence (health services are often destroyed during conflict) has left many women to deal with their traumas, physical injuries and diseases on their own. As a consequence, many women are still suffering every day. Unfortunately, the list of such situations is abundant: Sudan (Darfur), north-eastern Democratic Republic of Congo, northern Uganda, Central African Republic, Sierra Leone, Rwanda and the former Yugoslavia are just a few, yet extreme, examples in which the majority of victims of sexual violence, mostly women, have been left without any form of reparation, including adequate medical and psychological care.[10] It should be noted that all these situations are taken up either by the Court or by an *ad hoc* Tribunal.

Especially HIV/AIDS has become an issue of major concern, as many female victims of sexual violence have contracted the disease through sexual violence during conflict situations. It has been established that the increasing spread of HIV/AIDS among women and sexual violence are interlinked.[11] The risk of HIV transmission increases up to three-fold when sex is forced, especially for girls and young women, because their vaginal tracts are immature and tear easily.[12] Furthermore, women are more susceptible to HIV infection than men: 'male-to-female HIV transmission during

[10] On the Democratic Republic of Congo, see, *inter alia*, BBC, *Congo Rape Victims Seek Solace* (by Jackie Martens), 24 January 2004; BBC, *Report Shows DR Congo Rape Horror*, 26 October 2004; Amnesty International (2004e); Médecins Sans Frontières (2004); and Human Rights Watch (2002). On Rwanda, see, *inter alia*, African Rights (2004); Amnesty International (2004a); Human Rights Watch (2004b); and Nduwimana (2004). On Sudan, see, *inter alia*: Médecins Sans Frontières (2005); and Human Rights Watch (2005). On Sierra Leone, see, *inter alia*: Human Rights Watch (2003a); and Physicians for Human Rights (2002). On northern Uganda, see, *inter alia*, the Press Release by the Women's Initiatives for Gender Justice, in collaboration with Isis-WICCE and Ugandan Women Activists, 23 November 2004. On the former Yugoslavia, see, *inter alia*, Amnesty International (2004d). On the Central African Republic, see, *inter alia*, Amnesty International (2004f).

[11] UN Commission on Human Rights, Report of the Special Rapporteur on Violence Against Women, Its Causes and Consequences, Yakin Ertürk, *Integration of the Human Rights of Women and the Gender Perspective: Violence Against Women – Intersections of Violence Against Women and HIV/AIDS*, E/CN.4/2005/72, 17 January 2005; UN Commission on Human Rights, Resolution 2004/46, *Elimination of Violence Against Women*, 21 April 2004; UN Commission on Human Rights, Report of the Special Rapporteur on Violence Against Women, Its Causes and Consequences, *Towards an Effective Implementation of International Norms to End Violence Against Women*, E/CN.4/2004/66, 26 December 2003, p. 15; Amnesty International (2004g).

[12] World Health Organization Press Release, *Women and Girls Need Access to AIDS Treatment and Protection from Violence*, 30 November 2004.

sex is about twice as likely to occur as female-to-male transmission'.[13] Women are increasingly affected in each region of the world, and close to half of 37,2 million adults (aged 15-49) living with HIV are women.[14] In Sub-Saharan Africa, 57 percent of the adults living with the virus are women, and two thirds of young HIV-positive people are women and girls.[15] As the risk of HIV/AIDS transmission through sexual violence in times of genocide, crimes against humanity and armed conflict is believed to be high, especially for women and girls as they are often raped repeatedly and incessantly, without proper remedies, many of these women are literally left to die.

The need for reparation to victims of sexual violence will be addressed taking the situation of Rwanda as a case study (subsection 2.1).[16] It should, however, be stressed that, as was pointed out above, in many conflicts similar consequences of sexual violence and thus the need for reparation with respect to victims of sexual violence may be found, albeit to various levels and degrees.

2.1 Rwanda

Eleven years after the 1994 genocide which ravaged the tiny country of Rwanda, female survivors of sexual violence have hardly received any reparation from the Rwandese government, the genocidaires, the international community or the ICTR for the physical and psychological harm they suffered. Although several women's organisations, such as

---

[13] UNAIDS/WHO Press Release, *Number of Women Living with HIV Increases in Each Region of the World*, 23 November 2004.

[14] Annual Report by the Joint United Nations Programme on HIV/AIDS (UNAIDS) and the World Health Organization (WHO), *AIDS Epidemic Update 2004*, December 2004, p. 7.

[15] *Ibid.*

[16] The situation in the countries on the territory of the former Yugoslavia in respect of victims of sexual violence needs will not be addressed here. What can be noted, however, is that very few perpetrators of sexual violence who committed crimes in the former Yugoslavia have been brought to trial, denying most women's access to justice, and reparation has largely been unavailable. According to the Amnesty International report on Bosnia and Herzegovina (2003, p. 14): 'With the notable exceptions of the work of some women's non-governmental organizations, adequate medical and psycho-social support in general is unavailable.' For more information on justice for women in Bosnia-Herzegovina see, *inter alia*, Amnesty International (2004d); and Amnesty International (2003), in particular pp. 14-18. In general it can be said that there are serious problems in terms of prosecuting war criminals and enforcing victims' rights on reparation in the countries of the former Yugoslavia: (1) there is a lack of political will to investigate and prosecute crimes in national (cantonal and district) courts, and, in any event, criminal justice systems lack resources to process more than a handful of cases; (2) national laws are inadequate, i.e., not in conformity with international law standards; (3) there is an absence of effective victim and witness protection, participation and support; (4) the right to reparation is not fully guaranteed in national law and procedures for obtaining reparation are inadequate. The majority of the civilian victims of the war have never received any form of reparation for their suffering. See Amnesty International (2005). See further, *inter alia*, Organization for Security and Co-operation in Europe, *War Crimes Trials Before the Domestic Courts of Bosnia and Herzegovina: Progress and Obstacles*, March 2005; International Center for Transnational Justice (2002), (2004a) and (2004b).

the Association of Genocide Widows (AVEGA-AGAHOZO), do everything in their power to support survivors of sexual violence, the problem is so enormous that much more help in the form of, among other things, personnel, medicines and funding is needed.[17] While reparation could have met these women's needs for medical and psychological care, they are instead, still struggling to meet their own and their children's most basic needs, such as food, clothing, housing and education. Furthermore, besides dealing with their own injuries, traumas and illnesses, they are faced with the task of taking care of orphans, the sick and injured, and generating an income. These tasks have heavily impacted on women in the years following the genocide, considering that most survivors were women.[18] Furthermore, due to the conflict most women had lost not only their husbands, but also their homes that were looted and taken by others during the conflict and other property that was stolen. However, as a consequence of women's second-class status in Rwanda, women could not inherit property unless they were explicitly designated as the beneficiaries.[19] As a result, many widows and daughters had no legal claim to the homes of their killed husbands or fathers or to their male relatives' land or bank accounts.[20] Although a new law has enhanced women's rights to inheritance and land ownership, most women are still discriminated against in this respect, continue to live in extreme poverty, and remain vulnerable to sexual violence.[21]

In Rwanda, it is estimated that between 250,000 and 500,000 women were raped during the 1994 genocide, a large number of whom were also killed following their rape.[22] Pregnancies caused by rape have been estimated to amount to between 2,000 and

---

[17] African Rights (2004), Chapter 12 (discussing the activities of the women's organisations AVEGA, Abasa and SWAA). There are many more organisations that support women, including Solace Ministries, Ibuka, Rwanda Women's Network, Survivors Fund (SURF) and Women for Women International, but, on the whole, they all suffer from inadequate means. See also Hirondelle News Agency, *Silent Victims of Rwanda's Genocide* (by Gabriel Gabiro), 21 November 2003, on the 'Village of Hope', a community project established by Rwanda Women's Network in which victims of sexual violence live together and are given shelter, psychological assistance and medicines, including HIV/AIDS treatment. For an analysis on victim organisations in Rwanda and reparation generally, see the study prepared by Rombouts (2004).

[18] It has been estimated that 60-70 percent of the Rwandese population is women, of which 50 percent are widows. See the AVEGA-AGAHOZO, Association of Genocide Widows, website (under 'history') at http://www.avega.org.rw (last visited May 2005).

[19] Organization of African Unity, International Panel of Eminent Personalities Report, *Rwanda: The Preventable Genocide*, 2000, para. 16.11.

[20] *Ibid.*

[21] Amnesty International (2004a), pp. 4-5. According to this report, around 60 percent of the Rwandese are believed to live below the poverty line (with reference to the UNDP Human Development Index for 2003, in which it was recorded that 86.4 percent of the Rwandese lived on less than USD 2 per day from 1990-2001).

[22] UN Commission on Human Rights, *Report on the Situation of Human Rights in Rwanda Submitted by Mr. René Degni-Ségui Special Rapporteur of the Commission on Human Rights, under Paragraph 20 of Resolution S-3/1 of 25 May 1994*, E/CN.4/1996/68, 29 January 1996, para. 16. See further the Introduction in this study for a more complete overview of the sexual violence crimes committed in Rwanda during the 1994 genocide.

5,000,[23] but the number of pregnancies has also been estimated at 15,000.[24] Although the exact number of raped women and pregnancies resulting from these rapes will never be known, it has been held that 'almost all females who survived the genocide were direct victims of rape or other sexual violence, or were profoundly affected by it'.[25] The victims were mostly Tutsi women, but also moderate Hutu women were targeted. The perpetrators of the sexual violence were largely members of the Hutu militia, the *Interahamwe,* but rapes were also committed by soldiers of the Rwandan Armed Forces (FAR), including the Presidential Guard, and civilians. The sexual violence took on different cruel forms, including gang rapes, rapes with objects, sexual slavery, forced marriage, sexual mutilations and were often repeatedly committed over an extended period of time. Pregnant women were not spared, neither were young girls. Many unwanted pregnancies resulted from the rapes and thus many children of the ethnicity of the rapist were born, further adding to the victims' trauma. On many occasions, the sexual violence was conducted in public, and often family members of the rape victims were killed preceding, during or following the rapes.

In addition to the physical injuries and trauma resulting from the rapes, between 70 and 80 percent of the surviving women in Rwanda are estimated to have been infected with HIV.[26] Although not all cases of HIV/AIDS among rape survivors can be linked to the sexual violence they suffered during the genocide and an exact number can therefore not be given, it can be assumed that many women were infected with the virus as a result of these rapes in light of, for instance, the abnormally high incidence of HIV/AIDS infection among women raped during the genocide and the rapists not using condoms.[27] The mass rapes during the genocide contributed significantly to the spread

---

[23] *Ibid.* On the basis of the number of pregnancies the estimates of women raped during the genocide were extrapolated.

[24] Save the Children (2002), p. 5.

[25] Organization of African Unity, International Panel of Eminent Personalities Report, *Rwanda: The Preventable Genocide*, 2000, para. 16.20.

[26] In a survey of 1125 female genocide survivors carried out by AVEGA, it was found that some 80 percent remain severely traumatised, and about 70 percent of them have tested HIV positive. See the AVEGA-AGAHOZO, Association of Genocide Widows, website (under 'history') at http://www.avega.org.rw (last visited May 2005). See also Amnesty International (2004a), p. 3. Another survey, in which 2000 women were tested, found that 80 percent were HIV positive. See Save the Children (2002), p. 5 (with reference to E. Mujawayo and M. Kayitesi Blewitt, *Sexual Violence Against Women: Experiences from AVEGA's work in Kigali*, paper presented at the Silent Emergency Seminar in London, June 1999). It should be noted that in both cases the results were drawn from tests done by AVEGA, but the number of survivors tested differed.

[27] Nduwimana (2004), pp. 20-26. Nduwimana presents the following factors which strongly indicate that the majority of HIV/AIDS transmission had taken place through the rapes carried out during the genocide: (1) the abnormally high incidence of HIV/AIDS infection among women raped during the genocide; (2) the incubation period (in 1998 the first cases of HIV/AIDS among raped women became known, which corresponds with the incubation period of three to ten years); (3) rape-related health complications not experienced before the genocide; (4) children born before the rapes were healthy; (5) age of some women raped (some were still virgins, who could not have been affected by HIV/AIDS before the genocide); (6) rapists did not use condoms; and

of the virus in Rwanda, particularly as rates of HIV transmission during sexual violence are believed to be high.[28] In Rwanda, the HIV prevalence rate in rural areas dramatically increased from 1 percent before the start of the genocide to 11 percent in 1997.[29] Moreover, many women were raped by men who knew they were HIV-positive and deliberately tried to transmit the virus to Tutsi women and their families.[30] The number of patients clinically in need of life-prolonging anti-retroviral (ARV) therapy is estimated at between 50,000 and 100,000, but only about 2,000 Rwandese were treated with ARV drugs as of January 2004.[31] Approximately 50,000 Rwandese die of AIDS every year.[32] Transportation fees, consultation fees, medicines and tests are well beyond the means of most Rwandese.[33] Those few who have access to free ARV drugs are still required to pay their hospitalisation and consultation fees.[34] Many find themselves deciding between paying for medical expenses and buying food. One of the primary concerns of these women is what will happen to their children when they themselves die of AIDS. Many ill women have no relatives who may take care of their children (they often died during the genocide) and they have no houses of their own or other property they could leave to their children once they have died.[35] As there is generally no aftercare for these children, most of them end up living in the streets or in child-headed

---

(7) the ICTR confirmed that many victims had died before testifying and others were too sick to give testimony.

[28] Amnesty International (2004g).

[29] World Health Organization, *Violence against Women and HIV/AIDS: Critical Intersections, Sexual Violence in Conflict Settings and the Risk of HIV*, Information Bulletin Series, Number 2, 2004, p. 1.

[30] Organization of African Unity, International Panel of Eminent Personalities Report, *Rwanda: The Preventable Genocide*, 2000, para. 16.19. See also the AVEGA-AGAHOZO website, Association of Genocide Widows, under 'history', at http://www.avega.org.rw (last visited May 2005) ('Testimonies reveal that men who were HIV/AIDS positive deliberately infected women, using the social stigma attached to rape as an effective weapon in undermining the social fabric of these women'); UN Commission on Human Rights, Report of the Special Rapporteur on Violence against Women, Its Causes and Consequences, Ms. Radhika Coomaraswamy, Addendum, *Report of the Mission to Rwanda on the Issue of Violence against Women in Situations of Armed Conflict*, E/CN.4/1998/54/Add.1, 4 February 1998, para. 31 (one of Jeanne's rapists told her 'I have AIDS and I want to give it to you'); Nduwimana (2004), p. 19 ('I was raped by two gendarmes ... one of the gendarmes was seriously ill, you could see that he had AIDS, his face was covered with spots, his lips were red, almost burned, he had abscesses on his neck. Then he told me "take a good look at me and remember what I look like. I could kill you right now but I don't feel like wasting my bullet. I want you to die slowly like me"'). Paul Kagame, the President of Rwanda, furthermore claimed that during the genocide the former Hutu government released AIDS patients from the hospitals in order to rape and transmit the virus to Tutsi women. See New York Times Magazine, *A Woman's Work* (by Peter Landesman), 15 September 2002.

[31] Amnesty International (2004a), p. 3.

[32] *Ibid.* (with reference to the Government of Rwanda HIV/AIDS Treatment and Care Plan 2003-2007, developed with the William J. Clinton Foundation, p. 12).

[33] *Ibid.*, p. 18.

[34] *Ibid.*

[35] African Rights (2004), Chapter 8; and Amnesty International (2004a), pp. 29-30.

households. In both situations, girls are very vulnerable to sexual abuse and many see no alternative than to prostitute themselves in order to provide for their own and their brothers and sisters' basic needs.[36] Stigmatisation is also a serious problem for survivors of sexual violence and those living with HIV/AIDS. Women often refrain from seeking medical treatment following rape because of the risk that they will be identified as rape victims within their community and become ostracised, often by their own husbands. The stigmatisation attached to HIV/AIDS often leads to a denial of the women's property and inheritance rights, employment and access to finance, which further forces them into a very deplorable situation susceptible to further (sexual) violence.[37]

Owing to the lack of rehabilitation and support services, women and girls continue to die on a daily basis as a consequence of the diseases, in particular HIV/AIDS, inflicted upon them through sexual violence. According to AVEGA-AGAHOZO: 'AIDS has now become deadlier than war and genocide itself, and the social and economic consequences are felt widely among this already vulnerable and fragile population group. Amongst AVEGA's members, the issue of rape and the resulting infection of HIV/AIDS constitute the ultimate violation of human rights.'[38]

At the national level, compensation mechanisms for victims of crimes committed against them during the genocide are almost non-existent. In Rwanda, monetary claims have been awarded to victims by national courts on the basis of the Organic Law on the Organization of Prosecutions for Offences constituting the Crime of Genocide or Crimes against Humanity committed since 1 October 1990, which recognises victims' right to compensation.[39] However, no enforcement has resulted because those convicted simply do not have the money to pay the victims.[40] Although a statute which is to provide for the creation and governance of a reparations fund for genocide victims has been drafted, the *Fonds d'Indemnisation* (FIND), it still has not been adopted.[41] Lack of political will on the part of the government and problems inherent to the compensation process, including lack of means, have been said to be the main reasons for not adopting

---

[36] Amnesty International (2004a), pp. 29-30. The report refers to a study undertaken by the Johns Hopkins University in which it is reported that about 93 percent of girls living on the street have been sexually abused ('Rwanda: Sexual Activity among Street Children in Kigali, U.N. Integrated Regional Information Network, March 13, 2002'). In post-genocide Rwanda, a real concern has become the many rapes of children that take place. See Hirondelle News Agency, *Plus De 1.600 Cas De Viol De Janvier A Septembre Selon La Police*, 1 décembre 2004.

[37] Amnesty International (2004a), pp. 24-28.

[38] See the AVEGA-AGAHOZO, Association of Genocide Widows, website (under 'history') at http://www.avega.org.rw (last visited May 2005).

[39] See Articles 27-32 1996 Genocide Law.

[40] According to a report prepared by the International Crisis Group (2001, p. 33): 'Close to U.S. $ 100 million have been awarded after only some 4,000 people have been tried. In reality, however, not a single cent has been paid out because the defendants are all indigent.' See also Penal Reform International (2003), p. 15.

[41] Projet de loi No. ... du ... portent création, organisation et fonctionnement du fonds de réparation en faveur des rescapés du génocide ou des crimes contre l'humanité commis entre le 1er octobre 1990 et le 31 décembre 1994, 2002, Article 2, cited in Human Rights Watch (2004b), p. 57. The existence of such a law is also presupposed by the 1996 Genocide Law (Article 32), the 2001 Gacaca Law (Articles 90 and 91) and the 2004 Gacaca Law (Article 96).

the statute on compensation.[42] According to the requirements of the compensation fund, compensation may also be paid in the form of services, particularly in the field of education, health and housing. The State will pay 8 percent of internal revenue to feed the fund, which is somewhat more than the 5 percent it is currently paying to the *Fonds d'Assistance aux Rescapés du Génocide* (FARG).[43] At the time of writing this study, the FARG is aware of the needs of the survivors, but has been inadequate in meeting those needs. Today, its main contribution can be found in the implementation of affirmative or preferential measures of children survivors or children of survivors with respect to higher education.[44] However, the much needed HIV/AIDS treatment for rape survivors is lacking. Although community service – another form of reparation to victims in Rwanda – may work to reconstruct Rwandan society, community service is only applicable to category two offenders (murderers, attempted murderers, and those who caused serious bodily harm), not to those who committed sexual violence and other category one offenders (the masterminds of the genocide), which may impact on the general sense of reconciliation, especially by survivors of sexual violence.[45] Although 75 percent of the genocide survivors think that community service may promote reconciliation, lack of political will on the part of the government has resulted in delays in the establishment of a programme on community service.[46] Many survivors have lost all hope of compensation, either from the convicts or from the State, and therefore refuse to testify at Gacaca, as testifying may, in their eyes, create more enemies.[47]

On 10 December 2004, the UN General Assembly passed a resolution entitled 'Assistance to survivors of the 1994 genocide in Rwanda, particularly orphans, widows and victims of sexual violence'.[48] The resolution explicitly recognised that many victims of sexual violence are among those who face the greatest hardship in post-conflict Rwanda, even more than ten years after the conflict has ended: 'Recognizing the numerous difficulties faced by survivors of the 1994 genocide in Rwanda, particularly the orphans, widows and victims of sexual violence, who are poorer and more vulnerable as a result of the genocide, especially the many victims of sexual violence who have contracted HIV and have since either died or become seriously ill with AIDS....' The General Assembly invited:

> ... agencies, funds and programmes of the United Nations system to ensure that assistance is provided in the specific areas identified as priorities by the Government of Rwanda, notably education for orphans, medical care and treatment for victims of sexual violence, including HIV-positive victims, trauma and psychological counselling for

[42] Penal Reform International (2004), p. 16.

[43] *Ibid.*, p. 14.

[44] Mibenge (2005).

[45] *Ibid.* Mibenge points out that 'community service de-individualizes the harm committed and calls for the perpetrator to make public and tangible contributions to the reconstruction of society'.

[46] Penal Reform International (2004), p. 16.

[47] *Ibid.*, p. 55. See also Hirondelle News Agency, *The Limitations of Justice Without Compensation*, 18 April 2005.

[48] UN General Assembly, *Resolution 59/137 of 10 December 2004 on Assistance to Survivors of the 1994 Genocide in Rwanda, Particularly Orphans, Widows and Victims of Sexual Violence*, A/RES/59/137, 17 February 2004.

genocide survivors and skills training and microcredit programmes aimed at promoting self-sufficiency and alleviating poverty ...

Member States are also encouraged to provide assistance. The government and people of Rwanda, civil society organisations as well as international efforts are commended for providing support for and restoring the dignity of survivors, which helps to promote reconciliation and healing in Rwanda. In April 2005, the team of the *Hotel Rwanda* film, working in partnership with the United Nations Foundation, established the 'International Fund for Rwanda' to support Rwandese genocide survivors.[49] The Fund is to support genocide survivors and returning refugees, capacity-building for doctors and nurses, a gender-sensitive, HIV/AIDS income-generating project, give assistance to genocide orphans and support a Kigali-based film school.[50] The impact of the UNGA Resolution as well as the subsequent set-up of the International Fund for Rwanda on the lives of the genocide survivors, including the survivors of sexual violence, has yet to be awaited. As victims' rights to reparation are largely unenforceable at both the national level and the international level, victims, especially female survivors of sexual violence who constitute the larger part of the population, have been left uncompensated. Despite the fact that the genocide ended in 1994, for many women the genocide thus continues.

3 The ICTY and the ICTR

In this section, the possibilities that exist within the ICTY and the ICTR with regard to reparation to victims will be evaluated. In subsection 3.1, the legal bases for reparation claims before the Tribunals will be examined as well as the way in which they are used in practice. Subsection 3.2 will deal with the type of action that has been undertaken to improve victims' rights in terms of reparation before the Tribunals. Subsection 3.3 will focus on the Tribunals' role with regard to reparation, that is, the question is addressed whether compensation for and support to victims should fall within the Tribunals' mandate. These topics have been addressed in relation to the needs of and the support to victims of sexual violence.

3.1 Reparation possibilities

Although several forms of reparation to victims exist within both Tribunals – restitution, compensation and rehabilitation – the regime is far from comprehensive and effective on these matters.[51] While the restitution of property is laid down in the Statute with a direct role for the Tribunals to order such restitution, compensation is included in the RPE without any powers conferred upon the Tribunals themselves to order that compensation be awarded to victims of crimes. Instead, this is left to national courts or other competent bodies. In addition to reparation in the form of restitution of property and compensation to victims, the Tribunals may also decide on support measures, such

---

[49] See UN Press Release, *United Nations Welcomes Establishment of International Fund for Rwanda*, AFR/1133 IHA/1031, 4 April 2005; Hirondelle News Agency, *A New Fund to Assist Rwanda Genocide Survivors*, 6 April 2005.
[50] *Ibid.*
[51] On the Tribunals' reparation regime, see generally Malmström (2001) and Chifflet (2003).

as psychological and medical care (rehabilitation). Despite victims' need for such care before and after trial, support measures are generally only provided to victim-witnesses during their stay at the Tribunal.[52] These three forms of reparation will be discussed in subsection 3.1.1.

3.1.1 Restitution of property and proceeds

On the basis of Articles 24(3) of the ICTY Statute and 23(3) of the ICTR Statute, the Trial Chambers of the Tribunals are entitled, in addition to imprisonment, to 'order the return of any property and proceeds acquired by criminal conduct, including by means of duress, to their rightful owners'. The rule is inspired by the principle of unjust enrichment, found in many national jurisdictions, viz. that a perpetrator should not benefit from his crime and that property illegally acquired should therefore be returned. The provisions in the Statutes are further elaborated upon in Common Rule 105,[53] which, when read together with Rule 98*ter*(B) RPE ICTY/Rule 88 RPE ICTR, sets out three requirements for the restitution of property: (1) the accused is convicted and the unlawful taking of property has been established; (2) the property taken is 'associated with' the crime; and (3) either a request for restitution has been made by the Prosecutor or action has been taken by the Chamber *proprio motu*.[54] A victim thus has no standing

---

[52] See also Chapter 4 on protective and special measures.

[53] 'Common' refers to the fact that the relevant Rule is common to both the ICTY and the ICTR RPE.

[54] Rule 98*ter*(B) ICTY RPE ('Judgement') and the identical Rule 88(B) RPE ICTR ('Judgement'), state: 'If the Trial Chamber finds the accused guilty of a crime and concludes from the evidence that unlawful taking of property by the accused was associated with it, it shall make a specific finding to that effect in its judgement. The Trial Chamber may order restitution as provided in Rule 105.' Common Rule 105 ICTY/R RPE ('Restitution of Property') states:

(A) After a judgement of conviction containing a specific finding as provided in Rule 98 *ter* (B) [or Rule 88(B) in case of the ICTR], the Trial Chamber shall, at the request of the Prosecutor, or may, *proprio motu*, hold a special hearing to determine the matter of the restitution of the property or the proceeds thereof, and may in the meantime order such provisional measures for the preservation and protection of the property or proceeds as it considers appropriate.

(B) The determination may extend to such property or its proceeds, even in the hands of third parties not otherwise connected with the crime of which the convicted person has been found guilty.

(C) Such third parties shall be summoned before the Trial Chamber and be given an opportunity to justify their claim to the property or its proceeds.

(D) Should the Trial Chamber be able to determine the rightful owner on the balance of probabilities, it shall order the restitution either of the property or the proceeds or make such other order as it may deem appropriate.

(E) Should the Trial Chamber not be able to determine ownership, it shall notify the competent national authorities and request them so to determine.

before the Chamber to request restitution him- or herself. While in many civil law jurisdictions a victim has *locus standi* to initiate civil claims within criminal proceedings, before the Tribunals, as was mentioned before, the role of the victim is restricted to that of witness only.

If the abovementioned three requirements are met, a special hearing will be convened in order to determine the matter of restitution of unlawfully taken property or the proceeds thereof.[55] The most direct and accessible way for victims to receive restitution of property or the proceeds thereof seems to be by order of the Trial Chamber upon the determination of the rightful owner on the balance of probabilities.[56] In order for the Chamber to make such a determination, a sufficient level of investigation during the pre-trial or trial stages is needed, especially from the prosecution.[57] In this regard, it is interesting to note that there is no requirement that the determination of ownership be restricted to those victim-witnesses or witnesses who testify at the Tribunal proceedings only. If ownership cannot be determined by the Trial Chamber, the competent national authorities are required to do so, upon which the Trial Chamber will order the restitution of property or proceeds.[58] The latter procedure may prove to be more cumbersome, considering that national authorities will not always be able or willing to initiate restitution procedures.[59] In both situations, however, the Registrar bears the responsibility to transmit to the competent national authorities the orders for the restitution of property or proceeds, which are then responsible for the enforcement of the restitution orders received.[60]

Although in some cases either the issue was raised or evidence was brought that property was illegally taken from victims of a crime falling within the jurisdiction of the Tribunals for which the accused was found liable,[61] to date no restitution of property or

---

(F) Upon notice from the national authorities that an affirmative determination has been made, the Trial Chamber shall order the restitution either of the property or the proceeds or make such other order as it may deem appropriate.

(G) The Registrar shall transmit to the competent national authorities any summonses, orders and requests issued by a Trial Chamber pursuant to paragraphs (C), (D), (E) and (F).

[55] Rule 105 ICTY/R RPE.

[56] Rule 105(D) ICTY/R RPE. In Rule 105(D) mention is also made of the formulation 'or make such other order as it may deem appropriate'. According to Jones (2003, pp. 444-445), this formulation was inserted to allow the Chamber to award *compensation orders in favour of third parties* in case an order for restitution would be inappropriate or would not render justice to such third parties.

[57] Bottigliero (2004), p. 200.

[58] Rule 105(E), (F) and (G) ICTY/R RPE.

[59] Chifflet (2003, p. 102) refers, in this respect, to the potential absence of documents such as real-estate property records. Furthermore, it does not seem unlikely that States torn apart by conflict may find that they have other, more pressing priorities to take care of first than restitution of property to their rightful owners.

[60] Rule 105(G) ICTY/R RPE.

[61] See the cases mentioned in Malmström (2001), p. 377 (referring to the Aleksovski Judgment, paras. 87, 186, upheld on appeal; and the Bagosora case, which is still pending); and Chifflet

proceeds to the rightful owner has been ordered by the Chambers. In the *Bagasora* and *Musema* cases before the ICTR, the issue of restitution to and/or compensation for victims was raised by the governments of Rwanda and Belgium (*Bagasora*) as well as by the NGO African Concern (in both *Bagasora* and *Musema*) on the basis of a Rule 74 procedure ('Amicus Curiae').[62] However, in the Trial Chamber decisions the requests for reparation were denied on the ground that the applications by the *amici* were submitted too early in the process – a special hearing on restitution would only take place after a judgment of guilt with findings on the unlawful taking of property – and, moreover, the indictments should have included that the accused unlawfully took property. For these reasons, the submissions were held not to be relevant to the issues to be decided or in assisting the proper determination of the case, as required under Rule 74. The Tribunals do seem to have missed an opportunity here, however. The Prosecutor could have given the issue more attention by bringing it up. In those cases where the Trial Chamber found evidence of illegally taken property, it could at least have made such a determination. If ownership could not have been determined by the Trial Chamber, the competent national authorities might have done so. Such a determination could have been helpful for female victims of sexual violence in particular, who often face constraints in regaining access to their homes, land or other property taken during the conflict, as was demonstrated by the experiences of Rwandese women outlined above. Not only would proper housing be helpful for the general state of mind of survivors of sexual violence – as they have to worry about many other things (such as food and health) – for some women it would also have taken away one of their primary concerns, viz. that their children will not be left to live in the streets when she dies of AIDS contracted as a result of the sexual violence. As the determination of ownership is not restricted to those victim-witnesses or witnesses who testify at the Tribunal proceedings only, a potentially larger number of victims of sexual violence might have been reached by the provision on restitution. Apart from that, it may be questioned to what extent the procedure under Rule 105 will be an answer for the

(2003), p. 101 (referring to the Prosecutor's pre-trial brief in the Naletilić and Martinović case, Case No. IT-98-34-PT, 11 October 2000, para. 4.190). For example, in the Aleksovski case the Trial Chamber found that 'seven witnesses reported thefts during the search while the accused was present. According to Witness L, the thefts were committed on orders from the accused. Witness Osmancević, E, I, J, L, Garanović and Meho Sivro explained that the guards ordered the detainees to empty their pockets and that their belongings were seized. Some witnesses even said that they were robbed of their clothes and shoes.' The issue of restitution was, however, dropped on appeal.

[62] *The Prosecutor v. Alfred Musema*, Decision on an Application by African Concern for Leave to Appear as Amicus Curiae, Case No. ICTR-96-13-T, 17 March 1999 (restitution only); *The Prosecutor v. Théoneste Bagasora*, Decision on the Amicus Curiae Application by the Government of the Kingdom of Belgium, Case No. ICTR-96-7-T, 6 June 1998 (restitution and compensation); *The Prosecutor v. Théoneste Bagasora, Gratien Kabiligi, Aloys Ntabakuze and Anatole Nsengiyumva*, Decision on Amicus Curiae Request by African Concern, Case No. ICTR-98-41-T, 23 March 2004 (restitution only); *The Prosecutor v. Théoneste Bagasora, Gratien Kabiligi, Aloys Ntabakuze and Anatole Nsengiyumva*, Decision on Amicus Curiae Request by the Rwandan Government, Case No. ICTR-98-41-T, 13 October 2004 (restitution only). See further on Rule 74 and *amicus curiae* Chapter 5.

thousands of victims whose lost property (or the proceeds thereof) cannot be retrieved, especially in light of the lack of authority of the Tribunal to compensate them.

3.1.2 Compensation

Compensation is different from restitution of property and proceeds in that compensation to victims cannot be awarded by the Tribunals themselves. According to Common Rule 106, matters related to compensation are delegated to the 'national courts' or 'other competent bodies', which decide on compensation pursuant to their relevant national legislation.[63] The judgment is to be transmitted by the Registrar of the Tribunal to the competent authority and be considered final and binding as to the criminal responsibility of the convicted person for the injury caused to the victim.[64] Only a victim who has suffered injury as a result of a crime for which the accused has been convicted (or a person claiming on behalf of a victim) may claim compensation from the convict in a national court or other competent body, not the victims of crimes that have not been addressed by the Tribunals. The rationale behind Rule 106 not to provide for any direct compensation mechanism within the Tribunals can most probably be found in the fear that the Tribunals would not be able to handle a potentially high number of compensation claims themselves when, at the same time, they would also have to deal with the prosecution of individuals accused of the most serious crimes.[65] Instead, a claims commission for victims was considered to be a better solution.[66]

---

[63] Rule 106 ('Compensation to Victims') ICTY/R RPE, reads:

> (A) The Registrar shall transmit to the competent authorities of the States concerned the judgement finding the accused guilty of a crime which has caused injury to a victim.
> (B) Pursuant to the relevant national legislation, a victim or persons claiming through the victim may bring an action in a national court or other competent body to obtain compensation.
> (C) For the purposes of a claim made under paragraph (B) the judgement of the Tribunal shall be final and binding as to the criminal responsibility of the convicted person for such injury.

[64] Rule 106 ICTY/R RPE.

[65] Bottigliero (2004), p. 201. See also Resolution 827 (1993) of 25 May 1993 establishing the ICTY, where the UN Security Council stated that 'the work of the International Tribunal shall be carried out without prejudice to the right of the victims to seek, *through appropriate means*, compensation for damages incurred as a result of violations of international humanitarian law (italics added)'. According to Morris and Scharf (1995, pp. 167, 286-287), the UN Security Council thus wanted to exclude the possibility that the Tribunals themselves were going to deal with compensation claims of victims.

[66] Scharf (1997, p. 63), who co-drafted Resolution 827, commented: 'What we had in mind was a procedure similar to that devised for the victims of the Iraqi invasion of Kuwait, in which frozen Iraqi assets and proceeds from Iraq oil sales would be dispersed to victims through a UN Compensation Commission.' As can be seen in the preceding footnote, a clause was included in Security Council Resolution 827, declaring that the creation of the Tribunal was without prejudice to the future establishment of a victim compensation programme. See Security Council

Although the decision not to provide the Tribunal with the mandate to award compensation was opposed by some ICTY judges at the start of the operative phase of the Tribunal – in particular because they felt that it was highly inappropriate to give priority to the restitution of property over compensation, together with the fact that reparation before national courts in the circumstances would not be very likely[67] – this did not bring about any positive changes. As will be discussed below, to date the argument to give priority to prosecution still seems to be the main argument for Tribunal judges not to push for directly enforceable compensation mechanisms within the Tribunals and not to grant compensation awards to victims who appeared before the Tribunals.

As was the case with the restitution of property, an action under Rule 106 has not yet taken place[68] and compensation has thus never been granted to victims by national courts or other competent bodies.[69] Considering the state of jurisdictions in post-conflict situations, it is in general unlikely that compensation is awarded in the first few years after a State has fallen apart.[70] Apart from that, many convicted persons have no or little

---

Resolution 827, *Tribunal (Former Yugoslavia)*, S/RES/827 (1993), 25 May 1993. However, the Security Council later unfroze the assets of Serbia and the Bosnian Serbs, thereby ending any possibility of such a programme for the victims of the Balkans. See Security Council Resolution 1074, *The Situation in the Former Yugoslavia*, S/RES/1074 (1996), 1 October 1996.

[67] See comments made by Judge Cassese in Randelzhofer and Tomuschat (1999), p. 48.

[68] In this respect, see the request submitted by the government of Belgium to appear as *amicus curiae*, on, among other things, 'the right of Belgians or their rightful claimants, prejudiced by the massacres committed in 1994 in Rwanda, to appear before the Tribunal as plaintiffs and not as mere witnesses, in accordance with Rule 23(3) Statute [on penalties] and Rules 105-106 RPE [on restitution of property and compensation to victims, respectively]'. The request was denied as the Trial Chamber held that victims cannot appear as plaintiffs (the pre-sentencing procedure and penalties are phases open to the Prosecution and Defence only) and that the issue of reparation cannot arise before a determination of guilt. See *The Prosecutor v. Théoneste Bagasora*, Amicus Curiae: Letter from Geert Muylle to Mr. Agwu Ukiwe Okali, Case No. ICTR-96-7-T, 10 February 1998; *The Prosecutor v. Théoneste Bagasora*, Decision on the Amicus Curiae Application by the Government of the Kingdom of Belgium, Case No. ICTR-96-7-T, 6 June 1998. See further Chapter 5 on participation.

[69] In case victims with compensation claims do manage to appear before the competent (national) organ, Malmström (2001, p. 382) points out some difficulties which could be caused by the national law of the country where the claim is brought. For example, she refers to 'the relevant national jurisdiction [which] may not allow claims by anyone else than the victim and may not allow standing for relatives or family. Rule 106 does not provide for an obligation of the respective State to provide compensation and the scope of the compensation will depend on the respective national jurisdictions.' As to the phrase 'the judgement of the Tribunal shall be final and binding as to the criminal responsibility of the convicted person for such injury', she notes that 'it is doubtful what impact this provision has, as a judgement of the Tribunal in certain countries for example Germany, is not enforceable in the domestic legal system unless the judgement has been transformed into a domestic judgement'.

[70] Letter dated 12 October 2000 from the President of the International Tribunal for the Former Yugoslavia addressed to the Secretary-General, annex to a Letter dated 2 November 2000 from

money available to compensate for their crimes. If they do, they will usually try to find ways to dispose of their money, especially when they know that they are being searched for. An alternative suggested by Prosecutor Carla del Ponte in 2000 (then Chief Prosecutor of both the ICTY and the ICTR), viz. to pay compensation to victims from 'frozen assets' obtained from the accused in the course of international arrest warrants issued by the Tribunal against them, did not lead to any action and thus did not provide a solution to the problem of indigent accused or the compensation to victims either.[71]

Survivors of sexual violence could have used the compensation for such purposes as hospitalisation, medication including ARV drugs and counselling, but also, for instance, for education and rent. In the absence of a Rule 106 action (as well as direct compensation mechanisms within the Tribunals or claims commissions), however, survivors of sexual violence remain without compensation in spite of their pressing needs in post-conflict situations.

3.1.3 Rehabilitation

The possibilities within the ICTY and ICTR with regard to reparation in the form of restitution of property and compensation have clearly produced no positive results in terms of restorative justice for victims of crimes in the former Yugoslavia and in Rwanda. Against the background of the fact that many survivors of sexual violence

---

the Secretary-General addressed to the President of the Security Council, UN doc. S/2000/1063, 3 November 2000.

[71] 'If we cut off the funding – that is, the bank accounts – of the inductees, not only will we make their escape more difficult, but the money, according to the Chamber judges' decision, will also be used to provide compensation to the victims. ... It would be regrettable where we are unable to obtain such a decision from the judges. There is a problem, however. There is a loophole in our law. Our procedural rules do not provide access to confiscated sequestered funds. That is why we would request that a change be made in the rules' (Security Council Minutes from 4150th meeting, UN Doc. S/PV.4150, 2 June 2000, p. 5). See also the interview of 9 June 2000 with Carla del Ponte, in which she states that 'by saying that whenever a financial investigation takes place as part of a general investigation and we manage to freeze a defendant's money, the judges ought to decide what happens to that money. For me, there is only one proper response: give it to the victims. Of course, the pain does not go away. But if you are a victim and receive financial support, especially in the difficult conditions that we know about in Rwanda, then that's already a real bonus. According to the law governing international tribunals, all compensation claims must be made to the national legal system, which is the only body apt to judge. But just think of a civil action taken in a country like Rwanda or anywhere else: it takes a long time and costs a lot of money. Changing things on this front is a tricky business, since it requires changing the legal statutes, which means that the decision is down to the Security Council. That said, I have to say that there is a loophole in the law which might allow us to make some headway on the question. There is a rule which states that it is up to the judges to rule "on sentences and sanctions". I'm going to use the concept of sanctions to argue that sentences means prison and sanctions is the confiscation of money that has been sequestered. Let's say I'm making an interpretation. We're not quite there yet, but I've opened up the debate at least' (Diplomatie Judiciaire, *Compensating Victims With Guilty Money*, Interview with Carla del Ponte, The Hague, 9 June 2000).

were either too sick to testify or died before testifying,[72] the ICTR launched the 'Support Programme for Witnesses and Potential Witnesses' in September 2000.[73] The programme was set up by the Tribunal's Gender Issues and Assistance to Victims Unit to support victim-witnesses and witnesses of the ICTR in Rwanda through assistance programmes operated by NGOs, financed by the Voluntary Trust Fund of the Tribunal.[74] Support to witnesses was to be provided in the form of rehabilitation, such as legal guidance, psychological counselling, physical rehabilitation and reintegration assistance.[75] The restitutive character of the support programme was heralded by several participants at the launch, who stressed that the programme would contribute to national reconciliation and peace in Rwanda and would have a positive impact on the Rwandan people's perception of the relevance and reality of the Tribunal's justice for the victims of the genocide.[76] To a large extent the support was set up to meet the needs of victims of sexual violence. For this reason, the venue of the launch of the Support Programme was Taba commune, Gitarama Prefecture (Rwanda), chosen, in particular, to honour the victims of sexual violence in Taba, for which Akayesu, the mayor of this town during the genocide, was convicted. Another reason for choosing Taba as the venue for the launch of the programme was that Akayesu was the first person convicted by the Tribunal.

The Support Programme was based on Rule 34, which reads:

> (A) There shall be set up under the authority of the Registrar a Victims and Witnesses Support Unit consisting of qualified staff to:
>
> ...
>
> (i) ensure that they [the victims and witnesses] receive relevant support, including physical and psychological rehabilitation, especially counselling in cases of rape and sexual assault.
>
> ...
>
> (B) A gender sensitive approach to victims and witnesses protective and support measures should be adopted ...[77]

The Manual of Operational Guidance of the Witnesses and Victims Support Section (WVSS) further clarifies Rule 34 by stating that 'counselling and supporting the victims and witnesses particularly in cases of rape and sexual assault, is a major task, and the WVSS must rely on specialized services throughout the judicial proceedings as well as

---

72 Ngendahayo and Moledina (2000). Françoise Ngendahayo was the former ICTR Advisor on Gender Issues and Assistance to Victims.

73 ICTR Press Release, *ICTR Launches Victims Support Initiative in Rwanda*, ICTR/INFO-9-2-242.EN, 26 September 2000.

74 *Ibid.*

75 *Ibid.*

76 *Ibid.*

77 Ngendahayo and Moledina (2002). In the paper it is explained that Rule 34 was amended in order to clarify, among other things, the extent and type of counselling and support. The earlier version of Rule 34 read, in part, to 'provide counselling and support for them, in particular in cases of rape and sexual assault'. Rule 34 ICTY RPE still provides for the latter wording.

in the post-trial phase'.[78] Furthermore, 'the WVSS shall organize the necessary support services including legal counseling, which will explain to the witnesses how to present their testimony before the Tribunal. Trauma counseling and assistance will be provided to their relatives or dependants during the pre-trial, trial and post-trial phases.'[79] And 'medical and psychological services are provided to victims and witnesses who suffered extensive trauma as a result of the genocide, and became psychologically affected, or who contracted diseases which they were not able to overcome before testifying'.[80] Rule 34 and the explanatory Manual of Operational Guidance of the WVSS on this provision therefore clearly allow the ICTR to provide support to victims and witnesses (thus also potential witnesses) in terms of physical and psychological rehabilitation, including the treatment of women who contracted HIV/AIDS through rape, even in pre- and post-trial phases. Although the establishment of the Support Programme, based on Rule 34, was justified by the argument that it is inherent in the Tribunal's mandate to do justice, including restitutive justice,[81] this argument was later on severely questioned. Shortly after it was launched, concerns about the programme were raised, including the concern whether the programme was within the ambit of the ICTR's mandate or not, the concern about the lack of funding to support all witnesses, considering that the Trust Fund would be made up of voluntary contributions only and the concern that the support provided through the programme might be abused by individuals appearing as witnesses before the Tribunal while they were not.[82] Following the advice of the UN Office of Legal Affairs, the project was partly abandoned in 2002 as it was made clear that assistance was only allowed in the case of witnesses testifying before the Tribunal.[83] Moreover, in its short life span the Support Programme had not been able to respond to the pressing needs of HIV/AIDS treatment: 'The amounts received were so meagre that they did not even provide access to antibiotics to heal opportunistic infections.'[84]

Therefore, for a very long time (1995-2003) the support received by victim-witnesses during their stay at the Tribunal included, at the most, some medical and/or dental care, and sometimes a new pair of glasses.[85] The Tribunal chose not to offer medication for HIV/AIDS treatment, essentially because HIV/AIDS was not considered an 'opportunistic disease'.[86] In light of the many women dying of AIDS, victims 'needed' by the Tribunal as witnesses in the proceedings, such a decision is appalling, the more so when one considers the fact that HIV/AIDS-positive accused persons received ARV drug treatment during their detention in Arusha. This situation has often

[78] ICTR, Witnesses and Victims Support Section [WVSS], *Manual of Operational Guidance*, p. 41.
[79] *Ibid.*
[80] *Ibid.*, p. 51.
[81] Ngendahayo and Moledina (2002). See also Clark and Tolbert (1999), pp. 106-107.
[82] International Federation for Human Rights (2002), pp. 10-11. Nduwimana (2004, p. 25), refers to Akayesu's lawyers who criticised the project on the basis that the ICTR did not have the legal mandate to carry out a programme of restitutive justice and that the neutrality of the Registrar was compromised.
[83] ICTR Seventh Annual Report (2002), p. 14.
[84] Nduwimana (2004), p. 25.
[85] Interview with Trial Attorney at the ICTR, November 2003.
[86] Washington Square News, *Lawyer: Rwanda Rape Belittled* (by Kate Meyer), 23 March 2004.

been cited by victims as being beyond their comprehension.[87] Several potential witnesses have furthermore refused to cooperate with the Tribunal because of the lack of ARV treatment therapy.[88]

Yet, as of 2004, under the supervision of Elsie Effange-Mbella, the Gender Advisor of the ICTR, the tide seems to have changed somewhat. In February 2004, three medical specialists – a gynaecologist, a psychologist and a nurse-psychologist – were recruited for the Victims and Witnesses Medical Team, based at the ICTR in Kigali, to improve on access to medical support for and monitoring of victims, including HIV/AIDS treatment.[89] Such services had already been available through private clinics.[90] By setting up a medical unit aimed at monitoring the patients, the ICTR thus accepted a duty on the basis of Rule 34 to provide rape victims (including potential witnesses) testifying at the Tribunal not only with general medical services, but also with ARV treatment for those in need thereof, throughout the trial process as well as in the pre- and post-trial phases.[91] According to an ICTR document on improved access to ARV treatment and psychological counselling for ICTR witnesses with HIV/AIDS, 'mere psychological counselling on its own however, is not enough for the rehabilitation of witnesses, particularly victims of sexual assault. It has become increasingly important for the ICTR to access much needed support in order to adopt a systematic healthcare approach related to witnesses' physical conditions – HIV/AIDS, Malaria and other diseases, prevalent in Rwanda.'[92] Based on national statistics (the HIV/AIDS prevalence rate in Rwanda is 11 percent), out of the estimated 2,000 (prosecution and defence) witnesses testifying at the ICTR, about 220 persons are presumably infected with HIV/AIDS. In April 2004, 18 confirmed cases had been identified.[93] According to Effange-Mbella, the clinic in Kigali receives between 200 and

---

[87] See, *inter alia*, Nowrojee (2004b); Internews, *When Justice Takes Too Long* (by Mary Kimani), 1 September 2003; Nduwimana (2004), p. 11.

[88] ICTR Draft Report on Improved Access to Anti-Retroviral Treatment and Psychological Counselling for ICTR Witnesses with HIV/AIDS, prepared by Elsie Effange-Mbella, 2004, p. 2.

[89] ICTR Ninth Annual Report (2004), para. 60. In addition, the report mentions that a laboratory technician is being recruited to assist with the medical operation in support of witnesses in Rwanda.

[90] Hirondelle News Agency, *ICTR spent US$200,000 on HIV/AIDS Affected Witnesses in 2004*, 24 January 2005.

[91] ICTR Draft Report on Improved Access to Anti-Retroviral Treatment and Psychological Counselling for ICTR Witnesses with HIV/AIDS, prepared by Elsie Effange-Mbella, 2004, pp. 1-3. The report justifies this move on page 1 as follows: 'The ICTR by virtue of its mandate and the provisions of Article 21 of its Statute and Rule 34 of its Rules of Procedure and Evidence, has a fundamental and unique role to play in achieving peace, justice and national reconciliation in Rwanda, by creating inter-alia, conducive conditions for the maintenance of an adequate physical and psychological environment enabling the successful participation of witnesses to the process of testifying before the Tribunal particularly for victims of rape and sexual assault.'

[92] ICTR Draft Report on Improved Access to Anti-Retroviral Treatment and Psychological Counselling for ICTR Witnesses with HIV/AIDS, prepared by Elsie Effange-Mbella, 2004, p. 5. The document also recognises on page 4 the importance of protection, which, together with support, has become the greatest concern of most people willing to testify before the Tribunal.

[93] *Ibid.*, p. 3.

300 patients (ICTR witnesses) a week.[94] The Tribunal is also providing nutritional support for all Rwanda based witnesses with HIV/AIDS.[95] In September 2005, the clinic was caring for 43 confirmed HIV/AIDS patients, thirteen of whom are on ARV drugs as medically recommended.[96] Most of the people who are HIV-positive and are being treated at the clinic have already testified.[97] Furthermore, Effange-Mbella stated that the ICTR spent USD 200,000 on HIV/AIDS-affected witnesses in 2004.[98] The ICTR is also developing a medical support system that will link witnesses to available national services for treatment long after the ICTR has shut down in 2008 (Trial Chambers)/2010 (Appeals Chamber).[99] The current initiative is commendable. Yet, urgent testing of the cohort group of witnesses is needed to address their plight. In addition, family members too should be enabled to benefit from the support, especially if the raped women's children have contracted HIV/AIDS due to their mother's illness. Moreover, the funds for personnel costs at the clinic as well as medical support, including HIV/AIDS treatment, are largely dependent on the Tribunals' Trust Fund. In this respect, in October 2003, a glimmer of hope seemed to have accompanied the concept of support for victims, espoused by Najat Al Hajjaji, the President of the UN Human Rights Commission, during her visit to the ICTR, when she emphasised the need to establish a special Trust Fund for victims of the Rwandan genocide.[100] She called for contributions from Member States and individuals to the ICTR Trust Fund in order to support the Tribunal's Outreach Program in Rwanda entailing, *inter alia*, medical and psychological support to victims traumatised or sexually abused during the genocide.[101] Yet, according to Effange-Mbella the Voluntary Trust Fund resources are under depletion and no new substantive contributions to the Fund have been received from Member States for some time now.[102]

The situation as regards the ICTY is not much different: 'there is no follow-up counselling or material help for the witnesses who often come back to a country facing economic hardship.'[103] Like the ICTR, the Tribunal for the former Yugoslavia spends part of its voluntary contributions, alongside many other projects, to victim assistance in the field.[104] Over the years 2003-2004, the Tribunal hosted a series of conferences with health and welfare professionals (psychiatrists, medical doctors, psychologists and social workers) from Bosnia and Herzegovina, Serbia and Montenegro, Croatia and

---

94 Hirondelle News Agency, *ICTR Medical Support Programme Targets 2,300 Witnesses*, 28 January 2005.

95 *Ibid.* (as updated by Effange-Mbella).

96 *Ibid.* (as updated by Effange-Mbella).

97 Hirondelle News Agency, *ICTR spent US$200,000 on HIV/AIDS Affected Witnesses in 2004*, 24 January 2005.

98 *Ibid.*

99 *Ibid.*, p. 5.

100 ICTR Press Release, *The President of the UN Human Rights Commission to Lead a Campaign to Support Victims*, ICTR/INFO-9-2-363.EN, 7 October 2003.

101 *Ibid.*

102 Hirondelle News Agency, *ICTR Medical Support Programme Targets 2,300 Witnesses*, 28 January 2005.

103 Agence France-Presse, *Trauma and Isolation Await Many Witnesses of UN Court at Home*, 16 January 2004.

104 ICTY Ninth Annual Report (2002), paras. 331 and 334.

Kosovo aimed at providing physical, emotional and psychological support to witnesses who testified at the Tribunal upon their return home.[105] The idea behind the conferences was to discuss how the establishment of health and welfare networks throughout the former Yugoslavia could assist in providing preparation and follow-up services to meet the health needs of the witnesses who testified at the Tribunal.[106] It seems that the ICTY does not recognise any direct legal responsibility concerning victims' needs in terms of support before or after testimony, only during testimony at the Tribunal. Support after trial is left to the expertise of, for instance, NGOs and their personnel with expertise in this field. Therefore, the Tribunal seems to have accepted a moral duty to improvise and provide support measures to victims.

In order to support victims on a lasting, continuing basis, it is important that resources in the Voluntary Trust Fund are not depleted. The resources of the Trust Fund are, however, separate from the regular budgetary funds the Tribunal receives annually; the Fund depends on the voluntary contributions from Member States and other interested parties.[107] A lack of sufficient funds has threatened the existence of the Trust Fund time and time again and, as a result, projects financed by the Voluntary Trust Fund, such as witness support, could not be implemented on a continuing basis.[108]

---

[105] ICTY Press Release, *First Conference Between Health Professionals from the Former Yugoslavia and the ICTY on Witness Welfare*, CC/P.I.S./805-e, The Hague, 2 December 2003; ICTY Press Release, *Second Conference Between Health Professionals from the Former Yugoslavia and the ICTY on Witness Welfare*, WL/P.I.S./850-e, The Hague, 21 May 2004,; ICTY Press Release, *Conference Between Health Professionals from Croatia and the ICTY on Witness Welfare*, WL/P.I.S./855-e, The Hague, 4 June 2004; ICTY Press Release, *Fourth Conference Between Health Professionals from the Former Yugoslavia and the ICTY on Witness Welfare*, WL/P.I.S./894-e, The Hague, 13 September 2004.

[106] *Ibid.*

[107] At the end of 1998, cash contributions to the ICTR Voluntary Trust Fund amounted to USD 7,571,998.00. The following countries have contributed in various amounts to the ICTR Fund: Belgium, Canada, Chile, Denmark, Egypt, Finland, Greece, Holy See, Ireland, Israel, Lebanon, the Netherlands, New Zealand, Norway, Spain, Sweden, Switzerland, UK, and the USA. See ICTR Press Release, *Cooperation and Assistance of States Key to Success of ICTR*, ICTR/INFO-9-2-169, 9 March 1999. According to the Tribunal's spokesman, Kingsley Moghalu, the fund had received USD 8 million since its inception in 1995 and, in March 2002, these funds were almost exhausted. See Irin News, *Rwanda: ICTR to Embark on Fund-raising for Trust Fund*, 28 March 2002. Since 1994, the ICTY has received a total of USD 44,544,751 in donations from various Member States and institutions of the United Nations. See ICTY Ninth Annual Report (2002), para. 330.

[108] In an address by the Registrar, Adama Dieng, on the occasion of the visit of the Prime Minister of Norway to the ICTR on 11 October 2004, the Registrar mentioned that the Tribunal's Voluntary Trust Fund is depleted and that projects financed through the Trust Fund are severely threatened in their existence. See Address by the Registrar on the Occasion of the Visit of the Prime Minister of Norway to the International Criminal Tribunal for Rwanda, Arusha, 11 October 2004. Yet, in May 2004, the European Commission concluded an agreement with the ICTR, which foresees in the funding of special projects strengthening the managerial and operational capacity of the Tribunal. The total amount approved by the Commission was EUR 1,5 million, to be spend, *inter alia*, to projects aimed at assistance to victims and witnesses to receive adequate

Considering that the funds in the Voluntary Trust Fund have been used in respect of a multiplicity of projects that support the activities of the Court, the establishment of a special ICTR Voluntary Trust Fund, dedicated to the needs of victims only, is a clear advance, although resources are limited here as well.[109]

3.2 Pushing for compensation within the Tribunals?

In order to give an impetus to the Tribunals' indirect compensation regime, several attempts to improve the system were made by the Chief Prosecutor, Carla del Ponte. In 2000, Del Ponte raised the issue of compensation – as well as participation – for the first time before the ICTR judges. Although they basically favoured her proposal on compensation to victims, according to them compensation should only be granted on the condition that the Statute be amended: mere changes to the Rules were not considered sufficient.[110] In July 2000, during the 22nd Plenary Session of the ICTY, the Prosecutor sought the views of the ICTY on this matter for further guidance.[111] In the ICTY Plenary Session it was decided that the Rules Committee, with some assistance from the Registry, would further study the proposals made by the Prosecutor on compensation and to make recommendations to the Judges.[112] On 13 September 2000, the ICTY Judges subscribed to the conclusions laid down in the Report of the Rules Committee on 'Victims Compensation and Participation' and held that 'victims of crimes within the Tribunal's jurisdiction have a legal right to seek compensation for their injuries'.[113] The answer to the question where and how to implement such a right proved, however, not so straightforward. In the Report it was suggested that the Tribunal's President recommend to the Secretary-General and Security Council that 'methods of compensating victims of crimes in the former Yugoslavia, notably a claims commission, be considered by the appropriate organs of the United Nations'.[114] The Rules

---

psychological assistance, particularly witnesses who were victims of rape and other forms of sexual assault. See ICTR Press Release, *The European Commission to Fund Tribunal Projects*, ICTR/INFO-9-2-388.EN, Arusha, 10 May 2004. The amount was apparently not enough to cover all projects falling within the outreach programme of the Tribunal.

[109] 'Unsuccessful proposals were made for establishment of a fund for victims in the negotiations leading to the adoption of the statute of the ICTY. The National Alliance of Women's Organizations for instance proposed that the Security Council establish a fund for the benefit and compensation of victims of war crimes and crimes against humanity', cited in Ingadottir (2003), pp. 113-114.

[110] *Victims Compensation and Participation*, Report Prepared by the Rules Committee, 2000, Sections I and III.

[111] ICTY Press Release, *The 22nd Plenary Session of the International Criminal Tribunal for the former Yugoslavia*, JL/P.I.S./518-e, The Hague, 17 July 2000.

[112] *Ibid.*

[113] *Victims Compensation and Participation*, Report Prepared by the Rules Committee, 2000, Section IV.

[114] *Ibid.* The idea of a claims commission for victims was not new. As mentioned before, a claims commission was already considered as the right mechanism for compensation claims when the ICTY was first established.

Committee substantiated its recommendations not to change the compensation regime under the Tribunal as follows:

> While it would be possible for the Tribunal's Statute and Rules to be amended to provide for a procedure, akin to that envisaged in the ICC, there are a number of factors that make this approach very difficult to implement. These procedures would increase the Chambers' workload and further exacerbate the length of its proceedings, thus undermining its efforts to provide accused with fair and expeditious trials. Moreover, the Tribunal has now been in existence for a number of years, and the introduction of such procedures is likely to prove difficult to implement and run counter to the Tribunal's principal objective of prosecuting those responsible for the crimes in the former Yugoslavia. In view of the strenuous efforts that the Tribunal is making to address the length of its trials, it would not be wise to debate and adopt procedures which undermine those efforts. Moreover, there are serious questions as to how a compensation scheme could be adequately funded, particularly as many of the accused have few resources.[115]

In other words, the ICTY judges did not approve of a direct mechanism to administer compensation claims within the Tribunal, ancillary to the criminal trials of the accused. The judges concluded that other rights and policy considerations were at stake, including the accused's right to a fair and expeditious trial. Considering that the Tribunals were set up primarily to prosecute persons responsible for serious violations of international humanitarian law, the additional task of dealing with compensation claims, they held, would simply take up too much time and effort, which would only further delay trial proceedings. However, such a conclusion is not tenable. On a number of occasions, Groenhuijsen stated that 'quite a few jurisdictions have already proven that it is feasible as well as fruitful to transcend the distinction between punishment and court-ordered restitution'.[116] Van Boven summarises the advantages of the possibility of requesting and being awarded compensation during criminal proceedings as follows:

> First, it makes the criminal offender more aware that not only was a wrong committed against public order and public welfare but, in addition, an injury was inflicted on one or more human beings. Second, it establishes a link between punitive measures and measures of reparation. Third, it tends to facilitate and expedite the process of obtaining civil damages.[117]

However, while the proposals to amend the Statute to include direct ways of compensating victims was initially not rejected by the judges of the Rwanda Tribunal, the judges at the ICTY thus did not consider amendment of the Statute an option. Instead, it was proposed that an international claims commission be established. In this regard it was held that '... while the funding of such a commission would have to be determined by the appropriate international actors, in principle a commission provides a

[115] *Ibid.*
[116] Groenhuijsen (2004a), p. 73. See further, *inter alia*, Groenhuijsen (1985); Brienen, Groenhuijsen and Hoegen (2000), p. 138.
[117] Van Boven (1999b), p. 21.

much fairer and expeditious method of providing a measure of restorative justice to the victims of the wars in the former Yugoslavia'.[118]

The considerations in the Report were ultimately upheld by the ICTY judges and communicated to the Secretary-General, who subsequently sent the recommendations to the Security Council, and thus the Tribunal's tasks were not extended to deciding on the payment of compensation to victims of crimes committed by persons convicted by it.[119] The ICTR, in a similar fashion, proposed that other mechanisms be considered, such as a specialised agency within the UN or a scheme administered by some other agency or governmental entity.[120] The ICTR judges did, however, raise the possibility that the Tribunal, in tandem with one of those mechanisms, be vested with a limited power to decide on the payment of compensation to victims who appear as witnesses from a trust fund, on the condition that the Statute be amended.[121] On 21 November 2000, Del Ponte, this time in an address to the UN Security Council, again emphasised the deficits in the Tribunals' legal system as to the compensation and participation of victims, underlining that the present system falls short of delivering justice to the people of Rwanda and the former Yugoslavia.[122] In addition, she raised the possibility of using frozen assets in the personal accounts of the accused for the benefit of the victims.[123] Despite the Prosecutor's efforts to include compensation to victims in the Tribunals' mandate, the ICTY and ICTR judges remained unconvinced of a clear and specific role of the Tribunals in this respect. Moreover, no response from the Security Council on this matter has been received to date. The issue of direct compensation thus remains outside the scope of the Tribunals' mandate for the time being.

There are no realistic prospects that direct compensation to victims through a direct order of the Tribunals will be provided for in the Tribunals' Statutes before the completion of the Tribunals' work in 2008 (Trial Chambers)/2010 (Appeals Chamber). The debate on compensation to victims remains a lively one, however. In October 2002, the ICTR President, Judge Pillay, addressed the UN Security Council and General Assembly on the achievements of the ICTR during the year 2001-2002, and called for compensation to victims. She urged the Member States to help compensate victims if Rwanda is to recover from the genocide that was perpetrated in that country in 1994. She stated:

[118] *Ibid.*

[119] Letter dated 12 October 2000 from the President of the International Tribunal for the Former Yugoslavia addressed to the Secretary-General, annex to a Letter dated 2 November 2000 from the Secretary-General addressed to the President of the Security Council, UN doc. S/2000/1063, 3 November 2000.

[120] Letter of the President of the ICTR to the Secretary General of the United Nations, annex to a letter of 14 December 2000 by the UN Secretary-General, Kofi Annan, to the UN Security Council, UN Doc. S/2000/1198, 15 December 2000, para. 15.

[121] *Ibid.*

[122] ICTY Press Release, *Address to the Security Council by Carla del Ponte, Prosecutor of the International Criminal Tribunals for the former Yugoslavia and Rwanda, to the UN Security Council*, JL/P.I.S./542-e, The Hague, 24 November 2000.

[123] *Ibid.* See also Diplomatie Judiciaire, *Compensating Victims with Guilty Money,* Interview with Carla del Ponte, The Hague, 9 June 2000, where she raised the issue of 'frozen assets' before.

> Many Rwandans have questioned the ICTR's value and its role in promoting reconciliation where claim for compensation is not addressed. For every hour of every day over the past 7½ years, we have lived with the voices of the survivors of genocide and so we strongly urge the United Nations to provide compensation for Rwandan victims.[124]

Judge Pillay's message underlines the Tribunal's restrictive view on compensation, with no role for the Tribunal therein.[125] At the same time, she recognises and stresses the urgent need for and importance of compensation to victims, a matter which she – and thus the Tribunal – believes should be of major concern to the international community of States. In the same year, Prosecutor Del Ponte, however, again argued in favour of a role of the ICTR in matters of reparation as she specifically stated that she is 'supportive of the victims and survivors playing a greater part in the proceedings of the tribunal and hopes that the tribunal might have a freer hand in compensating survivors and victims'.[126] Van Boven once noted that the provisions on reparation were included in the Rules 'as a symbolic afterthought rather than being expected to produce concrete results'.[127] Indeed, any concrete results stayed out, nor was the reparation regime changed to the benefit of victims of crime, and today no compensation has been paid to victims. Victims of sexual violence are therefore left uncompensated.

3.3 The role of the Tribunals: The Tribunals at an impasse?

It is clear that the Tribunals have not invoked the provisions on restitution and compensation for the benefit of victims, although, on a number of occasions, it was recognised and expressed that reparation to victims is urgently needed, in particular with regard to compensation and support. A recent initiative by the ICTR Gender Advisor has led to improvements in relation to medical support, including HIV/AIDS treatment for rape survivors. The decision was expressly based on Rule 34 of the RPE, thus indicating that the ICTR accepts legal responsibility for support to witnesses. However, only witnesses who appear before the Tribunal are covered by this measure (no other victims of sexual violence) and only a small number of witnesses who have already testified before the Tribunal have received ARV drugs. Moreover, as support

---

124 ICTR, Office of the President, *Statement by the President of the ICTR to the United Nations General Assembly by Judge Navanethem Pillay, President*, 28 October 2002; ICTR, Office of the President, *Statement by the President of the ICTR to the United Nations Security Council by Judge Navanethem Pillay, President*, 29 October 2002.

125 This point of view was reiterated by the ICTR President, Judge Erik Møse, in an address to the UN General Assembly on 9 October 2003: 'Let me also recall that already in 2000, the ICTR expressed support for the principle of compensation, or rather reparation ('*indemnisation*'), for victims. *The responsibility for processing and assessing claims for such compensation is, however, not a task for the Tribunal.* I am pleased to note that this week, the President of the Human Rights Commission, who is presently in Arusha, committed herself to advocate for a special Trust Fund for victims of genocide, crimes against humanity and war crimes' (italics added). See ICTR, *Address by Judge Erik Møse, President of the International Criminal Tribunal for Rwanda, to the United Nations General Assembly*, 9 October 2003.

126 ICTR Seventh Annual Report (2002), para. 72.

127 Van Boven (1999a), pp. 81-82.

services are dependent on contributions to the Trust Fund, which is low on resources, its success is to be awaited. In light of the increasing weight that is given to victims' rights to restorative justice in a number of national criminal laws and procedures, the absence of directly enforceable rights for victims to reparation within the Tribunals seems old-fashioned. What both Tribunals should have done was to amend their Statutes to provide for a direct mechanism to award reparation to victims, similar to the ICC.[128] Thus, victims of crimes that were addressed by the Tribunal would have been able to apply for reparation themselves or, where they were unable to do so, the Chamber could have done this on their behalf. In addition, a special Trust Fund for victims and their families should have been set up, from which compensation to victims can be paid if the convicted perpetrators have no means to do so. Such a Trust Fund might also cover interim relief, which is especially useful for victims of sexual violence who need immediate treatment. The Trust Fund would then be receiving voluntary contributions from States and individuals, and the money would solely be spent on the compensation of victims, not to a plethora of different projects as is the case with the Voluntary Trust Funds of both Tribunals. In the absence of all of this, at least a mechanism outside the Tribunal could have been established to deal with the compensation to victims, as was suggested by the judges of both Tribunals in recognition of the right of victims to compensation.

4 The ICC

The drafters of the ICC clearly moved away from the inadequate and ineffective reparation provisions in the ICTY and ICTR Statutes and Rules. For the first time in the supranational criminal law context, the ICC gives victims independent status by providing them standing to request and receive reparation from the convicted person. In addition, a Trust Fund has been set up for the benefit of victims and their families. The Trust Fund will not only implement Court orders on reparation, it will most likely also have a complementary role to fulfil, especially where the rehabilitation of and support for victims is needed. The ICC thus aims to achieve not only retributive justice by punishing the perpetrator, but also restorative justice by providing reparation to victims.

4.1 The ICC: A necessary departure from the Tribunals?

Although at first the delegates in the Preparatory Commission were of the opinion that the Court should concentrate on the prosecution of perpetrators only – an argument similar to the one used by the Tribunals not to recognise a legal obligation to award compensation to victims in the context of the Tribunals' proceedings – it was primarily the experience before the Tribunals that brought one to realise that, in addition to retributive justice, more restorative approaches to victims should be included in the Court's work.[129] In particular France, the United Kingdom as well as a number of NGOs (such as Amnesty International, Human Rights Watch, Women's Caucus for Gender Justice and Redress) played an important role in the negotiations on the issue of

[128] As will be discussed in section 4.

[129] Muttukumaru (1999), pp. 263-264. See also Van Boven (1999b), p. 22.

reparation.[130] The fact that France (with its civil law system) and the United Kingdom (with its common law system) were able to reach a consensus on the issue of reparation in criminal proceedings evidences the importance given to reparation to victims in the ICC Statute and Rules. Whereas in common law systems victims are simply witnesses for the prosecution, in civil law jurisdictions victims generally have standing to bring a reparation claim before the court as part of the criminal trial. As reparation for victims of mass crimes has proved difficult to obtain by means of civil suits, the ICC's approach towards the issue of reparation can be considered to be a more victim-friendly mechanism.

The Tribunals, despite their ability to do so, never ordered the restitution of property, nor did they deliver judgments by which compensation could be awarded to victims through competent national authorities. Before the Tribunals, victims only served in their capacity as witnesses, an approach primarily based on common law. While the ICTR provided accused with HIV/AIDS with ARV drugs, many victims – many of whom contracted HIV/AIDS through sexual violence – have been left without proper care, despite recent efforts to address this situation. In addition, the Voluntary Trust Fund – a Fund which is constantly depleted – was never solely aimed at remedying victims. This situation, which is not much different for the victims in the former Yugoslavia, should have been remedied by an amendment to the Tribunals' Statutes to allow for direct mechanisms to request and be awarded compensation. At least as of 1998, when the ICC's reparation regime became the benchmark in the field of reparation in the supranational criminal law context, the Tribunals could have followed suit.

4.2 The ICC reparation regime for victims

The ICC reparation regime is laid down in Articles 75 and 79 of the ICC Statute and is further elaborated in Rules 94 to 99 of the ICC RPE.[131] The reparation regime for victims, including victims of sexual violence, is as follows and can be linked to the various stages of the trial. The Court can pass an order awarding reparation on the basis of the conviction of the accused. However, the creation of a Trust Fund allowed a broader system of reparation, which can be accessed at any stage in the trial, including the investigation, pre-trial and trial stages, at least in those cases where the Trust Fund will be able to operate in a complementary fashion to the Court. Apart from this, under Article 75(6) of the ICC Statute a victim may also look for and receive reparation from other sources.[132]

---

[130] Lewis and Friman (2001), pp. 475-477.

[131] The main features of the reparation possibilities under the ICC and the ways in which reparation can be of benefit to victims of sexual violence will be examined in this Chapter. For further general reading on the ICC and reparation, see, *inter alia*, Bottigliero (2004), pp. 212-247; Ingadottir (2003), pp. 111-144; Lewis and Friman (2001), pp. 474-491; and Heikkilä (2004), pp. 166-190.

[132] Article 75(6) ICC Statute reads: 'Nothing in this article shall be interpreted as prejudicing the rights of victims and witnesses under national or international law.'

4.2.1 Court orders to award reparation

After an individual has been convicted for one of the crimes under the ICC's jurisdiction, the Court may determine the scope and extent of any damage, losses and injuries suffered by the victims on the basis of principles relating to reparation, including restitution, compensation and rehabilitation.[133] The judges of the Court have full discretion in deciding whether or not the victim is to receive reparation,[134] and if it decides to award reparation, the Court itself is to determine the principles relating to reparation. A footnote attached to the final report of the Working Group on Procedural Matters of the Rome Conference, however, strongly indicates that the principles for reparation should be inspired by developing international standards on reparation, in particular the Van Boven/Bassiouni Principles.[135] The same footnote also indicates that 'victims' should be defined on the basis of the 1985 Declaration of Basic Principles of Justice for Victims of Crime and Abuse of Power and the Van Boven/Bassiouni Principles, which implies that not only those victims who are direct victims of crime should be awarded reparation, but also others, such as victims' families and successors.[136] Along this line, the term 'victims' has been defined in Rule 85 in a broad manner, that is 'natural persons who have suffered harm as a result of the commission of any crime within the jurisdiction of the Court'.[137]

While the type and modalities of reparation will thus be determined by the ICC judges, they may be assisted in this task by experts with knowledge of the needs of victims in a particular situation.[138] In any event, before deciding on an order concerning reparation, the Court may invite and is to take into account representations from or on behalf of the convicted person, victims, other interested persons or interested States.[139] Awards for reparations can be made on an individualised or collective basis or both, taking into account the scope and extent of any damage, loss and injury.[140] Where the number of victims is very high, the Court may be more inclined to award reparations on

---

[133] Articles 75(1) and 75(2) ICC Statute.

[134] Article 75(2) ICC Statute ('may').

[135] Footnote 5 to Article 73 on reparations to victims in the Final report of the Working Group on Procedural Matters, A/CONF.183/C.1/WGPM/L.2/Add.7, 13 July 1998. See also Lewis and Friman (2001), pp. 477-478; and Bonneau (2004). See further, including a description of the different types of reparation, section 1 of this Chapter.

[136] Footnote 5 to article 73 on reparations to victims in A/CONF.183/C.1/WGPM/L.2/Add.7, 13 July 1998. See also Bonneau (2004).

[137] Rule 85(a) ICC RPE. Also organisations or institutions may fall within the definition of 'victims'. See Rule 85(b) ICC RPE which reads: 'victims may include organizations or institutions that have sustained direct harm to any of their property, which is dedicated to religion, education, art or science or charitable purposes, and to their historic monuments, hospitals and other places and objects for humanitarian purposes'. Although such organisations and institutions can also be considered as 'victims', the wording 'may include' in subparagraph (b) implies that natural persons should be seen as those victims entitled to reparation first of all.

[138] Rule 97(2) ICC RPE.

[139] Article 75(3) ICC Statute; Rule 97(3) ICC RPE.

[140] Rule 97 ICC RPE.

a collective basis.[141] For example, where reparation to a victim of sexual violence is concerned, the Court may, for instance, award a certain amount of money in cash (to compensate for, for example, physical and mental harm, harm to reputation or dignity, costs required for medicines, including ARV drugs) and/or the restitution of the victim's house or other property and/or physical, medical and legal assistance. In the alternative or concurrently, the Court may decide on a collective award by ordering a school to be built for these women and/or their children and/or by ordering to set up treatment centres to provide psychological and medical assistance, including HIV/AIDS treatment.

With regard to compensation, it is not certain whether the Court will elaborate set scales for compensation to victims of genocide, crimes against humanity and war crimes. Within other frameworks, scales of compensation have been established, such as by the UN Compensation Commission, which was created in 1991 as a subsidiary organ of the UN Security Council to process claims and pay compensation for losses, damage and injury suffered as a direct result of Iraq's unlawful invasion and occupation of Kuwait. For example, a plaintiff who had been sexually assaulted or tortured could receive up to USD 5,000 per incident, with a total of claims not exceeding USD 30,000 per person or USD 60,000 per family.[142] In light of the many victims who may have suffered harm as a result of the commission of a crime within the jurisdiction of the Court, it may be wise for the Court to establish scales of compensation as well, such scales taking into account the level of income per country.

An application for reparation can be made by the victim through the Registrar by means of the Victims' Participation and Reparations Section (VPRS),[143] and exceptionally by the Chamber itself.[144] The latter case concerns situations in which victims are unable to apply for reparation themselves, for example where the victim is geographically secluded from the Court and has no access to information on reparation possibilities, and possibly is exposed to pressure from the State complicit in the

---

[141] Rule 98(3) ICC RPE.

[142] Taken from Reporters Without Borders (2003), pp. 79-80. See also the United Nations Compensation Commission's website at http://www2.unog.ch/uncc/ (last visited May 2005). On the national level, compensation scales have sometimes been set up as well. For example, the Dutch 'Schadefonds Geweldsmisdrijven' was set up to provide victims who sustained serious physical and/or psychological injury as a result of a violent crime taking place in the Netherlands with an amount of financial compensation. The scales range from 0 to 8: rape falls within scale 7 (maximum EUR 8,250) and rape with HIV transmission falls within scale 8 (maximum EUR 9,100). See http://www.schadefonds.nl (last visited May 2005).

[143] The Victims' Participation and Reparations Section will conduct outreach (in order to give as much publicity as possible to the reparation possibilities in order to enable victims to make their application) and receive applications for reparation orders. The Section is in the process of producing a standard form to make reparation applications by victims easier. See ICC website/Victims and witnesses/Participation of victims in proceedings and reparation, at http://www.icc-cpi.int/victimsissues/victimsparticipation.html (last visited 10 June 2005).

[144] Article 75(1) ICC Statute and Rules 94 ('Procedure when a Victim Requests Reparation') and 95 ('Procedure when the Court Raises the Issue of Reparations') ICC RPE. See also Regulation 88, 'Requests for reparations in accordance with rule 94', of the Regulations of the Court, Adopted by the judges of the Court on 26 May 2004, ICC-BC/01-01-04.

crimes.[145] Victims' entitlement to reparation is thus not restricted to their participation in the Court's proceedings. In order to have as many victims as possible to assert their reparation claims, the Court – in practice the Victims' Participation and Reparations Section – is required to give adequate publicity to the Court's reparation proceedings and may seek the assistance of States Parties and intergovernmental organisations for this purpose.[146] The VPRS has recognised the importance of gender sensitivity by the following: 'vulnerable groups, including women victims, will be disproportionately underrepresented as participants before the Court if steps are not taken to ensure that they are aware of their rights and granted full access to the Court's procedural regime'.[147] Therefore,

> In order to help ensure that women victims are able to benefit equally from the rights afforded them by the Court, the VPRS will reach out to international, national and local women's groups working in situations being analysed or investigated by the Prosecutor. These groups will act as intermediaries with female victim populations, helping to facilitate their participation and reparations rights under the Rome Statute by explaining to them their rights under the Rome Statute and assisting them in applying for participation and reparations in a sensitive and appropriate manner.[148]

It has, however, been established that by November 2004 the majority of the population in the Republic of Uganda – the first situation which was brought before the Court – were unaware about the existence of the ICC in general and the possibility of reparation in particular.[149] By February 2005, this situation was unchanged, both for northern Uganda and the Democratic Republic of Congo.[150] According to the Women's Initiatives for Gender Justice, who made a field mission to northern Uganda in November 2004 to meet women affected by the conflict and to hear their views and experiences as well as to provide them with information about the Court, adequate rehabilitation centres that could provide victims of sexual violence with trauma counselling or health facilities were grossly inadequate.[151] Therefore, in the case that victims of sexual violence in such a situation will not be able to make an application for

---

[145] Muttukumaru (1999), p. 269.

[146] Rule 96 ICC RPE.

[147] ICC Newsletter, *Registry: VPRS – Gender Sensitivity*, June 2005, #4, p. 6.

[148] *Ibid.* Mention is also made of 'gender sensitivity education', which the VPRS wants to provide to organisations working with women victims in the field, as well as guidelines on gender sensitivity for Court staff members.

[149] Press Release by the Women's Initiatives for Gender Justice, in collaboration with Isis-WICCE and Ugandan Women Activists, 23 November 2004. According to the Women's Initiatives for Gender Justice 'it seems that neither the Ugandan state nor the International Criminal Court cared to consult with or raise awareness about the ICC among the people of Northern Uganda'. Most of the people had little awareness about the referral of the Northern Uganda situation to the Court, nor had they seen or met any ICC officials in the field.

[150] See Victims Rights Working Group (2005), p. 10. The Court had been actively investigating the Northern Uganda situation since July 2004 and the DRC situation since June 2004.

[151] Press Release by the Women's Initiatives for Gender Justice, in collaboration with Isis-WICCE and Ugandan Women Activists, 23 November 2004.

reparation with the Court, the Chamber may do so itself on their behalf. On a final note, a victim may be represented in her claim for reparation by a legal representative, and where there are a number of victims, they will have to choose a common legal representative.[152] If victims lack the financial means to pay for a legal representative, they may receive financial assistance.[153]

After the determination of the damages, the Court has two options to award victims' reparation: it may make a reparation order directly against the convicted person[154] or it may order reparation to individual victims (where direct transfer to beneficiaries is 'impossible or impracticable'[155]) or a group of victims (by means of a collective award) through the ICC Trust Fund.[156] From Rule 98 it follows that in the case of individual reparation awards the Court prefers reparations to be transferred to the beneficiaries directly; in the case of collective awards, preference is given to making use of the Trust Fund.[157] The Trust Fund is considered to be the obvious body to administer collective awards. However, considering that the Trust Fund may not be the perfect body to distribute money or organise, for example, the set-up of a rehabilitation or support programme for women, the Court, after consultations with interested States and the Trust Fund, is allowed to call on intergovernmental, international or national organisations approved by the Trust Fund to carry out tasks on its behalf.[158] It is important to realise that in both situations the Trust Fund only acts as an intermediary; any reparation awards to victims ordered by the Court should therefore be distributed to victims through the Trust Fund in the manner decided by the Court.

It should be stressed that if Court orders concerning reparation are to have any meaning to victims, the Court will need the full cooperation of States Parties. In accordance with the procedures under their national laws, States Parties are obliged to ensure that orders of the Court related to reparation awards and fines or forfeiture are fully enforced.[159] It is, therefore, very important that States include in their

[152] Rule 90 ICC RPE.

[153] Rule 90(5) ICC RPE.

[154] Article 75(2) ICC Statute and Rule 98(1) ICC RPE.

[155] For instance where every victim of a determined group has not yet been identified or where the youth or mental incapacity of an individual victim makes it more appropriate to distribute the award until the young person becomes an adult or until a patient recovers from any mental incapacity. See Bonneau (2004); and Lewis and Friman (2001), p. 478.

[156] Article 75(2) ICC Statute and Rule 98(2) and (3) ICC RPE. When individual reparation awards are made through the Trust Fund, such fund 'shall be separated from other resources of the Trust Fund and shall be forwarded to each victim as soon as possible (Rule 98(2) ICC RPE)'.

[157] Compare Rule 98(2) with Rule 98(3) and (4) ICC RPE.

[158] Rule 98(4) ICC RPE.

[159] Article 75(5) together with Article 109 ICC Statute (reparation). A safeguard is contained in Rule 219 which states that 'giving effect to an order for reparations, the national authorities shall not modify the reparations specified by the Court, the scope or the extent of any damage, loss or injury determined by the Court or the principles stated in the order, and shall facilitate the enforcement of such order'. Article 109 originally applies to fines and forfeiture. Rule 220 states that judgments in which fines were imposed cannot be modified by the State. See generally Rules 217-222 ICC RPE. For the interplay between the Court and national courts on matters concerning reparation, see Ferstman (2002), pp. 667-686.

implementing legislation regulations on reparation.[160] Without the support of States Parties to obtain the money or fines or forfeiture of the convicted person, the beneficiaries will be left without reparation despite the Court's orders to award reparation.

4.2.2 The Trust Fund for victims and their families

The Trust Fund for victims and their families was officially established on 9 September 2002 under a Resolution of the Assembly of States Parties (ASP) pursuant to Article 79(1).[161] As will be explained below, the Trust Fund will be able to complement the work of the Court in respect of victims, rather than merely administer awards granted by the Court. The Trust Fund will be managed by a five-member independent Board of Directors.[162] At the first meeting of the Board of Directors (the Hague, 20 – 22 April 2004), the draft Regulations of the Trust Fund for victims (hereinafter draft Regulations), which develop further criteria for the management of the Trust Fund, were developed and approved by the Board of Directors and transmitted to the Assembly of States Parties for their consideration at the 3rd session of the Assembly of States Parties in September 2004.[163] At the 3rd session, the Assembly of States Parties established a Secretariat to provide assistance for the proper functioning of the Board of Directors in carrying out its tasks.[164] Yet it was decided that Parts I (Management and Oversight of the Trust Fund) and II (Receipt of Funds) of the draft Regulations of the Trust Fund for victims is to be applied provisionally, and that Part III of the draft

---

[160] To date, only few States have done so. For instance, see the International Criminal Court Act 2001 (Enforcement of Fines, Forfeiture and Reparation Orders), England, Wales and Northern Ireland, Regulations 2001, No. 2379, 29 June 2001, entered into force 1 August 2001; and Canada's Crimes Against Humanity and War Crimes Act, 2000, C.24, 24 June 2000.

[161] Resolution ICC-ASP/1/Res.6, *Establishment of a Fund for the Benefit of Victims of Crimes within the Jurisdiction of the Court, and of the Families of Such Victims*, Resolution ICC-ASP/1/Res.6, adopted at the 3rd plenary meeting by consensus, 9 September 2002.

[162] Annex to Resolution ICC-ASP/1/Res.6, *Establishment of a Fund for the Benefit of Victims of Crimes within the Jurisdiction of the Court, and of the Families of Such Victims*, 9 September 2002. The Board was elected by the Assembly of States Parties and is made up of five members, each elected for a three years term with a possibility to be re-elected once. The members of the Board all work on a voluntary basis. The Board is composed of Her Majesty Queen Rania Al-Abdullah of Jordan, His Excellency Dr. Oscar Arias Sánchez from Costa Rica, His Excellency Mr. Tadeusz Mazowiecki from Poland, Madam Minister Simone Veil from France (chair) and His Eminence Archbishop Emeritus Desmond Tutu from South Africa, who each represent their respective regions.

[163] Assembly of States Parties, *Report to the Assembly of States Parties on the Activities and Projects of the Board of Directors of the Trust Fund for Victims*, 2003-2004, Third session, The Hague, 6-10 September 2004, Annex A, *Draft Regulations of the Trust Fund for Victims*, First Meeting of the Board of Directors of the Trust Fund for Victims, 20-22 April 2004, The Hague (The Netherlands), ICC/ASP/3/14/Rev.1. See also ICC Press Release, *First Meeting of the Board of Directors of the Trust Fund for Victims*, The Hague, 22 April 2004.

[164] Resolution ICC-ASP/3/Res.7, *Establishment of the Secretariat of the Trust Fund for Victims*, adopted at the 6th plenary meeting by consensus, 10 September 2004, para. 1.

Regulations (The Activities and Projects of the Trust Fund) will be 'a reference point for further work'.[165] States Parties seemed to be unwilling to accept the draft Regulations at the 3rd ASP session because they had had insufficient time to review the draft Regulations in detail, in particular Part III, which governs the types of activities and projects the Trust Fund is to conduct as well as the scope of victims that may benefit therefrom.[166] Therefore, at the 4th session of the ASP (the Hague, 28 November – 3 December 2005) the draft Regulations will again be the topic of discussion with the aim to adopt the draft Regulations.[167] Adoption of the Regulations is imperative for the Board to start its work in a proper way.

According to Article 79(1) of the ICC Statute, the Trust Fund has been established 'for the benefit of victims of crimes within the jurisdiction of the Court, and of the families of such victims'. Draft Regulation 45 on 'beneficiaries' contains similar wording and refers to Rule 85. The term 'family' has not been defined, which, in the context of a Trust Fund with an international scope, allows the Board of Directors to respond in a range of situations involving varying family structures.[168] The Trust Fund will not only be funded by reparation awards and money or property collected from fines or forfeiture, but also by means of voluntary contributions by States, international organisations, NGOs, individuals, corporations and other entities, as well as resources, other than assessed contributions, as the ASP may decide to allocate to the Trust Fund.[169] The Trust Fund operates on a budget separate from that of the ICC, and in the likely event that fines, forfeiture and reparations ordered by the Court are minimal,[170] the voluntary contributions will be crucial to the Trust Fund's effective functioning. As past experiences of other Trust Funds have shown the difficulty to obtain funds, a real challenge here lies with the Board of Directors, whose prominence will hopefully contribute to the fund-raising. Following Rule 98(5), voluntary contributions are to be

---

[165] *Ibid*, para. 5.

[166] Victims Rights Working Group (2005), pp. 3 and 8.

[167] Resolution ICC-ASP/3/Res.7, *Establishment of the Secretariat of the Trust Fund for Victims*, 10 September 2004, para. 6.

[168] Victims Rights Working Group (2005), p. 6. During the 3rd session, some States raised their concern with regard to the fact that the term 'family' was not defined.

[169] See Article 79(2) ICC Statute; Rule 98 ICC RPE; Resolution ICC-ASP/1/Res.6, *Establishment of a Fund for the Benefit of Victims of Crimes within the Jurisdiction of the Court, and of the Families of Such Victims*, 9 September 2002; and the draft Regulations, Part II. Voluntary contributions for the benefit of victims and their families may be partially earmarked by the donor. However, the Trust Fund sees to an equitable distribution of the funds among groups of victims. See draft Regulations 25-33, and 31 and 33 in particular.

[170] Most of the accused before the ICTY and ICTR have been declared indigent. In theory, it might be easier to seize fines and forfeited property or assets than to get reparation. The ICC Statute provides for the possibility to request protective measures for the purposes of forfeiture in the form of freezing the accused's assets (Article 57(3)(e) and Rule 99). However, the freezing of assets requires cooperation of States and has unfortunately proven difficult to implement in the past (e.g., the freezing of assets of Milosević and Taylor). Contrary to the ICTY and ICTR, the ICC explicitly allows 'frozen assets' to be used for the benefit of the victims (Article 57(3)(e)). The Court cannot take similar provisional measures with regard to reparations until it has actually convicted the accused person (Article 75(4)).

used for the benefit of victims of crimes within the jurisdiction of the Court and their families. This rule is not associated with the reparative process of the Court, but aims at giving the Trust Fund the necessary flexibility to assist victims in a proper way, especially when the trial will take years. It is up to the Board of Directors to determine what programmes are set up under the Trust Fund. The draft Regulations propose that the funds be used: (1) to complement reparation orders of the Court; (2) to provide physical or psychological rehabilitation or material support for victims at the investigative stage; or (3) to provide such support in situations where the Prosecutor decides, in the interest of justice, not to investigate, or where an investigation is not commenced by the Court but by a State in accordance with the complementarity principle and reparations are otherwise unavailable.[171] Providing rehabilitation or support in the two situations mentioned under (3) can only be done in exceptional circumstances with the approval of the Pre-trial Chamber.

In light of the past experiences before the ICTR and ICTY, where the majority of the victims of sexual violence were left without medical care for the diseases they had contracted through sexual violence, especially HIV/AIDS, the Trust Fund should play an important role by allowing interim relief for victims.[172] Due to deteriorating health conditions, victims of sexual violence do not always have the time to await the conviction of the accused, which is an official requirement for reparation to be awarded by the Court. Furthermore, what happens in those cases in which the accused dies during trial? Should, in these circumstances, survivors of sexual violence be left to die or be abandoned without proper health care for themselves and their born or unborn children? To avoid repetition of the Rwandan and Yugoslav experiences, the Trust Fund should be given a role in providing medical and psychological assistance to victims of sexual violence (including HIV/AIDS treatment) early in the process, when assistance is most direly needed. As mentioned above, the draft Regulations of the Trust Fund contain such provisions; victims of sexual violence may receive physical or psychological rehabilitation or material support already in the investigative phase of the ICC proceedings (Rule 51(b)). However, it should be noted that even in the investigative phase the health of survivors of sexual violence may already be in a

---

[171] Draft Rules 50 and 51 of the draft Regulations. The second situation, raised concern among some States during the 3rd session of the ASP as they held that the Trust Fund could not conduct activities and projects during an investigation or trial but only after a conviction of the accused. For a discussion of the arguments raised by these States, see Victims Rights Working Group (2005), pp. 9-12.

[172] The Report on the International Seminar on 'Access of Victims to the International Criminal Court' noted that 'regarding the Trust Fund … provision of urgent interim relief, such as medical attention, for instance for victims such as those who contract AIDS or become pregnant as a result of rape, needed to be dealt with in the Rules of procedure and Evidence and that standard of care afforded to victims and witnesses when under the protection of the Court shall be at least that afforded to accused persons' (UN Doc. PCNICC/1999.WGRPE/INF/2, p. 8). A discussion paper proposed by the Coordinator on Rules of Procedure and Evidence related to Part 6 of the Statute proposed that the 'Court may, at any time before it has made a determination relating to reparations, order the Trust Fund to provide interim relief to victims, such as medical or psychological attention or other humanitarian assistance' (UN Doc. PCNICC/1999/WGRPE/RT.5/Rev.1/Add.3, Rule E).

deplorable state as it takes some time before the decision is taken by the Prosecutor to start to investigate the situation; moreover, the conflict may have been going on for weeks, months or years on end. For example, the first two situations under consideration by the Court are replete with testimonies of sexual violence which has been taking place for a very long time: the conflict in the DRC began in 1998, the situation was referred to the Court by the DRC in April 2004 and investigations began in June 2004. The conflict in northern Uganda started in 1987, was referred to the Court by the State itself in December 2003 and investigations began in July 2004.[173] As mentioned above, in northern Uganda, there were no adequate rehabilitation centres that could have provided trauma counselling or health facilities for victims of sexual violence. It is therefore imperative that situations are referred to the Court and investigations started by the Prosecutor as soon as possible if rehabilitation and support are to have any meaningful effect on victims' lives. The situation of the Darfur region in Sudan, where sexual violence is widespread, was referred by the Security Council to the Court in March 2005 (the conflict started in 2003), and investigations were opened by the Prosecutor in June 2005. In addition to the provision on rehabilitation and support services during the investigative phase, such care may also be extended to victims when the Prosecutor decides not to prosecute because doing so would not be in the interest of justice or where national courts are investigating and prosecuting the case in conformity with the complementarity principle and no reparation is likely to be available for victims (Rule 51(c)). The latter rule therefore allows for the possibility of addressing also the needs of those victims of sexual violence whose cases have not been dealt with by the Court itself, but whose conditions may not at all be very different from victims of sexual violence whose situations were taken up by the Court. To have any meaningful effect, also in these situations the Trust Fund should provide rehabilitation and support services to victims of sexual violence as soon as possible.

The Trust Fund is focused on 'priority activities and project areas' and the Board of Directors may consult victims and their families, as well as their legal representatives, and any competent expert or expert organisation on the situation of the potential beneficiaries and the ways to assist them.[174] Efficiency and effectiveness furthermore suggest that the Trust Fund should assist victims in a collective way rather than individually. The advantage of collective assistance is that it will reach unidentified victims who, due to their victimisation and/or social situation, cannot claim their right to reparations through formal procedures.[175] Due to the stigmatisation victims of sexual violence are confronted with in certain societies, collective assistance may thus be of particular importance to them. According to Rule 65 of the draft Regulations, 'the Trust Fund may invite proposals from international or national organizations which are specifically geared to addressing the enumerated priority activity and project areas'. Victims of sexual violence may in this way be helped through collective projects implemented at the national level which provide for, for instance, the establishment of

[173] Note that the Court has jurisdiction over genocide, crimes against humanity and war crimes as of July 2002.

[174] Rules 64 and 65 of the draft Regulations.

[175] Ingadottir (2003), p. 133. See also Wierda and De Greiff (undated). Wierda and De Greiff generally argue that the Trust Fund rather than the Court may be better suited to devise reparations for large numbers of victims.

treatment centres where the victims can get physical, psychological and medical assistance. Such assistance should be complementary to and provided in close coordination with the assistance provided by the Court's Victims and Witnesses Unit.[176] The Victims and Witnesses Unit is concerned with support services for victims who appear before the Court, whereas the Trust Fund's rehabilitation and support activities involve victims beyond those called to testify at the Court, thus no interference with each other's work is to be expected.

5 FINAL REMARKS

The ICC has made the progressive move of pursuing restorative justice for victims in addition to punishing the perpetrator. Unlike the Tribunals, the ICC gives victims standing to request and receive reparation from the convicted person through an order of the Court. The Court may order reparation awards in the form of restitution, compensation, rehabilitation or any other form, depending on the victims' needs. Reparation may be awarded either individually or collectively. To fulfil this task, the Court may consult experts and interesting parties in order to ascertain the needs of victims.

Victims will in most cases be helped with physical, psychological and medical care, including ARV drugs to treat HIV/AIDS, either through a court order on compensation or a court order on rehabilitation. In practice, the convicted person's money (supplemented with money from the Trust Fund, if needed) will, in most cases, be used by the victim to meet her rehabilitation needs, especially medical and psychological care. If the Court establishes the accused's guilt concerning intentional or foreseeable infection with HIV/AIDS, HIV/AIDS treatment should as a minimum be included in the reparation order. To obtain money from the convicted person, State cooperation is, however, an essential ingredient for success, though not without its difficulties.[177] A reparation order may, furthermore, be awarded not only individually, but also collectively, whether in the alternative or simultaneously. Especially if the number of victims is high, the Court may be inclined to order collective awards. In the case of victims of sexual violence, collective care, most probably by setting up treatment centres, will usually have to be implemented by international or national agencies that have experience with victims of sexual violence and their needs. However, also indirect victims of crime, for example the children of survivors of sexual violence, may benefit from the Court's order on rehabilitation. For example, the Court may decide to build schools for the benefit of these children. In addition to compensation and rehabilitation, the restitution of property and proceeds is essential to victims, including victims of sexual violence, as well. In order to be able to start building up their lives

---

[176] *Ibid.*, p. 132.

[177] In this respect it is interesting to mention Council Directive 2004/80/EC of 29 April 2004 relating to compensation to crime victims, Official Journal of the European Union, L 261/15, 6 August 2004. Under the Council Directive an 'assisting authority or authorities' shall be established in every Member State to assist in and facilitate access to compensation in cases where the crime was committed in a Member State other than that of the victim's residence. An initiative similar to the Council Directive may be helpful with regard to the enforcement of ICC reparation orders as well.

again, access to proper housing and stolen property is a basic requirement. Reparation is furthermore not restricted to victims who participated in the trial proceedings. The Chamber may therefore apply for reparation on behalf of victims of sexual violence in situations where they are unable to request for reparation themselves. If victims of sexual violence have no access to information on the reparation possibilities existent at the Court, and sexual violence has been so widespread and abhorrent that reparation is clearly needed, the Chamber could (and should) make such a request on their behalf. Such information may, for instance, have reached the Court by reports prepared by NGOs working with survivors of sexual violence. However, the main difficulty with reparation awards is that they are only awarded once the accused has been pronounced guilty, and victims of sexual violence may need physical, psychological and medical support much earlier. Although the Victims and Witnesses Support Section may be able to address some of the needs of victims of sexual violence testifying before the Court, they will not be in a position to meet the needs of victims of sexual violence who are not at the Court to testify.

In addition to the reparation possibilities attributed to the Court, a Trust Fund has been set up for the benefit of victims and their families. The Trust Fund should be considered to complement the work of the Court rather than only implement reparation orders by the Court. By enabling collective projects, the Trust Fund can reach many more victims of sexual violence than the Court, in particular because the ICC will primarily be concerned with prosecuting the main perpetrators, focusing on certain crimes, thus leaving aside victims of sexual violence not affected by the Prosecutor's prosecutorial strategy. Furthermore, the Trust Fund may be able to reach unidentified victims of sexual violence who, for instance, due to stigmatisation or trauma, have not been able to apply for reparation at the Court themselves. Through the establishment of the Trust Fund for victims and their families it may therefore, to some extent, be able to address the needs of victims of sexual violence on a broader scale. The Trust Fund is in particular useful for victims of sexual violence as it can, in principle and unlike the Court, provide interim relief. The draft Regulations of the Trust Fund for victims state that physical or psychological rehabilitation or material support during the investigation phase is possible. In addition, according to the draft Regulations such care should also be provided in certain exceptional circumstances, namely where the Prosecutor decides, in the interest of justice, not to investigate or where an investigation has been commenced by the relevant State in accordance with the complementarity principle but reparations are not available in that country. It is important that in all situations decisions as to whether or not to prosecute are made timely, as rehabilitation and support should be made available as soon as possible to have any significant effect on the lives of survivors of sexual violence. In order to implement rehabilitation and support services, the Trust Fund is to negotiate agreements with humanitarian agencies in the field to reach all victims of sexual violence. Collective humanitarian projects may include the set-up of centres with expertise in physical, psychological and medical care, including HIV/AIDS treatment, which have the potential to reach a large group of victims of sexual violence. In addition, school or income-generating projects may be set up for the victims and/or their children. Children may especially be in need of such support if their mother is disabled, died or will die as a result of the diseases she contracted through the sexual violence she endured. Interim relief in the form of physical, psychological or medical care, including HIV/AIDS treatment, is of particular importance if victims are not to suffer for many years after the crimes were committed against them. The right to request and to be awarded reparation under the ICC regime as well as the special Trust Fund for victims acknowledges the international community's responsibility to repair the wrongdoing and gives victims and their families a chance to start building up their lives again, which is unprecedented at the supranational criminal law level. The following words, spoken by His Eminence Archbishop Desmond Tutu on behalf of the Board of Directors of the Trust Fund for victims at the ceremony marking the first meeting of the Board of Directors of the Trust Fund for victims at The Hague on the 22nd of April 2004, testify to this:

> [T]his Trust Fund that you have set up, seeks to help, dear friends. What compensation could you ever give that would be adequate for the loss of a loved one? You could not possibly ever replace the one who is no longer there. But frequently, symbols can be powerful, and when a country, a nation, the international community says, symbolically, we cannot compensate you, but we want to show that we care, we want to show that we hope that this small thing we do for you will somehow pour balm on your wounds and help those wounds to heal.[178]

Despite these new reparation mechanisms at the supranational criminal level, it is clearly an understatement to say that not all victims of crimes within the jurisdiction of the Court, including victims of sexual violence, as well as their families will be fully assisted in their needs. Victims should therefore be cautioned against having great expectations of reparation beforehand; they should also consult other national and international venues of reparation. Much will depend on the effectuation of court orders on reparation, cooperation with humanitarian agencies in the field, as well as the resources that the Trust Fund will receive and the flexibility that the Trust Fund will be given in terms of utilisation of its resources and in what point in time.

---

[178] See the statement by Archbishop Desmond Tutu at the ceremony marking the first meeting of the Board of Directors of the Trust Fund for Victims at The Hague on the 22nd of April 2004 at http://www.icc-cpi.int/press/video.html (last visited May 2005).

EVALUATION OF PART III

The sentencing practice before the Tribunals has shown that the specific sentences imposed by the Tribunals for sexual violence as international crimes (genocide, crimes against humanity and war crimes), with the exception of Muhimana's conviction for rape as a crime against humanity and genocide, approximated (or not even approximated) the sentencing practice in the national courts of the former Yugoslavia and Rwanda for sexual violence as national crimes, as if the sexual violence had taken place in peace time situations. Moreover, the gravity of the sexual violence crimes, which needs to be assessed in light of their individual circumstances and consequences, thereby taking into account quantitatively the number of victims and qualitatively the suffering inflicted on the victims as well as the form and degree of the participation of the accused in the crimes, have often not explicitly been dealt with in the Tribunals' judgments. In addition, the aggravating circumstances relevant to sexual violence have in a considerable number of cases not or only to a small extent been addressed, despite the fact that they may severely impact on the sentence imposed. In particular, the repeated nature of sexual violence and the trauma associated with sexual violence has largely been left outside the realm of aggravating factors, even though the repetitiveness of rapes and the effects of sexual violence on its victim are such obvious features of wartime rape. These findings strongly suggest that the seriousness of sexual violence as genocide, crimes against humanity or war crimes has been undermined by the Tribunals when imposing sentences for these crimes. The ICC, which starts with a clean slate, should not take their approach, and should instead give more attention to the gravity and aggravating factors applicable to sexual violence when substantiating the sentence imposed.

While the ICTY and ICTR were primarily concerned with the prosecution of perpetrators, the ICC also has the possibility of addressing victims' rights to reparation. Victims of sexual violence may request reparation (restitution, compensation, rehabilitation) themselves; in exceptional circumstances, the Chamber may do so on behalf of victims. Thus the less empowered victims of sexual violence, who may not be in the position to request reparation themselves because of, for instance, the geographical distance to the Court or the stigmatisation or shame attached to the crime, may receive reparation. However, as the process of international justice is slow, victims of sexual violence may die of the consequences of the rapes or other forms of sexual violence they endured, in particular HIV/AIDS, prior or during trial proceedings. For this reason, victims of sexual violence are not always in the position to await the conviction of the accused. For this category of vulnerable victims, it should be possible to grant interim relief. If adopted, the draft Regulations of the Trust Fund meet some of their needs, and physical and psychological rehabilitation and support may, *inter alia*, be provided in the investigative phase. In light of the Rwanda experience, where victims of sexual violence died and are still dying of AIDS as a consequence of the rapes committed against them, the rehabilitation and support provided by the Trust Fund should be interpreted as including HIV/AIDS treatment. Reparation is essential for victims of sexual violence to be able to start building up a life for themselves and their families again. Reparation recognises the harm done to them. Collective projects, such as treatment centres and school projects, will most probably be the most pertinent and effective way to provide reparation to victims especially where the number of victims is high. This may not be any different when the Court awards reparation. Furthermore, collective projects potentially reach many more survivors of sexual violence, survivors who have not been identified before because of stigmatisation or shame. However, as convicted perpetrators may be indigent and the resources of the Trust Fund may be minimal, victims should not be given high hopes. This being said, reparation will be largely symbolic, but when it is provided in a timely manner it may have a positive effect on the lives of many women and their families.

Part IV
Concluding Observations and Recommendations

CHAPTER 8
TOWARDS A MORE COMPREHENSIVE SUPRANATIONAL CRIMINAL PROSECUTION OF SEXUAL VIOLENCE

1 INTRODUCTION

In this study, I have aimed to address supranational criminal prosecution of sexual violence from the point of view of the ICC, the benchmark for supranational criminal prosecutions, with reference to the ICTY and ICTR practice in the field of sexual violence prosecutions. The main question was: To what extent are the concerns and interests of victims of sexual violence integrated into the still rather young supranational criminal law system? In Part I of this study, the crimes under which sexual violence prosecutions can take place were examined, that is to say, genocide, crimes against humanity and war crimes. In Part II, the ways in which victims of sexual violence can benefit from protective and special measures were discussed, as well as their participationary status in the proceedings. In Part III of the study, the legal consequences of the supranational criminal law system, that is, sentencing and reparation, were examined. The ICC Statute, its Rules of Procedure and Evidence (RPE) and the Elements of Crimes (EoC), together with – and compared to – the ICTY and ICTR Statutes, their RPE and case law constituted the primary objects of research. This Chapter concludes, on the basis of the preceding Chapters, with several observations with respect to sexual violence prosecution on the supranational criminal law level. In addition, some recommendations as regards the possibilities that exist for a more comprehensive supranational criminal prosecution of sexual violence will be given.

2 SEXUAL VIOLENCE IN SUPRANATIONAL CRIMINAL LAW

No ICC, ICTY or ICTR treaty can remedy the suffering of victims of rape, sexual slavery, forced pregnancy or any other form of sexual violence taking place as constituent acts of genocide, crimes against humanity or war crimes. Yet, the explicit criminalisation in the ICC Statute of rape, sexual slavery, enforced prostitution, forced pregnancy, enforced sterilisation and other forms of sexual violence as crimes against humanity and war crimes (Articles 7 and 8 of the ICC Statute, respectively) provides another step in the direction of ending impunity for sexual violence on the supranational criminal law level. Rape and other forms of sexual violence can also be prosecuted as genocide under serious bodily or mental harm (Article 6 of the ICC Statute), as explained in a footnote in the Elements of Crimes on the definition of genocide. In addition, raping a person on the basis of his or her gender can now be prosecuted as the crime against humanity of persecution in the ICC Statute as well. With the exception of the crime of rape and enforced prostitution, these specific sexual violence crimes were never laid down in a treaty on the supranational criminal law level before. Therefore, with the exception of the definition of rape, which has been the subject of study in several ICTY and ICTR cases, most of these crimes had never been defined. The EoC provide meaningful guidance for the ICC judges in the determination of the elements of the crimes but, officially, this document is not binding. Therefore, the question that was raised was: What are or should be the definitions of the sexual violence crimes in the context of the supranational criminal law system?

With regard to the definition of rape, the ICC EoC are not focused on the issue of consent (as contained in the *Kunarac, Kovač and Vuković* Appeals Chamber definition of rape), but on force, threat of force, coercion or a coercive environment (as contained in the *Furundžija* and *Akayesu* cases). Lack of consent as an element of the crime of rape (or of any other sexual violence crime, for that matter) is immaterial within the supranational criminal law context, especially in light of the violent and oppressive context in which rapes as genocide, crimes against humanity or war crimes take place, and should therefore be rejected. To a large extent, the Tribunals took recourse to definitions of rape in national laws focusing on consent. However, the definitions of rape in those national laws were never written for the kind of situations the Court and Tribunals deal with and should therefore not be transposed to the supranational criminal law level easily. Introducing the concept of non-consent into the definition of rape would necessarily burden the Prosecutor with inquiring into the victim's state of mind. No matter how they are phrased ('Did you consent?' or 'Was it done against your will?'), questions about consent may insult victims of rape and may cause further traumatisation, especially if such questions are asked after the victim has explained to the court the totality of the sexual violence inflicted upon her and the coercive circumstances in which the sexual violence was committed. If it has been established that a crime has been committed, questions about consent are redundant. As has been explained in Part II, in those (presumably) rare cases in which the Defence may want to advance consent, this is still possible, but the relevance and admissibility of such evidence must first be established in an *in camera* procedure in order to spare the victim from painful propositions which have not been tested first. Including non-consent in the definition of rape is not in agreement with the nature of the crime and will cause victims of sexual violence to shun the Court. The ICC elements of rape have furthermore taken into account a larger number of prohibited sexual acts than as contained in the more restrictive *Furundžija* and *Kunarac, Kovač and Vuković* mechanical descriptions of body parts. The ICC definition of rape focuses not only on penetration of the vagina, anus and mouth with the penis and the penetration of the vagina and anus with an object, but also on penetration with the fingers or tongue and penetration with the penis of any other part of the body. At the same time, the ICC definition is not as broad as the *Akayesu* conceptual definition of rape, which makes it easier to distinguish between rape and sexual violence. The prohibited sexual acts constituting rape in the ICC EoC essentially focus on penetration and leave out sexual acts falling short thereof, such as forced nudity and forced masturbation. The latter sexual acts could then be prosecuted under 'any other form of sexual violence of comparable gravity'. This is not to say that crimes which are prosecuted under that heading are less serious than rape or any other of the explicitly mentioned sexual violence crimes in Article 7(1)(g) of the ICC Statute; the provision reads that these forms of sexual violence should be 'of comparable gravity'. Distinguishing between rape and other forms of sexual violence will make it possible not to cause injustice to those victims of rape who do fit the ICC mechanical definitional requirements of rape and who consider themselves the 'real victims of rape'.

Summarising, the definition of rape as found in the ICC EoC fits the reality of the crime well. The ICC has chosen, on the one hand, for incorporating the element of force, threat of force, coercion or a coercive environment (and not lack of consent) and, on the other hand, for a mechanical approach focusing on penetration (and not for a conceptual approach), albeit not in a restrictive manner. However, the developments with regard to the definition of rape since the coming into force of the EoC have not come to a standstill. Despite the non-uniformity as regards the definition of rape within the ICTY and ICTR, the *Kunarac, Kovač and Vuković* Appeals Chamber definition of rape, which includes the element of non-consent, seems to have been taken as the leading definition within the supranational criminal law context in a majority of cases. I have argued that this trend should not be followed by the ICC, as the *Kunarac, Kovač and Vuković* definition of rape does not reflect the reality of rapes taking place in situations over which the Court has jurisdiction. If rape is not defined in conformity with the nature of the crime, victims may be reluctant to come forward and testify at the Court. In that case, the crimes committed against them will not be recognised and punished.

As far as the other specific sexual violence crimes are concerned, the EoC have set out a rather workable framework as well. For the first time, sexual slavery has been laid down in an international instrument on the supranational criminal law level, that is, the ICC Statute. Of course, the crime itself is as old as war, one gruesome example being the rape camps during the Japanese occupation of parts of Asia during World War II. However, the criminal nature of the crime has now been explicitly recognised as a crime in and of itself and is as such prosecutable before the Court. The EoC define sexual slavery in conformity with the definition of enslavement (viz. 'exercise any or all of the powers attaching to the right of ownership over one or more persons'), with the addition that the perpetrator caused the victim to engage in one or more acts of a sexual nature. The examples mentioned in the EoC with regard to ownership – purchasing, selling, lending or bartering – might give the impression that some sort of commercial aspect must be involved. However, the footnote attached to the first element of sexual slavery makes it perfectly clear that sexual slavery also includes 'forced labour', 'reducing a person to a servile status' (including forced marriage) and 'trafficking in persons, in particular women and children'. On this basis, it can be concluded that sexual slavery does not necessarily require any financial benefits for the perpetrator or even confinement of the victim to a particular place. Sexual slavery should be distinguished from enslavement, but also from enforced prostitution, which does require that some pecuniary benefit is involved. In the ICTY, the sexual enslavement of women and girls was prosecuted as the crime against humanity of enslavement in the *Kunarac, Kovač and Vuković* case. Although the ICTY had no other option than to prosecute the sexual slavery as enslavement, the ICC will now be able to prosecute sexual slavery directly as sexual slavery, clearly recognising the sexual aspects of the slavery.

Like sexual slavery, enforced prostitution as a crime against humanity has also been included in a supranational criminal law instrument for the first time. Enforced prostitution, however, was already enumerated in Article 4(e) of the ICTR Statute as a violation of Article 3 Common to the 1949 Geneva Conventions and of 1977 Additional Protocol II, albeit no prosecutions on this basis have taken place. According to the ICC EoC, the elements of this crime require the perpetrator to have caused one or more persons to engage in one or more acts of a sexual nature under conditions of coercion (non-consent is not an element of the crime), and he obtained or expected to obtain pecuniary or other advantage in exchange for or in connection with these sexual acts. In wartime situations, it is important to distinguish the crime of enforced prostitution from the crime of sexual slavery. In many situations, the crime may be better charged as sexual slavery rather than as enforced prostitution. In times that genocide, crimes against humanity and war crimes take place, women are frequently captured for the prime purpose of sex without any financial benefits involved. The 'comfort women' were wrongly thought to have been captured for the purpose of enforced prostitution, whereas they were in fact sexual slaves. Situations falling short of sexual slavery are nevertheless prosecutable as enforced prostitution. Especially in times of peace, enforced prostitution takes place quite frequently and has now found a solid basis in supranational criminal law if it can be proven that the crime has taken place within the context of crimes against humanity or war crimes.

As sexual slavery and, partially, enforced prostitution, forced pregnancy was never before laid down in a supranational criminal instrument either. Due to contradictory opinions among ICC delegates, the definition in the ICC Statute and EoC are almost identical. This has left open some uncertainties, including whether confining a woman implies a specific amount of time or whether it includes any deprivation of physical liberty, no matter for how long, and whether confining a woman and forced impregnation are two separate acts not necessarily committed by the same person. It will be up to the judges of the ICC to interpret this crime. The realities of forced pregnancy as a constituent act of genocide, a crime against humanity or a war crime, however, require that no narrow interpretation of the crime of forced pregnancy should be made. In the case of the questions raised above, this means that no specific time frame should be required and that the confinement of the woman and the forced impregnation can be two separate acts committed by different persons.

The crime of enforced sterilisation has also been laid down in a supranational criminal law instrument, that is to say, the ICC Statute, for the first time. The crime concerns the deprivation of a person's biological reproductive capacity without any justified medical reason or this person's genuine consent. The crime would also entail situations in which women were raped so viciously that their reproductive system has been destroyed completely. Especially where women and girls have been raped multiple times by multiple perpetrators, their biological reproductive capacity may be injured beyond healing. Also the cutting off or taking out of genitals may come within the ambit of enforced sterilisation.

The category of 'any other form of sexual violence of comparable gravity' is a sort of rest category for sexual violence crimes not falling under any of the other specific sexual violence crimes mentioned in Article 7(g) or Articles 8(2)(b)(xxii) and 8(2)(e)(vi) (where it is referred to as 'any other form of sexual violence also constituting a grave breach of the Geneva Conventions' and 'any other form of sexual violence also constituting a serious violation of article 3 common to the four Geneva Conventions', respectively). This crime is new in supranational criminal law as well. In the crimes against humanity provision of the Tribunals, a similar rest category is found under 'other inhumane acts', but this category is applicable to all crimes against humanity, not to sexual violence crimes only. For an act to fall within the definition of 'any other form of sexual violence' the ICC EoC require that the perpetrator committed an act of a sexual nature under coercive circumstances (non-consent is not an element of the crime) and that the conduct be of a gravity comparable to the other crimes in Article 7(1)(g) of the ICC Statute. When interpreted strictly, this might lead to the conclusion that all other sexual violence crimes need some degree of penetration. Such an interpretation is unwanted and would not take into account case law by the Tribunals on this matter.

According to the case law of the Tribunals with regard to the 'other inhumane acts' category, sexual violence is not limited to physical invasion of the human body, but may include acts which do not involve penetration or even physical contact, like forced nudity. While concerns existed among ICC delegates with regard to the open-ended language contained in this provision, it is not always possible to capture all criminal acts in one definition, especially not in a rest category like this one, being drafted to take into account unforeseeable sexual violence crimes. This is also in conformity with national laws containing open-ended formulations of sexual assault crimes. For this reason, the category of 'any other form of sexual violence of comparable gravity' should not be interpreted restrictively. Furthermore, although the category of 'other inhumane acts' could serve as an additional rest category in cases where sexual violence would not fall under 'any other form of sexual violence of comparable gravity', it is suggested that this should not easily be the case because it would make the category of 'any other form of sexual violence of comparable gravity' completely superfluous. The rest category of 'other inhumane acts' does not take into account the specific sexual nature of the crimes as has been done by the category of 'any other form of sexual violence of comparable gravity'.

Another novelty with specific attention to sexual violence crimes committed on the basis of gender has been introduced at the Court through the crime of persecution. In general, persecution means the intentional and severe deprivation of fundamental rights by reason of a person's connection to a specific group. In a considerable number of cases, the Tribunals charged and convicted accused of the crime of persecution. Such charges and prosecutions are effective as the crime adequately covers a broad range of crimes (murder, torture, rape, etc.) and therefore make it possible for the Prosecutor not to charge each crime separately. For the first time ever, gender has now been added to the list of groups mentioned. Therefore, raping a woman solely for the reason that she is a woman can be prosecuted as the crime against humanity of persecution.

As far as the crime of genocide is concerned, the genocide definition as such does not include rape or any other forms of sexual violence (Article 6 of the ICC Statute). The (officially non-binding) EoC, however, do refer to rape and sexual violence in a footnote (which has the same standing as an element), explaining that these crimes come within the ambit of 'serious bodily or mental harm'. Despite such recognition in the EoC, the ICC has clearly missed the opportunity to outlaw rape, sexual slavery and other forms of sexual violence as constituent crimes of genocide in treaty law, that is to say, the ICC Statute. Furthermore, gender as a basis of group destruction has not been remedied either in the definition of genocide as contained in the ICC Statute. The evidence in both Tribunals has clearly shown that rape and sexual violence was a means to destroy a particular group by targeting the female members of that group. In order to bring the definition of genocide in conformity with the hard time reality of genocidal rapes taking place in contemporaneous conflicts around the world today, the definition of genocide should include specific sexual violence crimes as well as a reference to gender as a basis for group destruction. The specific sexual violence crimes laid down for crimes against humanity and war crimes (rape, sexual slavery, enforced prostitution, forced pregnancy, enforced sterilisation and any other form of sexual violence) could equally be applicable to genocide and should, for this reason, be transferred to the genocide definition. Such an explicit inclusion of sexual violence crimes would bring the law on the supranational criminal law level in uniformity with the crimes against humanity and war crimes provisions. More importantly, it would explicitly recognise the sexual violence crimes as genocidal crimes in and of themselves. Until that time, sexual violence may be prosecuted under any of the constituent acts of genocide, depending on the case at hand: i.e., killing members of the group; causing serious bodily or mental harm to members of the group; deliberately inflicting on the group conditions of life calculated to bring about its physical destruction in whole or in part; imposing measures intended to prevent births within the group; forcibly transferring children of the group to another group.

Apart from charging an accused under the specific sexual violence crimes, prosecutions can also still follow under the non-specific sexual violence crimes if this serves to establish the totality of the accused's conduct. For example, sexual violence could be prosecuted under the grave breaches of torture, inhuman treatment or wilfully causing great suffering or serious injury to body or health or under the violations of Article 3 Common to the 1949 Geneva Conventions of cruel treatment, torture or outrages upon personal dignity. In the case of crimes against humanity, it would be possible to prosecute sexual violence as enslavement, torture, or other inhumane acts of a similar nature in addition to the specific sexual violence crimes, including persecution on the basis of gender. Of particular interest could be the crime of torture as a war crime which imposes an additional purposive element. Rape could, for instance, be cumulatively prosecuted as the war crime of rape and the war crime of torture, the latter when the rapes were inflicted in order to humiliate, intimidate, punish and/or discriminate against the victim's gender. Although the Prosecutor in the ICTY and ICTR was more or less bound to prosecute under these non-specific sexual violence crimes in the absence of a number of specific sexual violence crimes, the ICC Prosecutor will have both options: non-specific sexual violence crimes and/or specific sexual violence crimes, of which the latter should come at the forefront of the prosecutorial strategy on sexual violence. Prosecuting sexual violence as sexual violence better recognises the nature of the crime.

Despite the prohibitions of rape, sexual slavery, enforced prostitution, forced pregnancy, enforced sterilisation and any other form of sexual violence as crimes against humanity and war crimes, contemporaneous conflicts have given insight into another form of sexual violence not expressly criminalised in the ICC Statute, that is, rape with the intent to transmit the HIV/AIDS virus to the victim. Depending on the circumstances of the case, this crime could be prosecuted as genocide, a crime against humanity or a war crime. It is important to recognise this crime as a crime in and of itself. For those who survive rape and/or other forms of sexual violence, the infliction of HIV/AIDS constitutes the ultimate violation of their human rights. In Rwanda, evidence of intentional HIV/AIDS transmission through rape was found, but not prosecuted before the ICTR. Therefore, the victims of these crimes have felt ignored as victims: the true nature of the crimes committed against them was not labelled as such, since their perpetrators were not prosecuted by the ICTR, nor by the Rwandan courts, for intentional HIV/AIDS transmission.

The elements common to genocide, crimes against humanity and war crimes all need to be fulfilled in order for rape or any other form of sexual violence to qualify as an international crime. In sexual violence cases, the specific intent for establishing genocide, can, in particular, be found in speeches of the accused calling for the rape of women of a particular group, in the disproportionate attack on the members of a particular group and in statements made by the rapists themselves during the sexual attack. In Rwanda, the majority of sexual violence perpetrators used language which clearly indicated that the intention underlying each specific act was to destroy the Tutsi group. Language such as 'the pride of the Tutsis will end today' or 'let us now see what the vagina of a Tutsi woman tastes like' was commonly used in the Rwanda of the 1994 genocide where women were raped *en masse* and otherwise sexually attacked. As far as crimes against humanity are concerned, it has been established in ICTY and ICTR case law that the act of rape or any other form of sexual violence does not need to be committed in a widespread or systematic manner; the act need simply form part of a widespread or systematic attack. Such an understanding of the common elements of crimes against humanity certainly facilitates the prosecution of sexual violence, as victims are not always able (they may, for instance, be dead, handicapped, or severely ill) or willing (they may, for instance, feel ashamed or stigmatised and/or fear reprisals) to testify, despite the mass rapes which may have taken place in a particular country or region. The elements common to war crimes include that the conduct took place in the context of and was associated with an international or non-international armed conflict, and that the perpetrator was aware of factual circumstances that established the existence of an armed conflict. Furthermore, in order to prove the elements common to war crimes, an unfortunate element has been added in Article 8 of the ICC Statute: war crimes will, in particular, be prosecuted when committed on a systematic or large-scale basis. This would leave serious, yet isolated cases of sexual violence outside the jurisdiction of the Court. It is suggested that, in principle, every serious case of rape, sexual slavery or any other form of sexual violence be taken up by the Court in the fulfilment of its mandate.

Accountability for sexual violence can naturally only be found if someone can be linked to the perpetration of the sexual violence crimes. Under the ICC Statute, a person can be held criminally responsible as a principal perpetrator, but also under other modes of criminal liability. As many accused before the Court may not be the physical perpetrators of sexual violence, their criminal liability may be derived from their status as a superior or their participation in a joint criminal enterprise. As a superior, someone can be held responsible if three conditions are fulfilled: (1) the existence of a superior-subordinate relationship of effective control between the accused and the perpetrator of the crime; (2) the knowledge, or constructive knowledge, of the accused that the crime was about to be, was being, or had been committed; and (3) the failure of the accused to take the necessary and reasonable measures to prevent or stop the crime, or to punish the perpetrators. Especially in the context of crimes against humanity, superior responsibility may be a perfect basis to prosecute someone for sexual violence. If sexual violence was so widespread or systematic that it would be almost impossible that someone could have failed to notice its occurrence, it can be argued that the superior knew or should have known that his subordinates were going to or were about to commit rapes, which he or she did not try to prevent, stop or punish. Evidence of widespread rapes and other forms of sexual violence may be submitted via NGO reports or through a database such as the one composed within the ICTR, viz., the 'OTP [Office of the Prosecutor] Rape Database'. The information in such a database could be submitted into evidence via a Rule 92*bis* procedure ('Proof of Facts Other Than by Oral Evidence') or it could be submitted into the record so that an expert witness can refer to it. In the case of the third variant of the joint criminal enterprise, someone can be convicted for sexual violence even if this conduct did not fall within the purpose of the joint criminal enterprise. Under the third variant of the joint criminal enterprise, a person can be convicted for sexual violence if the crimes were a natural and foreseeable consequence of the joint criminal enterprise. The joint criminal enterprise has been used in the Tribunals in leadership cases, but its (geographical) reach is still contested. The third variant of the joint criminal enterprise can be found in Article 25(3)(d) of the ICC Statute, although not directly, and the case law of the Tribunals may need to be used to interpret Article 25 to include the joint criminal enterprise in the third variant.

It can be argued that the recognition of specific sexual violence crimes in the ICC Statute has elevated the status of the crimes of rape, sexual slavery, enforced prostitution, forced pregnancy, enforced sterilisation (and any other form of sexual violence) at the very least to the level of international customary law crimes. The sexual violence crimes can also be considered *jus cogens* (fundamental norms from which no derogation is allowed[1]), at least where they are recognised as forming part of *jus cogens* crimes, such as genocide, slavery and torture. In addition, it has been questioned by lawyers and scholars why the prohibition of rape has not been recognised as a peremptory norm in and of itself. Viseur Sellers observes that rape and sexual violence are not only prohibited, but also that 'no circumstances exist in which rape can be authorized or tolerated or escape penal sanction under customary international law or international treaty law'.[2] After an elaborate survey of relevant codes and treaties, she concludes that rape, unfortunately, is not considered to be a *jus cogens* norm. She raises the question of whether 'the prohibition of rape's inability to meet international law's formalistic peremptory norm requirements [is] the gendered legacy of a patriarchal legal culture'.[3] It has been asserted by Askin, however, that sexual violence, at least rape and sexual slavery, are *jus cogens* crimes in and of themselves; not any longer because they form part of other *jus cogens* crimes.[4] Quénivet, on the other hand, has argued that '[t]he real question is whether we want sexual offenses to become a specific category of crime or whether it is appropriate to enumerate them as a type of crime that falls under the purview of a big crime. What must be ensured is that sexual offenses are included in each of these "bigger" crimes and prosecuted as grave breaches of the Geneva Conventions and Additional Protocol I, serious violations of the laws of war, acts of genocide, torture, crimes against humanity and slavery.'[5] On the supranational criminal law level this is certainly a first priority. As mentioned, specific sexual violence crimes are now listed as crimes against humanity, although such specific listing is not really found under the genocide and war crimes provisions (even though the latter provision refers to other form of sexual violence 'also constituting a grave breach of the Geneva

---

[1] Article 53 Vienna Convention on the Law of Treaties (1969) ('Treaties Conflicting with a Peremptory Norm of General International Law *(Jus Cogens)*') reads: 'A treaty is void if, at the time of its conclusion, it conflicts with a peremptory norm of general international law. For the purposes of the present Convention, a peremptory norm of general international law is a norm accepted and recognized by the international community of States as a whole as a norm from which no derogation is permitted and which can be modified only by a subsequent norm of general international law having the same character.' This article is generally regarded as having broader application, outside the Vienna Convention on the Law of Treaties itself.

[2] Viseur Sellers (1999), p. 324.

[3] Viseur Sellers (2002), p. 303. The gender bias of *jus cogens* was also raised by Charlesworth and Chinkin (1993), pp. 63-76.

[4] Askin (2003), p. 349.

[5] Quénivet (2005), p. 176.

Conventions' or 'a serious violation of article 3 common to the four Geneva Conventions'). Although sexual violence can be prosecuted under all three crimes, specific inclusion would further add to explicit recognition of the sexual violence crimes as genocide, crimes against humanity and war crimes.

The coming into force of the ICC Statute, recognising specific sexual violence crimes as grave breaches, violations of Common Article 3, crimes against humanity and genocide (the latter via the footnote in the EoC) calls for similar adjustments of the relevant treaties: the 1949 Geneva Conventions (and 1977 Additional Protocols), Common Article 3 in the 1949 Geneva Conventions and the 1948 Genocide Convention. Such adjustments are necessary in order to bring the law contained in these international (humanitarian) law treaties in conformity with the law on the supranational criminal level and would further acknowledge the seriousness of sexual violence crimes. These results can be achieved either via amendment of the relevant provisions themselves in the treaties or by additional protocol. Furthermore, prohibiting sexual violence as grave breaches in the 1949 Geneva Conventions (and 1977 Additional Protocol I) would be a strong impetus for compulsory universal jurisdiction for States: states are obliged to repress or prosecute the grave breaches of sexual violence. The same applies to genocide, as the 1948 Genocide Convention establishes a duty to prevent or punish perpetrators of genocide. Inclusion of rape and other forms of sexual violence as clear constituent acts of genocide would provide a clear signal, if the sexual violence amounts to genocide, that compulsory universal jurisdiction exists. Although no such clear requirements exist as to Common Article 3 and crimes against humanity, it should not matter in practice whether crimes are labelled as grave breaches or genocide, attracting a duty to prevent or punish. The acts committed will not be less grave. Although practice has shown that States are generally not quickly inclined to act upon their duties to repress or punish, inserting the sexual violence clauses into the international (humanitarian) law treaties will at least no longer deny their criminal nature.

3 Sexual Violence in Supranational Criminal Procedure

In the second part of this study, the status of victims of sexual violence in the ICC proceedings was examined, in particular, their status as witnesses and participants. In the ICTY and the ICTR, victims only serve as witnesses; they do not have any real participatory status. This changed with the establishment of the Court and, for the first time within the supranational criminal law context, victims can actually participate in the proceedings. The status of victims of sexual violence as witnesses was dealt with in Chapter 4. The main issue addressed was whether the protective and special measures offered by the Court take the needs of victims of sexual violence sufficiently into account, without compromising the rights of the accused. In other words, do anonymity and confidentiality measures and measures aimed at the prevention of retraumatisation adequately protect victims of sexual violence as regards their safety, dignity and privacy, and physical and psychological well-being? The ways in which victims of sexual violence have 'participated' at the Tribunals and the challenges faced by the Court to effectuate their participation in a gender-sensitive manner were addressed in Chapter 5.

3.1 Protective and special measures for victims of sexual violence

In the existence of the ICTY and the ICTR, quite a few incidents have revealed that testifying before the Tribunals is not completely without risks. NGO reports, press releases and official court documents on contempt of court have disclosed that victims have, *inter alia*, been intimidated, verbally assaulted, threatened and sometimes even killed. The situation has not been any different for victims of sexual violence. Intimidation and threats are, on the whole, not very surprising given the interests at stake in supranational criminal proceedings and can, depending of the case at hand, also be witnessed in national proceedings worldwide. The ICC is likely to face similar situations of witness intimidation. In order to protect victims and witnesses from any harm against their person, the Court has established a set of protective and special measures. After all, the Court was set up to prosecute perpetrators of egregious crimes of concern to the whole of mankind, a task which, in most cases, cannot be accomplished without witnesses' testimonies.

As opposed to most other victims, victims of rape, sexual slavery or any other form of sexual violence may not only have safety concerns to deal with, their concerns often relate to matters of dignity and privacy as well. In many societies, rape victims are still looked upon as if they did something wrong, as if they were to blame for what happened to them, instead of the perpetrators. Victims of sexual violence who come from such societies may therefore not want to testify, and if they do, they may only want to do so on the condition that their identity is concealed. For example, in Rwanda to be known as a genocide rape survivor may result in rejection and stigmatisation by community and family members and even by the fiancé or husband. If the rape survivor has children, the isolation may also befall them. At least in one reported case, a rape victim testified before the ICTR without telling her fiancé. She had never told him that she had been a victim of multiple rapes during the genocide. On her return from Arusha, it became clear that her identity details had been leaked. When her fiancé found out that she was a rape survivor, he immediately left her. The best remedy would obviously be to change the opinions about the survivors of rape in the societies concerned in order to take away the shame and stigmatisation attached to sexual violence crimes. Until that time, to shield rape victims from rejection and stigmatisation by their surroundings, the Court has several confidentiality measures at its disposal which are aimed to protect victims from having their identity details revealed to the public and the press.

Apart from the more obvious confidentiality measures such as withholding the victim's name from the Court's public records and the use of pseudonyms, Article 68(2) of the ICC Statute provides victims of sexual violence with an automatic right to conduct their testimony *in camera* or to have it presented by electronic or other special means, such as video conferencing or one-way closed circuit television. This provision is more far-reaching than the confidentiality measures offered under the ICTY and ICTR framework, where protective measures are an exception in all cases. The *in camera* proceedings at the Tribunals were usually restricted to those parts of the testimony of the rape victims which were most likely or certain to lead to the disclosure of the victim's identity. Other parts of the testimony were presented in open session and was therefore available to the public and the press. Although Article 68(2) also stipulates that *in camera* proceedings or presentation of testimony by electronic or other special means are justified 'unless otherwise ordered by the Court, having regard to all the circumstances, particularly the views of the victim or witness', it can be argued that a proper reading of the provision should direct the Court to automatically allow such confidentiality measures where the victim-witness of sexual violence herself prefers it. This requires an active role on the part of the Court in explaining the nature of the confidentiality measures available to the victim in order for that person to make an informed decision. It must also be noted that not all victims of sexual violence may want to have their identity concealed from the public and the press but instead want the world to know what happened to them.

Other confidentiality measures, such as video conferencing, can be particularly useful to victims of sexual violence as well, as it may not only prevent identification of the victim from the public or press, but it may also be useful in those cases where a victim is physically unable to testify in court. As victims of rape may have contracted very severe diseases resulting from the sexual violence inflicted upon them, such as HIV/AIDS, video conferencing may be a welcome solution for at least some victims of sexual violence. *In camera* proceedings and video conferencing are generally not seen as a violation of the accused's right to a fair and public trial. The accused's right to examine the witness is still retained in both situations, as only the public and the press are excluded from the proceedings, not the accused and his defence team. It has been furthermore been held in the Tribunals' case law that the public's right to information may yield to confidentiality when the protection of victims and witnesses is at stake.

In practice, however, victims of sexual violence have faced threats and rejection by family and community members after testifying. This has at least been so in Rwanda. As a consequence, some had to seek refuge and live in isolation. This makes one wonder to what extent confidentiality measures actually work in practice: are confidentiality measures not only a theoretical concept? On the one hand, the leaking of the victim's identity details can be explained by violations of court orders on non-disclosure of information to third parties. On the other hand, it has, in some cases, been extremely difficult to prevent the identity details of a witness from becoming known. For example, in villages where everybody knows everybody, it can be extremely difficult to cover up a survivor's absence during the trial of an accused from the same village, especially if people usually never leave their home for a few days or weeks. However, victims of sexual violence are often not informed by Tribunal staff members about the risk that their identity might become known in their own country and community. Although they were usually told that they would testify in confidentiality, they were often not explicitly told that this meant that their identification details were provided to the accused and his defence team in accordance with the rules. However, victims of sexual violence should be able to make a well-informed choice when it comes to testifying before the Tribunals or the Court. They should be informed about the possible risks involved in testifying. For victims of sexual violence, expose of their identity does not only have an impact on their security, it may also affect their status in society.

The ICC has not taken a clear stand on the issue of anonymity. The ICC provisions leave room for ambiguity. The negotiations during the ICC Preparatory Commission sessions were inconclusive on this point and seem to have left the issue open for the Court to decide. The ICC provisions and (inter)national (human rights) law allow the judges to follow either route. However, if concerns for safety as well as privacy and dignity are very real, the Court should not immediately refrain from granting anonymity. In particular on the basis of Rule 88, the Court is able to accept total anonymity as a special measure. Rule 88 states that the Chamber may 'order special measures *such as but not limited to* measures to facilitate the testimony of a ... victim or witnesses' (italics added). In addition, orders under this rule can be made *ex parte*. When special criteria and guidelines are followed – like those set out in the *Tadić Protective Measures Decision* – anonymity as a protective measure can be granted without violating the rights of the accused, especially his right to examine or to have the witness examined. European case law, however, has determined that a conviction may not be based either solely or to a decisive extent on anonymous testimony. For victims of sexual violence, the additional concern exists that, as long as confidentiality measures do not protect them from threats and stigmatisation, they will not come forward and justice will be categorically denied for this category of victims. In order to grant any significance to legislation penalising sexual violence crimes, the situation at the Court should not discourage this already underrepresented group of victims from testifying. Such reasoning is also in line with the equality and non-discrimination provision laid down in Article 21(3) of the ICC Statute. It must be noted in this respect that, in many cases that will appear before the Court, the accused will not be the physical perpetrator of the rape or any other form of sexual violence charged. In a situation where the accused was not present when the sexual violence was committed, it seems less relevant for the accused to know the identity of the victim than in situations where the accused was the physical perpetrator himself. Furthermore, at the time of the crime itself, the identity of the rape victim was generally of no importance to the perpetrator; most victims were chosen in a random fashion, irrespective of their identity. Some of the security concerns raised above, however, may be taken away if effective post-trial protection is offered. This can be realised through relocation and/or domestic witness protection programmes. It is important to construe a workable approach in order to protect victims and witnesses from threats or killings. This requires extensive collaboration between different actors, such as the Prosecutor, the Registry, the VWU, ICC field offices, NGOs and IGOs, and governments. In the past, however, States have not always been very cooperative as regards witness protection and it remains to be seen whether post-trial protection will be effective. However, as long as alternatives to anonymity, such as witness protection programmes, do not protect victims of sexual violence against threats and rejection by their society, family or partner, anonymity should be considered as a valuable tool for protection. It is furthermore suggested that, for each situation taken up by the Court, at least one ICC contact office should be set up in the country concerned, where victims and witnesses could seek help in cases of intimidation and threats.

Another category of protective and special measures to prevent further or increased traumatisation of the rape victim giving testimony addresses the physical and psychological well-being of the victim. In the ICTY *Tadić Protective Measures Decision*, the Chamber recognised that 'rape and sexual assault often have particularly devastating consequences' and that 'traditional court practice and procedures have been known to exacerbate the victim's ordeal during trial' which resulted in a general feeling of 'being raped a second time'.[6] Avoiding direct confrontation with the accused in court is one such measure which seeks to prevent further traumatisation and can consist of one-way closed circuit television (for the implementation of this measure, Article 68 of

[6] *Prosecutor v. Duško Tadić*, Decision on the Prosecutor's Motion Requesting Protective Measures for Victims and Witnesses, Case No. IT-94-1, 10 August 1995, para. 46.

the ICC Statute provides an automatic right for victims of sexual violence), the use of a screen in court, or removal of the accused from the court room. Although preferences for certain protective measures are clearly present, these measures have generally not been considered to violate the rights of the accused, who is still able to confront the witness and to hear and see the witness on the television monitors in the courtroom. Another option is giving testimony by means of prior recorded testimony, which may spare the victim from having to repeat testimony in court. In such cases, both parties should have had the opportunity to examine the witness during the recording. Some of the options mentioned, e.g., video conferencing, have the 'disadvantage' that the victim's demeanour cannot always be directly assessed. However, the measures are not prohibited and the weight given to such evidence, as for any evidence, should be evaluated in light of Article 69(4) of the ICC Statute. This provision requires that the relevance or admissibility of evidence, *inter alia*, the probative value of the evidence and any prejudice that such evidence may cause to a fair trial or to a fair evaluation of the testimony of a witness need to be taken into account.

The special evidentiary rules on sexual violence, on the other hand, restrict the admission of consent and prior or subsequent sexual conduct into evidence and therefore aim to protect the victim of sexual violence from retraumatisation in court as well (Rules 70-72 ICC RPE). In light of the nature of the crimes and the context in which they have been committed, it seems almost impossible to conceive of a situation in which consent or prior or subsequent sexual conduct may ever be raised by the counsel of the accused. However, Rule 71, which deals with prior or subsequent sexual conduct, does not totally preclude the introduction of evidence of prior or subsequent sexual conduct and refers to Article 69(4) of the ICC Statute on the relevance or admissibility of evidence. This is an unfortunate departure from Rule 96(iv) of the ICTY and ICTR RPE, its predecessor, where prior sexual conduct as a defence was not admissible under any circumstances. As far as the issue of consent is concerned, for those (presumably rare) cases in which the Defence may want to advance consent, an *in camera* procedure should first establish the relevance and admissibility of such evidence. This procedure shields the victim from being confronted with painful propositions that have not been tested first. The accused will be interrogated in order to establish relevance and credibility and the victim will not attend this session. In addition, as the ICC definition of rape (or any other form of sexual violence) as laid down in the ICC EoC does not explicitly include the element of consent – as opposed to the ICTY *Kunarac, Kovač and Vuković* Appeals Chamber definition of rape – the Prosecutor does not bear the burden of proving the element of absence of consent. Once the Prosecutor has proven that coercive circumstances existed, non-consent is presumed. In these circumstances, the Defence is not likely to raise the defence of consent. It must again be noted that including consent in the definition of rape is not relevant in cases of the nature the Court is dealing with and could keep victims of sexual violence away from testifying in court. It would place the burden of proof on the Prosecutor, who will necessarily need to inquire into the victim's state of mind. No matter how the question is phrased, such questioning is insulting and traumatising for most victims of sexual violence. As far as the corroboration rule is concerned, Rule 63(4) acknowledges that corroboration of evidence is not a requirement for any crime, particularly not with regard to crimes of sexual violence. When evidence on sexual violence of a single victim is relevant, probative, reliable and credible, a Trial Chamber may convict an accused for the crime charged. The special evidentiary rules thus specifically acknowledge that biases against victims of sexual violence, in particular women, are not accepted and that they are as reliable a witness as any other witness. This is again in line with the equality and non-discrimination provision.

Finally, other special measures that need to be mentioned include the manner of questioning, the length of time of the questioning and allowing a supports person to attend the proceedings. The practice before the Tribunals has shown some discouraging practices towards the treatment of victims of sexual violence during trial proceedings. It is therefore argued that guidelines dealing with the conduct of parties during testimony of a victim of sexual violence need to be established and implemented within both the Tribunals and the Court. Such guidelines are particularly necessary because they will set out one common approach towards the treatment of victims of sexual violence during testimony. Guidelines on the treatment of victims of sexual violence are important because the judges, prosecutors and defence lawyers come from different regions of the world, have different legal backgrounds (common and civil law), resulting in different approaches towards addressing and dealing with victims in court. The nature of the sexual violence crimes committed as constituent acts of genocide, crimes against humanity or war crimes does not allow rape victims to be treated in a more aggressive, common-law kind of style of cross-examination, without adequate intervention by the Prosecutor or the judges. Although it is certainly not argued that the treatment of victims of sexual violence has in been miserable in all Tribunal cases, it is obvious that a considerable amount of misunderstanding still exists as to what constitutes appropriate treatment. In short, the proposed guidelines or code of conduct on the treatment of victims of sexual violence in court would need to cover the following issues for the following actors:

Prosecutor
Preparation of the rape victim before trial in order to familiarise the victim with the sort of questions that the Prosecutor needs to pose to the victim in order to get the accused convicted on the sexual violence charges; knowledge of and sticking to the relevant facts to present the case in a succinctly manner; and active intervention during trial when rape victims are confronted with painful propositions by Defence Counsel.

Defence Counsel
Addressing the rape victim in an aggressive manner with irrelevant and painful questions is not allowed. Cross-examination needs to operate within the boundaries of establishing the truth and respect for the physical and psychological well-being of the rape victim. Once the victim has explained to the court, for instance, that she was held in sexual slavery, and that a crime was thus committed against her, questions as to whether or not she touched the rapist's penis or whether or not his penis was circumcised are irrelevant for the establishment of the truth and may cause secondary victimisation of the victim concerned.

Judges
An active role in the proceedings. This includes intervening when a Defence Counsel confronts a rape victim with unnecessary painful propositions. This does not mean that a Defence Counsel will be completely restricted in his or her cross-examination; it only means that clear directions are given by the judges in order to control the overall proceedings. On the basis of Article 64(8)(b), 64(9) and Rule 88(5) in particular, the judges have the power to do so.

It is important that victims of sexual violence are treated with respect and that their physical and psychological well-being is taken into account. Only then will they be willing to testify before the Court and will the record reflect the crimes that have been committed against them.

3.2 Participation of victims of sexual violence in the proceedings

For the first time within supranational criminal procedure, victims have the right to participate in the Court's proceedings, often through a legal representative. The ICC regime is therefore more victim-friendly than its Tribunal counterparts, where victims were not attributed any participatory rights. Although it has sometimes been suggested that the Prosecutor would also take care of victims' interests, it has been proven on a number of occasions that the interests of victims of sexual violence and those of the Prosecutor not always coincide. For example, whose interests did the Prosecutor take into account by entering into a plea agreement with the accused, dropping the count on rape in exchange for a guilty plea on the other counts, (*Serushago* and *Predrag Banović* cases)? What about the situation in which evidence of the accused's responsibility for sexual violence was available, but charges of sexual violence were not included in the indictments in spite of this (see, for example, the *Cyangugu* case and the *Butare* case with regard to the accused Kanyabashi, Ndayambaje, Ntezirayayo and Nsabimana)? Why did the Prosecutor fail to file for an appeal on the rape acquittals in the cases of *Niyitegeka*, *Kajelijeli* and *Kamuhanda*? In these kinds of situations, the Prosecutor may be giving precedence to other interests, such as time constraints to deal with the caseload, rather than the legitimate concerns of victims. While some mechanisms, such as *amicus curiae* interventions and directly addressing the OTP by sending letters, have been very helpful in addressing victims concerns and bringing the situation out in the open, their effectiveness is dependent on a number of issues, in particular judicial and/or prosecutorial discretion. Furthermore, the options of *amicus curiae* briefs or directly addressing the OTP are very much dependent on *amici* who care enough to take up the plight of victims and are therefore *ad hoc* mechanisms. The same is true for the victim impact statements which occasionally have been forwarded by the Prosecutor to the Chamber for sentencing purposes, but where, again, victims themselves do not have a right to submit such statements. This may be part of the reason why the impact of the crimes on victims of sexual violence has not been taken into account by the Chambers in a consistent and coherent manner.

This unsatisfactory situation for victims has now been remedied at the Court. At least victims can now, among other things, make opening and closing statements to tell their story. This will make it possible for victims of sexual violence to have the effects of the rapes recognised and taken into account for sentencing purposes. Victims also have the right to be informed about the progress of the proceedings and may be present when the Court reaches its verdict or, alternatively, be notified thereof when they cannot be there. In case of a guilty plea, the interests of victims are taken into account as well, and the Court may decide not to accept the plea because the interest of victims so dictate. Their views may also be sought where the indictment may be amended. These are just a few examples of victim participation recognised in the ICC Statute and RPE and where, in the past, victims of sexual violence have experienced difficulties in getting their voice heard. It is therefore no longer the Prosecutor who looks after victims' interests solely. In light of the complexity of cases, with potentially many victims participating, the Court will be able to keep control over the manner of participation and has the flexibility to make changes whenever appropriate. In most situations, a legal representative will be assigned to victims or a common legal representative if the number of victims is very high.

The Court has acknowledged that special attention must be given to victims of sexual violence. In particular Article 68(1) of the ICC Statute and Rule 16(5) of the ICC RPE contain such an obligation. These provisions require that participation of victims of sexual violence should be conducted in gender-sensitive circumstances which take into account the well-being, dignity and safety of the victim. This means, *inter alia*, that victims of sexual violence may be represented by a legal representative with experience in dealing with victims of sexual violence and/or trauma counselling. If the Court wants victims of sexual violence to participate, it is important that they are notified about the participation possibilities and the special arrangements that have been put into place to make their participation as gender-sensitive as possible. Exactly because of the stigmatisation, shame and fear disproportionately attached to these crimes, victims of sexual violence need extra attention so that they will be able to realise their participatory rights to the fullest extent. International, national or local women's organisations in the countries concerned will be instrumental in making participation of victims of sexual violence a reality. They will be able to locate victims of sexual violence and help them submit their applications for participation at the Court. If victims of sexual violence suffer from disease as a result of the sexual violence committed against them and are not capable of making the application themselves, someone else will be allowed to do this for them. Although the situation before the ICC is better in terms of participatory rights laid down in the legal instruments, it should be kept in mind that, if victims are not reached, they will not come. An important task lies ahead for the Victims Participation and Reparation Section (VPRS).

4 Sexual Violence and the Legal Consequences of the Supranational Criminal Law System

Part III of this study dealt with the legal consequences arising from supranational criminal prosecutions. In this phase of the proceedings, a victim of sexual violence may see the rape or other forms of sexual violence labelled publicly as a crime and see the perpetrator condemned by the international community and punished. A victim of sexual violence will see herself acknowledged by the international community as an innocent victim who deserves reparation. In both situations – sentencing and reparation – the judges of the respective Chambers exercise relatively wide discretionary powers. In the case of reparation, the Trust Fund for victims and their families may, moreover, complement the Court's powers on reparation. The issue of sentencing was addressed in Chapter 6 and mainly concerned the question of how the judges of the Tribunals had determined the sentences for persons convicted of sexual violence and whether this practice should be followed by the judges of the ICC. The issue of reparation to victims was not taken up by the Tribunals and the ICC Statute and RPE now contain an elaborate reparation regime. The subject of Chapter 7 of this study was the extent the reparation possibilities can be of help to victims of sexual violence.

4.1 Sentencing in cases of sexual violence

Witness 96, who testified in the *Kunarac, Kovač and Vuković* case, a case which exclusively dealt with rape, sexual slavery, and other forms of sexual violence, stated: 'I am disappointed with the sentences – given everything that they have done. I no longer believe in those sentences and will not testify before the tribunal.'[7] Feelings like these express the dissatisfaction felt by many victims and witnesses who came to the ICTY and the ICTR to testify about the rapes and other forms of sexual violence committed against them and others. Although feelings of the public at large or victims or witnesses in particular are not usually an indication of the length of a sentence to be imposed by a court, as sentencing falls within the discretionary powers of the judiciary, Witness 96, cited above, had legitimate reasons to be upset by the sentences imposed in that particular case. Why?

After an elaborate survey of the sentences imposed on a total of 29 ICTY and ICTR accused (in a total of 20 cases) convicted for rape and/or other forms of sexual violence to date, the overall conclusion was drawn that sentences for sexual violence imposed by the Tribunals have been rather lenient in light of the sentencing determinants applied by the two Tribunals. How can this be? According to the Tribunals' Statute and Rules of Procedure and Evidence, several factors need to be taken into account when the judges determine the sentence to be imposed on the person found guilty, including: (1) they must have recourse to the general practice regarding prison sentences in the courts of the former Yugoslavia or Rwanda, as applicable; (2) they must take into account such factors as the gravity of the crime and the individual circumstances of the convicted person; and (3) they must have regard to any aggravating or mitigating circumstances.[8] As an example of a mitigating circumstance, the substantial cooperation with the Prosecutor by the convicted person before or after conviction has been cited.

The interpretation of these sentencing determinants has overall been left to the discretion of the judges of the Tribunals, but some general remarks on the sentencing determinants can be made here. With regard to the first factor, recourse to the prison sentences imposed in the respective national jurisdictions, the Tribunal judges have consequently held that the national prison sentencing practice must be seen as a guiding, but not binding, tool to determine the penalty. However, if the Chambers divert from the national sentencing practice, they need to explain their reasons for doing so. The gravity of the crimes, the second factor mentioned, must be assessed in the light of their individual circumstances and consequences, taking into account quantitatively the number of victims and qualitatively the suffering inflicted on the victims[9] as well as the form and degree of the participation of the accused in the crimes.[10] The third and final factor mentioned, the aggravating and mitigating circumstances, have largely been developed in the Tribunals' case law and include such factors as the magnitude of the crimes, including the number of victims; the zeal in committing the crimes, including

---

[7] Institute for War & Peace Reporting, *Foca Rape Case* (by Mirko Klarin and Vjera Bogati), Issue 210, 28 February 2001.

[8] See Article 24 ICTY Statute, Article 23 ICTR Statute and Rule 101 ICTY/R RPE.

[9] Krstić Judgment, para. 701 (with reference to Čelebići Judgment, para. 1226).

[10] Kupreskić Judgment, para. 852.

the multiplicity of perpetrators; the heinousness of the crimes; the duration of the crimes; discriminatory intent; the vulnerability of the victims; the youth of the victims; the trauma of the surviving victims; and the abuse of trust or personal authority. As far as mitigating circumstances are concerned, circumstances that have been accepted by the judges of the Tribunals include a guilty plea; cooperation with the Prosecutor; remorse; voluntary surrender; no prior criminal record; assistance to victims; no active participation; family; youth; old age; subordinate rank; the context of the actions; cooperation with Defence Counsel; and post-conflict conduct. It must be noted that mitigating circumstances related specifically to sexual violence conduct are not easily found.

How have these factors been applied with regard to the sentences imposed on individuals convicted for sexual violence? Although the difficulties inherent to comparing crimes was recognised, it was possible to make some general as well as some case-specific and inter-case specific observations on the basis of the cases studied. Where sexual violence formed part of a larger package of other crimes, however, it was generally difficult to draw meaningful conclusions.

In the first place, it can be concluded that the study of the sentencing practice in the national courts of the former Yugoslavia and Rwanda established that specific sentences imposed by the Tribunals for sexual violence as international crimes (genocide, crimes against humanity or war crimes) only approximated – or not even approximated – sentences imposed for sexual violence as national crimes, as if the crimes had taken place in peace time situations instead of committed as constituent acts of genocide, crimes against humanity or war crimes. In Articles 360 and 361 of the Rwandan Penal Code, it is stipulated that rape should be punished with 5 to 10 years, or with 10 to 20 years if the rape is committed against a person under the age of sixteen.[11] These sentences may be doubled to 10 to 20 years and 20 to 40 years, respectively, if certain aggravating circumstances are established, like the position of authority of the accused, the multiplicity of perpetrators or the severity of the physical harm. Comparing this sentencing range to the ICTR practice, in which specific sentences of 7 and 15 years were imposed in cases where rape was charged as a crime against humanity, reveals similarities with sentences as they may be imposed by the Rwanda Penal Code for rape in times of peace. For example, in the *Akayesu* case, a sentence of only 15 years was imposed on Akayesu for the, often multiple, rapes of more than a dozen women and girls, some under the age of sixteen years old. In Rwanda, rape as a crime against humanity or genocide is prosecuted as a category 1 crime, which means that it is considered one of the most serious crimes for which the death penalty or life imprisonment may be imposed. A notable exception, however, forms the recently pronounced *Muhimana* Judgment, where, for the first time, the ICTR convicted a person for rape as genocide and a crime against humanity to life imprisonment on each count. The sentencing range for rape laid down in the Penal Codes of the countries in the former Yugoslavia vary between 3 and 10 to 15 years.[12] The sentences imposed by the ICTY, on the other hand, reveal that specific sentences imposed for sexual violence crimes range between 5 and 15 years imprisonment, with most crimes sentenced with between 7 and 10 years. An exception are the sentences imposed for Kunarac and

[11] For the applicable laws, see Chapter 6 on sentencing in cases of sexual violence.
[12] *Ibid.*

Kovač, who received 28 and 20-year sentences, respectively, for sexual violence conduct only. In the former Yugoslavia, rape as a war crime or genocide carries a sentence of imprisonment of between 5 and 20 years under the 1977 SFRY Criminal Code or even up to 40 to 45 years, or life imprisonment under more recent codes.[13] Although the actual sentencing practice in prosecuting sexual violence as genocide, crimes against humanity or war crimes is limited in both Rwanda and the countries of the former Yugoslavia, on the basis of the relevant sentencing provisions for sexual violence as international crimes, it can be reasonably assumed that the Tribunals' sentencing practice deviates from the sentences that would have been imposed for such crimes in national jurisdictions. Furthermore, in the cases examined, the Chambers have hardly offered any explicit reasons for their departure from the national sentencing laws or practices for sexual violence as genocide, a crime against humanity or a war crime, despite their promise to do so.

In the second place, where the sentence or sentences to be imposed are discussed in the Tribunal judgments, the gravity of rape or any other form of sexual violence is usually not mentioned at all. To be more precise, out of a total of 20 ICTY and ICTR cases dealing with sexual violence, only 3 cases refer to the gravity of rape or sexual violence in general (*Kvočka et al.*, *Češić*, and *Muhimana* cases), in spite of the Tribunals' recognition on a number of occasions that 'rape is one of the worst sufferings a human being can inflict upon another' and can cause 'victims severe mental and physical pain and suffering'.[14] In the *Stakić* Judgment, it was held that 'for a woman, rape is by far the ultimate offence, sometimes even worse than death because it brings shame on her'.[15]

Finally, in the third place, the same that has been said of the gravity of rape above can be said of aggravating circumstances: in most of the cases examined, the aggravating circumstances applicable to rape or other forms of sexual violence were discussed only to a certain extent, or not at all. Again, only 3 cases (out of a total of 20) refer to the aggravating circumstances applicable to the accused found guilty for sexual violence conduct (*Kunarac, Kovač and Vuković*, *Muhimana* and *Nikolić* cases), and even in these cases more aggravating factors could have been found. When sexual violence is committed in conflict situations, many aggravating factors are usually applicable, *inter alia*, the magnitude of crimes, the zeal in committing the rapes, including a multiplicity of perpetrators, the heinousness of the sexual violence crimes, the duration of the sexual violence, the discriminatory intent, including the commission of sexual violence on the basis of gender and/or ethnicity, the vulnerability of the victims, the youth of victims, the repeated nature of the rapes, and the trauma of the surviving victims and others, including the physical and emotional scars inherent to sexual violence, such as pregnancy and HIV/AIDS resulting from the sexual violence inflicted, but also social isolation and economic hardship. Kunarac and Kovač, for instance, were convicted for keeping women and young girls in sexual slavery conditions, sometimes for weeks or months on end. However, the repetitiveness of the rapes and the trauma resulting from the sexual violence were not addressed when the aggravating factors were discussed in the judgment. As far as the effects of the rapes or

---

[13] For the applicable laws, see Chapter 6 on sentencing in cases of sexual violence.

[14] Kunarac, Kovač and Vuković Judgment, para. 655. See also Čelebići Judgment, para. 495.

[15] Stakić Judgment, para. 803.

other forms of sexual violence on the victims is concerned, the fact that victims are no true participants in the trial has partly been the cause that the consequences of rape were not taken into account in the sentencing to the fullest extent.[16]

The above findings strongly give the impression that, on the whole, the seriousness of rape or other forms of sexual violence as genocide, crimes against humanity or war crimes have not been fully recognised by the judges of the Tribunals when imposing sentences for these crimes. If the three factors for determining a sentence (national sentencing practice, the gravity of the crime and aggravating circumstances) are not applied correctly, this will adversely affect the length of the sentence imposed. However, if the totality of the criminal conduct is not reflected in the sentence, justice may not prevail for those survivors of sexual violence who had the courage to come forward and testify at the Tribunal. This may, in turn, lead them and other victims of sexual violence not to appear before the Tribunal in any other cases in which charges of sexual violence may feature.

It is therefore argued that the ICC, which starts with a clean slate, should not follow the Tribunals' general approach when it comes to sentencing sexual violence in particular. For the Court, the sentencing determinants are laid down in Article 78(1) of the ICC Statute, further substantiated by Rule 145. Although the sentencing determinants are comparable to the ones found in the relevant ICTY and ICTR provisions, on paper, the ICC provisions are far more elaborate. The provisions refer to the gravity of the crime and the individual circumstances as factors for determining a sentence and include a non-exhaustive list of aggravating and mitigating circumstances. The circumstances mentioned largely reflect the ICTY and ICTR case law, and many of the aggravating circumstances can be found to be applicable to perpetrators of rape. For example, reference is made to 'the extent of the damage caused, in particular the harm caused to the victims and their families'. In the Tribunals' experience, the trauma experienced by surviving victims of sexual violence has only been raised twice, in the *Simić* and *Nikolić* cases, despite the myriad of consequences generally resulting from sexual violence. Even in cases replete with sexual violence, such as the *Kunarac, Kovač and Vuković* and *Muhimana* cases, the trauma experienced by the victims was not referred to when discussing aggravating circumstances. Another example is the reference to the 'commission of the crime for any motive involving discrimination on any of the grounds referred to in article 21, paragraph 3', which includes gender. As sexual violence is disproportionately often committed against women, gender discrimination as an aggravating factor should be taken up by the Court. This was never done by the Tribunals. It is to be hoped that the explicit mention of the aggravating circumstances in Rule 145 contributes to the fact that such circumstances are not easily overlooked. As the provision is non-exhaustive in nature, other aggravating circumstances, such as the repetitiveness of the rapes, should be taken into account when determining the sentence. Especially where victims have been held in sexual slavery or have become the victims of multiple (gang) rapes, each rape (whether vaginal, anal or oral) should count as one rape and thus add to the aggravation of the sentence.

It is not suggested that the discretionary power of the judiciary should be restricted by means of, for example, sentencing guidelines. Sexual violence charged as a war

[16] On this issue, see also Chapter 5 on participation of victims in the proceedings.

crime is not automatically less serious than sexual violence charged as a crime against humanity, and the latter as less serious than sexual violence charged as genocide, resulting in sentences matching the rank of the crimes. In this perspective, the ICTY and ICTR practice has shown, with the exception of *Muhimana*, that sentences imposed for sexual violence prosecuted as a war crime and a crime against humanity are more or less the same. What is argued here, however, is that each and every case needs to be well substantiated. This has not always been done in the ICTY and ICTR cases in which people were convicted of sexual violence crimes. Explanation of the sentence is even more significant for the Court as specific sentences for each count need to be imposed. This may more easily lead to comparisons between cases. It should be noted that the Court no longer needs to take into account the national sentencing practice, which will allow the Court to develop its own sentencing practice. Since the sentencing practice of the ICC may become the standard on the basis of which punishment of the most serious crimes in countries around the world will be meted on, including a standard on sexual violence crimes, it is important that the sentences are persuasively substantiated and are similar in more or less similar cases. If the Court is truly committed in its prosecution of sexual violence crimes, it is essential that sexual violence crimes are taken seriously by acknowledging the gravity and aggravating circumstances of the crimes concerned. Otherwise, victims may not feel recognised in the harm committed against them and may not want to cooperate with the Court in the long term.

4.2 Reparation to victims of sexual violence

In addition to victims' participatory rights, the Court brought in another restorative justice element on the supranational criminal law level: reparation to victims. In imitation of many national jurisdictions, in particular, those founded on civil law, the Court provides victims with the possibility to request and be awarded reparation. Keeping in mind that the Tribunals never awarded reparation, which would have been very welcome to the victims in the former Yugoslavia and Rwanda, the reparation regime at the Court is a major breakthrough in the field of supranational criminal law. Although the ICTY and ICTR provisions allow for restitution of property or proceeds to the rightful owner and make matters related to compensation subject to delegation to the 'national courts' or 'other competent bodies' in the countries concerned, for which the Tribunals' judgments on the criminal responsibility of the convict will be considered final and binding, the Tribunals have never applied these provisions.[17] Despite some efforts by Prosecutor Del Ponte to change the compensation regime in favour of those who need it most, the judges have largely remained unconvinced that compensation should come within the ambit of the work of the Tribunals. The Tribunals, they argued, are concerned with retributive justice mainly, that is, with prosecuting perpetrators of serious violations of international humanitarian law. Apart from Voluntary Trust Funds with depleting resources and, in the case of the ICTR, a start with providing HIV/AIDS-infected persons with anti-retroviral (ARV) drugs, the Tribunals have clearly missed an

[17] Article 24(3) of the ICTY Statute, Article 23(3) of the ICTR Statute, Rule 105 ICTY and ICTR RPE, Rule 98*ter*(B) ICTY RPE, Rule 88 ICTR RPE (restitution) and Rule 106 ICTY and ICTR RPE (compensation).

opportunity here, unfortunately to the detriment of those who needed reparation urgently.

As mentioned, the Court has given victims standing to request and receive reparation. In short, the reparation regime before the Court is as follows. The Court can pass an order awarding reparation after the conviction of the accused (Article 75 of the ICC Statute). Reparation to victims may consist of restitution, compensation and rehabilitation or any other form of reparation. The terms largely reflect the Basic Principles and Guidelines on the Rights to a Remedy and Reparation for Victims of Violations of International Human Rights and Humanitarian Law.[18] In addition, the creation of the Trust Fund for victims and their families (Article 79) has opened up a broader system of reparation, which can also be accessed at an earlier stage in the proceedings, including during the investigation phase. In the latter situation, the Trust Fund will operate in a complementary fashion to the Court. The ICC reparation regime is laid down in Articles 75 and 79 of the ICC Statute and further elaborated upon in Rules 94-99 of the ICC RPE.

To what extent can the newly established reparation regime on the supranational criminal law level be of any help to victims of sexual violence? In other words, what are their needs to which the Court and/or Trust Fund could (and should) respond in an adequate and timely manner? In order to find an answer to the latter question, the Rwandan situation was taken as a case study. In Rwanda, eleven years after the 1994 genocide, the persons who are still suffering from the genocide today are, in particular, the orphans, widows and survivors of sexual violence. In an UN General Assembly resolution passed on 10 December 2004, the General Assembly called on agencies, funds and programmes of the UN as well as Member States to assist orphans, widows and survivors of sexual violence 'who are poorer and more vulnerable as a result of the genocide, especially the many victims of sexual violence who have contracted HIV and have since either died or become seriously ill with AIDS'.[19] In Rwanda, it has been

[18] On 13 April 2005, the Commission on Human Rights, during its sixty-first session, adopted a resolution on the 'Basic Principles and Guidelines on the Right to a Remedy and Reparation for Victims of Gross Violations of International Human Rights Law and Serious Violations of International Humanitarian Law'. This is the latest version of the Basic Principles and Guidelines. See E/CN.4/2005/L.48. Principles 19 (restitution), 20 (compensation) and 21 (rehabilitation) describe the terms, as follows: 'Restitution should, whenever possible, restore the victim to the original situation before the gross violations of international human rights or serious violations of international humanitarian law occurred. Restitution includes, as appropriate: restoration of liberty, enjoyment of human rights, identity, family life and citizenship, return to one's place of residence, restoration of employment and return of property'; 'Compensation should be provided for any economically assessable damage, as appropriate and proportional to the gravity of the violation and the circumstances of each case, resulting from gross violations of international human rights law and serious violations of international humanitarian law, such as: (a) Physical or mental harm; (b) Lost opportunities, including employment, education and social benefits; (c) Material damages and loss of earnings, including loss of earning potential; (d) Moral damage; and (e) Costs required for legal or expert assistance, medicines and medical services, and psychological and social services'; 'Rehabilitation should include medical and psychological care as well as legal and social services.'

[19] A/RES/59/137, 17 February 2005.

estimated that in between 250,000 and 500,000 women were raped during the genocide, many of them killed following the rapes.[20] As a result of the rapes and other forms of sexual violence committed against them, they face dire physical, psychological, social and economical consequences. Many survivors of sexual violence have contracted sexually transmitted diseases, including HIV/AIDS, faced unwanted pregnancies and health complications resulting from botched abortions, and suffered sexual mutilation and other injuries, such as fistulas, uterine problems, vaginal lesions and scarring. Injuries to reproductive organs, unwanted pregnancies as well as diseases such as HIV/AIDS are typical consequences female victims of sexual violence face. It has been estimated that, of the Rwandese women who survived rape, between 70 and 80 percent have been infected with HIV.[21] Although it cannot be argued that all HIV infections were linked to the genocide, it can be reasonably assumed that many women were infected with the virus as a result of the rapes committed during the genocide. This can be concluded, for instance, in light of the abnormally high incidence of HIV/AIDS infections among women survivors raped during the genocide (the HIV prevalence rate in rural areas increased from 1 percent before the 1994 genocide to 11 percent in 1997[22]) and that the rapists did not wear condoms. Moreover, in Rwanda, a considerable number of rapists intentionally raped the women in order to transmit the HIV virus. Rapists made statements in this vein to the victims before, during or after the rapes. Several reports have furthermore held that the increasing spread of HIV/AIDS among women and sexual violence are interlinked.[23] The risk of HIV transmission increases up to three-fold when sex is forced, especially for girls and young women because their vaginal tracts are immature and tear easily.[24] This will in particular be the case where girls and women are raped multiple times, by multiple perpetrators, gang raped or held in sexual slavery. Furthermore, women are more physically susceptible to HIV infection than men: male-to-female HIV transmission during sex is about twice as likely to occur as female-to-male transmission.[25]

However, as reparation remains largely unavailable and unenforceable on both the national and international level, victims, especially female survivors of sexual violence who make up the largest part of the population (in Rwanda, the survivors of sexual

---

[20] Report on the situation of human rights in Rwanda submitted by Mr. René Degni-Ségui, Special Rapporteur of the Commission on Human Rights, under paragraph 20 of resolution S-3/1 of 25 May 1994, E/CN.4/1006/68, 29 January 1996, para. 16.

[21] See the AVEGA-AGAHOZO, Association of Genocide Widows, website (under 'history') at http://www.avega.org.rw (last visited May 2005) and Save the Children (2002), p. 5.

[22] World Health Organization, *Violence Against Women and HIV/AIDS: Critical Intersections, Sexual Violence in Conflict Settings and the Risk of HIV*, Information Bulletin Series, Number 2, 2004.

[23] UN Commission on Human Rights, Report of the Special Rapporteur on Violence Against Women, Its Causes and Consequences, *Towards an Effective Implementation of International Norms to End Violence Against Women*, E/CN.4/2004/66, 26 December, 2003, p. 15; Amnesty International (2004g).

[24] World Health Organization, *Women and Girls Need Access to AIDS Treatment and Protection from Violence*, 30 November 2004.

[25] Annual Report by the Joint United Nations Programme on HIV/AIDS (UNAIDS) and the World Health Organization (WHO), *AIDS Epidemic Update 2004*, December 2004.

violence are often also the widows and the ones who take care for orphans), have largely been left uncompensated. Many survivors of sexual violence, who live on less than USD 1 to 2 a day, find themselves stuck between paying for medical expenses to treat their diseases (if possible at all, as ARV treatment is beyond the means of most Rwandese people) and taking care of their own and their children's basic needs, like buying food or paying their children's school fees. Many survivors have furthermore lost their property during the genocide. As women's inheritance rights cannot be enforced as easily as those of men, they often have no claim to their house. Many women are extremely troubled by the thought what will happen with their children after they have passed away, in particular, because their death will cause their children to live on the streets, where exposure to maltreatment and sexual violence is not unlikely. Many girls end up in prostitution in order to survive. Despite the fact that the genocide ended in 1994, the genocide thus still lives on for many women. Without medical treatment, including ARVs, these women are still dying every day, while many have already died. As mentioned by the Association of Genocide Widows in Rwanda, AVEGA-AGAHOZO, 'amongst AVEGA's members, the issue of rape and the resulting infection of HIV/AIDS constitute the ultimate violation of human rights'.[26]

This short impression of the plight of survivors of sexual violence in Rwanda today is not unique to the context of Rwanda solely. In many conflicts around the world, where women are subjected to rapes, gang rapes, sexual slavery and other forms of sexual violence, the consequences are equally grave. Treatment centres are generally not available (especially during or just after the conflict), or if they are, they are outnumbered by the women who are in need of treatment. As a result, women suffer tremendously from the effects of the injuries inflicted upon them. A considerable number of NGO reports have highlighted the extremely bad conditions women survivors of rape find themselves in as a consequence of contemporaneous conflicts. Reports on Sudan (in particular Darfur), the Democratic Republic of Congo (DRC) (in particular the northeast), Uganda (in particular the north) and the Central African Republic all show the inadequacy of medical and psychological care available to women. If reparation is not made available to these women soon, their fate will not be so much different as the fate of many survivors of sexual violence in Rwanda today.

The reparation possibilities at the supranational criminal law level may be able to address some of the needs of victims of sexual violence. As mentioned above, reparation can be awarded by the Court and/or via the Trust Fund for victims and their families. In the first situation, the Court may order an award of reparation to the victim or victims concerned. This necessarily implies that victims have knowledge about the reparation possibilities at the Court. The VPRS is charged with the task of notifying victims thereof. Given the consequences of sexual violence for victims, the help needed in most situations will be physical, psychological and medical care, including HIV/AIDS medication, either through a court order on compensation or a court order on rehabilitation. In most cases, the convict's money (complemented with money from the Trust Fund, if needed) will be used by the victim to meet her rehabilitation needs, especially medical and psychological care. If the Court establishes the guilt of the accused for intentionally or foreseeably infecting the victim with HIV/AIDS,

[26] See the website of AVEGA-AGAHOZO, the Association of Genocide Widows, under 'history' at http://www.avega.org.rw (last visited May 2005).

HIV/AIDS treatment should as a minimum be included in the reparation order. In order to obtain money from the convict, State cooperation is an essential ingredient to success, but not without difficulties as history has shown.[27] Furthermore, a reparation order may be awarded both individually and collectively. Especially if the number of victims is high, the Court may be more inclined to order collective awards. In the case of victims of sexual violence, international and/or national agencies that have experience with victims of sexual violence and their needs are the most likely candidates to implement collective care programmes by setting up, for example, treatment centres. But also indirect victims of crime, for example the children of survivors of sexual violence, may benefit from the court order on rehabilitation. For example, a decision can be made that schools will be established for the benefit of these children.

In addition to compensation and rehabilitation, restitution of property and proceeds is also essential to victims, including victims of sexual violence. In order to start building up their lives again, access to proper housing and restitution of (other) stolen property is a basic requirement. Reparation is not restricted to victims who participated in the trial proceedings. The Chamber may apply for reparation on behalf of victims of sexual violence in situations where they are unable to request for reparation themselves. If victims of sexual violence suffer from a lack of information on reparation possibilities existent at the Court, and the sexual violence has been so widespread and abhorrent that reparation is clearly needed, the Chamber could (and should) make such a request on their behalf. However, the main difficulty with reparation awards is that they are only awarded once the accused has been pronounced guilty, and victims of sexual violence may urgently need physical, psychological and medical support. Although the Victims and Witnesses Support Section may be able to address some of the needs of victims of sexual violence testifying before the Court, they will not be in a position to meet the needs of victims of sexual violence who are not at the Court to testify.

For this reason, interim relief should be offered by the Trust Fund. The Draft Regulations of the Trust Fund provide for such a need, as it stipulates that physical and psychological rehabilitation and support may be provided already in the investigative phase.[28] In addition, in exceptional circumstances, such services may also be provided where, in the interest of justice, the Prosecutor decides not to investigate and in situations where national courts have started proceedings against the accused in light of

---

[27] In this respect, it is interesting to mention Council Directive 2004/80/EC of 29 April 2004 relating to compensation to crime victims, Official Journal of the European Union, L 261/15, 6 August 2004. Under the Council Directive, an 'assisting authority or authorities' must be established in every Member State to assist in and facilitate access to compensation in cases where the crime was committed in a Member State other than that of the victim's residence. An initiative similar to the Council Directive may be helpful with regard to the enforcement of ICC reparation orders as well.

[28] Assembly of States Parties, Report to the Assembly of States Parties on the activities and projects of the Board of Directors of the Trust Fund for Victims, 2003-2004, Third session, The Hague, 6-10 September 2004, Annex A, *Draft regulations of the Trust Fund for Victims*, First Meeting of the Board of Directors of the Trust Fund for Victims, 20-22 April 2004, The Hague (The Netherlands), ICC/ASP/3/14/Rev.1, Draft Rule 50.

the complementarity principle, but where reparation for victims is unavailable.[29] It is very important that rehabilitation and support measures include HIV/AIDS treatment, as forced sex and the spread of HIV/AIDS transmission are closely interlinked in conflict situations. This may be even more so in the case of Sudan, the DRC and Uganda, the first three situations taken up by the Court, as they lie at the hart of Africa's AIDS belt.[30] However, to have any meaningful impact on victims' lives, it is important for the Trust Fund to act as soon as possible. It is not unlikely that survivors of sexual violence may already be in bad health by the time the Prosecutor initiates an investigation: at that time, the conflict may have been going on for weeks, months or even years. This means that the Trust Fund will have to negotiate agreements with humanitarian organisations in the field which will be able to reach and know how to work with survivors of sexual violence. Collective projects for the benefit of victims of sexual violence could include setting up centres with expertise in physical, psychological and medical care, including HIV/AIDS treatment. A school or income generating projects could also be set up for victims and for their children. Children may especially be in need of such support if the mother is disabled, has died or will die as a result of the diseases she may have contracted as a result of the sexual violence. Collective projects will allow the Trust Fund to reach many more victims of sexual violence than the Court, as the Court will usually focus on certain crimes, areas and perpetrators and may therefore overlook victims of sexual violence not affected by the Prosecutor's prosecutorial strategy. In addition, the Trust Fund may be able to reach unidentified victims of sexual violence who, for instance, due to stigmatisation, fear or trauma, were not able to request reparation at the Court themselves. The establishment of the Trust Fund for victims and their families may therefore, to some extent, be able to address the needs of victims of sexual violence on a wider scale.

Although the reparation regime laid down in the ICC Statute and RPE gives reason for optimism, it must be acknowledged that previous experiences at the Tribunals and elsewhere have shown that convicts are often indigent and that resources in the Trust Fund are minimal. For this reason, the Court should make it clear to victims what they can reasonably expect from the Court and the Trust Fund as far as reparation is concerned, so that victims will not be too disappointed in the end. Collective awards, either by the Court or Trust Fund, therefore seem to be a good and effective option in reaching out to as many victims as possible. Again, it must be emphasised that interim relief in the form of physical, psychological or medical care, including HIV/AIDS treatment, is of particular importance to victims of sexual violence if they are not to suffer for many years to come. In this respect, it is important that the Trust Fund is given enough flexibility in how and when it uses its resources. With the experiences of the Rwandese survivors of sexual violence in mind, one would think that the same mistake will not be made again.

---

[29] *Ibid.*, Draft Rule 51.

[30] According to UNAIDS Sub-Saharan Africa (which includes Uganda and the DRC) has 'just over 10% of the world's population, but is home to more than 60% of all people living with HIV – some 25,4 million'. See http://www.unaids.org/EN/geographical+area/by+region/sub-saharan+africa.asp.

5 Final thoughts

The past ten years have seen major breakthroughs in the prosecution of sexual violence on the supranational criminal law level. Whereas once there was even discussion as to whether rape was actually a war crime, the ICC Statute now includes a number of specific sexual violence crimes as crimes against humanity and war crimes. The EoC on the definition of genocide contains a footnote in which it is held that rape and sexual violence can constitute the crime of genocide as well. In addition, supranational criminal procedure takes the interests of victims of sexual violence into account by providing for gender-sensitive measures and circumstances during trial. ICTY and ICTR practice has been instrumental in arriving where we stand today; both their shortcomings and their achievements have given great insight into how best to deal with sexual violence prosecutions. ICTY and ICTR staff members with expertise on sexual violence and gender issues have considerably contributed to the developments in sexual violence prosecutions; a practice which should be set forth at the ICC. But also the lobbying by NGOs and the writings of scholars have influenced the framework of sexual violence on the supranational criminal law level considerably.

In this study, I have tried to answer the question of whether the supranational criminal law system provides sufficient possibilities to comprehensively prosecute sexual violence crimes. Although I think that the tools for prosecuting sexual violence are quite well represented under the relevant instruments of the Court, the ICTY and ICTR practice has revealed that it is the application of the law that sometimes leaves more to wish for. On a number of occasions, it has become clear that the Tribunals did not sufficiently take into account such factors as the reality of the crimes, respectful treatment of victims of sexual violence in the proceedings, the seriousness of the crimes and the needs of victims of sexual violence. In order to come to a more comprehensive supranational criminal prosecution of sexual violence, such factors must clearly be taken into consideration more systematically. Taking into account such factors does not compromise other parties' rights and does not interfere with the rule of law; rather, they are an expression of dealing with victims of sexual violence in a humane and respectful manner, doing justice to people who were the victims of very serious crimes. In many societies, victims of sexual violence are still looked upon as if they were responsible for what happened to them. In the countries concerned, little attempt is usually made to bring the perpetrators of sexual violence to trial.[31] The shame and stigmatisation attached to sexual violence crimes needs to be shifted to the perpetrators once and for all. Although clearly initiatives from within the respective societies need to bring about such changes, the Court may also add to this development by taking up cases of sexual violence persistently, demonstrating that the perpetrators of such crimes will not escape with impunity.[32]

---

[31] See, for example, the Report of the United Nations High Commissioner for Human Rights, *Access to Justice for Victims of Sexual Violence*, 29 July 2005, on the situation in Darfur, Sudan.

[32] In a report prepared by the ICC Prosecutor to the Security Council, the Prosecutor announced that 'information also *suggests* a pervasive pattern of rape and sexual violence taking place throughout Darfur, including allegations of gang rape, as well as attacks on children and young girls' (emphasis added). Especially in light of the many NGO reports on sexual violence that has been taken place in Darfur, the cursory mention of rape and sexual violence in the Prosecutor's

I started this study with the story of Perpetue, a Tutsi survivor of sexual violence during the 1994 genocide in Rwanda. Perpetue was a victim of sexual violence among millions of other victims worldwide against whom sexual violence is being or was committed as a constituent act of genocide, a crime against humanity or a war crime. This study has been witness to some of their immense suffering. Yet, their suffering has not come to an end; many survivors of sexual violence are living in extremely bad conditions or are dying of the consequences of the sexual violence that was inflicted upon them. Moreover, each day, many other, new victims of sexual violence can be added to the list of victims. For example, NGO and other reports have exposed the sexual violence crimes inflicted upon women in Sudan, the DRC and northern Uganda. It is therefore important for the ICC to set a good precedent on sexual violence prosecutions; not only with regard to the laws and procedures before the Court, but also for the effect this may have on national courts. The standard set by the ICC on supranational criminal prosecution of sexual violence may well become the standard on the basis of which national courts will deal with sexual violence as well. It is not really any longer an issue of whether or not sexual violence *can* be prosecuted on the supranational criminal law level, but now it is time for lawyers and other practitioners *to act* on the basis of the law.

---

report has been interpreted by the Women's Initiatives for Gender Justice as a signal that the ICC may not take gender crimes seriously enough. See *Report of the Prosecutor of the International Criminal Court, Mr. Louis Moreno Ocampo, to the Security Council Pursuant to UNSCR 1593 (2005)*, 29 June 2005, p. 2; Women's Initiatives for Gender Justice Press Release, *ICC Must Demonstrate it Takes Gender Crimes Seriously*, 30 June 2005.

SUMMARY

The topic of this study is the supranational criminal prosecution of sexual violence, viz. how can or should sexual violence be prosecuted before the International Criminal Court (ICC), with a clear reference to the practice of the International Criminal Tribunal for the former Yugoslavia (ICTY) and the International Criminal Tribunal for Rwanda (ICTR) in this field? In order to present a picture that is as complete as possible regarding the role that the prosecution of sexual violence may play in the supranational criminal law system, this book is divided into four parts: sexual violence in supranational criminal law (Part I), sexual violence in supranational criminal procedure (Part II) and sexual violence and the legal consequences of the supranational criminal law system (Part III). Recommendations for a more comprehensive supranational criminal prosecution of sexual violence are given in Part IV. The central question focuses on whether the supranational criminal law system, which is still a relatively recent phenomenon, is adequate from the perspective of victims of sexual violence. The ICC Statute, its Rules of Procedure and Evidence (RPE) and the Elements of Crimes (EoC), together with – and compared to – the ICTY and ICTR Statutes, their RPE and case law constitute the primary objects of research.

Part I of this study thus deals with sexual violence in supranational criminal law. In the ICC Statute, rape, sexual slavery, enforced prostitution, forced pregnancy, enforced sterilisation and any other form of sexual violence are explicitly outlawed as crimes against humanity and war crimes (Articles 7 and 8, respectively). With the exception of the crime of rape and enforced prostitution, these specific sexual violence crimes were never laid down in a treaty on the supranational criminal law level before. The question which arose was: What are, or what should be, the definitions of sexual violence crimes in the context of the supranational criminal law system? Although the ICC EoC provide a detailed overview of the elements of these sexual violence crimes, the EoC are – officially – not binding. With regard to the definition of rape, the ICC EoC do not focus on the issue of non-consent, but rather on force, threat of force, coercion or a coercive environment. Indeed, lack of consent as an element of the crime of rape (or any other sexual violence crime for that matter) is immaterial within the supranational criminal law context, especially in light of the violent and oppressive context in which rapes take place during genocide, crimes against humanity or armed conflict, and should therefore be rejected. No matter how the question is phrased by the Prosecutor ('Did you consent?' or 'Was it done against your will?'), such questions may insult rape victims and may cause further traumatisation, especially if questions like these are asked after the victim has set out the coercive circumstances in which the sexual violence was inflicted upon him or her. If it has been established that a crime was committed, questions about consent are irrelevant. As explained in Part II, in those (presumably) rare cases in which the Defence may want to advance consent, this is still possible, but relevance and admissibility of such evidence must first be established in an *in camera* procedure in order to spare the victim from painful propositions which have not been tested first. The elements of the crime of rape, furthermore, enumerate certain prohibited sexual acts that constitute rape, essentially focusing on penetration. This makes it possible to distinguish rape from other forms of sexual violence, such as forced masturbation, and will therefore not cause injustice to those victims of rape that do fit the ICC definitional requirements of rape and who consider themselves the 'real victims of rape'. It has been argued that the ICC definition of rape, on the whole, fits the reality of the crime as a constituent act of genocide, a crime against humanity or a war crime and should therefore be taken as the leading definition of rape in supranational criminal law. For this reason, the *Kunarac, Kovač and Vuković* Appeals Chamber decision on the definition of rape (focusing on the issue of consent) should not be followed by the ICC. If rape is not defined in conformity with the nature of the crime, victims may be reluctant to come forward and testify at the Court.

As far as the crime of sexual slavery is concerned, the crime is defined in the EoC in conformity with the definition of enslavement (viz., 'exercise any or all of the powers attaching to the right of ownership over one or more persons'), with the addition that the perpetrator caused the victim to engage in one or more acts of a sexual nature. Although the definition may at first give the impression that some sort of commercial aspect is involved (viz., 'ownership' may be understood to refer to, e.g., purchasing and selling), a footnote attached to the first element of the crime of sexual slavery makes it perfectly clear that sexual slavery includes 'forced labour', 'reducing a person to a servile status' (including forced marriage), and 'trafficking in persons, in particular women and children'. It can therefore be concluded that sexual slavery does not necessarily require any financial benefits to the enslaver nor confinement of the victim in a particular place. The crime of enforced prostitution, on the other hand, focuses mainly on pecuniary advantages. However, in most situations, the act committed may be better charged as sexual slavery rather than enforced prostitution. When genocide, crimes against humanity or war crimes are committed, women are frequently captured for the prime purpose of sex without any financial benefits involved. Situations falling short of sexual slavery are nevertheless prosecutable as enforced prostitution. The crime of forced pregnancy was not substantially changed in the EoC, compared to the definition of this crime in the ICC Statute. It remains to be seen how the crime will be interpretated by the judges of the ICC, but it must be noted that a narrow interpretation (e.g., requiring that the confinement of a woman implies that a specific amount of time needs to have elapsed) will certainly not be in conformity with the reality of forced pregnancy as a constituent act of genocide, a crime against humanity or a war crime. The crime of enforced sterilisation may also capture sexual violence crimes, e.g., the situation in which women were raped so viciously that their reproductive system was completely destroyed. The rest-category of 'any other form of sexual violence of comparable gravity' need not be interpreted strictly as this might lead to the conclusion that all other sexual violence crimes need some degree of penetration. Such an interpretation is unwanted and would not take into account the Tribunals' case law on this matter, in which, for example, forced nudity was found to fall within the ambit of 'other inhumane acts'. Finally, the ICC Statute makes it possible that the rape of a woman on the basis of her gender alone be prosecuted as persecution. It should be observed that rape with the intent to transmit the HIV virus to the victim is not as such explicitly recognised in the ICC Statute, despite its frequent occurrence, and should therefore be added to the list of specific sexual violence crimes as well.

Apart from charging an accused under the specific sexual violence crimes, as commented on above, prosecutions at the ICC can also still take place under non-specific sexual violence crimes if this serves to establish the totality of the accused's conduct. Of particular interest could be the crime of torture as a war crime, which imposes an additional purposive element. Rape, for instance, could be cumulatively prosecuted as the war crime of rape and the war crime of torture, the latter when the rapes were inflicted in order to humiliate, intimidate, punish, and/or to discriminate on the basis of gender. Whereas the Prosecutor at the ICTY and ICTR was, to a certain extent, also bound to prosecute sexual violence under non-specific sexual violence crimes in the absence of such an elaborate list of specific sexual violence crimes as can now be found in the ICC Statute, the ICC Prosecutor has both options: prosecuting under non-specific sexual violence crimes and/or under specific sexual violence crimes, of which the latter should come at the forefront of the prosecutorial strategy on sexual violence. Prosecuting sexual violence as sexual violence better recognises the nature of the crime.

As far as the crime of genocide is concerned (Article 6 of the ICC Statute), the genocide definition as such does not include rape or any other forms of sexual violence. The EoC, however, do refer to rape and sexual violence in a footnote (which has the same standing as an element), explaining that these crimes come within the ambit of 'serious bodily or mental harm'. However, the specific sexual violence crimes laid down in the crimes against humanity and war crimes provisions (rape, sexual slavery, enforced prostitution, forced pregnancy, enforced sterilisation, and any other form of sexual violence) could equally be prosecuted as genocide and, for this reason, should be transferred to the genocide definition. Such an explicit inclusion of sexual violence crimes constituting genocide would make the law on the supranational criminal law level in uniformity with the crimes against humanity and war crimes provisions. Although prosecution of sexual violence under the five subheadings of the definition of genocide is possible, as ICTY and ICTR practice has shown, explicit reference to the specific sexual violence crimes would recognise the sexual violence crimes as genocidal crimes in and of themselves. In addition, the genocide definition should be amended to include a reference to group destruction on the basis of gender.

For a successful prosecution of sexual violence, the elements common to genocide, crimes against humanity, and war crimes all need to be fulfilled in order for rape or any other form of sexual violence to qualify as an international crime as well. Specific intent can, for example, be found in speeches of the accused calling for the rape of women of a particular group or in statements made by the rapists themselves during the rapes. As far as crimes against humanity are concerned, it has been established in ICTY and ICTR case law that the act of rape or any other form of sexual violence does not need to be committed in a widespread or systematic manner; the act need simply form part of a widespread or systematic attack. The elements common to war crimes include that the conduct took place in the context of and was associated with an international or non-international armed conflict, and that the perpetrator was aware of factual circumstances that established the existence of an armed conflict. Yet, an unfortunate element has been added to the war crimes provision: war crimes must, in particular, be prosecuted when committed on a systematic or large-scale basis. This could keep isolated cases of serious sexual violence outside the jurisdiction of the Court. It is suggested, however, that every serious case of rape, sexual slavery or any other form of sexual violence be taken up by the Court in the fulfilment of its mandate.

Naturally, for sexual violence to be attributed to the accused, a link between the crime and the accused needs to be established. The ICTY and ICTR practice revealed that this is not always an easy task. However, two options for establishing the criminal liability of the perpetrator seem not to have been used to the fullest extent. In the first place, especially in the context of crimes against humanity, superior responsibility may be a perfect basis to prosecute someone for sexual violence. If sexual violence was so widespread or systematic that it would be almost impossible that someone could have failed to notice its occurrence, it could be argued that the superior knew or should have known that his subordinates were going to or were about to commit sexual violence crimes and that he or she did not take any measures to prevent or stop the crime or to punish the perpetrators. The concept of the joint criminal enterprise also seems to give scope for prosecuting sexual violence more effectively since a person can be convicted of sexual violence under the third variant of the joint criminal enterprise if these crimes were a natural and foreseeable consequence of the joint criminal enterprise.

The coming into force of the ICC Statute, recognising specific sexual violence crimes as grave breaches, violations of Common Article 3, crimes against humanity and genocide (the latter via the footnote in the EoC) calls for similar adjustments of the relevant treaties: the 1949 Geneva Conventions (and the 1977 Additional Protocols), Common Article 3 of the 1949 Geneva Conventions and the 1948 Genocide Convention. Such adjustments would bring treaty law and supranational criminal law in conformity with each other and would further recognise the seriousness of sexual violence crimes. On the whole, the ICC Statute and EoC offer a workable framework for prosecuting sexual violence on the supranational criminal law level. As long as the crimes are interpreted in conformity with the reality of the crimes, the ICC will give a strong message that sexual violence crimes are taken seriously. This will, in turn, further attribute to the willingness of victims of sexual violence to come forward and to testify before the Court. By and large, it is no longer a question of criminalising sexual violence; it is a question of actually putting the law into effect.

Part II of this study focuses on sexual violence in supranational criminal procedure, viz., the status of victims of sexual violence as witnesses and as participants in ICC proceedings. The first issue is addressed in Chapter 4 and concerns the question of whether the 'protective and special measures' offered by the Court take into account the needs of victims of sexual violence, without compromising the rights of the accused to a fair trial. As opposed to most other victims, victims of sexual violence may not only have to deal with matters of dignity and privacy, their concerns often relate to safety as well.

One category of protective measures are confidentiality measures which aim to protect the witness from the public or the press. Article 68(2) of the ICC Statute gives victims of sexual violence an automatic right to present their testimony *in camera* or to have it presented by electronic or other special means, such as video conferencing or one-way closed circuit television. Although Article 68(2) also stipulates that *in camera* proceedings or presentation of testimony by electronic or other special means are justified 'unless otherwise ordered by the Court, having regard to all the circumstances, particularly the views of the victim or witness', it is suggested that a proper reading of the provision should direct the Court to automatically allow such confidentiality measures if the victim-witness of sexual violence herself is in favour thereof. This necessarily implies an active role of the Court in informing the victim-witness of the confidentiality measures available. Other confidentiality measures, such as video conferencing, can be particularly useful to victims of sexual violence as well: it may not only prevent identification of the victim by the public or the press, but it may also be useful in those cases where a victim is physically unable to testify in court. As victims of rape may have contracted very serious diseases resulting from the sexual violence inflicted upon them, such as HIV/AIDS, videoconferencing may be a welcome solution for at least some victims of sexual violence. *In camera* proceedings and video conferencing are generally not seen as a violation of the accused's right to a fair and public trial. The accused's right to examine the witness is retained in both situations, as only the public and the press are excluded from the proceedings, not the accused and his defence team. In practice, however, victims of sexual violence have faced threats and rejection by family and community members after testifying, a situation which is not unlikely to occur in cases before the Court. This leads to the question of whether confidentiality measures actually work in practice. At the very least, victims should be informed about the possible risks involved when testifying, a practice which has not always been implemented by the Tribunals. For victims of sexual violence, exposure of their identity does not only have an impact on their safety, it may also affect their status in society.

Although it is not clear from the ICC provisions what stand the drafters of the ICC took on anonymity measures (protection from the accused), the Court could accept total anonymity on the basis of Rule 88 as a special measure. When special criteria and guidelines are followed – like those set out in the *Tadić Protective Measures Decision* – anonymity as a protective measure can be granted without violating the rights of the accused, especially his right to examine the witness or to have the witness examined. In European case law, it has furthermore been determined that a conviction may not be based either solely or to a decisive extent on anonymous testimony. For victims of sexual violence, the additional concern exists that, as long as confidentiality measures do not protect them from threats and stigmatisation, they will not come forward and justice will be categorically denied for this category of victims despite legislation criminalising sexual violence. Moreover, in a situation where the accused was not present when the sexual violence was committed, it seems less relevant for the accused to know the identity of the victim than in situations where the accused was the physical perpetrator himself. Furthermore, at the time of the crime itself, the identity of the rape victim was of no importance to the perpetrator: most victims were chosen in a random fashion, irrespective of their identity. As long as alternatives to anonymity, such as witness protection programmes and relocation, do not protect victims of sexual violence against threats and rejection by their society, family or partner, anonymity should be considered by the Court as a valuable tool for protection.

A third category of protective and special measures seeks to prevent further or increased traumatisation of the rape victim giving testimony. Avoiding direct confrontation with the accused in court is one such measure, and can consist of one-way closed circuit television, the use of a screen in court, or removal of the accused from the court room. These measures have generally not been considered to violate the rights of the accused, who is still able to confront the witness and to hear and see the witness via television monitors. Another possibility is giving testimony by means of prior recorded testimony, in which case both parties must have had the opportunity to examine the witness during the recording. This measure may spare the victim from having to repeat testimony in court. A third possibility concerns the special evidentiary rules on sexual violence, which restrict the admission of consent and prior or subsequent sexual conduct into evidence and therefore aim to protect the victim of sexual violence from retraumatisation in court as well (Rules 70-72 ICC RPE). In light of the nature of the crimes and the context in which they have been committed, it seems almost impossible to think of a situation in which consent or prior or subsequent sexual conduct may ever be raised by the counsel for the accused in a meaningful way. However, Rule 71, which deals with prior or subsequent sexual conduct, does not totally forbid the introduction of evidence of prior or subsequent sexual conduct and constitutes an unfortunate departure from Rule 96(iv) of the ICTY and ICTR RPE where prior sexual conduct as a defence was under no circumstances admissible. For those (presumably rare) cases in which the Defence may want to advance consent, an *in camera* procedure should first establish the relevance or admissibility of such evidence. This procedure will shield the victim from having to be confronted with painful propositions that have not been tested first. The accused will be interrogated in order to establish relevance and credibility and the victim will not attend this session. As far as the corroboration rule is concerned, Rule 63(4) acknowledges that corroboration of evidence is not a requirement for any crime, particularly not with regard to crimes of sexual violence. The special evidentiary rules thus specifically acknowledge that biases against victims of sexual violence, in particular women, are not accepted and that they are as reliable as witnesses as any other witness.

Finally, other special measures that seek to prevent further or increased traumatisation and that need to be mentioned include the manner of questioning, the length of time of the questioning, and allowing a supports person to attend the proceedings. The practice before the Tribunals has shown some discouraging practices towards the treatment of victims of sexual violence during trial proceedings: at times, victims of sexual violence have been confronted with irrelevant and painful questions. It has therefore been suggested that guidelines dealing with the conduct of parties during testimony of a victim of sexual violence need to be established and implemented within both the Tribunals and the Court. Such guidelines are particularly necessary because they will set out one common approach towards the treatment of victims of sexual violence during testimony. Guidelines on the treatment of victims of sexual violence are important because judges, prosecutors and defence counsels come from different regions of the world, have different legal backgrounds (common and civil law), resulting in different approaches towards addressing and dealing with victims in court. It is important that victims of sexual violence are treated with respect for their physical and psychological well-being. Only then will they be willing to testify before the Court and will the record reflect the crimes that have been committed against them.

The ways in which victims of sexual violence have 'participated' at the Tribunals and the challenges faced by the Court to effectuate their participation in a gender-sensitive manner are addressed in Chapter 5. It has sometimes been argued, in respect of the Tribunals, that the Prosecutor should also take care of victims' interests. On a number of occasions, however, the interests of victims of sexual violence and those of the Prosecutor proved not to coincide, this to the detriment of victims of sexual violence. Some mechanisms, such as *amicus curiae* interventions and directly addressing the Office of the Prosecutor by sending letters, have been very helpful in addressing victims concerns and bringing the situation out in the open. However, their effectiveness is dependent on a number of issues, in particular judicial and/or prosecutorial discretion, but also on *amici* who care enough to take up the plight of victims. Furthermore victims themselves have no right to submit victim impact statements to the court.

This situation changed with the establishment of the ICC. For the first time within supranational criminal procedure, victims have the right to participate in the Court's proceedings, often through a legal representative. Victims can now, among other things, make opening and closing statements to tell their story. This will make it possible for victims of sexual violence to have the effects of the rapes recognised and taken into account for sentencing purposes. Victims also have the right to be informed about the progress of the proceedings, may be present when the Court reaches its verdict and, in case of a guilty plea (which in the past has, on occasion, resulted in dropping the sexual violence counts in favour of a guilty plea on the basis of the other counts), the interests of victims are taken into account as well. The overall control of the proceedings, however, remains with the judges of the Court. Yet, the Court has committed itself to having the participation of victims of sexual violence conducted in gender-sensitive ways which take into account the well-being, dignity and safety of the victim (Article 68(1) ICC Statute and Rule 16(5) ICC RPE). For victims of sexual violence, this means, *inter alia*, that they may be represented by a legal representative with experience in dealing with victims of sexual violence and/or trauma counselling. However, a prior condition is that victims of sexual violence are notified about their participatory rights and the gender-sensitive arrangements available to them. Exactly because of the stigmatisation, shame and fear disproportionately attached to these crimes, the Court should give victims of sexual violence extra attention so that they will be able to realise their participatory rights to the fullest extent. For this purpose, the Victims Participation and Reparation Section should, on behalf of the Court, also reach out to international and national women's groups working in the countries concerned.

Part III of this study deals with sexual violence and the legal consequences of the supranational criminal law system, viz., sentencing in cases of sexual violence and reparation to victims of sexual violence. The issue of sentencing is addressed in Chapter 6 and mainly concerns the question of how the judges of the Tribunals had determined the sentences for persons convicted of sexual violence and whether this practice should also be followed by the judges of the ICC. After an elaborate survey of the sentences imposed on a total of 29 ICTY and ICTR accused convicted of rape or any other form of sexual violence to date (in a total of 20 cases), the overall conclusion was drawn that sentences for sexual violence imposed by the Tribunals have been rather lenient in light of the sentencing determinants applied by the two Tribunals.

The first sentencing factor, the sentencing practice in the national courts of the former Yugoslavia and Rwanda, established that specific sentences imposed by the Tribunals for sexual violence as genocide, a crime against humanity or a war crime approximated – or not even approximated – sentences imposed for sexual violence as national crimes, as if the crimes had taken place in peace time situations instead of conflict. Muhimana's recent conviction before the ICTR for rape as genocide and a crime against humanity resulting in life imprisonment for each crime constituted a positive exception. In Rwanda and the former Yugoslavia, sentences for sexual violence in peace time situations were considerably lower than sentences imposed for sexual violence as genocide, a crime against humanity or a war crime. The Tribunal judges repeatedly held that the national prison sentencing practice must be seen as a guiding, not a binding, tool to determine the sentence and the Chambers committed themselves to explaining their reasons if they thought it necessary to diverge from the national sentencing practice. Yet, in most cases examined, no explicit reasons were given for the Chambers' departure from the national sentencing laws or practices for sexual violence as genocide, a crime against humanity or a war crime.

Following ICTY case law, the gravity of the crime, the second sentencing factor mentioned, must be assessed in the light of the individual circumstances and consequences, taking into account quantitatively the number of victims and qualitatively the suffering inflicted on the victims, as well as the form and degree of the participation of the accused in the crimes. Yet, the gravity of rape or other forms of sexual violence was not mentioned at all in most of the judgments, despite the Tribunals' recognition that 'rape is one of the worst sufferings a human being can inflict upon another' and can cause 'victims severe mental and physical pain and suffering'.[1] Out of the 20 ICTY and ICTR cases dealing with sexual violence examined, only 3 cases explicitly refer to the gravity of rape or sexual violence, viz. the *Kvočka et al.*, *Češić* and *Muhimana* cases.

As regards the third sentencing determinant, the aggravating circumstances, it can be said that, in most of the cases, the aggravating circumstances applicable to rape or other forms of sexual violence were not discussed, or only to a limited extent. Again, only 3 cases out of a total of 20 refer to the aggravating circumstances applicable to the accused found guilty for sexually violent conduct (*Kunarac*, *Kovač and Vuković*, *Muhimana* and *Nikolić* cases) and even, in these cases, more aggravating factors could have been found. This is remarkable especially because, when sexual violence is committed in conflict situations, many aggravating factors are usually applicable, *inter alia*: the magnitude of the crimes, the zeal in committing the rapes, including a multiplicity of perpetrators, the heinousness of the sexual violence crimes, the duration of the sexual violence, the discriminatory intent, including the commission of sexual violence on the basis of gender and/or ethnicity, the vulnerability of the victims, the youth of the victims, the repeated nature of the rapes, and the trauma of the surviving victims and others, including the physical and emotional scars inherent to sexual violence, such as pregnancy and HIV/AIDS resulting from the sexual violence, but also social isolation and economic hardship.

Although the difficulties inherent to comparing crimes was recognised before conducting the survey of sentences imposed for sexual violence conduct, the above findings strongly give the impression that the seriousness of rape or other forms of sexual violence as genocide, a crime against humanity or a war crime have, overall, not been fully recognised by the judges of the Tribunals when imposing sentences for sexual violence crimes. Indeed, if the three factors for determining a sentence (national sentencing practice, gravity of the crime, and aggravating circumstances) are not applied correctly, the length of the prison sentence imposed will be lower. If the totality of the criminal conduct is not reflected in the sentence, justice may not prevail for those survivors of sexual violence who had the courage to come forward and testify at the Tribunal. This may, in turn, lead them and other victims of sexual violence not to appear before the Tribunal in any other cases in which charges of sexual violence may feature.

---

[1] Kunarac, Kovač and Vuković Judgment, para. 655. See also Čelebići Judgment, para. 495. In the Stakić Judgment (para. 803), it was held that 'for a woman, rape is by far the ultimate offence, sometimes even worse than death because it brings shame on her'.

It has therefore been argued that the ICC, which starts with a clean slate, should not follow the Tribunals' general approach when it comes to sentencing in cases of sexual violence. For the Court, the sentencing determinants are laid down in Article 78(1) of the ICC Statute, further substantiated by Rule 145 of the ICC RPE. Although the sentencing determinants are comparable to the ones found in the relevant ICTY and ICTR provisions, on paper, the ICC provisions are far more elaborate. As far as aggravating circumstances are concerned, reference is made, *inter alia*, to 'the extent of the damage caused, in particular the harm caused to the victims and their families'. Another example is the reference to the 'commission of the crime for any motive involving discrimination on any of the grounds referred to in article 21, paragraph 3', which includes gender. These factors have largely been overlooked by the Tribunals in cases of sexual violence and should be given extra care by the Court. As the provision is non-exhaustive in nature, other aggravating circumstances, such as the repetitiveness of the rapes, should be taken into account when determining the sentence. Especially where victims have been held in sexual slavery or have become the victims of multiple (gang) rapes, each rape (whether vaginal, anal or oral) should count as one rape and therefore add to the sentence. It is to be hoped that the explicit mention of the aggravating circumstances in Rule 145 contributes to the fact that such circumstances cannot be easily overlooked. As the Court no longer needs to take into account the national sentencing practice, the Court will be able to develop its own sentencing practice. Since the sentencing practice of the ICC may become the standard against which punishment of the most serious crimes in countries around the world will be judged, it is important that the sentences are persuasively substantiated and similar in more or less similar cases from the very beginning. Otherwise, victims of sexual violence may not feel recognised in the harm committed against them and may not want to cooperate with the Court in the long run. If the Court is truly committed to its task of prosecuting sexual violence crimes, it is essential that sexual violence crimes are taken seriously by acknowledging the gravity and aggravating circumstances of the crimes concerned.

The subject of Chapter 7 of this study is to what extent the reparation possibilities at the Court and the Trust Fund for victims and their families can be of help to victims of sexual violence. Despite provisions on restitution of property or proceeds as well as compensation, the issue of reparation to victims has hardly been dealth with by the Tribunals. The judges of the Tribunals have instead always held that their primary task lies with retributive justice, that is, with prosecuting perpetrators for serious violations of international humanitarian law. The ICC's Statute and RPE, on the other hand, contain an elaborate reparation regime (Articles 75 and 79 of the ICC Statute and Rules 94-99 of the ICC RPE). For the first time in history, an international criminal court will be giving victims standing to request and receive reparation. In addition, a Trust Fund for victims and their families has been created which may complement the Court's work where reparation is concerned.

First of all, the special needs of victims of sexual violence were set out in Chapter 7, taking the Rwandan survivors of sexual violence as an example. Today, 11 years after the genocide, survivors of sexual violence, most of them women, are still suffering from the sexual violence committed against them during the 1994 genocide. Many survivors of sexual violence have contracted sexually transmitted diseases, including HIV/AIDS, faced unwanted pregnancies and health complications resulting from botched abortions, and suffered sexual mutilation and other injuries, such as fistulas, uterine problems, vaginal lesions and scarring. In Rwanda, of the surviving women raped, it has been estimated that between 70 and 80 percent have been infected with HIV. In most of the cases, the HIV infection was a result of the multiple rapes they suffered during the genocide. Sadly, the plight of the survivors of sexual violence in Rwanda today is not unique. In many conflicts around the world, where women are subjected to rapes, gang rapes, sexual slavery and other forms of sexual violence, the consequences are equally serious. This includes the first three situations investigated by the Court, viz., Sudan (Darfur), the north-eastern part of the Democratic Republic of Congo and northern Uganda. If no adequate reparation is provided to these women in time, their fate will not be much different from the women in Rwanda today.

In order to help victims of sexual violence, the Court may award reparation to the victim or victims concerned. Given the consequences of sexual violence for its victims, the help needed in most situations will be physical, psychological and medical care, including HIV/AIDS medication, either through a court order on compensation or a court order on rehabilitation. In most cases, the convict's money (complemented with money from the Trust Fund, if needed) will be used by the victim to meet her rehabilitation needs, especially medical and psychological care. If the Court establishes the guilt of the accused for intentionally or foreseeably infecting the victim with HIV/AIDS, HIV/AIDS treatment should as a minimum be included in the reparation order. Furthermore, a reparation order may be awarded both individually and collectively. Especially if the number of victims is high, the Court may be more inclined to order collective awards. In the case of victims of sexual violence, international and/or national agencies that have experience with victims of sexual violence and their needs are the most likely candidates to implement collective care programmes by setting up, for example, treatment centres. In order to reach as many victims as possible, victims need to have knowledge about the reparation possibilities provided by the Court. The Victims Participation and Reparation Section, which is, *inter alia*, charged with the task of notifying victims, faces immense challenges. Reparation will not necessarily be restricted to victims who participated in the trial proceedings. The Chamber may apply for reparation on behalf of victims of sexual violence in situations where they are unable to request reparation themselves. If victims of sexual violence suffer as a result of lack of information on reparation possibilities existent at the Court, and if the sexual violence has been so widespread and abhorrent that reparation is clearly needed, the Chamber could (and should) make such a request on their behalf.

However, the main difficulty with reparation awards is that they are only awarded once the accused has been pronounced guilty, and victims of sexual violence may need physical, psychological and medical support much earlier. For this reason, interim relief should be offered by the Trust Fund. The Draft Regulations of the Trust Fund contains provisions for this purpose, as it stipulates that physical and psychological rehabilitation and support may be provided already in the investigative phase (Draft Rule 50). In addition, in exceptional circumstances, such services may also be provided where, in the interest of justice, the Prosecutor decides not to investigate and in situations where national courts have started proceedings against the accused in light of the complementarity principle, but where reparation for victims is unavailable (Draft Rule 51). To have any meaningful impact on victims' lives, it is important for the Trust Fund to act as soon as possible. It is not unlikely that survivors of sexual violence are already in bad health by the time the Prosecutor, for instance, initiates an investigation: at that time, the conflict may have been going on for weeks, months or even years. This means that the Trust Fund will have to negotiate agreements with humanitarian organisations in the field that are able to reach and work with survivors of sexual violence. Collective projects for the benefit of victims of sexual violence could possibly include setting up centres with expertise in physical, psychological and medical care, including HIV/AIDS treatment. A school or income generating projects could also be set up for victims and for their children. Children may especially be in need of such support if the mother is disabled, has died or will die as a result of the diseases she may have contracted as a result of the sexual violence. Collective projects will allow the Trust Fund to reach many more victims of sexual violence than the Court, as the Court will usually focus on certain crimes, areas and perpetrators and may therefore ignore victims of sexual violence not affected by the Prosecutor's prosecutorial strategy. In addition, the Trust Fund may be able to reach unidentified victims of sexual violence who, for instance, due to stigmatisation, fear or trauma, were not able to request reparation at the Court themselves. The establishment of the Trust Fund for victims and their families may therefore, to some extent, be able to address the needs of victims of sexual violence on a wider scale. Much will depend on the next Assembly of States Parties' session in November-December 2005, in which the scope of the activities of the Trust Fund will be decided upon. With the Rwanda situation still fresh in mind, it is strongly suggested that interim relief by the Trust Fund is accepted as a means to meet the needs of victims of sexual violence.

In this study, it was concluded that, on the whole, the supranational criminal law system provides sufficient possibilities to comprehensively prosecute sexual violence crimes. However, in order to do so, the Court as well as the Tribunals should take into account such factors as the realities of the crimes, the respectful treatment of victims of sexual violence in the proceedings, the seriousness of the crimes and the needs of victims of sexual violence. The practice before the Tribunals, however, has not always sufficiently taken these factors into account. Yet, it is no longer really a question of having the possibility to prosecute sexual violence within the supranational criminal law context. It is rather a question of putting the law into effect in an appropriate way.

NEDERLANDSE SAMENVATTING (DUTCH SUMMARY)

SUPRANATIONALE STRAFVERVOLGING VAN SEKSUEEL GEWELD

Het Internationale Strafhof en de Praktijk van het Joegoslavië- en het Rwanda-tribunaal

Het onderwerp van deze studie is de supranationale strafvervolging van seksueel geweld. Om precies te zijn, hoe seksueel geweld kan of zou moeten worden vervolgd door het Internationale Strafhof (*International Criminal Court*, ICC) en met duidelijke verwijzingen naar de praktijk op dit gebied zoals gebezigd door het Joegoslavië-tribunaal (*International Criminal Tribunal for the former Yugoslavia*, ICTY) en het Rwanda-tribunaal (*International Criminal Tribunal for Rwanda*, ICTR). Om een zo volledig mogelijk beeld te geven van de rol die strafrechtelijke vervolging van seksueel geweld zou kunnen spelen in het supranationale strafrechtssysteem, is dit boek verdeeld in vier delen. Deel I behandelt seksueel geweld in het supranationale strafrecht, deel II seksueel geweld in supranationale strafvordering, deel III seksueel geweld en de juridische consequenties voortvloeiend uit het supranationale strafrechtssysteem. Deel IV geeft aanbevelingen voor een completere supranationale strafrechtelijke vervolging van seksueel geweld. De centrale vraag is of het supranationale strafrechtsysteem, een relatief nieuw verschijnsel, adequaat is vanuit het oogpunt van de slachtoffers van seksueel geweld. Het ICC Statuut, haar *Rules of Procedure and Evidence* (RPE) en de *Elements of Crimes* (EoC), samen met en vergeleken met de Statuten van het ICTY en het ICTR, hun RPE en jurisprudentie, zijn de hoofdonderdelen van het onderzoek.

Deel I van dit onderzoek behandelt dus seksueel geweld in het supranationale strafrecht. In het ICC Statuut worden verkrachting, seksuele slavernij, gedwongen prostitutie, gedwongen zwangerschap, gedwongen sterilisatie en enige andere vorm van seksueel geweld uitdrukkelijk strafbaar gesteld als misdaden tegen de menselijkheid en oorlogsmisdaden (respectievelijk artikel 7 en 8). Met uitzondering van de misdaden verkrachting en gedwongen prostitutie werden deze specifieke seksuele geweldsmisdrijven nog niet eerder opgenomen in een supranationaal strafrechtelijk verdrag. De vraag die zich aandiende was: wat zijn de definities van seksuele geweldsmisdrijven in de context van het supranationale strafrechtsysteem, of wat zouden deze moeten zijn? Hoewel de EoC van het ICC een gedetailleerd overzicht bevatten van de elementen van deze seksuele geweldsmisdrijven, zijn deze EoC (officieel) niet bindend.

Wat betreft de definitie van verkrachting, concentreert de definitie in de EoC van het ICC zich niet op afwezigheid van toestemming, maar op dwang, dreiging met dwang, dwangactie of een coërcitieve omgeving. Inderdaad is afwezigheid van toestemming als element van het misdrijf verkrachting (of van ieder ander seksueel geweldsmisdrijf) niet op haar plaats in de context van het supranationale strafrecht, gezien de gewelddadige en onderdrukkende situaties waarin verkrachtingen plaatsvinden bij genocide, misdaden tegen de menselijkheid of gewapende conflicten, en daarom zou het moeten worden afgekeurd. Ongeacht hoe de aanklager de vraag stelt ("Stemde u erin toe?" of "Gebeurde het tegen uw wil?"), dergelijke vragen kunnen slachtoffers van verkrachting beledigen of verder traumatiseren, vooral als deze vragen gesteld worden nadat het slachtoffer al uit de doeken heeft gedaan onder welke dwingende omstandigheden het seksueel geweld werd toegebracht. Indien reeds is vastgesteld dat een misdrijf werd gepleegd, zijn vragen over toestemming irrelevant. Zoals uitgelegd in deel II is dit nog steeds mogelijk in die (waarschijnlijk) zeldzame gevallen waarin de verdediging instemming wil aanvoeren, maar relevantie en ontvankelijkheid van dergelijk bewijs moet eerst worden vastgesteld in een *in camera* procedure om het slachtoffer pijnlijke confrontaties te besparen. Onder de elementen van het misdrijf "verkrachting" vallen een aantal verboden seksuele handelingen die verkrachting definiëren; deze handelingen zijn vooral gericht op penetratie. Dit maakt het mogelijk om verkrachting te onderscheiden van andere vormen van seksueel geweld, zoals gedwongen masturbatie en doet recht aan 'werkelijke verkrachtingsslachtoffers' volgens zowel de definitie van het ICC als van hen zelf. Betoogd wordt dat de ICC definitie van verkrachting over het algemeen de realiteit van het misdrijf in tijd van genocide, gewapend conflict, of misdaden tegen de menselijkheid goed benadert en daarom zou moeten worden gezien als een modeldefinitie van verkrachting in het supranationale strafrecht. Hierom zou het besluit over de instemminggerichte definitie van verkrachting zoals genomen door het Hof van Beroep in de zaak *Kunarac, Kovač en Vuković* niet door het ICC gevolgd moeten worden. Als verkrachting niet gedefinieerd wordt in overeenstemming met de aard van het misdrijf, zouden slachtoffers terughoudend kunnen zijn om zich bekend te maken en voor het Hof een verklaring af te leggen.

Het misdrijf van seksuele slavernij is in de EoC gedefinieerd volgens dezelfde lijnen als slavernij, namelijk "de uitoefening van enige of alle macht verbonden aan het eigendomsrecht over één of meerdere personen," met de toevoeging dat de beschuldigde het slachtoffer dwong om deel te namen aan één of meerdere seksuele handelingen. Hoewel de definitie de indruk zou kunnen wekken dat er een commercieel belang in het spel is, omdat "eigendom" zou kunnen worden opgevat in termen van kopen en verkopen, maakt een voetnoot bij het eerste element van seksuele slavernij het volledig duidelijk dat seksuele slavernij ook "dwangarbeid," "gedwongen onderwerping (inclusief gedwongen huwelijk)" en "mensenhandel, vooral vrouwen en kinderen" omvat. Er kan worden geconcludeerd dat seksuele slavernij niet noodzakelijk hoeft te leiden tot financieel voordeel voor de dader, noch dat het slachtoffer op een bepaalde plaats vastgehouden hoeft te worden. Het misdrijf van gedwongen prostitutie daarentegen richt zich voornamelijk op financieel voordeel. In de meeste gevallen kan de verrichte daad beter worden aangeklaagd als seksuele slavernij dan als gedwongen prostitutie. In tijden dat genocide, misdaden tegen de menselijkheid en oorlogsmisdrijven worden gepleegd, worden vrouwen vaak gevangen genomen voor seksuele doeleinden zonder dat daar enig financieel gewin van komt. Situaties die niet vallen onder seksuele slavernij kunnen niettemin worden vervolgd als zijnde gedwongen prostitutie. De misdaad van gedwongen zwangerschap was in de EoC niet noemenswaardig veranderd, vergeleken met de definitie van deze misdaad in het ICC Statuut. Het moet nog blijken hoe deze misdaad wordt gezien door de rechters van het ICC, maar er moet worden opgemerkt dat een nauwe interpretatie (zoals het eisen dat de gijzeling van een vrouw gedurende een bepaalde tijd moet hebben plaatsgevonden) zeker geen recht zal doen aan de realiteit van gedwongen zwangerschap in tijden van genocide, misdaden tegen de menselijkheid of gewapend conflict. De misdaad van gedwongen sterilisatie kan ook bepaalde vormen van seksueel geweld omvatten, zoals wanneer vrouwen dusdanig bruut verkracht worden dat hun voortplantingssysteem totaal vernietigd wordt. De overblijvende categorie "enig andere vorm van seksueel geweld van vergelijkbare ernst" moet niet strak gehanteerd te worden, omdat dit tot de conclusie zou kunnen leiden dat deze misdaden een vorm van penetratie vereisen. Een dergelijke interpretatie is ongewenst en zou de jurisprudentie van de Tribunalen op dit gebied negeren, waarin bijvoorbeeld gedwongen ontkleding werd vervolgd onder "andere inhumane activiteiten." Tot slot maakt het ICC Statuut het mogelijk dat de verkrachting van een vrouw uitsluitend vanwege haar geslacht vervolgd kan worden als het misdrijf "vervolging" onder misdaden tegen de menselijkheid. Het moet worden opgemerkt dat verkrachting met als doel het overdragen van het HIV-virus op het slachtoffer niet als zodanig genoemd wordt in het ICC Statuut, ondanks de vele gevallen daarvan, en zou daarom moeten worden toegevoegd aan de lijst van specifieke seksuele geweldsmisdrijven.

Naast het aanklagen van verdachten specifiek voor misdadig seksueel geweld zoals hierboven omschreven, kunnen vervolgingen door het ICC ook plaatsvinden voor niet-specifieke seksuele geweldsmisdrijven indien dit het volledige gedrag van een aangeklaagde beter in beeld brengt. Van speciaal belang is marteling als een oorlogsmisdaad, dat een ander doelgericht element inbrengt. Verkrachting kan bijvoorbeeld worden vervolgd voor de oorlogsmisdaden verkrachting én marteling, het laatste wanneer de verkrachtingen werden uitgevoerd ter vernedering, ter intimidatie, als straf, of ter discriminatie op basis van geslacht. Terwijl de aanklager van het ICTY en ICTR – bij gebrek aan een uitgebreide lijst specifieke seksuele geweldsmisdrijven, zoals die inmiddels gevonden kan worden in het ICC Statuut – min of meer gedwongen werd om seksueel geweld onder de niet-specifieke seksuele geweldsmisdrijven te scharen, heeft de ICC-aanklager beide opties. Hij kan zowel op niet-specifieke gronden als op specifieke gronden seksuele geweldsmisdrijven aanklagen, waarbij de laatste de voorkeur verdient bij de vervolgingsstrategie voor seksueel geweld. Het vervolgen van seksueel geweld als seksueel geweld doet beter recht aan de aard van de misdaad.

Wat betreft de misdaad van genocide (artikel 6 van het ICC Statuut) omvat de definitie daarvan niet verkrachting of enig andere vorm van seksueel geweld. De EoC noemen verkrachting en ander seksueel geweld wel in een voetnoot (met dezelfde status als een element), als verduidelijking dat deze misdaden allen het doel kunnen hebben om "ernstige lichamelijke of geestelijke schade toe te brengen." Omdat de specifieke seksuele geweldsmisdrijven zoals vastgelegd in de artikelen over misdaden tegen de menselijkheid en oorlogsmisdaden (verkrachting, seksuele slavernij, gedwongen prostitutie, gedwongen zwangerschap, gedwongen sterilisatie en enig andere vorm van seksueel geweld) evengoed kunnen worden vervolgd als genocide zouden deze ook moeten worden verplaatst naar de definitie van genocide. Een dergelijke expliciete opname van seksuele geweldsmisdrijven in het kader van genocide zou de wetgeving op supranationaal strafrechtniveau op één lijn brengen met die voor misdaden tegen de menselijkheid en oorlogsmisdaden. Hoewel vervolging voor seksueel geweld volgens de vijf onderverdelingen van genocide mogelijk is, wat de praktijk van het ICTY en het ICTR heeft laten zien, zou een uitdrukkelijke verwijzing naar de specifieke seksuele geweldsmisdrijven deze misdrijven beter aanduiden als genocidale misdrijven op zichzelf. Bovendien zou de definitie van genocide moeten worden aangepast met een verwijzing naar groepsvernietiging gebaseerd op geslacht.

Voor een succesvolle vervolging van seksueel geweld moet aan alle elementen die gemeenschappelijk zijn voor genocide, misdaden tegen de menselijkheid en oorlogsmisdaden voldaan zijn om verkrachting of enig andere vorm van seksueel geweld als een internationale misdaad te laten gelden. Oogmerk (een vereiste bij het misdrijf genocide) kan bijvoorbeeld worden gevonden in toespraken van de verdachte waarin hij oproept tot verkrachting van de vrouwen van een bepaalde groep, of in uitspraken van de verkrachters tijdens de verkrachtingen. Voor wat betreft misdaden tegen de menselijkheid, is in jurisprudentie van zowel het ICTY als het ICTR vastgelegd dat verkrachting of enig andere vorm van seksueel geweld niet hoeft te zijn gepleegd op een grootschalige of systematische manier; het is voldoende wanneer de misdaad gepleegd is als onderdeel van een grootschalige of systematische aanval. De gemeenschappelijke elementen van oorlogsmisdaden vereisen dat het wangedrag plaatsvond in de context van, en geassocieerd met een internationaal of nationaal gewapend conflict, en dat de verdachte op de hoogte was van feitelijke omstandigheden die het bestaan van het gewapende conflict bevestigden. Toch is er een ongelukkig element toegevoegd aan de voorwaarden voor oorlogsmisdaden: er kan alleen voor vervolgd worden als ze zijn gepleegd op een grootschalige en systematische manier. Dit zou geïsoleerde gevallen van serieus seksueel geweld buiten de jurisdictie van het Hof kunnen houden. Het is echter aan te raden dat ieder serieus geval van verkrachting, seksuele slavernij, of iedere andere vorm van seksueel geweld door het Hof aangepakt kan worden indien het binnen haar mandaat valt.

Om seksueel geweld toe te kunnen schrijven aan de beklaagde moet het verband tussen de misdaad en de beklaagde worden aangetoond. De praktijk van het ICTY en het ICTR heeft laten zien dat dit niet altijd eenvoudig is. Echter, twee mogelijkheden om de criminele aansprakelijkheid van de beklaagde aan te tonen lijken niet maximaal te zijn benut. Op de eerste plaats en speciaal in het geval van misdaden tegen de menselijkheid, kan strafbaar leidinggeven een uitstekende mogelijkheid zijn om iemand te vervolgen wegens seksueel geweld. Als seksueel geweld zo grootschalig of systematisch was opgezet dat het nagenoeg onmogelijk was om het niet op te merken, kan worden aangenomen dat de hoogst verantwoordelijke persoon er van wist of er van had moeten weten dat zijn ondergeschikten tot doel hadden om seksuele geweldsmisdrijven te gaan plegen terwijl hij of zij niets ondernomen heeft om dit geweld te stoppen of de plegers te straffen. Ten tweede kan het concept van een gezamenlijke criminele onderneming handvatten geven om seksueel geweld effectief te vervolgen. Een persoon kan voor seksueel geweld veroordeeld worden via de derde variant van deelname aan een criminele onderneming als dit geweld een natuurlijk en voorspelbaar gevolg was van de gezamenlijke criminele onderneming.

Het van kracht worden van het ICC Statuut, waarmee specifieke seksuele geweldsmisdrijven erkend worden als zware overtredingen van gemeenschappelijk Artikel 3, misdaden tegen de menselijkheid en (via de voetnoot in de EoC) genocide, nodigt uit tot het bijstellen van gelijkaardige verdragen, namelijk de Genocide Conventie uit 1948 en de Conventies van Genève uit 1949 (met de addities uit 1977). Zulke bijstellingen zouden verdragsrecht en supranationaal strafrecht met elkaar in overeenstemming brengen en verder bijdragen aan de erkenning van de ernst van seksuele geweldsmisdrijven. Alles bij elkaar genomen geven het ICC Statuut en de EoC een werkbaar raamwerk om seksueel geweld te vervolgen op het niveau van de supranationale strafrechtwetgeving. Zolang de misdaden worden beschouwd in samenhang met de realiteit van de misdrijven, kan het ICC een sterke boodschap uitdragen dat seksuele geweldsmisdrijven serieus worden genomen. Dit, op zijn beurt, zal de bereidheid van de slachtoffers van seksueel geweld bevorderen om aangifte te doen en te getuigen voor het Hof. Uiteindelijk gaat het niet meer zozeer om het strafbaar stellen van seksueel geweld, maar om het handhaven van de wet.

Deel II van deze studie richt zich op seksueel geweld in supranationale strafvordering, voornamelijk de status van slachtoffers van seksueel geweld als getuigen en als deelnemers aan ICC-procedures. Het eerste probleem dat wordt behandeld in hoofdstuk 4 gaat over de vraag of de “beschermende en speciale maatregelen,” aangeboden door het Hof, rekening houden met de behoeften van slachtoffers van seksueel geweld, zonder het recht van de beklaagden op een eerlijk proces aan te tasten. In tegenstelling tot de meeste andere slachtoffers, hebben slachtoffers van seksueel geweld vaak niet alleen te maken met aantasting van hun waardigheid en privacy, maar ook met die van hun veiligheid.

Eén categorie beschermende maatregelen betreft vertrouwelijkheidsmaatregelen die tot doel hebben om de getuige te beschermen tegen het publiek en de pers. Artikel 68(2) van het ICC Statuut geeft slachtoffers van seksueel geweld automatisch het recht om hun getuigenis *in camera* af te leggen, of om het op een andere manier te presenteren zoals via video conferencing of een gesloten TV-circuit. Hoewel Artikel 68(2) het Hof de mogelijkheid geeft om dit recht niet toe te staan, wordt geadviseerd dat het Hof al deze beschermende maatregelen automatisch toestaat indien het slachtoffer van seksueel geweld daar zelf om vraagt. Dit vraagt om een actieve rol van het Hof om de getuige correct te informeren over de beschikbare bescherming die zij kan genieten. Bepaalde maatregelen zoals video conferencing kunnen ook uitkomst bieden als een slachtoffer fysiek niet in staat is om voor het Hof een getuigenis af te leggen. Omdat slachtoffers van seksueel geweld mogelijk ernstige aandoeningen hebben opgelopen, zoals HIV/AIDS, kan video conferencing wellicht een uitkomst voor een aantal van hen bieden. *In camera* verhoren en video conferencing worden normaliter niet gezien als een inbreuk op het recht van de aangeklaagde op een eerlijk en openbaar proces. Het recht van de aangeklaagde om de getuige te verhoren wordt in beide situaties behouden, omdat alleen het publiek en de pers van de verhoren worden uitgesloten, niet de beklaagde en zijn verdediging. In de praktijk hebben slachtoffers van seksueel geweld echter regelmatig geleden onder bedreigingen en afwijzingen van familie en bekenden na hun verklaring voor het Tribunaal, en dit kan ook worden verwacht met betrekking tot zaken voor het Hof. Dit leidt tot de vraag of beschermende maatregelen ook werkelijk effect hebben. Op zijn minst moeten de slachtoffers geïnformeerd worden over de mogelijke gevaren van het afleggen van een getuigenis, hetgeen niet altijd gedaan is door de Tribunalen. Voor slachtoffers van seksueel geweld heeft bekendmaking van hun identiteit niet alleen invloed op hun veiligheid, maar ook kan het hun sociale status beïnvloeden.

Hoewel het niet duidelijk is welke mening de oprichters van het ICC hadden over anonimiserende maatregelen (bescherming tegen de aangeklaagde), kan het Hof volledige anonimiteit aanvaarden volgens regel 88. Als speciale procedures worden gevolgd, zoals in het geval van de *Tadić Protective Measures Decision*, dan kan anonimiteit worden toegekend zonder de rechten van de verdachte aan te tasten, in het bijzonder zijn recht om de getuige te horen of te laten verhoren. Europese jurisprudentie heeft bovendien uitgewezen dat een veroordeling niet mag worden gebaseerd op slechts (of grotendeels) een anonieme getuigenis.Voor slachtoffers van seksueel geweld betekent dit dat, zolang beschermende maatregelen hen niet beschermen tegen bedreigingen en stigmatisering, ze geen aanklacht zullen indienen en dat aan hen geen recht zal worden gedaan, ondanks specifieke strafrechtwetgeving aangaande seksueel geweld. Overigens is het minder belangrijk voor een aangeklaagde om de identiteit van een slachtoffer te kennen wanneer het seksuele geweld niet in zijn bijzijn werd gepleegd, dan wanneer hijzelf erbij betrokken was. Verder was ten tijde van het misdrijf de identiteit van het slachtoffer van geen belang voor de dader: de meeste slachtoffers worden lukraak gekozen. Zolang alternatieven voor anonimiteit, zoals getuigenbeschermingsprogramma's, slachtoffers van seksueel geweld niet beschermen tegen bedreigingen en afwijzingen uit hun eigen omgeving, van familie, of van hun partner, moet anonimiteit door het Hof worden beschouwd als een waardevol beschermingsinstrument.

Een derde categorie speciale en beschermingsmaatregelen probeert de slachtoffer-getuige zo min mogelijk extra traumatisering te bezorgen. Het vermijden van een directe confrontatie met de beklaagde voor het Hof is zo'n maatregel en deze kan bestaan uit een gesloten TV-circuit, een kamerscherm, of tijdelijke verwijdering van de beklaagde uit de rechtszaal. Dergelijke maatregelen worden normaliter niet gezien als een inbreuk op de rechten van de beklaagde, die de getuige nog steeds kan horen en zien via de TV. Een andere mogelijkheid is het afleggen van een van te voren opgenomen videoverklaring, waarbij beide partijen de mogelijkheid moeten hebben gehad om de getuige te horen gedurende de opname. Deze methode kan de getuige de druk van een herhaalde verklaring voor het Hof besparen. Een derde mogelijkheid maakt gebruik van speciale bewijslastregels aangaande seksueel geweld, die opname van instemming en eerder of later seksueel contact in het bewijsmateriaal beperken en zo beogen om de hertraumatisering van het slachtoffer voor het Hof te voorkomen (70-72 ICC RPE). Gezien de aard van de misdaden en de situatie in welke ze werden begaan, is het vrijwel onmogelijk om een situatie te verzinnen waarbij dergelijk bewijs door de verdediging van de beklaagde kan worden aangedragen. Toch laat regel 71 (eerder of later seksueel contact) het toe om bewijs te leveren voor eerder of later seksueel contact, en dit betekent een lastige tegenstelling met regel 96(iv) van de ICTY en ICTR RPE die eerder seksueel contact als verdediging niet toestaat. In die (waarschijnlijk zeldzame) gevallen waarin de verdediging instemming wil aanvoeren, zou een hoorzitting achter gesloten deuren eerst de relevantie en geldigheid van zulk bewijs moeten vaststellen. Een dergelijke procedure beschermt een slachtoffer tegen confrontatie met pijnlijke stellingen die niet eerder zijn aangevoerd. De beklaagde zal worden ondervraagd om relevantie en betrouwbaarheid vast te stellen terwijl het slachtoffer niet aanwezig is. Voor wat betreft de corroboratieregel, regel 63(4) bevestigt dat corroboratie van bewijsmateriaal niet verplicht is voor enig misdrijf, in het bijzonder niet voor seksuele geweldsmisdrijven. De speciale bewijslastregels voor slachtoffers van seksueel geweld, met name voor vrouwen, maken duidelijk dat getuigenissen van deze slachtoffers even betrouwbaar moeten worden geacht als enig andere getuigenis.

Als laatste zijn er nog enige maatregelen die verdere traumatisering van het slachtoffer proberen te beperken, zoals de wijze van ondervraging, de duur van de ondervraging en toestemming om een ondersteuner bij het proces toe te laten. De praktijk van de Tribunalen heeft een aantal vervelende manieren laten zien om slachtoffers van seksueel geweld te behandelen; zo werden slachtoffers soms geconfronteerd met irrelevante maar pijnlijke vragen. Daarom zijn in dit boek aanbevelingen gedaan voor richtlijnen inzake het gedrag van alle partijen tijdens de getuigenis van een slachtoffer van seksueel geweld, zowel voor beide Tribunalen als voor het Hof. Dergelijke richtlijnen zijn vooral nodig, omdat ze een gemeenschappelijke aanpak van getuigenissen van slachtoffers van seksueel geweld bevorderen. Ze zijn onontbeerlijk, omdat rechters, aanklagers en advocaten uit verschillende delen van de wereld komen, verschillende juridische achtergronden hebben en dus verschillend omgaan met slachtoffers voor het Hof. Het is belangrijk dat slachtoffers van seksueel geweld worden behandeld met respect voor hun fysiek en psychologisch welzijn. Alleen dan zullen ze toestemmen in een getuigenis voor het Hof en zullen de misdaden die tegen hen gepleegd zijn correct in de annalen terechtkomen.

Hoofdstuk 5 behandelt de manier waarop slachtoffers van seksueel geweld hebben "deelgenomen" aan de Tribunalen, en de uitdagingen waarvoor het Hof zich geplaatst ziet om hen op een geslachtsvriendelijke manier tot deelname uit te nodigen. Er wordt soms op gewezen dat de aanklager rekening zou moeten houden met de belangen van de slachtoffers, maar in verschillende (Tribunaal) gevallen bleken de belangen van de aanklager en de slachtoffers dusdanig uiteen te lopen dat de slachtoffers zeer benadeeld werden. Sommige methoden, zoals interventies van de *amicus curiae* en het rechtstreeks aanschrijven van het Bureau van de Aanklager, zijn erg behulpzaam geweest bij het oplossen van de problemen van de slachtoffers en het publiekelijk aankaarten van de situatie. De effectiviteit van deze methoden hangt echter van een aantal zaken af, voornamelijk van de discretionaire bevoegdheid van de rechters en/of de aanklagers, maar ook van *amici* die zich het lot van de slachtoffers aantrekken. De slachtoffers zelf hebben niet het recht om 'victim impact statements' voor te leggen aan het Tribunaal.
Deze situatie veranderde bij de oprichting van het ICC. Het is voor de eerste keer in supranationale strafrechtszittingen dat slachtoffers het recht hebben om te participeren in de zittingen van het Hof, meestal via een juridisch vertegenwoordiger. Zo kunnen slachtoffers openings- en sluitwoorden uitspreken om hun verhaal kwijt te kunnen. Dit maakt het mogelijk voor slachtoffers van seksueel geweld om de effecten van de verkrachtingen erkend te krijgen en mee te laten tellen bij de veroordelingen. Slachtoffers hebben ook recht om de voortgang van de zittingen te vernemen, mogen aanwezig zijn bij de uitspraak van het Hof, en in geval van een schuldbekentenis (die in het verleden soms leidde tot het laten vallen van de aanklacht voor seksueel geweld in ruil voor een bekentenis voor de andere misdrijven) wordt met de belangen van slachtoffers ook rekening gehouden. De algehele sturing van de zittingen blijft echter in handen van de rechters van het Hof, maar het Hof heeft zich verplicht om de deelname van slachtoffers van seksueel geweld op een geslachtsvriendelijke manier te organiseren en zorg te dragen voor het welbevinden, het eergevoel en de veiligheid van de slachtoffers (artikel 86(1) ICC Statuut en regel 16(5) ICC RPE). Voor slachtoffers van seksueel geweld betekent dit onder andere dat ze mogen worden vertegenwoordigd door een juridisch afgevaardigde met ervaring op het gebied van seksuele geweldszaken en/of traumatherapie. Het is belangrijk dat slachtoffers van seksueel geweld vooraf worden geïnformeerd over hun deelnamerechten en de geslachtsgevoelige arrangementen die hen ter beschikking staan. Precies vanwege de disproportionele stigmatisering, schaamte en angst die aan deze misdaden verbonden zijn, moet het Hof slachtoffers van seksueel geweld extra aandacht geven, zodat zij hun deelnamerechten ten volle kunnen uitoefenen. Voor dit doel zou de *Victims Participation and Reparation Section* uit naam van het Hof contact moeten leggen met nationale en internationale vrouwengroeperingen in de betrokken landen.

Deel III van deze studie behandelt seksueel geweld en de juridische consequenties van het supranationale strafrechtsysteem, in het bijzonder strafoplegging in het geval van seksueel geweld en schadeloosstelling van slachtoffers van seksueel geweld. Strafoplegging wordt beschreven in hoofdstuk 6, dat vooral aansnijdt hoe de rechters van de Tribunalen de strafmaat bepaalden in het geval van een veroordeling voor seksueel geweld, en of deze werkwijze ook gevolgd moet worden door de rechters van het ICC. Na een uitgebreid onderzoek van de veroordelingen van in totaal 29 door het ICTY en ICTR berechte verdachten van verkrachting of een andere vorm van seksueel geweld (in totaal 20 zaken) wordt geconcludeerd dat de strafmaat voor seksueel geweld, opgelegd door de Tribunalen, aan de lichte kant is, gezien de strafmaatbepalingen die ze volgen.

Onderzoek naar de eerste strafmaatbepaling, de geldende strafrechtspraktijk van de nationale rechtbanken in het voormalige Joegoslavië en Rwanda, wees uit dat straffen uitgesproken door de Tribunalen voor seksueel geweld als genocide, misdaden tegen de menselijkheid of oorlogsmisdaden, de straffen die werden uitgesproken voor seksuele misdrijven in voormalig Joegoslavië en Rwanda in vredestijd benaderden, maar vaak zelfs ook nog lager waren. Muhimana's recente veroordeling door het ICTR voor verkrachting als genocide en misdaden tegen de menselijkheid, leidend tot levenslange gevangenisstraf voor iedere misdaad, was hierop een uitzondering. In voormalig Joegoslavië en Rwanda waren straffen voor seksueel geweld in vredestijd aanzienlijk lager dan die voor seksueel geweld als genocide, misdaad tegen de menselijkheid of oorlogsmisdaad. De rechters van de Tribunalen stelden regelmatig dat de nationale strafpraktijk moest worden gezien als een richtlijn; niet als een bindende bepaling. De rechters beloofden daarbij uit te leggen waarom ze in voorkomende gevallen afweken van de nationale strafmaat. In de meeste gevallen werd echter niet uitgelegd waarom van de nationale strafmaat werd afgeweken.

Volgens ICTY-jurisprudentie moet de ernst van het misdrijf, de tweede strafmaatbepaling, gezien worden in het licht van individuele omstandigheden en consequenties, het aantal slachtoffers en hun lijden, en de betrokkenheid van de aangeklaagde bij de misdaden. Toch werd de ernst van verkrachting of andere vormen van seksueel geweld niet genoemd in de meeste vonnissen, ondanks de stelling van de Tribunalen dat "verkrachting één van de ernstigste vormen van lijden is die een mens een ander mens kan aandoen" en "bij slachtoffers ernstige geestelijke en fysieke pijn en lijden" kan veroorzaken.[1] Van de 20 bekeken ICTY- en ICTR-gevallen die over seksueel geweld gingen, noemden slechts 3 de ernst van verkrachting of seksueel geweld, namelijk de zaken *Kvočka et al.*, *Češić* en *Muhimana.*

Wat betreft de derde strafmaatbepaling, de verzwarende omstandigheden, kan worden gezegd dat ze in de meeste gevallen niet of nauwelijks genoemd werden. Slechts in 3 van de 20 zaken werd gewag gemaakt van verzwarende omstandigheden bij seksueel geweld (*Kunarac, Kovač en Vuković, Muhimana* en *Nikolić*) en zelfs in deze zaken hadden meer verzwarende omstandigheden aangevoerd kunnen worden. Dit is des te opmerkelijker, omdat, vooral wanneer seksueel geweld tot uiting komt in

[1] Kunarac, Kovač en Vuković uitspraak, paragraaf 655. Zie ook Čelebići uitspraak, paragraaf 495. In de Stakić uitspraak (paragraaf 803) werd gesteld dat "voor een vrouw, verkrachting met afstand de ultieme misdaad is, soms zelfs erger dan de dood, omdat hij met schaamte gepaard gaat."

conflictsituaties, er zoveel verzwarende omstandigheden zijn, waaronder: de schaal van de misdaden, de gedrevenheid bij de verkrachtingen waarbij inbegrepen meerdere daders, de gruwelijkheid van de seksuele geweldsmisdrijven, de duur van de misdrijven, het discriminerende karakter waaronder het aandoen van geweld op basis van geslacht of etnische afkomst, de kwetsbaarheid van de slachtoffers, hun jeugdigheid, het herhalen van de verkrachtingen en het trauma van de slachtoffers en anderen, zoals de fysieke en emotionele littekens die horen bij seksueel geweld, waaronder zwangerschap, HIV/AIDS-besmetting, sociale isolatie en emotioneel lijden.

Hoewel de moeilijkheden van het vergelijken van misdaden bekend waren voordat de veroordelingen vergeleken werden, geven de resultaten de sterke indruk dat de ernst van verkrachting of een andere vorm van seksueel geweld als genocide, misdaad tegen de menselijkheid of oorlogsmisdaad over het algemeen niet werd erkend door de rechters van de Tribunalen bij het opleggen van straffen voor seksuele geweldsmisdrijven. En inderdaad, als de drie richtlijnen voor de strafmaat (nationale strafrechtspraktijk, ernst van het misdrijf en verzwarende omstandigheden) niet correct worden toegepast, dan resulteert dat in een kortere opgelegde gevangenisstraf. Als het geheel van het misdadige gedrag niet voldoende wordt gereflecteerd in de strafmaat, wordt geen recht gedaan aan de slachtoffers van seksueel geweld die de moed hadden om aangifte te doen en op het Tribunaal te getuigen. Dit, op zijn beurt, kan leiden tot nog minder animo om voor het Tribunaal te verschijnen in andere gevallen.

Om voornoemde redenen is in dit onderzoek voorgesteld dat het ICC, beginnend met een schone lei, niet de aanpak van de Tribunalen moet volgen als het gaat over strafopleggingen voor seksueel geweld. De strafmaatbepalingen voor het Hof staan beschreven in artikel 78(1) van het ICC Statuut en zijn verder uitgewerkt in regel 145 van het ICC RPE. Hoewel de bepalingen vergelijkbaar zijn met die voor het ICTY het ICTR, zijn ze voor het ICC veel uitgebreider, op papier althans. Voor zover het verzwarende omstandigheden betreft, wordt onder andere verwezen naar "de omvang van de aangerichte schade, in het bijzonder de schade aan de slachtoffers en hun families." Een ander voorbeeld is de verwijzing naar "het begaan van een misdaad waarbij gediscrimineerd wordt op grond van artikel 21, paragraaf 3," die o.a. geslacht bevat. Deze factoren werden grotendeels genegeerd door de Tribunalen waar het ging om seksueel geweld en zouden extra aandacht van het Hof moeten krijgen. Omdat de bepaling niet uitputtend is, moeten extra verzwarende omstandigheden, zoals herhaaldelijke verkrachtingen, worden meegenomen bij het bepalen van de strafmaat. In het bijzonder wanneer slachtoffers ter seksuele slavernij werden vastgehouden, of het slachtoffer werden van meerdere (groeps)verkrachtingen dient iedere individuele verkrachting, zij het vaginaal, oraal of anaal, als zodanig mee te tellen bij de bepaling van de strafmaat. Het is te hopen dat de uitdrukkelijke opname van verzwarende omstandigheden in regel 145 er toe zal leiden dat dergelijke omstandigheden niet gemakkelijk over het hoofd worden gezien. Omdat het Hof niet langer de nationale strafrechtspraktijk bij de veroordeling hoeft te betrekken, kan zij haar eigen strafmaat gaan bepalen. Aangezien de strafmaat van het ICC de standaard zou kunnen worden waaraan bestraffing van de ernstigste misdaden in landen over de gehele wereld wordt afgemeten, is het belangrijk dat de veroordelingen goed worden onderbouwd en dat vergelijkbare zaken ook vergelijkbaar gestraft worden, meteen vanaf het begin. Zo niet, dan zouden slachtoffers van seksueel geweld zich niet voldoende erkend kunnen voelen en op termijn niet meer met het Hof willen samenwerken. Als het Hof werkelijk toegewijd is aan haar taak om seksuele geweldsmisdaden te vervolgen, dient zij ook serieus de ernst van de misdrijven en de verzwarende omstandigheden te erkennen.

Hoofdstuk 7 van deze studie beschouwt in hoeverre de schadeloosstellingmogelijkheden van het Hof en het Trust Fund voor slachtoffers en hun families van nut kan zijn voor slachtoffers van seksueel geweld. Ondanks voorzieningen voor de teruggave van zowel bezittingen of opbrengsten als schadeloosstellingen, heeft de schadeloosstelling van slachtoffers van de Tribunalen nauwelijks aandacht gehad. De rechters van de Tribunalen hebben altijd volgehouden dat hun taak primair in het vervolgen van aangeklaagden voor ernstige overtredingen van internationaal humanitair recht lag. Het ICC Statuut en de RPE daarentegen bevatten een uitgebreid schadeloosstellingregeling (artikelen 75 en 79 van het ICC Statuut en regels 94-99 van het ICC RPE). Voor de eerste keer in de geschiedenis kan een internationaal strafhof slachtoffers het recht geven schadeloosstelling te eisen en te ontvangen. Daarnaast is een Trust Fund voor slachtoffers en hun families opgericht, dat het werk van het Hof kan aanvullen als schadeloosstelling aan de orde is.

In hoofdstuk 7 worden allereerst de speciale behoeften van slachtoffers van seksueel geweld beschreven, met de Rwandese overlevenden van seksueel geweld als voorbeeld. Vandaag de dag, 11 jaar na de genocide, lijden de meeste vrouwelijke slachtoffers nog steeds onder het seksuele geweld uit 1994. Veel slachtoffers van seksueel geweld zijn besmet met seksueel overdraagbare aandoeningen, zoals HIV/AIDS, hebben ongewenste zwangerschappen gehad, gezondheidsproblemen gekend door mislukte abortussen en geleden onder seksuele verminkingen en andere aandoeningen zoals fistels, urinewegproblemen, vaginale snijwonden of littekenvorming. De schatting is dat, van de verkrachte vrouwen in Rwanda die de genocide van 1994 hebben overleefd, tussen 70 en 80 procent besmet is met HIV. In de meeste gevallen is de HIV-infectie een gevolg van de herhaaldelijke verkrachtingen die zij ondergingen tijdens de genocide. Het lot van de overlevenden van het seksuele geweld in Rwanda is niet uniek. In vele conflicten over de gehele wereld, waarin vrouwen het slachtoffer worden van (groeps) verkrachtingen, seksuele slavernij en andere vormen van seksueel geweld, zijn de gevolgen even ernstig. Voorbeelden zijn de eerste drie gevallen onderzocht door het Hof, namelijk Sudan/Darfur, het noordoosten van de Democratische Republiek Congo en het noorden van Uganda. Als geen goede schadeloosstelling aangeboden wordt aan deze vrouwen, zal hun lot even tragisch zijn als dat van de vrouwen in Rwanda vandaag de dag.

Om de slachtoffers van seksueel geweld tegemoet te komen, kan het Hof hen schadeloosstelling toekennen. Gegeven de gevolgen van seksueel geweld voor haar slachtoffers zal in de meeste gevallen de benodigde hulp bestaan uit fysieke, psychologische en medische zorg, waaronder HIV/AIDS-medicatie, via een gerechtelijke uitspraak over compensatie of rehabilitatie. In de meeste gevallen zal het geld van de veroordeelde, waar nodig aangevuld met geld uit het Trust Fund, door het slachtoffer worden gebruikt om haar rehabilitatie te bekostigen, vooral voor medische en psychologische zorg. Als het Hof vaststelt dat de aangeklaagde schuldig is aan opzettelijke of te voorziene besmetting van het slachtoffer met HIV/AIDS, dan moet minimaal behandeling van HIV/AIDS worden opgenomen in de schadeloosstelling. Schadeloosstelling kan verder zowel individueel als collectief worden toegekend. Vooral wanneer het aantal slachtoffers groot is, zal het Hof er toe neigen om collectieve schadeloosstelling te verordonneren. In het geval van slachtoffers van seksueel geweld zullen het vooral ervaren (inter)nationale organisaties zijn die zullen helpen bij het opzetten van collectieve zorgprogramma's zoals behandelcentra. Om zoveel mogelijk slachtoffers te bereiken, moeten die slachtoffers ook weten van de schadeloosstellingen die door het Hof worden aangereikt. De *Victims Participation and Reparation Section*, die onder andere als taak heeft de slachtoffers te benaderen, ziet zich voor een immense uitdaging geplaatst. Schadeloosstelling zal zich niet noodzakelijk beperken tot die slachtoffers die hebben meegewerkt aan de procesgang. De rechters kunnen schadeloosstelling eisen namens slachtoffers van seksueel geweld die hier zelf niet om kunnen vragen. Als slachtoffers lijden vanwege een gebrek aan informatie vanuit het Hof, en als het seksuele geweld zo wijd verbreid en ernstig was dat schadeloosstelling duidelijk nodig is, kan en moeten de rechters een dergelijk verzoek namens hen doen.

Helaas is het grootste probleem met schadeloosstellingen dat ze pas worden toegekend als de beklaagde schuldig is bevonden. Echter, de slachtoffers van seksueel geweld kunnen de fysieke, psychologische en medische hulp veel eerder nodig hebben. Hierom moet tussentijdse hulp worden aangeboden vanuit het Trust Fund. De voorlopige statuten van het Trust Fund bevatten voorzieningen hiervoor, namelijk dat fysieke en psychologische rehabilitatie en ondersteuning al in de onderzoeksfase mag worden verleend (ontwerpregel 50). In uitzonderlijke omstandigheden kan dergelijke ondersteuning ook worden verleend wanneer de aanklager op juridische gronden besluit geen onderzoek te starten, en wanneer nationale rechtbanken processen tegen de aangeklaagden zijn gestart, maar waar schadeloosstelling van slachtoffers niet beschikbaar is (ontwerpregel 51). Om een betekenisvolle invloed op het leven van slachtoffers te hebben moet het Trust Fund zo snel als mogelijk handelen. Het is niet onwaarschijnlijk dat slachtoffers van seksueel geweld al in slechte gezondheid verkeren op het moment dat de aanklager zijn onderzoek start; op dat moment kan het conflict al weken, maanden of zelfs jaren zijn beloop hebben gehad. Dit betekent dat het Trust Fund overeenstemming moet bereiken met humanitaire organisaties in het veld die in staat zijn om de overlevenden van seksueel geweld te bereiken en hen te helpen. Collectieve projecten om slachtoffers te helpen zouden centra op kunnen richten met ervaring in fysieke, psychologische en medische zorg waaronder HIV/AIDS-behandeling. Een school en geld opleverende projecten kunnen ook worden gestart, zowel voor de slachtoffers als voor hun kinderen. Kinderen kunnen dergelijke hulp hard nodig hebben, bijvoorbeeld als hun moeder gehandicapt is, reeds is overleden of snel zal overlijden aan ziektes die het gevolg zijn van seksueel geweld. Collectieve projecten zullen het Trust Fund in staat stellen om veel meer slachtoffers te helpen dan het Hof, omdat het Hof zich meestal zal richten op bepaalde misdaden, gebieden en beklaagden en daardoor slachtoffers over het hoofd zou kunnen zien die niet worden omvat door de strategie van de aanklager. Bovendien kan het Trust Fund onbekende slachtoffers bereiken die, bijvoorbeeld door stigmatisering, angst of trauma, niet in staat waren zelf om schadeloosstelling te vragen bij het Hof. De oprichting van het Trust Fund voor slachtoffers en hun families zou het daardoor mogelijk maken om de noden van slachtoffers van seksueel geweld op een grotere schaal te lenigen. Veel zal afhangen van de eerstvolgende zitting van de *Assembly of States Parties* in november-december 2005, waarin de grenzen van de activiteiten van het Trust Fund zullen worden vastgelegd. Met de situatie in Rwanda nog vers in het geheugen, wordt ernstig aanbevolen om tussentijdse zorg via het Trust Fund te accepteren als een manier om de slachtoffers van seksueel geweld te helpen.

In deze studie wordt geconcludeerd dat, over het geheel bezien, het supranationale strafrechtsysteem voldoende mogelijkheden levert om seksuele geweldsmisdrijven adequaat te vervolgen. Om dit ook werkelijk te doen, moeten zowel het Hof als de Tribunalen rekening houden met factoren als de realiteit van de misdaden, de respectvolle behandeling van slachtoffers van seksueel geweld tijdens de zittingen, de ernst van de misdaden en de behoeften van slachtoffers. De Tribunalen hebben niet altijd voldoende met deze factoren rekening gehouden. Het is daarom niet langer de vraag of seksueel geweld kan worden vervolgd middels het supranationale strafrecht; het is eerder een kwestie van de wet op de juiste manier toepassen.

APPENDIX
ICTY AND ICTR JUDGMENTS ON SEXUAL VIOLENCE

Up to 1 July 2005, the ICTY had convicted 21 individuals of, among other crimes, sexual violence, in a total of 14 cases, of which 2 cases (involving 4 individuals) were completely devoted to sexual violence charges. The ICTR, on the other hand, had convicted 9 persons of, among other charges, sexual violence, in a total of 7 cases, of which 1 case dealt with sexual violence primarily.[1] In this Appendix, an overview of these judgments is given.[2]

ICTY JUDGMENTS ON SEXUAL VIOLENCE

1 Tadić (7 May & 14 July 1997 / 15 July & 11 November 1999)

Tadić, a former Serbian camp guard at Omarska, Keraterm and Trnopolje camps (Prijedor, northwest Bosnia and Herzegovina), was found guilty of crimes against humanity (on 6 counts) and of violations of the laws or customs of war (on 5 counts): i.e., persecution, beatings and acts of sexual violence against Muslims and Croats.[3] Tadić was indicted under counts 5-11 for, *inter alia*, sexual violence: together with others, Tadić allegedly forced two male prisoners, G and H, to commit oral sexual acts on Harambasić and forced G to sexually mutilate him.[4] For this, Tadić was sentenced to 9 years under count 10 for cruel treatment as a violation of the laws or customs of war and under count 11 to 10 years for inhumane acts as a crime against humanity, both under Article 7(1) of the ICTY Statute. On appeal, Tadić was additionally sentenced to 9 years under count 8 for inhumane treatment as a grave breach and for 9 years under

[1] One individual, Musema, was acquitted on appeal of the charge related to sexual violence. Despite this acquittal, the Trial Chamber's findings on Musema's guilt and the determination of the sentence imposed are relevant for the purposes of this study, in particular with regard to Chapter 6 on sentencing, and have therefore been taken into account.

[2] Cases in which sexual violence charges were dropped before trial or where the accused were acquitted of all sexual violence charges on first instance, not altered on appeal, are not taken into account in this overview.

[3] The Trial Chamber found Tadić not guilty on 11 counts of grave breaches of the 1949 Geneva Conventions as they were considered to be not applicable. In addition, Tadić was not convicted on another 11 counts charging him with 13 murders, 5 beatings, 2 inhumane acts and one case of abuse of prisoners. On appeal, Tadić was convicted on several of these counts after all, including some grave breaches counts.

[4] Counts 2-4 were withdrawn at the Prosecutor's request. In these counts, Tadić was charged with forcing F to sexual intercourse at the Omarska camp under inhuman treatment as a grave breach, cruel treatment as a violation of the laws or customs of war, and rape as a crime against humanity.

count 9 for wilfully causing great suffering or serious injury to body or health as a grave breach for the same events, both under Article 7(1) of the ICTY Statute. The sentences for all crimes were to be served concurrently, which implied that Tadić was sentenced to twenty years in prison (in Germany). On appeal, Tadić was convicted on additional charges and therefore his sentence was increased to twenty-five years in prison. The *Tadić* case was the first case before the ICTY in which (male) sexual assault was prosecuted.

2 Delić and Mucić – *Čelebići* case (16 November 1998 / 20 February 2001; 9 October 2001 / 8 April 2003)

The *Čelebići* case concerned the case of four accused (Bosnian Muslims and Bosnian Croats) and the crimes they committed against Bosnian Serbs in the Čelebići prison camp in the Konjic municipality in central Bosnia and Herzegovina. Of the four individuals, three (Delalić, Delić and Mucić) were charged with sexual violence. One person, however, Delalić, was acquitted on all counts, including the sexual violence charge against him, on the basis of lack of evidence. The case is significant as it elaborates on the concept of command responsibility: i.e., not only military commanders, but also civilians holding positions of authority, and not only persons in *de jure* positions but also those in such position *de facto* are held responsible. In addition, the judgment also contains the first conviction for rape as torture (charged as a grave breach of the Geneva Conventions and a violation of the laws or customs of war) by the ICTY. Overall, Delić was convicted on 13 counts of grave breaches of the Geneva Conventions and violations of the laws or customs of war, e.g., for murder, torture, rape, causing great suffering or serious injury and inhumane acts.[5] Mucić, on the other hand, was convicted on 11 counts of grave breaches of the Geneva Conventions and violations of the laws or customs of war, for his superior responsibility for murder, torture, causing great suffering or serious injury, inhumane acts, and for his direct participation in the unlawful confinement of civilians in inhumane conditions.[6] In respect of sexual violence, Delić, a deputy commander at the Čelebići camp, was convicted on counts 18 and 19 for the repeated incidents of forcible sexual intercourse with Grozana Cecez by him and others at the camp premises. Delić personally raped Ms. Cecez twice, in front of others, and on another occasion she was raped again by multiple persons.[7] For Delić's acts and omissions, the Čelebići Chamber sentenced him to 15 years for torture as a grave breach and for another 15 years for torture as a violation of the laws or customs of war.[8] On counts 21-23, Delić was indicted for subjecting Witness A to repeated incidents of sexual intercourse, including both vaginal and anal intercourse. Delić raped her on three different occasions.[9] The Trial Chamber

[5] Delić was found not guilty on 23 counts of the grave breaches of the Geneva Conventions and violations of the laws or customs of war and several counts were dismissed.

[6] Mucić was found not guilty in respect of 3 counts of the grave breaches provisions and several counts were dismissed.

[7] Čelebići Judgment, paras. 925-943.

[8] Čelebići Judgment, para. 1285. The Chamber dismissed count 20, the sexual assaults as cruel treatment under Article 3(a), violations of the laws or customs of war.

[9] Čelebići Judgment, paras. 944-965.

found that both Ms. Cecez and Witness A were raped with the purpose of obtaining information as well as for the discriminatory purpose of being female. Additionally, the rapes did not only intimidate the rape victims, but also the other inmates by creating an atmosphere of fear and powerlessness in the camp. For his acts, the Chamber sentenced Delić to 15 years for torture punishable as a grave breach and 15 years for torture as a violation of the laws or customs of war, both under Article 7(1) of the ICTY Statute.[10] For all crimes charged, Delić has to serve a total of 20 years in prison (in Finland). With regard to Mucić, a commander at the camp, the Chamber convicted and sentenced him as a superior responsible (Article 7(3)) for placing a 'burning fuse cord around the genital areas' of 2 male detainees (counts 38 and 39 of the Indictment).[11] The Chamber sentenced the accused to 7 years for wilfully causing great suffering or serious injury to body or health as a grave breach. Mucić was sentenced to a further 7 years for this act of cruel treatment as a violation of the laws or customs of war. In addition, the Chamber found Mucić responsible as a superior for incidents of inhumane acts, 'including forcing persons to commit fellatio with each other' under counts 44 and 45.[12] On these counts, the accused was sentenced to 7 years for inhumane treatment as a grave breach and a further 7 years for cruel treatment as a violation of the laws or customs of war. The Trial Chamber found that Mucić was in a *de facto* position of superior authority over the Čelebići prison camp: in this position, Mucić knew or had reason to know of the violations of international humanitarian law committed in the Čelebići prison camp, but failed to prevent these acts or punish the perpetrators.[13] The Trial Chamber additionally noted that if the forced oral sex had been charged as rape, Mucić would have been convicted of rape as a war crime.[14] Mucić was eventually sentenced to 7 years in prison. On appeal, the sexual violence convictions for both accused were upheld, although the cumulative convictions under the violations of the laws or customs of war provisions were dismissed.[15] The sentences were subsequently adjusted by a new Trial Chamber, but the change in sentences did not relate to the dismissal of the violations of the laws or customs of war convictions.[16] Delić finally received a sentence of 18 years in prison and Mucić a sentence of 9 years in prison.[17] Mucić was granted early release (before transfer) on 18 July 2003.

---

[10] *Ibid.*, para. 1285. Count 23 (cruel treatment as a violation of the laws or customs of war) was dismissed and the accused was found not guilty under the remaining 8 counts.

[11] *Ibid.*, para. 1019-1040.

[12] *Ibid.*, paras. 1060-1072.

[13] Delić was initially indicted under counts 38-39 and 44-45 as well, but as Delić had been found not to have exercised superior authority over the Čelebići prison camp, the Trial Chamber found Delić not guilty of the acts charged in these counts.

[14] Čelebići Judgment, para. 1066.

[15] See Chapter 6 on cumulative convictions.

[16] Instead, on appeal, Delić was acquitted on two counts of wilful killing, while the sentence imposed on Mucić did not reflect the gravity of the crimes he had committed.

[17] Čelebići Sentencing Judgment; Čelebići Judgment on Sentence Appeal.

3 Furundžija (10 December 1998 / 21 July 2000)

The *Furundžija* case was the first case before the Tribunal (as well as in the history of international criminal prosecutions) in which the charges against the accused centred on sexual violence only. The entire trial lasted about eleven days and focused on the multiple rapes perpetrated against solely one woman. At the time, Furundžija was the commander of the Jokers, a special unit of the Croatian Defence Council (HVO).[18] At the Jokers Headquarters (in Nadioci, central Bosnia and Herzegovina), Furundžija interrogated Witness A, a civilian Bosnian Muslim woman who was naked, while Accused B (another commander of one of the HVO units) rubbed his knife against her inner thighs and threatened to cut out her private parts if she did not tell the truth in answer to the interrogation by the accused. Accused B then raped her orally, vaginally and anally and forced her to lick his penis clean. This happened in front of an audience of laughing soldiers.[19] Although Furundžija had not raped the woman himself, he was found as responsible as his colleague who did rape her as he had facilitated the rapes by allowing them to occur and continue. [forced observance] Furundžija was found guilty under Article 7(1) of the ICTY Statute and was sentenced to 10 years for sexual assault as torture (as a co-perpetrator) and 8 years for rape as part of outrages against personal dignity, both as violations of the laws or customs of war (as an aider and abetter). The sentences were to be served concurrently and thus Furundžija had to serve a prison term of 10 years in total (in Finland). These sentences were upheld on appeal. In conformity with the law in Finland, Furundžija was granted early release on 17 August 2004, after serving two-thirds of his sentence.[20]

4 Blaškić (3 March 2000 / 29 July 2004)

Blaškić, a former General of the HVO armed forces, was convicted of: grave breaches of the 1949 Geneva Conventions (Article 2: wilful killing; wilfully causing great suffering or serious injury to body or health; extensive destruction of property; inhuman treatment; taking civilians as hostages); violations of the laws or customs of war (Article 3: unlawful attack on civilians; unlawful attack on civilian objects; murder; violence to life and person; plunder of public or private property; destruction or wilful damage to institutions dedicated to religion or education; cruel treatment; taking of hostages); and crimes against humanity (Article 5: persecutions on political, racial or religious grounds; murder; inhumane acts) under both Article 7(1) and 7(3) of the ICTY Statute.[21] Blaškić was convicted of sexual violence committed as part of counts 15

[18] The Croatian Community of Herzeg-Bosna (HZ-HB) considered itself an independent political entity inside the Republic of Bosnia-Herzegovina. From at least January 1993 to at least mid-July 1993, the HZ-BZ armed forces, known as the Croatian Defence Council (HVO), were engaged in an armed conflict with the armed forces of the government of the Republic of Bosnia-Herzegovina (BiH).

[19] Furundžija Judgment, paras. 264-275.

[20] ICTY Press Release, *Anto Furundzija Granted Early Release*, CT/P.I.S./877e, The Hague, 30 July 2004.

[21] The only count he was not convicted on was count 2 (devastation not justified by military necessity as a violation of the laws or customs of war), which was withdrawn by the Prosecutor.

(inhumane treatment as a grave breach) and 16 (cruel treatment as a violation of the laws or customs of war) under Article 7(3) of the ICTY Statute. The Chamber found that the accused must have been aware of the acts of sexual violence that occurred in the Rotilj village (Kiseljak municipality) and Dubravica Primary School (Vitez municipality) by the HVO soldiers and Military police (over which he had effective control) and did not take the necessary and/or reasonable measures required to prevent the acts or punish the perpetrators.[22] The Chamber thus found Blaškić guilty of inhuman treatment as a grave breach under Article 2(b) and cruel treatment as a violation of the laws or customs of war under Article 3(a).[23] Blaškić was sentenced to a single sentence of 45 years. On appeal, his sentenced was reduced to 9 years. The sexual violence convictions were nonetheless upheld. Blaškić was granted early release (before transfer) on 2 August 2004.[24]

5 Kunarac, Kovač and Vuković – Foča (22 February 2001 / 12 June 2002)

The *Kunarac, Kovač and Vuković* case was the second case which concentrated on sexual violence crimes only. It was the first time that accused persons were convicted of rape as a crime against humanity before the ICTY and the first case in the history of international criminal prosecutions in which convictions for sexual enslavement were rendered. The three accused were members of the Bosnian Serb Army and were held responsible for, *inter alia*, the rapes, sexual enslavement, sexual torture and nude dancing of civilian Muslim women and girls kept in detention centres around Foča (East Bosnia). Some women and girls were held captive for weeks or months on end, completely at the mercy of their captors. Although none of the three individuals occupied high level positions, the Trial Chamber made it clear that no one should expect to escape prosecution, no matter how low their level of responsibility. Kunarac, a commander of a special volunteer unit of the Bosnian Serb Army (VRS), received a single prison sentence of 28 years (Germany) under Article 7(1) for counts 1 (crime against humanity, torture), 2 (crime against humanity, rape), 3 (violations of the laws or customs of war, torture), 4 (violations of the laws or customs of war, rape), 9 (crime against humanity, rape), 10 (violations of the laws or customs of war, rape), 11 (violations of the laws or customs of war, torture), 12 (violations of the laws or customs of war, rape), 18 (crime against humanity, enslavement), 19 (crime against humanity, rape) and 20 (violations of the laws or customs of war, rape).[25] Counts 1-4 apply to the

---

[22] Blaškić Judgment, paras. 692, 695, 732-734.

[23] Blaškić Judgment, at disposition.

[24] ICTY Press Release, *Tihomir Blaskic Granted Early Release*, CT/P.I.S./876-e, The Hague, 29 July 2004.

[25] Kunarac was acquitted of counts 5 (torture as a crime against humanity), 6 (rape as a crime against humanity), 7 (torture as a violation of the laws or customs of war), 8 (rape as a violation of the laws or customs of war), 13 (plunder as a violation of the laws or customs of war) and 21 (outrages upon personal dignity as a violation of the laws or customs of war). Note that some of the charges contained in counts 1-4 and 18-20 were not established beyond reasonable doubt either. The Trial Chamber further held that Kunarac was not accountable as a superior under Article 7(3), as the Prosecutor had failed to show that the soldiers who committed the offences

rapes of women at the House Ulica Osmana Dikica No. 16, the headquarters of a group of soldiers under Kunarac's command. Kunarac personally raped three women (Witnesses D.B., FWS-87, FWS-95) and aided and abetted the (gang) rapes of other women by soldiers at the house.[26] As to counts 9 and 10, it was proven that Kunarac went to a place called 'Karaman's house' in Miljevina where he took Witness FWS-87 to the upper floor and raped her.[27] Counts 11 and 12 concern the event where Kunarac and two other soldiers took Witness FWS-183 from her home to the banks of the Cehotina River in Foča, where she was raped by all three of them. Kunarac personally raped the woman and aided and abetted her rape by the two other soldiers by encouraging the other men while they were raping her.[28] Counts 18-20 cover the events in which Kunarac is held responsible for personally raping Witness FWS-191 in a house in Trnovace. He took FWS-191 and FWS-186 to this house and every time he visited the house he raped FWS-191. On one occasion, he aided and abetted the rape of FWS-186 by a soldier, DP6. Both women were kept at the house for several months, where they were treated as Kunarac's and DP6's private property.[29] Kovač, sub-commander of the military police and paramilitary leader in Foča, received a single prison sentence of 20 years (in Norway) under Article 7(1) for counts 22 (crime against humanity, enslavement), 23 (crime against humanity, rape), 24 (violations of the laws or customs of war, rape), 25 (violations of the laws or customs of war, outrages upon personal dignity).[30] The convictions were entered for the enslavement, naked dancing and multiple rapes of Muslim girls and women at the Brena apartment, Kovač's apartment. Kovač personally raped several women, some of them on a constant basis; aided and abetted their rapes by other soldiers who visited his house; handed them over to other Serb soldiers in the knowledge they would be raped; forced some of the women to dance naked on a table while watching them; and held them captive for several weeks on end.[31] Among the victims was the young girl A.B., only 12 years old at the time. Finally, Vuković, sub-commander of the military police and paramilitary leader in Foča, received a single prison term of 12 years (in Norway) under Article 7(1) for counts 33 (crime against humanity, torture), 34 (crime against humanity, rape), 35 (violations of the laws or customs of war, torture), 36 (violations of the laws or customs of war, rape).[32] Out of these counts, Vuković was convicted for the rape of a 15-year-old girl,

---

charged in the indictment were under the effective control of Kunarac *at the time they committed the offences*. Kunarac, Kovač and Vuković Judgment, paras. 626-629.

[26] Kunarac, Kovač and Vuković Judgment, paras. 630-687.

[27] *Ibid.*, paras. 699-704.

[28] *Ibid.*, paras. 705-715.

[29] *Ibid.*, paras. 716-745.

[30] Kovač was found guilty on all counts charged.

[31] *Ibid.*, paras. 746-782.

[32] Vuković was acquitted of counts 21 (torture as a crime against humanity), 22 (rape as a crime against humanity), 23 (torture as a violation of the laws or customs of war) and 24 (rape as a violation of the laws or customs of war). Note that some of the charges contained in counts 33-36 were not established beyond reasonable doubt either, namely, the rapes of Witnesses FWS-48 and FWS-87.

who was taken by Vuković from the Partizan Sports hall.[33] The judgment was upheld by the Appeals Chamber.

6 Todorović (31 July 2001, Guilty Plea)

On 29 November 2000, Todorović, a former Serbian Chief of Police in Bosanski Šamac (north-east Bosnia and Herzegovina), entered a guilty plea to Count 1 of the indictment (persecution as a crime against humanity, including sexual assaults)[34] and a withdrawal of all other counts against him.[35] In the plea agreement, the Prosecution and Todorović agreed on certain facts as being true and constituting the factual basis for the guilty plea. Todorović's conviction for persecution included, *inter alia*, his participation in the beating and murder of a man, the beatings of several other individuals, his participation in the unlawful detention and the deportation and forcible transfer of Bosnian Muslims, Bosnian Croats and other non-Serb civilians in the municipality of Bosanski Šamac. In relation to the allegations of sexual assault, Todorović accepted the following account of his conduct: (1) 'Witness A described how he was taken to the police station in Bosanski Šamac, where Todorović began to beat him and kick him in the genital area. Witness A was then taken over to another man and ordered by Todorović to "bit into his penis." After that he was beaten again and endured further mistreatment'; (2) 'Witness

[33] Kunarac, Kovač and Vuković Judgment, paras. 799-822.

[34] Paragraph 34 of the indictment (count 1) states: 'From on or about 17 April 1992 through at least 31 December 1993, Stevan TODOROVIC, while serving as Chief of Police of Bosanski Šamac and as a member of the Serb Crisis Staff, committed and aided and abetted the commission of the crime of persecutions as described in paragraphs 29 and 30 above, through his participation in the following acts or omissions, among others: (a) the forcible take-over of the municipality of Bosanski Šamac by Serb forces; (b) the murders, sexual assaults and repeated beatings of numerous Bosnian Croats, Bosnian Muslims and other non-Serb civilians detained in various detention camps in and around the Bosanski Šamac municipality; (c) the unlawful detention and confinement of Bosnian Croats, Bosnian Muslims and other non-Serb civilians under inhumane conditions on political, racial or religious grounds and not for their protection and safety; (d) the cruel and inhumane treatment of Bosnian Croats, Bosnian Muslims and other non-Serb civilians including beatings, torture, forced labour assignments and confinement under inhumane conditions; (e) the interrogation of Bosnian Croats, Bosnian Muslims and other non-Serb civilians who had been arrested and detained and forcing them to sign false and coerced statements; (f) the deportation, forcible transfer and expulsion of Bosnian Croats, Bosnian Muslims and other non-Serb civilians, including women, children and the elderly, from their homes and villages by force, intimidation and coercion; and (g) the issuance of orders and directives which violated the rights of the Bosnian Croat, Bosnian Muslim and other non-Serb civilians to equal treatment under the law and infringed upon their enjoyment of basic and fundamental rights.' See *Prosecutor v. Blagoje Simić, Milan Simić, Miroslav Tadić, Stevan Todorović and Simo Zarić*, Second Amended Indictment, Case No. IT-95-9, 25 March 1999. See also paragraphs 29 and 30.

[35] Todorović was initially charged with persecution on political, racial and religious grounds, deportation, murder, inhumane acts, rape and torture (as crimes against humanity); unlawful deportation or transfer, wilful killing, wilfully causing great suffering and torture or inhuman treatment (as grave breaches of the Geneva Conventions); and murder, cruel treatment, humiliating and degrading treatment and torture (violations of the laws or customs of war).

C stated that Todorović had telephoned and had required him to come to the police station in Bosanski Šamac. There, Witness C was beaten for about half and hour. In Witness C's words: "Only Todorović and me were present at the office and the beating lasted for about half and hour. After that Witness D was brought to the office and he continued beating both of us. The beating lasted for another hour. After that he ordered us to perform oral sex on each other;" (3) 'Witness E described how he was arrested on 9 or 10 May 1992 and taken to the police station in Bosanski Šamac. There he was beaten by Stevan Todorović, among others, for several hours. Witness E stated that: "After the beating Todorović ordered us (Witness E and Witness F) to do a blow job on each other. He was laughing when we were doing it."[36] Todorović received a prison sentence of 10 years (in Spain) for persecution as a crime against humanity, including ordering oral sex.

7 Kvočka, Prcać, Kos, Radić and Žigić (2 November 2001 / 28 February 2005)

The crimes which Kvočka (a policeman/(deputy) commander of Omarska camp), Prcać (a retired police forensic specialist/deputy commander of Omarska camp), Kos (a waiter/shift commander of guards at Omarska camp), Radić (a policeman/shift commander of guards at Omarska camp) and Žigić (taxi driver and musician/regularly visited Omarska, Keraterm and Trnopolje camp to beat, torture and kill prisoners) were convicted of persecution as a crime against humanity and violations of the laws or customs of war of murder, torture and cruel treatment. In respect of sexual violence, all the accused were convicted of persecution as a crime against humanity, including sexual assault and rape under Article 7(1). In addition, Radić personally raped a woman and further sexually assaulted female prisoners for which he was convicted under Article 7(1) of torture as a violation of the laws or customs of war.[37] The crimes were committed over a period of about three months against the non-Serb population in Prijedor, particularly against those held captive in the Omarska camp, where most of the accused worked. Although there was not much evidence that any of the accused, other than Radić, knew that women held in Omarska camp were raped or otherwise sexually assaulted, the Trial Chamber concluded that they nevertheless incurred individual criminal responsibility on the basis of the joint criminal enterprise theory. On the basis of this theory, those involved in a common purpose can be prosecuted. Here, this common purpose involved the persecution and mistreatment of the non-Serbs in the Omarska camp, which includes crimes which were an intended or a natural and foreseeable consequence of the common purpose, e.g., the rapes and sexual assault on the women held captive in the camp. Kvočka, Prcać, Kos, Radić and Žigić received single sentences of 7, 5, 6, 20 and 25 years, respectively. Kos was granted early release (before transfer) on 31 July 2002.[38] On appeal, the sentences imposed on Kvočka, Prcać, Radić and Žigić were all affirmed. However, the Appeals Chamber allowed Kvočka's ground of appeal in so far as it related to his conviction as a co-perpetrator of persecution for rape and sexual assault under count 1 of the indictment. Žigić's ground

---

[36] Todorović Sentencing Judgment, paras. 38-40.

[37] Kvočka et al. Judgment, paras. 546-561.

[38] ICTY Press Release, *The President of the ICTY Orders Release of Milojica Kos*, R.C./P.I.S./692e, The Hague, 31 July 2002.

of appeal concerning his responsibility for crimes committed in the Omarska camp generally were allowed and his conviction pursuant to Article 7(1) of the Statute under count 1 (persecution as a crime against humanity) in so far as this conviction related to the crimes committed in the Omarska camp were reversed. Prcać completed his sentence on 4 March 2005 and was subsequently released[39] and Kvočka was granted early release on 30 March 2005.[40]

8 Sikirica (13 November 2001, Guilty Plea)

Sikirica, the Commander of Security at the Keraterm camp in the municipality of Prijedor in north-western Bosnia and Herzegovina, made a guilty plea to the charge of persecution, a crime against humanity.[41] He admitted to a number of crimes, including killing one of the detainees in the camp, by shooting him in the head, as well as other killings in the Prijedor municipality and outside the camp, torture and beatings in the Prijedor municipality and outside the camp, sexual assault and rape in the Prijedor municipality and outside the camp, harassment, humiliation and psychological abuse in the Prijedor municipality and inside the camp and confinement in inhumane conditions in the camp.[42] The acts were discriminately committed against Bosnian Muslims, Bosnian Croats and other non-Serbs. With regard to the sexual assault and rapes, Sikirica had 'admitted that a small number of women were raped at Keraterm. There is no evidence that Sikirica knew of any such incidents or that he was in a position to know of their having happened after the event. He admits that there is evidence that certain detainees were forced to engage in sexual activities against their will.'[43] Sikirica was sentenced to <u>15 years</u> imprisonment (in Austria).[44]

9 Simić (17 October 2002, Guilty Plea)

On 13 May 2002, the Prosecutor and Simić, then President of the Executive Board of the Municipal Assembly of Bosanski Šamac (north-west Bosnia Herzegovina) and member of the Serb Crisis Staff, agreed to a plea agreement whereby Simić pleaded

---

[39] ICTY Press Release, *Completion of Sentence by Dragoljub Prcac*, CVO/MOW/941e, The Hague, 4 March 2005.

[40] ICTY Press Release, *Miroslav Kvocka Granted Early Release*, CVO/MOW/955e, The Hague, 31 March 2005.

[41] The other counts where withdrawn, namely, genocide and complicity to commit genocide (which included sexual violence), inhumane acts (including sexual violence) and murder, or in the alternative, inhumane acts as crimes against humanity; outrages upon personal dignity (including sexual violence) and murder, or, in the alternative, cruel treatment as violations of the laws or customs of war. Došen and Kolundžija also entered a guilty plea to persecution as a crime against humanity. Although they had also been charged with sexual violence as persecution and inhumane acts as crimes against humanity and outrages upon personal dignity as violations of the laws or customs of war, sexual violence did not form part of their plea agreement. See Sikirica Sentencing Judgment, paras. 26, 32.

[42] Sikirica Sentencing Judgment, para. 18.

[43] *Ibid.*, para. 125; see also para. 22.

[44] *Ibid.*, paras. 235, 245.

guilty to counts 4 and 7 of the indictment in which he was charged under Article 7(1) with acts of torture as crimes against humanity.[45] Simić therefore accepted certain facts as being true and constituting the factual basis of the guilty plea. The events related to acts of torture committed against Croats and Muslims at the Bosanski Šamac primary school. As far as sexual violence was concerned, Simić pleaded guilty to the following fact (as part of count 7): '(e) in an incident in June 1992, Safet Hadzialijagic was severely beaten by Milan Simić and the men accompanying him; it was common knowledge in Bosanski Šamac that Safet Hadzialijagic had a heart condition; Safet Hadzialijagic was forced to pull down his pants, and one of the men accompanying Milan Simić brandished a knife and threatened to cut off Safet Hadzialijagic's penis; the other assailants were challenging and exhorting the man wielding the knife to cut off Safet Hadzialijagic's penis; and at one point, the barrel of a handgun was pushed into Safet Hadzialijagic's mouth and Milan Simić fired gunshots over his head, before the victim was released and allowed to return to the gymnasium'.[46] With this judgment *the threat* of committing sexual violence was recognised for the first time as a crime (here torture) deserving punishment. Simić received two prison sentences of 5 years for each count of torture to be served concurrently: thus 5 years in total. Simić was granted early release (before transfer) on 27 October 2003.

10 Plavšić (27 February 2003, Guilty Plea)

At a hearing on 2 October 2002, Mrs. Plavšić, the former co-President of Bosnia and Herzegovina, pleaded guilty to count 3, persecution as a crime against humanity, which included acts of sexual violence. All other counts against her were dismissed.[47] A factual basis was agreed by the accused and the Prosecution and formed the basis upon which the Trial Chamber passed sentence: i.e., that, between 1 July 1991 and 30 December 1992, Plavšić, acting individually and in concert with others in a joint criminal enterprise, planned, instigated, ordered and aided and abetted persecutions of the Bosnian Muslim, Bosnian Croat and other non-Serb populations of 37 municipalities in Bosnia and Herzegovina. Mrs. Plavšić embraced and supported the objective of persecution and contributed to achieving it, but she did not participate in its conception and planning and had a lesser role in its execution than others: Bosnian Serb Forces and Bosnian Serb Political and Governmental Organs and their agents committed persecutions in the municipalities and detention centres, which were controlled by them. The persecutions were carried out by means of, amongst other charges, cruel or inhumane treatment during and after the attacks on towns and villages

[45] The other counts were withdrawn against Simić, i.e., persecution as a crime against humanity (count 1); deportation as a crime against humanity (count 2); unlawful deportation or transfer as a grave breach (count 3); inhumane acts as a crime against humanity (count 5); cruel treatment as a violation of the laws or customs of war (count 6); inhumane acts as a crime against humanity (count 8); cruel treatment as a violation of the laws or customs of war (count 9).

[46] Simić Sentencing Judgment, paras. 11 and 54.

[47] Genocide (count 1); complicity in genocide (count 2); extermination as a crime against humanity (count 4); murder as a crime against humanity (count 5); murder as a violation of the laws or customs of war (count 6); deportation as a crime against humanity (count 7); inhumane acts (forced transfer) as a crime against humanity (count 8).

in the municipalities including torture, physical and psychological abuse, sexual violence and forced existence under inhumane living conditions; and cruel or inhuman treatment in detention facilities, which included torture, physical and psychological abuse and sexual violence.[48] Mrs. Plavšić received a sentence of 11 years in prison (in Sweden).

11 Stakić (31 July 2003, Appeal Pending)

Stakić (both a member of the municipality of Prijedor Crisis Staff and the President of the Municipal Assembly of Prijedor during the period from 29 April 1992 to 31 December 1992) was found guilty of extermination as a crime against humanity, murder as a violation of the laws or customs of war and persecution as a crime against humanity, including, among other crimes, rapes and sexual violence.[49] The Trial Chamber ruled that rapes and sexual assaults were committed in the Trnopolje, Keraterm and Omarska camps, and that these crimes were committed with a discriminatory intent.[50] The Trial Chamber specifically stated: 'For a woman, rape is by far the ultimate offense, sometimes even worse than death because it brings shame on her.'[51] The Trial Chamber established that Stakić had the intent to discriminate against non-Serbs or those affiliated or sympathising with them because of their political or religious affiliations in the Prijedor municipality during the relevant time in 1992 and that he was therefore guilty as a co-perpetrator of the persecutorial acts, including rapes and sexual violence. For the above conduct, Stakić was sentenced to life imprisonment.

12 Nikolić (18 December 2003, Guilty Plea / 4 February 2005)

Nikolić, a former camp commander at Sušica detention camp, pleaded guilty to counts 1-4, i.e., persecutions, including sexual violence (count 1) and incorporating murder (count 2); aiding and abetting rape (count 3); and torture as a crime against humanity (count 4) under Article 7(1) of the ICTY Statute. Nikolić personally removed and otherwise facilitated the removal of female detainees from the hangar, which he knew was for purposes of rapes and other sexually abusive conduct. The sexual assaults were committed by camp guards, special forces, local soldiers and other men.[52] He was sentenced to a single prison term of 23 years. On appeal, his sentence was reduced to 20 years for the reason that the Trial Chamber erred in taking into account the time he would actually serve in detention.

[48] *Prosecutor v. Momcilo Krajisnik and Biljana Plavšić*, Amended Consolidated Indictment, Case No. IT-00-39 and 40-PT, 7 March 2002, paras. 18-23; Plavšić Sentencing Judgment, paras. 29, 34 and 126.

[49] Stakić Judgment, at disposition. He was acquitted of genocide, complicity in genocide (which included charges of rape and sexual assault) and other inhuman acts (forcible transfer) as a crimes against humanity.

[50] *Ibid.*, para. 806; also paras. 228-244, 791-806.

[51] *Ibid.*, para. 803.

[52] Nikolić Sentencing Judgment, paras. 86-90.

13 Češić (11 March 2004, Guilty Plea)

On 8 October 2003, Češić pleaded guilty to all twelve counts with which he was charged, i.e., six counts of crimes against humanity and six counts of violations of the laws or customs of war, five of which charged murder and one of which charged rape and humiliating and degrading treatment (based on the same events) under Article 7(1) of the ICTY Statute.[53] Češić, a member of the Bosnian Serb Police Reserve unit at the Brčko police station, admitted that he 'intentionally forced, at gunpoint, two Muslim brothers detained at Luka Camp to perform fellatio on each other in the presence of others. Ranko Češić acknowledged that he was fully aware that this was taking place without the consent of the victims.'[54] Češić was convicted on all counts and received a single prison term of 18 years.

14 Brđanin (1 September 2004, Appeal Pending)

Brđanin (elected First Vice-President of the Association of the Bosanska Krajina Municipalities Assembly in 1991 and appointed President of the Autonomous Region of Krajina (ARK) Crisis Staff in 1992) was found guilty under Article 7(1) of aiding and abetting persecution, incorporating sexual violence as torture, and torture as a grave breach, including sexual violence. Furthermore, Brđanin was convicted of deportation and inhuman acts (forcible transfer) as crimes against humanity; wilful killing; wanton destruction of cities, towns or villages, or devastation not justified by military necessity; and destruction or wilful damage done to institutions dedicated to religion.[55] With regard to the rapes and sexual violence, the Trial Chamber established that Brđanin aided and abetted members of the Bosnian Serb forces in the commission of rapes and sexual violence perpetrated against Muslim women amounting to torture in the Keraterm (July 1992), Trnopolje (May-October 1992) and Omarska camp (June 1992) in the municipality of Prijedor as well as the rapes of Bosnian Muslim women in Teslic municipality.[56] He furthermore aided and abetted the rapes and sexual assault by Bosnian Serb soldiers and policemen of Bosnian Muslims and Bosnian Croat women in the above-mentioned camps in the municipalities of Prijedor and Teslic, as well as the municipalities of Banja Luka, Bosanska Krupa, Donji Vakuf and Kotor Varos.[57] These rapes and acts of sexual assault were carried out with the intent to discriminate against Bosnian Muslim and Bosnian Croat women on racial, religious or political grounds and

[53] The Prosecutor also seemed to have evidence that Češić allegedly raped two women in May and June 1992, but chose not to indict him for these acts and instead put it forward to establish that Češić was not a man of good character meriting mitigation of his punishment. Češić Sentencing Judgment, para. 73.

[54] Češić Sentencing Judgment, para. 13. See also para. 14.

[55] Brđanin Judgment, para. 1152 (on these counts, he was not found guilty under Article 7(3) of the ICTY Statute). He was acquitted of genocide, complicity in genocide, extermination, and unlawful and wanton extensive destruction of property not justified by military necessity.

[56] *Ibid.*, paras. 512-518, 523-524, 535, 538.

[57] *Ibid.*, para. 1010.

amounted to persecution as a crime against humanity.[58] Brđanin was given a single sentence of 32 years imprisonment.

ICTR JUDGMENTS ON SEXUAL VIOLENCE

1 Akayesu (2 October and 2 September 1998 / 1 June 2001)

Akayesu, the former *bourgmestre* of Taba commune (Gitarama Prefecture), was convicted of genocide (count 1), extermination as a crime against humanity (count 3), murder as a crime against humanity (counts 5, 7, 9), torture as a crime against humanity (count 11), rape as a crime against humanity (count 13) and other inhumane acts as crimes against humanity (count 16).[59] With respect to sexual violence crimes, Akayesu was found guilty under Article 6(1) with respect to count 1 of genocide (life imprisonment); count 13 of rape as a crime against humanity (15 years); and count 14 of other inhumane acts as crimes against humanity (10 years).[60] Akayesu's guilt was based on the multiple acts of rape by *Interahamwe* and forced undressing and public naked marching on and near the Taba bureau communal premises. Akayesu, although not a principal perpetrator himself, ordered, instigated, and aided and abetted in these acts of sexual violence.[61] In respect of his conviction for rape as genocide, the Trial Chamber held that 'these rapes resulted in physical and psychological destruction of Tutsi women, their families and their communities. Sexual violence was an integral part of the process of destruction, specifically targeting Tutsi women and specifically contributing to their destruction and to the destruction of the Tutsi group as a whole.'[62] Akayesu had to serve all sentences concurrently and therefore received a single sentence

---

[58] *Ibid.*, paras. 1008-1013, 1055-1059.

[59] Akayesu was found not guilty of complicity in genocide (count 2), murder and cruel treatment as a violation of Common Article 3 to the Geneva Conventions (counts 6, 8, 10 and 12), and outrage upon personal dignity, in particular rape, degrading and humiliating treatment and indecent assault as a violation of Article 3 common to the Geneva Conventions and of Article 4(2)(e) of Additional Protocol II (count 15).

[60] With respect to Article 6(3) and counts 13 and 14, the Trial Chamber held that 'although the evidence supports a finding that a superior/subordinate relationship existed between the Accused and the Interahamwe who were at the bureau communal, the Tribunal notes that there is no allegation in the Indictment that the Interahamwe, who are referred to as 'armed local militia', were the subordinates of the Accused. This relationship is a fundamental element of the criminal offence set forth in Article 6(3). The amendment of the Indictment with additional charges pursuant to Article 6(3) could arguably be interpreted as implying an allegation of the command responsibility required by Article 6(3). In fairness to the Accused, the Tribunal will not make this inference. Therefore, the Tribunal finds that it cannot consider the criminal responsibility of the Accused under Article 6(3).' Akayesu was not charged under Article 6(3) with regard to the genocide count. See Akayesu Judgment, para. 691.

[61] Akayesu Judgment, paras. 416-460 (factual findings) and paras. 685-734 (legal findings).

[62] *Ibid.*, para. 731.

of life imprisonment (in Mali).[63] His sentence with respect to the sexual violence conduct was upheld on appeal.

2 Musema (27 January 2000 / 16 November 2001)

Musema, the former director of the Gisovu tea factory (Kibuye Prefecture), was convicted of genocide (count 1), extermination as a crime against humanity (count 5) and rape as a crime against humanity (count 7).[64] With respect to the sexual violence crimes, Musema was convicted on count 1 of rape as genocide and count 7 of rape as a crime against humanity, both under Article 6(1) of the ICTR Statute.[65] These convictions were based on the Trial Chamber's finding that Musema raped Nyiramusugi and by his example encouraged others to rape her. More specifically, on 13 May 1994, Musema ordered a policeman to bring Nyiramusugi to him, whereupon four youths held her down while Musema raped her. After Musema left, the four took turns raping her and then left her for dead.[66] No separate sentences for each count were imposed, but instead a single sentence of life imprisonment (in Mali) was rendered. However, on

---

[63] In addition, Akayesu was acquitted on count 15 of sexual violence as an outrage against personal dignity under Article 4(e) (violations of Article 3 common to the Geneva Conventions and of the Additional Protocols). The Chamber maintained that it had not been proven beyond a reasonable doubt 'that the acts perpetrated by Akayesu in the commune of Taba at the time of the events alleged in the Indictment were committed in conjunction with the armed conflict'. Moreover, the Chamber held that it was not proven beyond a reasonable doubt that Akayesu had been a member of the armed forces, or 'legitimately mandated and expected, as a public official or agent or person otherwise holding public authority or de facto representing the Government, to support or fulfil the war efforts'. See Akayesu Judgment, para. 643.

[64] He was found not guilty of complicity in genocide (count 2, as an alternative to genocide), conspiracy to commit genocide (count 3), murder as a crime against humanity (count 4), other inhumane acts as a crime against humanity (count 6), violations of Common Article 3 to the Geneva Conventions and the Additional Protocol II thereto, Article 4(a) of the Statute (count 8), and violations of Common Article 3 to the Geneva Conventions and the Additional Protocol II thereto, Article 4(e) of the Statute (count 9).

[65] The Trial Chamber found that it was not established that Musema incurred responsibility under Article 6(3) as it was not established that the assailants who attacked Nyiramusugi were Musema's subordinates (they were not employees of the Gisovu Tea Factory or other persons who were Musema's subordinates). Musema Judgment and Sentence, paras. 908-909 and 966-968. In addition, all other events relating to sexual violence were, according to the Trial Chamber, not proven by the evidence presented. In the first place, as regards the allegations that Musema ordered the rape of Tutsi women on Karongi hill on 18 April 1994, it was not proven that Musema was present at this meeting. In the second place, although it had been proven that Musema ordered the rape and cutting off of Annunciata Mujawayezu's breast to be fed to her son on 14 April 1994, there is no conclusive evidence that she was raped or that her breast was cut off. In the third place, the accused was not convicted of the rape and killing of Immaculée Mukankuzi and the rape and killing of others with her by his men and on his orders on 13 May 1994 because of unexplained inconsistencies in the testimony presented. Musema Judgment and Sentence, paras. 797-883.

[66] Musema Judgment and Sentence, paras. 847-853.

appeal, Musema's conviction for rape as a crime against humanity was quashed on the basis of additional evidence presented by two witnesses that contradicted the evidence given by Witness N, whose testimony was used before the Trial Chamber to convict Musema of rape.[67] The sentence of life imprisonment remained in place for the other crimes he had been convicted of (genocide and extermination as a crime against humanity). However, as a consequence of the contradictory evidence in relation to the rape of Nyiramusugi, Musema could no longer be held individually responsible for rape as genocide.

3 Semanza (15 May 2003 / 20 May 2005)

Semanza, the former *bourgmestre* of Bicumbi (Kigali Rural Prefecture), was convicted of complicity to commit genocide (count 3), and of extermination (count 5), rape (count 10), torture (count 11) and murder (counts 12 and 14) as crimes against humanity.[68] With respect to sexual violence crimes, Semanza was found guilty under count 10 of instigating rape as a crime against humanity (7 years) and count 11 of instigating torture by rape (and personally committing torture) as crimes against humanity (10 years), both under Article 6(1) of the ICTR Statute.[69] Both convictions were based on the finding that Victim A was raped by one of the assailants who heard Semanza encouraging a crowd in Gikoro Commune to rape Tutsi women before killing them. The rape immediately followed Semanza's speech. The Trial Chamber found that Semanza not

[67] In particular, the new statement described the rape as having been carried out by somebody other than Musema. See Musema Appeal Judgment, paras. 172-194. If additional evidence establishes that a reasonable tribunal of fact could not have reached a conclusion of guilt, the Appeals Chamber has to pronounce that an error of fact occasioned a miscarriage of justice. See Article 24 ICTR Statute and Rule 118(A) ICTR RPE.

[68] Semanza was acquitted of genocide, direct and public incitement to commit genocide, serious violations of Common Article 3 and Additional Protocol II of the Geneva Conventions, and persecution as a crime against humanity.

[69] The Chamber did not consider the charge of rape as a crime against humanity (Count 8) in its factual or legal findings. The count was based solely on paragraphs 3.15 and 3.16 of the indictment, which was held to be impermissibly vague and, for this reason, prejudiced the accused's ability to prepare his defence (paras. 41-62). Further, Semanza was found not guilty of the charges concerning serious violations of Article 3 Common the Geneva Conventions and Additional Protocol II, Articles 4(e) and 4(a) of the Statutes (counts 9 and 13). As to count 9, the Trial Chamber held that the Prosecutor had failed to introduce any evidence of the occurrence of rape or other forms of sexual violence at the sites mentioned (para. 539). In respect of count 13: although it was established that Semanza instigated the rape and torture of Victim A, the Trial Chamber held (Judge Williams dissenting) that no conviction could be entered because of an ideal concurrence with rape and torture as crimes against humanity charged in counts 10 and 11 (paras. 551-552). Semanza was also acquitted on count 7 of rape and other serious violations of Common Article 3 and Additional Protocol II listed in Article 4(a) of the Statute: even though Semanza urged people in a crowd to rape and kill Tutsi women before going to Musha church, a conviction on count 7 would create an ideal concurrence with the crime of complicity in genocide charged in count 3 (paras. 523-536). See the Separate and Dissenting Opinion of Judge Pavel Dolenc on cumulative convictions.

only instigated rape, but also rape for a discriminatory purpose and thus constituting torture: the rape, causing severe mental suffering, targeted women because of their ethnicity.[70] He received 25 years imprisonment, a sentence which was divided into both consecutive and concurrent jail terms.[71] On appeal, Semanza's sentence was increased to 35 years in prison. With regard to the sexual violence charges, the convictions for rape as a crime against humanity under count 10 and the conviction for torture as a crime against humanity under count 11 were affirmed. In addition, convictions for serious violations of Common Article 3 of the 1949 Geneva Conventions and of the 1977 Additional Protocol II thereto under, *inter alia*, count 13 (for instigating the rape and torture of Victim A and the murder of Victim B, and for committing torture and intentional murder of Rusanganwa) were entered (Article 4(a) ICTR Statute).

4 Niyitegeka (16 May 2003 / 9 July 2004)

Niyitegeka, the former Minister of Information, was convicted of the following crimes: genocide (count 1), conspiracy to commit genocide (count 3), direct and public incitement to commit genocide (count 4) and the crimes against humanity of murder, extermination and other inhumane acts (counts 5, 6 and 8, respectively).[72] In respect of sexual violence crimes, Niyitegeka was acquitted of rape as a crime against humanity, but found guilty of other inhumane acts as crimes against humanity under Article 6(1), which included the killing and subsequent decapitation and castration of a man and the sexual mutilation of a dead woman.[73] The Trial Chamber sentenced Niyitegeka to imprisonment for the remainder of his life. The sentence was upheld on appeal.

5 Nahimana, Ngeze and Barayagwiza – *Media* case (3 December 2003, Appeal Pending)

Three accused stood trial in the so-called '*Media* trial': Nahimana, the founder of RTLM Radio, Barayagwiza, member of the Steering Committee of RTLM Radio, and Ngeze, founder and editor-in-chief of the newspaper *Kangura*. Nahimana, Barayagwiza and Ngeze were convicted of conspiracy to commit genocide (count 1); genocide (count 2); direct and public incitement to commit genocide (count 3); persecution as a crime against humanity (count 5); and extermination as a crime against humanity (count 6).[74] In respect of sexual violence, all three accused were convicted of sexual violence as a

---

[70] Semanza Judgment and Sentence, paras. 475-485. Although the Trial Chamber found that Victim B was killed by two other men from the crowd, it held that there was insufficient evidence to conclude that Victim B was raped as well.

[71] The concurrent sentences for counts 10, 11, 12 and 14 were served consecutively to the concurrent sentences for counts 3 and 5.

[72] The Trial Chamber acquitted the Appellant on four counts: complicity in genocide (count 2), rape as a crime against humanity (count 7), and two counts of serious violations of Article 3 Common to the Geneva Conventions and of Additional Protocol II thereto (counts 9 and 10).

[73] Niyitegeka Judgment and Sentence, paras. 303-316.

[74] All three were acquitted of complicity in genocide and murder as a crime against humanity. In addition, Barayagwiza, who was also charged with violations of Article 3 Common to the Geneva Conventions and Additional Protocol II in counts 8 and 9, was acquitted thereof.

form of persecution as a crime against humanity under count 5 (Nahimana under Article 6(1) and 6(3)), count 7 (Barayagwiza under Article 6(1) and 6(3)) and count 6 (Ngeze under Article 6(1)). The Trial Chamber held that: 'Tutsi women, in particular, were targeted for persecution. The portrayal of the Tutsi woman as a *femme fatale*, and the message that Tutsi women were seductive agents of the enemy was conveyed repeatedly by RTLM and *Kangura*. *The Ten Commandments*, broadcast on RTLM and published in *Kangura*, vilified and endangered Tutsi women ... By defining the Tutsi woman as an enemy in this way, RTLM and *Kangura* articulated a framework that made the sexual attack of women a foreseeable consequence of the role attributed to them.'[75] Nahimana and Ngeze received a single sentence of life imprisonment and Barayagwiza received a single sentence of 35 years.

6 Gacumbitsi (17 June 2004, Appeal Pending)

Gacumbitsi, the former *bourgmestre* of Rusumo commune (Kibungo Prefecture), was found guilty of genocide (count 1), extermination as a crime against humanity (count 3) and rape as a crime against humanity (count 5).[76] In relation to sexual violence, Gacumbitsi was convicted of rape as a crime against humanity under Article 6(1), e.g., instigating, not under Article 6(3) and rape as a form of genocide, i.e., the Trial Chamber held that Gacumbitsi caused serious bodily harm to Tutsi women who were raped at his instigation, which manifested his genocidal intent.[77] The Chamber found that, on 17 April 1994, Gacumbitsi publicly incited the rape of Tutsi women and girls, by specifying that sticks should be inserted into their genitals in the event they resisted the rapes. Prosecution Witness TAQ testified that she and seven other Tutsi women and girls were raped by young men who heard the *bourgmestre*'s instigation, while he was in a caravan crossing the bridge between Kankobwa and Nyarubuye, in the direction of Nyarubuye. These rapes were the direct consequences of Gacumbitsi's instigation to rape Tutsi women.[78] Gacumbitsi received a single sentence of 30 years imprisonment.

7 Muhimana (28 April 2005, Appeal Pending)

For a substantial part, the Muhimana trial evolved around evidence of sexual violence, which occurred between April and June 1994 in the Bisesero area and in many locations in Gishyita commune, Kibuye Prefecture, where Muhimana was *conseiller*. The trial took only 34 trial days, in which the Chamber heard 52 witnesses, 19 for the Prosecution and 33 for the Defence. Muhimana was found guilty of genocide, which included sexual violence (count 1), rape as a crime against humanity (count 3) and

---

[75] Media Judgment, para. 1079.

[76] Gacumbitsi was found not guilty of complicity in genocide (count 2, as an alternative to count 1 on genocide) and murder as a crime against humanity (count 4).

[77] The Chamber found it not necessary to enquire whether Gacumbitsi was equally liable under Article 6(3) of the Statute, given the similarity of the facts and the absence of any evidence of a superior-subordinate relationship between the accused and the perpetrators of the rapes.

[78] Although the Chamber found that the rapes recounted by Prosecution Witnesses TAQ, TAS and TAP were established, it did not find that these rapes resulted from the instigation made by Gacumbitsi to rape Tutsi women.

murder as a crime against humanity (count 4) and was sentenced for each crime to life imprisonment, to be served concurrently.[79] With regard to sexual violence, Muhimana was sentenced to life imprisonment for raping seven women and girls (6 Tutsi girls and one Hutu girl whom he mistakenly believed was a Tutsi) and aiding and abetting others to rape a total of 5 Tutsi women and girls.

[79] The charge for complicity in genocide (count 2) was dismissed in light of Muhimana's conviction for genocide.

BIBLIOGRAPHY

Amann (1999)
Amann, D.M., Prosecutor v. Akayesu. Case ICTR-96-4-T. International Criminal Tribunal for Rwanda, September 2, 1998, *American Journal of International Law*, 93, 1999, 195-199.
Arnold (2003)
Arnold, R., The *Mens Rea* of Genocide under the Statute of the International Criminal Court, *Criminal Law Forum*, 14, 2003, 127-151.
Askin (1997)
Askin, K.D., *War Crimes Against Women: Prosecution in International War Crimes Tribunals*, Dordrecht: Martinus Nijhoff Publishers, 1997.
Askin (1999)
Askin, K., Sexual Violence in Decisions and Indictments of the Yugoslav and Rwandan Tribunals: Current Status, *American Journal of International Law*, 93(1), 1999, 97-123.
Askin (2003a)
Askin, K.D., Prosecuting Wartime Rape and Other Gender-Related Crimes Under International Law: Extraordinary Advances, Enduring Obstacles, *Berkeley Journal of International Law*, 21, 2003, 288-349.
Askin (2003b)
Askin, K.D., Commentary – ICTY, Judgement, Prosecutor v. Kunarac, Kovač and Vuković, Cases No. IT-96-23-T and IT-96-23/1-T, T. Ch. II, 22 February 2001, in: A. Klip and G. Sluiter (eds.), *Annotated Leading Cases of International Criminal Tribunals: The International Criminal Tribunal for the former Yugoslavia 2000-2001*, Volume 5, Antwerp/Oxford/New York: Intersentia 2003, pp. 806-817.
Askin (2003c)
Askin, K.D., The ICTY at Ten: A Critical Assessment of the Major Rulings of the International Criminal Tribunal Over the Past Decade: Reflections on Some of the Most Significant Achievements of the ICTY, *New England Law Review*, 37, 2003, 903-914.
Askin (2004a)
Askin, K., International Criminal Tribunals and Victim-Witnesses, in: S. R. Ratner and J.L. Bischoff (eds.), *International War Crimes Trials: Making a Difference?, Proceedings of an International Conference Held at the University of Texas School of Law, November 6-7, 2003*, Texas: The University of Texas at Austin School of Law 2004, pp. 49-59.
Askin (2004b)
Askin, K.D., The International Criminal Tribunal for Rwanda and Its Treatment of Crimes Against Women, in: J. Carey et al. (eds.), *International Humanitarian Law: Origins, Challenges and Prospects*, 2, Ardsley, New York: Transnational Publishers 2004, pp. 33-88.

Aydelott (1993)
Aydelott, D., Mass Rape During War: Prosecuting Bosnian Rapists Under International Law, *Emory International Law Review*, 7, 1993, 585-631.

Barnett (2002)
Barnett, M., *Eyewitness to a Genocide: The United Nations and Rwanda*, Ithaca and London: Cornell University Press, 2002.
Barrett and Little (2003)
Barrett, R.P. and L.E. Little, Lessons of the Yugoslav Rape Trials: A Role for Conspiracy Law in International Tribunals, *Minnesota Law Review*, 88, 2003, 30-85.
Bassiouni (1992)
Bassiouni, C.M., *Crimes Against Humanity in International Criminal Law*, Dordrecht: Martinus Nijhoff Publishers, 1992.
Bassiouni (1998)
Bassiouni, M.C., *The Statute of the International Criminal Court: A Documentary History*, Arsley, New York: Transnational Publishers, 1998.
Bassiouni and McCormick (1996)
Bassiouni, C.M. and M. McCormick, *Sexual Violence: An Invisible Weapon of War in the former Yugoslavia*, Occasional Paper No. 1, Chigago, IL: International Human Rights Institute, 1996.
Bassiouni and Manikas (1996)
Bassiouni, M.C. and P. Manikas, *The Law of the International Criminal Tribunal for the former Yugoslavia,* Irvington-on-Hudson, NY: Transnational Publishers, 1996.
Bedont and Hall Martinez (1999)
Bedont, B. and K. Hall Martinez, Ending Impunity for Gender Crimes Under the International Criminal Court, *Brown Journal of World Affairs*, VI(1), 1999, 65-85.
Beresford (2001)
Beresford, S., Unshackling the Paper Tiger – The Sentencing Practices of the Ad Hoc International Criminal Tribunals for the former Yugoslavia and Rwanda, *International Criminal Law Review*, 1, 2001, 33-90.
Beverly (1996)
Beverly, A., *Rape Warfare: The Hidden Genocide in Bosnia-Herzegovina and Croatia*, Minneapolis, MN: University of Minnesota Press, 1996.
Bitti and Friman (2001)
Bitti, G. and H. Friman, Participation of Victims in the Proceedings, in: R.S. Lee *et al.* (eds.), *The International Criminal Court: Elements of Crimes and Rules of Procedure and Evidence*, Ardsley, New York: Transnational Publishers 2001, pp. 456-474.
Boas (2000)
Boas, G., Comparing the ICTY and the ICC: Some Procedural and Substantive Issues, *Netherlands International Law Review*, 47(3), 2000, 267-292.
Bonneau (2004)
Bonneau, K., *The Reparation Regime of Victims Before the International Criminal Court, presentation held at the Grotius Center*, The Hague, 13 May 2004.
Boon (2001)
Boon, K., Rape and Forced Pregnancy Under the ICC Statute: Human Dignity, Autonomy, and Consent, *Columbia Human Rights Law Review*, 32, 2001, 624-675.

Boot (2002)
Boot, M., *Nullum Crimen Sine Lege and the Subject Matter Jurisdiction of the International Criminal Court: Genocide, Crimes Against Humanity, War Crimes,* Antwerp/Oxford/New York: Intersentia, 2002.
Boot, Hall and Dixon (1999)
Boot, M., C.K. Hall and R. Dixon, Article 7 – Crimes Against Humanity, in: O. Triffterer (ed.), *Commentary on the Rome Statute of the International Criminal Court: Observers' Notes, Article by Article*, Baden-Baden: Nomos 1999, pp. 117-172.
Bottigliero (2004)
Bottigliero, I., *Redress for Victims of Crimes Under International Law*, Leiden/Boston: Martinus Nijhoff Publishers, 2004.
Brady (2001)
Brady, H., Protective and Special Measures for Victims and Witnesses, in: R.S. Lee *et al.* (eds.), *The International Criminal Court: Elements of Crimes and Rules of Procedure and Evidence*, Ardsley, New York: Transnational Publishers, Inc., 2001, pp. 434-456.
Brienen and Hoegen (2000)
Brienen, M.E.I. and E.H. Hoegen, *Victims of Crime in 22 European Criminal Justice Systems: The Implementation of Recommendation (85) 11 of the Council of Europe on the Position of the Victim in the Framework of Criminal Law and Procedure*, Nijmegen: Wolf Legal Productions, 2000.
Brienen, Groenhuijsen and Hoegen (2000)
Brienen, M., M. Groenhuijsen and E. Hoegen, Evaluation and Meta-Evaluation of the Effectiveness of Victim-Oriented Legal Reform in Europe, *Criminologie*, 33(1), 2000, 121-144.
Brownmiller (1993)
Brownmiller, S., *Against Our Will: Men, Women, and Rape*, New York: Simon and Schuster, 1975.
Burg and Shoup (1999)
Burg, S.L., and P.S. Shoup, *The War in Bosnia-Herzegovina: Ethnic Conflict and International Intervention*, Armonk, New York: Sharpe, 1999.

Campanaro (2000)
Campanaro, J., Women, War and International Law: The Historical Treatment of Gender-Based War Crimes, *Georgetown Law Journal*, 89, 2001, 2557-2592.
Carcano (2002)
Carcano, A., Sentencing and the Gravity of the Offence in International Criminal Law, *International and Comparative Law Quarterly*, 51(3), 2002, 583-610.
Cassese (2003)
Cassese, A., *International Criminal Law*, Oxford: Oxford University Press, 2003.
Cavelius (2000)
Cavelius, A., *Leila: Een meisje uit Bosnië*, Baarn: Tirion Uitgevers BV, 2000.
Charlesworth and Chinkin (1993)
Charlesworth, H. and C. Chinkin, The Gender of Jus Cogens, *Human Rights Quarterly*, 15(1), 1993, 63-76.

Chifflet (2003)
Chifflet, P., The Role and Status of the Victim, in: G. Boas and W. Schabas (eds.), *International Criminal Law Developments in the Case Law of the ICTY*, The Netherlands: Koninklijke Brill NV 2003, pp. 75-111.
Chinkin (1994)
Chinkin, C., Rape and Sexual Abuse of Women in International Law, *European Journal of International Law*, 5(3), 1994, 326-341.
Chinkin (1996)
Chinkin, C., International Tribunal for the former Yugoslavia: Amicus Curiae Brief on Protective Measures for Victims and Witnesses, *Criminal Law Forum*, 7, 1996, 179-212.
Chinkin (2000)
Chinkin, C., The Protection of Victims and Witnesses, in: G.K. McDonald and O. Swaak-Goldman (eds.), *Substantive and Procedural Aspects of International Criminal Law: the Experience of International and National Courts*, Volume I: Commentary, The Hague: Kluwer Law International 2000, pp. 453-478.
Clark and Tolbert (1999)
Clark, R.S. and D. Tolbert, Toward an International Criminal Court, in: Y. Danieli, E. Stamatopoulou and C.J. Dias (eds.), *Universal Declaration of Human Rights: Fifty Years and Beyond*, Amityville, New York: Baywood Publishing Company 1999, pp. 99-112.
Cleiren and Tijssen (1994)
Cleiren, C.P.M. and M.E.M. Tijssen, Rape and Other Forms of Sexual Assault in the Armed Conflict in the former Yugoslavia: Legal, Procedural, and Evidentiary Issues, *Criminal Law Forum*, 5(1-2), 1994, 471-506.
Coan (2000)
Coan, C.B., Rethinking the Spoils of War: Prosecuting Rape as a War Crime in the International Criminal Tribunal for the former Yugoslavia, *North Carolina Journal of International Law and Commercial Regulation*, 26, 2000, 183-237.
Copelon (1995)
Copelon, R., Gendered War Crimes: Reconceptualizing Rape in Time of War, in: J. Peters and A. Wolper (eds.), *Women's Rights, Human Rights: International Feminist Perspectives*, New York: Routledge 1995, pp. 197-214.
Copelon (2000)
Copelon, R., Gender Crimes as War Crimes: Integrating Crimes against Women into International Criminal Law, *McGill Law Journal*, 46, 2000, 217-240.

Dallaire (2003)
Dallaire, R.A. (Lt.Gen.) and B. Beardsley, *Shake Hands with the Devil: The Failure of Humanity in Rwanda*, Toronto: Random House Canada, 2003.
Damrosch (1998)
Damrosch, L.F., Genocide and Ethnic Conflict, in: D. Wippman (ed.), *International Law and Ethnic Conflict*, Ithaca, New York: Cornell University Press 1998, pp. 256-279.
Danner (2001)
Danner, A.M., Constructing a Hierarchy of Crimes in International Criminal Law Sentencing, *Virginia Law Review*, 87, 2001, 415-501.

De Brouwer (1999)
De Brouwer, A., *Prosecuting Rape and Other Forms of Sexual Violence Against Women Under the ICTY, ICTR and ICC Statutes: What Has Been Accomplished So Far?*, LL.M. Dissertation Essex, 1999.
De Brouwer (2001)
De Brouwer, A., Case Law: The International Criminal Tribunal for the former Yugoslavia: Kunarac, Kovac and Vukovic case ("Foča"), *Tilburg Foreign Law Review*, 9(2), 2001, 221-236.
De Brouwer (2005)
De Brouwer, A., Commentary – Indictment (Hadzihasanović *et al.*; Blagojević *et al.*; Brdjanin and Talić; and Zec and Banović), in: A. Klip and G. Sluiter (eds.), *Annotated Leading Cases of International Criminal Tribunals: The International Criminal Tribunal for the former Yugoslavia 2001-2002*, Volume 8, Antwerp/Oxford: Intersentia 2005, pp. 130-138.
Fernandez de Gurmendi (2001)
A. Fernandez de Gurmendi, S.A., Definition of Victims and General Principle, in: R.S. Lee *et al.* (eds.), *The International Criminal Court: Elements of Crimes and Rules of Procedure and Evidence*, New York: Transnational Publishers 2001, pp. 427-433.
Dembour and Haslam (2004)
Dembour, M-B and E. Haslam, Silencing Hearings? Victim-Witnesses at War Crimes Trials, *European Journal of International Law*, 15(1), 2004, 151-177.
Des Forges (1999)
Des Forges, A., *Leave None to Tell the Story: Genocide in Rwanda*, New York/Washington/London/Brussels: Human Rights Watch and Paris: International Federation of Human Rights, 1999.
Dieng (2002a)
Dieng, A., II. Other Preparations for the Establishment of the Court: International Criminal Justice: From Paper to Practice – A Contribution from the International Criminal Tribunal for Rwanda to the Establishment of the International Criminal Court, *Fordham International Law Journal*, 25, 2002, 688-707.
Dieng (2002b)
Dieng, A., *The International Criminal Court: Lessons From the International Criminal Tribunal for Rwanda – Potential Problems for the Registrar*, Paper presented by Mr. Adama Dieng, UN Assistant S-G and Registrar ICTR, at the Conference on 'Towards Global Justice: Accountability and the International Criminal Court, held at Wilton Park, Sussex, UK, 4-8 February 2002.
Dixon (2002)
Dixon, R., Rape as a Crime in International Humanitarian Law: Where to from Here?, *European Journal of International Law*, 13(3), 2002, 697-719.
Donat-Cattin (1999a)
Donat-Cattin, D., Article 68 – Protection of Victims and Witnesses and Their Participation in the Proceedings, in: O. Triffterer (ed.), *Commentary on the Rome Statute of the International Criminal Court: Observers' Notes, Article by Article*, Baden-Baden: Nomos 1999, pp. 869-888.
Donat-Cattin (1999b)
Donat-Cattin, D., Article 75 – Reparation to Victims, in: O. Triffterer (ed.), *Commentary on the Rome Statute of the International Criminal Court: Observers' Notes, Article by Article*, Baden-Baden: Nomos 1999, pp. 965-978.

Dörmann (2001)
Dörmann, K., in: Article 8(2)(a)(ii) – Torture, Inhuman Treatment and Biological Experiments, in: R.S. Lee *et al.* (eds.), *The International Criminal Court: Elements of Crimes and Rules of Procedure and Evidence*, Ardsley, New York: Transnational Publishers 2001, pp. 125-130.
Dörmann (2004)
Dörmann, K., *Elements of War Crimes under the Rome Statute of the International Criminal Court: Sources and Commentary*, Cambridge: Cambridge University Press, 2004.
Drakulić (2000)
Drakulić, S., *Alsof ik er niet ben*, Breda: Uitgeverij de Geus, 2000.

Ellis (1997)
Ellis, M.S., Symposium: Justice in Cataclysm Criminal Trials in the Wake of Mass Violence: Comment: Achieving Justice Before the International War Crimes Tribunal: Challenges for the Defense Counsel, *Duke Journal of Comparative and International Law*, 7, 1997, 519-537.

Featherstone (1997)
Featherstone, Y.M.O., The International Criminal Tribunal for the former Yugoslavia: Recent Developments in Witness Protection, *Leiden Journal of International Law*, 10, 1997, 179-198.
Fein (1999)
Fein, H., Genocide and Gender: The Uses of Women and Group Destiny, *Journal of Genocide Research*, 1(1), 1999, 43-63.
Ferstman (2002)
Ferstman, C., The Reparation Regime of the International Criminal Court: Practical Considerations, *Leiden Journal of International Law*, 15, 2002, 667-686.
Fife (1999a)
Fife, Article 77 – Applicable Penalties, in: O. Triffterer (ed.), *Commentary on the Rome Statute of the International Criminal Court: Observers' Notes, Article by Article*, Baden-Baden: Nomos 1999, pp. 985-998.
Fife (1999b)
Fife, R., Article 80 – Non-Prejudice to National Application of Penalties and National Laws, in: O. Triffterer (ed.), *Commentary on the Rome Statute of the International Criminal Court: Observers' Notes, Article by Article*, Baden-Baden: Nomos 1999, pp. 1009-1014.
Fife (2001)
Fife, R., Penalties, in: R.S. Lee *et al.* (eds.), *The International Criminal Court: Elements of Crimes and Rules of Procedure and Evidence*, New York: Transnational Publishers 2001, pp. 555-574.
Fischer (1996)
Fischer, S.K., Occupation of the Womb: Forced Impregnation as Genocide, *Duke Law Journal*, 46, 1996, 91-133.
Fitzgerald (1997)
Fitzgerald, K., Problems of Prosecution and Adjudication of Rape and Other Sexual Assaults under International Law, *European Journal of International Law*, 8, 1997, 638-663.

Franke (1998)
Franke, K.M., Putting Sex to Work, *Denver University Law Review*, 75, 1998, 1139-1180.
Frulli (2001)
Frulli, M., Are Crimes Against Humanity More Serious than War Crimes?, *European Journal of International Law*, 12(2), 2001, 329-350.

Gardam (2001)
Gardam, J.G., and M.J. Jarvis, *Women, Armed Conflict and International Law*, The Hague/London/Boston: Kluwer Law International, 2001.
Garkawe (2001)
Garkawe, S., The Victim-Related Provisions of the Statute of the International Criminal Court: A Victimological Analysis, *International Review of Victimology*, 8, 2001, 269-289.
Garkawe (2003)
Garkawe, S., Victims and the International Criminal Court: Three Major Issues, *International Criminal Law Review*, 3(4), 2003, 345-367.
Garraway (2001)
Garraway, C., Elements of the Specific Forms of Genocide, in: R.S. Lee *et al.* (eds.), *The International Criminal Court: Elements of Crimes and Rules of Procedure and Evidence*, Ardsley, New York: Transnational Publishers 2001, pp. 49-55.
Gillard (2003)
Gillard, E-C., Reparation for Violations of International Humanitarian Law, *International Review of the Red Cross*, 85(851), September 2003, 529-553.
Goldstein (1993)
Goldstein, A.T., *Recognizing Forced Impregnation as a War Crime Under International Law*, The Center for Reproductive Law and Policy, 1993.
Goldstone (2002)
Goldstone, R., Prosecuting Rape as a War Crime, *Case Western Reserve Journal of International Law*, 34, 2002, 277-285.
Gordon and Crehan (2002)
Gordon, P. and K. Crehan, *Dying of Sadness: Gender, Sexual Violence and the HIV Apidemic*, 2002.
Gourevitch (1998)
Gourevitch, P., *We Wish to Inform You that Tomorrow we will be Killed with our Families: Stories from Rwanda*, New York: Picador USA, 1998.
Gow (2003)
Gow, J., *The Serbian Project and its Adversaries: A Strategy of War Crimes*, Montreal: McGill-Queen's University Press, 2003.
Green (2002)
Green, L.L., Gender Hate Propaganda and Sexual Violence in the Rwandan Genocide: An Argument for Intersectionality in International Law, *Columbia Human Rights Law Review*, 33, 2002, 733-776.
Green, Copelon, Cotter and Stephens (1994)
Green, J., R. Copelon, P. Cotter and B. Stephens, Affecting the Rules for the Prosecution of Rape and Other Gender-Based Violence Before the International Criminal Tribunal for the former Yugoslavia: A Feminist Proposal and Critique, *Hastings Women's Law Journal*, 5, 1994, 171-221.

Greenawalt (1999)
Greenawalt, A.K.A., Rethinking Genocidal Intent: Note, Rethinking Genocidal Intent: The Case for a Knowledge-Based Interpretation, *Columbia Law Review*, 99, 1999, 2259-2294.
Groenhuijsen (1985)
Groenhuijsen, M.S., *Schadevergoeding voor slachtoffers van delicten in het strafgeding*, PhD Thesis Leiden, Nijmegen: Ars Aequi Libri, 1985.
Groenhuijsen (1996)
Groenhuijsen, M.S., Straftoemeting en de consequenties van een delict voor het slachtoffer, *Delikt & Delinkwent*, 26(7), 1996, 605-613.
Groenhuijsen (2004a)
Groenhuijsen, M., Victims' Rights and Restorative Justice: Piecemeal Reform of the Criminal Justice System or a Change of Paradigm?, in: H. Kaptein and M. Malsch, *Crime, Victims and Justice: Essays on Principles and Practice*, Hampshire: Ashgate 2004, pp. 63-79.
Groenhuijsen (2004b)
Groenhuijsen, M.S., Herstel, schadevergoeding en normbevestiging. Naar een processuele vertaling van strafdoeleinden, in: B. van Stokkom (red.), *Straf en herstel: Ethische reflecties over sanctiedoeleinden*, Den Haag: Boom Juridische Uitgevers 2004, pp. 273-286.

Hall (1999)
Hall, C.K., Article 7(2)(b-e) – Definition of Crimes or Their Elements, in: O. Triffterer (ed.), *Commentary on the Rome Statute of the International Criminal Court: Observers' Notes, Article by Article*, Baden-Baden: Nomos 1999, pp. 160-164.
Haveman (2002)
Haveman, R., Rape and Fair Trial in Supranational Criminal Law, *Maastricht Journal of European and Comparative Law*, 9(3), 2002, 263-278.
Haveman (2003a)
Haveman, R., Introduction: A System Sui Generis, in: R. Haveman, O. Kavran and J. Nicholls (eds.), *Supranational Criminal Law: A System Sui Generis*, Antwerp/Oxford/New York: Intersentia 2003, pp. 1-8.
Haveman (2003b)
Haveman, R., The Context of the Law, in: R. Haveman, O. Kavran and J. Nicholls (eds.), *Supranational Criminal Law: A System Sui Generis*, Antwerp/Oxford/New York: Intersentia 2003, pp. 9-38.
Haveman (2004)
Haveman, R.H., De Rationaliteit van het Supranationale Straffen, *Justitiële Verkenningen*, 30(5), 2004, 67-78.
Haveman and Wijers (2002)
Haveman, R. and M. Wijers, Kroniek supranationaal strafrecht (1), *Nemesis*, 3, 2002, 61-66.
Heikkilä (2004)
Heikkilä, M., *International Criminal Tribunals and Victims of Crime*, Turku/Åbo: Institute for Human Rights, Åbo Akademi University, 2004.

Hoffman and Riemann (2004)
Hoffman, R. and F. Riemann, *Compensation for Victims of War*, Background Report, International Law Association, Committee on Compensation for Victims of War, 17 March 2004.
Home Office (2000)
Home Office, *Setting the Boundaries: Reforming the Law on Sex Offences*, Volume 1, Home Office, July 2000.
Hunt (2004)
Hunt, The Hon. D., AO, The International Criminal Court: High Hopes, 'Creative Ambiguity' and an Unfortunate Mistrust in International Judges, *Journal of International Criminal Justice*, 2, 2004, 56-70.

Ingabire (2004)
Ingabire, M.I., *The Rape of Tutsi Women: A Weapon of the 1994 Genocide*, April 2004 (filed under ICTR-95-1B-T, *Muhimana* case, 27 April 2004).
Ingadottir (2003)
Ingadottir, T., The Trust Fund for Victims (Article 79 of the Rome Statute), in: T. Ingadottir (ed.), *The International Criminal Court – Recommendations on Policy and Practice: Financing, Victims, Judges, and Immunities*, Ardsley, New York: Transnational Publishers 2003, pp. 111-144.
Ingadottir, Ferstman and Kristjanjsdottir (2003)
Ingadottir, T., C. Ferstman and E. Kristjanjsdottir, *Victims of Atrocities – Access to Reparations*, Paper Presented at the Conference Searching for Justice: Comprehensive Action in the Face of Atrocities, York University, Canada, 4-6 June 2003.
Ingadottir, Ngendahayo and Viseur Sellers (2003)
Ingadottir, T., F. Ngendahayo and P. Viseur Sellers, The Victims and Witnesses Unit (Article 43.6 of the Rome Statute), in: T. Ingadottir (ed.), *The International Criminal Court – Recommendations on Policy and Practice: Financing, Victims, Judges, and Immunities*, Ardsley, New York: Transnational Publishers 2003, pp. 1-46.

Jones, A. (2002)
Jones, A., Gender and Genocide in Rwanda, *Journal of Genocide Research*, 4(1), 2002, 65-94.
Jones, J.R.W.D. (2002a)
Jones, J.R.W.D., Protection of Victims and Witnesses, in: A. Cassese, P. Gaeta and J.R.W.D. Jones (eds.), *The Rome Statute of the International Criminal Court: A Commentary*, Oxford: Oxford University Press 2002, pp. 1355-1370.
Jones, J.R.W.D. (2002b)
Jones, J.R.W.D., The Registry and Staff, in: A. Cassese, P. Gaeta and J.R.W.D. Jones (eds.), *The Rome Statute of the International Criminal Court: A Commentary*, Oxford: Oxford University Press 2002, pp. 275-283.
Jones, J.R.W.D. (2003)
Jones, J., *The Practice of the International Criminal Tribunals for the former Yugoslavia and Rwanda*, Ardsley: Transnational Publishers, 2003.
Jorda and De Hemptinne (2002)
Jorda, C. and J. de Hemptinne, The Status and Role of the Victim, in: A. Cassese, P. Gaeta and J.R.W.D. Jones (eds.), *The Rome Statute of the International Criminal Court: A Commentary*, Oxford: Oxford University Press 2002, pp. 1387-1419.

Kalosieh (2003)
Kalosieh, A., Consent to Genocide?: The ICTY's Improper Use of the Consent Paradigm to Prosecute Genocidal Rape in Foca, *Women's Rights Law Reporter*, 24, 2003, 121-135.
Kalra (2001)
Kalra, M.S., Forced Marriage: Rwanda's Secret Revealed, *U.C. Davis Journal of International Law and Policy*, 7, 2001, 197-221.
Karagiannakis (1999)
Karagiannakis, M., The Definition of Rape and Its Characterization as an Act of Genocide – A Review of the Jurisprudence of the International Criminal Tribunals for Rwanda and the former Yugoslavia, *Leiden Journal of International Law*, 12, 1999, 479-490.
Keller (2001)
Keller, A.N., Punishment for Violations of International Criminal Law: An Analysis of Sentencing at the ICTY and ICTR, *Indiana International and Comparative Law Review*, 12, 2001, 53-74.
Kelt and Von Hebel (2001)
Kelt, M. and H. von Hebel, What are Elements of Crimes?, in: Roy S. Lee *et al.* (eds.), *The International Criminal Court: Elements of Crimes and Rules of Procedure and Evidence*, Ardsley: Transnational Publishers 2001, pp. 13-18.
Khan (2000)
Khan, S.M., *The Shallow Graves of Rwanda*, New York: I.B. Taurus and Co Ltd, 2000.
Kittichaisaree (2001)
Kittichaisaree, K., *International Criminal Law*, Oxford: Oxford University Press, 2001.
Klip (1995)
Klip, A., Interrogation of Witnesses Abroad through a Live Television Link: The Modernization of Mutual Legal Assistance in Criminal Matters, *Maastricht Journal of European and Comparative Law*, 2, 1995, 244-255.
Klip (1996)
Klip, A., Witnesses Before the International Criminal Tribunal for the former Yugoslavia, *International Review of Penal Law*, 67(1-2), 1996, 267-295.
Klip (1999)
Klip, A., Commentary – ICTY, Witnesses: Summons, Protections and Video-link Testimony, in: A. Klip and G. Sluiter (eds.), *Annotated Leading Cases of International Criminal Tribunals: The International Criminal Tribunal for the former Yugoslavia 1993-1998*, Volume 1, Antwerp/Groningen/Oxford/Vienna: Intersentia/Hart Publishing/Verlag Österreich 1999, pp. 225-226.
Koenig and Askin (2000)
Koenig, D.M. and K.D. Askin, International Criminal Law and the International Criminal Court Statute: Crimes Against Women, in: K.D. Askin and D. Koenig (eds.), *Women and International Human Rights Law*, Volume II, 2000, pp. 3-29.
Kok (2003)
Kok, R.A., Levenslange gevangenisstraf en het Joegoslavië Tribunaal, *Delikt en Delinkwent*, 33(9), 2003, 1059-1071.
Kok and Van der Wilt (2004)
Kok, R. and H. van der Wilt, Kanttekening bij de straftoemeting voor het Joegoslavië Tribunaal, *Strafblad*, 2004, 53-63.

Kreβ (2001)
Kreβ, C., Witnesses in Proceedings Before the International Criminal Court: An Analysis in the Light of Comparative Criminal Procedure, in: H. Fischer, C. Kreβ and S.R. Lüder (eds.), *International and National Prosecution of Crimes Under International Law: Current Developments*, Berlin: Berliner Wissenschafts-Verlag 2001, pp. 309-383.
Kuo (2002)
Kuo, P., Prosecuting Crimes of Sexual Violence in an International Tribunal, *Case Western Reserve Journal of International Law*, 34, 2002, 305-321.

La Haye (2001)
La Haye, E., Article 8(2)(b)(xxii) – Rape, Sexual Slavery, Enforced Prostitution, Forced Pregnancy, Enforced Sterilization, and Sexual Violence, in: R.S. Lee *et al.* (eds.), *The International Criminal Court: Elements of Crimes and Rules of Procedure and Evidence*, Ardsley, New York: Transnational Publishers 2001, pp. 184-199.
Lakatos (1995)
Lakatos, A.C., Evaluating the Rules of Procedure and Evidence for the International Tribunal in the former Yugoslavia: Balancing Witnesses' Needs Against Defendants' Rights, *Hastings Law Journal*, 46, 1995, 909-940.
Lehr-Lehnardt (2002)
Lehr-Lehnardt, R., One Small Step for Women: Female-Friendly Provisions in the Rome Statute of the International Criminal Court, *Brigham Young University Journal of Public Law*, 16, 2002, 317-354.
Leigh (1996)
Leigh, M., Editorial Comment: The Yugoslav Tribunal: The Use of Unnamed Witnesses Against Accused, *American Journal International Law*, 90, 1996, 235-238.
Leigh (1997)
Leigh, M., Editoral Comment: Witness Anonymity is Inconsistent with Due Process, *American Journal International Law*, 91, 1997, 80-83.
Letschert (2005)
Letschert, R.M., *The Impact of Minority Rights Mechanisms*, The Hague: T.M.C. Asser Press, 2005.
Lewis and Friman (2001)
Lewis, P. and H. Friman, Reparations to Victims, in: R.S. Lee *et al.* (eds.), *The International Criminal Court: Elements of Crimes and Rules of Procedure and Evidence*, Ardsley, New York: Transnational Publishers 2001, pp. 474-491.
Lyons (2001)
Lyons, M.A., Hearing the Cry Without Answering the Call: Rape, Genocide, and the Rwandan Tribunal, *Syracuse Journal of International Law and Commerce*, 28, 2001, 99-124.

MacKinnon (1991)
MacKinnon, C.A., Chapter 9: On Coercion and Consent, in: C.A. MacKinnon, *Toward a Feminist Theory of the State*, Cambridge, Mass. etc.: Harvard University Press, 1991, pp. 171-183.
MacKinnon (1993)
MacKinnon, C.A., Crimes of War, Crimes of Peace, *UCLA Women's Law Journal*, 4, 1993, 59-86.

MacKinnon (1994)
MacKinnon, C.A., Rape, Genocide, and Women's Human Rights, *Harvard Women's Law Journal*, 17, 1994, 5-16.
Mamdani (2001)
Madani, M., *When Victims Become Killers: Colonialism, Nativism, and the Genocide in Rwanda*, New Jersey: Princeton University Press, 2001.
Malmström (2001)
Malmström, S., Restitution of Property and Compensation to Victims, in: R. May, D. Tolbert, J. Hocking, K. Roberts, B. B. Jia, D. Mundis and G. Oosthuizen (eds.), *Essays on ICTY Procedure and Evidence: In Honour of Gabrielle Kirk McDonald*, The Hague/London/Boston: Kluwer Law International 2001, pp. 373-384.
May and Wierda (2002)
May, Judge R. and M. Wierda, *International Criminal Evidence*, Ardsley, New York: Transnational Publishers, Inc., 2002.
McDonald (1998)
McDonald, A., Prosecuting IHL Violations against Women: A Note on the Relevant Provisions of the ICC Statute, *Nemesis*, 5, 1998, 132-142.
McDonald (1999)
McDonald, A., Sex Crimes at the *ad hoc* Tribunals, *Nemesis*, 3, 1999, 72-82.
McDonald (2000)
McDonald, G.K., Friedmann Award Address Crimes of Sexual Violence: The Experience of the International Criminal Tribunal, *Columbia Journal of Transnational Law*, 39, 2000, 1-17.
McHenry (2002)
McHenry, J., Casenote – Justice for Foca: The International Criminal Tribunal for Yugoslavia's Prosecution of Rape and Enslavement as Crimes Against Humanity, *Tulsa Journal of Comparative and International* Law, 10, Fall 2002, 183-222.
McHenry III (2002)
McHenry III, J.R., Note: The Prosecution of Rape Under International Law: Justice That Is Long Overdue, *Vanderbilt Journal of Transnational Law*, 35, 2002, 1269-1311.
Meernik and King (2003)
Meernik, J., and K. King, The Sentencing Determinants of the International Criminal Tribunal for the former Yugoslavia: An Emperical and Doctrinal Analysis, *Leiden Journal of International Law*, 16, 2003, 717-750.
Melvern (2000)
Melvern, L., *A People Betrayed: The Role of the West in Rwanda's Genocide*, London/New York: Zed Books, 2000.
Meron (1993)
Meron, T., Rape as a Crime under International Humanitarian Law, *American Journal of International Law*, 87, 1993, 424-428.
Mibenge (2005)
Mibenge, C., The Right to Access to a Remedy for Victims of Wartime Sexual Violence: A Case Study of Rwanda (1994-2004), in: D. Zarkov (ed.), *Gender, Conflict Development: Challenges of Practice*, Zubaan Books 2005 (forthcoming).
Miller (2003)
Miller, A.A, From the International Criminal Tribunal for Rwanda to the International Criminal Court: Expanding the Definition of Genocide to Include Rape, *Penn State Law Review*, 108, 2003, 349-373.

Moghalu (2002)
Moghalu, K.C., International Humanitarian Law from Nuremberg to Rome: The Weighty Precedents of the International Criminal Tribunal for Rwanda, *Pace International Law Review*, 14, 2002, 273-305.
Momeni (1997)
Momeni, M., Balancing the Procedural Rights of the Accused Against a Mandate to Protect Victims and Witnesses: An Examination of the Anonymity Rules of the International Criminal Tribunal for the former Yugoslavia, *Howard Law Journal*, 41, 1997, 155-179.
Morris and Scharf (1995a)
Morris, V. and M.P. Scharf, *An Insiders Guide to the International Criminal Tribunal for the former Yugoslavia*, Volume 1, Irvington-on-Hudson, New York: Transnational Publishers, 1995.
Morris and Scharf (1995b)
Morris, V. and M.P. Scharf, *An Insider's Guide to The International Criminal Tribunal for the former Yugoslavia: A Documentary History and Analysis*, Volume 1, Irvington-on-Hudson, New York: Transnational Publishers, 1995.
Morris and Scharf (1998)
Morris, V. and M.P. Scharf, *The International Criminal Tribunal for Rwanda*, Volume 1, Irvington-on-Hudson, New York: Transnational Publishers, 1998.
Moshan (1998)
Moshan, B.S., Women, War, and Words: The Gender Component in the Permanent International Criminal Court's Definition of Crimes Against Humanity, *Fordham International Law Journal*, 22, 1998, 154-184.
Mukagasana (1997)
Mukagasana Y., *La Mort Ne Veut Pas De Moi*, Paris: Robert Laffont, 1997.
Mukagasana (1999)
Mukagasana Y., *N'aie pas peur de savoir – Rwanda: une rescapée tutsi raconte*, Paris: J'ai lu, 1999.
Mumba (2001)
Mumba, F., Ensuring a Fair Trial whilst Protecting Victims and Witnesses – Balancing of Interests?, in: R. May, D. Tolbert, J. Hocking, K. Roberts, B. B. Jia, D. Mundis and G. Oosthuizen (eds.), *Essays on ICTY Procedure and Evidence: In Honour of Gabrielle Kirk McDonald*, The Hague/London/Boston: Kluwer Law International 2001, pp. 359-371.
Muttukumaru (1999)
Muttukumaru, C., Reparation to Victims, in: R.S. Lee (ed.), *The International Criminal Court – The Making of the Rome Statute: Issues, Negotiations, Results*, The Hague/London/Boston: Kluwer Law International 1999, pp. 262-270.

Nahapetian (1999)
Nahapetian, K., Selective Justice: Prosecuting Rape in the International Criminal Tribunals for the former Yugoslavia and Rwanda, *Berkeley Women's Law Journal*, 14, 1999, 126-135.
Nduwimana (2004)
Nduwimana, F., *The Right to Survive: Sexual Violence, Women and HIV/AIDS*, Rights and Democracy (International Centre for Human Rights and Democratic Development), 2004.

Neier (1998)
Neier, A., *War Crimes: Brutality, Genocide, Terror and the Struggle for Justice*, New York: Times Books, 1998.
Nemitz (2001)
Nemitz, J.C., The Law of Sentencing in International Criminal Law: The Purposes of Sentencing and the Applicable Method for the Determination of the Sentence, in: H. Fischer and A. McDonald (eds.), *Yearbook of International Humanitarian Law*, 4, The Hague: T.M.C. Asser Press 2001, 87-127.
Ngendahayo and Shermin (2000)
Ngendahayo, F., and M. Shermin, *Gender and HIV/AIDS: ICTR Challenges*, Presented at the Expert Group Meeting on "The HIV/AIDS Pandemic and its Gender Implications", Windhoek, Namibia, 13-17 November 2000, EGM/HIV-AIDS/2000/OP 4, 16 November 2000.
Ni Aolain (1997)
Ni Aolain, F., Radical Rules: The Effects of Evidential and Procedural Rules on the Regulation of Sexual Violence in War, *Albany Law Review*, 60, 1997, 883-905.
Niarchos (1995)
Niarchos, C.N., Women, War and Rape: Challenges Facing the International Criminal Tribunal for the former Yugoslavia, *Human Rights Quarterly*, 17, 1995, 649-690.
Nicholls (2003)
Nicholls, J., Evidence: Hearsay and Anonymous Witnesses, in: R. Haveman, O. Kavran and J. Nicholls (eds.), *Supranational Criminal Law: A System Sui Generis,* Antwerp/Oxford/New York: Intersentia 2003, pp. 239-303.
Nikolić-Ristanović (1999)
Nikolić-Ristanović, V., Living Without Democracy and Peace: Violence Against Women in the former Yugoslavia, *Violence Against Women*, 5(1), 1999, 63-80.
Nikolić-Ristanović (2000)
Nikolić-Ristanović, V. (ed.), *Women, Violence and War: Wartime Victimization of Refugees in the Balkans*, Budapest: Central European University Press, 2000.
Nowrojee (1996)
Nowrojee, B., *Shattered Lives: Sexual Violence During the Rwandan Genocide and its Aftermath*, Human Rights Watch, HRW Index No.: 2084, September 1996.
Nowrojee (2004a)
Nowrojee, B., Expert Report, *Sexual Violence Crimes during the Rwandan Genocide*, Human Rights Watch, June 2004 (filed under the *Government II* case, Case No. ICTR-99-50-T, 25 October 2004).
Nowrojee (2004b)
Nowrojee, B., *We Can Do Better: Investigating and Prosecuting International Crimes of Sexual Violence*, presented at the OTP Colloquium, Arusha, November 2004.
Nowrojee (2005)
Nowrojee, B., *"Your Justice is Too Slow": Will the ICTR Fail Rwanda's Rape Victims?*, UNRISD Occasional Paper Series, No. 10, UNRISD, Geneva, 2005 (forthcoming).
Nowrojee and Ralph (2000)
Nowrojee, B. and R. Ralph, Justice for Women Victims of Violence: Rwanda after the 1994 Genocide, in: I. Amadiume and A. An-Na'im (eds.), *The Politics of Memory: Truth, Healing and Social Justice*, London: Zed Books 2000, pp. 162-175.

Ntanda Nsereko (2002)
Ntanda Nsereko, D., Commentary – Indictment, in: A. Klip and G. Sluiter (eds.), *Annotated Leading Cases of International Criminal Tribunals: The International Criminal Tribunal for the former Yugoslavia 1999-2000*, Volume 4, Antwerp/Oxford/New York: Intersentia/Hart Publishing 1999, pp. 58-68.

Oosterhoff (2000)
Oosterhoff, P., *Male Victims of Sexual Torture in the former Yugoslavia – Challenges in Identification and Treatment in Croatia*, Final Paper as part of the Master of Public Health Program of the Netherlands School of Public Health, June 2000.
Oosterveld (2001)
Oosterveld, V., The Elements of Genocide, in: R.S. Lee *et al.* (eds.), *The International Criminal Court: Elements of Crimes and Rules of Procedure and Evidence*, Ardsely, New York: Transnational Publishers 2001, pp. 41-48.

Pace and Schense (2001)
Pace and Schense, The Coalition for the International Criminal Court and at the Preparatory Commission, in: R.S. Lee *et al.* (eds.), *The International Criminal Court: Elements of Crimes and Rules of Procedure and Evidence*, Ardsely, New York: Transnational Publishers 2001, pp. 705-733.
Pickard (1997)
Pickard, D.B., Proposed Sentencing Guidelines for the International Criminal Court, *Loyola of Los Angeles International and Comparative Law Journal*, 20, 1997, 123-164.
Pictet (1958)
Pictet, J., *Commentary on IV Geneva Convention Relative to the Protection of Civilian Persons in Time of War*, Geneva: ICRC, 1958.
Pilch (1998)
Pilch, F.T., The Crime of Rape in International Humanitarian Law, *United States Air Force Academy Journal of Legal Studies*, 9, 1998/1999, 99.
Pilch (2003)
Pilch, F.T., Note: Sexual Violence as Genocide: The Developing Law of the International Criminal Tribunals and the International Criminal Court, *Michigan Journal of Race and Law*, 8, 2003, 503-527.
Piragoff (2001a)
Piragoff, D.K., Evidence, in: R.S. Lee *et al.* (eds.), *The International Criminal Court: Elements of Crimes and Rules of Procedure and Evidence*, New York: Transnational Publishers 2001, pp. 349-401.
Piragoff (2001b)
Piragoff, D.K., Procedural Justice Related to Crimes of Sexual Violence, in: H. Fischer, C. Kreβ and S.R. Lüder (eds.), *International and National Prosecution of Crimes Under International Law: Current Developments*, Berlin: Berliner Wissenschafts-Verlag 2001, pp. 385-421.
Prunier (1995)
Prunier G., *The Rwanda Crisis: History of a Genocide*, New York: Columbia University Press, 1995.

Quénivet (2005)
Quénivet, N.N.R., *Sexual Offenses in Armed Conflict and International Law*, Ardsley, New York: Transnational Publishers, 2005.

Randelzhofer and Tomuschat (1999)
Commentary by Judge Cassese, in: A. Randelzhofer and C. Tomuschat (eds.), *State Responsibility and the Individual, Reparation in Instances of Grave Violations of Human Rights*, The Hague: Martinus Nijhoff Publishers 1999, pp. 46-49.
Ray (1997)
Ray, A.E., The Shame of it: Gender-Based Terrorism in the former Yugoslavia and the Failure of International Human Rights Law to Comprehend the Injuries, *American University Law Review*, 46, 1997, 793.
Rijken (2003)
Rijken, C., *Trafficking in Persons: Prosecution from a European perspective*, The Hague: T.M.C. Asser Press, 2003.
Roberts and Guelff (2000)
Roberts, A. and R. Guelff (eds.), *Documents on the Laws of War*, Third Edition, Oxford: Oxford University Press, 2000.
Robinson (1999)
Robinson, D., Defining Crimes Against Humanity at the Rome Conference, *American Journal of International Law*, 93(1), 1999, 43-57.
Robinson (2001a)
Robinson, D., Article 7(1)(c) – Enslavement, in: R.S. Lee *et al.* (eds.), *The International Criminal Court: Elements of Crimes and Rules of Procedure and Evidence*, Ardsley, New York: Transnational Publishers 2001, pp. 84-85.
Robinson (2001b)
Robinson, D., Article 7(1)(f) – Torture, in: R.S. Lee *et al.* (eds.), *The International Criminal Court: Elements of Crimes and Rules of Procedure and Evidence*, Ardsley, New York: Transnational Publishers 2001, pp. 90-92.
Robinson (2001c)
Robinson, D., Article 7(1)(g) – Rape, sexual slavery, enforced prostitution, forced pregnancy, enforced sterilization, or any other form of sexual violence of comparable gravity, in: R.S. Lee *et al.* (eds.), *The International Criminal Court: Elements of Crimes and Rules of Procedure and Evidence*, Ardsley, New York: Transnational Publishers 2001, p. 93.
Rombouts (2004)
Rombouts, H., Chapter 7: Reparation Policies in Rwanda, in: H. Rombouts, *Victim Organisations and the Politics of Reparation: A Case-Study on Rwanda*, Antwerpen/Oxford: Intersentia 2004, pp. 301-395.
Rückert and Witschel (2001a)
Rückert, W. and G. Witschel, Genocide and Crimes Against Humanity in the Elements of Crimes, in: H. Fischer, C. Kreβ and S.R. Lüder (eds.), *International and National Prosecution of Crimes Under International Law: Current Developments*, Berlin: Berliner Wissenschafts-Verlag 2001, pp. 59-93.
Rückert and Witschel (2001b)
Robinson, D., Article 7(1)(h) – Persecution, in: R.S. Lee *et al.* (eds.), *The International Criminal Court: Elements of Crimes and Rules of Procedure and Evidence*, Ardsley, New York: Transnational Publishers 2001, pp. 94-97.

Rückert and Witschel (2001c)
Article 7(1)(k) – Other Inhumane Acts, in: R.S. Lee *et al.* (eds.), *The International Criminal Court: Elements of Crimes and Rules of Procedure and Evidence*, Ardsley, New York: Transnational Publishers 2001, pp. 106-108.
Russell-Brown (2003)
Russell-Brown, S.L., Rape as an Act of Genocide, *Berkeley Journal of International Law*, 21, 2003, 350-374.
Rydberg (1999)
Rydberg, Å., The Protection of the Interests of Witnesses – The ICTY in Comparison to the Future ICC, *Leiden Journal of International Law*, 12(2), 1999, 455-478.
Rydberg (2004)
Rydberg, Å., Victims and the International Criminal Tribunal for the former Yugoslavia, in: H. Kaptein and M. Malsch, *Crime, Victims and Justice: Essays on Principles and Practice*, Hampshire: Ashgate 2004, pp. 126-140.

Safferling (2001)
Safferling, C., *Towards an International Criminal Procedure*, Oxford: Oxford University Press, 2001.
Salzman (1998)
Salzman, T.A., Rape Camps as a Means of Ethnic Cleansing: Religious, Cultural, and Ethical Responses to Rape Victims in the former Yugoslavia, *Human Rights Quarterly*, 20(2), 1998, 348-378.
Sari Moshan (1998)
Sari Moshan, B., Women, War, and Words: The Gender Component in the Permanent International Criminal Court's Definition of Crimes Against Humanity, *Fordham International Law Journal,* 22, 1998, 154-183.
Schabas (1997)
Schabas, W.A., Sentencing by International Tribunals: A Human Rights Approach, *Duke Journal of Comparative and International Law*, 7, 1997, 461-517.
Schabas (2000a)
Schabas, W.A., Perverse Effects of the Nulla Poena Principle: National Practice and the Ad Hoc Tribunals, *European Journal of International Law*, 11(3), 2000, 521-539.
Schabas (2000b)
Schabas, W.A., *Genocide in International Law: The Crime of Crimes*, Cambridge: Cambridge University Press, 2000.
Schabas (2001)
Schabas, W.A., The Jelisic case and the Mens Rea of the Crime of Genocide, *Leiden Journal of International Law*, 14(1), 2001, 125-139.
Schabas (2001a)
Schabas, W., Commentary – ICTR, Prosecutor v. Akayesu, Case No. ICTR-96-4-T, T. Ch., 2 September 1998, in: A. Klip and G. Sluiter (eds.), *Annotated Leading Cases of International Criminal Tribunals: The International Criminal Tribunal for Rwanda 1994-1999*, Volume 2, Antwerp/Groningen/Oxford/Vienna: Intersentia/Hart Publishing/Verlag Österreich 2001, pp. 539-554.
Schabas (2001b)
Schabas, W., Commentary – ICTY, Judgement, Prosecutor v. Furundzija, Case No. IT-95-17/1-T, T. Ch., 10 December 1998, in: A. Klip and G. Sluiter (eds.), *Annotated Leading Cases of International Criminal Tribunals: The International Criminal*

Tribunal for the former Yugoslavia 1997-1999, Volume 3, Antwerp/Oxford/New York: Intersentia 2001, pp. 753-760.
Scharf (1997)
Scharf, M.P., *Balkan Justice: The Story Behind the First International War Crimes Tribunal Since Nuremberg*, Durham, North Carolina: Carolina Academic Press, 1997.
Scheffer (1998)
Scheffer, D.J., US Ambassador at Large for War Crimes Issues Address at Fordham University School of Law New York, *Witness and Victim Protection in International Criminal Courts*, New York, January 28, 1998.
Schindler and Toman (1988)
Schindler, D. and J. Toman (eds.), *The Laws of Armed Conflict: A Collection of Conventions, Resolutions and Other Documents*, Dordrecht: Nijhoff, 1988.
Shah (2002)
Shah, S.B., The Oversight of the Last Great International Institution of the Twentieth Century: The International Criminal Court's Definition of Genocide, *Emory International Law Review*, 16, 2002, 351-389.
Sharlach (2000)
Sharlach, L., Rape as Genocide: Bangladesh, the former Yugoslavia, and Rwanda, *New Political Science*, 22(1), 2000, 89-102.
Sharratt (1999)
Sharratt, S., Interview with Patricia Viseur-Sellers, Legal Officer on Gender Issues, in: S. Sharratt and E. Kaschak (eds.), *Assault on the Soul: Women in the former Yugoslavia*, New York/London/Oxford: The Haworth Press 1999, pp. 53-78.
Short (2003)
Short, J.M.H., Sexual Violence as Genocide: The Developing Law of the International Criminal Tribunals and the International Criminal Court, *Michigan Journal of Race and Law*, 8, 2003, 503-527.
Sieber (2004)
Sieber, U., *The Punishment of Serious Crimes: A Comparative Analysis of Sentencing Law and Practice*, Volume 1: Expert Report, Freiburg/Breisgau: Ed. Luscrim, 2004.
Silber and Little (1997)
Silber, L., and A. Little, *Yugoslavia: Death of a Nation*, New York: Penguin Books, 1997.
Smith and Hogan (1999)
Smith, J.C., and B. Hogan, *Criminal Law*, 9th ed., London: Butterworths, 1999.
Stapleton (1999)
Stapleton, S., Ensuring a Fair Trial in the International Criminal Court: Statutory Interpretation and the Impermissibility of Derogation, *New York University School of Law Journal of International Law and Politics*, 31, 1999, 535-609.
Steains (2000)
Steains, C., Gender Issues, in: R.S. Lee (ed.), *The International Criminal Court: The Making of the Rome Statute: Issues, Negotiations, Results*, The Hague/London/Boston: Kluwer Law International 2000, pp. 357-390.
Stevens (2002)
Stevens, L., *Strafrecht en seksualiteit. De misdrijven inzake aanranding van de eerbaarheid, verkrachting, ontucht, prostitutie, seksreclame, zedenschennis en overspel*, Antwerpen/Groningen: Intersentia, 2002.

Stiglmayer (1993)
Stiglmayer, A. (ed.), *Mass Rape: The War Against Women in Bosnia-Herzegovina*, Lincoln, NE: Nebraska University Press, 1993.
Strumpen-Darrie (2000)
Strumpen-Darrie, C., Rape: A Survey of Current International Jurisprudence, *Human Rights Brief*, 7, 2000, 12-17.
Stuckenberg (2004)
Stuckenberg, C-F, Multiplicity of Offences: Concursus Delictorum, in: H. Fischer, C. Kreβ and S.R. Lüder (eds.), *International and National Prosecution of Crimes Under International Law: Current Developments*, Berlin: Berliner Wissenschafts-Verlag 2004, pp. 559-604.
Survivors Fund (SURF) (2005)
Survivors Fund (SURF), *Survival Against the Odds: A Book of Testimonies from Survivors of the Rwandan Genocide*, 2005.
Swaak-Goldman (1997)
Swaak-Goldman, O.Q., The ICTY and the Right to a Fair Trial: A Critique of the Critics, *Leiden Journal of International Law*, 10, 1997, 215-221.

Thomas and Levi (1999)
Thomas, D.Q., and R.S. Levi, Common Abuses Against Women, in: K.D. Askin and D.M. Koenig (eds.), *Women and International Human Rights Law*, Ardsley, New York: Transnational Publishers 1999, Volume 1, pp. 139-176.
Timm (2001)
Timm, B., The Legal Position of Victims in the Rules of Procedure and Evidence, in: H. Fischer, C. Kreβ and S.R. Lüder (eds.), *International and National Prosecution of Crimes Under International Law: Current Developments*, Berlin: Berliner Wissenschafts-Verlag 2001, pp. 289-308.
Tochilovsky (1999)
Tochilovsky, V., Rules of Procedure for the International Criminal Court: Problems to Address in Light of the Experience of the *Ad Hoc* Tribunals, *Netherlands International Law Review*, XLVI, 1999, 343-360.
Tolbert and Rydberg (2001)
Tolbert, D. and Å. Rydberg, Enforcement of Sentences, in: R. May, D. Tolbert, J. Hocking, K. Roberts, B. B. Jia, D. Mundis and G. Oosthuizen (eds.), *Essays on ICTY Procedure and Evidence: In Honour of Gabrielle Kirk McDonald*, The Hague/London/Boston: Kluwer Law International 2001, pp. 533-543.

Van Boven (1999a)
Van Boven, T., The Position of the Victim in the Statute of the ICC, in: H.A.M. von Hebel, J.G. Lammers and A. Bos (eds.), *Reflections on the International Criminal Court: Essays in Honour of Adriaan Bos*. The Hague, T.M.C. Asser Press 1999, pp. 77-89.
Van Boven (1999b)
Van Boven, T., The Perspective of the Victim, in: Y. Danieli, E. Stamatopoulou, C.J. Dias, *The Universal Declaration of Human Rights*, Amityville, NY: Baywood 1999, pp. 13-26.

Van Boven (2003)
Van Boven, T., Foreword by Theo van Boven, The Special Rapporteur of the UN Commission on Human Rights on Torture, in: Redress, *Reparation for Torture: A Survey of the Law and Practice in Thirty Selected Countries*, April 2003, pp. iii-iv.
Van Genugten (1995)
Van Genugten, W.J.M., Het Joegoslavië-Tribunaal: Pervertering van het internationale recht?, *Nederlands Tijdschrift voor Rechtsfilosofie en Rechtstheorie*, 24(1), 1995, 49-56.
Van Sliedregt (2003)
Van Sliedregt, E., *The Criminal Responsibility of Individuals for Violations of International Humanitarian Law*, The Hague: T.M.C. Asser Press, 2003.
Verdirame (2000)
Verdirame, G., The Genocide Definition in the Jurisprudence of the *Ad Hoc* Tribunals, *International and Comparative Law Quarterly*, 49, 2000.
Verrijn Stuart (undated)
Verrijn Stuart, H.H.M., *Een beschrijving en waardering van de stand van zaken met betrekking tot relevante nieuwe ontwikkelingen als gevolg van de jurisprudentie van de ad hoc Tribunalen inzake voormalig Joegoslavië en Rwanda en de totstandkoming van het Statuut van het Internationaal Strafhof*, undated.
Villiger (1997)
Villiger, M.E., *Customary International Law and Treaties: A Manual on the Theory and Practice of the Interrelation of Sources*, The Hague/Boston/London: Kluwer Law International, 1997.
Viseur Sellers (1997)
Viseur Sellers, P. and K. Okuizumi, Intentional Prosecution of Sexual Assault, *Transnational Law and Contemporary Problems*, 7, 1997, 45-80.
Viseur Sellers (1999)
Viseur Sellers, P. The Cultural Value of Sexual Violence, *American Society of International Law Proceedings*, 93, 1999, 312-324.
Viseur Sellers (2001a)
Viseur Sellers, P., Rule 89(C) and (D): At Odds or Overlapping with Rule 96 and Rule 95?, in: R. May, D. Tolbert, J. Hocking, K. Roberts, B. B. Jia, D. Mundis and G. Oosthuizen (eds.), *Essays on ICTY Procedure and Evidence: In Honour of Gabrielle Kirk McDonald*, The Hague/London/Boston: Kluwer Law International 2001, pp. 275-290.
Viseur Sellers (2001b)
Viseur Sellers, P., *Sexual Violence Materials and ICTY/ICTR Jurisprudence*, August 2001 (on file with the author).
Viseur Sellers (2002)
Viseur Sellers, P., Sexual Violence and Peremptory Norms: The Legal Value of Rape, *Case Western Reserve Journal of International Law*, 34, 2002, 287-303.
Viseur Sellers (2004)
Viseur Sellers, P., Individual(s') Liability for Collective Sexual Violence, in: K. Knop (ed.), *Gender and Human Rights*, Oxford: Oxford University Press 2004, pp. 153-194.
Vohrah and Cina (2001)
Vohrah, L.C. and J. Cina, The Outreach Programme, in: R. May, D. Tolbert, J. Hocking, K. Roberts, B. B. Jia, D. Mundis and G. Oosthuizen, *Essays on ICTY Procedure and Evidence: In Honour of Gabrielle Kirk McDonald*, The Hague/London/Boston: Kluwer Law International 2001, pp. 547-557.

Von Hebel (2001)
Von Hebel, H., The Elements of War Crimes – Introduction, in: R.S. Lee *et al.* (eds.), *The International Criminal Court: Elements of Crimes and Rules of Procedure and Evidence*, Ardsley, New York: Transnational Publishers 2001, pp. 109-111.

Wierda and De Greiff (undated)
Wierda, M. and P. de Greiff, *Reparations and the International Criminal Court: A Prospective Role for the Trust Fund for Victims*, International Center for Transnational Justice, undated.

Yoshiaki (2000)
Yoshiaki, Y., *Comfort Women: Sexual Slavery in the Japanese Military During World War II*, New York: Columbia University Press, 2000.

Zappalà (2002)
Zappalà, S., The Rights of the Accused, in: A. Cassese, P. Gaeta and J.R.W.D. Jones (eds.), *The Rome Statute of the International Criminal Court: A Commentary*, Oxford: Oxford University Press, 2002, pp. 1319-1354.

Zegveld (2003)
Zegveld, L., Remedies for Victims of Violations of International Humanitarian Law, *International Review of the Red Cross*, 85(851), 2003, 497-526.

LIST OF DOCUMENTS

INTERNATIONAL CRIMINAL COURT

- Assembly of States Parties, *Report on Participation of and Reparations to Victims*, 25 August 2004, ICC-ASP/3/21, Third Session, The Hague, 6-10 September 2004.
- Assembly of States Parties, *Report to the Assembly of States Parties on the Activities and Projects of the Board of Directors of the Trust Fund for Victims 2003-2004*, Third Session, The Hague, 6-10 September 2004, including Annex A, *Draft Regulations of the Trust Fund for Victims*, First Meeting of the Board of Directors of the Trust Fund for Victims, ICC/ASP/3/14/Rev.1, The Hague (The Netherlands), 20-22 April 2004.
- *Decisions taken by the Preparatory Committee at its Session held in New York*, 11 to 21 February 1997, A/AC.249/1997/L.5 (1997), 12 March 1997.
- *Decisions taken by the Preparatory Committee at its Session held in New York*, 4 to 15 August 1997, A/AC.249/1997/L.8/Rev.1 (1997), 14 August 1997.
- *Decisions taken by the Preparatory Committee at is Session held in New York*, 1 to 12 December 1997, A/AC.249/1997/L.9/Rev.1 (1997), 18 December 1997.
- *Discussion Paper Proposed by the Coordinator on Rules of Procedure and Evidence Related to Part 6 of the Statute*, Second Session of the Preparatory Commission, UN Doc. PCNICC/1999/WGRPE/RT.5/Rev.1/Add.3, 11 August 1999.
- ICC, *Order Regarding Request for Additional Information (Concerning Applications for Participation of Victims). Confidential and Ex-parte*, 1 June 2005.
- ICC website, *Assembly of States Parties/The States Parties to the Rome Statute*, at http://www.icc-cpi.int/asp/statesparties.html.
- International Seminar 'Access of Victims to the International Criminal Court', Paris, 27-29 April 1999, *Report of Workshops*, 29 April 1999.
- Preparatory Committee Meeting, A/AC/249/1998/CRP.8, 2 April 1998.
- *Proceedings of the Preparatory Commission at its Fourth Session (13-31 March 2000)*, PCNICC/2000/L.1/Rev.1, 3 April 2000.
- Proposal for a draft Code of Professional Conduct for counsel before the International Criminal Court, ICC-ASP/3/11/Rev.1, 27 August 2004.
- Proposal Submitted by the Holy See, A/AC.249/1998/DP.13, 1 April 1998.
- Proposal Submitted by France, *Comments on the Proposal Submitted by the United States of America Concerning Article 6 Crime of Genocide*, PCNICC/1999/WGEC/DP.1, 18 February 1999.

- Proposal Submitted by the United States of America, *Draft Elements of Crimes*, PCNICC/1999/DP.4/Add.1, 4 February 1999.
- Proposal Submitted by the United States of America, *Draft Elements of Crimes*, PCNICC/1999/DP.4/Add.2, 4 February 1999.
- *Proposal Submitted by Costa Rica, Hungary and Switzerland on Certain Provisions of Article 8 Para. 2 (B) of the Rome Statute of the International Criminal Court, (VIII), (X), (XIV), (XV), (XVI), (XXI), (XXII), (XXVI)*, PCNICC/1999/WGEC/DP.8, 19 July 1999.
- Proposal Submitted by Colombia, *Comments on the Proposal by the Delegations of Costa Rica, Hungary and Switzerland Concerning Article 8, Paragraph 2(b) of the Rome Statute (PCNICC/1999/WGEC/DP.8)*, PCNICC/1999/WGEC/DP.16, 29 July 1999.
- *Proposal Concerning the Elements of Crimes Against Humanity Submitted by Bahrain, Iraq, Kuwait, Lebanon, The Libyan Arab Jamahiriya, Oman, Qatar, Saudi Arabia, The Sudan, The Syrian Arab Republic and United Arab Emirates*, PCNICC/1999/WGEC/DP.39, 3 December 1999.
- *Report on the International Seminar on Victims' Access to the ICC*, PCNICC/1999/WGRPE/INF/2, Second Session of the Preparatory Commission, 26 July-13 August, 6 July 1999.
- *Report of the Inter-Sessional Meeting from 19 to 30 January 1998*, Zutphen, The Netherlands, A/AC.249/1998/L.13 (1998), 4 February 1998.
- *Report of the Ad Hoc Committee on the Establishment of an International Criminal Court*, G.A. 50th Session, Supp. No. 22, A/50/22 (1995),1 January 1995.
- *Report of the Prosecutor of the International Criminal Court, Mr. Louis Moreno Ocampo, to the Security Council Pursuant to UNSCR 1593 (2005)*, 29 June 2005.
- *Report of the Preparatory Committee on the Establishment of an International Criminal Court, Proceedings of the Preparatory Committee during March-April and August 1996*, Volume 1, GA 51st Session, Supp. No. 22, A/51/22 (1996), 1 January 1996.
- *Report of the Preparatory Committee on the Establishment of an International Criminal Court*, A/CONF.183/2/Add.1, 14 April 1998.
- *Report of the Preparatory Commission for the International Criminal Court: Addendum*, PCNICC/2000/1/Add.2, 2 November 2000.
- *Request from the Governments of Belgium, Costa Rica, Finland, Hungary, The Republic of Korea and South Africa and the Permanent Observer Mission of Switzerland Regarding the Text Prepared by the International Committee of the Red Cross on Article 8, paragraph 2(B), (C), and (E) of the Rome Statute of the International Criminal Court*, PCNICC/1999/WGEC/INF.2, 14 July 1999.
- Resolution ICC-ASP/1/Res.6, *Establishment of a Fund for the Benefit of Victims of Crimes within the Jurisdiction of the Court, and of the Families of Such Victims*, 9 September 2002.

- Resolution ICC-ASP/3/Res.7, *Establishment of the Secretariat of the Trust Fund for Victims*, 10 September 2004.
- Statement by Archbishop Desmond Tutu at the Ceremony Marking the First Meeting of the Board of Directors of the Trust Fund for Victims at The Hague on the 22nd of April 2004, at http://www.icc-cpi.int/press/video.html.
- United Nations Diplomatic Conference of Plenipotentiaries on the Establishment of an International Criminal Court, *Final Act of the United Nations Diplomatic Conference of Plenipotentiaries on the Establishment of an International Criminal Court, done at Rome on 17 July 1998,* A/CONF.183/10*, 17 July 1997.
- Working Group on Procedural Matters, *Final Report of the Working Group on Procedural Matters*, A/CONF.183/C.1/WGPM/L.2/Add.7, 13 July 1998.
- Working Group on Procedural Matters, *Final Report of the Working Group on Procedural Matters,* A/CON.183/C.1/WGPM/L.63/Rev.1, 15 June-17 July 1998.

INTERNATIONAL CRIMINAL TRIBUNAL FOR THE FORMER YUGOSLAVIA

- ICTY, *Yearbook 1995*, The Netherlands, 1996.
- ICTY, *Third Annual Report of the International Tribunal for the Prosecution of Persons Responsible for Serious Violations of International Humanitarian Law Committed in the Territory of the Former Yugoslavia since 1991*, A/51/292-S/1996/665, 16 August 1996 (ICTY Third Annual Report (1996)).
- ICTY, *Ninth Annual Report of the International Tribunal for the Prosecution of Persons Responsible for Serious Violations of International Humanitarian Law Committed in the Territory of the Former Yugoslavia since 1991*, A/57/379-S/2002/985, 4 September 2002 (ICTY Ninth Annual Report (2002)).
- ICTY, *Eleventh Annual Report of the International Tribunal for the Prosecution of Persons Responsible for Serious Violations of International Humanitarian Law Committed in the Territory of the Former Yugoslavia since 1991*, A/59/215-S/2004/627, 16 August 2004 (ICTY Eleventh Annual Report (2004)).
- ICTY website, *The ICTY at a Glance/Key Figures of ICTY Cases*, at http://www.un.org/icty/cases-e/factsheets/procindex-e.htm.
- Letter dated 12 October 2000 from the President of the International Tribunal for the Former Yugoslavia addressed to the Secretary-General, Annex to a Letter dated 2 November 2000 from the Secretary-General addressed to the President of the Security Council, UN doc. S/2000/1063, 3 November 2000.
- *Victims Compensation and Participation*, Report Prepared by the Rules Committee, 2000, at http://www.un.org/icty/pressreal/tolb-e.htm.

INTERNATIONAL CRIMINAL TRIBUNAL FOR RWANDA

- *Completion Strategy of the International Criminal Tribunal for Rwanda*, 19 November 2004.
- ICTR, Witnesses and Victims Support Section [WVSS], *Manual of Operational Guidance*, Volume I, undated.
- ICTR website, Fact Sheet No. 1, *The Tribunal at a Glance*, at http://www.ictr.org/ENGLISH/factsheets/1.htm.
- ICTR, *Seventh Annual Report of the International Criminal Tribunal for the Prosecution of Persons Responsible for Genocide and Other Serious Violations of International Humanitarian Law Committed in the Territory of Rwanda and Rwandan Citizens Responsible for Genocide and Other Such Violations Committed in the Territory of Neighbouring States Between 1 January and 31 December 1994: For the Period from 1 July 2001 to 30 June 2002*, A/57/163-S/2002/733, 2 July 2002 (ICTR Seventh Annual Report (2002)).
- ICTR, Office of the President, *Statement by the President of the ICTR to the United Nations General Assembly by Judge Navanethem Pillay, President*, 28 October 2002.
- ICTR, Office of the President, *Statement by the President of the ICTR to the United Nations Security Council by Judge Navanethem Pillay, President*, 29 October 2002.
- ICTR, *Address by Judge Erik Møse, President of the International Criminal Tribunal for Rwanda, to the United Nations General Assembly*, 9 October 2003.
- ICTR, *Ninth Annual Report of the International Criminal Tribunal for the Prosecution of Persons Responsible for Genocide and Other Serious Violations of International Humanitarian Law Committed in the Territory of Rwanda and Rwandan Citizens Responsible for Genocide and Other Such Violations Committed in the Territory of Neighbouring States Between 1 January and 31 December 1994*, A/59/183-S/2004/601, 27 July 2004 (ICTR Ninth Annual Report (2004)).
- ICTR, *Address by the Registrar on the Occasion of the Visit of the Prime Minister of Norway to the International Criminal Tribunal for Rwanda*, Arusha, 11 October 2004.
- ICTR Draft Report on Improved Access to Anti-Retroviral Treatment and Psychological Counselling for ICTR Witnesses with HIV/AIDS, prepared by Elsie Effange-Mbella, 2004 (on file with the author).
- Kamuhanda, *Kamuhanda Jean de Dieu, Innocent Mais Condamné*, 11 février 2004.
- Letter of the President of the ICTR to the Secretary General of the United Nations, Annex to a Letter of 14 December 2000 by the UN Secretary-General, Kofi Annan, to the UN Security Council, UN Doc. S/2000/1198, 15 December 2000.

- Letter dated 19 November 2004 from the President of the International Criminal Tribunal for the Prosecution of Persons Responsible for Genocide and Other Serious Violations of International Humanitarian Law Committed in the Territory of Rwanda and Rwandan Citizens Responsible for Genocide and Other Such Violations Committed in the Territory of Neighbouring States Between 1 January and 31 December 1994 Addressed to the President of the Security Council, Annexed the Completion Strategy of the International Criminal Tribunal for Rwanda, S/2004/921, 22 November 2004.
- Letter from Dr. Alex Obote-Odora, Special Assistant to the Prosecutor, to Ms. Brunet, 11 February 2005.

NGO REPORTS

- **African Rights (1995a)**
  African Rights, *Death, Despair and Defiance*, rev. ed., 1995.
- **African Rights (1995b)**
  African Rights, *Rwanda Not So Innocent: When Women Become Killers*, August 1995.
- **African Rights (2004)**
  African Rights, *Broken Bodies, Torn Spirits, Living With Genocide, Rape and HIV/AIDS*, April 2004.
- **Amnesty International (1993)**
  Amnesty International, *Bosnia-Herzegovina: Rape and Sexual Abuse by Armed Forces,* January 1993.
- **Amnesty International (1998)**
  Amnesty International, *Rwanda: Major Step Back for Human Rights as Rwanda Stages 22 Public Executions*, AI Index: AFR 47/14/98, 24 April 1998.
- **Amnesty International (1999)**
  Amnesty International, The International Criminal Court: Preliminary Comments Concerning the Elements of War Crimes Other Than Grave Breaches of the Geneva Conventions – Part I, July 1999.
- **Amnesty International (2003)**
  Amnesty International, *Bosnia-Herzegovina: Shelving Justice – War Crimes Prosecutions in Paralysis,* AI Index: EUR 63/018/2003, 12 November 2003.
- **Amnesty International (2004a)**
  Amnesty International, *Rwanda: Marked for Death*, AI Index: AFR 47/007/2004, 5 April 2004.
- **Amnesty International (2004b)**
  Amnesty International, *Sudan – Darfur: Rape as a Weapon of War: Sexual Violence and its Consequences*, AI Index: AFR 54/076/2004, 19 July 2004
- **Amnesty International (2004c)**
  Amnesty International, *Sudan – Mass Rape, Abduction and Murder*, AI Index: AFR 54/125/2004, 12 October 2004.

- **Amnesty International (2004d)**
  Amnesty International, *Justice Shelved – Impunity for Rape in Bosnia Herzegovina*, AI Index: EUR 63/005/2004, 12 October 2004.
- **Amnesty International (2004e)**
  Amnesty International, *Democratic Republic of Congo: Mass Rape – Time for Remedies*, AI Index: AFR 62/022/2004, 26 October 2004.
- **Amnesty International (2004f)**
  Amnesty International, *Central African Republic: Five Months of War Against Women*, AI Index: AFR 19/001/2004, 10 November 2004.
- **Amnesty International (2004g)**
  Amnesty International, *Women, HIV/AIDS and Human Rights*, AI Index: ACT 77/084/2004, 24 November 2004.
- **Amnesty International (2005)**
  Amnesty International, *Amnesty International's Concerns on the Implementation of the "Completion Strategy" of the International Criminal Tribunal for the former Yugoslavia*, AI Index: EUR 05/001/2005, 6 June 2005.
- **Coalition for Women's Human Rights in Conflict Situations (1997a)**
  Coalition for Women's Human Rights in Conflict Situations, *The Prosecutor v. Jean-Paul Akayesu, Amicus Brief Respecting Amendment of the Indictment and Supplementation of the Evidence to Ensure the Prosecution of Rape and Other Sexual Violence Within the Competence of the Tribunal*, Case No. ICTR-96-4-T, 29 May 1997 (also filed in the ICTR Database).
- **Coalition for Women's Human Rights in Conflict Situations (1997b)**
  Coalition for Women's Human Rights in Conflict Situations, *Witness Protection, Gender and the ICTR*, A report prepared by Connie Walsh, as a result of investigations in Rwanda in June and July 1997, for the Centre for Constitutional Rights (CCR), International Centre for Human Rights and Democratic Development (ICHRDD), International Women's Law Clinic (IWHR) and MADRE, 1997.
- **Coalition for Women's Human Rights in Conflict Situations (1998a)**
  Coalition for Women's Human Rights in Conflict Situations, *Application to File an Amicus Curiae Brief in the Case of the Prosecutor v. Anto Furundzija*, Case No. IT-95-17/1-T, 5 November 1998.
- **Coalition for Women's Human Rights in Conflict Situations (1998b)**
  Coalition for Women's Human Rights in Conflict Situations, *Prosecutor v. Anto Furundzija, Amicus Curiae Brief Respecting the Decision and Order of the Tribunal of 16 July 1998 Requesting that the Tribunal Reconsider its Decision Having Regard to the Rights of Witness "A" to Equality, Privacy and Security of the Person and to Representation by Counsel*, Case No. IT-95-17/1-T, 5 November 1998.
- **Coalition for Women's Human Rights in Conflict Situations (2001a)**
  Coalition for Women's Human Rights in Conflict Situations, *The Prosecutor v. Samuel Imanishimwe, Emmanuel Bagambiki and André Ntagerura, Amicus Curiae Brief Respecting the Need to Include Sexual Violence Charges in the Indictment*, Case No. ICTR-99-46-T, 1 March 2001 (also filed in the ICTR Database).

- **Coalition for Women's Human Rights in Conflict Situations (2001b)**
  Coalition for Women's Human Rights in Conflict Situations, *The Prosecutor v. Samuel Imanishimwe, Emmanuel Bagambiki and André Ntagerura, Request for Reconsideration of the Decision on Amici's Application to File an Amicus Curiae Brief According to Rule 74 of the Rules of Procedure and Evidence Filed on Behalf of the NGO Coalition for Women's Human Rights in Conflict Situations*, Case No. ICTR-99-46-T, 12 July 2001 (also filed in the ICTR Database).
- **Human Rights Watch (1993)**
  Human Rights Watch, *War Crimes in Bosnia-Hercegovina (Volume II)*, HRW Index No.: 0979, 1 April 1993.
- **Human Rights Watch (1999)**
  Human Rights Watch, *Commentary to the Second Preparatory Commission on Rules of Procedure and Elements of Crimes*, July 1999.
- **Human Rights Watch (2000a)**
  Human Rights Watch, *Federal Republic of Yugoslavia – Kosovo: Rape as a Weapon of Ethnic Cleansing*, HRW Index No.: D1203, 1 March 2000.
- **Human Rights Watch (2000b)**
  Human Rights Watch, *Commentary to the Fifth Preparatory Commission Meeting on the International Criminal Court*, June 2000.
- **Human Rights Watch (2002)**
  Human Rights Watch, *The War Within the War: Sexual Violence against Women and Girls in Eastern Congo*, June 2002.
- **Human Rights Watch (2003a)**
  Human Rights Watch, *We'll Kill You if You Cry: Sexual Violence in the Sierra Leone Conflict*, January 2003.
- **Human Rights Watch (2003b)**
  Human Rights Watch, *Abducted and Abused: Renewed Conflict in Northern Uganda*, July 2003.
- **Human Rights Watch (2004a)**
  Human Rights Watch, *Memorandum to the International Criminal Court*, 3 March 2004.
- **Human Rights Watch (2004b)**
  Human Rights Watch, *Struggling To Survive: Barriers to Justice for Rape Victims in Rwanda*, September 2004.
- **Human Rights Watch (2004c)**
  Human Rights Watch, *Foca Confronts its Past: Human Rights Activists and Tribunal Officials Discuss War Crimes with Residents of Notorious Bosnian Serb Town*, 15 October 2004.
- **Human Rights Watch (2005)**
  Human Rights Watch, *Sexual Violence and its Consequences Among Displaced Persons in Darfur and Chad*, April 2005.
- **International Center for Transitional Justice (2002)**
  International Center for Transitional Justice, *A Casualty of Politics: Overview of Acts and Projects of Reparation on the Territory of the Former Yugoslavia* (prepared by D. Djordjević), July 2002.

- **International Center for Transitional Justice (2004a)**
International Center for Transnational Justice, *Bosnia and Herzegovina: Selected Developments in Transitional Justice* (prepared by M. Freeman), October 2004.
- **International Center for Transitional Justice (2004b)**
International Center for Transnational Justice, *Serbia and Montenegro: Selected Developments in Transitional Justice* (prepared by M. Freeman), October 2004.
- **International Committee of the Red Cross (1999a)**
International Committee of the Red Cross, *Working Paper on Article 8, Paragraph 2 (b) (viii), (x), (xiii), (xiv), (xv), (xvi), (xxi), (xxii), and (xxvi) of the Statute*, 18 June 1999.
- **International Committee of the Red Cross (1999b)**
International Committee of the Red Cross, *Working Paper on Article 8, Paragraph 2 (e) (v), (vi), (vii), (viii), (xi), and (xii) of the Statute*, 29 June 1999.
- **International Crisis Group (2001)**
International Crisis Group, *International Criminal Tribunal for Rwanda: Justice Delayed*, Nairobi/Arusha/Brussels: Africa Report No. 30, 7 June 2001.
- **International Federation for Human Rights (2002)**
International Federation for Human Rights, *Report: Victims in the Balance, Challenges Ahead for the International Criminal Tribunal for Rwanda*, No. 329/2, November 2002.
- **International Helsinki Federation for Human Rights (2000)**
International Helsinki Federation for Human Rights, *Women 2000: An Investigation into the Status of Women's Rights in Central and Sourth-Eastern Europe and the Newly Independent States*, 9 November 2000.
- **Médecins Sans Frontières (2004)**
Médecins Sans Frontières, *I Have No Joy, No Peace of Mind: Medical, Psychosocial, and Socio-Economic Consequences of Sexual Violence in Eastern DRC*, 2004.
- **Médecins Sans Frontières (2005)**
Médecins Sans Frontières, *The Crushing Burden of Rape: Sexual Violence in Darfur*, 8 March 2005.
- **Penal Reform International (2003)**
Penal Reform International, *Research on the Gacaca: Report V*, September 2003.
- **Penal Reform International (2004)**
Penal Reform International, *Research Report on the Gacaca: Report VI: From Camp to Hill, the Reintegration of Released Prisoners*, May 2004.
- **Physicians for Human Rights (2002)**
Physicians for Human Rights, *War-Related Sexual Violence in Sierra Leone: A Population Based Assessment*, 2002.
- **Reporters Without Borders (2003)**
Reporters Without Borders, *Victims' Guide to the International Criminal Court*, 2003.
- **Save the Children (2002)**
Save the Children, *HIV and Conflict: A Double Emergency*, 2002.
- **Save the Children (2005)**
Save the Children, *Forgotten Casualties of War: Girls in Armed Conflict*, April 2005.

- **Victims Rights Working Group (2003)**
  Victims Rights Working Group, *Victim Participation at the International Criminal Court: Summary of Issues and Recommendations*, November 2003.
- **Victims Rights Working Group (2005)**
  Victims Rights Working Group, *Comments on the Draft Regulations of the ICC Trust Fund for Victims*, February 2005.
- **Women Caucus for Gender Justice (1999)**
  Women Caucus for Gender Justice, Women's Caucus Advocacy in ICC Negotiations, *Recommendations and Commentary for the Elements Annex*, Submitted to the July 26 – August 13, 1999, Preparatory Commission for the International Criminal Court.
- **Women Caucus for Gender Justice (2000)**
  Women's Caucus for Gender Justice, *Recommendations and Commentary for the Elements of Crimes and Rules of Procedure and Evidence: Submitted to the Preparatory Commission for the International Criminal Court*, Commentary to the 5th PrepCom, 12 June 2000.

Press Releases

- Agence France-Presse, *Trauma and Isolation Await Many Witnesses of UN Court at Home*, 16 January 2004
- BBC News, *Rwanda Going Ahead with Genocide Executions*, 24 April 1998.
- BBC News, *Japan Rejects Sex Slave Appeal*, 25 March 2003.
- BBC News, *Genocide Witnesses Being Killed: The Rwandan Government Has Been Urged to Halt the Murder and Intimidation of Potential Witnesses to the Genocide in 1994 During which 800,000 People Died*, 16 December 2003.
- BBC News, *Congo Rape Victims Seek Solace* (by Jackie Martens), 24 January 2004.
- BBC News, *Rwanda Still Searching for Justice*, 30 March 2004.
- BBC News, *Woman Soldier in Abuse Spotlight*, 7 May 2004.
- BBC News, *DR Congo's Shameful Sex Secret*, 3 June 2004.
- BBC News, *US Soldier Jailed for Prison Abuse*, 22 October 2004.
- BBC News, *Report Shows DR Congo Rape Horror*, 26 October 2004.
- BBC News, *Japan to End WWII Sex Slave Fund*, 24 January 2005.
- BBC News, *UN's Darfur Death Estimates Soars*, 14 March 2005.
- Coalition for Women's Human Rights in Conflict Situations News Release, *Rwanda: Akayesu Sentencing a Victory for Women's Rights*, 2 October 1998.
- Coalition for Women's Human Rights in Conflict Situations News Release, *Women's Group Congratulate ICTY on Charges of Sexual Violence Against Slobodan Milosevic*, 29 October 2001.
- Diplomatie Judiciaire, *Témoin Non Protégé*, No. 80, Décembre 2001, pp. 14-17.
- Diplomatie Judiciaire, *Compensating Victims with Guilty Money*, Interview with Carla del Ponte, The Hague, 9 June 2000.

- Hirondelle News Agency, *Rwanda Tribunal's Witness Protection in Question* (by Julia Crawford), 10 December 2001.
- Hirondelle News Agency, *Survivors Accused 14 Defence Investigators of Genocide Crimes*, 25 March 2002.
- Hirondelle News Agency, *Analysis: Confronting Genocide with Country's Regular Courts* (by Gabriel Gabiro), 17 September 2003.
- Hirondelle News Agency, *Silent Victims of Rwanda's Genocide* (by Gabriel Gabiro), 21 November 2003.
- Hirondelle News Agency, *Prosecution Witness Assassinated in Rwanda*, 20 October 2004.
- Hirondelle News Agency, *Plus De 1.600 Cas De Viol De Janvier A Septembre Selon La Police*, 1 décembre 2004.
- Hirondelle News Agency, *ICTR Spent US$200,000 on HIV/AIDS Affected Witnesses in 2004*, 24 January 2005.
- Hirondelle News Agency, *ICTR Medical Support Programme Targets 2,300 Witnesses*, 28 January 2005.
- Hirondelle News Agency, *First Testimonies via Video Link from Kigali Next Week*, 9 February 2005.
- Hirondelle News Agency, *Alibi Witness Testifies via Video Conference from The Hague*, 21 February 2005.
- Hirondelle News Agency, *Witness Fearing for His Safety Gives Entire Testimony In Camera*, 22 February 2005.
- Hirondelle News Agency, *ICTR/Muvunyi – New Genocide Trial Opens in Arusha*, 2 March 2005.
- Hirondelle News Agency, *ICTR/Muvunyi – Prosecutor to Call 20 Witnesses on Rape Charges against Former Officer*, 5 March 2005.
- Hirondelle News Agency, *Simba Trial Hits Snag as Key Witnesses Refuse to Testify*, 7 March 2005.
- Hirondelle News Agency, *Over 80 People Flee Rwanda as Gacaca Trials Begin*, 14 March 2005.
- Hirondelle News Agency, *700 Hundred Gacaca Judges Accused of Taking Part in the Genocide*, 17 March 2005.
- Hirondelle News Agency, *On Day One of Trials, Gacaca Courts Deliver First Genocide Judgements*, 11 March 2005.
- Hirondelle News Agency, *A New Fund to Assist Rwanda Genocide Survivors*, 6 April 2005.
- Hirondelle News Agency, *The Limitations of Justice Without Compensation*, 18 April 2005.
- Hirondelle News Agency, *Six Hundred Flee to Burundi Over Gacaca*, 19 April 2005.
- Hirondelle News Agency, *Villagers Flee as Genocide Courts Press on*, 25 April 2005.

- Hirondelle News Agency, *Muhimana Gets Life Sentence for Multiple Rapes in Rwanda Genocide*, 28 April 2005.
- Hirondelle News Agency, *Investigations into Allegations of Interference of Witnesses Ordered*, 27 May 2005.
- Hirondelle News Agency, *ICTR/Muvunyi – Witness Describes Horror of Being Raped by Soldiers*, 9 June 2005.
- Hirondelle News Agency, *Rwandan Journalist Cleared of Contempt of Court Charges*, 13 June 2005.
- Hirondelle News Agency, *Judge Intervenes to Quell Heated Exchange in Soldiers' Trial*, 21 June 2005.
- Hirondelle News Agency, *Gacaca Tribunals Officially Launched in Rwanda*, 24 June 2004.
- ICC Newsletter, *Registry: VPRS – Gender Sensitivity*, June 2005, #4, p.6.
- ICC Press Release, *President of Uganda Refers Situation Concerning the Lord's Resistance Army (LRA) to the ICC*, The Hague, 29 January 2004.
- ICC Press Release, *Prosecutor Receives Referral of the Situation in the Democratic Republic of Congo*, The Hague, 19 April 2004.
- ICC Press Release, First Meeting of the Board of Directors of the Trust Fund for Victims, The Hague, 22 April 2004.
- ICC Press Release, The Office of the Prosecutor of the International Criminal Court Opens its First Investigation, The Hague, 23 June 2004.
- ICC Press Release, *Prosecutor of the International Criminal Court Opens an Investigation into Northern Uganda*, The Hague, 29 July 2004.
- ICC Press Release, *Prosecutor Receives Referral Concerning Central African Republic*, The Hague, 7 January 2005.
- ICC Press Release, *The Prosecutor of the ICC Opens Investigation in Darfur*, The Hague, 6 June 2005.
- ICTR Press Release, *Cooperation and Assistance of States Key to Success of ICTR*, ICTR/INFO-9-2-169, Arusha, 9 March 1999.
- ICTR Press Release, *ICTR Launches Victims Support Initiative in Rwanda*, ICTR/INFO-9-2-242.EN, Arusha, 26 September 2000.
- ICTR Press Release, *Statement of Judge Pillay, President of the Tribunal*, ICTR/INFO-9-3-07, Arusha, 14 December 2001.
- ICTR Press Release, *ICTR President Calls for Compensation for Victims*, ICTR/INFO-9-2-326.EN, Arusha, 31 October 2002.
- ICTR Press Release, *The President of the UN Human Rights Commission to Lead a Campaign to Support Victims*, ICTR/INFO-9-2-363.EN, Arusha, 7 October 2003.
- ICTR Press Release, *The European Commission to Fund Tribunal Projects*, ICTR/INFO-9-2-388.EN, Arusha, 10 May 2004.
- ICTR Newsletter, *ICTR Seminar on Gender Sensitivity*, June 2004, pp. 10-15.
- ICTR Newsletter, *ICTR Completion Strategy*, June 2004, pp. 4-6.

- ICTY Press Release, *The 22nd Plenary Session of the International Criminal Tribunal for the former Yugoslavia*, JL/P.I.S./518-e, The Hague, 17 July 2000.
- ICTY Press Release, *The Judges of the ICTY Acknowledge the Right of Victims of Crimes Committed in the Former Yugoslavia to Seek Compensation*, JL/P.I.S./528-e, The Hague, 14 September 2000.
- ICTY Press Release, *Address to the Security Council by Carla del Ponte, Prosecutor of the International Criminal Tribunals for the Former Yugoslavia and Rwanda, to the UN Security Council*, JL/P.I.S./542-e, The Hague, 24 November 2000.
- ICTY Press Release, *Judgement of Trial Chamber II in the Kunarac, Kovac and Vukovic case*, JL/P.I.S./566-e, The Hague, 22 February 2001.
- ICTY Press Release, *The ICTY and the Truth and Reconciliation Commission in Bosnia and Herzegovina*, JL/P.I.S./591-e, The Hague, 17 May 2001.
- ICTY Press Release, *The President of the ICTY Orders Release of Milojica Kos*, R.C./P.I.S./692e, The Hague, 31 July 2002.
- ICTY Press Release, *First Conference Between Health Professionals from the Former Yugoslavia and the ICTY on Witness Welfare*, CC/P.I.S./805-e, The Hague, 2 December 2003.
- ICTY Press Release, *Second Conference Between Health Professionals from the Former Yugoslavia and the ICTY on Witness Welfare*, WL/P.I.S./850-e, The Hague, 21 May 2004.
- ICTY Press Release, *Conference Between Health Professionals from Croatia and the ICTY on Witness Welfare*, WL/P.I.S./855-e, The Hague, 4 June 2004.
- ICTY Press Release, *Tihomir Blaskic Granted Early Release*, CT/P.I.S./876-e, The Hague, 29 July 2004.
- ICTY Press Release, *Anto Furundzija Granted Early Release*, CT/P.I.S./877e, The Hague, 30 July 2004.
- ICTY Press Release, *Fourth Conference Between Health Professionals from the Former Yugoslavia and the ICTY on Witness Welfare*, WL/P.I.S./894-e, The Hague, 13 September 2004.
- ICTY Press Release, *Foca Conference: Bridging the Gap Between the ICTY and Communities in Bosnia and Herzegovina*, RC/P.I.S./901-e, The Hague, 13 October 2004.
- ICTY Press Release, *Completion of Sentence by Dragoljub Prcac*, CVO/MOW/941e, The Hague, 4 March 2005.
- ICTY Press Release, *Gojko Jankovic Transferred to ICTY Detention Unit*, JP/MOW/948e, The Hague, 14 March 2005.
- ICTY Press Release, *Initial Appearance of Gojko Jankovic Scheduled for 18 March 2005*, CVO/MOW/PA213e, The Hague, 16 March 2005.
- ICTY Press Release, *Miroslav Kvocka Granted Early Release*, CVO/MOW/955e, The Hague, 31 March 2005.
- ICTY Press Release, *Two Indictments for Contempt of the Tribunal Confirmed and Released to the Public*, CT/MOW/967e, The Hague, 27 April 2005.

- ICTY Press Release, *Judgement in the Case The Prosecutor v. Beqa Beqaj*, CT/MOW/968e, The Hague, 5 May 2005
- Institute for War & Peace Reporting, *Foca Rape Case* (by Mirko Klarin and Vjera Bogati), Issue 210, 28 February 2001.
- Internews, *When Justice Takes Too Long* (by Mary Kimani), Kigali, 1 September 2003.
- Internews, *Living a Death Sentence: Rape Victims of the Rwanda Genocide* (by Mary Kimani), Kigali, 1 September 2003.
- Irin News, *Rwanda: ICTR to Embark on Fund-raising for Trust Fund*, Nairobi, 28 March 2002.
- Irin News, *Rwanda: Traditional Courts Inaugurated*, Kigali, 24 June 2004.
- New York Times, *Court Rejects Any Liberty for Milosevic, Citing Threats* (by Marlise Simons), 7 March 2002.
- New York Times Magazine, *A Woman's Work* (by Peter Landesman), 15 September 2002.
- The Guardian, *Mass Rape Ruled a War Crime* (by Andrew Osborn), Brussels, 23 February 2001.
- The New Times, *Gacaca Witnesses Murdered*, Kigali, 25 April 2005.
- The New Times, *Survivors' Houses Burnt*, Kigali, 28-29 June 2004.
- UN Press Release, *Juan E. Mendez of Argentina Appointed Special Advisor on Prevention of Genocide*, SG/A/880/BIO/3580, 14 July 2004.
- UN Press Release, *United Nations Welcomes Establishment of International Fund for Rwanda*, AFR/1133 IHA/1031, 4 April 2005.
- UNAIDS/WHO Press Release, *Number of Women Living with HIV Increases in Each Region of the World*, 23 November 2004.
- Washington Square News, *Lawyer: Rwanda Rape Belittled* (by Kate Meyer), 23 March 2004.
- Women's Initiatives for Gender Justice Press Release, in Collaboration with Isis-WICCE and Ugandan Women Activists, without title, 23 November 2004.
- Women's Initiatives for Gender Justice Press Release, *ICC Must Demonstrate it Takes Gender Crimes Seriously*, 30 June 2005.
- World Health Organization Press Release, *Women and Girls Need Access to AIDS Treatment and Protection from Violence*, 30 November 2004.

UN COMMISSION ON HUMAN RIGHTS

- UN Commission on Human Rights, *Report on the Situation of Human Rights in the Territory of the Former Yugoslavia Prepared by Mr. Tadeusz Mazowiecki, Special Rapporteur of the Commission on Human Rights, Pursuant to Paragraph 15 of Commission Resolution 199/S-1/1 and Economic and Social Council Decision 1992/305*, A/47/666, 17 November 1992.
- UN Commission on Human Rights, *Report on the Situation of Human Rights in the Territory of the Former Yugoslavia, Submitted by Tadeusz Mazowiecki, Special Rapporteur of the Commission on Human Rights, Pursuant to Paragraph 15 of Commission Resolution 1992/S-1/1 of 14 August 1992,* E/CN.4/1993/50, 10 February 1993 (UN Doc. E/CN.4/1993/50 (1993)).
- UN Commission on Human Rights, *Situation of Human Rights in the Territory of the Former Yugoslavia: 5th Periodic Report on the Situation of Human Rights in the Territory of the Former Yugoslavia, Submitted by Tadeusz Mazowiecki, Special Rapporteur of the Commission on Human Rights, Pursuant to Paragraph 32 of Commission Resolution 1993/7 of 23 February 1993*, E/CN.4/1994/47, 17 November 1993.
- UN Commission on Human Rights, *Situation of Human Rights in the Territory of the Former Yugoslavia: 6th Periodic Report on the Situation of Human Rights in the Territory of the Former Yugoslavia, Submitted by Tadeusz Mazowiecki, Special Rapporteur of the Commission on Human Rights, Pursuant to Paragraph 32 of Commission Resolution 1993/7 of 23 February 1993,* E/CN.4/1994/110, 21 February 1994.
- UN Commission on Human Rights, *Report on the Situation of Human Rights in Rwanda Prepared by the Special Rapporteur of the Commission on Human Rights, in Accordance with Commission Resolution S-3/1 and Economic and Social Council Decision 1994/223,* S/1994/1157, Annexes I and II, 13 October 1994.
- UN Commission on Human Rights, *Ninth Periodic Report on the Situation of Human Rights in the Territory of the Former Yugoslavia, Pursuant to Paragraph 37 of Commission Resolution 1994/72 of 9 March 1994 and Economic and Social Council Decision 1994/262 of 22 July 1994,* A/49/641, Annex to *Human Right Questions: Human Rights Situations and Reports of Special Rapporteurs and Representatives*, A/49/641, S/1994/1252, 4 November 1994.
- UN Commission on Human Rights, *Report on the Situation of Human Rights in Rwanda*, Submitted by Mr. René Degni-Segui, Special Rapporteur of the Commission on Human Rights, under Paragraph 20 of Resolution S-3/1 of 25 May 1994, E/CN.4/1996/68, 29 January 1996.
- UN Commission on Human Rights, *Systematic Rape, Sexual Slavery and Slavery-like Practices During Armed Conflict: Final Report Submitted by Gay J. McDougall, Special Rapporteur,* E/CN.4/Sub.2/1998/13, 22 June 1998.
- UN Commission on Human Rights, Report of the Special Rapporteur on Violence Against Women, Its Causes and Consequences, Ms. Radhika Coomaraswamy, Addendum, *Report of the Mission to Rwanda on the Issue of Violence Against Women in Situations of Armed Conflict*, E/CN.4/1998/54/Add.1, 4 February 1998.

- UN Commission on Human Rights, Report of the Special Rapporteur on Violence Against Women, Its Causes and Consequences, *Towards an Effective Implementation of International Norms to End Violence Against Women*, E/CN.4/2004/66, 26 December 2003.
- UN Commission on Human Rights, Resolution 2004/46, *Elimination of Violence Against Women*, E/CN.4/2004/L.11/Add.5, 21 April 2004.
- UN Commission on Human Rights, Report of the Special Rapporteur on Violence Against Women, Its Causes and Consequences, Yakin Ertürk, *Integration of the Human Rights of Women and the Gender Perspective: Violence Against Women – Intersections of Violence Against Women and HIV/AIDS*, E/CN.4/2005/72, 17 January 2005.

UN General Assembly

- UN General Assembly, *Resolution 95(I) Affirmation of Principles of International Law Recognized by the Charter of the Nürnberg Tribunal,* UN Doc. A/64/Add.1, 11 December 1946.
- UN General Assembly, *Resolution 488 (V) Formulation of the Nürnberg Principles*, 12 December 1950.
- UN General Assembly, *Resolution 39/46 of 10 December 1984 on the Convention Against Torture and Other Cruel, Inhuman or Degrading Treatment or Punishment*, A/RES/39/46, 10 December 1984.
- UN General Assembly, *Resolution 59/137 of 10 December 2004 on Assistance to Survivors of the 1994 Genocide in Rwanda, Particularly Orphans, Widows and Victims of Sexual Violence*, A/RES/59/137, 17 February 2005.

UN Secretary-General

- *Report of the Secretary-General on the Establishment of the Commission of Experts Pursuant to Paragraph 2 of Security Council Resolution 780 (1992),* S/24657, 14 October 1992.
- *Report of the Secretary-General Pursuant to Paragraph 2 of Security Council Resolution 808 (1993),* UN Doc. S/25704, 3 May 1993.
- *Report of the Secretary-General Pursuant to Paragraph 5 of Security Council Resolution 955 (1994),* UN Doc. S/1995/134, 13 February 1995.
- *Outline of the Mandate for the Special Advisor on the Prevention of Genocide,* Annex to Letter dated 2004/07/12 from the Secretary-General addressed to the President of the Security Council, S/2004/567, 13 July 2004.

UN SECURITY COUNCIL

- *Final Report of the Commission of Experts Established Pursuant to Security Council Resolution 780 (1992)*, S/1994/674, 27 May 1994.
- Final Report of the United Nations Commission of Experts Established Pursuant to Security Council Resolution 780 (1992), *Annex II – Rape and Sexual Assault: A Legal Study*, S/1994/674/Add.2 (Vol. 1), 28 December 1994.
- *Final Report of the Commission of Experts Established Pursuant to Security Council Resolution 935 (1994),* S/1994/1405, 9 December 1994.
- *Interim Report of the Commission of Experts Established Pursuant to Security Council Resolution 780 (1992)*, Annex to *Letter Dated 93/02/09 from the Secretary-General Addressed to the President of the Security Council*, S/25274, 11 February 1993.
- *Preliminary Report of the Independent Commission of Experts Established Pursuant to Security Council Resolution 935 (1994)*, S/1994/1125, 4 October 1994.
- Security Council Minutes from 4150th meeting, UN Doc. S/PV.4150, 2 June 2000.
- Security Council Resolution 764, *on Bosnia and Herzegovina,* S/RES/764, 13 July 1992.
- Security Council Resolution 771, *on the Former Yugoslavia*, S/RES/771, 13 August 1992.
- Security Council Resolution 780, *on the Establishment of a Commission of Experts for the former Yugoslavia*, S/RES/780 (1992), 6 October 1992.
- Security Council Resolution 808, *on the Establishment of the ICTY,* S/RES/808 (1993), 22 February 1993.
- Security Council Resolution 820, *Bosnia and Herzegovina*, S/RES/820, 17 April 1993.
- Security Council Resolution 827, *on the Establishment of the ICTY*, S/RES/827 (1993), 25 May 1993.
- Security Council Resolution 955, *on the Establishment of the ICTR,* S/RES/955, 8 November 1994.
- Security Council Resolution 1074, *on the Situation in the former Yugoslavia*, S/RES/1074 (1996), 1 October 1996.
- Security Council Resolution 1503, *on the International Criminal Tribunal for the former Yugoslavia and International Criminal Tribunal for Rwanda*, S/RES/1503 (2003), 28 August 2003.
- Security Council Resolution 1593, *Reports of the Secretary-General on Sudan*, S/RES/1593 (2005), 31 March 2005.

Miscellaneous

- Annual Report by the Joint United Nations Programme on HIV/AIDS (UNAIDS) and the World Health Organization (WHO), *AIDS Epidemic Update 2004*, December 2004.
- Center for Civil and Human Rights, Notre Dame Law School, *Amicus Curiae Brief on Protective Measures for Victims or Witnesses of Sexual Violence and Other Traumatic Event*, 6 November 1998.
- Coalition for Women's Human Rights in Conflict Situations, *Letter to Carla del Ponte, Prosecutor, Regarding the Urgent Need to Include Charges of Sexual Violence in the Indictment Against Milosevic*, 14 August 2001.
- Coalition for Women's Human Rights in Conflict Situations, Rights and Democracy, and International Centre for Human Rights and Democratic Development, *Letter to Carla del Ponte*, 12 March 2003.
- Coalition for Women's Human Rights in Conflict Situations, *Letter to Kofi Annan, Secretary General of the United Nations, Concerning the Reappointment of Carla Del Ponte as Prosecutor of the International Criminal Tribunal for Rwanda*, 24 July 2003.
- Coalition for Women's Human Rights in Conflict Situations, *Letter to Prosecutor Hassan Jallow*, 8 February 2005.
- Coalition for Women's Human Rights in Conflict Situations, *Sexual Violence in Cyangugu: A Testimonial* (by Monique Kankera), undated.
- Council of Europe, *Legislation in the Member States of the Council of Europe in the Field of Violence Against Women*, EG (2001) 3 rev., Volumes I and II, Strasbourg, November 2002.
- Council of the European Union, *Council Directive 2004/80/EC of 29 April 2004 Relating to Compensation to Crime Victims*, Official Journal of the European Union, L 261/15, 6 August 2004.
- *General Comment adopted by the Human Rights Committee under Article 40, paragraph 4, of the ICCPR*, CCPR/C/21/Rev.1/Add.6, 11 November 1994.
- Netherlands Institute for War Documentation, *Srebrenica – A 'Safe' Area*, Part I, Chapter 9, 10 April 2002.
- Organization for Security and Co-operation in Europe, *War Crimes Trials before the Domestic Courts of Bosnia and Herzegovina: Progress and Obstacles*, March 2005.
- Organization of African Unity, International Panel of Eminent Personalities Report, *Rwanda: The Preventable Genocide*, 2000.
- *Report of the International Commission of Inquiry on Darfur to the United Nations Secretary General: Pursuant to Security Council Resolution 1564 of 18 September 2004*, Geneva, 25 January 2005.
- *Report of the International Law Commission on the Work of Its Forty-Eight Session*, A/51/10 (SUPP), 1 January 1996.
- United Nations High Commissioner for Human Rights, *Access to Justice for Victims of Sexual Violence*, 29 July 2005.

- United Nations Division for the Advancement of Women, *Report of the Expert Group Meeting*, EGM/GBP/1997/Report, Toronto, Canada, 9-12 November 1997.
- United Nations Office for Drug Control and Crime Prevention, Center for International Crime Prevention, *Handbook on Justice for Victims: On the Use and Application of the Declaration of Basic Principles of Justice for Victims of Crime and Abuse of Power*, New York, 1999.
- World Health Organization, *Violence Against Women and HIV/AIDS: Critical Intersections, Sexual Violence in Conflict Settings and the Risk of HIV*, Information Bulletin Series, Number 2, 2004.

OVERVIEW OF CASES

INTERNATIONAL COURTS AND TRIBUNALS

EUROPEAN COURT OF HUMAN RIGHTS

- *Doorson v. The Netherlands*, Judgment, Publications of the European Court of Human Rights, Series A: Judgments and Decisions, Vol. 330, 26 March 1996.
- *Kostovski v. The Netherlands*, Judgment, Publications of the European Court of Human Rights, Series A: Judgments and Decisions, Vol. 166, 20 November 1989.
- *Ludi v. Switzerland*, Judgment, Publications of the European Court of Human Rights, Series A: Judgments and Decisions, Vol. 330, 15 June 1992.
- *Van Mechelen v. The Netherlands*, Judgment, Publications of the European Court of Human Rights, Series A: Judgments and Decisions, Vol. 674, 23 April 1997.

INTERNATIONAL COURT OF JUSTICE

- *Reservations to the Convention on the Prevention and the Punishment of the Crime of Genocide*, Advisory Opinion, ICJ Reports 1951, 28 May 1951.
- *North Sea Continental Shelf Cases (Federal Republic of Germany v. Denmark; Federal Republic of Germany v. The Netherlands)*, Judgment, ICJ Reports 1969, 20 February 1969.
- *Case Concerning the Continental Shelf (Libyan Arab Jamahiriya/Malta)*, Judgment, ICJ Reports 1985, 3 June 1985.
- *Military and Paramilitary Activities in and against Nicaragua (Nicaragua v. US)*, Judgment, ICJ Reports 1986, 27 June 1986.
- *Application of the Convention on the Prevention and Punishment of the Crime of Genocide (Bosnia and Herzegovina v. Serbia and Montenegro)*, Further Requests for the Indication of Provisional Measures, ICJ Reports 1993, 13 September 1993.

International Criminal Tribunal for the former Yugoslavia

Aleksovski

- *Prosecutor v. Zlatko Aleksovski,* Décision Portant Condamnation Pour Outrage Au Tribunal, Case N° IT-95-14/1-T, 11 décembre 1998.
- *Prosecutor v. Zlatko Aleksovski*, Judgment, Case No. IT-95-14/1-A, 24 March 2000 (Aleksovski Appeal Judgment).
- *Prosecutor v. Zlatko Aleksovski,* Judgment on Appeal by Anto Nobilo against Finding of Contempt, Case No. IT-95-14/1-AR77, 30 May 2001.

Banović, Banović, Fustar and Knežević

- *Prosecutor v. Nenad Banović, Predrag Banović, Dusan Fustar and Dusko Knežević*, Decision on Motion by the Prosecution for Withdrawal of Indictment against Nenad Banović, Case No. IT-95-8/1-PT, 10 April 2002.
- *Prosecutor v. Predrag Banović*, Sentencing Judgment, Case No. IT-02-65/1-S, 28 October 2003 (Banović Sentencing Judgment).

Blagojević and Jokić

- *Prosecutor v. Vidoje Blagojević and Dragan Jokić*, Transcripts, Case No. IT-02-60, 22 July 2003.

Blaškić

- *Prosecutor v. Tihomir Blaškić*, Decision on the Application of the Prosecutor dated 17 October 1996 Requesting Protective Measures for Victims and Witnesses, Case No. IT-95-14-T, 5 November 1996.
- *Prosecutor v. Tihomir Blaškić*, Decision of Trial Chamber I on the Requests of the Prosecutor of 12 and 14 May 1997 in Respect of the Protection of Witnesses, Case No. IT-95-14, 6 June 1997.
- *Prosecutor v. Tihomir Blaškić*, Judgment on the Request of the Republic of Croatia for Review of the Decision of Trial Chamber II of 18 July 1997, Case No. IT-95-14-AR108*bis*, 29 October 1997.
- *Prosecutor v. Tihomir Blaškić*, Judgment, Case No. IT-95-14-T, 3 March 2000 (Blaškić Judgment).
- *Prosecutor v. Tihomir Blaškić*, Judgment, Case No. IT-95-14-A, 29 July 2004 (Blaškić Appeal Judgment).

Brđanin

- *Prosecutor v. Radislav Brđanin and Momir Talić*, Decision on Form of Further Amended Indictment and Prosecution Application to Amend, Case No. IT-99-36, 26 June 2001.
- *Prosecutor v. Radoslav Brđanin,* Decision on Motion of Acquittal Pursuant to Rule 98*bis*, Case No. IT-99-36-T, 28 November 2003.
- *Prosecutor v. Radoslav Brđanin,* Sixth Amended Indictment, Case No. IT-99-36-T, 9 December 2003.
- *Prosecutor v. Radoslav Brđanin,* Prosection's Appeal from Trial Chamber's Decision Pursuant to 98*bis*, Case No. IT-99-36-T, 10 December 2003.
- *Prosecutor v. Radoslav Brđanin,* Decision on Interlocutory Appeal, Case No. IT-99-36-T, 19 March 2004.
- *Prosecutor v. Radoslav Brđanin*, Judgment, Case No. IT-99-36-T, 1 September 2004 (Brđanin Judgment).

Češić

- *Prosecutor v. Ranko Češić*, Sentencing Judgment, Case No. IT-95-10/1-S, 11 March 2004 (Češić Sentencing Judgment).

Delalić, Mucić, Delić and Landžo (Čelebići)

- *Prosecutor v. Zejnil Delalić, Zdravko Mucić, Hazim Delić and Esad Landžo*, Decision on the Motions by the Prosecution for Protective Measures for Prosecution Witnesses pseudonymed "B" through to "M", Case No. IT-96-21-T, 28 April 1997.
- *Prosecutor v. Zejnil Delalić, Zdravko Mucić, Hazim Delić and Esad Landžo*, Decision on the Motion to Allow Witnesses K, L and M to give Their Testimony by Means of Video-Link Conference, Case No. IT-96-21-T, 28 May 1997.
- *Prosecutor v. Zejnil Delalić, Zdravko Mucić, Hazim Delić and Esad Landžo*, Decision on the Prosecution's Motion for Redaction of the Public Record, Case No. IT-96-21-T, 5 June 1997.
- *Prosecutor v. Zejnil Delalić, Zdravko Mucić, Hazim Delić and Esad Landžo*, Judgment, Case No. IT-96-21-T, 16 November 1998 (Čelebići Judgment).
- *Prosecutor v. Zejnil Delalić, Zdravko Mucić, Hazim Delić and Esad Landžo*, Judgment, Case No. IT-96-21-A, 20 February 2001 (Čelebići Appeal Judgment).
    - *Prosecutor v. Zejnil Delalić, Zdravko Mucić, Hazim Delić and Esad Landžo,* Separate and dissenting Opinion of Judge David Hunt and Judge Mohamed Bennouna, Case No. IT-96-21-A, 20 February 2001.
- *Prosecutor v. Zejnil Delalić, Zdravko Mucić, Hazim Delić and Esad Landžo*, Sentencing Judgment, Case No. IT-96-21-T*bis*-R117, 9 October 2001 (Čelebići Sentencing Judgment).

- *Prosecutor v. Zdravko Mucić, Hazim Delić and Esad Landžo*, Judgment on Sentence Appeal, Case No. IT-96-21-A*bis*, 8 April 2003 (Čelebići Judgment on Sentence Appeal).

Delić

- *Prosecutor v. Rasim Delić*, Indictment, Case No. IT-04-83-PT, 17 March 2005.

Erdemović

- *Prosecutor v. Drazen Erdemović*, Judgment, Case No. IT-96-22-A, 7 October 1997 (Erdemović Appeal Judgment).
  - *Prosecutor v. Drazen Erdemović*, Separate and Dissenting Opinion of Judge Cassese, Case No. IT-96-22-A, 7 October 1997.
- *Prosecutor v. Drazen Erdemović*, Decision on the Defendant's Motion to Dismiss Counts 13 and 14 of the Indictment (Lack of Subject Matter Jurisdiction), Case No. IT-95-17/1, 29 May 1998.
- *Prosecutor v. Drazen Erdemović*, Sentencing Judgment, Case No. IT-96-22-A, 5 March 1998 (Erdemović Sentencing Judgment).

Furundžija

- *Prosecutor v. Anto Furundžija*, Prosecutor's Pre-Trial Brief, Case No. IT-95-17/1-PT, 22 May 1998.
- *Prosecutor v. Anto Furundžija*, Decision on the Defendant's Motion to Dismiss Counts 13 and 14 of the Indictment (Lack of Subject Matter Jurisdiction), Case No. IT-95-17/1, 29 May 1998.
- *Prosecutor v. Anto Furundžija*, Decision on Prosecutor's Motion Requesting Protective Measures for Witnesses "A" and "D" at Trial, Case No. IT-95-17/1-T, 11 June 1998.
- *Prosecutor v. Anto Furundžija*, Order Granting Leave to File *Amicus Curiae* Brief, Case No. IT-95-17/1-T, 10 November 1998.
- *Prosecutor v. Anto Furundžija*, Corrigendum to Order Granting Leave to File *Amicus Curiae* Brief, Case No. IT-95-17/1-T, 11 November 1998.
- *Prosecutor v. Anto Furundžija*, Order Granting Leave to File *Amicus Curiae* Brief, Case No. IT-95-17/1-T, 11 November 1998.
- *Prosecutor v. Anto Furundžija*, Judgment, Case No. IT-95-17/1-T, 10 December 1998 (Furundžija Judgment).
- *Prosecutor v. Anto Furundžija*, Respondent's Brief of the Prosecution (Public Version), Case No. IT-95-17/1-A, 30 September 1999.
- *Prosecutor v. Anto Furundžija*, Judgment, Case No. IT-95-17/1-A, 21 July 2000 (Furundžija Appeal Judgment).

Haradinaj, Balaj and Brahimaj

- *Prosecutor v. Ramush Haradinaj, Idriz Balaj and Lahi Brahimaj*, Indictment, Case No. IT-04-84-I, 4 March 2005.

Jelisić

- *Prosecutor v. Goran Jelisić*, Pre-Trail Brief, Case No. IT-95-10-T, 19 November 1998 (Jelisić Pre-Trail Brief).
- *Prosecutor v. Goran Jelisić*, Judgment, Case No. IT-95-10-T, 14 December 1999 (Jelisić Judgment).
- *Prosecutor v. Goran Jelisić*, Prosecution's Appeal Brief (Public Redacted Version), Case No. IT-95-10-A, 14 July 2000.
- *Prosecutor v. Goran Jelisić*, Judgment, Case No. IT-95-10-A, 5 July 2001 (Jelisić Appeal Judgment).

Karadžić and Mladić

- *Prosecutor v. Radovan Karadžić and Ratko Mladić*, Transcripts, Case No. IT-95-18-R61 and Case No. IT-95-5-R61, 2 July 1996.
- *Prosecutor v. Radovan Karadžić and Ratko Mladić*, Review of the Indictments Pursuant to Rule 61 of the Rules of Procedure and Evidence, Case No. IT-95-5-R16 and IT-95-18-R61, 11 July 1996 (Karadžić and Mladić Rule 61 Decision).
- *Prosecutor v. Radovan Karadžić*, Amended Indictment, Case No. IT-95-5/18-I, 28 April 2000.
- *Prosecutor v. Ratko Mladić*, Amended Indictment, Case No. IT-95-5/18-I, 10 October 2002.

Kordić and Čerkez

- *Prosecutor v. Dario Kordić and Mario Čerkez*, Judgment, Case No. IT-95-14/2-T, 26 February 2001 (Kordić and Čerkez Judgment).

Kovačević

- *Prosecutor v. Milan Kovačević*, First Amended Indictment, Case No. IT-97-24-I, 28 January 1998.

Krajisnik

- *Prosecutor v. Momcilo Krajisnik and Biljana Plavšić*, Amended Consolidated Indictment, Case No. IT-00-39 and 40-PT, 7 March 2002.

Krnojelac

- *Prosecutor v. Milorad Krnojelac*, Judgment, Case No. IT-97-25-T, 15 March 2002 (Krnojelac Judgment).
- *Prosecutor v. Milorad Krnojelac*, Judgment, Case No. IT-97-25-A, 17 September 2003 (Krnojelac Appeal Judgment).

Krstić

- *Prosecutor v. Radislav Krstić*, Judgment, Case No. IT-98-33-T, 2 August 2001 (Krstić Judgment).
- *Prosecutor* v. *Radislav Krstić*, Judgment, Case No. IT-98-33-A, 19 April 2004 (Krstić Appeal Judgment).

Kunarac, Kovač and Vuković (Foča)

- *Prosecutor v. Dragan Gagović, Gojko Janković, Janko Janjić, Radomir Kovač, Zoran Vuković, Dragan Zelenović, Dragoljub Kunarac and Radovan Stanković*, Decision on Prosecution Motion to Protect Victims and Witnesses, Case No. IT-96-23 and 23/1, 29 April 1998.
- *Prosecutor v. Dragoljub Kunarac and Radomir Kovač*, Amended Indictment, Case No. IT-96-23-PT, 8 November 1999.
- *Prosecutor v. Dragoljub Kunarac and Radomir Kovač,* Prosecutor's Pre-Trail Brief, Case No. IT-96-23-PT, 9 December 1999.
- *Prosecutor v. Dragoljub Kunarac, Radomir Kovač and Zoran Vuković,* Transcripts, Case No. IT-96-23-T and IT-96-23/1-T, 19 April 2000.
- *Prosecutor v. Dragoljub Kunarac, Radomir Kovač and Zoran Vuković,* Transcripts, Case No. IT-96-23-T and IT-96-23/1-T, 25 April 2000.
- *Prosecutor v. Dragoljub Kunarac, Radomir Kovač and Zoran Vuković,* Transcripts, Case No. IT-96-23-T and IT-96-23/1-T, 18 May 2000.
- *Prosecutor v. Dragoljub Kunarac, Radomir Kovač and Zoran Vuković*, Prosecutor's Final Trial Brief, Case No. IT-96-23-T and IT-96-23/1-T, 8 November 2000.
- *Prosecutor v. Dragoljub Kunarac, Radomir Kovač and Zoran Vuković,* Transcripts, Case No. IT-96-23-T and IT-96-23/1-T, 20 November 2000.
- *Prosecutor v. Dragoljub Kunarac, Radomir Kovač and Zoran Vuković*, Judgment, Case No. IT-96-23 and IT-96-23/1, 22 February 2001 (Kunarac, Kovač and Vuković Judgment).
- *Prosecutor v. Dragoljub Kunarac, Radomir Kovač and Zoran Vuković*, Judgment, Case No. IT-96-23-A and IT-96-23/1-A, 12 June 2002 (Kunarac, Kovač and Vuković Appeal Judgment).

Kupreškić, Kupreškić, Kupreškić, Josipović, Papić and Santić (Kupreškić et al.)

- *Prosecutor v. Zoran Kupreškić, Mirjan Kupreškić, Vlatko Kupreškić, Drago Josipović, Dragan Papić and Vladimir Santić*, Judgment, Case No. IT-95-16-T, 14 January 2000 (Kupreškić, Kupreškić, Kupreškić, Josipović, Papić and Santić Judgment).
- *Prosecutor v. Zoran Kupreškić, Mirjan Kupreškić, Vlatko Kupreškić, Drago Josipović and Vladimir Santić*, Appeal Judgment, Case No. IT-95-16-A, 23 October 2001 (Kupreškić, Kupreškić, Kupreškić, Josipović and Santić Appeal Judgment).

Kvočka, Kos, Radić, Žigić and Prcać (Kvočka et al.)

- *Prosecutor v. Miroslav Kvočka, Milojica Kos, Mlado Radić, Zoran Žigić and Dragoljub Prcać,* Judgment, Case No. IT-98-30/1-T, 2 November 2001 (Kvočka et al. Judgment).
- *Prosecutor v. Miroslav Kvočka, Mlado Radić, Zoran Žigić and Dragoljub Prcać,* Judgment, Case No. IT-98-30/1-A, 28 February 2005 (Kvočka et al. Appeal Judgment).

Limaj, Bala, and Musliu (Limaj et al.)

- *Prosecutor v. Beqa Beqaj*, Indictment, Case No. IT-03-66-R77, 21 October 2004.

Martić

- *Prosecutor v. Milan Martić,* Amended Indictment, Case No. IT-95-11, 18 December 2002.

Milosević

- *Prosecutor v. Slobodan Milosević*, Indictment (Croatia), Case No. IT-01-50-I, 8 October 2001.
- *Prosecutor v. Slobodan Milosević*, Indictment (Bosnia), Case No. IT-01-51-I, 22 November 2001.

Milutinović, Šainović and Ojdanić

- *Prosecutor v. Slobodan Milosević, Milan Milutinović, Nikola Šainović, Dragoljub Ojdanić and Vlajko Stojiljković*, Second Amended Indictment, Case No. IT-99-37-PT, 29 October 2001.
- *Prosecutor v. Milan Milutinović, Nikola Šainović and Dragoljub Ojdanić*, Decision on Dragoljub Ojdanic's Motion Challenging Jurisdiction – Joint Criminal Enterprise, Case No. IT-99-37-AR72, 21 May 2003.

Mrkšić, Radić, Šljivančanin and Dokmanović

- *Prosecutor v. Mile Mrkšić, Miroslav Radić, Veselin Šljivančanin and Slavko Dokmanović*, Decision on the Prosecutor's Motion for Deposition Evidence, Case No. IT-95-13a, 11 March 1998.
- *Prosecutor v. Mile Mrkšić, Miroslav Radić, Veselin Šljivančanin and Slavko Dokmanović*, Decision on the Defence Motions for Video-Conference Link, Case No. IT-95-13a, 29 April 1998.
- *Prosecutor v. Mile Mrkšić, Miroslav Radić, Veselin Šljivančanin and Slavko Dokmanović*, Decision on Defence Motion for Video Link Conference, Case No. IT-95-13a, 18 May 1998.
- *Prosecutor v. Mile Mrkšić, Miroslav Radić, Veselin Šljivančanin and Slavko Dokmanović*, Scheduling Order, Case No. IT-95-13a, 8 June 1998.

Naletilić and Martinović

- *Prosecutor v. Mladen Naletilić and Vinko Martinović*, Judgment, Case No. IT-98-34-T, 31 March 2003 (Naletilić and Martinović Judgment).

Nikolić

- *Prosecutor v. Dragan Nikolić*, Sentencing Judgment, Case No. IT-94-2-S, 18 December 2003 (Nikolić Sentencing Judgment).
- *Prosecutor v. Dragan Nikolić*, Judgment on Sentencing Appeal, Case No. 94-2-A, 4 February 2005 (Nikolić Judgment on Sentencing Appeal).

Plavšić

- *Prosecutor v. Momcilo Krajisnik and Biljana Plavšić*, Amended Consolidated Indictment, Case No. IT-00-39 and 40-PT, 7 March 2002.
- *Prosecutor v. Biljana Plavšić*, Sentencing Judgment, Case No. IT-00-39 and 40/1-S, 27 February 2003 (Plavšić Sentencing Judgment).

Sikirica, Došen and Kolundžija

- *Prosecutor v. Duško Sikirica, Damir Došen and Dragan Kolundžija*, Prosecutor's Second Revised Pre-Trail Brief, Case No. IT-95-8-PT, 13 October 2000 (Sikirica Pre-Trial Brief).
- *Prosecutor v. Duško Sikirica, Damir Došen and Dragan Kolundžija*, Sentencing Judgment, Case No. IT-95-8-S, 13 November 2001 (Sikirica Sentencing Judgment).

Simić

- *Prosecutor v. Milan Simić*, Sentencing Judgment, Case No. IT-95-9/2-S, 17 October 2002 (Simić Sentencing Judgment).

Stakić

- *Prosecutor v. Milomir Stakić,* Decision on Rule 98*bis* Motion for Judgment of Acquittal, Case No. IT-97-24-T, 31 October 2002.
- *Prosecutor v. Milomir Stakić*, Fourth Amended Indictment, Case No. IT-97-24-PT, 10 April 2002.
- *Prosecutor v. Milomir Stakić,* Judgment, Case No. IT-97-24-T, 31 July 2003 (Stakić Judgment).

Stanković

- *Prosecutor v. Radovan Stanković*, Decision of Referral of Case Under Rule 11*bis*, Case No. IT-96-23/2-PT, 17 May 2005.

Tadić

- *Prosecutor v. Duško Tadić,* Decision on the Defense Motion on Jurisdiction, Case No. IT-94-1, 10 August 1995 (Tadić Jurisdiction Decision).
- *Prosecutor v. Duško Tadić*, Decision on the Prosecutor's Motion Requesting Protective Measures for Victims and Witnesses, Case No. IT-94-1, 10 August 1995 (Tadić Protective Measures Decision).
- *Prosecutor v. Duško Tadić*, Separate Opinion of Judge Stephen on the Prosecutor's Motion Requesting Protective Measures for Victims and Witnesses, Case No. IT-94-1, 10 August 1995.
- *Prosecutor v. Duško Tadić*, Decision on the Defence Motion to Summon and Protect Defence Witnesses, and on the Giving of Evidence by Video-Link, Case No. IT-94-1-T, 25 June 1996.
- *Prosecutor v. Duško* Tadić, Decision on Prosecutor's Motion Requesting Protective Measures for Witness R, Case No. IT-94-1-T, 31 July 1996.
- *Prosecutor v. Duško Tadić*, Decision on the Defence Motion Requesting Video-Link for Defence Witnesses, Case No. IT-94-1-T, 16 October 1996.
- *Prosecutor v. Duško Tadić*, Decision on the Defence Motion Requesting Video-Link for Defence Witness Jelena Gajić, Case No. IT-94-1-T, 17 October 1996.
- *Prosecutor v. Duško Tadić,* Decision on Prosecution Motion to Withdraw Protective Measures for Witness L, Case No. IT-94-1-T, 5 December 1996.
- *Prosecutor v. Duško Tadić,* Opinion and Judgment, Case No. IT-94-1-T, 7 May 1997 (Tadić Opinion and Judgment).
- *Prosecutor v. Duško Tadić,* Sentencing Judgment, Case No. IT-94-1-T, 14 July 1997 (Tadić Sentencing Judgment).
- *Prosecutor v. Duško Tadić*, Decision on Appellant's Motion for the Extension of the Time-limit and Admission of Additional Evidence, Case No. IT-94-1-A, 15 October 1998.
- *Prosecutor v. Duško Tadić*, Judgment, Case No. IT-94-1-A, 15 July 1999 (Tadić Appeal Judgment).

- *Prosecutor v. Duško Tadić*, Sentencing Judgment, Case No. IT-94-1-T*bis*-R117, 11 November 1999.
- *Prosecutor v. Duško Tadić*, Judgment in Sentencing Appeals, Case No. IT-94-1, 26 January 2000 (Tadić Judgment in Sentencing Appeals).

Talić

- *Prosecutor v. Radislav Brđanin and Momir Talić*, Decision on Form of Further Amended Indictment and Prosecution Application to Amend, Case No. IT-99-36, 26 June 2001.

Todorović

- *Prosecutor v. Blagoje Simić, Milan Simić, Miroslav Tadić, Stevan Todorović and Simo Zarić*, Second Amended Indictment, Case No. IT-95-9, 25 March 1999.
- *Prosecutor v. Stevan Todorović*, Sentencing Judgment, Case No. IT-95-9/1-S, 31 July 2001 (Todorović Sentencing Judgment).

International Criminal Tribunal for Rwanda

Akayesu

- *The Prosecutor v. Jean-Paul Akayesu*, Judgment, Case No. ICTR-96-4-T, 2 September 1998 (Akayesu Judgment).
- *The Prosecutor v. Jean-Paul Akayesu*, Sentencing Judgment, Case No. ICTR-96-4-T, 2 October 1998 (Akayesu Sentencing Judgment).
- *The Prosecutor v. Jean-Paul Akayesu*, Judgment, Case No. ICTR-96-4-A, 1 June 2001 (Akayesu Appeal Judgment).

Bagosora, Kabiligi, Ntabakuze, Nsengiyumva (Military I)

- *The Prosecutor v. Théoneste Bagosora*, Amicus Curiae: Letter from Geert Muylle to Mr. Agwu Ukiwe Okali, Case No. ICTR-96-7-T, 10 February 1998.
- *The Prosecutor v. Théoneste Bagosora*, Prosecutor's Memorial (In Response to the Motion Filed by the Kingdom of Belgium on 10 February 1998 to Appear at the Trial and Lead Evidence as *Amicus Curiae*), Case No. ICTR-96-7-T, 10 February 1998.
- *The Prosecutor v. Théoneste Bagosora*, Withdrawal of Prosecutor's Memorial (In Response to the Motion Filed by the Kingdom of Belgium on 10 February 1998 to Appear at the Trial and Lead Evidence as *Amicus Curiae*), Case No. ICTR-96-7-T, 9 March 1998.
- *The Prosecutor v. Théoneste Bagosora,* Request to Appear Before the Tribunal and to Testify as Amicus Curiae in the Case of Théoneste Bagosora and Others, Case No. ICTR-96-7-T, 20 April 1998.

- *The Prosecutor v. Théoneste Bagosora*, Decision on the Amicus Curiae Application by the Government of the Kingdom of Belgium, Case No. ICTR-96-7-T, 6 June 1998.
- *The Prosecutor v. Théoneste Bagosora, Gratien Kabiligi, Aloys Ntabakuze and Anatole Nsengiyumva*, Decision on Prosecutor's Motion for Deposition of Witness OW, Case No. ICTR-98-41-I, 5 December 2001.
- *The Prosecutor v. Théoneste Bagosora, Gratien Kabiligi, Aloys Ntabakuze and Anatole Nsengiyumva*, Decision on the Prosecution Motion Ex Parte in the Matter of Violation of the Trial Chamber's Witness Protection Orders, and Contempt of Court, Case No. ICTR-98-41-T, 5 July 2002.
- *Le Procureur c. Théoneste Bagosora, Gratien Kabiligi, Aloys Ntabakuze et Anatole Nsengiyumva*, Transcription Caviardee, Affaire N° ICTR-98-41-T, 20 janvier 2004.
- *The Prosecutor v. Théoneste Bagosora, Gratien Kabiligi, Aloys Ntabakuze and Anatole Nsengiyumva*, Transcripts, Case No. ICTR-98-41-T, 3 February 2004.
- *The Prosecutor v. Théoneste Bagosora, Gratien Kabiligi, Aloys Ntabakuze and Anatole Nsengiyumva*, Decision on Amicus Curiae Request by African Concern, Case No. ICTR-98-41-T, 23 March 2004.
- *The Prosecutor v. Théoneste Bagosora, Gratien Kabiligi, Aloys Ntabakuze and Anatole Nsengiyumva*, Transcripts, Case No. ICTR-98-41-T, 12 July 2004.
- *The Prosecutor v. Théoneste Bagosora, Gratien Kabiligi, Aloys Ntabakuze and Anatole Nsengiyumva*, Decision on Amicus Curiae Request by the Rwandan Government, Case No. ICTR-98-41-T, 13 October 2004.

Bagilishema

- *The Prosecutor v. Ignace Bagilishema*, Judgment, Case No. ICTR-95-1A-T, 7 June 2001 (Bagilishema Judgment).

Bizimungu, Mugenzi, Bicamumpaka, Mugiraneza (Government II)

- *The Prosecutor v. Casimir Bizimungu, Justin Mugenzi, Jérôme-Clément Bicamumpaka and Prosper Mugiraneza*, Decision on the Prosecutor's Motion and Notice Pursuant to Rule 92*bis*(E), Case No. ICTR-99-50-T, 17 November 2004.

Gacumbitsi

- *The Prosecutor v. Sylvestre Gacumbitsi*, Transcripts, Case No. ICTR-2001-64, 3 April 2002.
- *Le Procureur c. Sylvestre Gacumbitsi*, Transcription Caviardee, Affaire N° ICTR-2001-64-T, 6 août 2003.
- *The Prosecutor v. Sylvestre Gacumbitsi*, The Prosecutor's Closing Brief, Case No. ICTR-2001-64-I, 22 December 2003.
- *The Prosecutor v. Sylvestre Gacumbitsi*, Judgment, Case No. ICTR-2001-64-T, 17 June 2004 (Gacumbitsi Judgment).

- *The Prosecutor v. Sylvestre Gacumbitsi*, Appelant's Brief, Case No. ICTR-2001-64-A, 28 September 2004.

Kajelijeli

- *The Prosecutor v. Juvénal Kajelijeli*, Closing Brief, Case No. ICTR-98-44A-T, 16 June 2003.
- *The Prosecutor v. Juvénal Kajelijeli*, Judgment and Sentence, Case No. ICTR-98-44A-T, 1 December 2003 (Kajelijeli Judgment and Sentence).

Kambanda

- *The Prosecutor v. Jean Kambanda*, Judgment and Sentence, Case No. ICTR 97-23-S, 4 September 1998 (Kambanda Judgment and Sentence).
- *Jean Kambanda v. The Prosecutor*, Judgment, Case No. ICTR-97-23-A, 19 October 2000 (Kambanda Appeal Judgment).

Kamuhanda

- *The Prosecutor v. Jean de Dieu Kamuhanda*, Judgment, Case No. ICTR-95-54A-T, 22 January 2004 (Kamuhanda Judgment).

Karemera, Ngirumpatse and Nzirorera (Government I)

- *The Prosecutor v. Édouard Karemera, Mathieu Ngirumpatse, Joseph Nzirorera and André Rwamakuba,* Decision on the Preliminary Motions by the Defence of Joseph Nzirorera, Edouard Karemera, André Rwamakuba and Mathieu Ngirumpatse Challenging Jurisdiction in relation to Joint Criminal Enterprise, Case No. ICTR-98-44-T, 11 May 2004.
- *The Prosecutor v. Édouard Karemera, Mathieu Ngirumpatse and Joseph Nzirorera*, Amended Indictment, Case No. ICTR-98-44-I, 23 February 2005.

Kayishema and Ruzindana

- *The Prosecutor v. Obed Ruzindana*, Decision on the Motion filed by the Prosecutor on the Protection of Victims and Witnesses, 4 March 1997.
- *The Prosecutor v. Clément Kayishema and Obed Ruzindana*, Judgment, Case No. ICTR-95-1-T, 21 May 1999 (Kayishema and Ruzindana Judgment).
- *The Prosecutor v. Clément Kayishema and Obed Ruzindana*, Judgment (Reasons), Case No. ICTR-95-1-A, 1 June 2001 (Kayishema and Ruzindana Appeal Judgment).

Muhimana

- *The Prosecutor v. Mika Muhimana*, The Prosecutor's Closing Brief, Case No. ICTR-95-1B-T, 25 October 2004.
- *The Prosecutor v. Mikaeli Muhimana*, Judgment and Sentence, Case No. ICTR-95-1B-T, 28 April 2005 (Muhimana Judgment and Sentence).

Musema

- *The Prosecutor v. Alfred Musema*, Decision on an Application by African Concern for Leave to Appear as Amicus Curiae, Case No. ICTR-96-13-T, 17 March 1999.
- *The Prosecutor v. Alfred Musema*, Judgment and Sentence, Case No. ICTR-96-13-T, 27 January 2000 (Musema Judgment and Sentence).
- *Alfred Musema v. The Prosecutor*, Judgment, Case No. ICTR-96-13-A, 16 November 2001 (Musema Appeal Judgment).

Muvunyi

- *The Prosecutor v. Tharcisse Muvunyi*, Decision on the Prosecutor's Motion for Leave to File an Amended Indictment, Case No. ICTR-2000-55A-PT, 23 February 2005.

Nahimana, Barayagwiza and Ngeze (Media)

- *The Prosecutor v. Ferdinand Nahimana, Jean-Bosco Barayagwiza and Hassan Ngeze*, Decision on the Prosecutor's Application to Add Witness X to its List of Witnesses and for Protective Measures, Case No. ICTR-99-52-I, 14 September 2001.
- *The Prosecutor v. Ferdinand Nahimana, Jean-Bosco Barayagwiza and Hassan Ngeze,* Judgment, Case No. ICTR-99-52-T, 3 December 2003 (Media Judgment).

Niyitegeka

- *The Prosecutor v. Eliézer Niyitegeka*, Judgment and Sentence, Case No. ICTR-96-14-T, 16 May 2003 (Niyitegeka Judgment and Sentence).
- *The Prosecutor v. Eliézer Niyitegeka,* Prosecutor's Final Trial Brief, Case No. ICTR-96-14-T, 13 December 2003.
- *Eliézer Niyitegeka v. The Prosecutor*, Judgment, Case No. ICTR-96-14-A, 9 July 2004 (Niyitegeka Appeal Judgment).

Ntagerura, Bagambiki and Imanishimwe (Cyangugu)

- *The Prosecutor v. André Ntagerura, Emmanuel Bagambiki, Samuel Imanishimwe and Yussuf Munyakazi,* Notice of the Prosecutor to Withdraw All Pending Motions, Case No. ICTR-99-46-T, 14 February 2000.

- *The Prosecutor v. André Ntagerura, Emmanuel Bagambiki and Samuel Imanishimwe,* Transcripts, Case Nos. ICTR-99-10A-T, ICTR-97-36-T, ICTR-99-46-T, 13 February 2001.
- *The Prosecutor v. André Ntagerura, Emmanuel Bagambiki and Samuel Imanishimwe,* Transcripts, Case Nos. ICTR-99-10A-T, ICTR-97-36-T, ICTR-99-46-T, 14 February 2001.
- *The Prosecutor v. André Ntagerura, Emmanuel Bagambiki and Samuel Imanishimwe,* Prosecutor's Response to Application for Leave to File an Amicus Brief, Case No. ICTR-99-46-T, 8 May 2001.
- *The Prosecutor v. André Ntagerura, Emmanuel Bagambiki and Samuel Imanishimwe,* Decision on the Application to File an Amicus Curiae Brief According to Rule 74 of the Rules of Procedure and Evidence Filed on Behalf of the NGO Coalition for Women's Human Rights in Conflict Situations, Case No. ICTR-99-46-T, 24 May 2001.
- *The Prosecutor v. André Ntagerura, Emmanuel Bagambiki and Samuel Imanishimwe,* Prosecutor's Response to a Request for Reconsideration of the Decision of the Application to File an Amicus Curiae Brief by Coalition for Women's Human Rights in Conflict Situations, Case No. ICTR-99-46-T, 7 September 2001.
- *The Prosecutor v. Samuel Imanishimwe, Emmanuel Bagambiki and André Ntagerura,* Decision on the Coalition for Women's Human Rights in Conflict Situation's Motion for Reconsideration of the Decision on Application to File an Amicus Curiae Brief, Case No. ICTR-99-46-T, 24 September 2001.
- *The Prosecutor v. André Ntagerura, Emmanuel Bagambiki and Samuel Imanishimwe,* Judgment, Case No. ICTR-99-46-T, 25 February 2004 (Cyangugu Judgment).

Ntakirutimana and Ntakirutimana

- *The Prosecutor v. Elizaphan Ntakirutimana and Gérard Ntakirutimana*, Judgment and Sentence, Case No. ICTR-96-10-T & ICTR-96-17-T, 21 February 2003 (Ntakirutimana and Ntakirutimana Judgment and Sentence).

Nyiramasuhuko, Ntahobali, Nteziryayo, Nsabimana, Ndayambaje, Kanyabashi (Butare)

- *The Prosecutor v. Pauline Nyiramasuhuko and Shalom Ntahobali,* Amended Indictment, Case No. ICTR-97-21-I, 1 March 2001.
- *The Prosecutor v. Pauline Nyiramasuhuko, Arsène Shalom Ntahobali, Alphonse Nteziryayo, Sylvain Nsabimana, Elie Ndayambaje and Joseph Kanyabashi,* Transcripts, Case No. ICTR-98-42-T, 24 October 2001.
- *The Prosecutor v. Pauline Nyiramasuhuko, Arsène Shalom Ntahobali, Alphonse Nteziryayo, Sylvain Nsabimana, Elie Ndayambaje and Joseph Kanyabashi,* Transcripts, Case No. ICTR-98-42-T, 25 October 2001.

- *The Prosecutor v. Pauline Nyiramasuhuko, Arsène Shalom Ntahobali, Alphonse Nteziryayo, Sylvain Nsabimana, Elie Ndayambaje and Joseph Kanyabashi*, Transcripts, Case No. ICTR-98-42-T, 29 October 2001.
- *The Prosecutor v. Pauline Nyiramasuhuko, Arsène Shalom Ntahobali, Alphonse Nteziryayo, Sylvain Nsabimana, Elie Ndayambaje and Joseph Kanyabashi*, Transcripts, Case No. ICTR-98-42-T, 31 October 2001.
- *The Prosecutor v. Pauline Nyiramasuhuko, Arsène Shalom Ntahobali, Alphonse Nteziryayo, Sylvain Nsabimana, Elie Ndayambaje and Joseph Kanyabashi*, Transcripts, Case No. ICTR-98-42-T, 1 November 2001.
- *The Prosecutor v. Pauline Nyiramasuhuko, Arsène Shalom Ntahobali, Alphonse Nteziryayo, Sylvain Nsabimana, Elie Ndayambaje and Joseph Kanyabashi*, Transcripts, Case No. ICTR-98-42-T, 3 April 2002.
- *The Prosecutor v. Pauline Nyiramasuhuko, Arsène Shalom Ntahobali, Alphonse Nteziryayo, Sylvain Nsabimana, Elie Ndayambaje and Joseph Kanyabashi*, Transcripts, Case No. ICTR-98-42-T, 24 October 2002.
- *The Prosecutor v. Pauline Nyiramasuhuko, Arsène Shalom Ntahobali, Alphonse Nteziryayo, Sylvain Nsabimana, Elie Ndayambaje and Joseph Kanyabashi*, Transcripts, Case No. ICTR-98-42-T, 11 March 2003.
- *The Prosecutor v. Pauline Nyiramasuhuko, Arsène Shalom Ntahobali, Alphonse Nteziryayo, Sylvain Nsabimana, Elie Ndayambaje and Joseph Kanyabashi*, Decision on Prosecutor's Motion for Leave to Be Authorised to Have Admitted the Affidavits Regarding the Chain of Custody of the Diary of Pauline Nyiramasuhuko Under Rule 92*bis*, Case No. ICTR-98-42-T, 14 October 2004.

Ruggiu

- *The Prosecutor v. Georges Ruggiu*, Judgment and Sentence, Case No. ICTR-97-32-I, 1 June 2000 (Ruggiu Judgment and Sentence).

Rutaganda

- *The Prosecutor v. Georges Anderson Nderubumwe Rutaganda*, Judgment and Sentence, Case No. ICTR 96-3-T, 6 December 1999 (Rutaganda Judgment and Sentence).

Rwamakuba

- *The Prosecutor v. Édouard Karemera, Mathieu Ngirumpatse, Joseph Nzirorera and André Rwamakuba,* Decision on the Preliminary Motions by the Defence of Joseph Nzirorera, Edouard Karemera, André Rwamakuba and Mathieu Ngirumpatse Challenging Jurisdiction in relation to Joint Criminal Enterprise, Case No. ICTR-98-44-T, 11 May 2004.
- *André Rwamakuba v. The Prosecutor*, Decision on Interlocutory Appeal Regarding Application of Joint Criminal Enterprise to the Crime of Genocide, Case No. ICTR-98-44-AR72.4, 22 October 2004.

Semanza

- *The Prosecutor v. Laurent Semanza*, Judgment and Sentence, Case No. ICTR-97-20-T, 15 May 2003 (Semanza Judgment and Sentence).
- *The Prosecutor v. Laurent Semanza*, Prosecution Appeal Brief, Case No. ICTR-97-20-A, 1 September 2003.
- *Laurent Semanza v. The Prosecutor*, Judgment, Case No. ICTR-97-20-A, 20 May 2005 (Semanza Appeal Judgment).

Serushago

- *The Prosecutor v. Omar Serushago*, Sentence, Case No. ICTR 98-39-S, 5 February 1999 (Serushago Sentence).

WOMEN'S INTERNATIONAL WAR CRIMES TRIBUNAL ON JAPAN'S MILITARY SEXUAL SLAVERY

- The Women's International War Crimes Tribunal 2000 for the Trial of Japanese Military Sexual Slavery' in the matter of THE PROSECUTORS AND THE PEOPLES OF THE ASIA-PACIFIC REGION V. EMPEROR HIROHITO et al. AND THE GOVERNMENT OF JAPAN, Summery of Findings, 12 December 2000 (on file with the author).
- Transcript of Oral Judgment delivered on 4 December 2001 by the Judges of the Women's International War Crimes Tribunal on Japan's Military Sexual Slavery, Tokyo, Japan (on file with the author).

NATIONAL COURTS

United Kingdom

- *Islam (A.P.) v. Secretary of State for the Home Department, Regina v. Immigration Appeal Tribunal and Another Ex Parte Shah (A.P.)(Conjoined Appeals)*, 25 March 1999, House of Lords.
- *R. v. Watford Magistrates* (1993), TLR 285.
- *R. v. Taylor* (1994), TLR 484.

The Netherlands

- Hoge Raad, Staat der Nederlanden v. T.J., 21 april 1998, *NJ* 1998, 781 ('Tongzoen-arrest')
- Hoge Raad, Staat der Nederlanden v. D. Bouterse, 18 september 2001, 00749/01 *CW* 2323.

Australia

- *Jarvie and Another v. The Magistrates' Court of Victoria at Brunswick and Others* (1994), VR 88.

Overview of Legislation

International Treaties and Other Legislation

1863 Instructions for the Government of Armies of the United States in the Field by Order of the Secretary of War, 24 April 1863, reprinted in Schindler and Toman (1988) (Lieber Code).

1899 Hague Convention (II) with Respect to the Laws and Customs of War on Land, 29 July 1899, 32 Stat. 1803, TS No. 403, reprinted in Schindler and Toman (1988), p. 63 (1899 Hague Convention (II) with Respect to the Laws and Customs of War on Land).

1904 International Convention for the Suppression of the White Slave Traffic, 18 May 1904, 35 Stat. 426, 1 LNTS 83, as amended by the Protocol of 4 May 1949, 92 UNTS 19.

1907 Hague Convention (IV) Respecting the Laws and Customs of War on Land (and Annex Regulations Concerning the Laws and Customs of War on Land), 18 October 1907, 36 Stat. 2277, TS No. 539, reprinted in Roberts and Guelff (2000), p. 67 (1907 Hague Convention (IV) Respecting the Laws and Customs of War on Land).

1910 International Convention for the Suppression of White Slave Traffic, 4 May 1910, III LNTS 278.

1921 International Convention for the Suppression of the Traffic in Women and Children, 30 September 1921, 9 LNTS 416, as amended by Protocol, 93 UNTS 43.

1926 Slavery Convention, 25 September 1926, 60 LNTS 253 (1926 Slavery Convention).

1930 Convention Concerning Forced or Compulsory Labour (ILO No. 29), 28 June 1930, 39 UNTS 55 (1930 Forced or Compulsory Labour Convention).

1933 International Convention on the Suppression of the Traffic in Women of Full Age, 11 October 1933, 150 LNTS 431, as amended by the Protocol of 12 November 1947, 53 UNTS 39.

1945
- Charter of the United Nations, San Francisco, 26 June 1945.
- Statute of the International Court of Justice, San Francisco, 26 June 1945.
- Charter of the International Military Tribunal for the Trial of the Major War Criminals, appended to the Agreement for the Prosecution and Punishment of Major War Criminals of the European Axis, 8 August 1945, London, as amended, Protocol to Agreement and Charter, 6 October 1945, 82 UNTS 279 (Nuremberg Charter).

1946 - Nuremberg Trials Final Report Appendix D: Allied Control Council Law No. 10, Punishment of Persons Guilty of War Crimes, Crimes Against Peace and Humanity, 20 December 1945, published in Official Gazette of the Control Council for Germany, No. 3, Berlin, 31 January 1946 (Control Council Law No. 10 or CCL 10).

- Charter of the International Military Tribunal for the Far East, 19 January 1946 (General Orders No. 1), Tokyo, as amended, General Orders No. 20, 26 April 1946, TIAS No. 1589, 4 Bevans 20 (Tokyo Charter).

1947 First Draft of the Genocide Convention, prepared by the UN Secretariat, May 1947, UN Doc. E/447.

1948 - Convention on the Prevention and Punishment of the Crime of Genocide, UN General Assembly Res. 260 A (III) (9 December 1948), 78 UNTS 277 (Genocide Convention).

- Universal Declaration of Human Rights, UN General Assembly Res. 217 (A) (10 December 1948), UN GAOR, Third Session, UN Doc. A/RES/3/217 (1948) (1948 Universal Declaration of Human Rights).

1949 - Convention for the Amelioration of the Condition of the Wounded and Sick in Armed Forces in the Field, 12 August 1949, 75 UNTS 31 (1949 Geneva Convention I).

- Convention for the Amelioration of the Condition of the Wounded, Sick and Shipwrecked Members of Armed Forces at Sea, 12 August 1949, 75 UNTS 85 (1949 Geneva Convention II).
- Convention Relative to the Treatment of Prisoners of War, 12 August 1949, 75 UNTS 135 (1949 Geneva Convention III).
- Convention Relative to the Protection of Civilian Persons in Time of War, 12 August 1949, 75 UNTS 287 (1949 Geneva Convention IV).
- Convention for the Suppression of the Traffic in Persons and of the Exploitation of the Prostitution of Others, 2 December 1949, 96 UNTS 272.

1950 European Convention for the Protection of Human Rights and Fundamental Freedoms, Rome, 4 November 1950, ETS No. 5 (1950 European Convention on Human Rights or ECHR).

1951 Convention Relating to the Status of Refugee, Geneva, 28 July 1951, 189 UNTS 137.

1956 Supplementary Convention on the Abolition of Slavery, the Slave Trade, and Institutions and Practices Similar to Slavery, 7 September 1956, 266 UNTS 3 (1956 Supplementary Slavery Convention).

1957 Convention Concerning the Abolition of Forced Labour (ILO No. 105), 25 June 1957, 320 UNTS 291 (1957 Convention Concerning the Abolition of Forced Labour).

1965 International Convention on the Elimination of All Forms of Racial Discrimination, UN General Assembly Resolution 2106 A (XX) (21 December 1965), 660 UNTS 195.

1966 International Covenant on Civil and Political Rights, UN General Assembly Resolution 2200 (XXI) (16 December 1966), 999 UNTS 171 (1979) (1966 International Covenant on Civil and Political Rights or ICCPR).

1969 - Vienna Convention on the Law of Treaties, 23 May 1969, 1155 UNTS 331 (1969 Vienna Convention on the Law of Treaties).

- American Convention on Human Rights, San José, 22 November 1969, OAS Treaty Ser. No. 36, OAS Off. Rec. OEA/Ser.L/V/II.23 doc. 21 rev. 6 (1979) (1969 American Convention on Human Rights or ACHR).

1977 - Protocol Additional to the Geneva Conventions of 12 August 1949 and Relating to the Protection of Victims of International Armed Conflicts, 8 June 1977, 1125 UNTS 3 (1977 Additional Protocol I).

- Protocol Additional to the Geneva Conventions of 12 August 1949 and Relating to the Protection of Victims of Non-International Armed Conflicts, 8 June 1977, 1125 UNTS 609 (1977 Additional Protocol II).

1979 - Statute of the Inter-American Commission on Human Rights, General Assembly Res. No. 447, La Paz, Bolivia, October 1979.

- Convention on the Elimination of All Forms of Discrimination Against Women, UN General Assembly Res. 34/180 (18 December 1979), reprinted in United Nations, *A Compilation of International Instruments*, UN Doc. ST/HR/1/Rev. 5 (Vol.1/Part 1) (1994), p. 150 (1979 Convention on the Elimination of All Forms of Discrimination Against Women).

1981 African Charter on Human and Peoples' Rights, Banjul, 26 June 1981, OAU Doc. CAB/LEG/67/3 Rev. 5 (1981 African Charter on Human and Peoples' Rights).

1984 Convention against Torture and Other Cruel, Inhuman or Degrading Treatment or Punishment, UN General Assembly Res. 39/46 (10 December 1984), 1465 UNTS 85 (1984 Torture Convention).

1985 - Declaration of Basic Principles of Justice for Victims of Crime and Abuse of Power, UN General Assembly Res. 40/34, 29 November 1985, UN Doc. A/RES/40/34 (1985 Victims Declaration).

- Recommendation No. R (85) 11 of the Committee of Ministers to Member States of the Council of Europe on the Position of Victims in the Framework of Criminal Law and Procedure, 28 June 1985, Rec. 85(11) E.

1989 Convention on the Rights of the Child, UN General Assembly Res. 44/25 (20 November 1989) reprinted in 28 *ILM* 1448 (1989 Convention on the Rights of the Child).

1991 Draft Code of Crimes Against Peace and Security of Mankind, Report of the International Law Commission, 43rd Session, 29 April – 19 July 1991, 46th Session, Supp. No. 10, UN Doc. A/46/10 (1991) (1991 Draft Code of Crimes Against Peace and Security of Mankind 1991).

1993 - Statute of the International Tribunal for the Prosecution of Persons Responsible for Serious Violations of International Humanitarian Law Committed in the Territory of the Former Yugoslavia since 1991, established by the Security Council acting under Chapter VII of the United Nations Charter, 25 May 1993,

Security Council Resolution 827 (1993), United Nations Security Council Official Records, Forty-eight Session, 3217th Meeting, UN Doc. S/RES/827 (1993) (ICTY Statute).

- Draft Principles on the Right to Restitution, Compensation and Rehabilitation for Victims of Gross Violations of Human Rights and Fundamental Freedoms, annexed to the Final Report Submitted by Mr. Theo van Boven, Special Rapporteur, *Study Concerning the Right to Restitution, Compensation and Rehabilitation for Victims of Gross Violations of Human Rights and Fundamental Freedoms* (2 July 1993), UN Doc. E/CN.4/Sub.2/1993/8.
- Vienna Declaration and Programme of Action, 12 July 1993, UN Doc. A/Conf.157/23.

1994 - Statute of the International Criminal Tribunal for the Prosecution of Persons Responsible for Genocide and Other Serious Violations of International Humanitarian Law Committed in the Territory of Rwanda and Rwandan Citizens Responsible for Genocide and Other Such Violations Committed in the Territory of Neighbouring States, Between 1 January 1994 and 31 December 1994, Established by the Security Council Acting Under Chapter VII of the United Nations Charter, 8 November 1994, Security Council Resolution 955 (1994), United Nations Security Council Official Records, Forty-Ninth Session, 3453rd Meeting, UN Doc. S/RES/955 (1994) (ICTR Statute).

- International Criminal Tribunal for the former Yugoslavia, Rules of Procedure and Evidence, adopted on 11 February 1994 and amended up to 11 March 2005, UN Doc. IT/32/Rev. 36.

1995 - International Criminal Tribunal for Rwanda, Rules of Procedure and Evidence as adopted on 29 June 1995, as amended up to 21 May 2005.

- Beijing Declaration and Platform for Action, Fourth World Conference on Women, 15 September 1995, UN Doc. A/Conf.177/20.

1996 - The Administration of Justice and the Human Rights of Detainees: *Revised Set of Basic Principles and Guidelines on the Right to Reparation for Victims of Gross Violations of Human Rights and Humanitarian Law*, Prepared by Mr. Theo van Boven Pursuant to Sub-Commission Decision 1995/117, 24 May 1996, UN Doc. E/CN.4/Sub.2/1996/17.

- Titles and Texts of Draft Articles on the Draft Code of Crimes Against the Peace and Security of Mankind, adopted by the Drafting Committee on 2nd Reading at its 47th and 48th Sessions, 31 May 1996, UN Doc. A/CN.4/L.522 (1996) (1996 Draft Code of Crimes Against Peace and Security of Mankind 1996).

1997 - Question of the Human Rights of All Persons Subjected to Any Form of Detention or Imprisonment, *Basic Principles and Guidelines on the Right to Reparation for Victims of Violations of Human Rights and International Humanitarian Law*, 16 January 1997, UN Doc. E/CN.4/1997/104.

- Recommendation No. R (97) 13 of the European Council's Committee of Ministers to Member States Concerning Intimidation of Witnesses and the Rights of the Defence, 10 September 1997.

1998 Statute of the International Criminal Court, Rome 17 July 1998, UN Doc. A/CONF.183/9*, as corrected by the *procès-verbaux* of 10 November 1998 and 12 July 1999.

1999 - International Criminal Tribunal for the former Yugoslavia, *Practice Direction on the Procedure for the Determination of Applications for Pardon, Commutation of Sentence and Early Release of Persons Convicted by the International Tribunal*, 7 April 1999, IT/146.

- Resolution of the International Association of Penal Law, adopted by the International Association of Penal Law at its Budapest session 'The Criminal Justice Systems Facing the Challenge of Organized Crime', 1999.

2000 Basic Principles and Guidelines on the Rights to a Remedy and Reparation for Victims of Violations of International Human Rights and Humanitarian Law, annexed to the Final Report of the Special Rapporteur, Mr. M. Cherif Bassiouni, *The Right to Restitution, Compensation and Rehabilitation for Victims of Gross Violations of Human Rights and Fundamental Freedoms*, 18 January 2000, UN Doc. E/CN.4/2000/62.

2002 - Assembly of States Parties, *Rules of Procedure and Evidence*, adopted by the Assembly of States Parties, First Session, New York, 3-10 September 2002, Official Records, 9 September 2002, ICC-ASP/1/3.

- Assembly of States Parties, *Elements of Crimes*, adopted by the Assembly of States Parties, First Session, New York, 3-10 September 2002, Official Records, 9 September 2002, ICC-ASP/1/3.

2004 *Regulations of the Court*, Adopted by the Judges of the Court on 26 May 2004, Fifth Plenary Session, The Hague, 17-28 May 2004, ICC BD/01-01-04.

2005 Basic Principles and Guidelines on the Right to a Remedy and Reparation for Victims of Gross Violations of International Human Rights Law and Serious Violations of International Humanitarian Law, 13 April 2005, UN Doc. E/CN.4/2005/L.48.

National Laws

1879 French Penal Code, as amended up to 15 September 2003. Available at http://www.preventgenocide.org

1881 Dutch Penal Code, 3 March 1881, as amended up to 9 December 2004, *Staatsblad* 645.

1889 The Penal Code of Finland, 39/1889, as amended up to 650/2003. Available at http://www.preventgenocide.org

1921 Dutch Code of Criminal Procedure, 15 January 1921, as amended up to 9 December 2004, *Staatsblad* 645.

1976 Criminal Code of Socialist Republic of Yugoslavia, *Official Gazette of SFRJ*, No. 44, 8 October 1976.

1977 Criminal Code of the Socialist Republic of Bosnia and Herzegovina, *Official Gazette of the Socialist Republic of Bosnia and Herzegovina*, No. 16/77.

1978 Rwandan Penal Code, Decree-Law No. 21/77 (18 August 1977), *Journal Officiel de la République Rwandaise*, 1 July 1978.

1987 German Code of Criminal Procedure, 7 April 1987, BGBl. I, S. 1074, 1319.

1988 Criminal Justice Act 1988 (England). Available at http://www.opsi.gov.uk/acts/acts1988/Ukpga19880033_en_1.htm

1993 Wet van 11 november 1993 tot wijziging van het Wetboek van Strafvordering, het Wetboek van Strafrecht en enige andere wetten (getuigenbescherming), 11 November 1993, *Staatsblad* 603 (Witness Protection Act); and Memorie van Toelichting (Explanatory Memorandum), Tweede Kamer, vergaderjaar 1991-1992, 22 483, nr. 3.

1995 Spanish Penal Code (del Código Penal), Jefartura del Estado, Organic Law (Ley Organica) 10/1995, 23 November 1995. Available at http://www.preventgenocide.org

1996 Organic Law No. 08/96 of 30 August 1996 on the Organization of Prosecutions for Offences Constituting the Crime of Genocide or Crimes against Humanity Committed Since 1 October 1990, published in the Gazette of the Republic of Rwanda, 35th year, No. 17, 1 September 1996 (Rwandan Organic Law No. 08/96).

1997
- Evidence (Witness Anonymity) Amendment Act 1997 (NZ) (New Zealand).
- Polish Code of Criminal Procedure, Act of 6 June 1997, Dz.U.97.89.555.

1998 Law No. 02/98 of 22/01/1998 Establishing a National Assistance Fund for Needy Victims of Genocide and Massacres Committed in Rwanda Between October 1, 1990 and December 31, 1994.

2000 Canada's Crimes Against Humanity and War Crimes Act, 2000, C.24, 24 June 2000.

2001
- The International Criminal Court Act 2001 (Enforcement of Fines, Forfeiture and Reparation Orders), England and Wales and Northern Ireland, Regulations 2001, No. 2379, 29 June 2001.
- Organic Law No. 40/2000 of 26/01/2001 Setting Up 'Gacaca Jurisdictions' and Organizing Prosecutions for Offences Constituting the Crime of Genocide or Crimes against Humanity Committed Between October 1, 1990, and December 31, 1994 (Gacaca Organic Law No. 40/2000).
- Organic Law No. 33/2001 of 22/6/2001 Modifying and Completing Organic Law No. 40/2000 Setting Up 'Gacaca Jurisdictions' and Organizing Prosecutions for Offences Constituting the Crime of Genocide or Crimes against Humanity Committed Between October 1, 1990, and December 31, 1994.

2004 Organic Law No. 16/2004 of 19/6/2004 Establishing the Organisation, Competence and Functioning of Gacaca Courts Charged with Prosecuting and Trying the Perpetrators of the Crime of Genocide and Other Crimes Against Humanity Committed Between October 1, 1990, and December 31, 1994, *Official Gazette of the Republic of Rwanda*, Year No. 43, Special of 19 June 2004 (Gacaca Organic Law No. 16/2004).

INDEX

CURRICULUM VITAE

Anne-Marie de Brouwer (1975) studied law at Tilburg University (The Netherlands) and La Sapienza (Italy). She graduated in International Law at Tilburg University in 1998. In 1998/1999 she did an LL.M. in International Human Rights Law at the University of Essex (United Kingdom). In 2000 she was employed as a PhD researcher and lecturer in international law and supranational criminal law at the Department of European and International Law at Tilburg University. Since then, she has been a member of the School of Human Rights Research. Currently, she works as a University Lecturer in supranational criminal law and international law at Tilburg University.

SCHOOL OF HUMAN RIGHTS RESEARCH SERIES

The School of Human Rights Research is a joint effort by human rights researchers in the Netherlands. Its central research theme is the nature and meaning of international standards in the field of human rights, their application and promotion in the national legal order, their interplay with national standards, and the international supervision of such application. The School of Human Rights Research Series only includes English titles that contribute to a better understanding of the different aspects of human rights.

Published titles within the Series:

1 Brigit C.A. Toebes, *The Right to Health as a Human Right in International Law*
ISBN 90-5095-057-4

2 Ineke Boerefijn, *The Reporting Procedure under the Covenant on Civil and Political Rights. Practice and Procedures of the Human Rights Committee*
ISBN 90-5095-074-4

3 Kitty Arambulo, *Strengthening the Supervision of the International Covenant on Economic, Social and Cultural Rights. Theoretical and Procedural Aspects*
ISBN 90-5095-058-2

4 Marlies Glasius, *Foreign Policy on Human Rights. Its Influence on Indonesia* under Soeharto
ISBN 90-5095-089-2

5 Cornelis D. de Jong, *The Freedom of Thought, Conscience and Religion or Belief in the United Nations (1946-1992)*
ISBN 90-5095-137-6

6 Heleen Bosma, *Freedom of Expression in England and under the ECHR: in Search of a Common Ground. A Foundation for the Application of the Human Rights Act 1998 in English Law*
ISBN 90-5095-136-8

7 Mielle Bulterman, *Human Rights in the External Relations of the European Union*
ISBN 90-5095-164-3

8 Esther M. van den Berg, *The Influence of Domestic NGOs on Dutch Human Rights Policy. Case Studies on South Africa,Namibia, Indonesia and East Timor*
ISBN 90-5095-159-7

9 Ian Seiderman, *Hierarchy in International Law: the Human Rights Dimension*
ISBN 90-5095-165-1

10 Anna Meijknecht, *Towards International Personality: the Position of Minorities and Indigenous Peoples in International Law*
ISBN 90-5095-166-X

11 Mohamed Eltayeb, *A Human Rights Approach to Combating Religious Persecution. Cases from Pakistan, Saudi Arabia and Sudan*
ISBN 90-5095-170-8

12 Machteld Boot, *Genocide, Crimes Against Humanity, War Crimes: Nullum Crimen Sine Lege and the Subject Matter Jurisdiction of the International Criminal Court*
ISBN 90-5095-216-X

13 Corinne Packer, *Using Human Rights to Change Tradition. Traditional Practices Harmful to Women's Reproductive Health in sub-Saharan Africa*
ISBN 90-5095-226-7

14 Theo R.G. van Banning, *The Human Right to Property*
ISBN 90-5095-203-8

15 Yvonne M. Donders, *Towards a Right to Cultural Identity?*
ISBN 90-5095-238-0

16 Göran K. Sluiter, *International Criminal Adjudication and the Collection of Evidence: Obligations of States*
ISBN 90-5095-227-5

17 Nicola Jägers, *Corporate Human Rights Obligations: in Search of Accountability*
ISBN 90-5095-240-2

18 Magdalena Sepúlveda, *The Nature of the Obligations under the International Covenant on Economic, Social and Cultural Rights*
ISBN 90-5095-260-7

19 Mitsue Inazumi, *Universal Jurisdiction in Modern International Law: Expansion of National Jurisdiction for Prosecuting Serious Crimes under International Law*
ISBN 90-5095-366-2

20 Anne-Marie L.M. de Brouwer, *Supranational Criminal Prosecution of Sexual Violence: The ICC and the Practice of the ICTY and the ICTR*
ISBN 90-5095-533-9

www.ingramcontent.com/pod-product-compliance
Ingram Content Group UK Ltd.
Pitfield, Milton Keynes, MK11 3LW, UK
UKHW051918100926
8556IPUK00021B/1238

9 789050 955331